T0217779

Communications in Computer and Information Science 1163

Commenced Publication in 2007
Founding and Former Series Editors:
Phoebe Chen, Alfredo Cuzzocrea, Xiaoyong Du, Orhun Kara, Ting Liu, Krishna M. Sivalingam, Dominik Ślęzak, Takashi Washio, Xiaokang Yang, and Junsong Yuan

More information about this series at http://www.springer.com/series/7899

Hong Shen · Yingpeng Sang (Eds.)

Parallel Architectures, Algorithms and Programming

10th International Symposium, PAAP 2019
Guangzhou, China, December 12–14, 2019
Revised Selected Papers

Editors
Hong Shen
Sun Yat-sen University
Guangzhou, China

Yingpeng Sang
Sun Yat-sen University
Guangzhou, China

ISSN 1865-0929 ISSN 1865-0937 (electronic)
Communications in Computer and Information Science
ISBN 978-981-15-2766-1 ISBN 978-981-15-2767-8 (eBook)
https://doi.org/10.1007/978-981-15-2767-8

This Springer imprint is published by the registered company Springer Nature Singapore Pte Ltd.
The registered company address is: 152 Beach Road, #21-01/04 Gateway East, Singapore 189721, Singapore

Preface

Welcome to PAAP 2019, the 10th International Symposium on Parallel Architectures, Algorithms and Programming. PAAP is an annual international conference for scientists and engineers in academia and industry to present their research results and development activities in all aspects of parallel architectures, algorithms, and programming techniques.

Following the successful PAAP 2008 in Hefei, PAAP 2009 in Nanning, PAAP 2010 in Dalian, PAAP 2011 in Tianjin, PAAP 2012 in Taipei, PAAP 2014 in Beijing, PAAP 2015 in Nanjing, PAAP 2017 in Haikou, and PAAP 2018 in Taiwan, PAAP 2019 will be held in Guangzhou, which is the third largest Chinese city and serves as an important national transportation hub and trading port.

This year we received 121 submissions from 6 different countries and regions across the world. Out of these submissions, we accepted 47 papers. This represents an acceptance rate of 39.7%. The submissions were in general of high quality, making paper selection a tough task. The paper review process involved all Program Committee members and 15 external reviewers. To ensure a high-quality program and provide sufficient feedback to authors, we made great effort to have each paper reviewed by three independent reviewers on average. All accepted papers are included in the proceedings.

It would not have been possible for PAAP 2019 to take place without the help and support from various people. The efforts of authors, Program Committee members, and reviewers are essential to the conference's quality, and all deserve our utmost appreciation. We also wish to thank the Local Organization Committee members for all their hard work in making PAAP 2019 a great success, and thank our sponsors, Sun Yat-sen University and *Communications in Computer and Information Science* (CCIS) of Springer, for their support. Last but not least, we wish to thank Guoliang Chen from Nanjing University of Posts and Telecommunications and Shenzhen University, China; Depei Qian from Sun Yat-sen University and Beihang University, China; Manu Malek as the Editor-in-Chief of the Elsevier *International Journal of Computers and Electrical Engineering*; Ajay Gupta from Western Michigan University, USA; and Keqiu Li from Tianjin University, China, who delivered keynote speeches and helped in obtaining the objectives of the conference.

We hope that all participants enjoyed PAAP 2019 and had a great time in Guangzhou.

December 2019

Hong Shen
Geoffrey Fox
Ajay Gupta
Manu Malek
Nong Xiao

Organization

Organizing Committee

General Chair

Hong Shen	Sun Yat-sen University, China

Program Chairs

Geoffrey Fox	Indiana University, USA
Ajay Gupta	Western Michigan University, USA
Manu Malek	Stevens Institute of Technology, USA
Nong Xiao	Sun Yat-sen University, China

Publications Chairs

Yingpeng Sang	Sun Yat-sen University, China
Hui Tian	Griffith University, Australia

Publicity Chair

Xu Chen	Sun Yat-sen University, China

Local Arrangement Chair

Shangsong Liang	Sun Yat-sen University, China

Registration and Finance Chair

Xiangyin Liu	Sun Yat-sen University, China

Workshop and Tutorial Chair

Zonghua Zhang	Institut Mines-Télécom, France

Program Committee

Zhanmao Cao	South China Normal University, China
Yaodong Cheng	Institute of High Energy Physics, Chinese Academy of Sciences, China
Guoliang Chen	Nanjing University of Posts and Telecommunications and Shenzhen University, China
Xu Chen	Sun Yat-sen University, China
Yawen Chen	Otago University, New Zealand
Karl Fuerlinger	University of California, Berkeley, USA
Teofilio Gonzalez	University of California, Santa Barbara, USA

Huaxi Gu	Xidian University, China
Longkun Guo	Fuzhou University, China
Shi-Jin Horng	National Taiwan University of Science and Technology, Taiwan
Haiping Huang	Nanjing University of Posts and Telecommunications, China
Zhiyi Huang	Otago University, New Zealand
Mirjana Ivanovic	University of Novi Sad, Serbia
Graham Kirby	University of St Andrews, UK
Kai-Cheung Leung	The University of Auckland, New Zealand
Kenli Li	Hunan University, China
Keqiu Li	Tianjin University, China
Shuangjuan Li	South China Agricultural University, China
Yamin Li	Hosei University, Japan
Shangsong Liang	Sun Yat-sen University, China
Haixiang Lin	Delft University of Technology, The Netherlands
Xiaola Lin	Sun Yat-sen University, China
Xingcheng Liu	Sun Yat-sen University, China
Zhongzhi Luan	Beihang University, China
Rui Mao	Shenzhen University, China
Ge Nong	Sun Yat-sen University, China
Depei Qian	Sun Yat-sen University and Beihang University, China
Yingpeng Sang	Sun Yat-sen University, China
Neetesh Saxena	Bournemouth University, UK
Guangzhong Sun	University of Science and Technology of China, China
Jiande Sun	Shandong Normal University, China
Shaohua Tang	South China University of Technology, China
Haibo Tian	Sun Yat-sen University, China
Hui Tian	Griffith University, Australia
Ye Tian	University of Science and Technology of China, China
Jigang Wu	Guangdong Polytechnic University, China
Weigang Wu	Sun Yat-sen University, China
Di Wu	Sun Yat-sen University, China
Xin Wang	Fudan University, China
Yan Wang	Soochow University, China
Jian Yin	Sun Yat-sen University, China
Fangguo Zhang	Sun Yat-sen University, China
Haibo Zhang	Otago University, New Zealand
Xianchao Zhang	Dalian University of Technology, China
Yu Zhang	University of Science and Technology of China, China
Yunquan Zhang	Institute of Software, Chinese Academy of Sciences, China
Zonghua Zhang	Institut Mines-Télécom, France
Cheng Zhong	Guangxi University, China

Organizers

Hosted by

Sun Yat-sen University

In cooperation with

Springer

Contents

Architectures

High Performance Systems

Algorithms

Security and Privacy

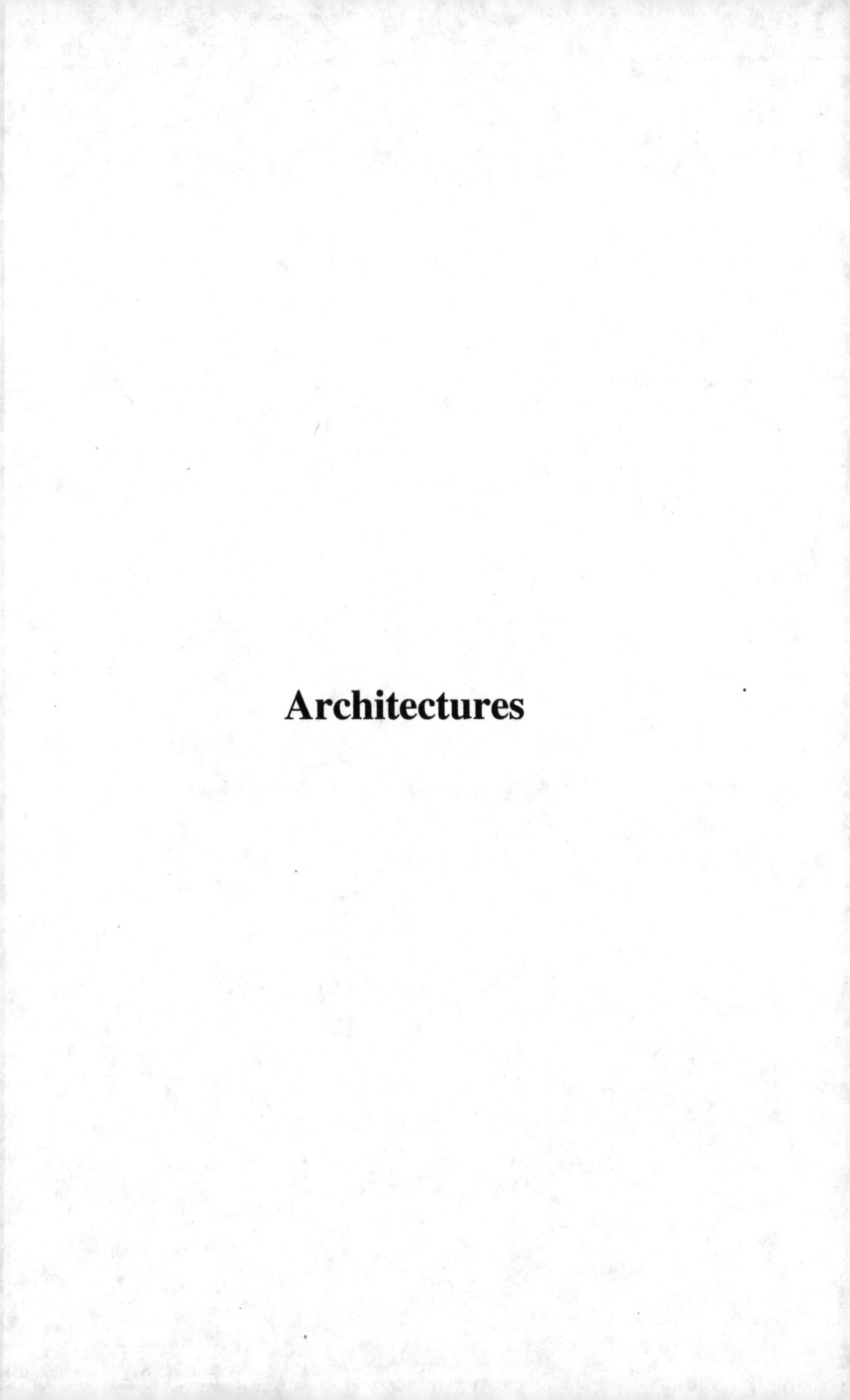

Architectures

On a Coexisting Scheme for Multiple Flows in Multi-radio Multi-channel Wireless Mesh Networks

Zhanmao Cao[1(✉)], Qisong Huang[1], Chase Q. Wu[2], Wenkang Kong[1], and Aiqin Hou[3]

[1] School of Computer, South China Normal University, Zhongshan, Guangzhou 510631, China
{caozhanmao,qshuang,kongwenkang}@m.scnu.edu.cn

[2] Department of Computer Science, New Jersey Institute of Technology, Newark, NJ 07102, USA
chase.wu@njit.edu

[3] School of Information Science and Technology, Northwest University Xi'an, Xi'an 710127, Shaanxi, China
houaiqin@nwu.edu.cn

Abstract. Multi-radio multi-channel (MRMC) wireless mesh networks (WMNs) hold the promise to become the next-generation networks to provide the service of ubiquitous computing, access to the Internet, and support for a large number of data flows. Many applications in WMNs can be modeled as a multi-flow coexistence problem. Assembling links distributed in orthogonal channels to support multiple flows is essentially a combinatorial optimization problem, which concerns channel assignment, path finding, and link scheduling. To make full use of network resources, links in different channel layers should be concatenated to compose data transfer paths for multiple flows with awareness of nodes' free interfaces and available channels. Based on the analysis of traffic behaviors, this paper designs a coexisting algorithm to maximize the number of flows. Simulations are conducted in combinatorial cases with various traffic requests of multiple pairs, and the results show the efficacy of the proposed algorithm over a random network topology. This scheme can be used to develop routing and scheduling solutions for multi-flow network tasks through prior computing.

Keywords: Multiple flows · Routing and scheduling · Coexisting links · Wireless mesh networks

1 Introduction

With rapid popularization of smart mobile terminals, data traffic requests converge to mesh routers, which form multiple data flows between multiple pairs.

H. Shen and Y. Sang (Eds.): PAAP 2019, CCIS 1163, pp. 3–11, 2020.
https://doi.org/10.1007/978-981-15-2767-8_1

Wireless Mesh Networks (WMNs) have inherent advantages to serve ubiquitous communication as a broadband backbone. Increasingly, Multi-radio Multi-Channel (MRMC) WMNs are believed to be the next-generation wireless backbone to address the challenge of heavy data flows [8]. Almost all applications in such network environments can be modeled as multi-flow tasks in a global wireless mesh topology. This leads to an important problem: How to assemble links to support multiple data flows with optimal performance in a coexisting manner, considering the limited resources in WMNs?

For traffic requests of multiple pairs $(s_i, d_i), i = 1, 2, ..., n$, a basic task is to enable continuous transmission without wireless interference. This is a fundamental and challenging problem, which naturally boils down to a coexistence problem of multiple flows, which must coexist and be activated along the paths for these specific pairs. Hence, the problem has a general meaning for different applications. As the data volume continues to increase, many applications need to transmit data between different pairs of nodes and it has become a common task to support multiple flows concurrently. Due to the limited transmitting media and the wireless interference that obstructs the usage of radios, it is challenging to design an efficient method that takes into consideration various factors such as interfaces, channels, interference, topology, traffic requests, and data size [11].

The challenge also arises from the problem's computational complexity. If we consider maximizing the number of flows or the throughput of source-destination pairs, the problem has been proved to be NP-complete [12]. To optimize congestion control by considering channel assignment (CA) and traffic allocation, even in a simpler combinatorial case of multi-radio networks to realize a given set of rate demands, the problem still remains NP-hard [13]. Energy efficiency is another concern as massive flows consume significant energy [4]. Cao *et al.* designed a joint routing and scheduling algorithm for multi-pair traffic requests based on a Cartesian Product of Graphs (CPG) model [5].

To develop a coexisting scheme for multiple flows in WMNs, we consider the most important factors, i.e., the number R of node interfaces, the number C of available orthogonal channels, time slot t, topology G, and traffic requests T_r. This research sheds lights on several key points as follows:

- Model the problem as a combinatorial optimization problem for maximum capacity of coexisting flows.
- Design a coexisting algorithm to support multiple flows simultaneously.
- Evaluate the performance in terms of capacity, throughput, and delay in various combinatorial cases.

The remaining sections are organized as follows: Sect. 2 provides a brief summary of research work. Section 3 builds an optimization model for maximum capacity and designs a coexisting algorithm. Section 4 evaluates the performance of the coexisting algorithm. Section 5 draws a conclusion of the work.

2 Related Work

Channel Assignment (CA) for interference avoidance has been investigated in-depth through the use of graph coloring. The impact of network topology on channel resource utilization has been well recognized [1]. Interference-aware topology control has also been extensively studied [2,9]. Cao *et al.* developed a Cartesian product of graphs (CPG) model to simplify channel assignment [10].

There is very limited study on the efficiency of combinatorial cases considering the number of interfaces, the number of channels, network topology, time slots, and traffic distributions. Cao *et al.* addressed combinatorial routing using CPG model [7], which is useful to discuss CA. Resource utilization also depends on the communication scheme. MRMC is able to significantly improve network capacity and reduce the cost of broadband WMN deployment [3]. The number of orthogonal channels and the number of interface cards per node determine the mesh capacity. The combined cases of critical resources should be compared to understand the relationship between throughput and other metrics.

Most of the existing work considered one aspect of routing, scheduling, or channel assignment. There is some limited work considering two or more of them. Jin showed that the routing and packet scheduling problem in general graphs is NP-complete [14]. The subproblem only considering CA in mesh networks is similar to the least coloring problem of graph, which is NP-complete [12]. The joint routing and scheduling problem in WMNs is obviously more complicated. Even in a directional radio case, the transmission of multiple concurrent flows, which can be formulated as a mixed integer nonlinear problem, is inherently difficult to solve [6].

The shortest path routing scheme only considers the least resource consumption for one stream, while neglecting the fact that overlapped nodes may exhaust resources quickly [15]. If one node has no free resource, it cannot forward any packet. Kim *et al.* discussed resource sharing by quantifying node resource usage [16]. Although there exist some efforts in this direction, resource-aware routing still remains largely unexplored.

To avoid interferences between links and to reduce heavy congestion on intersected nodes, path finding/selection and link scheduling should be carried out based on the actual available resources. Hence, a joint scheduling and routing scheme with CA is deeply coupled with the network topology, the number of node interfaces, and the number of available channels.

3 Multi-flow Coexistence

A data flow is carried over a path between a node pair (s_i, d_i), where s_i denotes the source node, and d_i denotes the destination node. A traffic request from one mesh node to another with data size z_i, $i = 1, 2, ..., \rho$, is denoted as $T_r = \{(s_i, d_i; z_i) | i = 1, 2, ..., \rho\}$. Typical examples include FTP or some other real-time data transfer requests. The set of all traffic requests within a given period defines the traffic situation.

To support the transmission for multi-pair traffic requests, we need to analyze several main factors. According to the Cartesian Product of Graphs (CPG) model [10], a routing and scheduling scheme should consider the number R of interfaces, the number C of available channels, the topology of the multi-radio multi-channel (MRMC) wireless mesh network (WMN), and traffic requests T_r.

3.1 Model for Coexisting Links

We consider a WMN topology $G = (V, E), |V| = n, |E| = m$, where E denotes the set of effective communications between neighbor nodes, not actual links in the wireless mesh. Only when a pair of nodes (u, v) in V are communicating with each other over the same channel c_j, $(u, v) \in E$ becomes a link at an assigned time slot t, denoted as $l_{c_j,t}^{(u,v)}$. If the channel c_j has bandwidth ω_j, the maximum capacity of the link is ω_j. Obviously, the flow data rate of $l_{c_j,t}^{(u,v)}$ is bounded by ω_j.

The maximum capacity depends on several critical factors: the traffic situation T_r, the resources of the mesh represented by R and C, the topology, and the scheme for routing and scheduling multiple flows of multiple pairs. $T_r = \{(s_i, d_i; z_i)|i = 1, 2, ..., \rho\}$ is the initial traffic situation. The resources of a mesh include interfaces R_i of node v_i and the set $C = \{c_1, c_2, ..., c_q\}$ of available channels, where q is the total number of orthogonal channels. Of course, the topology is another important input of the problem as it affects routing selection and node/link interference relation.

The path of node pair (s_i, d_i) is denoted as $P_{(s_i,d_i)}$, or simply as P_i. The number of hops along P_i from s_i to d_i is denoted as ϱ_i. We denote the jth hop of P_i as $\hbar_j^{P_{(s_i,d_i)}}$, or $\hbar_j^{P_i}$ for brevity. The channel assigned to link $\hbar_j^{P_i}$ is denoted as $c_{ij} \in C$, and its corresponding bandwidth is denoted as ω_{ij}. The capacity of $P_{(s_i,d_i)}$ is the sum of link capacities along P_i, denoted as $Cap(P_{(s_i,d_i)})$. The lower bound of $Cap(P_{(s_i,d_i)})$ is the minimum link capacity along P_i multiplied by ϱ_i. Similarly, the upper bound of $Cap(P_{(s_i,d_i)})$ is the maximum link capacity multiplied by ϱ_i. The capacity of an active path P_i is calculated as

$$Cap(P_{(s_i,d_i)}) = \sum_{j=1}^{\varrho_i} \omega_{ij}. \tag{1}$$

Over a certain channel layer in the CPG model, the maximum number of links is determined by the topology. The choice of maximum links may not be unique, but the maximum number of coexisting links must match with the number of node-pairs at all times. Let λ be the maximum number of coexisting links in one channel layer. Then, the number of possible links over all q channels in a given mesh can be estimated by its upper bound $q \cdot \lambda$.

However, the traffic situation may contain not only one-hop communications, but also many-hop communications for P_i. Generally, we need to concatenate several links, which are distributed in different channel layers, to assemble the paths for the current $T_r = \{(s_i, d_i; z_i)|i = 1, 2, ..., \rho\}$. We have $\hbar_{j,c_k,t}^{P_i} = 1$, if the link is scheduled; else, $\hbar_{j,c_k,t}^{P_i} = 0$. Obviously, the capacity is also limited by the size of T_r. Hence, the maximum capacity, as the optimization objective, is calculated as

$$\max \sum_{i=1}^{\rho} \sum_{k=1}^{q} \sum_{t=1}^{T} \hbar_{j,c_k,t}^{P_i} \cdot \omega_k. \tag{2}$$

Clearly, the link count of a node is limited by its interfaces. If node v_i is a link's receiver over c_j, we denote this link as $l_{c_j,t}^{\triangleright,v_i}$; if node v_i is a link's sender, we denote this link as $l_{c_j,t}^{v_i,\triangleright}$. Hence, $l_{c_j,t}^{\triangleright,v_i} + l_{c_j,t}^{v_i,\triangleright} \leq R_i, \forall i$. Here, $\triangleright$ denotes the direction of the radio from/to a certain node.

If there are several paths sharing one connection over channel c_j, say $l_{c_j,t}^{(u,v)}$, then the minimum sum of the link capacities for those sharing paths must be less than ω_j.

In the CPG model, the links of a path are distributed in various channel layers as shown in [5,7]. The links in one channel layer are collected in a greedy way to have sufficient interference-free links for an initial path and other interference-free links to support other paths. The critical step is to find the best fit for path edges and interference-free links. However, the combinations of links in different layers are restricted by the paths of multiple pairs. The combinatorial nature makes the problem extremely challenging.

We attempt to design a heuristic scheme to find as many required links as possible and generate multiple coexisting link groups. Based on the model and the coexisting properties discussed above, we design our scheme as shown in Algorithm 1, where the coexisting links are combined to maximize the number of coexisting paths.

3.2 The Link Coexistence Algorithm

To simultaneously activate as many paths as possible, it is necessary to make full use of the network resources. In the CPG model, we understand that one-hop paths cannot meet the demands for real multiple flows. Let $C(v_i)$ denote the set of all available channels of router v_i, and let $c_j(v_i)$ denote the channel assignment operation, which assigns channel c_j to router v_i. We use I_{Free} to denote the set of links without interference over a certain channel, i.e., every two links in I_{Free} satisfy interference-free relation. In fact, for a specific topology, I_{Free} holds over any channels.

We use L_t to denote the set of all links that satisfy I_{Free} at time t, i.e., $L_t \bowtie I_{Free}$. Here, $\bowtie$ means "satisfy the right-side relation". If new links are added into L_t, the interferences have to be screened.

Based on the models constructed in Sect. 3.1, we design Algorithm 1 to optimize the resource use. It produces the maximum link groups at time t. As a result, the links in L_t are combined to form as many paths as possible for multiple pairs $(s_i, d_i), i = 1, 2, ..., \rho$.

Algorithm 1. Link coexistence algorithm for multiple flows
Input: Topology G, the set R of node interfaces, and the set C of available channels, traffic requests $T_r = \{(s_i, d_i; z_i)|i = 1, 2, ..., \rho\}$.
Output: L, the set of coexisting links combined to support multiple flows.

Require: $R \geq 0 \wedge |C| \geq 0$;
Ensure: $\omega_i \geq 0$;
$t := 0$;
$i := 1$;
$j := 1$;
for $(t = 0 \text{ to } T)$ **do**
  while $(i < \rho)$ **do**
    if $(\exists$ path $P_i \wedge \forall v_h \in P_i, r(v_h) > 0$ **then**
      if $(\forall i, h, (v_h \in P_i) \wedge (v_h \neq s_i) \wedge (v_h \neq d_i) \wedge (c(v_h) > 0)$ **then**
        Choose $c_j \in C(v_{i_{h-1}}) \cap C(v_{i_h})$, and let $c_j(l_t^{(v_{i_{h-1}}, v_{i_h})})$;
        if $L_t \cup_i \{l_{c_j,t}^{(v_{i_{h-1}}, v_{i_h})}\} \bowtie I_{Free}$ **then**
          $L_t := L_t \cup \{l_{c_j,t}^{(v_{i_{h-1}}, v_{i_h})}\}$;
      else $\{P_i$ has a node with no free resources$\}$
        $i := i + 1$;
  $t := t + 1$;
output $L := \bigsqcup_t \{L_t\}, \{t \in (0, T)\}$.

4 Performance Evaluation

To valuate the performance of Algorithm 1, we conduct a series of combinatorial simulations of $R \times C = \{4, 8, 12, 16, 20\} \times \{8, 16, 32, 64\}$ in an MRMC WMN topology with 77 nodes, as shown in Fig. 1.

The number of coexisting links for the combinations is plotted in Fig. 2. As links for multiple pairs are simultaneously activated, the more links activated, the more packets forwarded. The simulation also presents an interesting phenomenon: when $|R| = 12$, channel count $|C| = 32$ is sufficient to use the interface resources. Having more channels may not improve the number of simultaneous links with $|R| = 12$. Also, increasing the number of interfaces may not improve the number of simultaneous links with $|C| = 32$ as shown in Fig. 2. We refer to the situation $|R| = 12 \wedge |C| = 32$ as a shake-hand match. Similarly, $|R| = 16 \wedge |C| = 64$ is another shake-hand match. The best use of free resources may sustain nearly up to 290 links in the given mesh.

The average capacities are measured to estimate the performance of the coexisting algorithm for the combinations of $R \times C = \{4, 8, 12, 16, 20\} \times \{8, 16, 32, 64\}$. The multi-pair requests form a random group of 80 pairs, i.e., $|Tr| = 80$. Generally, more resources equipped in the mesh promise higher capacity. However, we note that if there are only 8 available channels, the capacity cannot be improved further by increasing the number of radios. Furthermore, in the case of $|C| = 16$ or $|C| = 32$, the upper capacity limit can be reached with $|R| = 12$. Similarly, in the case of $|C| = 64$, the upper capacity limit can be reached with $|R| = 16$. Generally, the mesh provides a large capacity as shown in Fig. 3.

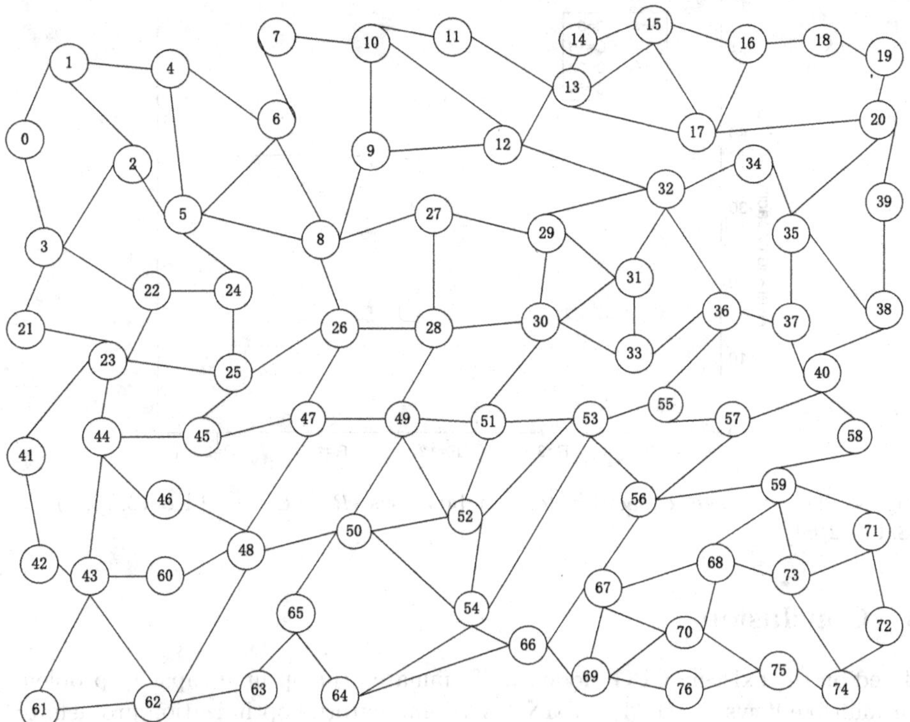

Fig. 1. The WMS topology with 77 routers.

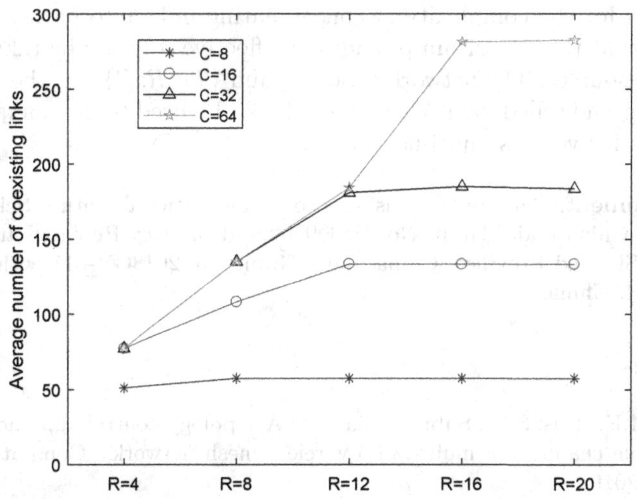

Fig. 2. The average number of activated links in the topology.

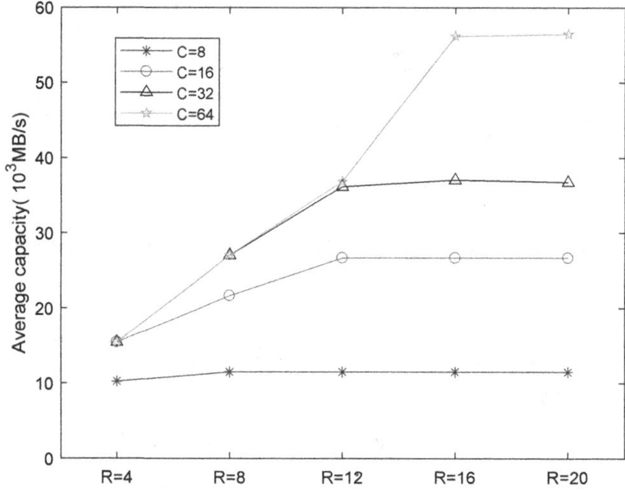

Fig. 3. The average capacities for combinations $R \times C = \{4, 8, 12, 16, 20\} \times \{8, 16, 32, 64\}$.

5 Conclusion

Based on the existing CPG model, we formulated the optimal capacity problem for multiple flows in MRMC WMNs as a combinatorial optimization problem to maximize the number of coexisting links over different channel layers. We analyzed the optimization objective and the corresponding constraints, and designed a link coexistence algorithm to meet the demands for maximum transmission. The proposed algorithm is based on a heuristic greedy strategy, which specifically accounts for the complexity of concatenating links into paths. Simulation results show that this algorithm provides an effective solution by taking full use of available resources. The network topology and $\{Tr, R, C\}$ together determine a joint routing and scheduling scheme, which can be used to pre-compute routes and schedules for various multi-flow tasks.

Acknowledgement. This research is sponsored by National Nature Science Union Foundation of China under Grant No. U1609202 and the Key Research and Development Plan of Shaanxi Province, China under Grant No. 2018GY-011 with Northwest University, P.R. China.

References

1. Marina, M.K., Das, S.R., Subramanian, P.: A topology control approach for utilizing multiple channels in multi-radio wireless mesh networks. Comput. Netw. **54**, 241–256 (2010)
2. Maleki, E.N., Mirjalily, G.: Fault-tolerant interference-aware topology control in multi-radio multi-channel wireless mesh networks. Comput. Netw. **110**, 206–222 (2016)

3. Liu, Q., Jia, X., Zhou, Y.: Topology control for multi-channel multi-radio wireless mesh networks using directional antennas. Wireless Netw. **17**(1), 41–51 (2011)
4. Shu, T., Wu, C.Q.: Energy-efficient mapping of large-scale workflows under deadline constraints in big data computing systems. FGCS (2018). https://doi.org/10.1016/j.future.2017.07.050
5. Cao, Z., Wu, C.Q., Berry, M.L.: An optimization scheme for routing and scheduling of concurrent user requests in wireless mesh networks. Comput. Sci. Inf. Syst. **14**(3), 661–684 (2017)
6. Roh, H.-T., Lee, J.-W.: Channel assignment, link scheduling, routing, and rate control for multi-channel wireless mesh networks with directional antennas. J. Commun. Netw. **18**(6), 884–891 (2016)
7. Cao, Z., Wu, Q., Zhang, Y., Shiva, S.G., Gu, Y.: On modeling and analysis of MIMO wireless mesh networks with triangular overlay topology. Math. Probl. Eng. **2015**, 11 (2015). Article ID 185262
8. Larsson, E.G., Edfors, O., Tufvesson, F., Marzetta, T.L.: Massive MIMO for next generation wireless systems. IEEE Commun. Mag. **52**(2), 186–195 (2014)
9. Jang, H.-C., Fang, R.-W.: Interference-aware topology control in wireless mesh network. In: Proceedings of the International Conference on Mobile Technology, Applications, and Systems, vol. 76, pp. 1–7 (2008)
10. Cao, Z., Xiao, W., Peng, L.: A mesh×chain graph model for MIMO scheduling in IEEE802. 16 WMN. In: Proceedings of the 2nd IEEE International Conference on Computer Modeling and Simulation, Sanya, vol. 2, pp. 547–551. Computer Society (2010)
11. Cao, Z., Wu, C.Q., Berry, M.L.: On routing of multiple concurrent user requests in multi-radio multi-channel wireless mesh networks. In: 17th International Conference on Parallel and Distributed Computing, Applications and Technologies, Guangzhou, China, pp. 24–29 (2016)
12. Ramachandran, K.N., Belding-Royer, E.M., Almeroth, K.C., Buddhikot, M.M.: Interference-aware channel assignment in multi-radio wireless mesh networks. In: INFOCOM, vol. 6, pp. 1–12 (2006)
13. Giannoulis, A., Salonidis, T., Knightly, E.: Congestion control and channel assignment in multi-radio wireless mesh networks. In: 5th Annual IEEE Communications Society Conference on Sensor, Mesh and Ad Hoc Communications and Networks, SECON 2008, pp. 350–358 (2008)
14. Jin, F., Arora, A., Hwang, J., Choi, H.A.: Routing and packet scheduling in WiMAX mesh networks. In: Proceedings of the 4th IEEE International Conference on Broadband Communications, Networks and Systems (BROADNETS), pp. 574–582 (2007)
15. Jun, J., Sichitiu, M.L.: MRP: wireless mesh networks routing protocol. Comput. Commun. **31**(7), 1413–1435 (2008)
16. Kim, T.-S., Yang, Y., Hou, J.C., Krishnamurthy, S.V.: Joint resource allocation and admission control in wireless mesh networks. In: 2009 7th International Symposium on Modeling and Optimization in Mobile, Ad Hoc, and Wireless Networks. WiOPT 2009, pp. 1–10. IEEE (2009)

Non-linear K-Barrier Coverage in Mobile Sensor Network

Zijing Ma[1], Shuangjuan Li[1(✉)], Longkun Guo[2], and Guohua Wang[1]

[1] College of Mathematics and Informatics, South China Agricultural University, Guangzhou, China
mazijingscau@hotmail.com, lishj2013@hotmail.com, w.guohuascut@gmail.com
[2] School of Computer Science and Technology, Qilu University of Technology (Shandong Academy of Sciences), Jinan, China
forkun@mail.ustc.edu.cn

Abstract. Intrusion detection is an important application of wireless sensor network. A belt region is said to be k-barrier covered if any intruder crossing the width of this region can be detected by at least k sensors. After initial random sensor deployment, k-barrier coverage can be achieved by relocating mobile sensors to construct k barriers appropriately. Due to energy limit of mobile sensors, it is important to reduce the amount of movements of mobile sensors. Existing algorithms focused on forming k linear barriers energy-efficiently. However, large redundant sensor movement are needed by mobile sensors to move to linear barriers. In this paper, we will study how to form k non-linear barriers energy-efficiently, which can result smaller sensor movement than linear barriers. We define a notion of horizontal virtual force by considering the euclidean distance and also horizontal angle and then propose an energy-efficient algorithm to form k non-linear barriers based on the initial deployment of mobile sensors. The algorithm first divides the region into several subregions and then constructs k sub-barriers from the left boundary of each subregion to the right boundary respectively by always choosing the mobile sensor chain with the largest horizontal virtual force and also flattening it and finally connects the sub-barriers in neighbor subregions for forming k barriers in the whole region. Simulation results show that this algorithm efficiently decreases the movements of mobile sensors compared to a linear k-barrier coverage algorithm and it can be applicable to large scale sensor networks.

Keywords: Wireless sensor networks · K-barrier coverage · Virtual force · Non-linear barrier

1 Introduction

Wireless Sensor Networks (WSNs) have been widely applied in many fields such as intrusion detection and border protection and environment monitoring. Nowadays, many problems in WSNs have been widely studied such as topology control,

H. Shen and Y. Sang (Eds.): PAAP 2019, CCIS 1163, pp. 12–23, 2020.
https://doi.org/10.1007/978-981-15-2767-8_2

localization technology, data aggregation and coverage problem. The coverage problem includes area coverage, target coverage, barrier coverage and sweep coverage. Barrier coverage [9] is a significant problem in coverage problems. It is often used to detect intruders by forming a sensor chain in a belt region of interest (ROI) so that any intruder will be detected when passing through the ROI along any crossing paths. K-barrier coverage is a kind of barrier coverage which means that a belt region is said to be k-barrier covered if any intruder crossing the width of this region can be detected by at least sensors. Due to environmental constraints, mobile sensors are often deployed randomly in ROI. It is not likely to form k-barrier coverage after initial random sensor deployment, as shown in Fig. 1(a). Fortunately, mobile sensors can be relocated to the desired positions for forming k barriers after initial random sensor deployment.

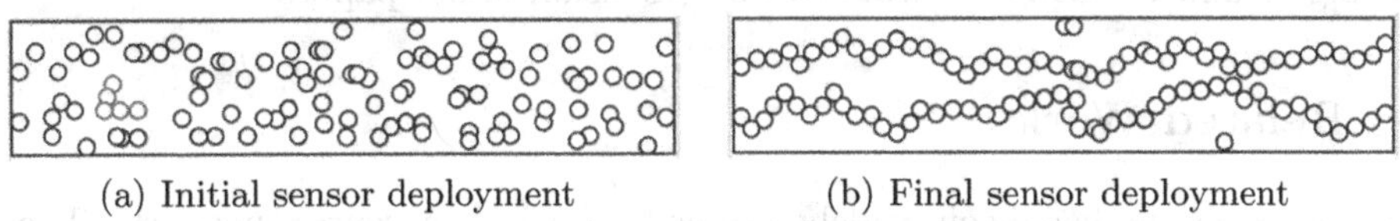

(a) Initial sensor deployment (b) Final sensor deployment

Fig. 1. Initial sensor deployment and final sensor deployment

However, mobile sensors are energy-limited since they are equipped with the batteries and it costs much more energy during the movement of sensors than the sensing of sensors. Thus, it is important to minimize the sensor movement while achieving k barrier coverage. Many algorithms [2,4,5,10,13,15,16] are proposed to form linear barriers using mobile sensors. The barrier is a line segment and mobile sensors are relocated to the line barrier to cover it. However, large redundant sensor movement are needed by mobile sensors to move to a line barrier. The work [1,12,15,17] formed a non-linear barrier energy-efficiently, which proved that the sensor movement for forming a non-linear barrier can be smaller than that for forming a line barrier. Non-linear means the barrier formed by the algorithm might not be straight but curving, as shown in Fig. 1(b). The barrier is formed by a chain of sensors whose sensing range overlap with each other and cross from the left boundary of the region to the right boundary. However, very few work studied how to form k non-linear barriers energy-efficiently, which is a challenging problem. This paper tries to propose a solution to solve this problem.

The work [1] proposed an algorithm for forming a non-linear barrier energy-efficiently, which outperformed other existing algorithms. However, this algorithm cannot be extended to the case of k-barrier coverage directly. Inspired by the work [1], we propose an energy-efficient algorithm to form k non-linear barriers based on the initial deployment of mobile sensors. In the work [1], virtual force has been proposed to pull one sensor chain to touch another sensor chain. This traditional virtual force only focuses on the euclidean distance of two sensors, which might cause part of barriers are formed vertically. We define horizontal virtual force by considering the euclidean distance and also horizontal angle. The algorithm first divides the region into several subregions and then constructs k sub-barriers from the left boundary of each subregion to the right boundary respectively by always choosing the mobile sensor chain with the largest horizontal virtual force and also flattening it and finally connects the sub-barriers in adjacent subregions together for forming k barriers in the whole region. Simulation results show that this algorithm efficiently decreases the movements of mobile sensors compared to a linear k-barrier coverage algorithm and is quite scalable.

The rest of the paper is organized as follows. Section 2 reviews some related works about barrier coverage using mobile sensors. In Sect. 3 we will establish the networks model and give some terms. Section 4 describes an algorithm of forming one sub-barrier in a subregion. In Sect. 5 we propose an algorithm of forming k barriers in the whole region. Section 6 evaluates the performance of the algorithm. In Sect. 7 we will draw a conclusion of our paper.

2 Related Work

Barrier coverage has been widely studied in wireless sensor network. The notion of k-barrier coverage was first proposed by the work [9]. The work [1–5, 7, 8, 10, 12–16, 18] proposed algorithms for achieving barrier coverage with mobile sensors, which can be divided into two kinds, centralized algorithms and distributed algorithms.

The centralized algorithms are under the assumption of all the information of region and the accurate locations of mobile sensors should be known beforehand. A central device can compute the final location of each mobile sensor so that sensors can move directly to their final location, avoiding redundant movements. The work [2] constructed k linear barriers by dividing the region into subregions and forming a baseline grid barrier and an isolation grid barrier in each subregion. A lot of redundant sensors are needed for constructing isolation grid barriers. The work [15] proposed a central algorithm to first compute the location of linear barrier and then move the sensors to the grid points of the barrier. The work [13] tried to move the sensors to the grid points while minimizing the maximum sensor movement. The work [10] proposed a polynomial-time algorithm to move the sensors to cover the barrier line while minimizing the maximum sensor movement, which can reduce the sensor movement. All the above algorithms formed linear barriers. The work [1] proposed an energy-efficient algorithm to form a non-linear barrier, which outperformed the linear barrier algorithms in the work [2, 15]. The work [3] solved the problem of moving mobile sensors to the circle barrier energy-efficiently for achieving barrier coverage. The work [17] proposed a central algorithm to form barriers with mobile sensors under both sunny and rainy day. The work [14] studied the hybrid network consisting of stationary sensors and mobile sensors and proposed an algorithm of relocating mobile sensors to improve barrier coverage by filling the gap resulted by stationary sensors.

However, the performance of the central algorithms might be limited by the central device. Some researchers studied the distributed algorithms. Mobile sensor adjusts its location according to its environment and it does not need to know all the information of other sensors. However, these algorithms might cause redundant movements of mobile sensors in practical application. The work [5] tried to solve the problem of establishing barrier coverage between two landmarks, which was inspired from the animal aggregations. The work [8] proposed a fully distributed algorithm based on virtual force to relocate the sensors from the original positions to uniformly distribute on the convex hull of the region. The work [16] presented a distributed algorithm called MobiBar to form k linear barriers. The work [12] proposed two distributed algorithms for self-adjustment of mobile sensors to form barriers based on virtual force. However, it was not aimed for energy-efficiency. The work [4] studied the sensors' movement in barrier coverage with a game theoretic approach.

3 Network Model

Assuming that there is a rectangular belt region of length L and width H, which is $L \gg H$. A set of mobile sensors are deployed randomly in this region. The sensing range of these sensors is R_s and the number of the sensors is N. The initial position of mobile sensor s_i is (x_i, y_i). Each sensor can move in all the direction. The moving distance of each sensor is the euclidean distance of its initial position and final position.

In this paper, we focus on how to form k barriers energy-efficiently using mobile sensors. K barriers are formed by k chains of sensors whose sensing range overlap with each other and cross from the left boundary of the region to the right boundary. We study how to find the sensors' final positions so that the sensors can move to the final positions for forming k barriers crossing the region while minimizing the average sensor moving distances.

Before showing the algorithm, we will define some terms below.

Definition 1. ***Mobile Sensor Chain:*** *A mobile sensor chain is a set of mobile sensors in which the sensing range of each sensor should intersect with that of another sensor in this set, which means the distance between these two mobile sensors is less than or equal to* $2 \times R_s$.

A mobile sensor chain, denoted in red, can be seen in Fig. 1(a). Note that a mobile sensor chain can have only one sensor. A barrier is formed when there is a mobile sensor chain in which there are two mobile sensors whose sensing ranges intersect the left boundary and the right boundary respectively.

Definition 2. ***Main Mobile Sensor Chain:*** *A main mobile sensor chain is a kind of mobile sensor chain in which the sensing range of one sensor intersects with the left boundary.*

We form a barrier by constructing a main mobile sensor chain from the left boundary to the right boundary of the region. We choose the mobile sensor chain with the largest horizontal virtual force to extend the main mobile sensor chain.

Now we'll define the notion of horizontal virtual force by considering the euclidean distance and also horizontal angle.

Let N represent the set of all sensors deployed in the region and N_c represent all the mobile sensors in the main mobile sensor chain. For each mobile sensor $c \in N_c$ and $v \in N - N_c$, we define horizontal virtual force $h(c, v)$ from v to c as follows:

$$h(c, v) = \frac{\alpha}{distance(c, v)} \times \cos\theta$$

$$c \in N_c, v \in N - N_c, \theta \in (0, \frac{\pi}{2})$$

In the formula, $distance(c, v)$ is the Euclidean distance between mobile sensor c and mobile sensor v.The direction of $h(c, v)$ starts from v and points to c. θ is the included angle of the horizontal line and the line of mobile sensor c and v . Note that $\theta \in (0, \frac{\pi}{2})$ and α is a scaling parameter.

For each sensor $c \in N_c$, we can calculate the maximum horizontal virtual force $H\left(c\right)$ as follows:

$$H\left(c\right) = \max_{v} h(c, v)$$

$$c \in N_c, v \in N - N_c, \theta \in (0, \frac{\pi}{2})$$

The action point is defined as the sensor $c_m \in N_c$ which satisfies that $H\left(c_m\right) = \max_{c} H(c)$, $\forall c \in N_c$. The reaction point is defined as the sensor $v_m \in N - N_c$ whose horizontal virtual force to sensor c_m is $H\left(c_m\right)$.

4 Forming One Sub-barrier

The main idea of our algorithm of forming k barriers is to first divide the region into several subregions and then construct k sub-barriers from the left boundary of each subregion to the right boundary by always choosing the mobile sensor chain with the largest horizontal virtual force and finally connect the sub-barriers in adjacent subregions for forming k barriers in the whole region.

In this section we will show the algorithm of forming a sub-barrier in one subregion.

The main idea of forming a sub-barrier can be described in three phases. First we will find out the leftmost mobile sensor chain and then pull it to left boundary and regard it as the main mobile sensor chain. Then we will compute the mobile sensor chain with the largest horizontal virtual force, and pull the mobile sensor chain towards the main mobile sensor chain. Once the main mobile sensor chain touches the right boundary, it implies that one sub-barrier is formed. If a sub-barrier isn't formed and no redundant sensors can be used, we'll pull the main mobile sensor chain straight to the right boundary of the subregion.

Before showing the detail of these three phases, we first present the flattening algorithm.

4.1 Flattening Algorithm

The flattening algorithm is used when a mobile sensor chain is selected to move to the target which may be the left boundary of the region or the main mobile sensor chain. The main idea of this flattening algorithm is that we first compute the horizontal path of this mobile sensor chain and then pull the sensors in this chain toward the target one by one by extending the horizontal path.

The detail of this algorithm is described as follows:

Algorithm 1. Flattening Algorithm

```
Input: main mobile sensor chain M, mobile sensor chain G
Output: updated main mobile sensor chain M
Compute the reaction point and action point.
if the action point is the rightmost sensor of M then
   Compute the horizontal path H starting from the reaction point.
   action point = the rightmost sensor of M
   for each mobile sensor c ∈ H
      moving mobile sensor = c
      Let moving mobile sensor move towards action point along the shortest way.
      action point = moving mobile sensor
      if the action point intersects with the mobile sensor chain then
         return M
      end if
      if moving mobile sensor's degree ≥ 2 then
         for each mobile sensor d ∈ redundant mobile sensor chain R
            moving mobile sensor = d
            Let moving mobile sensor move to action point along the shortest way.
            action point = moving mobile sensor
            if the action point intersects with the mobile sensor chain then
               return M
            end if
         end for
      end if
   end for
else
   insert the reaction point of the mobile sensor chain into the main mobile sensor chain
return M
```

First, compute the reaction point. If the target is the left boundary of the region, then the reaction point should be the sensor with the smallest x-coordinate. If the target is the main mobile sensor chain, then the reaction point should be the sensor with the largest horizontal virtual force. Let N denote all mobile sensors and N_c denote those mobile sensors in the main mobile sensor chain. For each mobile sensor c in the main mobile sensor chain and each sensor $v \in N - N_c$, compute the largest horizontal virtual force from v to c and the corresponding sensor c is action point and sensor v is reaction point. If the action point is just the rightmost sensor of the main mobile sensor chain, we'll extend the main mobile sensor chain by pulling the mobile sensor chain towards it.

Second, compute the horizontal path of this mobile sensor chain. Enumerate all possible paths starting from this reaction point by doing depth-first search and calculate the variance of Y coordinate of these paths and find the lowest path as the horizontal path of this mobile sensor chain.

Third, move the sensors in the mobile sensor chain towards the target by extending the horizontal path. We first compute the degree of the reaction point and then move the reaction point to touch the action point of the target. Then the reaction point becomes the new action point. If its degree is greater than or equal to two, it means there is at least one redundant mobile sensor chain R_G connecting the reaction point before it moves. Thus, moving R_G is preferential and we will move the sensors in R_G towards the action point one by one until the new action point intersects with the mobile sensor chain or all mobile sensors in R_G have been moved. If the new action point intersects with the mobile sensor chain, the procedure stops; If all mobile sensors in R_G have been moved, then we will continue moving those mobile sensors in the horizontal path. The procedure is repeated until it stops.

However, if the action point is not the rightmost sensor of the main mobile sensor chain, we need to insert the reaction point of the mobile sensor chain into the main mobile sensor chain.

To illustrate the algorithm more clearly, we will show a simple example. Figure 2(a) shows the initial deployment of the main mobile sensor chain and another mobile sensor chain D_G. As is shown in the figure, the rightmost mobile sensor in main mobile sensor chain is selected as the action point and the reaction point in D_G is selected as the moving mobile sensor. By traversing the horizontal path, we can move the moving mobile sensor towards action point and keep their sensing ranges just intersect at one point. After this, the moving mobile sensor will become new action point and the next mobile sensor in horizontal path will be new moving mobile sensor. In Fig. 2(b), we can find the degree of moving mobile sensor is two, which means there is a redundant mobile sensor chain touching moving mobile sensor, so we need to record this redundant mobile sensor chain, and then move the moving mobile sensor. When it comes to Fig. 2(c), since we have recorded a redundant mobile sensor chain, we have to move the redundant mobile sensor chain instead of mobile sensors in the horizontal path. For each mobile sensor in the redundant mobile sensor chain, we will move it towards the action point and then become the new action point until all mobile sensors are added to the main mobile sensor chain. In Fig. 2(d), the redundant mobile sensor chain has been moved to the main mobile sensor chain. Note that adding the redundant mobile sensor chain increases the horizontal length of the main sensor chain. Next, we keep moving the mobile sensors in horizontal path until there is another redundant mobile sensor chain or no mobile sensors in the horizontal path. Figure 2(e) shows the result of the flattening algorithm. We can see the main mobile sensor chain merges the other mobile sensor chain and extends in horizontal direction.

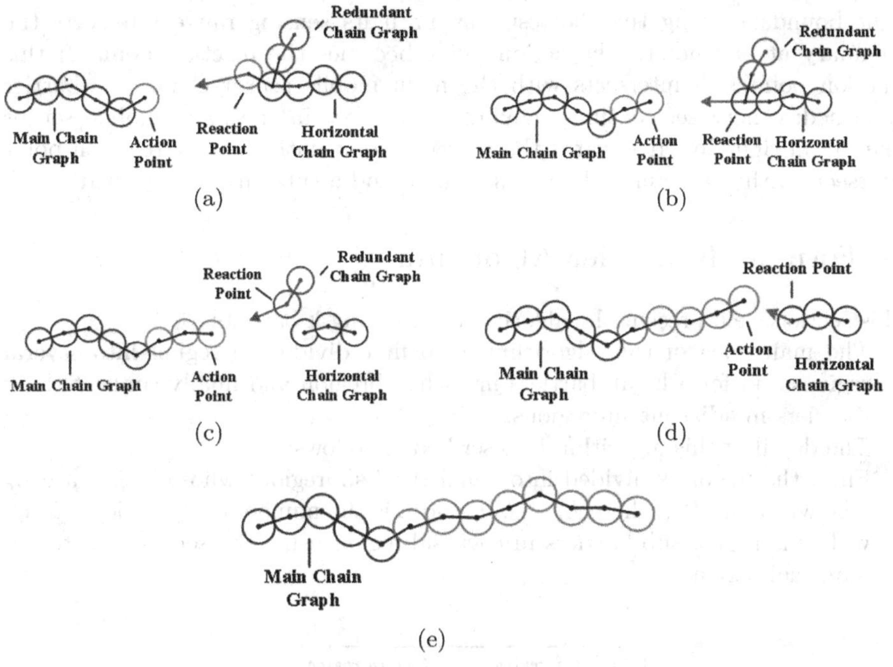

Fig. 2. An example of flattening algorithm

4.2 The Algorithm of Forming One Sub-barrier

Now we'll show the whole algorithm of forming one sub-barrier. The algorithm is divided into three phases: Left-Fix Phase, Extending Phase and Right-Fix Phase.

In the Left-Fix Phase, we will identify the main mobile sensor chain in the subregion. We find out the leftmost mobile sensor chain, which is the closest mobile sensor chain L_G to the left boundary of the subregion. Next we will move L_G to the left boundary, making the leftmost mobile sensor in L_G touching the left boundary and flattening it. In the end, we regard L_G as the main mobile sensor chain.

In the Extending Phase, we try to extend the main mobile sensor chain by moving other mobile sensor chains towards it. We will first calculate the reaction point and the action point, where the reaction point is the sensor with the largest horizontal virtual force. Move the mobile sensor chain containing reaction point to the main mobile sensor chain and also flatten it. We continue iterating this phase until a barrier is formed or no redundant sensor can be selected. The sub-barrier is formed if the rightmost sensor in the main mobile sensor chain touches the right boundary of the subregion. If no redundant sensor can be selected, we will go to the Right-Fix phase.

In the Right-Fix phase, we will pull the main mobile sensor chain towards the right boundary of the subregion. We first move the action point to the right boundary along the shortest way until its sensing range intersects the boundary at one point. The action point becomes the reaction point. If this reaction point still intersects with the main mobile sensor chain, the barrier is formed; otherwise, continue moving the sensors in the main mobile sensor chain from right to left towards the reaction point until the new reaction point intersects with the main mobile sensor chain and a sub-barrier is formed.

5 Forming K-Barrier Algorithm

This section we'll present the algorithm of forming k barriers.

The main idea of this algorithm is to first divide the region into several subregions and form k sub-barriers in each subregion and finally connect the k sub-barriers in adjacent subregions.

The detail of this algorithm is described as follows:

First, the region is divided into equal-sized subregions whose length are L_r and the width are W, where $L_r = L/n$ and n is the number of subregions. Then we will construct k sub-barriers in each subregion using the sensors located in the same subregion.

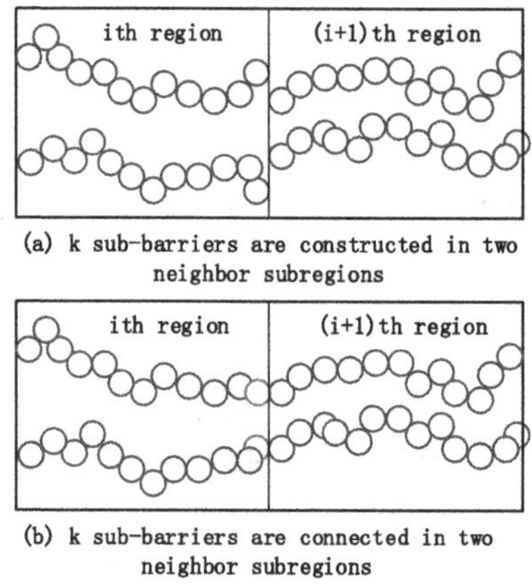
ith region
(i+1)th region
(a) k sub-barriers are constructed in two neighbor subregions
ith region
(i+1)th region
(b) k sub-barriers are connected in two neighbor subregions

Fig. 3. Connecting two sub-barriers in two adjacent subregion

Second, form k sub-barriers in each region independently by running the algorithm of forming one sub-barrier k times. The number of sensors constructing one barrier is limited to be N_i/k, avoiding that there is not enough sensor to construct the kth sub-barrier, where N_i is the number of sensors deployed in ith subregion. After completing k sub-barriers in each subregion, it can be observed that these sub-barriers in two adjacent subregions may be not connected, as shown in Fig. 3(a).

Third, we connect the k sub-barriers in adjacent subregions. For simplicity, k sub-barriers in one subregion is called the left k sub-barriers while k sub-barriers in its right neighbor subregion is called the right k sub-barriers. The left or right k sub-barriers are numbered increasingly by their locations on the right or left boundary of their subregion respectively. Each left sub-barrier connects with the same number of the right sub-barrier by pulling the sensors in left sub-barriers towards the right sub-barriers. For example, sensors denoted in red are moved to connect sub-barriers in adjacent subregions, as shown in Fig. 3(b).

Finally, k barriers are formed in the whole region. The time complexity of the algorithm is $O(n^2)$.

6 Simulation Results

We simulate our proposed algorithm using Eclipse, compared with one existing algorithm CBIGB in the work [2]. The CBIGB algorithm constructs k barriers by dividing the region into equal-sized subregions and forming a baseline grid barrier and an isolation grid barrier in each subregion. The result obtained are the average of running the experiments 100 times.

Sensors are deployed in a 50 m×8 m belt region randomly. Each subregion is 25 m. The sensing range of sensors is 0.5 m. The number of sensors varies from 130 to 155 with a step 5. Figure 4 shows that the average moving distance decreases as the number of sensors increases. The average moving distance obtained by our algorithm decreases from 2.1 m to 1.6 m when the number of sensors increases from 130 to 155. The reason is that nearer sensor can be chosen to form barriers when more sensors are deployed in the region. The average moving distance by our proposed algorithm is better than that by CBIGB algorithm. It implies that our algorithm is more energy-efficient. Thus it can prolong the lifetime of the mobile sensor network.

Figure 5 shows that the average moving distance resulted by our proposed algorithm is smaller than that by CBIGB algorithm when the sensor density is 0.35. The length of the region varies from 50 m to 90 m with a step 10 m and the width is 8 m. The sensing range of sensors is 0.5 m. The average moving distance

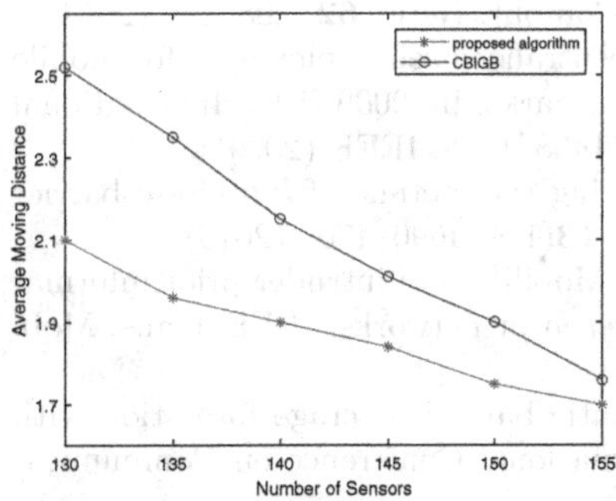

Fig. 4. Average moving distance vs number of sensors

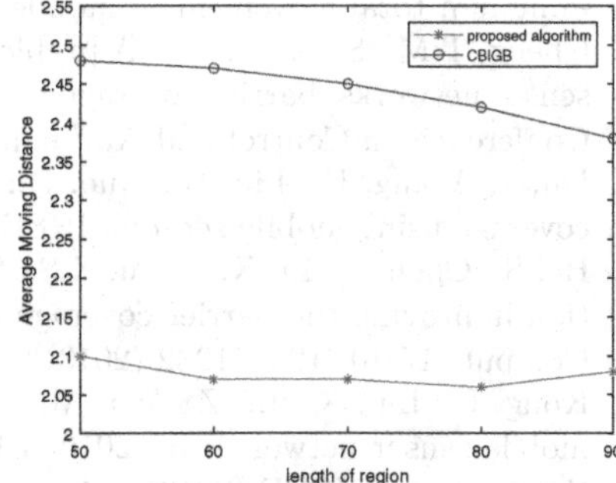

Fig. 5. Average moving distance vs length of region

by our algorithm is 2.1 m when the length of region is 50 m, while the average moving distance is 2.08 m when the length of region is 90 m. The average moving distance obtained by our algorithm is almost the same as the length of region increases. It implies that our algorithm is scalable and can be applied to large scale sensor networks.

7 Conclusion

In this paper, we propose an algorithm to form k non-linear barriers in mobile sensor network. We define horizontal virtual force by considering the euclidean distance and also horizontal angle and then propose an energy-efficient algorithm to form k non-linear barriers. Simulation results show that this algorithm efficiently decreases the movements of mobile sensors compared to a linear barrier algorithm and can be applicable to large scale sensor networks. In the future, we will design a distributed algorithm for achieving k-barrier coverage using horizontal virtual force.

Acknowledgment. This work is supported by National Natural Science Foundation of China (Grant No. 61702198 and 61772005). The corresponding author is Shuangjuan Li.

References

1. Baheti, A., Gupta, A.: Non-linear barrier coverage using mobile wireless sensors. In: 2017 IEEE Symposium on Computers and Communications (ISCC), pp. 804–809. IEEE (2017)
2. Ban, D., Jiang, J., Yang, W., Dou, W., Yi, H.: Strong k-barrier coverage with mobile sensors. In: Proceedings of the 6th International Wireless Communications and Mobile Computing Conference, pp. 68–72. ACM (2010)
3. Bhattacharya, B., Burmester, M., Hu, Y., Kranakis, E., Shi, Q., Wiese, A.: Optimal movement of mobile sensors for barrier coverage of a planar region. Theoret. Comput. Sci. **410**(52), 5515–5528 (2009)
4. Cheng, C.F., Wu, T.Y., Liao, H.C.: A density-barrier construction algorithm with minimum total movement in mobile WSNs. Comput. Netw. **62**, 208–220 (2014)
5. Cheng, T.M., Savkin, A.V.: A problem of decentralized self-deployment for mobile sensor networks: barrier coverage between landmarks. In: 2009 IEEE International Conference on Control and Automation, pp. 1438–1442. IEEE (2009)
6. Du, J., Wang, K., Liu, H., Guo, D.: Maximizing the lifetime of k-discrete barrier coverage using mobile sensors. IEEE Sens. J. **13**(12), 4690–4701 (2013)
7. He, S., Chen, J., Li, X., Shen, X.S., Sun, Y.: Mobility and intruder prior information improving the barrier coverage of sparse sensor networks. IEEE Trans. Mob. Comput. **13**(6), 1268–1282 (2013)
8. Kong, L., Liu, X., Li, Z., Wu, M.Y.: Automatic barrier coverage formation with mobile sensor networks. In: 2010 IEEE International Conference on Communications, pp. 1–5. IEEE (2010)
9. Kumar, S., Lai, T.H., Arora, A.: Barrier coverage with wireless sensors. In: Proceedings of the 11th Annual International Conference on Mobile Computing and Networking, pp. 284–298. ACM (2005)

10. Li, S., Shen, H.: Minimizing the maximum sensor movement for barrier coverage in the plane. In: 2015 IEEE Conference on Computer Communications (INFOCOM), pp. 244–252. IEEE (2015)
11. Qiu, C., Shen, H., Chen, K.: An energy-efficient and distributed cooperation mechanism for k-coverage hole detection and healing in WSNs. IEEE Trans. Mob. Comput. **17**(6), 1247–1259 (2018)
12. Rout, M., Roy, R.: Self-deployment of randomly scattered mobile sensors to achieve barrier coverage. IEEE Sens. J. **16**(18), 6819–6820 (2016)
13. Saipulla, A., Liu, B., Xing, G., Fu, X., Wang, J.: Barrier coverage with sensors of limited mobility. In: Proceedings of the Eleventh ACM International Symposium on Mobile Ad Hoc Networking and Computing, pp. 201–210. ACM (2010)
14. Saipulla, A., Westphal, C., Liu, B., Wang, J.: Barrier coverage with line-based deployed mobile sensors. Ad Hoc Netw. **11**(4), 1381–1391 (2013)
15. Shen, C., Cheng, W., Liao, X., Peng, S.: Barrier coverage with mobile sensors. In: 2008 International Symposium on Parallel Architectures, Algorithms, and Networks (i-span 2008), pp. 99–104. IEEE (2008)
16. Silvestri, S.: MobiBar: barrier coverage with mobile sensors. In: 2011 IEEE Global Telecommunications Conference-GLOBECOM 2011, pp. 1–6. IEEE (2011)
17. Tian, J., Liang, X., Wang, G.: Deployment and reallocation in mobile survivability-heterogeneous wireless sensor networks for barrier coverage. Ad Hoc Netw. **36**, 321–331 (2016)
18. Yang, G., Zhou, W., Qiao, D.: Defending against barrier intrusions with mobile sensors. In: International Conference on Wireless Algorithms, Systems and Applications (WASA 2007), pp. 113–120. IEEE (2007)

Interrupt Responsive Spinlock Mechanism Based on MCS for Multi-core RTOS

Jingqiu Zheng(✉), Jiali Bian, and Jian Kuang

Beijing Key Laboratory of Intelligent Telecommunication Software and Multimedia, Beijing University of Posts and Telecommunications, Beijing 100876, China
{niqiu1683,jlbian,jkuang}@bupt.edu.cn

Abstract. The kernel spinlock has a non-negligible influence on the real-time performance of the multi-core RTOS. In order to protect mutual exclusive kernel data accessed in both task context and interrupt context by CPU-cores, the RTOS kernel uses existing FIFO spinlock algorithm as kernel spinlock must disable interrupt before acquiring lock, which will increase the interrupt response latency in the case of fierce competition for spinlock. In this work, the Interrupt Responsive Spinlock (IRS) mechanism based on MCS algorithm allows the CPU-cores to respond to interrupt during spin waiting, disable interrupt while holding spinlock, therefore the system can respond to interrupts in time without damaging OS kernel critical section. Besides, MCS-IRS maintains the compatibility with MCS semantics so that is transparent to the caller. Experiments show that MCS-IRS can eliminate the impact of spinlock fierce contention on Worst-Case Interrupt Response Latency, and has better multi-core scalability than MCS on Worst-Case Interrupt Disable Time, which can improve the real-time performance of multi-core RTOS.

Keywords: Spinlock · Multi-core · RTOS · Interrupt response

1 Introduction

With the popularity of multi-core processors in the field of real-time embedded systems, the Real-Time Operating System (RTOS) for multi-core processors has become a research hotspot in recent years [1, 2]. As an indispensable mechanism in multi-core operating system, kernel spinlock provides the only way to protect operating system kernel data (such as Task Control Block) shared between CPU-cores [3], which has a non-negligible impact on the real-time performance of multi-core RTOS [4].

The simplest spinlock algorithm (Naive Spinlock) makes per CPU-core busy waiting for a shared variable in memory, and determines which CPU-core first acquires spinlock through bus arbitration. Unordered competition lacks fairness, and there is a possibility that a certain CPU-core will not acquire spinlock for a long time, which is unacceptable for real-time system. Therefore, multi-core RTOS often adopts spinlock algorithms with fairness such as TKT, MCS and CLH [5, 6]. However, these spinlock algorithms have been proposed as a single mechanism, without considering the impact on other parts of RTOS. Some research works proposed optimized spinlock scheme considering the factor

H. Shen and Y. Sang (Eds.): PAAP 2019, CCIS 1163, pp. 24–34, 2020.
https://doi.org/10.1007/978-981-15-2767-8_3

of task scheduling with application knowledge, so that the system real-time performance can be improved [7, 8].

In addition to the task scheduling latency, the system real-time performance also depends on the interrupt response latency. The operating system must ensure that the kernel data will not accessed concurrently, not only by other CPU-cores, but also by the interrupt of the same core. Therefore, before acquiring the spinlock, it is necessary to disable interrupt of the CPU-core. This will increase the Worst-Case Interrupt Response Latency (WCIRL) if the interrupt is allocated to the inappropriate CPU-core. On the other hand, with the number of CPU-cores growing, the Worst-Case Interrupt Disable Time (WCIDT) will increase linearly when the spinlock contention is fierce [9]. In short, the existing kernel spinlock mechanism in RTOS may reduce the real-time performance to respond interrupts.

In this work, after analyzing the problem of spinlock affecting the interrupt response latency, we proposes an Interrupt Responsive Spinlock (IRS) mechanism that can respond to the interrupt in time, and implements the MCS-IRS lock based on the MCS algorithm. MCS-IRS lock allows the CPU-core is able to respond to the interrupts during the spin waiting, disable interrupt to protect kernel critical section while holding the spinlock. In addition, the new mechanism is compatible with existing spinlock interface by guaranteeing the CPU-core can rejoin the spinlock waiting queue after handling the interrupt. The comparison experiment proves that the MCS-IRS spinlock mechanism can mitigate the impact of the spinlock fierce contention on the WCIRL of RTOS and has better multi-core scalability of WCIDT under the premise of ensuring the correct execution of the OS kernel critical section code.

The rest of this paper is organized as follows. In Sect. 2 we discuss related works and summarize the relevant methods for implementing spinlock preemption in the existing research. Section 3 analyses the real-time performance of existing OS kernel spinlock mechanism and proposes the IRS mechanism. Section 4 describes how to implement MCS-IRS lock based on MCS lock. Experimental results for a comparison between IRS-MCS and MCS are reported in Sect. 5. Section 6 gives the conclusion.

2 Related Work

In order to alleviate the impact of the FIFO spinlock on the interrupt response latency, one way is to allow the hardware to interrupt the CPU-core that is busy waiting for the spinlock. However, this CPU-core may acquire spinlock during the response to the interrupt but cannot release the spinlock in time, thereby delaying other CPU-core that waiting for the spinlock. This problem is similar to the anti-pattern problem proposed in [10], where a spinlock holder thread running a long critical section is scheduled by OS, so that all its successors in the queue are affected. Whether it is scheduled or interrupted, it can be defined as the problem that lock holder is preempted.

One solution is upgrading the spinlock to a blocking lock when preemption occurs [10] to avoid the spinlock being acquired by the preempted task. In [11, 12], Sara Afshar proposes a Flexible Spinlock Model based on the task priority, allowing high priority tasks to seize and block low-priority spin tasks. However, this method of upgrading the spinlock requires support of the operating system and cannot be used as a kernel spinlock to protect the critical section of the OS kernel.

Another solution is to allow the successor nodes in the waiting queue to perceive whether the lock holder is preempted and seize the spinlock. Preemption Adaptive Spinlock proposed in [13] uses timestamps as heuristics into queue-based lock such as MCS and CLH, to perceive whether the lock holder is deprived of the CPU-core usage rights, so that the successor node can preempt the spinlock when timeout. In addition, this approach maintains the state transitions of spinlock to identify whether the lock is preempted. To solve LWP problem and LHP problem in VMM scheduling [14], Preemptable Ticket Spinlock algorithm is proposed in [15], which combining the ticket spinlock and naive spinlock. The timeout method was also used to perceive whether the lock holder is preempted. Note that both of the above schemes use timeout approach to perceive preemption, which need to determine the timeout parameter by knowing the duration of the critical section, so they are not suitable approach to solve the problem proposed in this paper, because it will still cause waste of CPU time if the timeout parameter is set too large.

In summary, it can be seen that the existing spinlock mechanism cannot satisfy the demand proposed in this paper well, where the CPU-core can respond to the interrupt in time during spin waiting, but does not delay other CPU-cores that are waiting for the spinlock.

3 IRS Mechanism

3.1 Real-Time Analysis

Although the real-time analysis of RTOS using Worst-case Execution Time (WCET) in multi-core environment becomes more and more complicated [16], the Worst-Case Response Time (WCRT) [17] is still an valuable metrics to evaluate the real-time performance of RTOS, which reflects the degree of rapid sensitivity of the system to respond to external event input. WCRT is affected by many factors including task scheduling latency and interrupt response latency, where the interrupt response latency is the time between the occurrence of an interrupt and the execution of the first ISR instruction, which is affected by the interrupt disable time. Since it is difficult to determine when an interrupt occurs in the real world, the WCIDT is usually used instead of WCIRL as a metrics of the real-time performance of the RTOS.

In multi-core environment, the operating system must first disable the interrupt and then acquire the spinlock to ensure the mutual exclusion of the kernel data that may accessed in the task context and interrupt context. This causes the WCIDT (defined as Ti_{max}) to be affected by the Maximum Spin Time (MST) of the spinlock. In order to avoid the starvation problem caused by the disordered contention of spinlocks by each CPU-core, spinlock algorithm with fairness is used to improve the predictability of the RTOS kernel. Each CPU-core acquires the spinlock in FIFO order, so the MST is equal to the number of CPU-cores (defined as N_c) multiplied by the MST (defined as Ts_{max}), as shown in

$$Ti_{max} = N_c * Ts_{max} \tag{1}$$

In the actual RTOS, Ts_{max} is related to the kernel critical section size, and there is an upper bound for it, thus the influencing factor is only the CPU-core number N_c Therefore, it can be concluded that the existing queue-based spinlock algorithm will increase the WCIDT linearly with the increase of CPU-cores number when the spinlock contention is fierce, resulting in an increase in the interrupt response latency. In short, the existing spinlock mechanism implemented in RTOS kernel will affect the WCRT of the entire system.

3.2 Interrupt Responsive Spinlock

The solution to the above problem is analyzed as follows: Firstly, it can be found for all spinlock algorithm that the process of acquiring spinlock can be divided into two phases: the doorway section and the waiting section [18]. The doorway section consists of a limited number of steps to modify the spinlock state, usually using CAS (Compare and Swap) operation to ensure the atomicity of the lock state modification. The waiting section includes an infinite number of spin waiting operations.

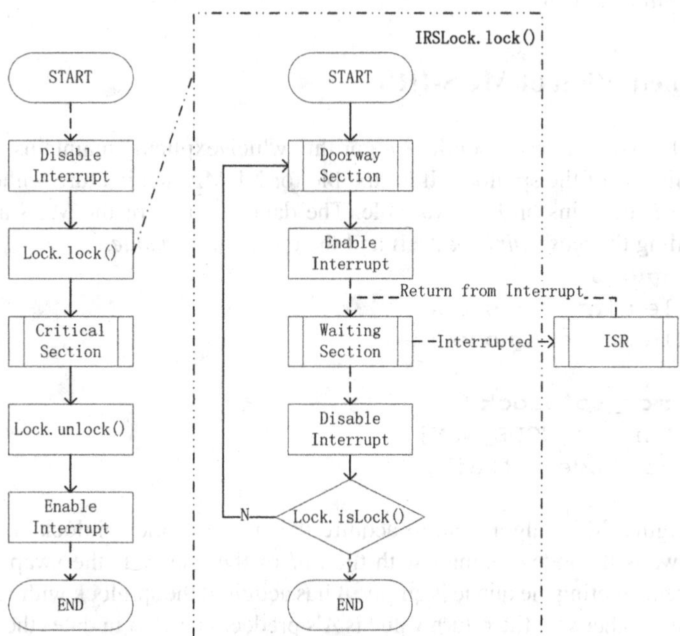

Fig. 1. The locking and unlocking process of IRS mechanism. (The dashed line indicates that the process is possible to be interrupted. The solid line indicates that the process is impossible to be interrupted)

Secondly, as shown in the left side of Fig. 1, in order to guarantee the correctness of accessing the kernel mutual resource shared between the CPU-cores, the existing kernel spinlock mechanism disables interrupt before LOCK operation, then enters critical section, and finally enables interrupt after UNLOCK operation. Careful analysis of this process, only the lock holder who actually executes the critical section code need to disable interrupt. Other CPU-cores in wait section can make use of these CPU time, which are destined to be wasted, to handle interrupt events which have higher priority than tasks in RTOS.

Based on the above analysis, we propose the Interrupt Responsive Spinlock mechanism to spin wait with interrupt enabled and disable interrupt while executing critical section code. The right part of Fig. 1 shows the process of the IRS LOCK operation which is transparent to the kernel developer. The key point of the IRS mechanism is to allow the spinlock to enable interrupt before entering the waiting section, and to disable interrupt again before entering the critical section. When an interrupt occurs, the CPU-core in waiting section can enter Interrupt Service Routine (ISR) and return from interrupt to the waiting section after the interrupt service ends.

It is noted that it is still possible to be interrupted while exiting the waiting section to enter the critical section. So in order to ensure the correctness of the spinlock itself, it is necessary to test the state of the spinlock after disabling interrupt. If the spinlock is released because of the interrupt, it needs to go back to the doorway section and try to acquire the spinlock again.

4 Implementation of MCS-IRS

The MCS [5] is a queue-based spinlock algorithm which explicitly maintains a queue to ensure the fairness of the spinlock. It is suitable for NUMA architecture without cache because each node spins on local variable. The data structure of the MCS are shown below, including the *mcs_spinlock* itself and the queue node *qnode*.

```
struct qnode {
volatile uint32_t status;
volatile struct qnode *next;
}
struct mcs_spinlock {
qnode_t nodes[NODE_NUM];
volatile qnode_t *tail;
}
```

In the original MCS algorithm, to acquire the spinlock, the spinlock contender *A* atomically swaps its node's pointer with the *tail* of the queue. If the swap operation returns *null* representing the queue is empty, *A* has acquired the spinlock without through waiting section; otherwise the return value is *A*'s predecessor *B*. *A* updates the *next* field of *B*'s node to point to itself, and spins on the *status* field of its own node until *B* explicitly modifies the *status* from *waiting* to *available*. All above steps are doorway section except that the node waiting on the *status* field is waiting section.

To release the lock, *A* reads its next pointer to find a successor node. If there is no successor node, *A* atomically updates the queue's *tail* pointer to *null*.

4.1 State Transitions of MCS-IRS

We extend the set of states based on the MCS algorithm to implement the IRS mechanism. These states represent the different stages of acquiring and releasing spinlock. Figure 2 shows the state transitions of the MCS-IRS spinlock node.

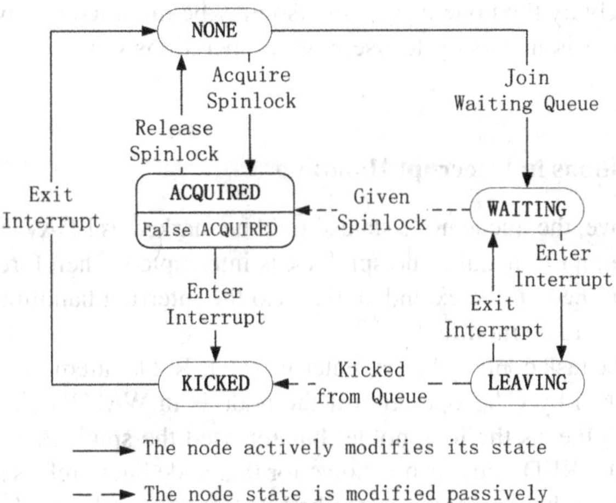

Fig. 2. State transitions for MCS-IRS queue nodes

NONE is the initial state of the queue node. In the case that the spinlock is available, the first applicant can change its node state from NONE to ACQUIRED directly after doorway section and acquire the spinlock without entering waiting section. After exiting the critical section, the lock holder releases spinlock and changes its node state from ACQUIRED to NONE.

In the case that the spinlock is already locked, the CPU-core puts its node into linked queue tail and modifies its node state from NONE to WAITING. After completing these doorway section operations, the CPU-core enters waiting section with interrupt enabled, which means that there are two execution paths:

Under normal progress, the CPU-core waits for the predecessor node to release the spinlock until its node state is modified from WAITING to ACQUIRED by predecessor node. Note that it is still possible to be interrupted between exiting waiting section loop and disabling interrupt again, called as False ACQUIRED state. The solution is that the node will actively release the spinlock and modify its node state to KICKED if the node state is ACQUIRED in the interrupt context. So it is necessary to check whether the node status is ACQUIRED after exiting from waiting section and disabling interrupt. If not, the node needs to go back to the initial state NONE and try to acquire the spinlock again.

Another execution path under the WAITING state is to be interrupted while spin waiting. The node state is modified to LEAVING while entering the interrupt context. Before exiting the interrupt, the LEAVING state is changed to WAITING representing this node is attempting to back to the wait queue in original order. However, if during the interrupt handling, the lock holder (predecessor node) hands over spinlock to this node but finds that this node is in the LEAVING state, it will skip this node and pass the spinlock to the successor node of this node. Then this node state is passively marked as KICKED, which means this node was "kicked" out of the waiting queue. This node also need retry to acquire the spinlock from NONE state.

Note that under the WAIRING and LEAVING states, the node state will not only be modified actively by the node itself, but also may be modified passively by the lock holder. Therefore, it is necessary to use atomic operations CAS to modify these two states.

4.2 State Transitions in Interrupt Handling

As mentioned above, the queue node state should be marked as LEAVING from WAITING when the attempt to acquire the spinlock is interrupted. Therefore, not only does the MCS algorithm need to be extended, but also the interrupt handling mechanism of the OS kernel needs to be modified.

After saving the task context, before entering the ISR, OS attempts to swap the node state with LEAVING by CAS operation if the node is in WAITING state. Once CAS return false, which means the lock holder has released the spinlock and modified this node state to ACQUIRED, there is no choice for this node but to release the spinlock to its successor node, so that the interrupt can be handled while other node in queue won't be delayed.

After returning from ISR, before resuming the task context, OS attempts to modify the node state from LEAVING back to WAITING by CAS operation too. If failed, which means this node is kicked from the waiting queue, this node has to retry to acquire the spinlock from NONE state after returning to the spinlock context.

5 Experiment Analysis

5.1 Design of Experiments

In order to eliminate the influence of other factors in the operating system on the interrupt disable time and interrupt response latency, this paper builds the experiments environment on the NXP iMX6Q hardware development board with 4 cores 799 MHz ARM Cortex-A9MP, 2 GB of RAM. Except the necessary hardware and stack initialization procedures, the test program is compiled by the GNU GCC compiler and runs directly on the bare board.

In this paper, two sets of experiments are designed to compare the effects of the MCS-IRS and MCS on the WCIDT and the WCIRL.

Experiment I

In the first experiment, we simulate the scenario where the operating system enters the kernel critical section to access the mutual exclusive resources. First, disable the interrupt and then acquire the spinlock. After exiting the critical section, the spinlock is released and the interrupt is enabled. In the experiment, each CPU-core loops 1000 times to compete for acquiring spinlock, and the critical section duration parameter is set to 200 μs to create a scene in which CPU-cores queue for the spinlock. Finally, the WCIDT of each CPU-core is measured in this experiment.

Experiment II

In the second experiment, on the basis of the spinlock queuing scenario, interrupt events is added to simulate the scenario in which the operating system responds to the interrupt. We use EPIT (Enhanced Periodic Interrupt Timer) as the interrupt source to generate external interrupts periodically at a frequency of 100 Hz. Four CPU-cores have the same priority to respond to the interrupt. Finally, which CPU-core responds to the interrupt is determined by the hardware GIC (Generic Interrupt Controller).

The EPIT counter generates an interrupt when the count value is decremented to zero and reloads the initial value T_0 to start the next round countdown. In the interrupt service routine, the current value T_1 of the EPIT counter is read, so the difference between T_0 and T_1 is the interrupt response latency.

In order to simulate critical sections of different sizes, the fixed critical section duration is not set in Experiment II. Instead, the upper bound of the critical section duration is set in each round of testing, and the test program randomly generates critical section of different duration within this upper bound range. We measure the WCIRL of system in Experiment II.

5.2 Worst-Case Interrupt Disable Time

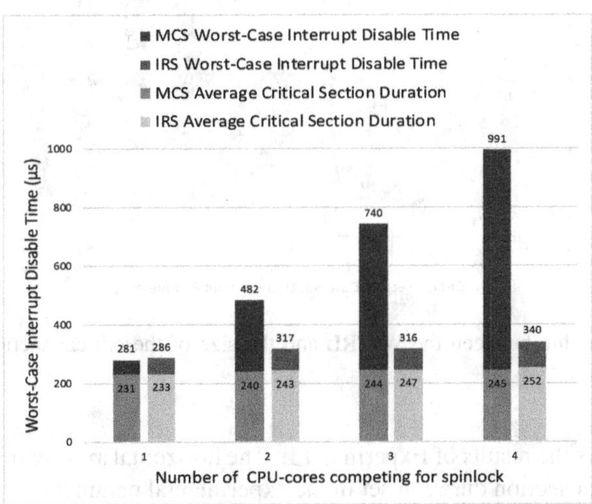

Fig. 3. The relationship between the WCIDT and the length of the spinlock queue (Color figure online)

Figure 3 shows the results of Experiment I. The horizontal axis of the graph represents the number of CPU-cores participating in the spinlock competition, and the vertical axis represents the WCIDT and the average critical section duration. Blue (shown on left-hand) column represents MCS, red (shown on right-hand) column represents MCS-IRS, and the light-colored portion of the column in histogram represents the actual measured average critical section duration.

It can be seen that when MCS lock is used, the WCIDT increases linearly with the increase of the queue length of the spinlock, and the numerical relationship is in accordance with the conclusion derived from the (1) in Sect. 3.1. While the MCS-IRS is used, regardless of the spin queue length, the WCIDT is only related to the critical section duration, because the IRS mechanism allows the CPU-core to respond to interrupt in time during spin waiting, disabling interrupt only when the spinlock is actually acquired.

The experiment results show that MCS-IRS lock has better multi-core scalability on WCIDT than MCS lock, which means better real-time performance.

5.3 Worst-Case Interrupt Response Latency

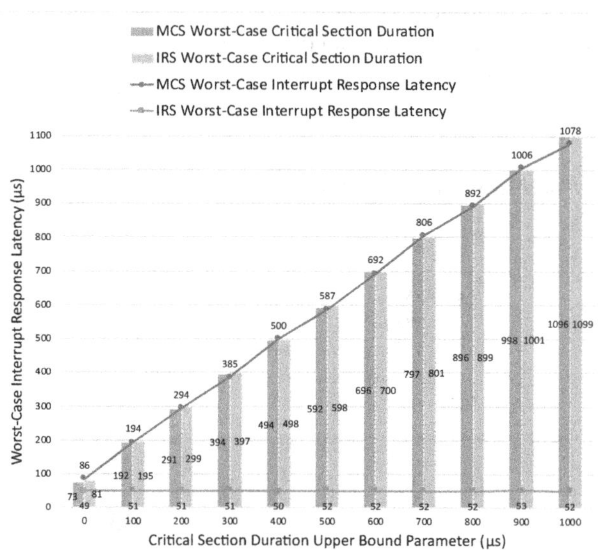

Fig. 4. The relationship between the WCIRL and the size of the critical section (Color figure online)

Figure 4 shows the results of Experiment II. The horizontal axis represents the upper limit of the critical section duration set in the experimental parameters, and the vertical axis represents the WCIRL (represented by line graph) and the actual measured worst-case critical section duration (represented by histogram). The blue (shown on left-hand) and red (shown on right-hand) histogram shows the worst-case critical section duration measured while using the MCS lock and the MCS-IRS lock respectively, and it can be found that both of them increase as the critical section duration upper bound parameter increases.

Focus on the WCIRL represented by the line graph. The blue round dot line represents MCS lock, and the red square dot line represents MCS-IRS lock. It can be seen that when MCS lock is used, the WCIRL will increase linearly with the increase of the critical section duration; when the MCS-IRS lock is used, the WCIRL is independent of the critical section duration. This is because the IRS mechanism can respond to interrupts in time during the spin waiting, while the MCS disable the interrupt response of all CPU-cores when all CPU-cores are waiting in queue. Only after the lock holder releases the spinlock, the interrupt can be responded. This results in a positive correlation between WCIRL and the critical section duration.

The experiment results show that the MCS-IRS can still respond to the interrupt in time when the spinlock contention is fierce, without the fluctuation of the interrupt response latency due to the size of the critical section. This feature is suitable to be applied in a multi-core system that is prone to spinlock contention due to a small number of CPU-cores, and can reduce the impact of spinlock contention on the interrupt response latency.

6 Conclusion

In this paper, we analyze the following problem: the existing spinlock mechanism applied in the multi-core RTOS will affects the real-time performance of the interrupt response. To solve this problem, The IRS mechanism is proposed to allow the CPU-core to respond to the interrupt during the spin waiting and disable the interrupt during the lock holding. Finally, The MCS-IRS lock are implemented on the basis of the MCS algorithm in this work.

Experimental comparison shows that MCS-IRS lock has better real-time performance than MCS, thanks to IRS mechanism which has better multi-core scalability on WCIDT, and can reduce the impact of spinlock contention on WCIRL. Furthermore, MCS-IRS lock is transparent to the caller.

As future work, it is considered to implement the IRS mechanism based on other spinlock algorithms to avoid the disadvantage of the MCS algorithm which has too many locking and unlocking steps. Besides, how to reduce the loss of the fairness due to the introduction of the IRS mechanism is the next problem to be solved.

References

1. Chen, G., Guan, N., Lü, M.S., Wang, Y.: State-of-the-art survey of real-time multicore system. Ruan Jian Xue Bao/J. Softw. **29**, 2152–2176 (2018). https://doi.org/10.13328/j.cnki.jos.005580. (in Chinese)
2. Kuo, T.W., Chen, J.J., Chang, Y.H., Hsiu, P.C.: Real-time computing and the evolution of embedded system designs. In: Proceedings of Real-Time Systems Symposium, pp. 1–12. IEEE (2019). https://doi.org/10.1109/rtss.2018.00011
3. Lochmann, A., Borghorst, H.: LockDoc : trace-based analysis of locking in the Linux kernel. In: EuroSys 2019 (2019). https://doi.org/10.1145/3302424.3303948
4. Dinh, S., Li, J., Agrawal, K., Gill, C., Lu, C.: Blocking analysis for spin locks in real-time parallel tasks. IEEE Trans. Parallel Distrib. Syst. **29**, 789–802 (2018). https://doi.org/10.1109/TPDS.2017.2777454

5. Mellor-Crummey, J.M., Scott, M.L.: Algorithms for scalable synchronization on shared-memory multiprocessors. ACM Trans. Comput. Syst. (TOCS) 21–65. (1991). https://doi.org/10.1145/103727.103729
6. Magnusson, P., Landin, A., Hagersten, E.: Queue locks on cache coherent multiprocessors. In: Proceedings of International Conference on Parallel Processing, pp. 165–171 (1994). https://doi.org/10.1109/ipps.1994.288305
7. Zhang, D., et al.: Efficient implementation of application-aware spinlock control in MPSoCs. Int. J. Embed. Real-Time Commun. Syst. **4**, 64–84 (2013). https://doi.org/10.4018/jertcs.2013010104
8. Block, A., Leontyev, H., Brandenburg, B.B., Anderson, J.H.: A flexible real-time locking protocol for multiprocessors. In: Proceedings of 13th IEEE International Conference on Embedded and Real-Time Computing Systems and Applications, RTCSA 2007, pp. 47–56 (2007). https://doi.org/10.1109/rtcsa.2007.8
9. Cui, Y., Wang, Y., Chen, Y., Shi, Y.: Requester-based spin lock: a scalable and energy efficient locking scheme on multicore systems. IEEE Trans. Comput. **64**, 166–179 (2015). https://doi.org/10.1109/TC.2013.196
10. Marotta, R., Tiriticco, D., Di Sanzo, P., Pellegrini, A., Quaglia, F.: Mutable locks: combining the best of spin and sleep locks. arXiv preprint arXiv:1906.00490 (2019)
11. Afshar, S., Behnam, M., Bril, R.J., Nolte, T.: Flexible spin-lock model for resource sharing in multiprocessor real-time systems. In: Proceedings of the 9th IEEE International Symposium on Industrial Embedded Systems, SIES 2014, pp. 41–51 (2014). https://doi.org/10.1109/sies.2014.6871185
12. Afshar, S., Behnam, M., Bril, R.J., Nolte, T.: An optimal spin-lock priority assignment algorithm for real-time multi-core systems. In: RTCSA 2017 - 23rd IEEE International Conference on Embedded and Real-Time Computing Systems and Applications (2017). https://doi.org/10.1109/rtcsa.2017.8046310
13. He, B., Scherer, W.N., Scott, M.L.: Preemption adaptivity in time-published queue-based spin locks. In: Bader, D.A., Parashar, M., Sridhar, V., Prasanna, V.K. (eds.) HiPC 2005. LNCS, vol. 3769, pp. 7–18. Springer, Heidelberg (2005). https://doi.org/10.1007/11602569_6
14. Teabe, B., Nitu, V., Tchana, A., Hagimont, D.: The lock holder and the lock waiter pre-emption problems: nip them in the bud using informed spinlocks (I-Spinlock). In: Proceedings of 12th European Conference on Computer Systems, EuroSys 2017 (2017). https://doi.org/10.1145/3064176.3064180
15. Ouyang, J., Lange, J.R.: Preemptable ticket spinlocks. ACM SIGPLAN Not. **48**, 191 (2013). https://doi.org/10.1145/2517326.2451549
16. Wilhelm, R., et al.: The worst-case execution-time problem-overview of methods and survey of tools. Trans. Embed. Comput. Syst. **7**, 1–47 (2008). https://doi.org/10.1145/1347375.1347389
17. Zhi-Hua, G., Zhi-Min, G.: WCET-aware task assignment and cache partitioning for wcrt minimization on multi-core systems. In: Proceedings of International Symposium on Parallel Architectures, Algorithms and Programming, PAAP, January 2016, pp. 143–148 (2016). https://doi.org/10.1109/paap.2015.36
18. Herlihy, M., Shavit, N.: The Art of Multiprocessor Programming, 1st edn. Morgan Kaufmann, San Francisco (2012)

A Novel Speedup Evaluation for Multicore Architecture Based Topology of On-Chip Memory

XiaoJun Wang[1,2(✉)], Feng Shi[1(✉)], and Hong Zhang[2]

[1] Beijing Institute of Technology, Beijing 100081, China
wxjred9915@163.com, bitsf@bit.edu.cn
[2] Henan University of Economics and Law, Zhengzhou 450046, Henan, China
gracezxkl@126.com

Abstract. Speedup is measured as parallel program potential for evaluation in CMP. Researchers made a lot of contributions in evaluating the speedup of multicore, however the specific architecture is not taken into consideration yet. This article presents a novel method ETOM (Evaluation on Topology of On-chip Memory) to evaluate the speedup of multicore. This method obtains the speedup based on the specific architecture and the memory organization. For verifying the legitimacy of this approach, existing speedup laws and our method are compared in this research work. The use of the method can be more easily to obtain the speedup of multicore architecture, especially at the initial phase of designing a new multicore architecture. Using ETOM, a novel multicore architecture TriBA can be obtained which performance is better than 2DMesh. In the processing of experiments, a lot of detailed characteristics of 2DMesh be found, such as different speedup of each core in different locations. However, each core has the same speedup in TriBA by using ETOM and the performance of speedup in it more than in 2DMesh. So the method is very fit for evaluating performance of specific architectures. And the new architecture TriBA has a reasonable topology of on-chip memory than 2DMesh.

Keywords: Performance evaluation · Multicore architecture · Topology · On-chip memory

1 Introduction and Motivation

As is known to all, parallel processing has become a main stream approach for achieving high performance, however, performance evaluation techniques of parallel processing are weak. Performance evaluation weakness limits the growth of parallel computation. Speedup is the most important factor as performance metric for parallel processing, which gives the performance comparison of parallel processing versus sequential processing. However, with different emphases, the speedup has been defined differently. Among the different defined speedups, the

H. Shen and Y. Sang (Eds.): PAAP 2019, CCIS 1163, pp. 35–47, 2020.
https://doi.org/10.1007/978-981-15-2767-8_4

relative speedup most probably is the one which has had the most influence on parallel processing. These relative speedup formulations only use a single parameter, the sequential of a parallel algorithm. However, a lot of facts show that on-chip memory architecture (OCMA) is one of the important factors affecting speedup of multicore architecture.

On the one hand, finding a suitable performance evaluation method of multicore architecture is not an easy task. Although many methods based on software testing (MBST) or on Amdahl, Gustafson and Sun-Ni's laws (Method Based on the Laws (MBL)) are used in evaluating speedup, these methods are not fit for the initial designing stage due to the following reasons.

Firstly MBST is only used at the completed stage of design multicore architecture, because none of the existing simulators and the related tools supports new multicore architecture directly, so that the modeling and simulating cost for designing new multicore architecture would spend too much time and money.

Secondly MBST's results are affected by several aspects, such as execution, schedule model, application algorithm and multicore architecture. Even if experienced researchers may not be able to make sure of which aspect mainly induced the result, so this type of evaluations is less helpful to OCMA designer for new multicore architecture design.

Thirdly, in fact, even if a test set fully embodied characteristics of a specified multicore architecture that gives a real performance evaluation, which doesn't implies that a new multicore architecture should be performed the same results except the two architectures are identical, otherwise the results from different test sets are not comparable with each other.

Finally MBLs are also not fit for evaluating performance of multicore architecture at the initial stage for measuring the speedup at a high and abstract level. The models in MBLs are based on the sequential of a parallel algorithm which are generally not associated with any specific architecture, so the results from MBLs have slightly small reflect the architecture details and are definitely not much helpful for the OCMA designer.

On the other hand, it needs to find a method to evaluate performance of new OCMA in the initial stages of designing a new multicore architecture. So it is significantly essential how rapid, inexpensive and slightly rough evaluate performance be impacted/affected by the OCMA.

On the basis of above mentioned reasons, it is important to find a new method which satisfies the demand of a new OCMA design. So this paper proposes an evaluation method ETOM (Evaluation on Topology of On-chip Memory) for evaluating speedup of multicore architecture. According to ETOM speedup model, the corresponding cores are placed directly with the topology characteristics of the OCMA in designing. Then the speedup model is used to assess the reasonability of the OCMA by its impact value on the speedup. In this paper, an ETOM evaluation methodology is taken as an example to realize the validity of ETOM with contrast to the results from other evaluations. The impact of the OCMA between 2D-mesh and TriBA on speedup of a core (SPoC) is revealed with the analysis of the ETOM results in order to show the utility of ETOM in designing new OCMA (the initial stages in particular). The two evaluations of TriBA and 2D-mesh in this paper explain the principle and course of ETOM evaluation.

2 Related Work

Speedup could be achieved ideal performance when all cores execute the tasks parallel simultaneously, whilst this may cause in reducing the efficiency. In the past researches, the speedup is estimated on a fixed-size work and fixed-time work with MBLs, which executed on single processor as well as multiple processors, and evaluated the execution time ratio of one over the many.

In 1967, Gene Amdhal proposed an overlooked speedup law for the special case of using n processors in parallel, limitation in performance improvement for any enhancement, which is adopted by modern multicore architecture evaluation till date [1]. He draws the computational performance of multicore system which only analyses the percentage of parallel and serial aspect. After Amdhal research published, many researchers make an effort to extended that work but few have also reservations on his idea [2–4].

Hill and Marty [2] extended Amdahl's law with a corollary for multicore hardware and obtained optimal multicore performance, but ignore the effects of memory and interconnection network. Whereas quite contrary to the Amdhal's, John Gustafson has revealed that speedup should be measured by scaling the problem to the number of processors, not fixing problem size. Because massively parallel machines didn't be justified by Amdhal's law due to the fact that those machines permit computations formerly intractable in the specified time constraints. Gustafson's law was significant difference and renewed efforts in scaled parallel problem size research [5,6]. Sun and Ni [7,8] proposed another speedup evaluation model, the memory-bounded model, which explained parallel processing comparative speedup performance with memory-bounded and overlooked the context switching in model. Those researchers claimed that the performance of multicore system possibly be increased with the proportion of higher parallel to serial execution and with the number of more processors.

Different from the above rules, E.F. Rent in 1960's found a rule, which focused on the wire-length prediction in the homogenous circuitry for communication with respect to group of gates and number of terminal. Rent's law presents the relation of average number of terminals of a part of any circuit to the average number of logic gates inside the module as $T = kG^{\gamma}$ [9–11]. In [12], authors explored the use of Rent's rule as a complexity metric for improving the placement of circuits on a target FPGA architecture. Haldun drew the origin of Rent's rule from the embedding of a high-dimensional information flow graph to two- or three-dimensional physical space and applied these concepts to free-space optically interconnected systems [13,14]. Greenfield et al. [15] applied the principles of Rent's rule to the analysis of networks-on-chip, and proposed a new type of router to evaluate mutability and the impact on congestion by further use of the hop-length distributions. Taking into consideration these rules, Cassidy et al.

in [16–18] present analytical model evaluating CMPs with shared memory and interconnection network by means of objective function using Matlab with particular applications, considering cache hit rate, interconnection area constraint, processor performance and number of cores . In contrast to Cassidy's opinion, where he only considers the high level architecture assessment of CMPs, ETOM is intensely useful at the lowest/primary level. These rules are used to evaluate speedup since last century from multi computers to multicore, however, they didn't involve all the resources as well as specific architecture at all. Sun and Ni are the only authors, who consider the memory bounded in their research. Although they illustrate few rules about multicore in topology level, these rules hardly calculate the specific architecture directly. Typically all of these speedup evaluation methodologies partition software/task to the serial part and the parallel part, which is used to calculate and evaluate the processor performance mainly from the software aspect. But these evaluation methodologies don't indicate that the serial part in software/task will always be executed in the hardware serially, such as the instruction pipeline. So these methodologies don't accurately reveal the characteristic of the specified multicore architecture. This reason diverts our interesting towards obtaining the accurate speedup evaluation for the specified multicore architectures. Speedup has been evaluated from Amdhal's law in various ways, authors in [19] analyzed speedup with two models which based on fixed time and memory bounded. They did researches to calculate speedup formula ($S_{ft} = 1+(n-1)\beta$) in fixed time for certain number of instructions executed and analyzed the results from 1 to 1024 cores. Through the above formula derivation, if the cache hit rate is 10% then the speedup is around 104, while for 90% cache hit rate with 1024 cores speedup is measured around 922. The researcher's graph trend shows that the speedup isn't increase adequately weather hit rate is 10% or 90% when the core number value is 16. It is also drew a conclusion that fixed time constraint execution obtain better performance than fixed size limitation. The research also showed that speedup of memory bounded even performs better than fixed size constraint. Whereas authors in [20] analyzed speedup factor as function of the number of processor and drew a trend with respect to fixed time and various data-set sizes. The work was divided into serial, parallel portion and stated that if half portion was processed parallel on 1024 cores the speedup was measured as 512x for multicore and 1+512x for uniprocessor applying John Gustafson law. In [21], the authors calculated speedup with considering to parallel and sequential operations by using fixed number of n processors. The authors calculated speedup by using 2 serial operations and 98 parallel operations with more than 100 processors, however, the value of speedup is not more than 50. As mentioned above, these authors measured speedup keeping in view some specific characteristics of multi-processor systems, whereas ETOM evaluate speedup based on other properties such as SPoC (speedup of cores), SPoA (speedup of multi-core architecture) and inter-core communication of SPoA as described in the following section.

3 Principle of ETOM Evaluation

The Base Core Equivalent (BCE) has been defined in this article. BCE is the baseline processor which is supposed to be without L1 private cache compared to "Core" in multi-core System. A common unicore processor with two-level cache can be formed as a BCE and on-chip memory modules (OMMs), which is to be used as the referenced processor in computing SPoC in multicore processor. Similarly, an N-core processor with multi-level cache scan also is formed as $N-BCE_s$ and OMMs connected each other with a dedicated on-chip network. In addition, unless otherwise specified, the memories and caches refer to on-chip resources.

3.1 The Limitations and Assumptions

In this paper we are concerned only with symmetric multicore architecture with uniform interconnected network, which implies that the resources are shared equally by all cores. The elapsed time of accessing a cache module from a node is composed of two parts: the access delay of writing or reading the cache module; and the transfer delay of data go through the path which connects the source node to the target cache module. This path is ordinarily path made up of more than one node except the two end-nodes. The competitions in multicore architecture for paths and memory ports make the computation of transfer delay more complex; in order to simplify the problem we make the following assumptions.

First, the access delay of on-chip Li cache is $\tau_i = 2i \times \tau$, and the sum of transfer delay and access delay of accessing off-chip memory is $\tau_off = 20\tau$. Although these two assumptions may be very different from the actual situation, the same values are used in both of the measurements for multicore and the reference, thus the impact on the assessment results is limited.

Second, the pure transfer delay between two physically adjacent nodes is $\iota \times \tau$, where ι is the path length in basic unit and the node can be cache module, the on-chip interconnected node, etc., for example the delay for neighbor nodes of 2D-mesh interconnect is τ.The physical channel in OCMA is always shared by multiple concurrent transfers, which often causes data left into pending state. The pure delay here refers to the amount of time for a flit of data to travel through the path between neighbor nodes, it does not include the waiting time.

Third, at last the amount of time for a BCE to finish tasks is proportional to the elapsed time for accessing all the caches during the same period of time. This assumption is special for investigating the impact of accessing on the performance of cores, which is consistent with the access-intensive executions.

Additionally, for simplification we do not distinguish between read and write operation for access and communication. It is also assumed that the CPI (Cycle Per Instruction) of BCE, hit rate of each level of the caches and the access delay of L_i cache are independent of the architecture and the number of cores.

3.2 Computing the Speedups

We compute the speedup in a way similar to the usual one. SPoC in multi-core architecture is as the ratio S_r of the time T_r^1 spent by a BCE in unicore architecture for K accesses over the time T_r^N spent by a BCE in the multi-core architecture with N nodes network for the same K accesses. Let a N-core processor be of L levels of on-chip caches and η_i be the hit rate of L_i cache for BCE_r, where BCE_r belongs to the core numbered r and connected to a node of OCMA. The access requests missed in L_{i-1} caches will continue to access L_i cache with an access delay of τ_i and an average transfer delay of $\overline{T_i}$ from L_{i-1} cache module to L_i cache module. The average elapsed time for BCE_r to access memory K times is

$$\begin{aligned} T_r^N &= K \times \left[\tau_1 + (1-\eta_1)(\overline{T_2} + \tau_2) + \cdots + (1-\eta_1)\ldots(1-\eta_L)(\overline{T_{L+1}} + \tau_{L+1})\right] \\ &= K \times \sum_{i=1}^{L+1} \left[(\overline{T_2} + \tau_2) \times \prod_{j=1}^{i} (1-\eta_{j-1}) \right] \end{aligned} \tag{1}$$

where $\overline{T_1} = 0$, $\eta_0 = 0$ and $L+1$ is specially for off-chip memory so $\overline{T_{L+1}} + \tau_{L+1} = \tau_{off}$.

Moreover, the average elapsed time for BCE_r in a unicore processor with two-level cache to access memory K times is $T_r^1 = K \times \left[\tau_1 + (1-\eta_1)(\overline{T_2} + \tau_2) + (1-\eta_1)(1-\eta_2)\tau_3)\right]$. From assumptions in the above section, the speedup ($S_r = \frac{T_r^1}{T_r^N}$) of BCE_r (i.e. SPoC) located in a multicore processor is

$$S_r = \frac{\tau_1 + (1-\eta_1)(\overline{T_2} + \tau_2) + (1-\eta_1)(1-\eta_2)\tau_{off})}{\sum_{i=1}^{L+1} \left[(\overline{T_i} + \tau_i) \times \prod_{j=1}^{i} (1-\eta_{j-1}) \right]} \tag{2}$$

In addition, the speedup of the multi-core architecture (SPoA) that S_r belongs to $\sum_{r=1}^{N} S_r$, here the additions is reasonable because that all impacts from the other cores on S_r is taken into account in computing S_r. Note that the deduction of (1) is just a general principle of ETOM; a customized deduction for special architecture may be needed in an actual application of ETOM.

We plot in Fig. 1 the values of speedups for evaluation methods in [19–21] and ETOM. The speedups have similar trends with number of core, but each of them has its own rate at which the speedup increases. Among the speedups shown in Fig. 1 at the "same" number of cores, Gustafson-based speedup is highest whereas the ETOM-based has lowest value. These results are taken in the case of Gustafson's all parallel-executable tasks, which are perfectly parallel executed without any competition for the resources and according to [21] sequential and parallel operation. ETOM takes too much of access into account because of the third assumption in Sect. 3.1. This implies that ETOM is not suitable for those specific executions with little accesses.

Despite the differences among the rising rates, the similar rising trend elucidates the validity of ETOM to some extent.

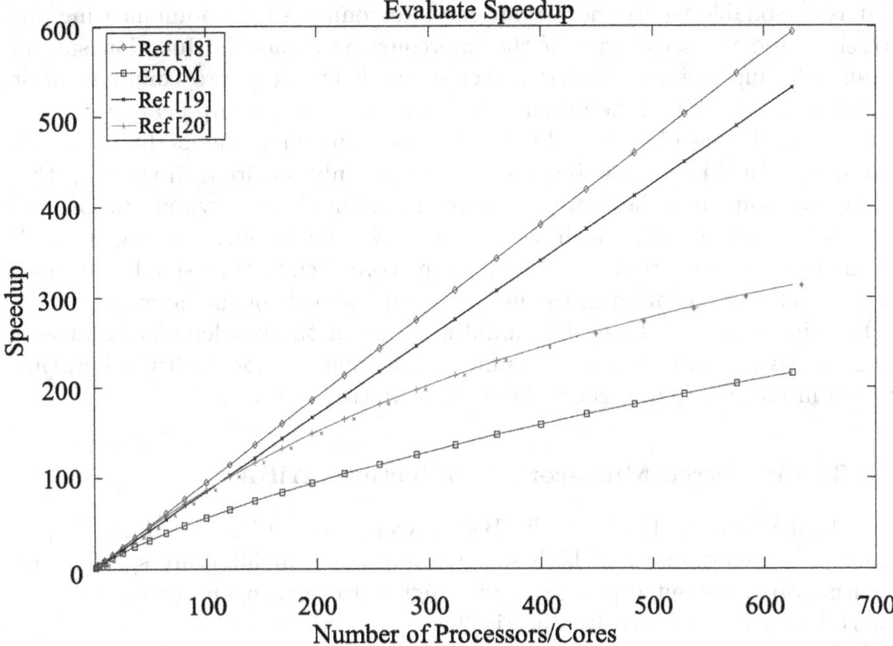

Fig. 1. Speedups of the architecture: ETOM vs. the other evaluating methods

4 An Application Instantiation of ETOM

ETOM is most appropriate at the primary stages of designing a new architecture; it is a simple and revealing evaluation method despite a slightly rough result. The ETOM model is very useful; it is applied on 2D-mesh and found some ambiguities in that architecture. We can get a conclusion from the ETOM about 2DMesh that a novel OCMA of TriBA architecture can obtain better performance than 2DMesh at the ETOM's standpoint.

4.1 Enlightenments from ETOM

From the modeling prospective and computation of speedup, a few problems are found in previous research with the application of the 2D-mesh network in Fig. 1, these problems are described below.

The global sharing of on-chip cache modules makes the cache access path longer with increase of network size, which decreases SPoC and SPoA and works against improving memory performance following the principle of locality.

As going through the shared channel means transfer delay multiplication, 2D-mesh has a node degree of 4, where the least node degree of 2 appears in the linear structure only, so the simplest 2D network with better performance should be of 3°.

It is reasonable to use more than one interconnects for communicating and accessing, and the topologies of the interconnects should be function specific because sharing the same interconnect network by inter-core communication and accessing on-chip cache modules will decrease the speedup heavily.

Cores in 2D-mesh have equal rights to access on-chip cache modules, namely Symmetric Multi-Processor, but one core commonly has its own speedup that is different from the other cores, so cores in 2D-mesh are asymmetric or non-uniform in performance, which is a disadvantage for resource management. It is clear that the preferred OCMA for multi-core architecture should be SPoC independent of its location in the network and the scale of the network.

The single port of L_2 cache modules is one of the bottlenecks because of being shared by more than one channels with time division multiplexing, time division in multi-core means cores are often waiting to access.

4.2 The Preferred Multi-core Architecture, TriBA

In the light of section IV.A, Triplet Based Architecture (TriBA) [22,23], is presented, it is easy-to-use and high scalable multi-core architecture specially for executing object-oriented programs with high performance, energy-efficient and powerful security, as illustrated in Fig. 2.

TriBA uses two different on-chip interconnects for inter-core communication and memory access respectively, the inter-core communication network is depicted in Figs. 2(a) and 3(a) and the on-chip memory network is depicted in Figs. 2(b) and 3(b). It is observed that the communication path lengths between two neighbour nodes are identical (as 3BU, see Fig. 3(a)), while the access path lengths between the two cache modules of level L_{i-1} and L_i is 2^{i-2} units (1 unit = 1.5 BU, see Fig. 3(b).

The on-chip memory network with ternary tree topology forms the Hierarchical Group Shared on-chip memory architecture for TriBA. Except L_1 cache, all cache modules consist of the Weakly Dependent Parallel Quad Port Memory modules with proper arbitration to itself. The two distinct networks of TriBA are both hierarchical; a $N - level$ TriBA is of 3^N communicating nodes and at most $N+1$ levels of on-chip cache modules, where L_1 cache modules are private and locate inside the core, making it different from the other cache modules.

The FPGA based implementation has been completed for the intercore communication network and the on-chip memory network in TriBA, while the 3D IC based implementation is in study phase [24].

4.3 The ETOM Speedup of TriBA

For simplification, let an $N - level$ TriBA be of the highest level (i.e. $N+1$) of on-chip cache. As the transfer delay for 1 unit of path length has been assumed as τ in Sect. 3.1, the length of path between two adjacent cache modules of L_{i-1} and L_i level is 2^{i-2} from the illustration of Fig. 2, and all uplinks above level L_2 are shared by three downlinks, the average transfer delay between neighbor

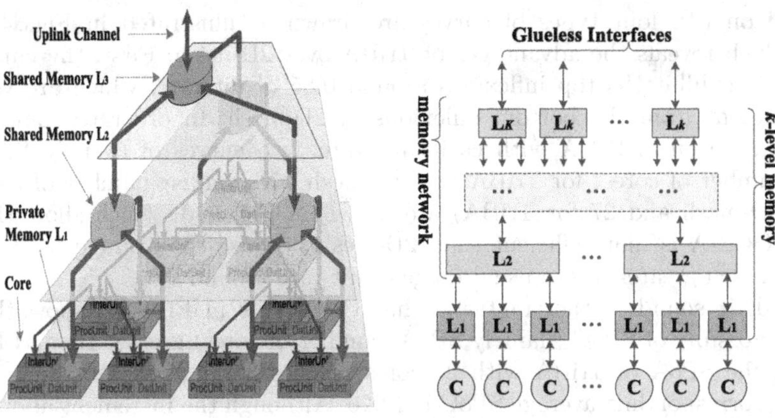

(a) Scheme for TriBA architecture (b) Abstract structure of the memory network

Fig. 2. Schemes for TriBA architecture with 9-cores and its memory network

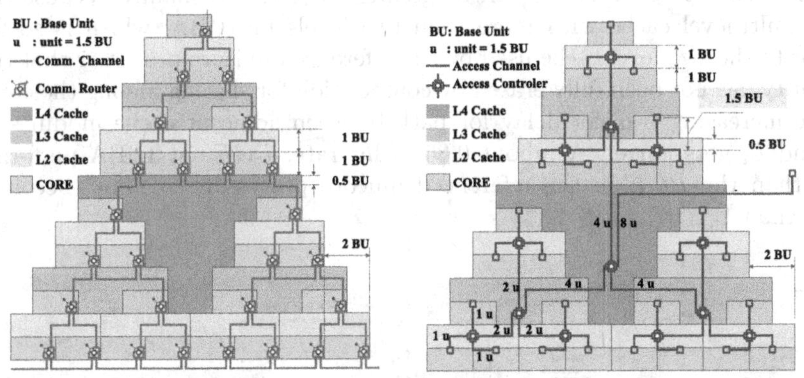

(a) Schematic diagram of Inter-core communication network for physical layout and wiring (b) Schematic diagram of Memory network for physical layout and wiring

Fig. 3. Physical layout and wiring for TriBA's interconnects (take 27-cores as the example)

cache modules can be written as $3 \times 2^{i-2} \times \tau$ for $i \geq 3$ .The speedups for TriBA architecture (SPoA) are obtained as followings:

$$\begin{cases} S = 3^N \times S_r \\ S_r = \dfrac{2 + 5(1-\eta_1) + 20(1-\eta_1)(1-\eta_2)}{2 + 5(1-\eta_1) + \sum\limits_{i=3}^{N+1}\left[(3 \times 2^{i-2} + 2i) \times \prod\limits_{j=1}^{i-1}(1-\eta_1)\right] + 60 \times \prod\limits_{j=1}^{N+1}(1-\eta_1)} \end{cases} \quad N \geq 1 \tag{3}$$

Based on (3), four types of curves are drawn as illustrated in Figs. 4, 5 and 6, which reveals the advantages of TriBA over 2D-mesh. First, the curves in Fig. 4(a) exhibit the top inflexions around 0.85 of hit rate, which are very much different from the bottom inflexions of 2D-mesh. In order to compare the two variation of SPoA with cache hit rate, two curves of average SPoC (SPoA/number of cores) for TriBA and 2D-mesh with similar number of cores (25 for 2D-mesh and 27 for TriBA) are drawn in Fig. 4(b), which show that TriBA's OCMA is more efficient than 2D-mesh because the average SPoC of TriBA is much greater in the usual range of hit rate around 0.8.

Second, it sounds rather fantastic that the curves in Fig. 4(a) show that TriBA is possibly of SPoC (namely SPoA/number of cores) greater than 1! For example, the SPoA of TriBA with 27 cores reaches 27.71 at 0.85 of hit rate, while the corresponding average SPoC is 1.026. Although the increment above 1 is small, is it possible to be magnified and what will it take? The TriBA ETOM modeling shows that it is true that decreasing the transfer delay of adjacent nodes in TriBA's memory network will enlarge the increment by some ways such as increasing the width of wires, using 3D IC technology, etc.

As for why SPoC of TriBA can be greater than 1, it is mainly because the use of multi-level cache with more than two levels in TriBA, which is so far superior to the two-level cache used by the referenced unicore processor that the superiority has not been fully erased by competition for sharing among the cores and the increasing transfer delay for path between adjacent cache modules of L_{i-1} and L_i gets longer. At about 0.85 of hit rate, BCE_s in TriBA performs better than the BCE in the referenced unicore processor, so SPoC becomes greater than 1.

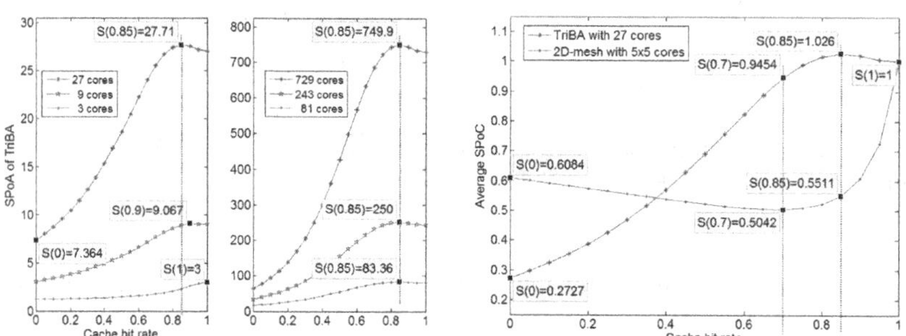

(a) SPoAs of TriBA for various hit rates

(b) Average SPoC for TriBA and 2D-mesh

Fig. 4. Speedups of TriBA VS the identical hit rate for each level of caches ($\eta_i = \eta_j$ and $\alpha = 1$)

Third, it is clear from the curves in Fig. 5(a) and (b) that TriBA is much more scalable than 2D-mesh, because TriBAs with more than 27 cores are of high and nearly invariant SPoC, while the SPoC of 2D-mesh with similar number of cores is much lower than TriBA and becomes lower and lower with increase of number of cores. Especially, SPoC of 2D-mesh decreases sharply to about 40% when number of cores increases in the range of 4 to 100 and then goes slowly to the lower limit about 10%, on the contrary, SPoC of TriBA rises abruptly and rapidly reaches the maximum value closed to 100%.

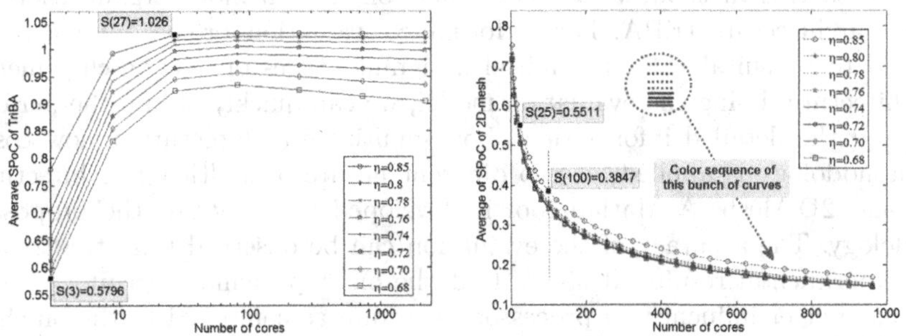

(a) Average SPoCs of TriBA with different number of cores (b) Average SPoCs of 2D-mesh with different number of cores

Fig. 5. Comparisons of average SPoC for TriBA and 2D-mesh ($\eta_i = \eta_j$)

Finally, TriBA possesses much better performance in speedup than 2D-mesh which can be seen from Fig. 6, at similar number of cores SPoA of TriBA is much greater than 2D-mesh, except the hit rate of each level of cache for 2D-Mesh is bigger than about 0.96 which implies the total hit rate of the 2D-mesh is 0.9984, nearly 1. In addition, the rising speed of SPoC in TriBA is greater than 2D-mesh.

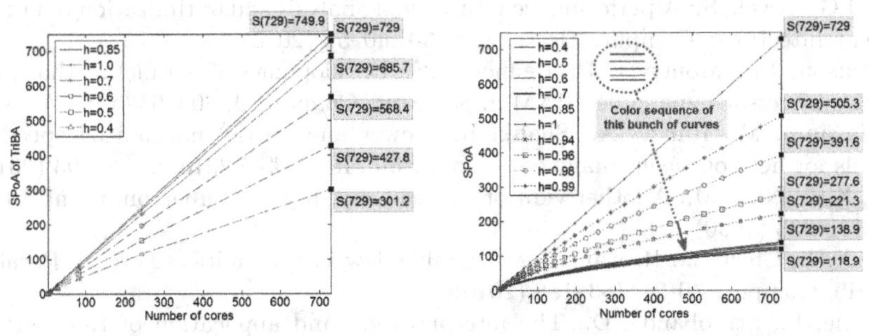

(a) SPoAs of TriBA with 729 cores (b) SPoAs of 2D-mesh with 729 cores

Fig. 6. Comparisons of SPoAs for TriBA and 2D-mesh in same coordinate scale

5 Conclusion

To evaluate speedup for multicore architecture on the topological characteristic of on-chip memory, this paper proposes an effective methodology ETOM. The proposed methodology merges the specific multicore architecture and the topology of the memory organization used for evaluating the speedup of CMP. According to this method, we obtain a new on-chip memory organization of multicore architecture TriBA. The performance evaluation for speedup has been confirmed to be suitable for the initial designing stages of new on-chip memory architecture. Using the evaluation model, we can quickly obtain the performance and the detailed information about multicore architecture at low cost. This methodology is applied on two different nature of multicore architecture TriBA and 2D-Mesh. A Matlab tool is developed to carry out the proposed methodology. The accuracy of the evaluation can be observed from the trends of the experimental results. It shows that the on-chip memory architecture of TriBA has better influence on processor's speedup as compared to the on-chip memory architecture of 2D-mesh. The experimental results reveal that TriBA speedup is more than the 2D-mesh, which confirm that TriBA has better multicore architecture and on-chip memory for future CMP.

References

1. Amdahl, G.M.: Validity of the single processor approach to achieving large scale computing capabilities. In: SJCC 1967, April 1967
2. Hill, M.D., Marty, M.R.: Amdahl's law in the multicore era. Computer **41**(1), 33–38 (2008)
3. Zeigler, B.P., Nutaro, J.J.: What's the best possible speedup achievable in distributed simulation: Amdahl's law reconstructed. In: DEVS 2015, pp. 189–196 (2015)
4. Lee, J.G., Kwak, S.: A performance-aware yield analysis and optimization of many-core architectures. Comput. Electr. Eng. **54**, 40–52 (2016)
5. Gustafson, J.L., Montry, G.R., Benner, R.E.: Development of parallel methods for a 1024-processor hypercube. SIAM J. Sci. Stat. Comput. **9**, 609–638 (1988)
6. Al-Hayanni, M., Rafiev, A., Shafik, R.: Power and energy normalized speedup models for heterogeneous many core computing. In: ACSD 2016, pp. 84–93 (2016)
7. Sun, X.H., Ni, L.M.: Another view on parallel speedup. In: Supercomputing 1990, pp. 324–333 (1990)
8. Sun, X.H., Chen, Y.: Reevaluating Amdahl's law in the multicore era. J. Parallel Distrib. Comput. **70**(2), 183–188 (2010)
9. Christie, P., Stroobandt, D.: The interpretation and application of Rent's rule. IEEE Trans. VLSI Syst. **8**, 639–648 (2000)
10. Bezerra, G.P., Forrest, S., Forrest, M.: Modeling NoC traffic locality and energy consumption with rent's communication probability distribution. In: SLIP 2010, pp. 3–8 (2010)
11. Li, W.S., Yao, Z.B.: Multicore architecture speedup computation based on Amdahl's law and Rent's rule. Acta Electronica Sinica **40**(2), 230–234 (2012)
12. Parthasarathy, G., Marek-Sadowska, M., Mukherjee, A.: Interconnect complexity-aware FPGA placement using Rent's rule. In: SLIP 2001, pp. 115–121 (2001)

13. Orsila, H., Salminen, E., Timo, D.: Parameterizing simulated annealing for distributing Kahn process networks on multiprocessor SoCs. In: SOC 2009, pp.19–26 (2009)
14. Ozaktas, H.M.: Information flow and interconnections in computing: extensions and applications of Rent's rule. J. Parallel Distrib. Comput. **64**(12), 1360–1370 (2004)
15. Greenfield, D., Banerjee, A., Lee, J.G.: Implications of Rent's rule for NoC design and its fault-tolerance. In: NOCS 2007, pp. 283–294 (2007)
16. Cassidy, A., Andreou, A.G.: Analytical methods for the design and optimization of chip-multiprocessor architectures. In: CISS 2009, pp. 482–487 (2009)
17. Cassidy, A., Yu, K., Zhou, H., Andreou, A.G.: A high-level analytical model for application specific CMP design exploration. In: DATE 2011, pp. 1–6 (2011)
18. Cassidy, A.S., Andreou, A.G.: Beyond Amdahl's Law: an objective function that links multiprocessor performance gains to delay and energy. IEEE Trans. Comput. **61**, 1110–1126 (2012)
19. Sun, X.H., Chen, Y., Byna, S.: Scalable computing in the multicore era. In: PAAP 2008, pp. 1–12 (2008)
20. Levitan, S.P., Chiarulli, D.M.: Massively parallel processing: it's Déjà Vu all over again. In: DAC 2009, pp. 534–538 (2009)
21. Touati, S.A., Worms, J., Briais, S.: The Speedup-Test: a statistical methodology for programme speedup analysis and computation. Concurr. Comput.: Pract. Exp. **25**(10), 1410–1426 (2013)
22. Shi, F., Ji, W., et al.: A triplet-based computer architecture supporting parallel object computing. In: IEEE ASSAP 2007, pp. 192–197, July 2007
23. Khan, H.-U.-R., et al.: Computationally efficient locality-aware interconnection topology for multi-processor system-on-chip (MP-SoC). Chin. Sci. Bull. **55**, 3363–3371 (2010)
24. Xue, L., Shi, F., Ji, W., Khan, H.-U.-R.: 3D floorplanning of low-power and area-efficient Network-on-Chip architecture. Microprocess. Microsyst. **35**, 484–495 (2011)

Improving the Performance of Collective Communication for the On-Chip Network

Slo-Li Chu(✉), Wen-Chih Ho, and Yi-Jie Jiang

Department of Information and Computer Engineering, Chung Yuan Christian University, Chung Li District, Taoyuan City, Taiwan
{slchu,g9877606,g10577021}@cycu.edu.tw

Abstract. Efficiently executing the massively parallel applications has become an important goal of developing a modern high-performance multicore computer. In these parallel programs, the collective communication among these cores consume a large portion of inter-core communication. In order to prevent the collective communication from the performance bottleneck of the on-chip network, this paper proposed a new on-chip network, call Hierarchy Self Similar Cubic (HSSC), to reduce the latency of the collective communication on the multicore system. The corresponding transmission mechanisms and packet scheduling mechanism are proposed to analyze and grouping the packets, and determine a suitable transmission mechanism for each packet group on-the-fly. The experiments compare the performance of several on-chip networks. The advantages of proposed transmission mechanisms and packet scheduling mechanism are also discussed.

Keywords: Multicore architecture · On-Chip network · Packet transmission mechanism · Collective communication

1 Introduction

As the requirements for the high performance computation makes the number of processor cores integrated into a single chip, so designing a suitable on-chip network for integrating these cores has brought great challenge. As the number of cores increases, the exchange of messages between cores becomes more complicated and busy. The delivery of messages in the massively parallel programs can be simply divided into two categories, one is the one-to-one data transfer between the two cores, the other is the exchange of data among multiple cores, also known as collective communication, such as one-to-many, many-to-one, many-to-many…etc. Among these two kinds of communication, collective communications among multiple cores seriously affect the overall performance, because when collective transmission occurs, the simultaneously transmission will easily lead to resource contention on the interconnection network, resulting increase the transmission time of the packets [1]. Therefore, how to design an on-chip network and transmission mechanism that are suitable for collective transmission will be an important challenge.

H. Shen and Y. Sang (Eds.): PAAP 2019, CCIS 1163, pp. 48–57, 2020.
https://doi.org/10.1007/978-981-15-2767-8_5

In order to improve the transmission efficiency of inter-core communication, we propose a new on-chip network architecture based on the previous work Self Similar Cubic (SSC) [2], and provide new transmission mechanisms for collective communication. The SSC has the advantage of local communication among the cores within the same block. While the massively collective communication among the foreign cores, the limited bandwidth of cross block link degrades the communication performance. But it inevitably to communicate among the foreign cores in the parallel programs. Accordingly, we propose a new on-chip network architecture, called Hierarchy Self Similar Cubic (HSSC), which preserves the advantages of local cores transmission via SSC, provides new transmission paths, and design a set of transmission mechanisms to improve the performance of communication among foreign cores. Besides, in order to improve the speed of collective communication, a new transmission mechanism, called Packet Analysis and Decision Mechanism (PADM), are proposed to analyze and partition the packets into group on-the-fly, and then determine suitable transmission mechanism for the packet group, according to its characteristic. Hence the transmission categories and the corresponding transmission mechanism will be assigned to the packet group to improve the efficiency of the transmission.

2 Related Works

The collective communication is very useful in parallel applications which can exchange data globally and synchronize the execution among nodes. The most widely used collective communication operations are broadcasting, multicast, scatter, gather and barrier synchronization [3]. However, the frequent use of collective communication has a huge impact on the overall efficiency of the interconnection network. Therefore, hardware or/and software acceleration support for collective communication can improve the performance and the resource utilization. Software-based approaches may increase the processing cost of the computer. Depending on required performance, the hardware-based support for collective communication is a better choice. In the architecture of Tofu2 [4] is a successful case of hardware acceleration, in order to improve the transmission performance of in collective communication, a Session-Mode Control Queue is proposed which uses the continuous data transmission of neighboring nodes to reduce the delay time of data transmission.

In addition, in [3], the author designed a circuit for multicast (One-to-Many) in wormhole network and developed a three-stage transmission process for high-speed multicast transmission to improve packet throughput. In [5], in order to reduce the transmission delay from replying acknowledgement packets to a core (Many-to-One), the researchers proposed a message composition framework to integrate the acknowledgement packet and reduce transmission overhead in the interconnection network. The proposed Balanced Adaptive Multicast (BAM) routing algorithm manages the traffic through the congestion of the output port, and controls the transmission path of the packet. It also balances the buffer resource in the interconnected network and reduces the delay of packet transmission. Although the schemes mentioned above may improve performance, the complicated data transmission from collective communication also affect the overall performance of the interconnection network.

3 Hierarchy Self Similar Cubic Network

The performance of the on-chip network dominates the data exchange latency in the multicore architectures, the overall system performance is effected dramatically. In this study, we propose a new on-chip network, called Hierarchy Self Similar Cubic (HSSC), which is based on the previous SSC [2] on-chip network, inherits its high scalability topology and high performance transmission within local cores. The advantage of HSSC comes from the low hop count transmission paths to avoid the network resource contention that may be encountered when the remote transmissions are dominated. The corresponding packet transmission mechanisms of HSSC help to transmit the variant types of packet efficiently. Figure 1 illustrates the proposed HSSC architecture.

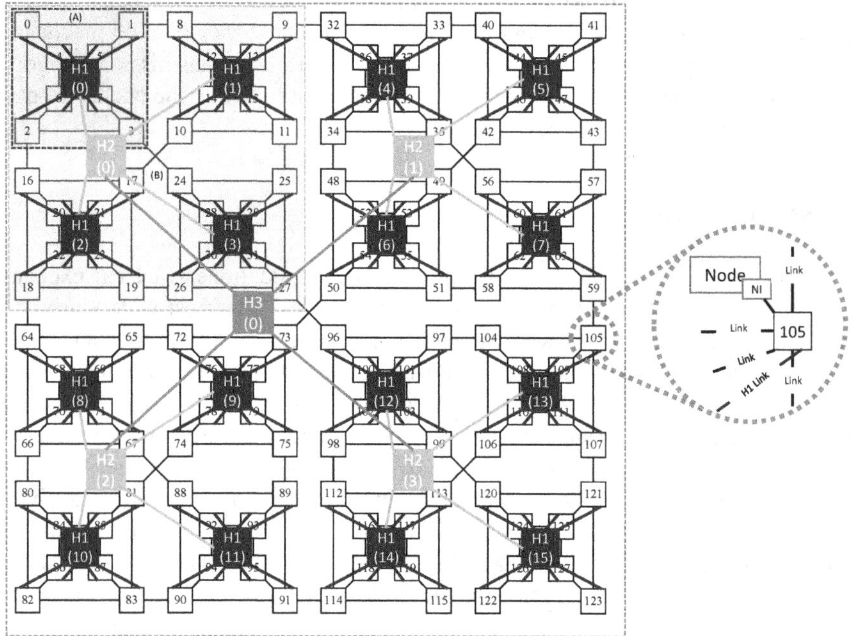

Fig. 1. The topology of HSSC on-chip network.

3.1 Self Similar Cubic Network

The layers of SSC network is represented by SSC(n). The first layer of SSC network is SSC(0), which contains 8 nodes with the links that connect to each other and form a cubic topology. The second layer is SSC(1), which consists of 4 SSC(1) blocks with the cross links to connect to each other. As with the above process, SSC(2) can be constructed to constitute 128 nodes. The topologies of SSC(0), SSC(1), SSC(2) are illustrated in Fig. 1.

Although SSC on-chip network has the advantage of transmitting within SSC(0) block, while a huge amount of packets need to be send beyond the SSC(0) block, the

SSC may have a high transmission delay due to the fact that SSC(0) has fewer external connections to other SSC(0) blocks. The transmission of the packet has to wait for resource to be released before it can be transmitted. However, in many parallel programs, the collective transmission requirements are often encountered, such as synchronizing data when the program start and collecting the calculation results of all nodes. This demand usually does not only need the local nodes communication but also require more about foreign communication with other nodes. The overall performance is degrading accordingly.

3.2 Hierarchy Self Similar Cubic on-Chip Network

In order to solve the above problem of SSC network, we propose a new Hierarchy Self Similar Cubic (HSSC) architecture that consist of original SSC network and additional hierarchical transmission paths for the foreign blocks, as shown in Fig. 1. In HSSC architecture, every 8 nodes (SSC(0)) will be connected to the new H1 switch, every 4 H1 switches (SSC(1)) will be connected to the H2 switch, and every 4 H2 switches (SSC(2)) will be connected to the top H3 switch. With these new transmission paths, the pressure of foreign transmission that occurs by collective communication can be relaxed. The performance of overall packets can be improved accordingly.

In addition to the improvement of foreign transmission in topology, HSSC has also improved transmission performance in terms of module design and packet transmission. In the module design, unlike the SSC, the modules in the HSSC are re-designed with pipelined behavior. In the node module, in order to improve the transmission performance, a packet analysis and decision mechanism, called PADM, is added to partition and classify the packets, and then assign different transmission mechanism to each packet group based on packet's characteristics. Two fundamental transferring methods between two nodes, single transfer mode and burst transfer mode are implemented. The single transfer mode is implemented by three-way handshaking for packet transmission requirement. The burst transfer mode will reduce a lot of handshaking operation for one transmission requirement to get better performance. The packet transfer between any two nodes is handled by the two transmission mechanisms, H-Single and H-Burst, which will transmit the data through the new transmission path of the HSSC. The mentioned PADM mechanism and the transmission mechanisms will be further explored in Sect. 4.

4 HSSC Transmission Mechanisms

In the application of parallel programs, according to the transmission behavior of data, it can be divided into two classes. The first class is one-to-one communication which means that the two cores communicate with each other. The second class is collective communication that means all of the cores that are participated in this transmission, may communicate among others. The collective communication can be divided into three categories, as shown in Fig. 2. The first category is One-to-Many, which means one core transmits data to other cores, such as Broadcast and Scatter. The second category is Many-to-One that denotes multiple cores transmit to one core, such as Reduce and Gather.

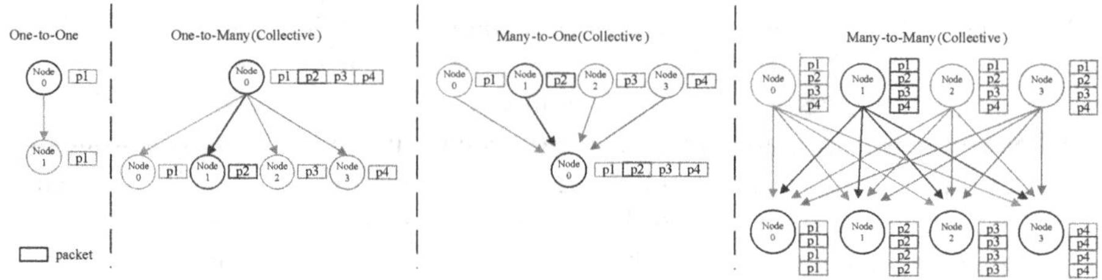

Fig. 2. One-to-one and collective communication categories.

The third category Many-to-Many, which means multiple cores transmit to other cores, such as All Reduce and All Gather.

Based on collective communication behaviors, we propose several high-performance transmission mechanisms for One-to-Many communication. The Many-to-Many communication can be divided into multiple One-to-Many communications, they can apply the same transmission mechanism. Besides, Many-to-One communication is a sequence of One-to-One communication, so it can adopt One-to-One communication.

4.1 High-Performance Transmission Mechanisms

In this paper, two high-performance transmission mechanisms, Centralized Distribution and Adaptive Distribution, are proposed to improve the performance of One-to-Many communications. The Centralized Distribution (CD) mechanisms collect the transmitted packets in the H3 switch. While the packets are collected completely, the packets are transmitted to the destination nodes in parallel. The Adaptive Distribution (AD) mechanisms firstly group the packets according to their destinations, then transmits to the suitable H2 switch, instead of forwarding all packets via H3 switch. Hence the transmission distance of the packets can be reduced. According to the message length of the transmitted packet, the CD and AD transmission mechanisms are divided into two types, the single transmission mechanisms (CD-Single and AD-Single) and the burst transmission mechanisms (CD-Burst and AD-Burst), respectively.

The CD mechanisms are designed for concurrently distributing the packets with distinct target nodes. Since the packet lengths can be short or long, the required packet collecting, buffer management, and packet distributing mechanisms are different. Therefore the CD mechanisms are divided into two types, CD-Single and CD-Burst, according to the length of the message that attempt to transmit.

Although the proposed CD mechanisms can distribute packets concurrently, the packet collecting steps will enlarge the potential transmission distance. While the packets that are attempted to transfer concurrently are located in the neighbor regions, the overhead of the packet that are collected in the H3 switch will reduced the performance of CD mechanisms. Accordingly, the AD mechanisms are proposed to deal with this situation. The AD mechanisms group the transmitted packets according to the target nodes, then decide the suitable H2 or H3 switches as the target switch to collects the packet group. While the packets in this group are collected completely, the packet group will be distributed concurrently to the target nodes. Since not all of the packet groups require to be collected and distributed via H3 switch, the transmission distance of the packets can be reduced while transmitting to the target nodes that are near the source nodes. According to the long or short messages of the packets that are attempted to transmit, the AD mechanism are divides into AD-Single and AD-Burst respectively.

4.2 Packet Analysis and Decision Mechanism

The proposed transmission mechanisms for HSSC on-chip network are suitable for different packet transmission scenarios. To achieve better performance and utilize the HSSC network, a Packet Analysis and Decision Mechanism (PADM) is proposed to analyze the packets, partition the packets into several groups according to their characteristics. Then the transmission scheduling mechanism is adopted to find a suitable transmission mechanism to improve communication performance. The transmission scheduling mechanism is as listed in Algorithm 1.

In PADM mechanism, the packets that attempt to transfer will be analyzed, according to their payload size ($P_{payload\_size}$), the target nodes (P_{target}), and other characteristics. Then the packets will be partitioned into several packet groups and stored into the packet grouped buffer (PG[]). While all the packets are analyzed, the partitioned packets in the packet grouped buffer will be sent to the transmission scheduling mechanism for further scheduling.

The transmission decision algorithm can determine the appropriate transmission mechanism for the grouped packet to improve the performance. The adopted transmission mechanisms that includes several basic transmission mechanisms and high-performance transmission mechanism mentioned before, and the transmission mechanism [6] to provide alternative transmission path while encountering the congestion in the hierarchical paths in HSSC.

In this algorithm, the H_{status} is firstly obtained that indicates the packet transmission status between H0 and H1. If H0 waits for the grant of H1 for a long time, it will be set as congestion then the mechanism will adopt the basic transmission mechanism for this packet group, to reduce the number of packets transmitted via the hierarchical interconnection network; if it is not set as congestion, then the mechanism checks $P_{payload\_size}$. If $P_{payload\_size}$ is higher than B_{length} * L_{width}, H-Burst is applied to this packet group to improve the performance of packet transmission. The remained mechanisms will be selected according to R_{target} (the ratio of the total number of different destination nodes to the total number of nodes in the interconnection network). If the R_{target} is smaller than the threshold $T_{covered}$, it means that the packets are not widely dispersed, therefore the parallel transmission are not suitable. In this case, the CD-based transmission mechanisms are not considered and other mechanisms are determined according to R_{remote} (the ratio of the total number of nodes that the packet destination needs to cross H3 to the total number of distinct destination nodes). When R_{remote} is greater than the threshold T_{remote}, it means that most of the packets are transmitted to the remote nodes, so H-Single will be used. Otherwise, according to L_{width}, it will be divided into two cases, the short message packets and the long message packets. In order to make packet transmission to be collected and spread at the same time, AD-Single will be used for the short message packets, otherwise AD-Burst will be selected. The AD-Single transmission is suitable for the local transmission.

If R_{target} exceeds $T_{covered}$, then it will be divided into two cases, according to L_{width}. In the case of a short message packet, if the value of $H3_{empty}$ is true, it means that H3 does not serve any packet, so CD-Single is selected to make the packet transmission achieve the effect of simultaneous transmission. However, if it is false, AD-Single is used, so that the local packet transmission is concentrated first and the packet contention is reduced. In the case of long message packets, $H3_{empty}$ is also used to determine the buffer status of H3. If $H3_{empty}$ is true, CD-Burst is used otherwise AD-Burst is applied.

Algorithm 1：Transmission Decision Algorithm

Input：PG[] /* packet grouped buffer */
N_{total} /* total number of nodes in the HSSC */
L_{width} /* Bus Link Width */
B_{length} /* Transfer Burst Length */
H_{status} /* Switch H0 to H2 Traffic Congestion Status */
$H3_{empty}$ /* H3 Buffer status */
$T_{covered}$, T_{remote} /* threshold value, in our work is 50%*/

Output：Mechanism

```
begin
if H_status == true then
  Mechanism ← Basic
else
  P_payload_size ← PG[first]_payload_size
  R_target ← (Number of packets in PG[]) / N_total
  R_remote ← (Number of packet in PG[] that need passing through H3) / (Number of packets in PG[])

  if P_payload_size >= B_length * L_width then
    Mechanism ← H-Burst
  else
    if R_target < T_covered then
      if R_remote > T_remote then
        Mechanism ← H-Single
      else
        if P_payload_size <= L_width then
          Mechanism ← AD-Single
        else
          Mechanism ← AD-Burst
        endif
      endif
    else
      if P_payload_size <= L_width then
        if H3_empty == true then
          Mechanism ← CD-Single
        else
          Mechanism ← AD-Single
        endif
      else
        if H3_empty == true then
          Mechanism ← CD-Burst
        else
          Mechanism ← AD-Burst
        endif
      endif
    endif
  endif
endif
end
```

5 Experiment Results

In this section, the experimental environment and the adopted benchmarks will be mentioned first. Then the experiment results of HSSC and PADM will be discussed.

5.1 Experimental Environment

In order to evaluate the performance of HSSC on-chip network, the proposed HSSC on-chip network and three conventional on-chip networks, Mesh, Torus, and SSC, are implemented by using SystemC [7] modeling language, to simulate the configuration of 128 nodes multicore architectures. The link width of the on-chip networks are 4 bytes. The implemented burst length for the HSSC model is set as 8 packets. The proposed PADM mechanism with a set of the packet transmission mechanisms are also implemented. The Mesh and Torus on-chip networks adopts XY-routing, and SSC adopts Tree-routing to avoid deadlock situations.

The evaluated benchmarks, BT, CG, LU, FT, are selected from NAS Parallel Benchmarks (NPB) [9], which can evaluate the performance of multi-nodes supercomputer. In this experiment, we apply EZTrace [8] to record and obtain trace of the communication among these cores that performs the benchmarks for evaluate the performance of target on-chip networks. The adopted version is MPI [10] version NPB 3.3.1. The configurations of node number and problem size of these benchmarks are as listed in Table 1.

Table 1. The configurations of four benchmarks.

Application	Class	Node numbers
BT	A	121
CG	S	128
LU	W	121
FT	S	128

5.2 The Performance of HSSC On-Chip Network

Figure 3 compares the execution time difference among four benchmarks and four on-chip networks. In BT, CG, and LU benchmarks, when the programs startup and finish, they perform some one-to-many transmissions with small payload size. And many of the remained transmissions belong to one-to-one transmissions with larger payload size. Accordingly, the proposed PADM mechanism may assign AD-Burst and H-Burst to suit this situation. Hence the HSSC on-chip network with PADM mechanism (HSSC(PADM)) performs better than other on-chip network, as shown in Fig. 3. The FT benchmark has different transmitting behavior from other applications. It contains a lot of many-to-many transmission. Since the payload size of the transmissions are much larger than the length of the burst transmission, the PADM will choose the H-Burst to transmit, instead of other transmission mechanisms. The result of this decision achieve extreme performance, as shown in Fig. 3.

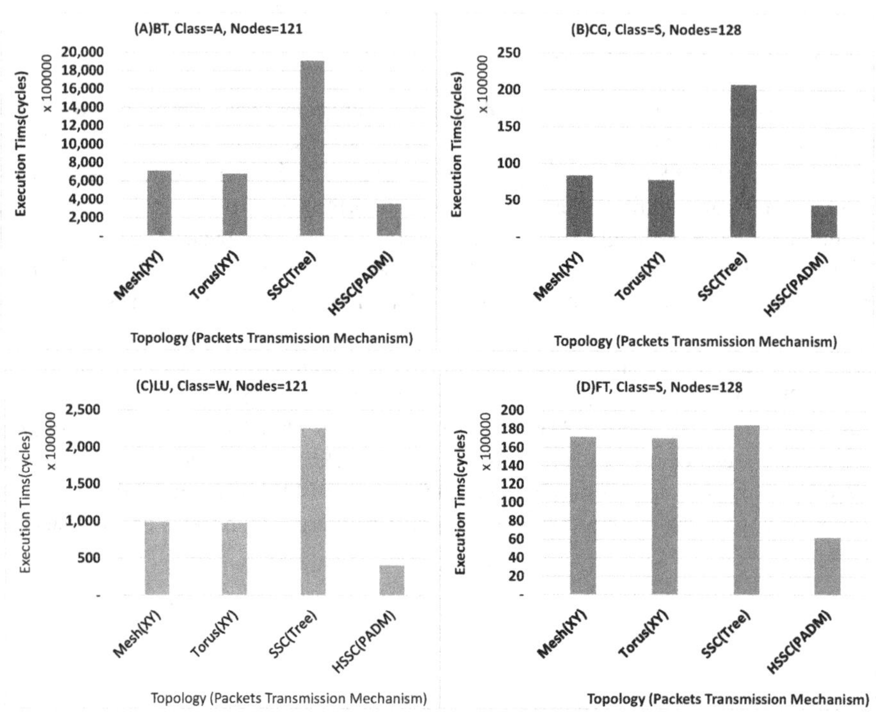

Fig. 3. The execution time comparison among four benchmarks.

6 Conclusions

This study proposed a novel on-chip network, called Hierarchy Self Similar Cubic (HSSC), to improve the transmission performance of collective communications. It retains the advantages of local transmission and improves the disadvantage of remote data transmission in the original SSC network, so that the transmission latency of the collective transmission can be reduced, whether it is local or remote transmissions. In addition to the proposed HSSC, we also proposed the corresponding transmission mechanism for determining the suitable transmission mechanisms by Packet Analysis and Decision Mechanism (PADM), so that the packets can be on-the-fly grouped and determined the appropriate transmission mechanism according to the attributes of the packets and other information to improve the transmission efficiency. From the experimental results, HSSC and PADM can effectively improve the transmission performance of collective transmission, compared to other three on-chip networks.

Acknowledgments. This work is supported in part by the Ministry of Science and Technology of Republic of China, Taiwan under Grant MOST 105-2221-E-033-047.

References

1. Dvorak, V., Jaros, J.: Optimizing collective communications on 2D-mesh and fat tree NoC. In: 2010 Ninth International Conference on Networks, pp. 22–27. IEEE, Menuires (2010)
2. Chu, S.L., Lee, G.S., Peng, Y.W.: Self similar cubic: a novel interconnection network for many-core architectures. In: 2012 Fifth International Symposium on Parallel Architectures, Algorithms and Programming, pp. 303–310. IEEE, Taipei (2012)
3. Moadeli, M., Vanderbauwhede, W.: A communication model of broadcast in wormhole-routed networks on-chip. In: 2009 International Conference on Advanced Information Networking and Applications, pp. 315–322. IEEE, Bradford (2009)
4. Ajima, Y., et al.: Tofu interconnect 2: system-on-chip integration of high-performance interconnect. In: Kunkel, J.M., Ludwig, T., Meuer, H.W. (eds.) ISC 2014. LNCS, vol. 8488, pp. 498–507. Springer, Cham (2014). https://doi.org/10.1007/978-3-319-07518-1_35
5. Ma, S., Jerger, N. E., Wang, Z.: Supporting efficient collective communication in NoCs. In: IEEE International Symposium on High-Performance Comp Architecture, pp. 1–12. IEEE, New Orleans (2012)
6. Liu, M.H.: The mechanisms for improving performance of SSC on-chip network. Master Thesis, Department of Information & Computer Engineering, CYCU (2017)
7. Black, D.C., Donovan, J., Bunton, B., Keist, A.: SystemC: From the Ground Up. Springer, Boston (2009). https://doi.org/10.1007/978-0-387-69958-5
8. Trahay, F., Rue, F., Faverge, M., Ishikawa, Y., Namyst, R., Dongarra, J.: EZTrace: a generic framework for performance analysis. In: 2011 11th IEEE/ACM International Symposium on Cluster, Cloud and Grid Computing, pp. 618–619. IEEE, Newport Beach (2011)
9. Bailey, D.H.: NAS parallel benchmarks. In: Padua, D. (ed.) Encyclopedia of Parallel Computing, pp. 1254–1259. Springer, Boston (2011). https://doi.org/10.1007/978-0-387-09766-4_133
10. Snir, M., Gropp, W., Otto, S., Huss-Lederman, S., Dongarra, J., Walker, D.: MPI–The Complete Reference: The MPI Core. MIT Press, London (1998)

A Survey of Multicast Communication in Optical Network-on-Chip (ONoC)

Wen Yang[1(✉)], Yawen Chen[1], Zhiyi Huang[1], Haibo Zhang[1], Huaxi Gu[2], and Cui Yu[3]

[1] Department of Computer Science, University of Otago, Dunedin 9016, New Zealand
{yangwen,yawen,hzy,haibo}@cs.otago.ac.nz

[2] State Key Laboratory of ISN, Xidian University, Xi'an 710071, China
hxgu@xidian.edu.cn

[3] Key Laboratory of Electromagnetic Wave Information Technology and Metrology of Zhejiang Province, China Jiliang University, Hangzhou 310018, China
yucui8712@126.com

Abstract. Optical Network-on-Chip (ONoC) is an emerging chip-level optical interconnection technology to realise high-performance and power-efficient inter-core communication for many-core processors. For on-chip networks, multicast communication is an important communication pattern, which is not only widely used in parallel computing applications in Chip Multi-Processors (CMPs), but also commonly adopted in emerging areas such as neuromorphic computing. However, the optimisation of multicast communication in an ONoC is not well studied and there is a significant room to improve the performance. In this paper, we present a comprehensive survey of the multicast communication in an ONoC, covering the development of both architecture design and networking design as well as our recent research outcomes. Moreover, we propose the design challenges and future research directions for optimising multicast in an ONoC, which can provide guidance and insight for the future researchers and chip developers.

Keywords: Optical Network-on-Chip · Multicast communication · Routing and wavelength assignment

1 Introduction

As the cores integrated into a single chip increase rapidly, inter-core communication is becoming an essential component for many-core processors. An Electrical Network-on-Chip (ENoC) is considered as the most viable solution to deal with inter-core communication issues that affect the future development of many-core Chip Multi-Processors (CMPs). However, as hundreds or even thousands of processing cores will be integrated into one processor chip, an ENoC will no longer fulfill the high demands on communication bandwidth and power consumption because of its inherent problems such as wire delay and signal interference.

H. Shen and Y. Sang (Eds.): PAAP 2019, CCIS 1163, pp. 58–70, 2020.
https://doi.org/10.1007/978-981-15-2767-8_6

An Optical Network-on-Chip (ONoC) is an emerging communication architecture to overcome the drawbacks of an ENoC due to the development of nanophotonic technologies. By integrating silicon nanophotonics into on-chip interconnection networks, ONoC, a chip-level inter-core optical network, can utilise the unique merits of optical communication (e.g., high bandwidth density, immunity to electro-magnetic effects) to improve network performance [5,8]. Compared to an ENoC, an ONoC has many advantages, such as high bandwidth by utilising Wavelength-Division-Multiplexing (WDM) [33], low power consumption, low end-to-end communication delay, and CMOS compatibility. While an ONoC has many benefits, inter-core communication is still a challenging problem because of its influence on communication performance, hardware cost and energy efficiency [30].

Among all inter-core communication patterns in an ONoC, multicast communication, where packets from one source need to be delivered simultaneously to multiple destinations, is one of the most important traffic patterns. It is not only common in parallel computing applications in CMPs (e.g., cache coherency and barrier synchronization), but also widely used in emerging areas such as neuromorphic computing [3] and computational genomics [9]. Previous experiments have shown that multicast traffic contributes to a large percentage of the total traffic. For example, the multicast traffic takes about 14.3% and 52.4% on average for HyperTransport and Token Coherence, respectively, in a 64-core system [25]. Moreover, the percentage of multicast traffic and the average number of destinations both increase with the increase of cores in CMPs, according to the analysis in [2]. Therefore, multicast communication is a vital traffic pattern in many-core processors.

The traditional method can be used in an ONoC by treating multicast communication as repeated unicasts, where a multicast packet can be replicated multiple times and sent to each of the destinations separately [16]. However, this method easily leads to the following problems: (*i*) The increase of global congestion. Sending multiple copies of the same packet into the network causes a significant amount of traffic and competition for the same network resource among repeated unicast packets. (*ii*) The increase of serialisation delay. This is because of the queuing of repeated unicast packets on the same communication fabric, and every copy of the packet suffers from the startup latency at the source node. (*iii*) The increase of power consumption. Redundant packets that transmit on the network will consume more power. As a result, even a small percentage of multicast traffic (e.g., 1%) will have severe effects on the ONoC performance and cost [2]. Therefore, the design of a high performance and scalable interconnection architecture and a routing protocol to support multicast communication is vital for the many-core processors.

In this paper, a comprehensive survey of multicast communication in an ONoC is provided. The multicast communication problem in an ONoC can be classified into two categories: architecture design and networking design. The architecture design is a hardware-based design, which studies the multicast support architectures, such as the topology and on-chip devices. The networking design is the routing and wavelength assignment design for multicast communication, which includes the optimisation of a single multicast and multiple multicasts. The classification for multicast communication in an ONoC is presented in Fig. 1. The rest of the paper is structured as follows. Section 2 discusses the issues of architecture design. Section 3 introduces the research about the networking design. Section 4 proposes the design challenges and future research directions. Finally, conclusions are given in Sect. 5.

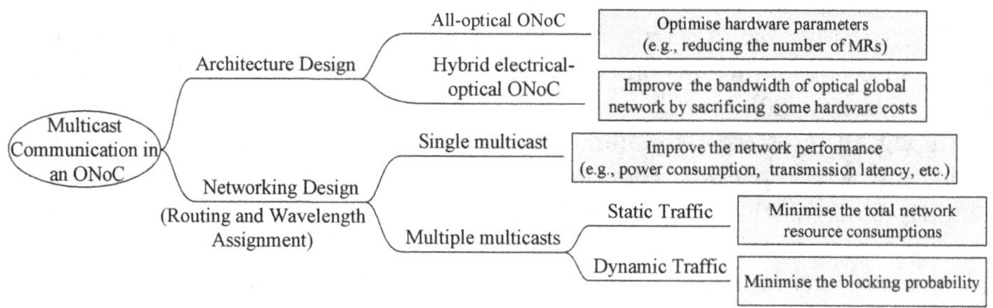

Fig. 1. Classification of the multicast communication problem in an ONoC

2 Architecture Design

The optimisation on ONoC architecture design that supports the multicast communication focuses mainly on *hardware parameters*, such as the power loss induced by the optical devices, commercial availability, and fabrication complexity. In an ONoC, many waveguided optical interconnects have been thoroughly investigated, and several state-of-the-art architectures have been proposed for multicast communication. *All-optical ONoC* and *hybrid electrical-optical ONoC* are two basic network architectures supporting the multicast communication, which we introduce as follows.

2.1 All-Optical ONoC

An all-optical ONoC only utilises the optical signal to implement the multicast communication without any electrical links involved. In an all-optical ONoC, Micro-ring Resonators (MR)-based routing architectures supporting WDM are used, and the routing is performed based on their wavelengths. In [1], a Multicast Rotary Router (MRR) which is able to perform the on-chip multicast support was proposed. It uses a fully adaptive tree to distribute multicast traffic, and performs the on-chip congestion control by extending the range of network utilisation. The authors in [41] proposed a generic wavelength-routed optical architecture, namely WRON, which uses cascaded MRR-based 2×2 optical switches.

WRON is a WDM-supported passive ONoC with a non-blocking routing. Similarly, a wavelength-routed multi-stage passive optical routing structure that uses multiple 2×2 switching elements, called λ router, was designed in [10]. Corona is an all-photonic crossbar-based CMPs architecture, which comprises 256 general purpose cores that are organised in 64 clusters [35]. Although Corona can provide significant bandwidth support, it suffers from high static power dissipation, due to the high complexity of the photonic layer. In [28], a nanophotonic broadcast tree-based network has been proposed for snoopy cache coherent multicores. This tree-topology requires splitters and combiners to fork and join the optical signals. A bus-based topology that utilises WDM was derived in [15]. It uses a bank of microring modulators, which can be configured to listen to a selected channel. Although the all-optical ONoC can achieve non-blocking optical communication for multicast using different wavelengths, this architecture based on global crossbars requires a large number of MRs, thus consuming considerable MR tuning power. Moreover, the requirements of laser power are also too large, due to the excessive number of required wavelengths. In addition, MRs have a fairly large footprint, compared to their electronic counterparts, thus leading to higher manufacturing costs. Therefore, an all-optical ONoC is not suitable for supporting a large number of cores, in terms of the cost and limitation of available lasers.

2.2 Hybrid Electrical-Optical ONoC

A hybrid electrical-optical ONoC combines both electrical and optical links in the architecture, which can provide a more practical solution by using optical signaling for long distance communication, while electrical signaling is used for local communication. As such, it has the advantages of optical signaling in bandwidth and power consumption, while keeping the low cost and flexibility of electrical signaling. The authors in [31] designed a hybrid hierarchical architecture, where an intra-cluster communication was based on the electrical signaling and an inter-cluster communication was carried on multiple optical crossbars. In this method, the crossbar was partitioned into multiple smaller crossbars and the arbitration was localised, to avoid the global switch arbitration. Another switch-based hybrid on-chip optical network that uses source-based routing and reconfigurable optical switches was derived in [13]. The authors in [7] designed an ONoC, based on the mesh and global crossbar, where the optical interconnect was used for high throughput traffic and metallic interconnect for local and fast switching. In [20], a fat-tree structure was proposed based on a circuit-switched ONoC, where an extra layer for tuning and controlling was required to be integrated with optical signal transmissions. The authors in [26] proposed a three-plane hierarchical ONoC architecture: all cores were contained in a core plane; an optical control plane was utilised to achieve centralised routing and wavelength allocation; an optical forwarding plane was used to provide non-blocking transmission for massive multicast packets. In general, combining electrical and optical links can take the load off the optical network, and allows for lower MR counts and throughput requirements in the optical part of the network. However, a hybrid electrical-optical ONoC may introduce extra processing delay, hardware cost, and power consumption, especially by using an electrical control network to establish the optical path in a hop-by-hop manner.

2.3 3D ONoC

As the two-dimensional (2D) chip fabrication technology is facing several challenges in the deep submicron regime (e.g., the limited floor-planning choices and the increase of wire delay), a three-Dimensional (3D) integration has emerged as a potential solution to further improve the ONoC performance. In 3D integration technology, Through-Silicon-Via (TSV) [32] is used to stack multiple device layers together with direct vertical interconnects. By combining 3D integration technology with the ONoC, a 3D ONoC will bring further performance improvements compared to its 2D counterparts, such as decreasing transmission latency, reducing low power consumption, and providing high routing diversity. In a 3D ONoC, there are also some studies on architectures supporting the multicast communication. The authors in [12] presented a new network architecture dedicated to the multicast service, aimed at reducing the effect of the rapid saturation of the network for an acceptable cost. The authors in [24] proposed a Single-Cycle Multi-hop Asynchronous Repeated Traversal (SMART) 3D ENoC architecture that is capable of achieving high-performance collective communication. The authors in [34] proposed a 3D-stacked wavelength-routed multi-core architecture by photonically integrating bandwidth-rich DRAM devices. Despite the significant advantages of a 3D ONoC, some challenges remain, such as thermal mitigation [4], interconnect modeling and crosstalk noise [21].

Overall, the power-efficient design and cost-efficient design of constructing a multicast-capable ONoC under hardware constraints are the main considerations in the architecture design to solve multicast communication problem in an ONoC.

3 Networking Design

In an ONoC, the routing and wavelength assignment algorithm plays a critical role in the multicast support since it determines the direction of the transmitted packet and the transmitting carrier. In the networking level design, the major focus is to investigate the efficient routing and wavelength assignment methods for multicast communication, which involves various modeling and optimisation processes. According to the complexity of the optimisation, we classify the modeling as two specific domains: (1) single multicast optimisation; (2) multiple multicasts optimisation, as illustrated in Fig. 1.

3.1 Design for a Single Multicast

For implementing single multicast in an ONoC, the optimisation objective is to *maximise network performance*, by reducing power consumption and transmission latency. The simplest case for a single multicast is based on the assumption that the network has full light splitting capability and no wavelength conversions are supported. Parallel tree-based and serial path-based routings are two major methods used in an ONoC for a single multicast, as illustrated in Fig. 2.

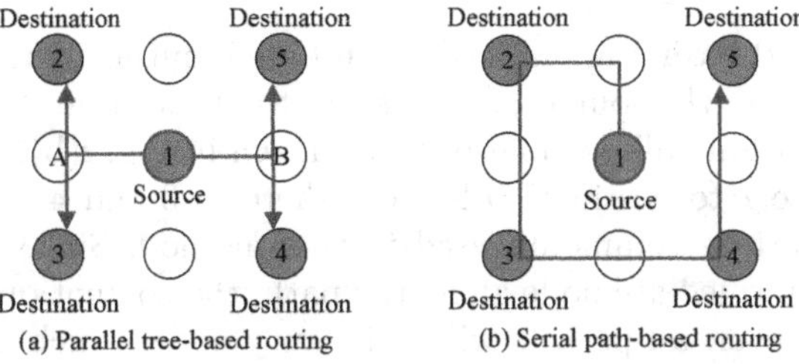

Fig. 2. Two main routing methods for a single multicast in an ONoC

Parallel Tree-Based Routing. In parallel tree-based routing methods [37], a packet is first transmitted to a common path from the source (the root of the tree). When the common path ends, the packet is replicated and the new copies also follow a recursive tree method, replicating multiple times to reach the destinations (the leaves of the tree). As illustrated in Fig. 2(a), a packet gets replicated at the source 1, one copy is delivered to nodes 2 and 3, and the other copy is sent to nodes 4 and 5. Each of these two copies is duplicated further at intermediate nodes A and B, and finally, forwarded to the destinations 2, 3, 4 and 5. The authors in [23] proposed a multicast support named Virtual Circuit Tree Multicasting (VCTM), which uses a virtual circuit table to construct the multicast tree incrementally, by sending a unicast packet to the next closest multicast destination. Although this method can achieve low latency for the transmission of packets, it is not power efficient due to maintaining a table at every switch to store a virtual tree. Another two tree-based multicast routing schemes called Optimize Tree (OPT) and Left-xy-Right-Optimized Tree (LXYROPT) were designed, based on VCTM [22]. OPT uses the west-first turn model to optimise the multicast tree with fewer links, thus avoiding a deadlock, while LXYROPT partitions destinations into two subsets. For the first subset that contains destinations left to the source node, XY routing is used to construct the multicast tree. For the destinations on the right of the source node, the west-first turn model is used. These two algorithms both use the minimum number of links to achieve the low multicast latency and power consumption. Switch Tree-Based Algorithm (STBA) [29] is a newly proposed multicast routing method that supports the construction of a multicast tree on a reconfigurable mesh NoC. It uses switches in a reconfigurable network to construct a minimal spanning tree with a Kruskal minimal spanning tree algorithm and west-first routing algorithm. A STBA can improve power consumption and packets' latency by dividing the channel-width and traffic. Overall, the tree-based routing can achieve low network latency due to constructing the tree by the shortest paths. However, for the branch node, the packet will be duplicated and forwarded to multiple outputs. When a branch occurs, if either output is blocked, the others must wait. In this case, if the packet does not proceed, many channels may be in lockstep for extended periods, resulting in increased network contentions [18].

Serial Path-Based Routing. In serial path-based routing methods, one packet is serially routed from the source to its first destination, from there to the next, and so on until reaching all destinations. As shown in Fig. 2(b), a packet is first routed from source 1 to destination 2, from there to 3 and 4, and finally to 5. A Hamiltonian path is commonly used in this method. Since packets do not replicate at the intermediate node along the path, the contention of packets will be decreased. However, all packets will visit every node, which may suffer from long latency. In order to overcome this shortcoming, a destinations-partitioning method has been derived according to the label of each node. The popular partitioning methods are Dual-Path (DP), Multi-Path (MP) and Column-Path (CP) [11,14]. DP (Fig. 3(a)) is a base method where destinations are divided into two parts. One part contains destinations that have higher labels than the source node, while the other has the remaining destinations. A packet will be sent along an ascending or descending order, respectively, according to the label of every destination. The DP performs well when the network size is small (e.g., tens of cores). As the network size enlarges, the DP has no effect on reducing latency. In order to reduce the path length, the MP partitioning (Fig. 3(b)) has been proposed by dividing destinations into four parts, based on the DP. In the CP (Fig. 3(c)), destinations are divided into more subsets, depending on the number of vertical columns. Each packet will transmit along a shorter path, compared to the DP and MP approaches; therefore, the CP can achieve a high level of parallelism and reduce the network latency. Based on these basic path-based routing methods, some modified path-based routing algorithms have been derived to further improve network performance. The authors in [11] presented a deadlock-free adaptation of a dual-path multicast algorithm for a mesh-based ENoC. However, this method cannot provide any adaptiveness for routing the multicast packets and has the disadvantage of high network latency due to the creation of long paths. In [17], a new adaptive routing model based on a Hamiltonian path for both the multicast and unicast (HAMUM) was presented, based on a partition to reduce latency and energy consumption. A hybrid multicast routing approach that combines the path-based and tree-based methods was proposed in [38], which is a deadlock-free multicast routing, without requiring additional virtual channels or large buffers to hold large packets. Overall, the path-based routing is attractive due to its simplified hardware design and is deadlock-free by means of the Hamiltonian path. However, if the destination nodes spread widely, the path-based routing may suffer from a great amount of latency, compared to tree-based routing.

Overall, current studies about realising a single multicast in an ONoC have mainly focused on improving network performance, such as reducing power consumption, achieving low latency, and avoiding a deadlock.

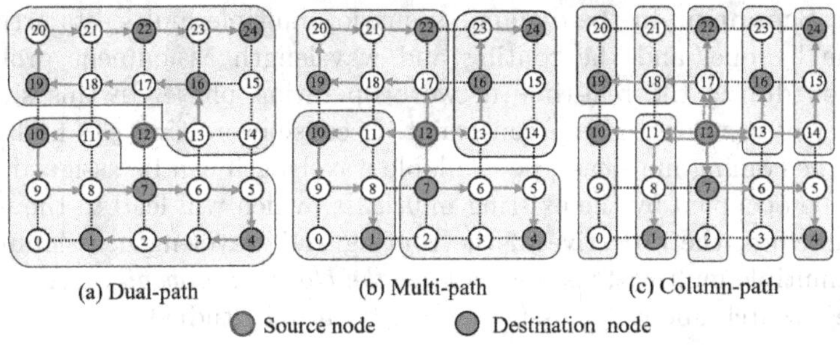

Fig. 3. Example of the path-based routings for multicast communication in a 5×5 2D mesh-based ONoC

3.2 Design for Multiple Multicasts

Instead of dealing with one multicast, the routing and wavelength assignment for multiple multicasts attempts to arrange a set of multicasts where each multicast has its own source node and a set of destination nodes. For a single multicast, the problem mainly focuses on satisfying one multicast. However, in the case of multiple multicasts required by the applications at the same time, the problem should not only try to optimise an individual multicast, but also consider the whole set of multicasts as a combined optimisation problem. The routing and wavelength assignment problem for multiple multicasts can be classified into two categories: **static scenario** and **dynamic scenario**.

Static Scenario. If the multiple multicasts are known in advance and any traffic variations take place over a long timescale, the routing and wavelength assignment problem for these multicasts is considered as a static multicast problem. In this situation, the most important optimisation objective is to *minimise the total network resource consumptions* (e.g., physical links and wavelengths). Specifically, the objective of the routing and wavelength assignment should be either that the number of wavelengths required to accommodate all multicasts is minimised or the number of multicasts established is maximised for a limited number of wavelengths. In [36], an Alternative Recursive Partitioning Multicasting (AL + RPM) was proposed to deal with multiple applications with applicable traffic isolation constraints in an ENoC. The basic idea of AL + RPM is to find the output directions following the basic RPM algorithm, and then decide to replicate the packets in the original output directions or the alternative (AL) output directions, based on the shape of the sub-network. In [39], we proposed a group-partitioning routing and wavelength assignment algorithm to accommodate all given multicasts in an ONoC. We investigated this problem according to the distribution of multicast nodes in a mesh-based ONoC, which can reduce the number of wavelengths used significantly. Due to the low manufacture complexity requirement of an ONoC, we also designed a path-based routing for multiple multicasts in [40] with low wavelengths requirements.

Dynamic Scenario. In the dynamic scenario, multiple multicasts arrive randomly one by one, and the routing and wavelength assignment problem is encountered during the real-time network operation phase. In this situation, the number of wavelengths is a constraint. Because even if we can find routing paths for the coming multicast, no available wavelength can be assigned to it as they may be occupied by the existing multicast, which will lead to the network block. Therefore, the objective of the routing and wavelength assignment for dynamic multiple multicasts is to *minimise the blocking probability*. As far as we know, the research about this issue has not been well studied.

4 Design Challenges and Future Work

4.1 Design Challenges

Despite the above schemes can solve multicast communication problem to some extent, there are still design challenges to achieve high-performance multicast communication in an ONoC which are shown as follows.

Wavelength Challenge. An ONoC offers orders-of-magnitude bandwidth improvement by leveraging on Wavelength-Division-Multiplexing (WDM) technology, that allows multiple optical signals to be transmitted concurrently, using different wavelengths through a single waveguide [33]. Although WDM can significantly improve communication throughput, the maximum number of supported wavelengths per waveguide is limited in realistic scenarios, since the maximum optical power which can be injected into the optical interconnect without non-linear effects is limited. For example, at most, 62 wavelengths can be used in a 10 Gbps data rate network as reported in [27]. More importantly, more used wavelengths will lead to a higher complexity of ONoC components (e.g., optical routers), resulting in lower energy efficiency. Furthermore, most existing research about multicast communication only focuses on electrical interconnects and improving the conventional criteria of routing design (e.g., shortest path and transmission delay), which are not suitable for an ONoC. Conversely, those important routing criteria for an ONoC, such as wavelength consumption, are not considered. *Therefore, the challenge is how to optimise the use of limited wavelength resources to provide guaranteed multicast communication performance.*

Complexity Challenge. Despite the significant advances achieved in silicon photonics in the past decades, the optical interconnect is still a costly alternative. Some of the optical devices (e.g., laser sources) might need to be placed off-chip, which creates issues with manufacture complexity (e.g., packaging and pin number requirements) and high coupling losses that might dominate the power consumption budget [6]. Moreover, the complexity of a routing and wavelength assignment scheme is also a critical design factor in an ONoC, which impacts performance (e.g., power and wavelength usage) and thermal regulation. *Therefore, the complexity of architecture and algorithms is another challenge for high performance and scalable multicast design in an ONoC.*

Multiple Multicasts Challenge. While some studies have been proposed to improve the performance of multicast in an ONoC, most of them only consider one multicast. For example, in [26], DWRMR is a multicast routing method for an ONoC, which is based on dynamical-established and wavelength-reused multicast rings. It can achieve low packet delay and the same performance, using half the number of wavelengths compared to existing schemes. However, they only consider the optimisation of one multicast, without considering the optimisation of multiple multicasts, which limits the practical applications because real systems often have to handle multiple multicasts requested from various applications. For example, multiprogrammed and server workloads (e.g., TPC-H or SPECweb99) imply the simultaneous execution of various instances of a set of simple applications [3]. Distributed shared cache systems, single program multiple data programming models, and data parallel programming models all need supports for multiple multicasts [19]. If the methods originally designed for one multicast are used for multiple multicasts, they are very likely to cause high contentions without considering other multicasts, thereby increasing the number of wavelengths used. *Hence, an effective multiple multicasts support in an ONoC is the third challenge.*

4.2 Future Directions

In the future, the research about the multicast communication in ONoC will focus on the following areas by taking into account the above challenges, as shown in Table 1.

Table 1. Future research directions for multicast in an ONoC

System-level design	Low complexity of architecture
	Large fanout capability
	Low power consumption
Network-level design	Low complexity routing algorithm
	Minimisation of the number of wavelengths
	Optimisation of multiple multicasts
Application-level design	Optimal routing for the communication pattern in Convolutional Neural Networks (CNNs)
	Optimal routing for the communication pattern in computational genomics
	Optimisation of mapping the tasks to ONoC-based architecture

System-Level Design. Despite optical interconnects show obvious advantages than their electrical counterparts, it still faces some challenges, such as architecture complexity, thermal regulation and power consumption. Therefore, how to design an ONoC architecture supporting multicast with low complexity and low power consumption is a future direction.

Network-Level Design. Since an ONoC differs from traditional large-scale optical network and even from multi-chip interconnects, how to design efficient routing schemes to support multiple multicasts in an ONoC is a vital consideration, aiming at reducing the utilisation of wavelengths.

Application-Level Design. If there are multiple tasks exist simultaneously, how to map the tasks on ONoC-based architecture is complex because there are a number of combinations of task positions. Therefore, the method to determine the best task mapping is desired in order to improve the performance of an ONoC.

5 Conclusion

In this paper, we provide a comprehensive review for multicast communication in an ONoC, including architecture design and networking design. For the architecture level, we present the current architectures supporting the multicast communication, including all-optical ONoC, hybrid electrical-optical ONoC and 3D ONoC. For the networking level, we introduce the existing studies from the perspectives of optimising single multicast and multiple multicasts. Furthermore, we point out the design challenges and the future research directions for multicast design in an ONoC, which is expected to provide guidance and insight for future researchers and developers on this research topic.

References

1. Abad, P., Puente, V., Gregorio, J.A.: MRR: enabling fully adaptive multicast routing for CMP interconnection networks. In: HPCA, pp. 355–366 (2009)
2. Abadal, S., Martínez, R., Alarcón, E., Cabellos-Aparicio, A.: Scalability-oriented multicast traffic characterization. In: IEEE/ACM international Symposium on NoCS, pp. 180–181 (2014)
3. Abadal, S., Mestres, A., Martinez, R., Alarcon, E., Cabellos-Aparicio, A.: Multicast on-chip traffic analysis targeting manycore NoC design. In: 23rd Euromicro International Conference on PDP, pp. 370–378 (2015)
4. Achballah, A.B., Othman, S.B., Saoud, S.B.: An extensive review of emerging technology networks-on-chip proposals. Global J. Res. Eng. **17**(6), 16–40 (2017)
5. Shacham, A., Bergman, K., Carloni, L.P.: Photonic networks-on-chip for future generations of chip multiprocessors. IEEE Trans. Comput. **57**(9), 1246–1260 (2008)
6. Association, S.I., et al.: International Technology Roadmap for Semiconductors 2.0 (2015 edn.) (2015). http://www.itrs2.net/
7. Batten, C., et al.: Building many-core processor-to-DRAM networks with monolithic CMOS silicon photonics. IEEE Micro **29**(4), 1 (2009)
8. Batten, C., Joshi, A., Stojanovć, V., Asanović, K.: Designing chip-level nanophotonic interconnection networks. In: O'Connor, I., Nicolescu, G. (eds.) Integrated Optical Interconnect Architectures for Embedded Systems, pp. 81–135. Springer, New York (2013). https://doi.org/10.1007/978-1-4419-6193-8_3

9. Bogdan, P., Majumder, T., Ramanathan, A., Xue, Y.: NoC architectures as enablers of biological discovery for personalized and precision medicine. In: IEEE/ACM International Symposium on NoCS, p. 27 (2015)
10. Briere, M., et al.: System level assessment of an optical NoC in an MPSoC platform. In: DATE, pp. 1–6 (2007)
11. Carara, E.A., Moraes, F.G.: Deadlock-free multicast routing algorithm for wormhole-switched mesh networks-on-chip. In: IEEE ISVLSI. pp. 341–346 (2008)
12. Chatmen, M.F., Baganne, A., Tourki, R.: A new network on chip design dedicated to multicast service. J. Adv. Comput. Sci. Appl. **7**(4), 104–116 (2016)
13. Cianchetti, M.J., Kerekes, J.C., Albonesi, D.H.: Phastlane: a rapid transit optical routing network. ACM SIGARCH Comput. Archit. News **37**(3), 441–450 (2009)
14. Daneshtalab, M., Ebrahimi, M., Xu, T.C., Liljeberg, P., Tenhunen, H.: A generic adaptive path-based routing method for MPSoCs. J. Syst. Archit. **57**(1), 109–120 (2011)
15. Dong, P., Chen, Y.K., Gu, T., Buhl, L.L., Neilson, D.T., Sinsky, J.H.: Reconfigurable 100 Gb/s silicon photonic network-on-chip. J. Opt. Commun. Netw. **7**(1), A37–A43 (2015)
16. Duraisamy, K., Xue, Y., Bogdan, P., Pande, P.P.: Multicast-aware high-performance wireless network-on-chip architectures. IEEE Trans. Very Large Scale Integr. (VLSI) Syst. **25**(3), 1126–1139 (2017)
17. Ebrahimi, M., Daneshtalab, M., Liljeberg, P., Tenhunen, H.: HAMUM-A novel routing protocol for unicast and multicast traffic in MPSoCs. In: The 18th Euromicro International Conference on PDP, pp. 525–532. IEEE (2010)
18. Ebrahimi, M., et al.: An efficient dynamic multicast routing protocol for distributing traffic in NOCs. In: DATE, pp. 1064–1069. IEEE (2009)
19. Gong, L., Zhou, X., Liu, X., Zhao, W., Lu, W., Zhu, Z.: Efficient resource allocation for all-optical multicasting over spectrum-sliced elastic optical networks. J. Opt. Commun. Netw. **5**(8), 836–847 (2013)
20. Gu, H., Mo, K.H., Xu, J., Zhang, W.: A low-power low-cost optical router for optical networks-on-chip in multiprocessor systems-on-chip. In: IEEE ISVLSI, pp. 19–24 (2009)
21. Guo, P., Hou, W., Guo, L., Yang, Q., Ge, Y., Liang, H.: Low insertion loss and non-blocking microring-based optical router for 3D optical network-on-chip. IEEE Photon. J. **10**(2), 1–10 (2018)
22. Hu, W., Lu, Z., Jantsch, A., Liu, H.: Power-efficient tree-based multicast support for networks-on-chip. In: The 16th ASP-DAC, pp. 363–368. IEEE (2011)
23. Jerger, N.E., Peh, L.S., Lipasti, M.: Virtual circuit tree multicasting: a case for on-chip hardware multicast support. In: The 35th IEEE International Symposium ISCA, pp. 229–240 (2008)
24. Joardar, B.K., Duraisamy, K., Pande, P.P.: High performance collective communication-aware 3D network-on-chip architectures. In: DATE, pp. 1351–1356. IEEE (2018)
25. Krishna, T., Peh, L.S., Beckmann, B.M., Reinhardt, S.K.: Towards the ideal on-chip fabric for 1-to-many and many-to-1 communication. In: The 44th IEEE/ACM International Symposium on MICRO, pp. 71–82 (2011)
26. Liu, F., Zhang, H., Chen, Y., Huang, Z., Gu, H.: Dynamic ring-based multicast with wavelength reuse for optical network on chips. In: IEEE International Symposium on MCSoC (2016)
27. Liu, F., Zhang, H., Chen, Y., Huang, Z., Gu, H.: Wavelength-reused hierarchical optical network on chip architecture for manycore processors. IEEE Trans. Sustain. Comput. **4**(2), 231–244 (2019)

28. Morris, R., Jolley, E., Kodi, A.K.: Extending the performance and energy-efficiency of shared memory multicores with nanophotonic technology. IEEE Trans. Parallel Distrib. Syst. **25**(1), 83–92 (2014)
29. Nasiri, F., Sarbazi-Azad, H., Khademzadeh, A.: Reconfigurable multicast routing for networks on chip. Microprocess. Microsyst. **42**, 180–189 (2016)
30. Nychis, G.P., Fallin, C., Moscibroda, T., Mutlu, O., Seshan, S.: On-chip networks from a networking perspective: congestion and scalability in many-core interconnects. In: ACM SIGCOMM, pp. 407–418 (2012)
31. Pan, Y., Kumar, P., Kim, J., Memik, G., Zhang, Y., Choudhary, A.: Firefly: illuminating future network-on-chip with nanophotonics. ACM SIGARCH Comput. Archit. News **37**, 429–440 (2009)
32. Pavlidis, V.F., Savidis, I., Friedman, E.G.: Three-dimensional Integrated Circuit Design. Newnes (2017)
33. Pile, D.: Integrated photonics: compact multiplexing. Nat. Photonics **9**(2), 78 (2015)
34. Ramini, L., Bertozzi, D., Carloni, L.P.: Engineering a bandwidth-scalable optical layer for a 3D multi-core processor with awareness of layout constraints. In: IEEE/ACM International Symposium NoCS, pp. 185–192 (2012)
35. Vantrease, D., et al.: Corona: system implications of emerging nanophotonic technology. ACM SIGARCH Comput. Archit. News **36**, 153–164 (2008)
36. Wang, X., Yang, M., Jiang, Y., Liu, P.: On an efficient NoC multicasting scheme in support of multiple applications running on irregular sub-networks. Microprocess. Microsyst. **35**(2), 119–129 (2011)
37. Wang, Z., Gu, H., Yang, Y., Zhang, H., Chen, Y.: An adaptive partition-based multicast routing scheme for mesh-based networks-on-chip. Comput. Electr. Eng. **51**, 235–251 (2016)
38. Wu, C.W., Lee, K.J., Su, A.P.: A hybrid multicast routing approach with enhanced methods for mesh-based networks-on-chip. IEEE Trans. Comput. **1**, 1 (2018)
39. Yang, W., Chen, Y., Huang, Z., Zhang, H.: RWADMM: routing and wavelength assignment for distribution-based multiple multicasts in ONoC. In: IEEE International Conference on ISPA/IUCC, pp. 550–557 (2017)
40. Yang, W., Chen, Y., Huang, Z., Zhang, H., Huaxi, G.: Path-based routing and wavelength assignment for multiple multicasts in an ONoC. In: IEEE International Conference on HPCC (2019)
41. Zhang, L., Yang, M., Jiang, Y., Regentova, E.: Architectures and routing schemes for optical network-on-chips. Comput. Electr. Eng. **35**(6), 856–877 (2009)

Virtual Network Embedding Based on Core and Coritivity of Graph

Jie Yang and Chenggui Zhao(✉)

School of Information, Yunnan University of Finance and Economics, Kunming 650221, China
zhaochenggui@126.com

Abstract. Network virtualization is an effective approach to solve the problem of high cost of reconstructing underlying hardware facilities. Network virtualization enables a substrate network to share multiple virtual networks. In order to achieve higher performance with a lower cost, how to effectively embed virtual network to substrate network has become a key issue. Regarding this, we design and implement a heuristic virtual network embedding algorithm based on core and coritivity of graph. This algorithm finds the core nodes in the virtual network and embeds them to the substrate network. The performance of the proposed algorithm is evaluated in comparison with three other algorithms in experiments. Consequently, proposed algorithm is more efficient and improves apparently the runtime of virtual network requests.

Keywords: Network virtualization · Virtual network embedding · Core and coritivity

1 Introduction

The increasing network applications have expanded the requirements of underlying network hardware facilities in the past few years. Traditional underlying network facilities cannot satisfy the demand for resource of these applications due to the problem of fixed network facilities. The cost of building network hardware facilities is generally expensive. Network virtualization [4], as one of the most prospective Internet technologies in the future, is attracting more attention from research communities. As a key part, the Internet Service Providers (ISPs) maximize the utilization of substrate network (SN) resources by allocating resources of one or more substrate networks to satisfy the operation of as many virtual networks (VNs) as possible. Although network virtualization technology is promising to improve the current network, it also encounters a major challenge: how to improve the number of VN successfully embedded in SN with limited resources and guarantee the profit and quality of service (i.e. how to

Supported by National Nature Science Foundation of China under Grants No. 61562089.

H. Shen and Y. Sang (Eds.): PAAP 2019, CCIS 1163, pp. 71–82, 2020.
https://doi.org/10.1007/978-981-15-2767-8_7

allocate resources in the SN to the VN high efficiently). The process of embedding VN into SN is called Virtual Network Embedding (VNE) problem [6]. The objective of the VNE is to make full use of the limited resources of the SN to provide services for more virtual network requests (VNRs).

The VNE problem has been proved to be NP-Hard [1], and researchers have proposed different solutions to the VNE problem [3,5,7,9,12,13]. Chowdhury et al. [3,5] aimed on two-stage dynamic mapping scheme for coordination nodes and links. They proposed deterministic D-ViNE and randomized R-ViNE algorithms through mixed integer programming (MIP), respectively. Yu et al. [13] focused on maximal resource utilization in the SN. The virtual nodes are mapped onto the substrate nodes with maximum available resources.Then each virtual link is mapped to the shortest substrate path. Hu et al. [7] presented a path-based model called P-VNE. And they designed a column generation process, which can be embedded into branch-and-bound framework to efficiently obtain an optimal solution for the VNE problem. Yao et al. [12] designed and implemented a strategy network, in which reinforcement learning is used to make node mapping decisions. The node mapping process is optimized through reinforcement learning agent(RLA). Nguyen et al. [9] proposed an efficient dynamic VNE strategy for cloud network: an RT-VNE algorithm was designed by embedding virtual nodes and links of each VNR to the substrate infrastructure at the same time.

There are always some extremely core network nodes whether in the SN or VN. Core nodes mean that they can change the structure of the whole network substantially if the core nodes are deleted. Inspired by this, this paper proposes a virtual network embedding algorithm BCVNE. The algorithm aims to find the core nodes in the network. Then, the core nodes is mapped prior to the ordinary nodes. Particularly, this paper introduces average link resource of core nodes, which can prejudge whether link mapping can be carried out. Consequently, the success of link mapping can be improved. The experimental results validate that, the runtime of BCVNE algorithm is shorter than the existing embedding methods while without degradation of the acceptance ratio of VNR.

2 Model and Problem Description

2.1 Substrate Network and Virtual Network Request

The SN is abstracted to an undirected weighted graph $H = (V(H), E(H))$, where $V(H)$ represents the set of substrate nodes with CPU resource, and $E(H)$ denotes the set of substrate links with bandwidth resource. For each $v \in V(H)$, the CPU resource of v is denoted as $c(v)$. For any two nodes i and j, $e_{i,j}$ ($e_{i,j} \in E(H)$) presents the link between i and j. The bandwidth of link $e_{i,j}$ is denoted as $w(e_{i,j})$. Meanwhile, the average link bandwidth resource of node v is defined as $w(v)$, which will be described detail in Sect. 4.3.

For example, Fig. 1(a) shows a SN, consisting of five nodes include A, B, C, D, E and seven links include $e_{A,B}$, $e_{A,C}$, $e_{A,D}$, $e_{A,E}$, $e_{B,E}$, $e_{C,D}$ and $e_{D,E}$. The number next to the link represents the bandwidth resource constraint of the link,

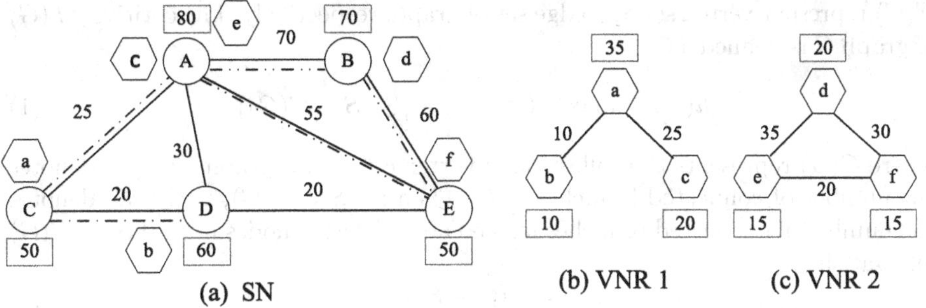

(a) SN (b) VNR 1 (c) VNR 2

Fig. 1. VN mapping

and the number in the box near the node indicates the CPU resource constraint of the node.

Also, the VN is modeled as an undirected weighted graph $G = (V(G), E(G))$, where $V(G)$ represents the set of substrate nodes with CPU demand, and $E(G)$ denotes the set of substrate links with bandwidth demand. The CPU demand of v is denoted as $c(v)$, $v \in V(G)$. The bandwidth of link $e_{i,j}$ is denoted as $w(e_{i,j})$, $e_{i,j} \in E(G)$. Figures 1(b) and 1(c) list two different VNRs, respectively.

2.2 Description of the VNE Problem

When users issue VNRs, the ISP needs to allocate the SN resources to respond the quest. The virtual network embedding is represented as φ: $G = (V(G), E(G)) \to H = (V(H), E(H))$, i.e. the VN Embedding into the SN, which includes node mapping and link mapping.

An example of the VNE problem is shown in Fig. 1. Figures 1(b) and 1(c) show two different VNRs. When a VNR arrives, if CPU resources of the substrate nodes and bandwidth resources meet the demand of the VNR: the virtual nodes a, b, c of VNR 1 are mapped onto the substrate nodes C, D and A, and the virtual links $e_{a,b}$ and $e_{a,c}$ of VNR 1 are mapped onto the substrate path $e_{C,D}$ and $e_{C,A}$. The virtual nodes d, e, f of VNR 2 are mapped onto the substrate nodes B, A and E, and the virtual links $e_{d,e}$, $e_{d,f}$ and $e_{e,f}$ of VNR 2 are mapped onto the substrate path $e_{B,A}$, $e_{B,E}$ and $e_{A,E}$, respectively. Among them, the CPU resources occupied by c and e nodes in A node are 35 less than 80. The CPU resources and bandwidth resources of the substrate nodes are still left (i.e. the total capacity of the VNs do not exceed the capacity of the SN) after two VNRs are embedded. So the two VNRs can be embedded into the SN and used.

3 Core and Coritivity of Graph

The core and coritivity theory of system is first proposed in [8, 10, 11], which seeks for the set of relatively core nodes in a connected graph by deleting some nodes with them edges associated. Given an undirected connected graph G, and let $V(G)$ and

$E(G)$ represent vertex set and edge set of graph, respectively. The coritivity $h(G)$ of graph G is defined as

$$h(G) = \max\{\omega(G - S) - |S|\,; S \in C(G)\} \tag{1}$$

where $C(G)$ represents the collection of vertex cut sets of graph G; $\omega(G)$ denotes the number of connected branches of G. Then for $S \subseteq V(G)$, $\omega(G - S)$ denotes the number of connected branches formed after deleting nodes in S. If $S^* \in C(G)$ and satisfied

$$h(G) = \omega(G - S^*) - |S^*| \tag{2}$$

then S^* is called the core set of graph G.

The core and coritivity theory plays an essential role in discovery of the core nodes in the network. Similarly, both VN and SN can be abstracted as graph to discover the sets of the core nodes. Since there are a large number of vertex cut sets in $C(G)$, in order to delete some not key vertex cut sets in $C(G)$, the concept of cut-vertex is introduced to optimize $C(G)$. Cut-vertex, i.e. a node affects the connectivity of the graph when this node is removed from graph. The cut-vertex denotes $c_n(c_n \in V(G))$, c_n satisfies $\omega(G - c_n) > 1$ through core and coritivity theory. Using D_g represents the set of cut-vertexes, where $D_g \in C(G)$. For $C_i \in C(G)$, if $D_g \not\subset C_i$, then delete C_i from $C(G)$. $C(G)$ is optimized by cut-vertexes, and reduces the computational complexity of $h(G)$.

4 Algorithm

Using the core and coritivity theory, we can abstract the VN into a connected graph G, the initialization of its coritivity can be assigned as $h(G) = 1$. Then we will ignore $h(G) < 1$ when calculating the coritivity of network graph.

Theorem 1. *Give a N-order connected undirected graph G, if $h(G) > 0$, then the number of node in S is*

$$|S| < N/2 \tag{3}$$

Proof. Suppose $|S| \geq N/2$, it holds that

$$\omega(G - S) \leq N/2. \tag{4}$$

Substitute Eqs. (4) into (2), it follows than

$$h(G) = \omega(G - S) - |S| \leq N/2 - |S| \leq 0 \tag{5}$$

According to Theorem 1, only the number of nodes of core set $|S| < N/2$ needs to be considered in N-order graph when designing the algorithm. That is not significance to analyze the coritivity calculation of network graph when $h(G) \leq 0$, in which $N/2 \leq |S| \leq N$. Restricting the number of nodes in S can greatly reduce the runtime of the algorithm.

Table 1. Formulation and algorithm notation

Y	candidate node set
S_{now}	current core set of H_{max}
S_{tem}	current core set of H_{tem}
addnum	number of candidate nodes to add
addnode	all combinations of candidate nodes of *addnum* number
$nodenum_{max}$	maximum number of candidate nodes to add
$d(i)$	degree of node i

4.1 The Main Algorithm

We list the notations used in our formulation and algorithm in Table 1, for ready reference.

For each VN that needs to be embedded, it can be abstracted to a N-order undirected connected graph $G(V(G), E(G))$, where $|V(G)|$ is N. There are always some edge nodes in the graph G, regarded as leaf nodes, i.e. the nodes with degree 2. These leaf nodes are at the edge of the graph, and their influence on the coritivity are almost zero. Inspired by this, these leaf nodes should be excluded accordingly when considering candidate nodes. Similarly, the cut-vertexes in the graph G can directly affect the connectivity of this graph. We first add the cut vertex set D_g with high priority to the set S of core nodes, and then consider other nodes, that is because cut-vertexes have much higher priority than other nodes during the process of finding the core set. The pseudo-code for finding the core set S is shown in Algorithm 1.

In Algorithm 1, lines 1–3 initialize the coritivity, candidate node set and other parameters. Lines 4–19 calculate the coritivity and continuously update the corresponding core node set. In line 15, $addnum_{abi}$ is a parameter, which indicates the number of temporary nodes added when the value of coritivity after adding candidate node set H_{tem} is higher than the current maximum of coritivity H_{max} in the next cycle. The loop of lines 4–19 searching core nodes can be optimized to a large extent, according to the judgement formula of $addnum_{abi}$. The decision formula $addnum_{abi}$ is deduced as follows.

In the N-order connected graph G, if the value of coritivity H_{max} is the largest when the current core node set is C, then the coritivity satisfies

$$H_{\max} = \omega(G - C) - |C| \tag{6}$$

According to the algorithm, the value of $|C|$ is

$$|C| = |D_g| + addnum_C \tag{7}$$

where $addnum_C$ denotes the number of candidate nodes added when the core set is C.

Algorithm 1: FindCore(G, D_g)

Input: Graph $G(V(G), E(G))$ and cut-vertex set D_g;
Output: Core S;

$H_{\max} \leftarrow \omega(G - D_g) - |D_g|$, $S_{now} \leftarrow D_g$;
$Y \leftarrow V(G) - D_g - \{v_i; d(i) \leq 2, v_i \in V(G)\}$;
$nodenum_{\max} \leftarrow N/2$;
for *addnum from 1 to* $nodenum_{max}$) **do**
  $addnode \leftarrow$ { all combinations of nodes of *addnum* number from Y} ;
  for *i from 1 to length(addnode)* **do**
    $addnode_{now} \leftarrow addnode(i)$;
    $C \leftarrow D_g \cup addnode_{now}$;
    $H_{tem} \leftarrow \omega(G - C) - |C|$;
    if $H_{tem} \geq H_{\max}$ **then**
      $H_{\max} \leftarrow H_{tem}$;
      $S_{now} \leftarrow C$;
    end
    $addnum_{abi} \leftarrow (N - H_{\max})/2 - length(D_g)$;
    if $addnum \geq addnum_{abi}$ **then**
      break ;
    end
  end
end
$S \leftarrow S_{now}$;
return S;

Suppose $\exists C' \in C(G)$ makes its corresponding coritivity $H_{C'}$ satisfies

$$H_{C'} > H_{\max} \tag{8}$$

And the coritivity $H_{C'}$ is

$$H_{C'} = \omega(G - C') - |C'| \tag{9}$$

According to the algorithm, the value of $|C'|$ should satisfies

$$|C'| = |D_g| + addnum_{abi} \tag{10}$$

Combining Eqs. (8), (9) and (10), it follows than

$$H_{\max} < \omega(G - C') - |C'| < (H_{C'} - |C'|) - |C'| < N - 2|C'| \tag{11}$$

where $H_{C'}$ satisfies $H_{C'} \leq N$. Combining Eqs. (7), (10) and (11), it holds that

$$addnum_{C'} = |C'| - |GD| < (N - H_{\max})/2 - |GD| \tag{12}$$

According to the final derivation Eq. (12), $addnum_{abi}$ can be used as a valid judgment condition to terminate the loop of the core set, which makes the algorithm avoid more calculating when more candidate nodes are added.

4.2 Calculation of the Continuous Branch Number

The core and coritivity theory involves the calculation of the connected branch number after removing the nodes of core set and the corresponding edges. For the VN graph, the corresponding adjacency matrix is generated for analysis. The algorithm for calculating the connected branch number is shown in Algorithm 2. In Algorithm 2, the graph is composed of the remaining nodes after deleting the node in S_{now}.

Algorithm 2: FindCount(G, D_g)

```
Input: Graph G(V(G), E(G)) and cut vertex set GD;
Output: Number of connected branches count;
Initialize count, matrix A and array Mark to 0 ;
for each (u, v) ∈ E(G) do
    A[u][v]←1 ;
end
for each v_i ∈ C do
    for j from 0 to N-1 do
        A[i][j]←0 ;
        Mark[i]←1;
    end
end
for each v_i ∈ V(G) do
    if Mark[v_i]==0 then
        DFS(v_i) ;
        count++ ;
    end
end
return count;
```

In Algorithm 2, the array *Mark* is used to mark whether this node is accessed in the depth-first search function (DFS(v_i)), to find the number of connected branch. The function of DFS(v_i) is shown in Algorithm 3.

4.3 Optimization of BCVNE Algorithm

The links around one node may fail to be embedded due to not meet the demand resources of links, if only consider the CPU resource of this core node. The average link resource of node n $w(n)$, representing the average resource of link bandwidth resources within 3-layers of links around a node, is given to improve the success ratio of link mapping. The core node determines the weight coefficient of each link resource. Proceeding from the core nodes, it is each hop neighbor's link weight coefficients denote as k_1, k_2, k_3 and $\sum_{i=1}^{3} k_i=1$, respectively.

Algorithm 3: DFS(v_i)

```
Input: v_i of Graph G;
for j from 0 to length(A) do
    for each A[v_i][j]==1 do
        Mark[j] ← 1 ;
        A[v_i][j] ← 0 ;
        DFS(j) ;
    end
end
```

The two network diagrams shown in Fig. 2, we assume that the node f in Fig. 2(a) network 1 and the node o in Fig. 2(b) network 2 are core nodes in their respective network. The link resources of the two nodes are calculated as shown in Eqs. (13) and (14) respectively. Equation (13) shows a calculation of the average resources of core node f, which on behalf of 3-layers link resources. Equation (14) shows a calculation of the average resources of o, which representing link resources of one layer, and $k_2 = k_3 = 0$ due to the absence of links in the other two layers.

$$w(f) = k_1 * (w(e_{f,d}) + w(e_{f,e}))/2 + k_2 * w(e_{c,d}) + k_3 * (w(e_{a,c}) + w(e_{b,c}))/2 \quad (13)$$

$$w(o) = k_1 * (w(e_{o,p}) + w(e_{o,r}) + w(e_{o,q}))/3 \quad (14)$$

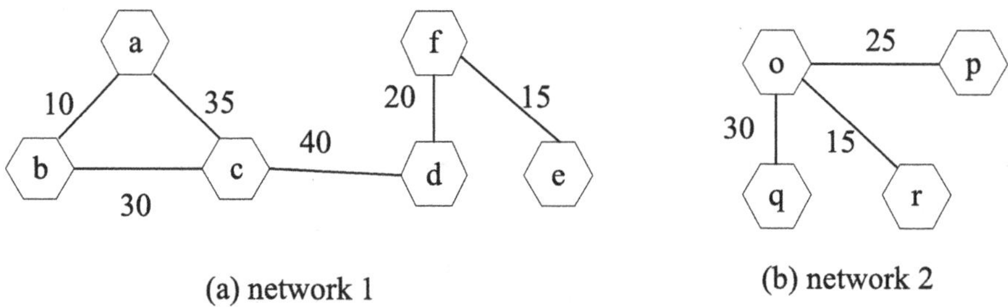

Fig. 2. Network diagram

5 Evaluation

This section describes the evaluation setting and the main evaluation results; and discusses the results of experiments using some performance parameters to evaluate VNE algorithms, such as runtime, acceptance ratio, cost/revenue ratio, and node utilization ratio. The generation and execution of experimental data rely on recently updated Alevin 2.2 [2], a simulation framework provided by Beck et al., recognized as a significant simulation framework for evaluating virtual network embedding.

5.1 Evaluation Setting

In our experiments, the SNs and VNs are generated dynamically and randomly in Alevin framework. The size of SN is set to 100 nodes, and node computing CPU resources and link bandwidth resources are generated randomly as real numbers in the interval [10,100]. The number of VN is set to 10, and the size of each VN nodes are generated randomly as integer numbers in the interval [4, 16]. The CPU and link bandwidth resources are generated randomly as real numbers in the interval [1, 10]. Random SN and VN topologies are generated with a probability 0.5 of each connecting a pair of nodes.

5.2 Compared Algorithms

To evaluation of performance and quality of BCVNE algorithm, BCVNE compared with three representative algorithms: DViNE-SP, RW-MM-SP and GAR-SP. Notations for different algorithms are listed in Table 2 and give each algorithm a brief description. All algorithms chosen for evaluation will run 20 times of experiments under the same evaluation setting, in order to avoid the randomness of experimental results.

Table 2. Compared algorithms

Notation	Algorithms description
DViNE-SP [5]	Node mapping by mixed integer programming(MIP) and link mapping with k-shortest paths
RW-MM-SP [9]	Node mapping by topology properties and link mapping with k-shortest paths
GAR-SP [3]	Node mapping by available resources and link mapping with k-shortest paths
BCVNE	Proposed scheme based on core and coritivity

5.3 Evaluation Results

The evaluation data is received using experiments, under evaluation setting in 5.1. The results of comparisons with other algorithms are depicted in Fig. 3 and Table 3. The BCVNE algorithm can get some improvements compare with other algorithms in Table 2.

1. **BCVNE improves the embedding efficiency compared with other algorithms.** Fig. 3a shows the runtime of each comparison algorithm experiment. Compared with the other two algorithms DViNE-SP and RW-MM-SP, the runtime of BCVNE algorithm and GAR-SP algorithm is much shorter than them, while the runtime of BCVNE algorithm is the shortest of the four algorithms. Table 3 shows the average results of each optimization parameter in 20 experiments of the comparison algorithm. In Table 3, it can be

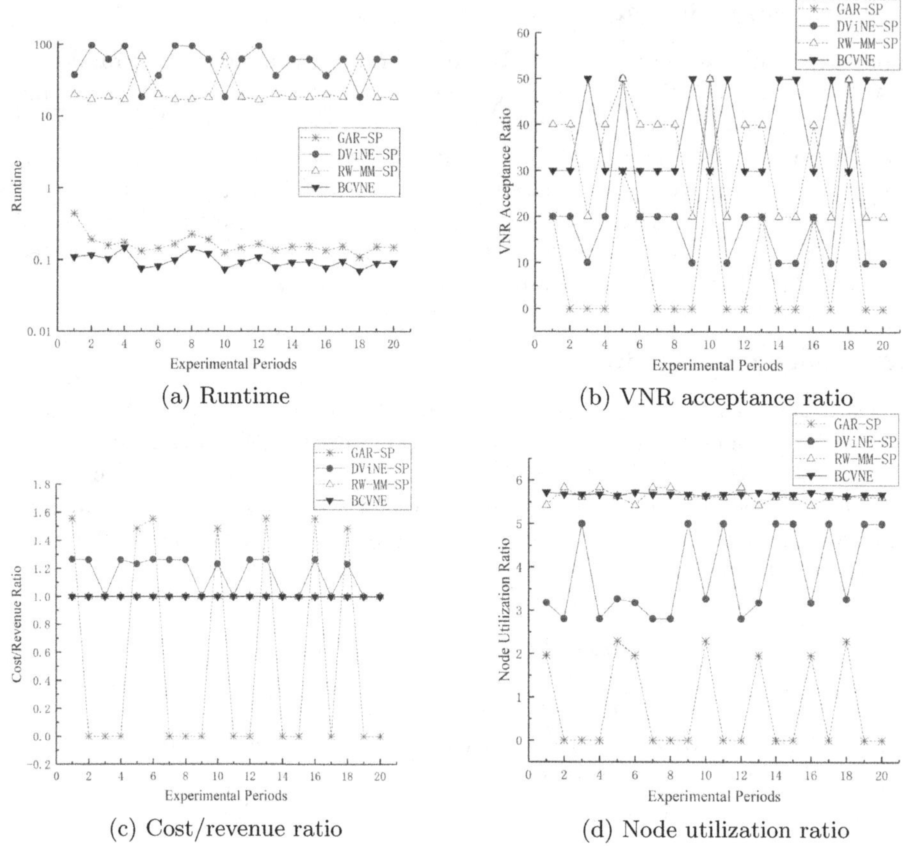

(a) Runtime

(b) VNR acceptance ratio

(c) Cost/revenue ratio

(d) Node utilization ratio

Fig. 3. Performance and quality comparisons of BCVNE with three representative VNE schemes for embedding.

seen that the BCVNE embedding the VN into SN within 0.10 s. The runtime of BCVNE algorithm is shortened by more than 100 times compared with DViNE-SP's 58.80 s and RW-MM-SP's 25.73 s. The two algorithm DViNE-SP and RW-MM-SP exhibited poor efficiency in the same conditions. The runtime of BCVNE algorithm is also clearly less than GAR-SP's 0.17 s. Therefore, BCVNE algorithm greatly improves the operation efficiency of VNE.

2. **BCVNE improves the acceptance ratio of virtual network requests under improving the embedding efficiency.** Figure 3b shows the VNR acceptance ratio results of each comparison algorithm experiment. In Fig. 3b, the acceptance ratio of BCVNE algorithm is significantly better than that of GAR-SP algorithm and DViNE-SP algorithm. According to the average acceptance rate of each algorithm in Table 3, the acceptance ratio of BCVNE algorithm is 38%, which is better than that of RW-MM-SP's 33.5%. The acceptance ratio of BCVNE algorithm is not as good as that of RW-MM-SP

algorithm under some conditions from Fig. 3b, but it can be seen with Table 3 that the acceptance ratio of VNR of BCVNE is better than that of RW-MM-SP in general. This is because the BCVNE algorithm designed in this paper is an embedding algorithm based on core and coritivity theory. Core and coritivity theory mainly look for core nodes in the network, and the number of core nodes is limited. Once all the CPU resources of the core node are used, subsequent VNRs cannot embed with the core node, which may cause embedding failure. In summary, BCVNE improves the VNR acceptance ratio under improving the embedding efficiency, although the embedding failure process in some special cases is inevitable.

Table 3. The average results of comparison algorithms of 20 experiments

Algorithm	Runtime(s)	VN request ratio	Cost/Revenue ratio	Node utilization ratio
GAR-SP	0.17	8.50	1.53	0.74
DViNE-SP	58.80	20.50	1.15	3.83
RW-MM-SP	25.73	33.50	1.00	5.63
BCVNE	0.10	38.00	1.00	5.68

3. **BCVNE algorithm has better embedding quality compared with other three algorithms.** Figure 3c shows the cost/revenue ratio results of each comparison algorithm experiment. The cost/revenue ratio of DViNE-SP and GAR-SP are higher than BCVNE and RW-MM-SP, as seen in Fig. 3c. The average cost/revenue ratio of BCVNE and RW-MM-SP are both 1.00, which is better than GAR-SP's 1.53 and DViNE-SP's 1.15, as seen in Table 3. Figure 3d shows the utilization ratio results of SN nodes. Combined with the analysis about Fig. 3c, Fig. 3d and Table 3, the utilization ratio of substrate nodes of BCVNE is stable and better than that of RW-MM-SP when the cost/revenue ratio is the same (in the experimental data, it is shown as 1.00). Meanwhile, we conclude that BCVNE not only greatly reduces the runtime of VNE, but also improves the acceptance ratio of VN requests, combined with Figs. 3a and 3b. In conclusion, BCVNE can achieve better VNE results and better embedding quality.

6 Conclusion

This paper proposed BCVNE, a virtual network embedding based on core and coritivity. The embedding is conducted through core and coritivity theory to find the core nodes in the virtual network. Considering the process of the next link mapping stage, the algorithm optimizes the link mapping by using the average link resource of nodes. Evaluation results show that proposed algorithm generates a better embedding result compared with some previous algorithms. Future work is planed to use the tool of neural network to analyze the relationship between core nodes and corresponding links, to achieve better embedding result.

References

1. Authors, C.L.O.: IEEE/ACM Transactions on Networking (2013)
2. Beck, M.T., Linnhoff-Popien, C., Fischer, A., Kokot, F., de Meer, H.: A simulation framework for virtual network embedding algorithms. In: 2014 16th International Telecommunications Network Strategy and Planning Symposium (Networks), pp. 1–6. IEEE (2014)
3. Chowdhury, M., Rahman, M.R., Boutaba, R.: Vineyard: virtual network embedding algorithms with coordinated node and link mapping. IEEE/ACM Trans. Netw. **20**(1), 206–219 (2012)
4. Chowdhury, N.M.K., Boutaba, R.: A survey of network virtualization. Comput. Netw. **54**(5), 862–876 (2010)
5. Chowdhury, N.M.K., Rahman, M.R., Boutaba, R.: Virtual network embedding with coordinated node and link mapping. In: IEEE INFOCOM 2009, pp. 783–791. IEEE (2009)
6. Fischer, A., Botero, J.F., Beck, M.T., De Meer, H., Hesselbach, X.: Virtual network embedding: a survey. IEEE Commun. Surv. Tutorials **15**(4), 1888–1906 (2013)
7. Hu, Q., Wang, Y., Cao, X.: Resolve the virtual network embedding problem: a column generation approach. In: 2013 Proceedings on IEEE INFOCOM, pp. 410–414. IEEE (2013)
8. Jin, X.: A new method of studying system core and coritivity. Syst. Eng. Electron. **6**, 1–10 (1994)
9. Nguyen, D.L., Byun, H., Kim, N., Kim, C.K.: Toward efficient dynamic virtual network embedding strategy for cloud networks. Int. J. Distrib. Sensor Netw. **14**(3), 1550147718764789 (2018)
10. Xu, J., Xi, Y., Wang, Y.: The core and coritivity of a system (i). J. Syst. Sci. Math. Sci. **13**(2), 102–110 (1993)
11. Xu, J., et al.: The core and coritivity of a system (ii) optimization design and reliable communication network. J. Syst. Eng. **9**(1), 1–11 (1994)
12. Yao, H., Chen, X., Li, M., Zhang, P., Wang, L.: A novel reinforcement learning algorithm for virtual network embedding. Neurocomputing **284**, 1–9 (2018)
13. Yu, M., Yi, Y., Rexford, J., Chiang, M.: Rethinking virtual network embedding: substrate support for path splitting and migration. ACM SIGCOMM Comput. Commun. Rev. **38**(2), 17–29 (2008)

Non-time-Sharing Full-Duplex SWIPT Relay System with Energy Access Point

Zhou Yening[1], Li Taoshen[1,2(✉)], Wang Zhe[1], and Ye Jin[1]

[1] School of Computer Electronic and Information, Guangxi University, Nanning 530004, China
tshli@gxu.edu.cn

[2] School of Information Engineering, Nanning University, Nanning 530004, China

Abstract. Utilizing the idle wireless devices with energy as an additional energy access point (EAP) to supplement energy for the relay, a non-time-sharing full-duplex amplification and forwarding (AF) relay system with energy access points based on radio frequency (RF) signals in wireless networks is proposed. Using AF protocol to cooperative transmit information and simultaneous wireless information and power transfer (SWIPT) technology to realize information and energy synchronous transmission in the energy-constrained relay system. The relay can eliminate the self-interference signal through self-energy recycling in the loop channel, and adopts power splitting scheme for information decoding and energy harvest for RF signals. Moreover, due to the non-time-sharing transmission characteristics, information transmission, energy harvest and cooperative transmission are completed synchronously in a time block. Taking maximize system throughput as optimization target, jointly optimizing the relay transmit power, the relay transmit beamforming vector and the power splitting ratio, and the system transforms the original multivariate non-convex problem into a semi-definite programming problem by using quadratic optimization, variable reduction methods and Lagrange method. Simulation experiments show that under the condition that the total energy harvested is fixed, the operation rate of the system can be promoted effectively by increasing the energy harvested from EAP. And the self-energy recycling of the relay can promote the throughput gain of the system. The experimental results also verify that our proposal the system based on applying non-time-sharing transmission protocol and SWIPT technology has more significant gains in improving system performance than HD-SWIPT and FD-no-SWIPT relay systems.

Keywords: Simultaneous wireless information and power transfer · Non-time-sharing transmission · Energy access point · Self-energy recycling · Semi-definite programming

1 Introduction

Information transmission and energy harvesting based on radio frequency (RF) signals have become an alternative method for transmitting data and power in a new generation of wireless communication networks, moreover, and based on radio frequency signals

H. Shen and Y. Sang (Eds.): PAAP 2019, CCIS 1163, pp. 83–97, 2020.
https://doi.org/10.1007/978-981-15-2767-8_8

in wireless networks, the use of SWIPT technology to realize the transmission of RF signals carrying information waves and energy waves in wireless networks has become a research trend in the future. In [1, 2], it is proposed that the RF signal is an important carrier for transmitting information and transmitting energy, and information decoding (ID) and energy harvest (EH) can be performed on the received RF signal by applying SWIPT technology. The literature provides a theoretical basis for powering wireless devices through energy harvesting[2]. Based on the wireless communication transmission system, the actual receiver structure for time switching (TS) and power splitting (PS) of realizing SWIPT technology is described in [4–10], and investigating the performance of wireless communication systems that use harvested wireless energy to power wireless devices. Moreover, the application of SWIPT technology in energy-constrained half-duplex (HD) relay systems is also beginning to be considered[5–7]. Maximizing throughput as an optimization goal to describe the system performance, and the method of solving problem by using the semi-determined relaxation (SDR) has been applied in the latest research [8–10].

Recently, the technology for self-energy recycling in wireless transmission networks has been the subject of many researchers. The application of self-recycling technology in point-to-point wireless communication systems and wireless relay systems has been initially explored. Energy-constrained nodes use only proprietary energy and self-recycling energy harvested from access points for information transmission [11–15]. In the latest research, a wireless power supply full-duplex relay system with self-energy recycling is proposed [14, 16–19], and a novel two-stage transmission protocol is proposed based on the traditional three-phase transmission protocol. Among them, in the literature [14], the method of self-energy recycling through the loop channel is proposed for the first time, and multi-antenna beamforming technology is adopted to suppress system self-interference and improve system transmission efficiency. In [18], the point-to-point broadcasting system using SWIPT technology is considered, under the condition of signal-to-noise ratio (SNR) and harvesting energy constraints, applying the SDR technology to solve the non-convex optimization problem. The combination of SWIPT and self-energy recycling in a full-duplex relay system is a new research direction and challenge.

Based on the above research, this paper proposes that SWIPT technology be adopted in non-time-sharing full duplex relay system with energy access point, and makes full use of idle wireless storage energy devices in the complex network near the relay as EAP. The system applies SWIPT technology to transmit RF signals carrying information and energy from the source node to relay, and the energy-constrained relay cooperatively transmits data to the destination node by harvesting the proprietary energy from the source node and the supplement energy from the EAP. Due to the full-duplex transmission mode of the relay, the system can harvest part of the self-energy caused by the loop channel at relay, and due to the non-time-sharing transmission characteristics of the system, let the information transmission, energy transmission and cooperative transmission process can completed in a time slot block. This paper maximizing system throughput as the optimization goal to describes the performance of the proposed system, and jointly optimizes the relay transmit power, relay transmit beamforming vector and power splitting ratio. The original multivariate non-convex problem is transformed into a semi-definite programming problem by quadratic optimization, SDR and variable reduction methods, and using the Lagrange method to solve the problem.

The remaining organizations in the paper are as follows: Sect. 2 describes the proposed system model of full-duplex SWIPT relay system with Energy Access Point. Section 3 describes the optimization object function problem and optimal solution. Section 4 briefly describes two comparison relay systems. Section 5 provides simulation experiment results and analysis. Finally, it is summarized in Sect. 6. Table 1 describes the meaning of the notations involved in the article.

Table 1. Description of notations in the article.

Notation	Denote
Boldface lowercase letters	vectors
Boldface uppercase letters	matrices
$\mathbb{C}^{M\times N}$	complex $M \times N$ matrix
$(\cdot)^{\mathrm{H}}$	Hermitian transpose
$(\cdot)^{\mathrm{T}}$	transpose
$\mathrm{Tr}(\cdot)$	trace of complex matrix
$\mathrm{Rank}(\cdot)$	rank of complex matrix
$\|\cdot\|$	Euclidean norm of a complex vector
$\lvert\cdot\rvert$	absolute value of a complex scalar
$(\cdot)\succeq\mathbf{0}$	the matrix is positive semi-definite
$\boldsymbol{I}_N$	$N \times N$ identity matrix
$\sim CN(0,\sigma^2)$	a symmetric complex Gaussian random variable with zero mean and variance σ^2

2 System Model

In this section, we describe the model and structure of the proposed system in detail. A non-time-sharing full-duplex SWIPT relay system structure with self-energy recycling and energy access point is proposed as shown in Fig. 1. In the system structure, the source node (S) equipped with M transmit antennas adopts SWIPT technology to transmit RF signals to the relay (R). The relay equipped with dual receive antennas and N transmit antennas, one receive antenna of the relay is used to receive the signal from S, and the other antenna harvests the energy transmitted by the EAP, and the information sent by S is forwarded by the relay to the destination node (D) equipped with a single receiving antenna. The relay system uses amplifying and forwarding protocol to transmit data cooperatively, and the single EAP acts as an energy supplement station for energy-constrained relay [2].

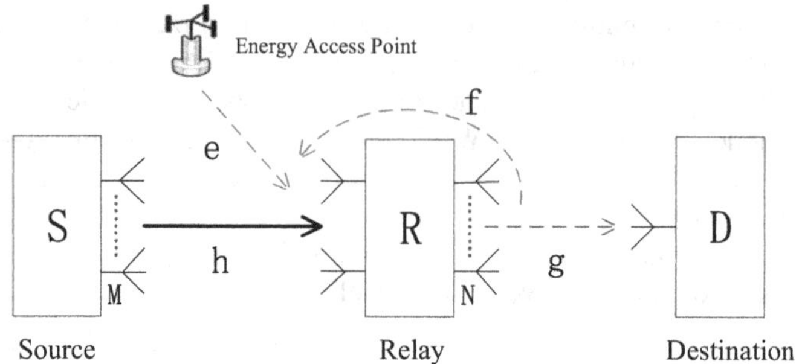

Fig. 1. SWIPT Full-duplex relay system structure with energy access point

Setting the EAP is a storable power wireless device in the vicinity of R in a complex network. When the wireless device has energy remaining, it can supply power to the relay, so that the excess energy stored by the wireless device is not wasted. And the relay can carried out self-energy recycling through the loop channel, so there is no need to configure additional hardware or adopt other methods to eliminate self-interference. Moreover, it can guarantee the continuous and stable operation of the system.

Figure 2 shows the logical structure of the system relay receiver. According to the existing research application PS scheme, the received RF signal is divided into information flow and energy flow through the power splitter. The energy flow is converted into electric energy and stored in the battery, and the information flow is transmitted to the destination node through the information transmitter. The allocation rates for ID and EH are ρ and $1 - \rho$, respectively, where $\rho \in (0, 1)$ [18]. The energy harvested by S and EAP is converted into electric energy for the system operation by the proprietary energy harvester and stored in the storable battery.

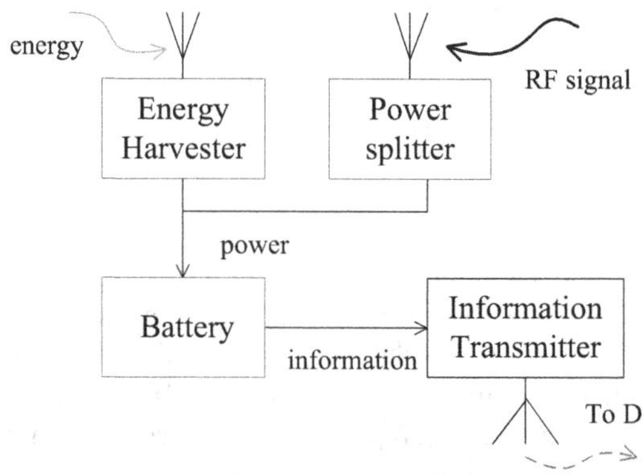

Fig. 2. SWIPT full-duplex relay receiver logical structure

As shown in Fig. 3, the non-time-sharing transmission protocol of the relay system is presented. Through this diagram, we can have a clearer understanding of the operation process of the proposed system. Different from the traditional slotted phase transmission information and energy relay system, the system realizes information transmission, energy harvest and cooperative transmission are completed synchronously in the entire transmission time slot block.

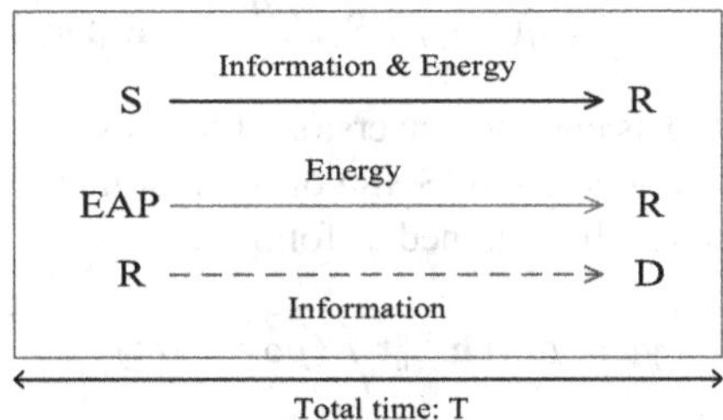

Fig. 3. Transmission protocol for relay system with energy access point

Assuming that all channels are static fading channels, channel state information (CSI) has already been obtained. From S to R using the Maximum Ratio Transmission (MRT) scheme [14], then the S transmits the beamforming vector $\mathbf{w} = \mathbf{h}/\|\mathbf{h}\|$, its downlink channel is denoted as $\mathbf{h} \in \mathbb{C}^{M\times1}$, and the uplink channel from the R to the D is denoted as $\mathbf{g} \in \mathbb{C}^{N\times1}$, the loop channel at R is denoted by $\mathbf{f} \in \mathbb{C}^{N\times1}$, and the duration block is normalized for easy calculation. The channel where the energy access point transmits energy to the relay is represented by $\mathbf{e}$. The energy harvested by R from the EAP is represented by q, and the noise from the EAP to R is ignored. Then the signal sent from S to R is given by

$$\mathrm{y_R} = \sqrt{\mathrm{P}_s}\|\mathbf{h}^H\|\boldsymbol{x} + \sqrt{\mathrm{P_r}}\mathbf{f}\boldsymbol{v}\boldsymbol{y} + n_1 \tag{1}$$

Where $\boldsymbol{x} \sim CN(0, 1)$ and P_s are the transmit symbol and transmit power at the S, respectively, and $\boldsymbol{y} \sim CN(0, 1)$,$\mathrm{P}_r$, $\boldsymbol{v} \in \mathbb{C}^{N\times1}$ and $n_1 \sim CN(0, \sigma_1^2)$ are the transmit symbol, transmit power, transmit beamforming vector and antenna noise at the R, respectively. The second term on the right side of the equation is self-interference signal generated by the loop channel at the relay.

The received signal is divided into two streams by ID and EH, the expressions are

$$\mathrm{y}_R^{ID} = \sqrt{\rho}\mathrm{y}_R + n = \sqrt{\rho \mathrm{P}_s}\|\mathbf{h}^H\|\boldsymbol{x} + \sqrt{\rho \mathrm{P_r}}\mathbf{f}\boldsymbol{v}\boldsymbol{y} + \sqrt{\rho}n_1 + n \tag{2}$$

$$\mathrm{y}_R^{EH} = \sqrt{1-\rho}\mathrm{y}_R = \sqrt{1-\rho}(\sqrt{\mathrm{P}_s}\|\mathbf{h}^H\|\boldsymbol{x} + \sqrt{\mathrm{P_r}}\mathbf{f}\boldsymbol{v}\boldsymbol{y} + n_1) \tag{3}$$

With perfect self-interference cancellation, the residual signal can be expressed as

$$\mathrm{y}_R^{ID-SIC} = \sqrt{\rho \mathrm{P}_s}\|\mathbf{h}^H\|\boldsymbol{x} + \sqrt{\rho}n_1 + n \tag{4}$$

Where $n \sim CN(0, \sigma^2)$ is the additional additive white Gaussian noise (AWGN) introduced by ID at R. Then the expression of the signal received at the D is

$$\mathrm{y_D} = \sqrt{\mathrm{P_r}}\mathbf{g}\boldsymbol{v}\boldsymbol{y} + n_2 \tag{5}$$

Where $n_2 \sim CN(0, \sigma_2^2)$ is the AWGN generated at the destination node receiver.

Ignoring the energy carried by the noise signal, the total energy harvested by the relay can be expressed as

$$\begin{aligned} Q_{th} &= \eta(E[|\sqrt{1-\rho}(\sqrt{P_s}\|\mathbf{h}^H\|\boldsymbol{x} + \sqrt{P_r}\mathbf{f}\boldsymbol{v}\boldsymbol{y})|^2] + q) \\ &= \eta(1-\rho)(P_s\|\mathbf{h}^H\|^2 + P_r|\mathbf{f}\boldsymbol{v}|^2) + \eta q \end{aligned} \tag{6}$$

Where $\eta \in (0, 1)$ is denoted as energy conversion efficiency.

Therefore, the signal-to-noise ratio (SNR) of the first hop (S to R) and the second hop (R to D) of the system can be obtained as follows:

$$\gamma_1 = \rho P_s\|\mathbf{h}^H\|^2 \Big/ (\rho\sigma_1^2 + \sigma^2) \tag{7}$$

$$\gamma_2 = P_r|\mathbf{g}\boldsymbol{v}|^2 \Big/ \sigma_2^2 \tag{8}$$

An amplification and forwarding protocol is adopted in the proposed system, neglect time delay τ, and the signal-to-noise ratio between S and D is expressed as γ:

$$\begin{aligned} \gamma &= \gamma_1\gamma_2 / (1 + \gamma_1 + \gamma_2) = \gamma_1 / [1 + (1+\gamma_1)/\gamma_2] \\ &= \rho P_s\|\mathbf{h}^H\|^2 \Bigg/ [(\rho\sigma_1^2 + \sigma^2) + \frac{\sigma_2^2(\rho A + \sigma^2)}{P_r|\mathbf{g}\boldsymbol{v}|^2}] \end{aligned} \tag{9}$$

where $A = P_s\|\mathbf{h}^H\|^2 + \sigma_1^2$. So, the throughput of the system can be expressed as

$$R = \log_2(1+\gamma) = \log_2(1 + \rho P_s\|\mathbf{h}^H\|^2 \Bigg/ [(\rho\sigma_1^2 + \sigma^2) + \frac{\sigma_2^2(\rho A + \sigma^2)}{P_r|\mathbf{g}\boldsymbol{v}|^2}]) \tag{10}$$

3 Problem Description

Maximizing system throughput as a more general objective function of optimization problems, but because the throughput equation is complex and difficult to solve, the goal of maximizing throughput is translated into an equivalent and more easily solved minimum objective function:

$$Z = \sigma^2 \Big/ \rho + \sigma_2^2(\rho A + \sigma^2) \Big/ \rho P_r|\mathbf{g}\boldsymbol{v}|^2 \tag{11}$$

In addition, considering the system benefits of self-energy recycling and energy-rate balance, P_r and ρ are jointly optimized in the objective function. In order to ensure continuous information transmission of the system and prolong the lifetime of the relay, the energy harvested by the relay needs to be higher than the given energy target threshold ε, and P_r should be lower than ε to make sure continuous and stable operation of the relay. So, the optimization problem can be described as

P0:

$$\min_{\boldsymbol{v},\mathrm{P_r},\rho} \quad \mathrm{Z} = \sigma^2 \Big/ \rho + \sigma_2^2 \mathrm{A} \Big/ \mathrm{P}_r |\mathbf{g}\boldsymbol{v}|^2 + \sigma_2^2 \sigma^2 \Big/ \rho \mathrm{P}_r |\mathbf{g}\boldsymbol{v}|^2$$

$$\text{S.T.} \quad \eta(1-\rho)(\mathrm{P}_s \|\mathbf{h}^H\|^2 + \mathrm{P_r}|\mathbf{f}\boldsymbol{v}|^2) + \eta q \geq \varepsilon \tag{12}$$

$$0 < \mathrm{P}_r \leq \varepsilon \tag{13}$$

$$0 < \rho < 1 \tag{14}$$

Obviously, because the coupled of the P_r, ρ and beamforming vector $\boldsymbol{v}$ and the quadratic term of $\boldsymbol{v}$ in the constraint make the original problem non-convex, a semi-definite programming scheme is used to solve the original optimization problem.

The variable reduction method is used to simplify the optimization problem, and using ρ_r, v_r as substitute symbols for the calculation variables. Let $\rho_r = \sigma^2 / \rho$, $v_r = \sqrt{\mathrm{P}_r} v$, derive $\mathbf{v} = \mathbf{v_r} / \|\mathbf{v_r}\|$, $\mathrm{P}_r = \|\mathbf{v_r}\|^2$. Denote $\mathbf{V_r} = \boldsymbol{v}_\mathbf{r}\boldsymbol{v}_\mathbf{r}^H \in \mathbb{C}^{N \times N}$, $\mathbf{G} = \boldsymbol{g}\boldsymbol{g}^H \in \mathbb{C}^{N \times N}$ and $\mathbf{F} = \mathbf{f}\mathbf{f}^H \in \mathbb{C}^{N \times N}$, all being rank-one matrices. Since the rank-one constraint is non-convex and difficult to deal with, therefore, the matrix rank-one constraint is discarded, and then the SDR method is used to convert the problem P0 into a more easily solved semi-determined relaxation optimization problem P0-SDR is described as:

P0-SDR:

$$\min_{\mathbf{V_r},\rho_r} \quad \rho_r + \sigma_2^2(\mathrm{A} + \rho_r) \Big/ \mathrm{Tr}(\mathbf{G}\mathbf{V_r})$$

$$\text{S.T.} \quad \mathrm{Tr}(\mathbf{F}\mathbf{V_r}) + \mathrm{P}_s \|\mathbf{h}^H\|^2 \geq \rho_r(\varepsilon - \eta q) \Big/ \eta(\rho_r - \sigma^2) \tag{15}$$

$$0 < \mathrm{Tr}(\mathbf{V_r}) \leq \varepsilon \tag{16}$$

$$\sigma^2 < \rho_r \tag{17}$$

$$\mathbf{V_r} \succeq \mathbf{0} \tag{18}$$

It is studied in [13] that if the optimal beamforming matrix $\mathbf{V}_r^*$ of the semi-determined programming problem satisfies $\mathrm{Rank}(\mathbf{V}_r^*) = 1$, then the optimal solution of the original problem P0 should be equivalent to the problem P0-SDR. In this paper, utilizing the Lagrange method of solving the inequality constrained optimization, and set the Lagrange function to solve the constrained optimization according to the KKT condition.

Defining the Lagrange multiplier variables $\lambda_1 \geq 0$, $\lambda_2 \geq 0$, $\lambda_3 \geq 0$ and $\mathbf{\Phi} \geq \mathbf{0}$ for each constraint, then the Lagrange function corresponding to the P-SDR problem is:

$$\begin{aligned} L(\mathbf{V}_r, \rho_r, \lambda_1, \lambda_2, \lambda_3, \mathbf{\Phi}) &= \rho_r + \sigma_2^2(\mathrm{A} + \rho_r) \Big/ \mathrm{Tr}(\mathbf{G}\mathbf{V_r}) \\ &- \lambda_1(\mathrm{Tr}(\mathbf{F}\mathbf{V_r}) + \mathrm{P}_s \|\mathbf{h}^H\|^2 - \rho_r(\varepsilon - \eta q) \Big/ \eta(\rho_r - \sigma^2)) \\ &- \lambda_2(-\mathrm{Tr}(\mathbf{V_r}) + \varepsilon) - \lambda_3(\rho_r - \sigma^2) - \mathrm{Tr}(\boldsymbol{\Phi}\mathbf{V_r}) \end{aligned} \tag{19}$$

The optimal dual solution of the problem P0-SDR is denoted by λ_1^*, λ_2^*, λ_3^*, $\mathbf{\Phi}^*$ and ρ_r^*, $\mathbf{V}_r^*$, respectively. According to the optimal solution of the K.K.T condition, the following necessary equations can be listed:

$$\partial L / \partial \mathbf{V}_r = \lambda_2^* \mathbf{I_N} - \lambda_1^* \mathbf{F} - \mathbf{\Phi}^* - \mathbf{G}\sigma_2^2(\mathrm{A} + \rho_r^*) \Big/ [\mathrm{Tr}(\mathbf{G}\mathbf{V_r^*})]^2 = \mathbf{0} \tag{20}$$

$$\partial L / \partial \rho_r = 1 - \lambda_3 + \sigma_2^2 \Big/ \mathrm{Tr}(\mathbf{G}\mathbf{V_r^*}) - \lambda_1^* \sigma^2(\varepsilon - \eta q) \Big/ \eta(\rho_r^* - \sigma^2)^2 = 0 \tag{21}$$

$$\lambda_1^*(\mathrm{Tr}(\mathbf{F}\mathbf{V_r^*}) + \mathrm{P}_s \|\mathbf{h}^H\|^2 - \rho_r^*(\varepsilon - \eta q) \Big/ \eta(\rho_r^* - \sigma^2)\,) = 0 \tag{22}$$

$$\lambda_3^*(\rho_r^* - \sigma^2) = 0 \tag{23}$$

$$\mathbf{\Phi}^* \mathbf{V_r^*} = \mathbf{0} \tag{24}$$

According to Eq. (23), if $\lambda_3^* > 0$, there is $\rho_r^* = \sigma^2$, which contradicts the constraint (17), so there is $\lambda_3^* = 0$. And according to Eqs. (20) and (21), the equation for the optimal solution of ρ_r^* and Lagrange multiplier $\mathbf{\Phi}^*$ can be derived:

$$\mathbf{\Phi}^* = \lambda_2^* \mathbf{I_N} - t\mathbf{G} - \lambda_1^* \mathbf{F} \tag{25}$$

$$\rho_r^* = \sqrt{\frac{\lambda_1^* \sigma^2(\varepsilon - \eta q)\mathrm{Tr}(\mathbf{G}\mathbf{V_r^*})}{\eta(\mathrm{Tr}(\mathbf{G}\mathbf{V_r^*}) + \sigma_2^2)}} + \sigma^2 \tag{26}$$

Where t is $\sigma_2^2(\mathrm{A} + \rho_r^*) / [\mathrm{Tr}(\mathbf{G}\mathbf{V_r^*})]^2$. From the Eq. (26), it is obvious that if $\lambda_1^* = 0$, there is $\rho_r^* = \sigma^2$, which contradicts the constraint (17), so there is $\rho_r^* = \sigma^2$.

Considering the complementary relaxation of Eq. (22), it can be obtained

$$\mathrm{Tr}(\mathbf{F}\mathbf{V_r^*}) + \mathrm{P}_s \|\mathbf{h}^H\|^2 - \rho_r^*(\varepsilon - \eta q) \Big/ \eta(\rho_r^* - \sigma^2) = 0 \tag{27}$$

That is, the constraint (15) of the problem P-SDR satisfies the equation at the optimal solution point. It can be derived according to formula (25)

$$\begin{aligned} \mathrm{Rank}(\lambda_2^* \mathbf{I_N}) &= \mathrm{Rank}(t\mathbf{G} + \lambda_1^* \mathbf{F} + \mathbf{\Phi}^*) \\ &\le \mathrm{Rank}(t\mathbf{G} + \lambda_1^* \mathbf{F}) + \mathrm{Rank}(\mathbf{\Phi}^*) \end{aligned} \tag{28}$$

Since $\lambda_1^* > 0$ and $\mathbf{G} = \boldsymbol{g}\boldsymbol{g}^H$, $\mathbf{F} = \mathbf{f}\mathbf{f}^H$, there must be $\mathrm{Rank}(t\mathbf{G}) = 1$, $\mathrm{Rank}(\lambda_1^* \mathbf{F}) = 1$, and therefore $\mathrm{Rank}(\mathbf{\Phi}^*) \ge N - 1$ can be obtained from (28). According to the Lagrange dual complementary relaxation of (24), it can be inferred that the rank satisfies $\mathrm{Rank}(\mathbf{V_r^*}) \le 1$. Because $\mathrm{Rank}(\mathbf{V_r^*}) = 0$ is in conflict with (16), it can be known $\mathrm{Rank}(\mathbf{V_r^*}) = 1$.

Since the relay optimal beamforming vector satisfies $\mathrm{Rank}(\mathbf{V_r^*}) = 1$, the optimal solution of the problem P0-SDR is equivalent to the original problem P0, and the optimal solution P_r^*, ρ^*, $\mathbf{V}^*$ of the original problem P0 can be obtained from the optimal solution ρ_r^*, $\mathbf{V_r^*}$ of P0-SDR.

4 Contrast System

In this section, we briefly introduces the half-duplex relay system and the traditional full-duplex relay system, which are all time-sharing transmission AF relay systems. Except whether the power splitter is used or not and apply the different system transport protocols, other hardware configurations and conditional assumptions are identical to the proposed system.

4.1 Half-Duplex Relay System with SWIPT (HD-SWIPT)

The system is simply referred to as HD-SWIPT, which uses the PS scheme to perform ID and EH, respectively. The half-duplex relay system is still adopting SWIPT technology, but the system does not have the conditions for self-energy recycling due to the half-duplex transmission characteristics. The total transmission time slot block T is divided into two T/2 time slots. In the first stage, the source node synchronously transmits information and energy based on RF signals to relay node, while relay receiver harvests the energy from EAP. And in the second phase, the harvested energy is used to cooperative transmit information to the destination node.

For the sake of simplicity, only the main optimization issues are listed. Ignoring the time delay τ, the system throughput expression is

$$\mathrm{R} = \frac{1}{2}\log_2(1+\gamma) = \frac{1}{2}\log_2(1+\rho \mathrm{P}_s\|\mathbf{h}^H\|^2 \Big/ [(\rho\sigma_1^2+\sigma^2)+\frac{\sigma_2^2(\rho \mathrm{A}+\sigma^2)}{\mathrm{P}_r|\mathbf{g}\boldsymbol{v}|^2}]) \tag{29}$$

Then, optimization goal can be converted into an equivalent optimization problem as follows:

P1:

$$\min_{\boldsymbol{v},\mathrm{P_r},\rho} \quad \mathrm{Z} = \sigma^2\Big/\rho + \sigma_2^2\mathrm{A}\Big/\mathrm{P}_r|\mathbf{g}\boldsymbol{v}|^2 + \sigma_2^2\sigma^2\Big/\rho\mathrm{P}_r|\mathbf{g}\boldsymbol{v}|^2$$

$$\text{S.T.} \quad 1\big/2\eta(1-\rho)\mathrm{P}_s\|\mathbf{h}^H\|^2 + 1\big/2\eta q \geq \varepsilon \tag{30}$$

$$0 < \mathrm{P}_r \leq \varepsilon \tag{31}$$

$$0 < \rho < 1 \tag{32}$$

Similarly, applying the SDR, rank relaxation and Lagrange methods to solve problems, the conversion and solution process of the P1 problem is omitted for brevity.

4.2 Traditional Full-Duplex Relay System Without SWIPT (FD-no-SWIPT)

The traditional full-duplex relay system is simply referred to as FD-no-SWIPT, and its transmission process is divided into two phases. The traditional full-duplex relay system does not using SWITP technology, but it can harvest self-energy from the loop channel due to the full-duplex transmission characteristics. In the first T/2, information is transmitted from source node to relay node. In the second T/2, the relay harvests energy from source node and EAP, and simultaneously transmits information to destination node.

Again, only the main optimization issues are listed here. Ignoring the time delay τ, the throughput of the system is given by

$$R = \frac{1}{2}\log_2(1+\gamma) = \frac{1}{2}\log_2(1 + P_s\|\mathbf{h}^H\|^2 \Big/ (\sigma_1^2 + \sigma_2^2 A \Big/ P_r|\mathbf{g}\boldsymbol{v}|^2)\ ) \tag{33}$$

Optimization goal can be converted into an equivalent optimization problem as:

P2:

$$\min_{\boldsymbol{v},P_r} \quad Z = \sigma_2^2 A \Big/ P_r|\mathbf{g}\boldsymbol{v}|^2$$

$$\text{S.T.} \quad 1\Big/2\eta(P_s\|\mathbf{h}^H\|^2 + P_r|\mathbf{f}\boldsymbol{v}|^2 + q) \geq \varepsilon \tag{34}$$

$$0 < P_r \leq \varepsilon \tag{35}$$

Similarly, the conversion and solution process for the P2 problem is omitted.

5 Simulation Results

In this section, simulation results are given to evaluate the performance of the proposed system and the trend change is analyzed in detail based on the simulation experiment results. Assuming the system available bandwidth for the WPR system be 10 MHz, the receiver's AWGN power spectrum density is −140 dBm/Hz. The parameters are set to $\sigma_1^2 = \sigma_2^2 = -80$ dBm, $\sigma^2 = -60$ dBm and $\eta = 0.5$. According to Rayleigh fading to simulate channel between S and D in the system, and the signal attenuation is set to 40 dBm every 5 m between source and destination node [10]. So the channel is described by an expression as:

$$\mathbf{h} = \sqrt{\frac{k}{1+k}}\mathbf{h}^{LoS} + \sqrt{\frac{1}{1+k}}\mathbf{h}^{NLoS}$$

where the light-of-sight (LOS) channel is modeled as a far-field uniform linear antenna array model with $\mathbf{h}^{Los} = 10^{-2}[1, e^{j\theta}, e^{j2\theta}, \ldots\ldots, e^{j(M-1)\theta}]^T$ and $\theta = 2\pi d\sin(\phi)/\lambda_{wave}$, and $d = \lambda_{wave}/2$ is the spacing of the continuous antenna elements at the R, where λ_{wave} is the carrier wavelength, and $\phi = 60^{\circ}$ is the angle-of-departure (AOD) of the R to D, and the Rayleigh fading factor k is set to 5 dB. Each element of the non-light-of-sight (NLOS) channel simulating the Rayleigh fading channel is subject to a Gaussian distribution random variable with zero mean and covariance of −60 dB. Since the channel model **g** is the same as **h**, a detailed description about them is omitted. Meanwhile, the loop channel model f can be expressed as $\mathbf{f} = \sqrt{\beta}[1, 1, \cdots, 1]^T$ by the loop path loss β_{mm}, where $\beta_{mm} = -15$ dB and **f** represents an $N \times 1$ matrix. Generally there is $P_s = 20$ dBm.

In this experiment, we explore the optimal power splitting ratio ρ^* when the rate-energy at the relay reaches equilibrium on the premise of maximizing the system throughput, and simulate the trend function of throughput changing with power splitting ratio ρ

under different energy thresholds. Set ε to -8, -6, -4, -2 and 0 dBm, respectively, ρ is scanned from -30 dB to -1 dB, and the energy supplemented by the EAP is $q = 1/3\varepsilon$. The optimal power splitting rate can be derived according to the curve change corresponding to different fixed energy thresholds. As shown in Fig. 4, the system throughput is proportional to energy target threshold. And with the increase of power splitting ratio, the system throughput first shows a slow decline trend and then gradually tends to be stable. This is because the larger the ρ value, the greater the proportion of information decode in the power splitting than the energy harvest, resulting in a larger throughput fluctuation and the energy-rate imbalance. Therefore, it is more meaningful to take the value of ρ at the energy-rate balance point.

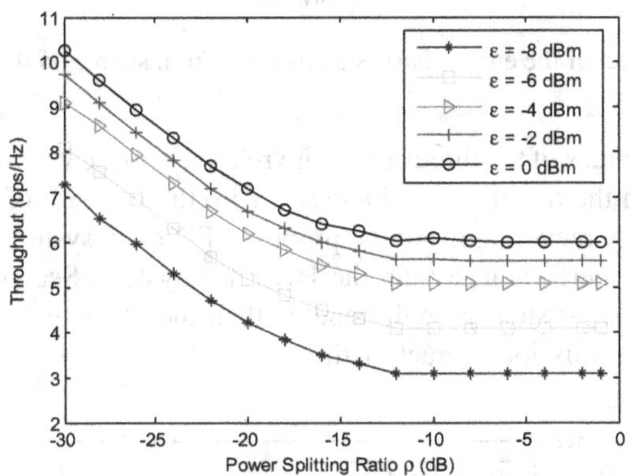

Fig. 4. Throughput and power splitting rates at different energy thresholds

In Fig. 5, we simulates the change in the relationship between the energy harvested $Q_{th} - \eta q$ by the relay from the source node and the system throughput, and explore the influence of external harvested energy value q on maintaining the continuous and stable operation of relay system. Set the $Q_{th} - \eta q$ value being from -10 to 2 dBm, and the external supplementary energy q is -14, -12, -10, -8 dBm respectively. As shown in Fig. 5, increasing the energy harvested by the relay from the source node has a significant effect on improving system throughput. And increasing the total energy harvested by the system can promote the performance of the system. That is to say, this numerical result reflects from the side that the energy threshold within a certain range of values is proportional to the system throughput. It can be seen from the graph that at point $Q_{th} - \eta q = -4$ dbm, the curve of $q = -8$ dbm begins to change and the value is the largest. Under the condition that the total energy harvested is fixed, when the energy harvested by the relay from the source node is limited, the system increases the energy value q harvested from the EAP, which can increase the system operating rate more effectively.

Figure 6 compares the proposed system with a half-duplex (HD-SWIPT) relay system with SWIPT and a traditional full-duplex (FD-no-SWIPT) relay system without SWIPT, and the experiment simulates the trend of throughput variation of each system under given energy target threshold, set the ε value is scanned from -10 to 2 dBm. As shown

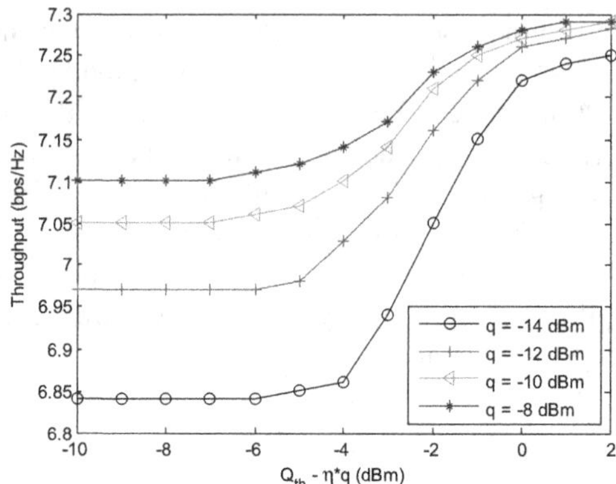

Fig. 5. Effect of the energy harvested by relay from source on throughput

in Fig. 6, the target values of the three curves are relatively close when the ε value is low, and the gap between the target values increases with the increase of ε. Obviously, the benefits of self-energy recycling make the proposed FD relay system more meaningful in promoting system performance than the HD relay system. Secondly, the proposed relay system has better system growth benefits than the other two systems due to its non-time-sharing transmission characteristics.

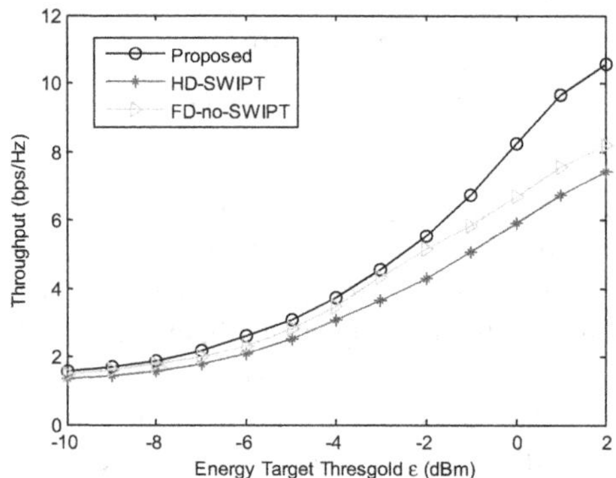

Fig. 6. Variations in different system throughputs as energy target thresholds increase

Finally, in order to compare the system performance of the proposed system and the comparison relay system in the same environment, the experiment simulates the variation trend of the throughput of the three relay systems with the increase of the transmission power of the source node. Under different fixed ε values, set the ε value is -5, 0 dBm, respectively, q is $1/3\varepsilon$, and the source transmit power P_s is between 0 to 30 dBm. As can be seen from Fig. 7, the source node transmit power is proportional to the system throughput. When the transmit power of the source node increases to 20 dBm, the target value shows a smooth and steady growth trend. Obviously, the benefit of self-energy recycling makes the proposed FD relay system more meaningful in promoting system

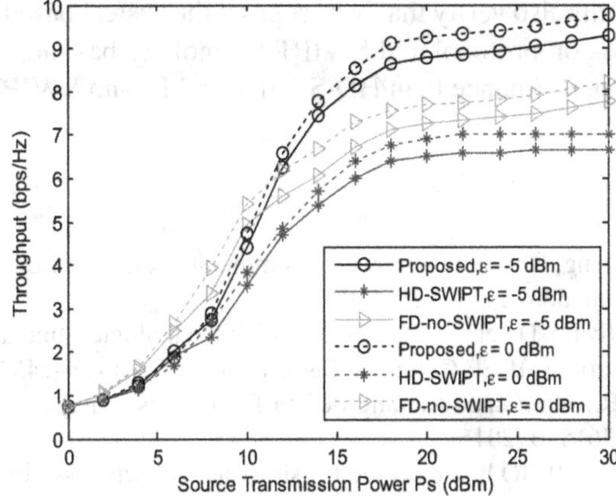

Fig. 7. Effect of source transmit power variation on system performance

performance than the HD relay system. Moreover, compared with different full-duplex relays, the proposed amplification and forwarding relay system with energy access points has significant effectiveness in improving system performance due to adopting SWIPT technology to realize information and energy synchronous transmission based on RF signals.

6 Conclusion

This paper proposes a non-time-sharing full-duplex amplification and forwarding (AF) relay system with energy access points adopting SWIPT technology in wireless networks. Utilizing SWIPT technology to realize information and energy synchronous transmission based on RF signals, and the energy-constrained relays harvest energy mainly from source nodes and external EAP. The relay can eliminate the self-interference signal through self-energy recycling in the loop channel, and jointly optimizing the relay transmit power, the relay transmit beamforming vector and the power splitting ratio. This paper take maximizing system throughput as optimization objective, adopting AF transmission protocol and power splitting scheme for ID and EH at the relay. Furthermore, due to the non-time-sharing transmission characteristics, information transmission, energy harvest and cooperative transmission are completed synchronously in a time block. The system transforms the original multivariate non-convex problem into a semi-definite programming problem by using quadratic optimization and SDR methods, and the variable reduction method is utilized to simplify the complex variables, and uses Lagrange method to solve optimization problems. Simulation experiments show that increasing the total energy harvested by the system can promote the performance of the system. Under the condition that the total energy harvested is fixed, the operation rate of the system can be promoted effectively by increasing the energy harvested from EAP. And the self-energy recycling of the relay can promote the throughput gain of the system.

The experimental results also verify that our proposal the system based on applying non-time-sharing transmission protocol and SWIPT technology has more significant gains in improving system performance than HD-SWIPT and FD-no-SWIPT relay systems.

References

1. Bi, S., Ho, C.K., Zhang, R.: Wireless powered communication: opportunities and challenges. IEEE Commun. Mag. **53**(4), 117–125 (2015)
2. Lu, X., Wang, P., Niyato, D., et al.: Wireless charging technologies: fundamentals, standards, and network applications. IEEE Commun. Surv. Tutor. **18**(2), 1413–1452 (2015)
3. Zeng, Y., Zhang, R.: Optimized training design for wireless energy transfer. IEEE Trans. Commun. **63**(2), 536–550 (2015)
4. Zhang, R., Ho, C.K.: MIMO broadcasting for simultaneous wireless information and power transfer. IEEE Trans. Wireless Commun. **12**(5), 1989–2001 (2013)
5. Wang, D.X., Zhang, R.Q., Cheng, X., et al.: Full-duplex energy-harvesting relay networks: capacity-maximizing relay selection. J. Commun. Inf. Netw. **3**(3), 79–85 (2018)
6. Sun, Q., Zhu, G., Shen, C., et al.: Joint beamforming design and time allocation for wireless powered communication networks. IEEE Commun. Lett. **18**(10), 1783–1786 (2014)
7. Kim, J., Lee, H., Song, C., et al.: Sum throughput maximization for multi-user MIMO cognitive wireless powered communication networks. IEEE Trans. Wireless Commun. **16**(2), 913–923 (2017)
8. Mohammadali, M., Chalise, B.K., Suraweera, H.A., et al.: Throughput analysis and optimization of wireless-powered multiple antenna full-duplex relay systems. IEEE Trans. Commun. **64**(4), 1769–1785 (2016)
9. Nasir, A.A., Zhou, X.Y., Durrani, S., et al.: Relaying protocols for wireless energy harvesting and information processing. IEEE Trans. Wireless Commun. **12**(7), 3622–3636 (2013)
10. Hwang, D., Nam, S.S., Yang, J.: Multi-antenna beamforming techniques in full-duplex and self-energy recycling systems: opportunities and challenges. IEEE Commun. Mag. **55**(10), 160–167 (2017)
11. Hwang, D., Hwang, K.C., Kim, D.I., et al.: Self-energy recycling for RF powered multi-antenna relay channels. IEEE Trans. Wireless Commun. **16**(2), 812–824 (2017)
12. Nasir, A.A., Zhou, X., Durrani, S., et al.: Relaying protocols for wireless energy harvesting and information processing. IEEE Trans. Wireless Commun. **12**(7), 3622–3636 (2013)
13. Hu, Z.W., Yuan, C.Y., Zhu, F.C., et al.: Weighted sum transmit power minimization for full-duplex system with SWIPT and self-energy recycling. IEEE Access **4**(1), 4874–4881 (2016)
14. Zeng, Y., Zhang, R.: Full-duplex wireless-powered relay with self-energy recycling. IEEE Wireless Commun. Lett. **4**(2), 201–204 (2015)
15. Dong, Y.J., Shafie, A.E., Hossain, M.J., et al.: Secure beamforming in full-duplex SWIPT systems with loopback self-interference cancellation. In: 2018 IEEE International Conference on Communications (ICC), pp. 1–6. IEEE, Kansas City (2018)
16. Wang, Z.L., Yue, X.W., Peng, Z.Y., et al.: Full-duplex user relaying for NOMA system with self-energy recycling. IEEE Access **6**(1), 67057–67069 (2018)
17. Kim, H., Kang, J., Jeong, S., et al.: Secure beamforming and self-energy recycling with full-duplex wireless-powered relay. In: 2016 13th IEEE Annual Consumer Communications & Networking Conference (CCNC), pp. 662–667. IEEE, Las Vegas (2016)
18. Shi, Q.J., Liu, L., Xu, W.Q., et al.: Joint transmit beamforming and receive power splitting for MISO SWIPT systems. IEEE Trans. Wireless Commun. **13**(6), 3269–3280 (2014)

19. Shi, Q.J., Xu, W.Q., Chang, T., et al.: Joint beamforming and power splitting for MISO interference channel With SWIPT: an SOCP relaxation and decentralized algorithm. IEEE Trans. Signal Process. **62**(23), 6194–6208 (2014)
20. Nguyen, D.D., Liu, Y., Chen, Q.C., et al.: On the energy efficient multi-pair two-way massive MIMO AF relaying with imperfect CSI and optimal power allocation. IEEE Access **6**(1), 2589–2603 (2018)

Recent Developments in Content Delivery Network: A Survey

Jiaming Zhao[1], Pingjia Liang[1], Weiming Liufu[1], and Zhengping Fan[2(✉)]

[1] School of Data and Computer Science, SUN Yat-Sen University, Guangzhou, China
[2] School of Intelligent Systems Engineering, SUN Yat-Sen University, Guangzhou, China
fanzhp@mail.sysu.edu.cn

Abstract. With the development of computer networks, the amount of network information continues to grow. To facilitate the transfer of the increasing information, a content distribution network (CDN) is developed by adding an intermediate layer on the existing network. Technically, Caching strategy of CDN is the most important mechanism, which heavily impacts the CDN performance. On the other hand, considering the cost of operating CDN, some strategies have been proposed, aiming to save the CDN cost in terms of, e.g., power energy. This paper makes a brief review on the recent developments of CDN in terms of its caching strategy and operation cost, and discusses some potential development directions of CDN.

Keywords: Content delivery network · Cache strategy · Cost

1 Introduction

In the past decades, with the wide use of the Internet and the mobile network, the amount of Internet information has been increasing at an explosive rate. A report by Cisco network company [1] has shown that the Internet traffic may grow nearly three times in the next five years. It also indicates that by 2021 the Internet traffic of the entire world will be 127 times of that of 2005. Meanwhile, the traffic carried by CDN [2] will account for 71% of all Internet traffic by then. Technically, CDN caches files near the user location, which significantly accelerates the response speed and thus reducing the delayed time.

The key strategies of CDN are the placement of replica server and content caching strategy. The placement of the Replica [3] is to find the best location from some candidate client nodes for the Replica by maximizing the CDN performance. For the content caching strategy, contents have different popularity, CDN needs to determine which caches should be chosen to store a given content such that the end users can reach the content with a high speed and less delayed time. For example, a fluid queue model in CDN was proposed by balancing the content caching strategy with redirect proximity in [4]. For each redistributed request, CDN utilizes the difference between the computational caches to select the appropriate replica server. In addition, since the algorithm limits the migration distance of each request, the latency cost is also greatly reduced. Note that the optimization method can also be used to determine the content location.

H. Shen and Y. Sang (Eds.): PAAP 2019, CCIS 1163, pp. 98–106, 2020.
https://doi.org/10.1007/978-981-15-2767-8_9

For example, the method of optimizing the CDN content caching strategy was proposed in [5], which significantly improves the CDN cache hit rate. A hybrid integer linear programming (MILP) optimization model was proposed in [6], which considered three issues of replica server placement and content caching and allocations.

Operation cost is another factor that should be considered in designing CDN. Although some strategies such as increasing server cache capacity, can improve the performance of CDN, it definitely increases the operating cost of service providers, creating an additional burden. Therefore, reducing cost of CDN is also very important for CDN providers.

In this paper, we give a brief review on the recent developments of CDN by focusing our attention on the impact of CDN caching strategy and operation cost. The paper is organized as follows. In Part Two, we investigate several caching strategies. In Part Three, we discuss the effect of operating costs on CDN and explore how CDN performance can be optimized at a limited cost. Finally, we conclude our review in Part Four.

2 Cache Strategy

In CDN, nodes often cooperate with each other. One of the most important things is to choose which node to cache which file. Common caching strategies are LCE, LCD, etc. [7]. Most of the caching nodes selected by these strategies are based on the path of content transmission. For example, LCE caches content at every point of the content transmission path. These strategies are intuitive and easy to implement, but the performance is often not satisfied. In order to adapt to the network structure to achieve better cache performance, some new strategies are proposed, in which cache nodes are chosen according to centrality, or have cooperation among caches.

2.1 Centrality-Measures Based Algorithm

It is shown [8] that better performance can be achieved by caching on a subset of content routers rather than on all routers in the content delivery path. The selection of a subset of content routers should achieve the goal of maximizing cache performance. Based on this observation, an algorithm based on centrality measure was proposed. The centrality can be determined by:

Closeness-centrality is the inverse of farness. The farness of a content router (CR) is defined as the summation of its shortest path distances to all other CRs. a CR which contains high Closeness-centrality is the most central CR in the network

Reach-centrality (RC) defines how many numbers of hops, a particular CR reaches to another CR in a network topology. A CR having a high value of RC indicates that it can reach to other CRs in a less hop count. A CR having a high value of RC can easily reach to the consumers with less number of hops.

Degree-centrality plays a very important role in Centrality-measures. This value of centrality defines how central a CR is in terms of nearby CRs. A CR having high degree contains a large number of the CRs in its range, and so it can easily distribute content items among various CRs to satisfy the customer requests.

Betweenness-centrality defines how many times a particular CR lies on the path between a consumer and server.

When delivering a user's request package, the maximum centrality value and the corresponding CR's ID that the package has passed through are recorded. All passed CRs need to check and decide whether to modify the request package information according to centrality. When the request packet is responded, the data packet will have the CR's ID with the largest centrality. When the data packet returns along the original path, if CR is the same router as the ID stored in the data packet, it caches the content, otherwise it does not cache, but only transfers packet. For example, in the Fig. 1, the request package is sent from A to D, and the Table 1 shows the changes in the package content during the process.

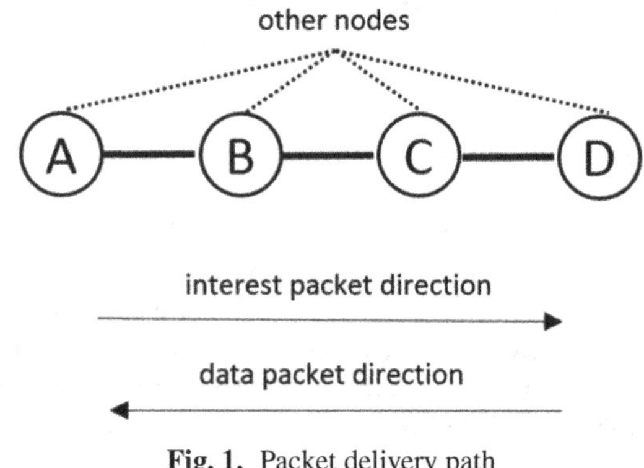

Fig. 1. Packet delivery path

Table 1. Changes in the contents of the packet

Node	A	B	C	D
Centrality	2	3	5	4
(ID, centrality) in interest parket	(A,2)	(B,3)	(C,5)	(C,5)
Data packet cached	×	×	√	×

As can be seen from the above, if the network structure is taken into account, the caching performance is improved. Note that in a real network it may be grouped into some clusters. In such networks, one can develop a community-based caching strategy, which may further improve the CDN performance.

2.2 Cooperative Caching

In [9], the author studies the user-centered cooperative edge caching problem in content delivery networks to improve the quality of experience by utilizing service provisioning at the edge of the network and minimizing end-to-end latency. They introduced a caching algorithm, a group of small base stations (SBS) collaboratively shared storage, and jointly decided on the caching strategy to cache as much content as possible under capacity constraints. In collaborative caching, nearby SBS forms a group and caches files based on user preference matrix. The purpose is to use the storage capacity of all SBS in the group to cache all files. A portion of each SBS storage space is used to cache the most popular files, while the rest is used to cache the most popular files that are not cached by other nodes (Fig. 2).

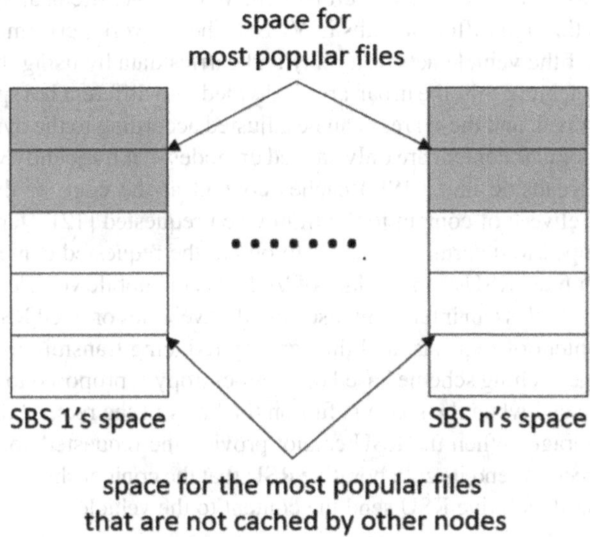

Fig. 2. SBS caching algorithm

In addition, in the user-centered delivery scheme, an improved matching theory is used to match users and SBS to ensure that more users can be served satisfactorily. Usually, a user requests a service from the nearest SBS, and if it has the requested file and sufficient service channels, the service will serve. Otherwise, other SBSs in the pre-allocation group will automatically check whether they meet the two requirements of serving the user. If there is no SBS in the group that can provide such services, the user request will be directed to the path that is not cached.

2.3 Mobile Edge Caching

The traditional CDN-content-based allocation mechanism is usually designed for the traditional wired communication network architecture. However, in today's increasingly mobile networks, resources (e.g., storage, bandwidth and computing power) and the location of deployed servers are limited. More importantly, due to content dynamics, user mobility and the limitation of the number of users in the cell, the hit rate of cached content in the mobile network may be very low. In [10], the author studies content distribution in the rapidly developing mobile network. They proposed a learning-based cooperative caching framework for mobile edge caching servers, which does not require prior knowledge of content requirements and content popularity matrices. They first use artificial neural networks to observe real-time requirements over a period of time, and then represent the content cache of the minimum latency problem as a 0–1 integer programming problem. Furthermore, they prove that the problem is NP-hard and propose a greedy algorithm to solve it.

In the Vehicular content networks (VCN), it is similar to the mobile network. It is pointed out that due to the mobility of vehicles, it is quite inefficient to establish end-to-end connections in VCNs [11]. Therefore, content packages are usually sent back to requesting nodes through different paths in VCNs. The network performance of VCNs can be improved if the vehicle acts as a relay and carries data by using the mobility of nodes. In order to achieve this, the urban area is divided into different hot spots according to the way users travel, and these areas can be adjusted according to the dynamic vehicle density. Finally, popular content are only cached on nodes that frequently visit hot spots.

In VCN, the roadside unit (RSU) caches content at the edge of the network to facilitate timely delivery of content to the train when requested [12]. Here a model for vehicles is developed to determine whether to obtain the requested content from other mobile vehicles or fixed RSUs on the edges of VCN. When mobile vehicles issue content requests, mobile vehicles can intelligently select other vehicles or fixed RSUs to connect to retrieve the content of requests, and thus greatly reducing transmission delay. For a fixed RSU, an edge caching scheme based on cross-entropy is proposed to determine the content to be replaced when the space is full on the basis of the request decision of the vehicle in its coverage. When the RSU cannot provide the requested content solely, it can identify and recommend its collaborative RSU that the content should be transferred to, and then this collaborative RSU send the content to the vehicle.

3 The Cost of CDN

In CDN deployment, it definitely needs energy. How to save energy is another very important issue in operating CDN.

3.1 The Energy Consumption Cost of CDN

A CDN is a large distributed system that consists of hundreds of thousands of servers [13]. These servers are implemented as clusters, which consume a lot of power in the content delivery system [14]. An intuitive way to reduce energy consumption is to reduce the number of CDN servers, but this will lead to performance degradation and other cost increases accordingly. The most of methods in reducing energy consumption of traditional CDN is to reduce cluster energy consumption by “adjusting” its service capacity [13, 15–17]. Its basic idea is to switch idle servers to energy-saving mode when the load is low, so as to reduce energy consumption [13]. However, it is pointed out [13] that in traditional CDN where a large number of edge servers are deployed, reducing service capacity will increase the flow of data between ISPs, which results in more cross-ISP traffic expenditure. He et al. [13] proposed a capacity allocation algorithm based on the workload prediction, especially considering ISP traffic expenditure. Through this method, the overall operating cost of CDN is reduced and frequent server switching is effectively avoided. That is, the traffic between ISPs is reduced. Another scheme is proposed on the basis of smart grid technology [14]. Here the smart grid technology with low complexity is integrated with online Lyapunov optimization for an energy/QoE efficient CDN. Compared with other methods without real-time energy management, this method can converge to the optimal convergence point at a faster speed. In fact, the dynamic prediction and real-time management methods are very common ideas to solve the problem of CDN energy consumption. Especially with the emergence and development of cloud-based CDN, real-time management method has more development space. The main reason is that cloud-based vCDNs are more flexible so that the size of CDNs can be dynamically adjusted to reduce energy consumption. Liao et al. [18] proposed an approximate algorithm of maximum flow prediction (MMF) by combining dynamic prediction and real-time management. This method can determine the best capacity of CDN components in real time, and dynamically adjust the scale of CDN to reduce energy consumption.

3.2 The Delivery Cost and Storage Cost of CDN

In CDN, when a request asking for a movie arrives at some node v, the CDN may select any other node u (as in a P2P network) which currently has a copy of that movie, and instructs u to send a copy to v [19]. In this process, both the movie content sent by u to v and the control information sent by CDN to u (although this is almost negligible compared with the bandwidth occupied by the content sent by u) occupy bandwidth, which constitutes the delivery cost of CDN. In order to reduce the delivery cost, two solutions are often given (as showed in Fig. 1): (1) to make u closer to v [19], and (2) to choose a better transit path [20], such as a transit route with better performance and lower price. In solution one, due to the limited caching space of the nodes near v, when there are many requests for different files, some of the cached contents need to be replaced. If more files are wanted to be close to v, the storage capacity of node v has to be increased, which leads to an increase in storage costs.

On the other hand, in the solution one, there is an obvious problem- the balance between the delivery cost and storage cost. It has been shown that finding a cache placement method that minimizes both costs is NP-hard [19], which is also confirmed by [21]. To deal with this, an O (log δ)- competitive algorithm is proposed in [19], where δ is the normalized diameter of the network. The caching strategy is: If node v gets a copy of the file from u, the time of the file kept in node v is positively correlated with the distance between u and v. In [21], a genetic algorithm (GA) is applied to solve the problem of dynamically placing copies to minimize the total cost including storage and delivery costs. Here the needed solved problem is expressed as a mixed integer programming (MIP) problem that takes into account the service level agreement (SLA) of CDN and the multicast transfer feature for the delivery. Compared with the current popular optimization algorithms, including random add, random delete, random delete all, zero greedy delete and one greedy delete, the GA algorithm is superior to these algorithms in reducing the total cost of delivery and storage (Fig. 3).

For the solution two, that is, to choose a better transit path, this method has nothing to do with the storage cost, but can reduce the delivery cost. It is clearly that the solution two is compatible with the solution one, which indicates that the solution two can be further

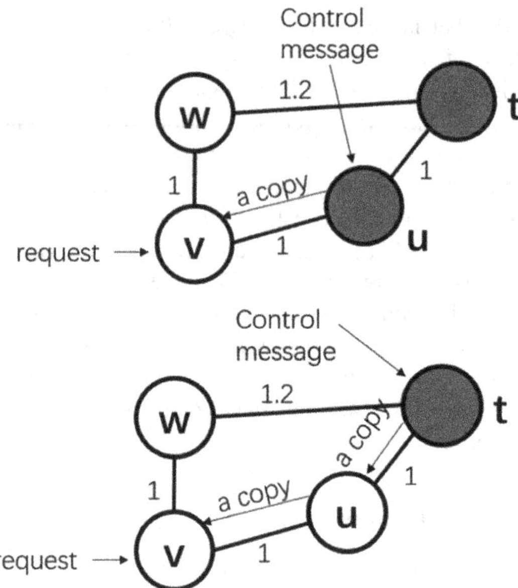

Fig. 3. The node t-w is CDN servers. The dark node indicates that the requested file is cached by the node. The white node indicates that the node has no requested file. The weight of the connection between the nodes indicates the cost of the file when it passes through the path. In Idea 1, considering the left and right graphs, the cost of the left graph is 1, and the cost of the right graph is 2. When the node nearer to v has the file, the delivery cost is lower. However, the cost of route is also very important. According to idea 2, considering the right figure, when t sends information to v, the cost of selecting path t-u-v is lower than that of path t-w-v.

optimized on the basis of the solution one. One application of such idea is discussed in [20]. In the Internet, there are many Internet Exchange Points (IXPs), which connect a large number of ISPs. But as mentioned in [13], this kind of content transmission across ISPs incurs a high cost, and thus it is particularly important to choose a lower cost transmission path. Through the optimal selection strategy, CDN deployed on IXPs can reduce transmission cost by 57% on average without sacrificing performance.

4 Conclusion

Nowadays, CDN has evolved from the original blank to the current bloom, and the role of CDN has become more prominent. In latest years, there have also been derivations of peer-assisted CDN [22], cloud-based CDN [23, 24], etc., all aimed at improving the performance of CDN. However, No matter what CDN have been developed, the most two important technical issues are the placement of the replica server and the selection of the content caching strategy. On the other hand, from the standpoint of CDN providers, the operating cost should be reduced as much as possible. In this paper, we have given a brief survey on CDN in terms of these topics. In the days to come, there may be more variants of CDN. For example, we can combine various topological properties of complex networks into CDN to improve the performance of CDN. The question is: Which topological property of a network should be chosen to achieve the best performance of CDN? It is worth of further investigation in our work.

References

1. Cisco. https://www.cisco.com/c/dam/global/zh_cn/solutions/collateral/service-provider/visual-networking-index-vni/complete-white-paper-c11-481360-CN.pdf?oid=wprsi001573&elqTrackId=8c75641ee1b443fea18d8278a77ea927&elq=&elqaid=5964&elqat=2&elqCampaignId=&elqcst=272&elqcsid=2374&_gscu_=69512337n7nuz341&_gscs_=t69815000lsxmmb41. Accessed 20 Sept 2019
2. Stocker, V., Smaragdakis, G., Lehr, W., Bauer, S.: The growing complexity of content delivery networks: challenges and implications for the internet ecosystem. Telecommun. Policy **41**(2), 1003–1016 (2017)
3. Sahoo, J., et al.: A survey on replica server placement algorithms for content delivery networks. IEEE Commun. Surv. Tutorials **19**(2), 1002–1026 (2016)
4. Shuai, Q., Wang, K., Miao, F., Jin, L.: A cost-based distributed algorithm for load balancing in content delivery network. In: 2017 9th International Conference on Intelligent Human-Machine Systems and Cybernetics (IHMSC), Hangzhou, China, pp. 11–15. IEEE (2017)
5. Kyryk, M., Pleskanka, N., Pleskanka, M.: The analysis of the optimal data distribution method at the content delivery network. In: 2019 IEEE 15th International Conference on the Experience of Designing and Application of CAD Systems (CADSM), Polyana, Ukraine, pp. 1–4. IEEE (2019)
6. Xu, K., Li, X., Bose, S.K., Shen, G.: Joint replica server placement, content caching, and request load assignment in content delivery networks. IEEE Access **6**(2), 17968–17981 (2018)
7. Zhang, G., Li, Y., Lin, T.: Caching in information centric networking: a survey. Comput. Netw. **57**(16), 3128–3141 (2013)
8. Lal, K.N., Kumar, A.: A centrality-measures based caching scheme for content-centric networking (CCN). Multimedia Tools Appl. **77**(14), 17625–17642 (2018)
9. Tang, S.Y., Alnoman, A., Anpalagan, A., Woungang, I.: A user-centric cooperative edge caching scheme for minimizing delay in 5G content delivery networks. Trans. Emerg. Telecommun. Technol. **29**(8), e3461 (2018)
10. Sun, S.S., Jiang, W., Feng, G., Qin, S., Yuan, Y.: Cooperative caching with content popularity prediction for mobile edge caching. Tehnicki Vjesnik-Technical Gazette **26**(2), 503–509 (2019)
11. Yao, L., Chen, A.L., Deng, J., Wang, J.B., Wu, G.W.: A cooperative caching scheme based on mobility prediction in vehicular content centric networks. IEEE Trans. Veh. Technol. **67**(6), 5435–5444 (2018)
12. Su, Z., Hui, Y.L., Xu, Q.C., Yang, T.T., Liu, J.Y., Jia, Y.J.: An edge caching scheme to distribute content in vehicular networks. IEEE Trans. Veh. Technol. **67**(6), 5346–5356 (2018)
13. He, H.J., Zhao, Y., Wu, J.F., Tian, Y.: Cost-aware capacity provisioning for internet video streaming CDNs. Comput. J. **58**(12), 3255–3270 (2015)
14. Simulation-transactions of the society for modeling and simulation international. http://sage.cnpereading.com/paragraph/article/10.1177/0037549719862023. Accessed 30 Sept 2019
15. Lin, M.H., Wierman, A., Andrew, L.L.H., Thereska, E.: Dynamic right-sizing for power-proportional data centers. IEEE/ACM Trans. Networking **21**(5), 1378–1391 (2013)
16. Mathew, V., Sitaraman, R.K., Shenoy, P.: Energy-aware load balancing in content delivery networks. In: IEEE INFOCOM, vol. 12, pp. 954–962. IEEE Press, Orlando (2012)

17. Tchernykh, A., Cortes-Mendoza, J.M., Pecero, J.E., Bouvry, P., Kliazovich, D.: Adaptive energy efficient distributed VoIP load balancing in federated cloud infrastructure. In: 3rd IEEE International Conference on Cloud Networking, pp. 1–6. IEEE Press, Luxembourg (2014)
18. Liao, D., Sun, G., Yang, G.H., Chang, V.: Energy-efficient virtual content distribution network provisioning in cloud-based data centers. Future Gener. Comput. Syst. Int. J. Sci. **83**, 347–357 (2018)
19. Bar-Yehuda, R., Kantor, E., Kutten, S., Rawitz, D.: Growing half-balls: minimizing storage and communication costs in content delivery networks. SIAM J. Discrete Math. **32**(3), 1903–1921 (2018)
20. Ahmed, F., Shafiq, M.Z., Khakpour, A.R., Liu, A.X.: Optimizing internet transit routing for content delivery networks. IEEE-ACM Trans. Netw. **26**(1), 76–89 (2018)
21. Fatin, H.Z., Jamali, S., Fatin, G.Z.: Data replication in large scale content delivery networks: a genetic algorithm approach. J. Circ. Syst. Comput. **27**(12), 1850189 (2018)
22. Tseng, L., DeAntonis, J., Higuchi, T., Altintas, O.: Peer-assisted content delivery network by vehicular micro clouds. In: 2018 IEEE 7th International Conference on Cloud Networking (CloudNet), Tokyo, Japan, pp. 1–3. IEEE (2018)
23. Salahuddin, M.A., Sahoo, J., Glitho, R., Elbiaze, H., Ajib, W.: A survey on content placement algorithms for cloud-based content delivery networks. IEEE Access **6**(8), 91–114 (2018)
24. Mahesh, G., Maheswara Rao, V.V.R., Shankar, R.S., Sirisha, G.V.G.: Primal-dual parallel algorithm for optimal content delivery in cloud CDNs. In: 2017 IEEE International Conference on Computational Intelligence and Computing Research (ICCIC), Coimbatore, India, pp. 1–6. IEEE (2017)

High Performance Systems

Weighted Mean Deviation Similarity Index for Objective Omnidirectional Video Quality Assessment

Mengzhen Zhong, Junhao Chen, and Yuzhen Niu(✉)

College of Mathematics and Computer Science, Fuzhou University, Fuzhou, China
1292824862@qq.com, fz.junhao.chen@gmail.com, yuzhenniu@gmail.com

Abstract. Objective quality assessment for omnidirectional videos is essential for the watching experience and optimization processes of Virtual Reality (VR) technologies. Currently, the most used objective video quality assessment (VQA) metrics for omnidirectional videos are based on PSNR. Because PSNR usually shows weak consistency with human perception, we adapt the mean deviation similarity index (MDSI) for omnidirectional VQA, and present a weighted mean deviation similarity index (WS-MDSI) for objective omnidirectional VQA. Because an omnidirectional video usually has a large frame resolution and a large number of frames, we also investigate the influence of temporal sampling on VQA. The proposed index WS-MDSI is evaluated on an omnidirectional VQA database. Experimental results show that, compared with the state-of-the-art methods based on PSNR, WS-MDSI increases the performance by 23.5% and 23.25% on the indicators of SROCC and PLCC, respectively. We also found that a 1/4 reduction in temporal resolution does not significantly affect the performance of the objective VQA for omnidirectional video.

Keywords: Omnidirectional video · Video quality assessment · Temporal sampling

1 Introduction

In recent years, we have witnessed the rapid development of virtual reality (VR). As an important development direction of VR [19], omnidirectional video is expected to have a huge impact on VR, automatic robots, monitoring systems, and other fields soon. The omnidirectional video provides the ability to view in all directions within the scene. The user can freely change the viewing direction by moving the head or device, the accessible field of view can cover the entire sphere with the support of a head-mounted display (HMD). The omnidirectional video brings immersive and interactive visual experience [10], but at the cost of extraordinarily high resolution. As reported in the mpeg survey [4], the quality of experience (QoE) [5] of omnidirectional video degrades when present at low resolutions will make humans feel uncomfortable. But due to limitations in

H. Shen and Y. Sang (Eds.): PAAP 2019, CCIS 1163, pp. 109–117, 2020.
https://doi.org/10.1007/978-981-15-2767-8_10

technologies such as storage and transmission [3,9], it tends to reduce the visual experience of omnidirectional video. Therefore, it is necessary to study VQA for omnidirectional video.

More recent attention has focused on the provision of VQA on omnidirectional video which based on PSNR by taking into account the characteristics of omnidirectional videos [12,17,18]. Yu et al. [17] proposed a spherical peak signal-to-noise ratio (S-PSNR), which calculates PSNR on a set of uniformly sampled points. Zakharchenko et al. [18] employed Craster parabolic projection PSNR (CPP-PSNR) to measure resampled pixel distortion. [12] applied weight allocation in the calculation of PSNR (WS-PSNR). To data, a great deal of previous research into omnidirectional VQA has focused on omnidirectional video features. However, several studies have investigated PSNR does not consider the content of an image and the characteristics of the human visual system (HVS). So these metrics usually result in a weak consistency with human perception. Many experiments indicated that SSIM and MDSI are more consistent with subjective quality evaluation than PSNR [7,14,15], which opens up opportunities to improve omnidirectional VQA. We adapted SSIM [14] and MDSI [8] for omnidirectional VQA. Through conducted multiple sets of experiments, we found that these methods improve the performance of VQA on omnidirectional video.

The remaining part of the paper proceeds as follows. We introduce related work on omnidirectional video quality assessment in Sect. 2. Section 3 is concerned with the methodology used for this paper. We describe experimental datasets and analyze experimental results in Sect. 4. We conclude the paper in Sect. 5.

2 Related Work

2.1 Video Quality Assessment on Omnidirectional Video

In recent years, many studies have begun to examine VQA on omnidirectional video. For subjective VQA, many subjective VQA methods [11,16,20] were presented. For example, subjective assessment of multimedia panoramic video quality (SAMPVIQ) [20], modified absolute category rating (M-ACR) [11] and a pair of overall DMOS (O-DMOS) and vectorized DMOS (V-DMOS) [16] was proposed. For objective VQA, there are several works [12,17,18], all base on PSNR. Yu [17] proposed a quality metric for spherical surface (S-PSNR), which averages the error of the set of sampling points to obtain the objective quality score of this omnidirectional video. Zakharchenko [18] developed CPP-PSNR to measure distortion based on resampled pixels on Craster parabolic projection. In [12] presented a Weighted-to-Spherically-uniform Peak Signal-to-Noise Ratio (WS-PSNR) which provided different weights for pixel distortion at different locations to realize uniform weights on a spherical surface. To date, WS-PSNR has been utilized as a typical quality metric in omnidirectional video coding by the joint video exploration team (JVET) [1]. The method proposed in [2] is adapted to SSIM in the spherical domain for omnidirectional VQA. Moreover, through some subjective experiments, finding some human behavior while people watching the omnidirectional video. Then, [6] developed a deep learning model, which embeds head movement (HM) and eye movement (EM) for objective quality assessment on omnidirectional video.

2.2 SSIM and MDSI on 2D Image

SSIM is a classic 2D image quality assessment method, and MDSI is currently the most effective algorithm without using deep learning methods in 2D image quality assessment.

The Structural Similarity Index (SSIM). Wang and Bovik believed that human eyes get image information through luminance, contrast, and structural information [14], and put forward a universal image quality index (UQI) [13] and the structural similarity index (SSIM). Specifically, the luminance, contrast and structural information constitute a similarity map for the SSIM index and then uses average pooling to compute the final similarity score.

The Mean Deviation Similarity Index (MDSI). Nafchi et al. presented a mean deviation similarity index (MDSI). It uses gradient magnitude to measure structural distortions and chrominance features to measure color distortions. These two similarity maps are combined to form a gradient-chromaticity similarity map, then use a deviation pooling strategy to compute the final quality score.

3 Proposed Method

The most used objective VQA for omnidirectional video is based on traditional PSNR. However, PSNR does not consider the content of an image and the characteristics of the human visual system (HVS). So these metrics usually result in a weak consistency with human perception. To address this, we proposed to develop the MDSI for omnidirectional VQA and applied weight to its error map. In this section, we describe WS-MDSI in detail. At the same time, we explored the influence on omnidirectional video objective quality assessment when its time resolution dropped by 1/4.

3.1 Weighted Mean Deviation Similarity Index

First, we calculated the error map of the distorted image. The gradient magnitude was computed to measure structural distortions, the chrominance features were computed to measure color distortions. These two similarity maps were then combined to form a gradient-chromaticity similarity map, this map represents the distortion of the image, which is defined as follow

$$\widehat{GCS}(x) = \alpha \widehat{GS}(x) + (1 - \alpha) \widehat{CS}(x) \tag{1}$$

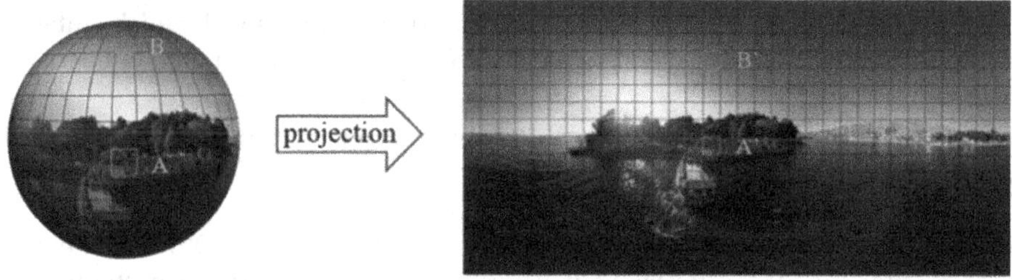

Fig. 1. A map from spherical surface to equirectangular.

where the $\widehat{GS}$ is the gradient similarity of the graph and the $\widehat{CS}$ is the color similarity of the graph. The parameter $0 \leq \alpha \leq 1$ adjusts the relative importance of the gradient and chromaticity similarity maps. $\widehat{GCS}$ is the pixel error map.

Second, we computed the weight for each pixel in the error map. Due to existing stretching and condensation at a various level according to its location on projection plane when mapped from representation space to observation space. Therefore, it is unreasonable that the weights of each pixel are equal on the projection plane. For example, there are very few pixels in two poles of the observation space while there are many pixels in the corresponding representation space (such as ERP projection), the equal weight of each pixel means that the pixel error of the two poles will be greatly enlarged. As projection planes are commonly uniformly sampled, weights of pixels can be calculated using a stretching ratio of the area from representation space to observation space. As shown in Fig. 1 the B on observation space is corresponded to the B' on representation space. The weight of pixel is given by:

$$w = \frac{Area(B)}{Area(B')} \tag{2}$$

the weight function should be discretized to be applied for a digital image. A pixel in the digital image was modeled as a little square. For equirectangular projection, the weights are calculated as

$$w(i,j)_{erp} = \cos\frac{(j + 0.5 - N/2)\,\pi}{N} \tag{3}$$

here (i, j) represents the position of the pixel in representation space, and N is the height of the image.

As mentioned earlier, we have got the weights of pixels, after that, embed the weights into the error map. The WS-MDSI is dened as follows:

$$WS - MDSI = \left[\frac{\sum_{i=1}^{N} w(i)\left|\widehat{GCS}_i^{\frac{1}{4}} - \left(\frac{1}{N}\sum_{i=1}^{N}\widehat{GCS}_i^{\frac{1}{4}}\right)\right|}{\sum_{i=1}^{N} w(i)}\right]^{\frac{1}{4}} \tag{4}$$

Fig. 2. Dataset samples. From top-left to bottom-right: *(dianying; fengjing1; fengjing3; hangpai1; hangpai2; hangpai3; tiyu1; tiyu2; tiyu3; xinwen1; xinwen2; yanchanghui1; yanchanghui2)*.

where N is the number of pixels of the error map, and w(i) is the weight of the pixel of the corresponding projection plane in the error map. Final, we applied deviation pooling to form the final score, it is worth noting deviation pooling considers both magnitude and the spread of the distortions across the image, which is more in line with HVS.

3.2 Investigated Temporal Sampling on Objective Omnidirectional VQA

The omnidirectional video needs to contain the information from all 360° . Therefore, the omnidirectional video should be with a very high spatial resolution even higher than 8k to maintain relatively good visual quality. Such high-resolution videos will bring many challenges to omnidirectional video storage and transmission. Therefore, we explored the influence of temporal sampling on objective quality assessment of omnidirectional video. For temporal sampling, we compared the quality evaluation result between frame by frame and took one frame every four frames.

Table 1. Experimental results of database. The top three performance values for metrics are formatted in bold, italic and bold italic.

Metric	SROCC	PLCC	RMSE
PSNR	0.4314	0.4600	10.9935
S-PSNR	0.5266	0.5492	10.3624
CPP-PSNR	0.5004	0.5231	10.5519
WS-PSNR	0.4983	0.5176	10.5856
SSIM	0.532	0.5137	10.6194
WS-SSIM	**0.6100**	**0.5959**	**9.9263**
MDSI	*0.7243*	*0.7499*	*8.1709*
WS-MDSI	***0.7616***	***0.7817***	***7.7167***

4 Experimental Results

We verified our method on a subjective omnidirectional video quality assessment database [16]. The dataset and experimental results are analyzed as follows.

4.1 Omnidirectional Video Quality Assessment Database

The subjective omnidirectional video quality assessment database we use was provided in [16], which contains viewing direction data and DMOS of 48 subjects on viewing omnidirectional videos. In all, there are 48 sequences of omnidirectional videos in our dataset, all videos last for 12 s with 25 frames per second all the sequences are mapped to the 2D plane by ERP with a resolution of 40962048. The dataset used the HTC Vive as the HMD and a software virtual desktop (VD) as the omnidirectional video player. In total, 48 subjects (30 males and 18 females) participated in the experiment. For each subject, all of 48 sequences were played at random order. During the experiment, the subjects were seated on a swivel chair, being allowed to turn around freely, such that all regions of omnidirectional videos are accessible. Besides, to avoid eye fatigue and motion sickness, there was a 5-minute interval after viewing each session of 16 sequences. Figure 2 shows one frame of each series of videos in our dataset.

4.2 Performance Evaluation

We computed three evaluation metrics for performance comparison, i.e. SROCC (Spearman rank order correlation coefficient), PLCC (Pearson linear correlation coefficient) and RMSE (root mean squared error). SROCC and PLCC indicators are positively correlated with human subjective visual perception, the greater the absolute value of these indicators, the higher the correlation between the objective quality assessment index and the subjective visual perception. RMSE is the root mean square error between objective score and subjective visual

Table 2. Comparison of objective quality assessment results of omnidirectional video which are original and after temporal sampling.

Original	Temporal sampling		
	SROCC	PLCC	RMSE
PSNR	0.4314/0.4641	0.4600/0.4848	10.9935/10.8283
S-PSNR	0.5266/0.5444	0.5492/0.5568	10.3624/10.2844
CPP-PSNR	0.5004/0.5102	0.5231/0.5446	10.5519/10.3845
WS-PSNR	0.4983/0.5058	0.5176/0.5292	10.5856/10.5045
SSIM	0.5320/0.5568	0.5137/0.5549	10.6194/10.2888
WS-SSIM	0.6100/0.6237	0.5959/0.6282	9.9263/9.6078
MDSI	0.7243/0.6777	0.7499/0.6865	8.1709/8.9758
WS-MDSI	0.7616/0.7102	0.7817/0.7190	7.7167/8.6055

perception after nonlinear regression. The value of RMSE is positive and the smaller the value, the higher the similarity between objective score and subjective visual perception. We can see from Table 1, the proposed method outperformed state-of-the-art PSNR-based algorithms specially designed for omnidirectional video, which achieved the first of each indicator, and the WS-MDSI method in SROCC and PLCC was 23.5% and 23.25% higher than the S-PSNR which was the best PSNR-based method in the experiment. The WS-SSIM was got by applied weight to SSIM, the weight calculation is the same with WS-MDSI.

4.3 Influence of Temporal Sampling on Objective Omnidirectional VQA

Besides, we investigated the influence of temporal sampling on the objective quality assessment performance of the omnidirectional video. The experimental results are shown in Table 2. From the chart, it can be seen that the temporal resolution decreased by 1/4, which hardly affected the objective quality evaluation performance of the omnidirectional video. These results suggested that using the omnidirectional video after temporal sampling to replace the original omnidirectional video to explore the objective VQA on omnidirectional video is a good solution. It does not only reduce the storage space occupied by omnidirectional video but also significantly increases computational efficiency.

5 Conclusion

In this paper, we presented a weighted mean deviation similarity index (WS-MDSI) for objective omnidirectional video quality assessment (VQA). The proposed index was verified on a subjective omnidirectional VQA database and compared with state-of-the-art PSNR-based metrics especially designed for omnidirectional video. Experimental results indicated that the proposed index achieved superior performance. Moreover, we investigated the influence of temporal sampling on the performance of VQA. The experimental results show that the omnidirectional videos after temporal sampling can achieve similar performance with the original omnidirectional videos. Further research might explore some other characteristics of the human visual system for omnidirectional VQA. For example, there are some high-level features, such as local motion and salient objects, which can be incorporated in predicting viewing direction to improve the performance of VQA metrics for omnidirectional video.

References

1. Boyce, J., Alshina, E., Abbas, A., Ye, Y.: JVET common test conditions and evaluation procedures for 360 video. In: Joint Video Exploration Team of ITU-T SG, vol. 16 (2017)
2. Chen, S., Zhang, Y., Li, Y., Chen, Z., Wang, Z.: Spherical structural similarity index for objective omnidirectional video quality assessment. In: 2018 IEEE International Conference on Multimedia and Expo (ICME), pp. 1–6. IEEE (2018)
3. Corbillon, X., Devlic, A., Simon, G., Chakareski, J.: Optimal set of 360-degree videos for viewport-adaptive streaming. In: Proceedings of the 25th ACM International Conference on Multimedia, pp. 943–951. ACM (2017)
4. The MPEG Virtual Reality Ad-hoc Group: Summary of survey on virtual reality. In: ISO/IEC JTC 1/SC 29/WG 11 N16542 (2016)
5. Konrad, R., Cooper, E.A., Wetzstein, G.: Novel optical configurations for virtual reality: evaluating user preference and performance with focus-tunable and monovision near-eye displays. In: Proceedings of the 2016 CHI Conference on Human Factors in Computing Systems, pp. 1211–1220. ACM (2016)
6. Li, C., Xu, M., Du, X., Wang, Z.: Bridge the gap between VQA and human behavior on omnidirectional video: a large-scale dataset and a deep learning model. arXiv preprint arXiv:1807.10990 (2018)
7. Li, Q., Lin, W., Fang, Y.: No-reference quality assessment for multiply-distorted images in gradient domain. IEEE Signal Process. Lett. **23**(4), 541–545 (2016)
8. Nafchi, H.Z., Shahkolaei, A., Hedjam, R., Cheriet, M.: Mean deviation similarity index: efficient and reliable full-reference image quality evaluator. IEEE Access **4**, 5579–5590 (2016)
9. Nasrabadi, A.T., Mahzari, A., Beshay, J.D., Prakash, R.: Adaptive 360-degree video streaming using scalable video coding. In: Proceedings of the 25th ACM International Conference on Multimedia, pp. 1689–1697. ACM (2017)
10. Sarmiento, W.J., Quintero, C.: Panoramic immersive videos-3D production and visualization framework. In: SIGMAP, pp. 173–177 (2009)
11. Singla, A., Fremerey, S., Robitza, W., Lebreton, P., Raake, A.: Comparison of subjective quality evaluation for HEVC encoded omnidirectional videos at different bit-rates for UHD and FHD resolution. In: Proceedings of the on Thematic Workshops of ACM Multimedia 2017, pp. 511–519. ACM (2017)
12. Sun, Y., Lu, A., Yu, L.: Weighted-to-spherically-uniform quality evaluation for omnidirectional video. IEEE Signal Process. Lett. **24**(9), 1408–1412 (2017)
13. Wang, Z., Bovik, A.C.: A universal image quality index. IEEE Signal Process. Lett. **9**(3), 81–84 (2002)

14. Wang, Z., Bovik, A.C., Sheikh, H.R., Simoncelli, E.P., et al.: Image quality assessment: from error visibility to structural similarity. IEEE Trans. Image Process. **13**(4), 600–612 (2004)
15. Wang, Z., Li, Q.: Information content weighting for perceptual image quality assessment. IEEE Trans. Image Process. **20**(5), 1185–1198 (2010)
16. Xu, M., Li, C., Liu, Y., Deng, X., Lu, J.: A subjective visual quality assessment method of panoramic videos. In: 2017 IEEE International Conference on Multimedia and Expo (ICME), pp. 517–522. IEEE (2017)
17. Yu, M., Lakshman, H., Girod, B.: A framework to evaluate omnidirectional video coding schemes. In: 2015 IEEE International Symposium on Mixed and Augmented Reality, pp. 31–36. IEEE (2015)
18. Zakharchenko, V., Choi, K.P., Alshina, E., Park, J.H.: Omnidirectional video quality metrics and evaluation process. In: 2017 Data Compression Conference (DCC), p. 472. IEEE (2017)
19. Zakharchenko, V., Choi, K.P., Park, J.H.: Quality metric for spherical panoramic video. In: Optics and Photonics for Information Processing X, vol. 9970, p. 99700C. International Society for Optics and Photonics (2016)
20. Zhang, B., Zhao, J., Yang, S., Zhang, Y., Wang, J., Fei, Z.: Subjective and objective quality assessment of panoramic videos in virtual reality environments. In: 2017 IEEE International Conference on Multimedia & Expo Workshops (ICMEW), pp. 163–168. IEEE (2017)

Tire X-ray Image Defects Detection Based on Adaptive Thresholding Method

Yuxiang Zhang[1], Naijie Gu[1](✉), Xiaoci Zhang[1], and Chuanwen Lin[2]

[1] Department of Computer Science and Technology, University of Science and Technology of China, Jinzhai Road No. 96, Hefei, China
gunj@ustc.edu.cn

[2] Department of Computer Science and Technology, Hefei University, Hefei 230601, China

Abstract. Thin line defect is a common and critical kind of tire defect, which may result in serious accidents. This paper proposes a novel adaptive threshold based model for thin line defects detection in tire X-ray images. First, a new adaptive binarization algorithm using column based threshold selecting is proposed. The proposed algorithm outperforms previous algorithms in hard examples, without introducing extra spots or distortions to the original defect area. Next, a tire X-ray image segmentation algorithm is developed, which can divide the image into sectors with different texture features. Finally, an adaptive criterion algorithm is introduced for thin line defection, which can deal with images from different angles of shooting. The proposed model is evaluated on a tire X-ray data set composed of tire images of various thin line types. Experimental results demonstrate that the proposed model obtains significant improvement in terms of both recall rate and precision rate compared with conventional models.

Keywords: Tire defects · Thin line detection · Adaptive binarization · Image segmentation

1 Introduction

Tires are one of the most commonly used industrial products and their quality are firmly connected with public safety. With the widespread popularization of automobiles and the rapid development of the industry, the quantity of new tire produced in China has been significantly springing up. Many reports indicate that tire defects are the main causes of traffic accidents [1, 2]. Thus, the responsibility of the motor vehicle safety falls on the tire production company to some extent. Therefore, it is essential to ensure the quality of the tire put into the market.

Traditional method to exclude tire with defect is by manual detection, causing high consumption in time and money. Furthermore, the accuracy of manual detection can be unstable due to the fatigue of the inspectors. To deal with the uneconomical and inaccurate method of manual detection, automatic detection technology has been developed for years. The main purpose of automatic detection is to detect the defect of tire accurately and rapidly, taking the advantages of great computing ability of computers.

H. Shen and Y. Sang (Eds.): PAAP 2019, CCIS 1163, pp. 118–129, 2020.
https://doi.org/10.1007/978-981-15-2767-8_11

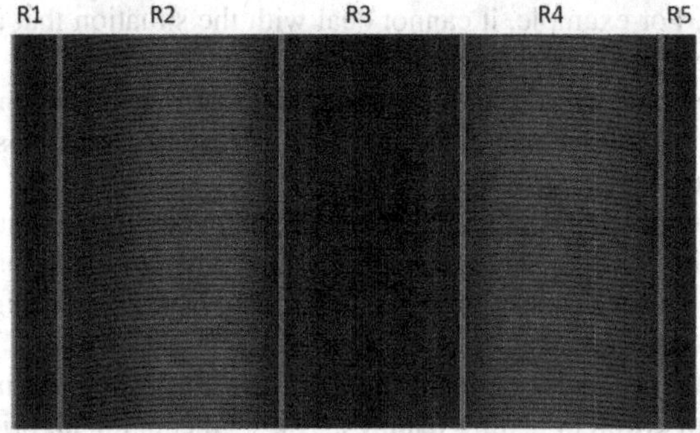

Fig. 1. Five regions of 3 types of a tire X-ray image. (1) R1 and R5 are of tire ring. (2) R2, R4 are of the tire body. (3) R3 are of the tire crown.

Since the detection algorithm is dependent on the appearance region of a defect. Every X-ray image of a tire is divided into 5 regions of 3 types (Fig. 1).

Among the defect types in tires, shoulder bent, thin line and dense line only occur in the tire body, corresponding to R3 in Fig. 1. In contrast, sundries would occur not only in the tire body, but also in the tire crown, corresponding to R2, R3 and R4 of Fig. 1.

Thin line defect is a common defect that may affect the quality of tire seriously. To give a clear concept of the defect, a standard image of thin line defect (Fig. 2a) is provided and it is described in a morphology point of view in a meticulous perspective (Fig. 2b).

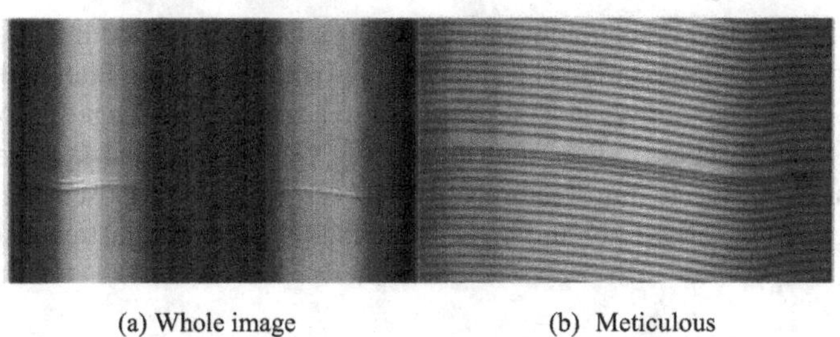

(a) Whole image (b) Meticulous

Fig. 2. (a) An overall view of a tire with thin line defect. (b) A close-up perspective of thin line defect.

Thin line detection can be described as an image feature extraction problem. Many algorithms have been proposed and proved efficient on some dataset so far. Zhang proposed an algorithm by calculating the center of gravity of the cord, and set a threshold to judge whether there is a big gap between two cords [3]. Guo proposed an algorithm, which use the texture feature of images to capture the anomalies [4]. Taking many abnormal pictures into consideration, the performance of existing algorithm rely on the robustness of the binarization algorithm, which is usually an adaptive threshold algorithm using a Gaussian kernel. However, the traditional algorithm cannot deal with some common situations. For example, it cannot deal with the situation that a big gap occur between two adjacent cords, meaning an extreme case of thin line.

In order to overcome the difficulties occurred in former algorithms, we propose a novel tire defect detection model. The major contributions of this paper can be summarized as follows:

(1) This paper proposes a column based adaptive binarization algorithm with strong robustness and fidelity. Unlike the traditional adaptive binarization algorithm, our algorithm would hardly produce dirty spots in the situation that some big gaps existing between adjacent cords.

(2) An edge based image segmentation algorithm is introduced. An image is divided into five sectors with different texture features. The segmentation algorithm is aimed at distinguish the tire crown, which has fixed texture feature. Thus under the assumption that pixels in a same column of an image have a similar grayscale distribution, which is quite normal, a vertical projection on grayscale could separate the image precisely.

(3) By designing an adaptive criterion, a thin line detection algorithm is proposed. In order to make a distinction between thin line and broken line, morphological operations are applied on the images. Based on the binarized image provided by (1) and (2), our algorithm computes a score for each column of the image, and combines them as the feature vector of the image. Then the feature vector is leveraged as the criterion for final threshold judgement.

2 Related Work

2.1 Tire X-ray Image Segmentation

Algorithms of tire defect detection usually contains a key step named image segmentation. Zhu proposed a segmentation algorithm by applying smoothing filter and grayscale correction on the image and then set a threshold to segment the image [5]. Manjunath introduced a texture segmentation algorithm using Gabor filter and k-means clustering [6]. Considering the texture feature of the tire crown, the proposed segmentation algorithm adopts the Gabor filter and make some field-specified adjustments on the tire image.

2.2 Adaptive Threshold Binarization

Many algorithms adopt adaptive threshold binarization to extract the information of key pixels. Otsu proposed an adaptive threshold algorithm by selecting the threshold through maximizing the separability of the resultant classes in gray levels [7]. Wang put forward an algorithm by computing the weighted mean of the neighborhood region to set an adaptive threshold [8]. Michael proposed a Gaussian-weighted moving-window strategy in which threshold is computed at the smallest scale of sufficient reliability [9]. These methods only utilize local information to minimize the calculations and will certainly lose some global information.

2.3 Morphology Open/Close Operations

The concept and mathematical foundation of morphology operations are first mentioned by Serra [10]. The main purpose of morphology open/close operation is to eliminate black or white outliers. In the process of many algorithm, there might be some side effects in the mid product. Moreover, the most common side effects are producing some black or white outliers. Morphology open/close is such an algorithm to eliminate the by-product.

2.4 Image Thinning Algorithm

Many state-of-the-art detection algorithms work better with a thinning algorithm done on the image. Michel proposed a parallel thinning algorithm to extract the skeleton of a grayscale image [11]. Khalid put forward a universal algorithm for image skeletonization [12]. An instance off the shelf is the algorithm mentioned in [3], it would work fairly worse without thinning operation. Similarly, a thinning algorithm after the proposed column based adaptive threshold binarization algorithm will make the following detection much easier.

3 Proposed Algorithms and Implementation Details

In this paper, we propose a novel adaptive threshold based model to enhance the performance of tire defect detection algorithms. First, a new column based adaptive threshold algorithm is proposed that can cope with most situations. Second, an image segmentation algorithm based on grayscale vertical projection is proposed. Third, an adaptive criterion is designed to do final judgment and in order to get a reliable criterion some morphological operations are also included.

3.1 Column Based Adaptive Threshold Binarization Algorithm

Previous algorithms on tire defect detection mainly apply a binarization algorithm on the segmented X-ray picture. However, the traditional adaptive binarization algorithm have their drawbacks whether it uses a kernel with arithmetic average or weighted average.

Due to the shape of the threshold-computing kernel, which is set to be a kernel with odd side length, it is hard to fix the drawback above by increasing the scale of the kernel. Moreover, increasing the scale of the kernel might even lead to a worse outcome i.e. mixing more background and foreground pixels up.

Another typical case is processing an image with exaggerated thin line feature, which means some adjacent cords with big gap occur in the image. The former algorithms are very likely to produce some dirty spots as fore ground which are supposed to be background in ideal case. Figure 3 shows that circumstance intuitively. Likewise, increasing the scale of threshold computing kernel is useless.

To analyze the cause of these unsatisfactory results, there are some formula illustrating the principle of traditional adaptive threshold binarization algorithm. Considering a kernel with a scale of n * n in which n is a positive odd number, its weight is recorded as

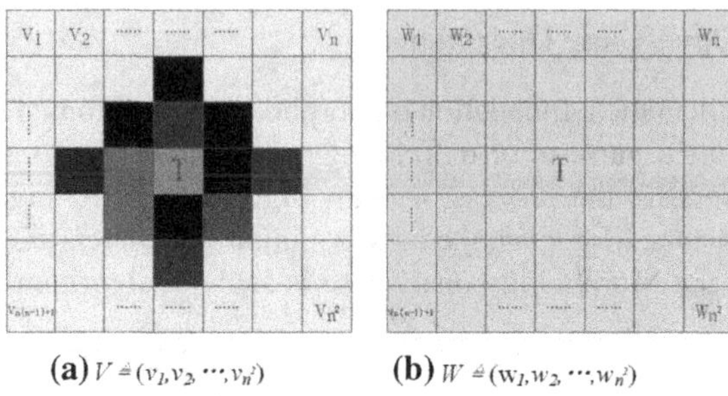

(a) $V \triangleq (v_1, v_2, \cdots, v_{n^2})$ (b) $W \triangleq (w_1, w_2, \cdots, w_{n^2})$

Fig. 3. (a) The target region to be computed. (b) The weighted kernel. Particularly in arithmetic average case, $w_1 = w_2 = \ldots = w_{n*n}$.

vector ***W*** and the corresponding region of image under computing is recorded as vector *V* (Fig. 3). Meanwhile, it is worth noting that the target of an iteration of threshold computing and binarization is always at the center of the given kernel. Based the regulations above, a threshold of a target pixel can be computed as formula (3.1).

$$\text{Threshold}_{Target} = V^T \cdot W \; s.t. \text{w}_t = 0 \tag{3.1}$$

Either theoretically or practically, a weighted kernel is more reasonable than an arithmetic average kernel. An obvious reason is that the capacity of the arithmetic average kernel is a subset of the weighted kernel. More vitally, a target pixel should depend more on those pixel with a small Euclidean distance rather than remote pixel. Therefore, a Gaussian weighted kernel is mostly applied to do binarization jobs. An important property of Gaussian weighted kernel is shown as formula (3.2).

$$W_{neighbor} \propto \frac{1}{||C_T - C_{neighbor}||_2} \tag{3.2}$$

However, viewing the closest pixel as such an important role may bring in some side effects, and that is the cause of the poor performance of previous methods shown Fig. 4. In Fig. 3(a), around the target pixel T there is a dirty region with an area of 13 pixels. The grayscale of the dirty region is uncommonly deeper than other pixel. Nevertheless, the center target pixel would be regarded as a background due to that its neighbor pixels are even deeper than it is. The unideal result in Fig. 4 can be explained in the same way.

To deal with those problems, a column based adaptive threshold binarization algorithm is designed.

In algorithm 1, the ratio of the cords is computed on the dataset in advance. This algorithm takes two advantages of the X-ray tire image. Firstly, the grayscale distribution of a column is regular so that binarization algorithm can restore the shape of the cord finely. Secondly, the proposed algorithm would not be so sensitive to the grayscale vibration in background. Applying the proposed model on the same image that previous model did not work well with, and Fig. 5 shows the improvements.

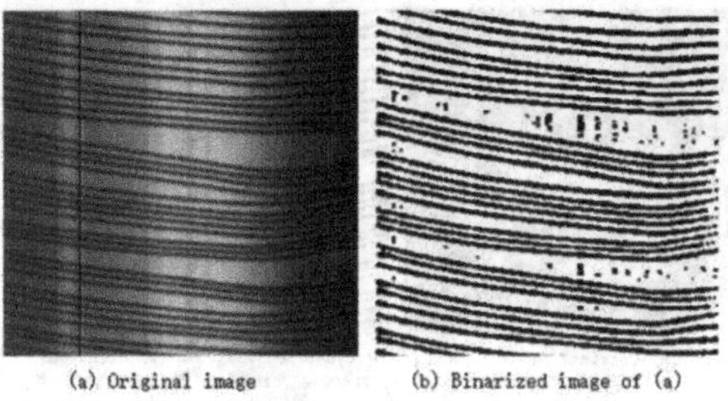

Fig. 4. (a) original thin line image. (b) binarized image of (a) using conventional algorithm.

Algorithm 1 Column Based adaptive threshold binarization algorithm

```
Inputs: grayscale image: img, ratio of cords: rt
output: corresponding binarized image of img
for i = 0, 1, ... , img.width do
    base ← minimum grayscale of image.column i
    for j = 0, 2, 4,..., 256 do
      thro ← base + j
      for k = 0, 1, ... , img.height do
        if img(j, i) <= thro do
          result(j, i) ← 0
          count ← count + 1
        else do
          result(j, i) ← 255
      if count / img.height > rt do
        break
return result
```

As is shown in Fig. 5, the dirty spots are removed. Though some morphology operations could be helpful to solve dirty spots phenomenon in Fig. 4(b), they are very likely to distort the shape of the cord if the kernel is not controlled perfectly. So algorithm is much robust in many ways and it lay a solid foundation for the afterwards detection.

3.2 Texture Feature Based Segmentation Algorithm

Method proposed in [6] is of general use and accurate though, it did not take the advantages of the distribution feature of tire X-ray image. Reference to Appendix I, after the filter of Gabor kernel with horizontal orientation, the tire body tends to get extremely shinning. And the grayscale distribution on each column is such distinguished that people

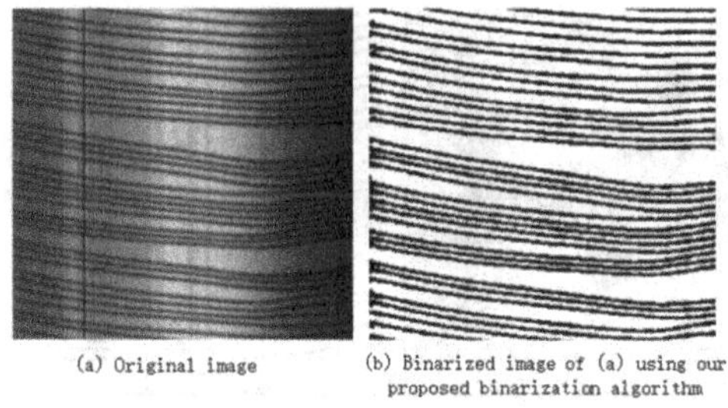
(a) Original image
(b) Binarized image of (a) using our proposed binarization algorithm

Fig. 5. (a) original thin line image. (b) binarized image of (a) using the proposed algorithm.

can do the segmentation with a glance. In order to make it understandable for machine, the proposed segmentation algorithm applies a vertical projection on the filtered image, so that the edge of each sector can be easily found with numerical judgment. After the projection, segmentation algorithm would select the edge of the sectors by slope comparison.

Algorithm 2 Slope comparison segmentation algorithm based on Gabor filter

```
Inputs: grayscale image: img, Gabor kernel: g_kernel,
output: edges of tire body and tire crown: edges
img ← do Gaussian smoothing on img
img ← do Gabor filter on img
mean ← average grayscale of img
for i = 0, 1, ..., img.width do
    count ← #(pixel p with p > mean)
    append count to projection
dx ← derivative of projection[x]
limit ← x with dx[x] in the largest four of dx
return limit
```

3.3 A Thin Line Detection Algorithm

In thin line detection, the proposed algorithm is based on spacing statistics. Get straight to the point of thin line defect and an intuitively way to characterize the feature of thin line is to do statistics on the vertical distance of adjacent cords. With a binarized image of tire body to be detected, a series of vertical line are drew through the cords, then the distances between each pairs of adjacent cords is counted. Finally, a score computed by the distances got last step is defined for each line to judge whether a thin line defect occurs in current column. A schematic diagram can be seen in Fig. 6. Equation (3.3), show the principle of the algorithm.

Having the scores of these columns, a threshold is set to judge whether a thin line defect occurs in a certain column. Since the standard of the defect may be changing between different types of tires, so this threshold could be adaptive to company requirements. In addition, designing the equation as a proportional form is adaptive to different types of tires to some extent.

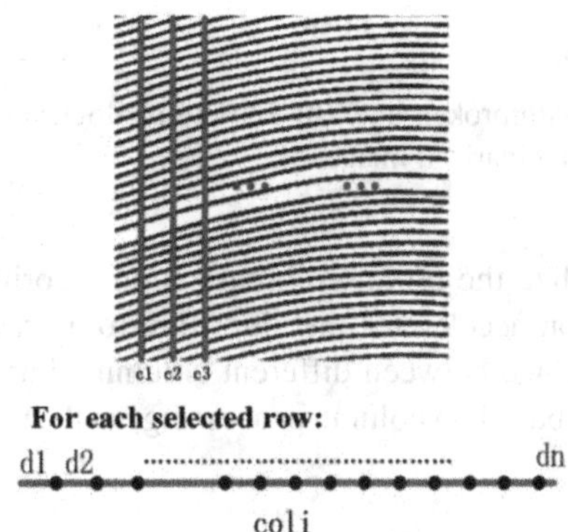

Fig. 6. Schematic diagram of thin line feature.

$$score = \frac{\max(d1,\ d2, \ldots,\ dn)}{median(d1,\ d2, \ldots,\ dn)} \tag{3.3}$$

Finally, a tire is judged to have thin line if any column of it is judged to be bad. Taking the advantages of the proposed adaptive threshold binarization algorithm and texture feature based segmentation algorithm, the proposed thin line detection algorithm would not miss the defect in edge of the cord and would not be unstable when processing some images with dark background.

3.4 Implementation Details

After the step of binarization, an optional step is image thinning. Since the thickness of cord may bias the compute of d_i in (3,3), an image thinning procedure may bring some enhancement. So a detection algorithm adding an image thinning step after the binarization step is also added as a comparison experiments.

Another defect should be considered is broken line for the reason that it may effect the result of thin line detection. More specifically, broken line defect has similar local feature with thin line, and it could be a cause of judging a broken line image as a thin line image. To deal with this confusion, a morphological open operation is applied on a binarized image with a rectangle kernel shaped as 1 × n. And experiment shows it helps to decrease the false positive rate. The applied kernel and an example are illustrated as Fig. 7.

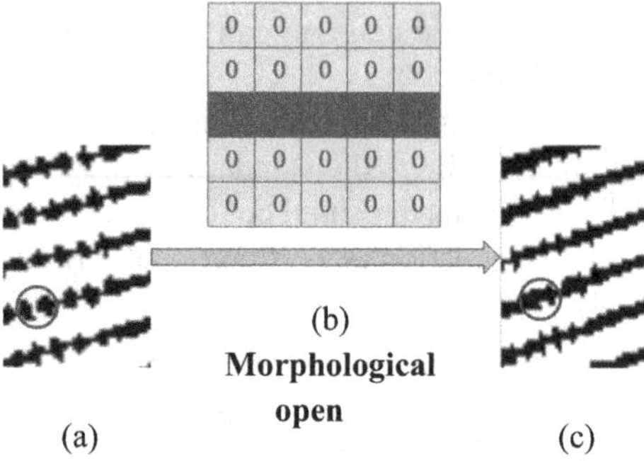

Fig. 7. (a) Binarized image with broken line. (b) The morphological open kernel. (c) Result of morphology open operation on binarized image.

In practice, we parallelize the proposed binarization algorithm to further improve its efficiency. Parallelization accelerates the algorithm to a great extent since there is no data conflict or dependence between different columns. Furthermore, algorithm of image segmentation is also based on column processing, so the parallelization can easily done.

4 Experiments

In this section, experimental results on a large scale self-made dataset are presented. The proposed algorithms with or without image thinning is compared to previous algorithms, then analysis on different pairs of comparisons is given.

4.1 Data

MTXD (Multi-category tire X-ray image data set) is a tire X-ray image data set. It is a data set labeled by us on a series of tire X-ray images provided by a tire production company. Each defect category contains different situations that may occur in actual production. For instance, the thin line category is consisted of images with different shapes of gaps in different positions. Other categories are similar.

4.2 Experimental Details

Four detection models are here included in the comparative experiment. First, a model proposed by Zhu taking absolute distance between two cords as the criterion, which uses a weighted average adaptive threshold binarization algorithm [13]. Next a model introduced by Zhang changing the criterion to weighted vertical distance between two cords [3]. Then a dictionary-based model proposed by Xiang [14] is also selected as a comparison. Finally a morphological-based method put forward by Mak [15] is taken into consideration.

4.3 Test Results and Analysis

The test results on MTXD dataset can be seen in Tables 1 and 2. For each model, a threshold that attain a recall around 90% is chosen, since the duty of the detection algorithm is to avoid failed tires being put into the market. Some results that applying conventional binarization algorithms is shown in Fig. 8.

The proposed model reach the highest precision with a recall over 90%. There are four differences in the proposed model contributing to get a better result. First, targeted binarization algorithm (Algorithm 1) prevents the image from being contaminated. Second, a meticulous image segmentation algorithm (Algorithm 2) divides tire image into parts with different texture precisely. Then, based on former work, an adaptive criterion is computed for different kinds of tire images. Last but not the least, some morphology operations such as open operation and image thinning helps to combine the sub-algorithms smoothly.

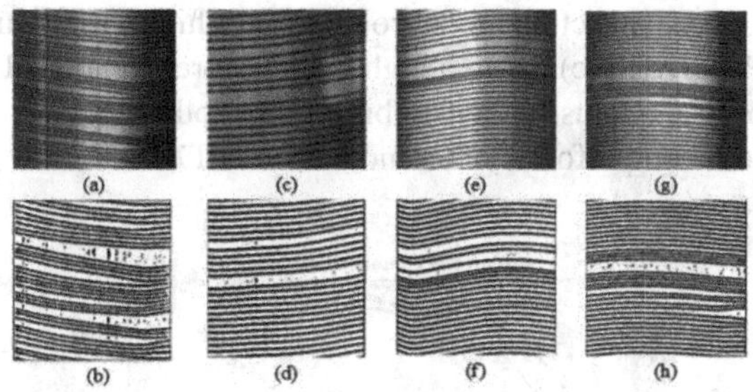

Fig. 8. Some result that applying conventional binarization algorithms may lead to. Image above is the original image and below is a binarized.

To inspect the effects of each step of the proposed model, Table 2 provides an explicit view. Test set contains 200 images with half positive and half negative. Conclusions can be drawn as follows. (1) The column based adaptive threshold binarization algorithm helps to increase the recall. (2) The proposed segmentation algorithm also contributes to increasing the recall, though a little side effect follows as decreasing the precision. (3) Image thinning can increase the precision but may decrease the recall.

Table 1. The test results of several compared models on MTXD dataset

Model	TP	TN	FP	FN	Precision	Recall	Number of samples
Khalid et al. [13]	91	21	79	9	50.55%	91%	200
Zhang et al. [3]	91	76	24	9	79.13%	91%	200
Xiang et al. [14]	93	71	29	7	76.22%	93%	200
Mak et al. [15]	92	88	12	8	88.46%	92%	200
Proposed final	96	91	9	4	**91.42%**	**96%**	200

Table 2. Result of ablation study, in which proposed_1 uses weighted binarization, proposed_2 uses direct threshold segmentation and proposed_3 includes an image thinning step. (Proposed model adopts the proposed binarization algorithms and segmentation algorithm if not specified.)

Model	TP	TN	FP	FN	Precision	Recall	Number of samples
Proposed_1	90	92	8	10	91.83%	90%	200
Proposed_2	88	93	7	12	**92.63%**	88%	200
Proposed_3	95	92	8	5	92.23%	95%	200
Proposed final	96	91	9	4	91.42%	**96%**	200

In the experiment, a receiver operating characteristic (ROC) curve is plotted to do a specific view of how the proposed model exceed previous models. The results are illustrated in Fig. 9. The ROCs of threshold-based models are drew in Fig. 9. It can be observed that the proposed detection model could reach a high TPR (True Positive Rate) before FPR (False Positive Rate) get to a high value. Moreover, the AUC (Area Under Curve) of the proposed model is obviously bigger than other models, which indicates that the proposed model outperforms other models on MTXD.

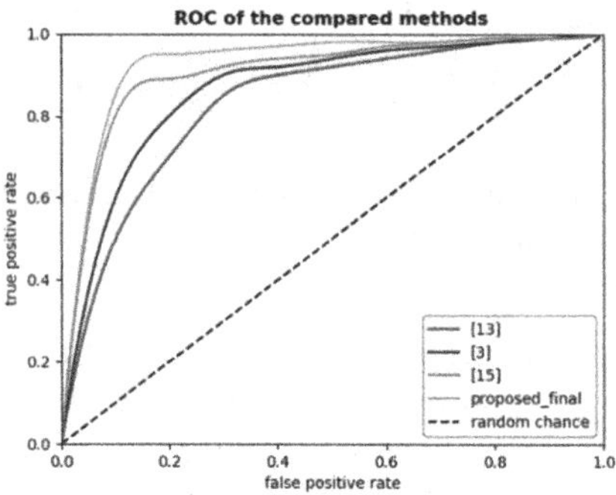

Fig. 9. ROC of compared methods

5 Conclusion

Compared with current method on tire defect detection tasks, this paper proposed a model on thin line detection based on adaptive thresholding. The model mainly has three innovations in different steps of the detection procedure. First, a column based adaptive threshold binarization algorithm is designed, which sets an adaptive threshold to distinguish the cords and background in a certain column. Next, an edge based image segmentation algorithm based on edge detection and vertical projection is developed. Unlike conventional edge detection algorithm, the proposed algorithm is designed for searching the ends of a fixed texture. Finally, the feature of thin line is extracted using the result of former step and an adaptive criterion is designed to do the final judgement.

In order to handle a case of blending thin line with blend line, a morphological open operation is adopted. In addition, for the purpose of eliminating the effects of cord thickness, an optional image-thinning step is optional to be added after the morphological open step. Experimental result shows that our model have advantages over existing methods.

References

1. Technical Research Centre of Finland (VTT) Intelligent tyre systems – state of the art and potential technologies; Deliverable D7 (2001)
2. Koornstra, M.K.: Transport safety performance in the EU [EB/OL]. European Transport Safety Council, Brussels, 20 November 2012
3. Zhang, Y., Lefebvre, D., Li, Q.: Automatic detection of defects in tire radiographic images. IEEE Trans. Autom. Sci. Eng. **14**(3), 1378–1386 (2017)
4. Guo, Q., Zhang, C., Liu, H., et al.: Defect detection in tire X-ray images using weighted texture dissimilarity. J. Sens. **1**, 1–12 (2016)
5. Yue, Z., Wenyao, L., Hua, Y., et al.: A defect extraction and segmentation method for radial tire X-ray image. J. Optoelectron. **21**(05), 758–761 (2010)
6. Aradhya, V.N.M.: A comprehensive of transforms, Gabor filter and k-means clustering for text detection in images and video. Appl. Comput. Informatics **12**(2), 109–116 (2016)
7. Ostu, N.: A threshold selection method from gray-level histograms. IEEE Trans. Syst. Man Cybern. **9**(1), 62–66 (1979)
8. Wang, J., Hong, J.: A new self-adaptive weighted filter for removing noise in infrared images. In: International Conference on Information Engineering and Computer Science (2009)
9. Michael, H.F.W.: Gaussian-weighted moving-window robust automatic threshold selection. In: International Conference on Computer Analysis of Images and Patterns (2003)
10. Serra, J.: Image Analysis and Mathematical Morphology. Academic Press, Inc., Orlando (1983)
11. Couprie, M., Bezerra, N., Bertrand, G.: A parallel thinning algorithm for grayscale images. In: Gonzalez-Diaz, R., Jimenez, M.-J., Medrano, B. (eds.) DGCI 2013. LNCS, vol. 7749, pp. 71–82. Springer, Heidelberg (2013). https://doi.org/10.1007/978-3-642-37067-0_7
12. Saeed, K., Tab, M., Rybnik, M., Adamski, M.: K3M: a universal algorithm for image skeletonization and a review of thinning techniques. Int. J. Appl. Math. Comput. Sci. **20**(2), 317–335 (2010)
13. Yue, Z.: Study on X-ray image inspection technology of engineering radial tire. Tianjin University, Tianjin (2009)
14. Xiang, Y., Zhang, C., Guo, Q.: A dictionary-based method for tire defect detection. In: Proceeding of the IEEE International Conference on Information and Automation, Hailar, China, July 2014
15. Mak, K.L., Peng, P., Yiu, K.F.C.: Fabric defect detection using morphological filters. Image Vis. Comput. **27**, 1585–1592 (2009)

Halftone Image Reconstruction Based on SLIC Superpixel Algorithm

Xinhong Zhang[1], Boyan Zhang[2], and Fan Zhang[2(✉)]

[1] School of Software, Henan University, Kaifeng 475001, China
[2] School of Computer and Information Engineering, Henan University, Kaifeng 475001, China
zhangfan@henu.edu.cn

Abstract. This paper proposes a halftone image reconstruction based on the SLIC (Simple Linear Iterative Clustering) superpixel algorithm and the affinity propagation algorithm. Firstly, the halftone image is segmented based on SLIC superpixel algorithm. Secondly, the affinity propagation algorithm is used to clustering the regions segmented by superpixel Algorithm. After deleting the background, the image is vectorized. The smooth background image is obtained by the linear smoothing filter and nonlinear smoothing filters. Finally, the vectored boundary and smooth background are combined together to get the reconstructed image. The boundary information is effectively retained during the reconstruction. The proposed method can effectively remove the halftone patterns and screen patterns.

Keywords: Image reconstruction · Halftone · SLIC superpixel · Affinity propagation

1 Introduction

With the development of computer technology and network technology, a large number of printing documents are converted to electronic documents on the internet. In the printing industry, halftone dot printing technology is widely used. Halftone technology is to control dot size (amplitude modulation screening) or ink dot density (FM screening) to represent the gray-scale or color of image [1, 2]. By the use of dots, varying either in size or in density, halftone technology simulates continuous tone image to display the grayscale or color of image [3, 4]. That is to say, Halftone images represent continuous changes with dot size or density dots.

When a halftone image is scanned into an electronic document, scanner will produce halftone mesh (halftone pattern) or screen pattern, which will affect quality of scanned images, so the inverse halftoning algorithm is necessary for the post scanning processing. This is a kind of the image reconstruction algorithm [5]. Halftoning methods may be classified into two main groups [6]: amplitude modulation (AM) methods that respond to changes in tone by changing the size of the dots, and frequency modulation (FM) methods that locally adjust the density of the dots. The inverse halftoning algorithm can be divided into three categories: spatial domain method, frequency domain method,

H. Shen and Y. Sang (Eds.): PAAP 2019, CCIS 1163, pp. 130–139, 2020.
https://doi.org/10.1007/978-981-15-2767-8_12

frequency domain and spatial domain hybrid method [7–9]. Common used image reconstruction algorithms for inverse halftoning include local average algorithm, time domain Gauss filter algorithm, B-spline function algorithm and so on. The scanning software of the scanner also has functions for removing the screen pattern. However, some algorithms can cause blurred image after removing the halftone pattern or screen pattern, and some edges and details of the image are lost, and it is difficult to achieve the ideal descreening effect [10, 11]. Simple low pass filtering can remove most of the noise due to halftoning, however, descreening requires more than just using a low pass filter to smooth the image. A low pass filter can remove halftone patterns or screen patterns but also causes blurring in the image [12, 13].

Generally, an image reconstruction algorithm for inverse halftoning only appropriates to a specific kind of screen pattern. There are several techniques to generate the patterns that create the illusion of a continuous-tone image. The corresponding image reconstruction algorithms use the appropriate pattern to optimize image reconstruction. In this paper, an image reconstruction algorithm for inverse halftoning based on the SLIC superpixel algorithm and the affinity propagation algorithm is proposed.

2 Inverse Halftonging Algorithm

The inverse halftoning algorithm of scanned document remove the halftone patterns or the screen patterns. Halftoning H is a process of introducing noises or screen patterns, therefore the descreening or the inverse halftoning H^{-1} is a process of removing noises. If the input continuous tone image is x, the output halftone image is b, the ordered dither matrix or the error diffusion kernel is θ, then the halftone system model can be expressed as

$$b = H(x, \theta), \tag{1}$$

where, $b = \{b_{i,j} | b_{i,j} \in [0, 1], 1 \le i \le M, 1 \le j \le N\}$; The size of image is $M \times N$.

Assuming that the halftone image b is processed by an inverse halftoning system H^{-1}, and get the continuous tone image $\hat{x}$. The inverse halftone system H^{-1} has two different solution methods.

For the first solution method, the requirement is that b and $\hat{x}$ are similar when observing two images at a certain distance, that is, seeking a map H_1^{-1} to satisfy the

$$\hat{x} = [H_1^{-1}(b)] \cap [\hat{x} \approx b]. \tag{2}$$

For the second solution method, the requirement is that if $\hat{x}$ is re-processed by halftoning, the result halftone image is still b, that is, seeking a map H_1^{-1} to satisfy the

$$\hat{x} = [H_2^{-1}(b)] \cap [H(\hat{x}, \theta) = b]. \tag{3}$$

Driven by the application requirements of inverse halftoning, some achievements have been made in the study of inverse halftoning. The methods of inverse halftoning can be mainly divided into three categories: the filter method, the machine learning method and the optimal estimation method. Among of them, the filter method and the machine learning method are usually based on Eq. 2, and the optimal estimation method is usually based on Eq. 3.

Halftone process belongs to the many-to-one mapping method. Therefore, the solution of inverse halftoning is not unique, which is an uncertain problem. In addition, the noise introduced by halftone processing is mainly distributed in the middle and high frequency components of the result image, which is confused with the details and edges of the image, and these noise increase the difficulty of solving the inverse halftoning problem. If we want to improve the quality of inverse halftone image, we must have enough prior halftoning knowledge, and make full use of these knowledge to eliminate the noise in halftoning process and minimize the loss of image detail information.

Some inverse halftoning algorithms have been proposed. For example, the low-pass filter algorithm [14], the fast algorithm [15], the wavelet based algorithm [16], the maximum posteriori probability algorithm [17], the LUT algorithm [18], and the deconvolution based inverse halftoning algorithm [19].

This paper proposes an image reconstruction algorithm for inverse halftoning to remove the halftone pattern or the screen pattern. The scanned image is segmented based on SLIC superpixel algorithm, and the affinity propagation algorithm is used to extract the boundaries of image. The boundary regions of the image are vectored. The smooth background image is obtained by the linear smoothing filter and nonlinear smoothing filters. Finally, the vectored boundary and smooth background are combined together to get the reconstructed image.

3 Image Segmentation Based on SLIC

Superpixels algorithms group pixels into perceptually meaningful atomic regions which can be used to replace the rigid structure of the pixel grid. Superpixels algorithms can capture image redundancy, provide a convenient form to compute image features, and greatly reduce the complexity of subsequent image processing tasks [20–22]. Superpixels segmentation algorithm can be roughly divided into two categories: the graph based algorithms and the gradient based algorithms. In the graph based algorithms, the segmentation problem is transformed to the minimization problem of energy function. The graph was divided into superpixels using a variety of segmentation criterions. The basic idea of the gradient based algorithms is clustering of pixels. Starting from a rough initial clustering of pixels, gradient based algorithms iteratively modify the clustering results until the convergence condition is satisfied.

Superpixels algorithms can reduce the complexity of the images from thousands of pixels to only a few hundred superpixels. Each of these superpixels will then contain some sort of perceptual. Pixels that belong to a superpixel group share some sort of commonality, such as similar color or texture distribution. Most superpixel algorithms over-segment the image. This means that most of important boundaries in the image are found.

SLIC (Simple Linear Iterative Clustering) algorithm is a kind of superpixel segmentation method based on clustering [23–27]. For color images, the clustering procedure of SLIC algorithm uses five-dimensional feature vectors in CIELAB color space and position coordinate space, thereby can effectively improves the performance of segmentation. Despite its simplicity, SLIC algorithm adheres to boundaries as well as other segmentation algorithms, and it is faster and more memory efficient. Figure 1 is an example of image segmentation based on SLIC.

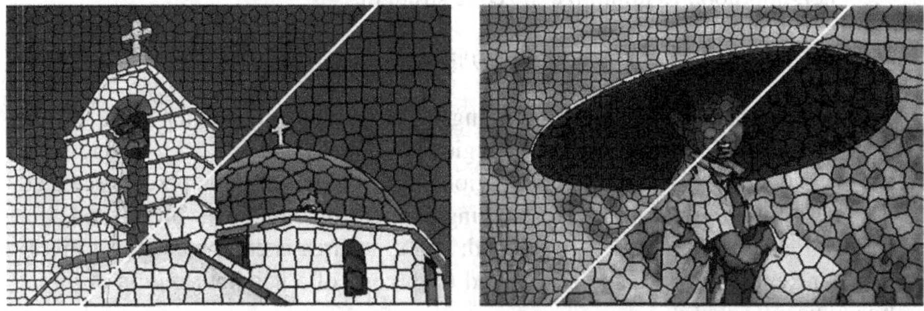

Fig. 1. Segmented image based on SLIC superpixels algorithm.

The specific implementation process of SLIC algorithm is as follows:

(1) Assuming that there are M pixels, and there are K initial clustering centers (superpixels). The size of each superpixel is M/K, then the distance between of each superpixel center is approximately. In order to avoid the superpixels centering in the position of image boundaries, the clustering centers are moved to the location that corresponding to the lowest gradient in a 3×3 neighborhood.

(2) For each pixel, the similarity measure is the distance between the pixel and the nearest clustering centers. The similarity measure is as follows:

$$D_{lab} = \sqrt{(l_k - l_i)^2 + (a_k - a_i)^2 + (b_k - b_i)^2}, \tag{4}$$

$$D_{xy} = \sqrt{(x_k - x_i)^2 + (y_k - y_i)^2}, \tag{5}$$

$$D = \sqrt{\left(\frac{D_{lab}}{m}\right)^2 + \left(\frac{D_{xy}}{\sqrt{M/K}}\right)^2}, \tag{6}$$

where D_{lab} is color difference between pixels; D_{xy} is the Euclidean distance between pixels; D is the similarity of two pixels; m is the balance parameter, which is used to control the proportion of color difference and spatial distance in the measure of similarity, the range of m is [1, 20], usually 10. The value of D is proportional to the degree of acquaintance, and the larger the value, the higher the similarity of the two pixels.

(3) According to the similarity formula, each pixel is assigned a label of the nearest cluster center.

(4) Compute new cluster centers and compute the residual error.

(5) Repeat step 3 and step 4 until the residual error is sufficient small, then the superpixels segmentation is done.

SLIC starts by dividing the image domain into a regular grid with $M \times N$ tiles. A region (superpixel or k-means cluster) is initialized from each grid center. In order to avoid placing these centers on top of image discontinuities, the centers are then moved in a 3×3 neighborhood to minimize the edge strength,

$$\text{edge}(x, y) = \|I(x+1, y) - I(x-1, y)\|_2^2 + \|I(x, y+1) - I(x, y-1)\|_2^2. \quad (7)$$

Then the regions are obtained by running k-means clustering. After k-means has converged, SLIC eliminates any connected region whose area is less than minRegionSize pixels. This is done by greedily merging regions to neighbor ones: the pixel is scanned in lexicographical order and the corresponding connected components are visited. If a region has already been visited, it is skipped; if not, its area is computed and if this is less than minRegionSize its label is changed to the one of a neighbor region at p that has already been visited.

4 Affinity Propagation Algorithm

The purpose of this paper is to remove halftone patterns or screen patterns, and preserve boundaries information at the same time. Therefore, boundaries information should be extracted from screened image firstly.

Superpixels are an over-segmentation of an image. Many state-of-the-art superpixel segmentation algorithms rely on minimizing special energy functions or clustering pixels in the effective distance space to track the boundaries of image. Clustering is a method of grouping similar types of data.

Affinity propagation (AP) algorithm was published by Frey and Dueck in 2007 [28]. Affinity propagation is a clustering algorithm based on the concept of message passing between data points. Unlike clustering algorithms such as k-means or k-means, affinity propagation does not require the number of clusters to be determined or estimated before running the algorithm. Similar to k-means, affinity propagation finds exemplars, members of the input set that are representative of clusters.

Let x_1 to x_n be a set of data points, and let s be a function that quantifies the similarity between any two points. For this example, the negative squared distance of two data points was used i.e. for points x_i and x_k,

$$s(i, k) = -\|x_i - x_k\|^2. \quad (8)$$

Affinity propagation algorithm proceeds by alternating two message passing steps, to update two matrices [29]:

The responsibility matrix R has values $r(i, k)$ that quantify how well-suited x_k is to serve as the exemplar for x_i, relative to other candidate exemplars for x_i.

The availability matrix A contains values $a(i, k)$ that represent how appropriate it would be for x_i to pick x_k as its exemplar, taking into account other points' preference for x_k as an exemplar.

Both matrices are initialized to all zeroes, and can be viewed as log-probability tables. The algorithm then performs the following updates iteratively:

Firstly, responsibility updates are sent around:

$$r(i,k) \leftarrow s(i,k) - \max_{k' \neq k}\{a(i,k') + s(i,k')\}. \tag{9}$$

Then, availability is updated by,

$$a(i,k) \leftarrow \min\left(0, r(k,k) + \sum_{i' \notin \{i,k\}} \max(0, r(i',k))\right) \; for \; i \neq k$$

and

$$a(k,k) \leftarrow \sum_{i' \neq k} \max(0, r(i',k)). \tag{10}$$

The iterations are performed until either the cluster boundaries remain unchanged over a number of iterations, or after some predetermined number of iterations.

The inventors of affinity propagation showed it is better for certain computer vision and computational biology tasks [30, 31], e.g. clustering of pictures of human faces and identifying regulated transcripts, than k-means, even when *k*-means was allowed many random restarts and initialized using PCA.

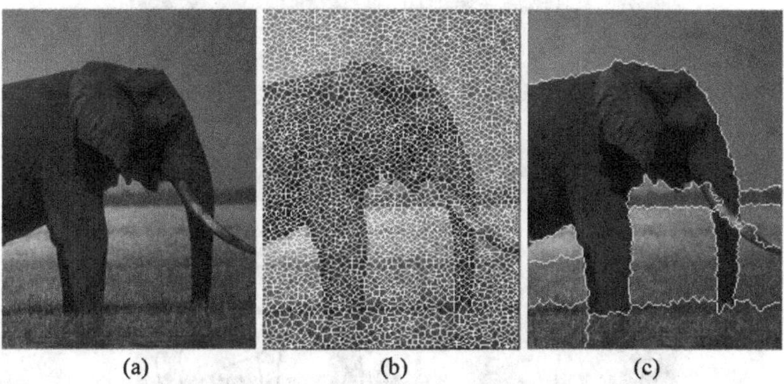

Fig. 2. (a) Original image. (b) SLIC superpixels' algorithm. (c) The result of affinity propagation clustering.

Figure 2 shows the boundaries extracted by the SLIC superpixels' algorithm and the affinity propagation clustering algorithm. The Euclidean distance $r(i, k)$ of any two superpixels is calculated by Eq. 8, and the similarity matrix is obtained as the input of AP algorithm. According to Eqs. 9 and 10, the responsibility and availability of each segmentation region after superpixel segmentation are calculated. The clustering center is determined according to:

$$k = \arg\max\{a(i,k) + r(i,k)\}. \tag{11}$$

After clustering based on AP algorithm, the clustering center divides the image into several main regions. According to the results of image segmentation, the foreground and background regions of the image are determined. Linear or non-linear smoothing filters are used to remove halftone meshes in the background area. For the foreground region, this paper uses the vectorization method to process.

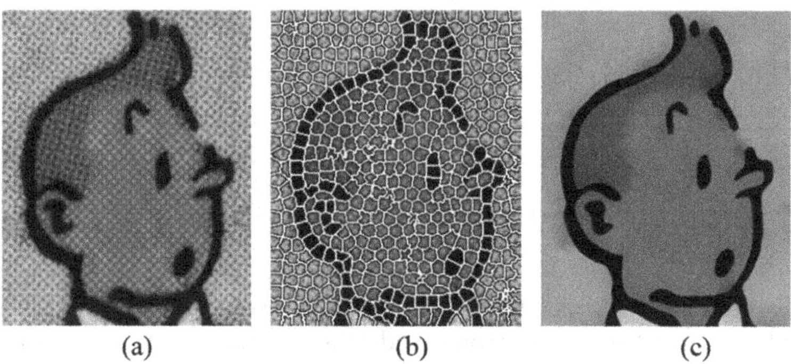

Fig. 3. The experimental results. (a) Original image. (b) Vectorization. (C) Reconstructed image.

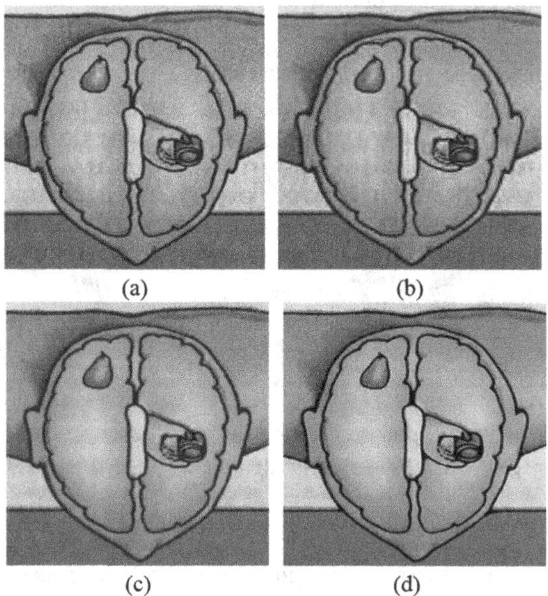

Fig. 4. The comparison of experimental results. (a) Original image. (b) Wavelet based image reconstruction. (c) Image reconstruction by scanner software processing. (d) Processing by our algorithm.

5 Image Reconstruction

When the boundaries have been extracted, the remaining part of screened image is smoothed to be a continuous tone image. In this paper, we select a linear smoothing filter and a nonlinear smoothing filter to get the smooth background. The linear filter is a 9×9 Gaussian low-pass filter, $\sigma^2 = 1.4$. The nonlinear filter is a 3×3 median filter. Both of them are used to eliminate screen patterns.

Vector graphics have been typically used for encoding abstract visual forms such as fonts, charts, maps and cartoon arts. There has been a recent trend to enhance the representation power of vector graphics so that they can more faithfully represent full-color raster images. A primary goal is to design powerful vector primitives that can accurately approximate raster images with as few vector primitives as possible. Since curvilinear features are important visual cues delineating silhouettes and occluding contours, they help users better interpret images.

The vectorization algorithms can be divided into two categories: the structural vectorization of raster images, and the polygon-based tracing. In this paper, we using the structural vectorization algorithm.

The image is reconstructed by combining the smooth background and the vector representation of image boundaries. Halftone patterns or screen patterns are removed from the reconstructed image while boundaries of image are retained at the same time.

Figure 3 is the experimental result of proposed method. Figure 4 is the experimental comparison of proposed method with other methods. The experimental results of our algorithm are compared with mean filtering processing, Gaussian filtering processing, Wavelet based inverse halftoning processing and inverse halftoning by scanner software processing respectively. Experimental results show that the proposed method can effectively removes the halftone patterns or screen patterns while retains boundaries information perfectly.

6 Conclusions

This paper proposes a halftone image reconstruction based on the SLIC superpixel algorithm and the affinity propagation algorithm. The reconstructed image combines the smooth background and the vector representation of image boundaries. Screen patterns are removed while boundaries of image are retained. Experimental results show that the proposed image reconstruction has good performance.

Acknowledgement. This research was supported by the Natural Science Foundation of China (No. U1504621) and the Natural Science Foundation of Henan Province (No. 162300410032).

References

1. Liu, Y.F., Guo, J.M.: Dot-diffused halftoning with improved homogeneity. IEEE Trans. Image Process. **24**(11), 4581–4591 (2015)
2. He, Z., Bouman, C.A.: AM/FM halftoning: digital halftoning through simultaneous modulation of dot size and dot density. J. Electron. Imaging **13**(2), 286–302 (2004)
3. Liao, J.R.: Theoretical bounds of direct binary search halftoning. IEEE Trans. Image Process. **24**(11), 3478–3487 (2015)
4. Son, C.H., Choo, H.: Local learned dictionaries optimized to edge orientation for inverse halftoning. IEEE Trans. Image Process. **23**(6), 2542–2556 (2014)

5. Kopf, J., Lischinski, D.: Digital reconstruction of halftoned color comics. ACM Trans. Graph. (TOG) **31**(6), 140–149 (2012)
6. Kipphan, H.: Handbook of Print Media: Technologies and Production Methods. Springer, New York (2001). https://doi.org/10.1007/978-3-540-29900-4
7. Guo, J.M., Prasetyo, H.: Content-based image retrieval using features extracted from halftoning-based block truncation coding. IEEE Trans. Image Process. **24**(3), 1010–1024 (2015)
8. Kopf, J., Lischinski, D.: Digital reconstruction of halftoned color comics. ACM Trans. Graph. **31**(6), 439–445 (2012)
9. Fung, Y.H., Chan, Y.H.: Blue noise digital color halftoning with multiscale error diffusion. J. Electr. Imaging **23**(6), 063013 (2014)
10. Zhou, Y., Jiang, Z., Zheng, L.: Image analysis based on noise power spectrum. Packag. Eng. **2014**(21), 91–95 (2014)
11. Qu, X., Zhang, F., Liu, B., et al.: Survey on image inverse halftoning and its quality evaluation. Comput. Sci. **43**(6A), 110–114 (2016)
12. Brauchart, J.S., Grabner, P.J.: Distributing many points on spheres: minimal energy and designs. J. Complex. **31**(3), 293–326 (2015)
13. Son, C.H., Choo, H.: Color recovery of black-and-white halftoned images via categorized color-embedding look-up tables. Digit. Signal Proc. **28**(1), 93–105 (2014)
14. Sun, B., Li, S., Sun, J.: Scanned image descreening with image redundancy and adaptive filtering. IEEE Trans. Image Process. **23**(8), 3698–3710 (2014)
15. Tang, L., Ni, J., Wang, C., Zhang, R.: A modified kernels-alternated error diffusion watermarking algorithm for halftone images. In: Shi, Y.Q., Kim, H.-J., Katzenbeisser, S. (eds.) IWDW 2007. LNCS, vol. 5041, pp. 382–394. Springer, Heidelberg (2008). https://doi.org/10.1007/978-3-540-92238-4_30
16. You, X., Du, L., Cheung, Y., et al.: A blind watermarking scheme using new nontensor product wavelet filter banks. IEEE Trans. Image Process. **19**(12), 3271–3284 (2010)
17. Stevenson, R.L.: Inverse halftoning via MAP estimation. IEEE Trans. Image Process. **6**(4), 574–583 (1997)
18. Mese, M., Vaidyanathan, P.P.: Look-up table (LUT) method for inverse halftoning. IEEE Trans. Image Process. **10**(10), 1566–1578 (2001)
19. Katkovnik, V., Foi, A., Egiazarian, K., et al.: Directional varying scale approximations for anisotropic signal processing. In: 2004 12th European Signal Processing Conference, pp. 101–104. IEEE (2004)
20. Wei, X., Yang, Q., Gong, Y., Ahuja, N., Yang, M.H.: Superpixel hierarchy. IEEE Trans. Image Process. **27**(10), 4838–4848 (2018)
21. Ban, Z., Liu, J., Cao, L.: Superpixel segmentation using Gaussian mixture model. IEEE Trans. Image Process. **27**(8), 4105–4117 (2018)
22. Akyilmaz, E., Leloglu, U.M.: Segmentation of SAR images using similarity ratios for generating and clustering superpixels. Electron. Lett. **52**(8), 654–656 (2016)
23. Achanta, R., Shaji, A., Smith, K., et al.: SLIC superpixels compared to state-of-the-art superpixel methods. IEEE Trans. Pattern Anal. Mach. Intell. **34**(11), 2274–2282 (2012)
24. Chu, J., Min, H., Liu, L., et al.: A novel computer aided breast mass detection scheme based on morphological enhancement and SLIC superpixel segmentation. Med. Phys. **42**(7), 3859–3869 (2015)
25. Jia, S., Wu, K., Zhu, J., et al.: Spectral-spatial Gabor surface feature fusion approach for hyperspectral imagery classification. IEEE Trans. Geosci. Remote Sens. **99**, 1–13 (2018)
26. Yang, H., Huang, C., Wang, F., et al.: Robust semantic template matching using a superpixel region binary descriptor. IEEE Trans. Image Process. **28**, 3061–3074 (2019)
27. Pun, C.M., Chung, J.L.: A two-stage localization for copy-move forgery detection. Inf. Sci. **463**, 33–55 (2018)

28. Frey, B.J., Dueck, D.: Clustering by passing messages between data points. Science **315**(5814), 972–976 (2007)
29. Wikipedia: Affinity propagation (2019). https://en.wikipedia.org/wiki/Affinity_propagation
30. Liu, R., Wang, H., Yu, X.: Shared-nearest-neighbor-based clustering by fast search and find of density peaks. Inf. Sci. **450**, 200–226 (2018)
31. Xu, Z., Gao, M., Papadakis, G.Z., et al.: Joint solution for PET image segmentation, denoising, and partial volume correction. Med. Image Anal. **46**, 229–243 (2018)

Study on the Method of Extracting Diabetes History from Unstructured Chinese Electronic Medical Record

Chengzhi Niu[1](✉) and Xiaofan Zhao[2]

[1] The First Affiliated Hospital of Zhengzhou University, Beijing, China
nczfkb@126.com

[2] People's Public Security University of China, Zhengzhou, China

Abstract. In this paper, based on the real electronic medical record data of the hospital, a customized method of rule-based learning and information extraction is designed, and three steps are adopted to realize the extraction of Chinese information: sampling and labeling. The medical history information of 600 electronic medical records (including current medical history, past history, personal history, family history, etc.) were randomly selected, and the information needed to be extracted (taking diabetes history as an example) was marked by the labeling platform developed in this study. According to the annotation results, the extraction template is summarized, and the extraction template can be directly used to extract the regular expression extraction rules, and these rules can be used to extract the actual information. The method of manual verification and automatic verification is used to verify the effectiveness of the method. By using the method of natural language processing and rule-based information extraction, an algorithm for extracting customized information from unstructured Chinese electronic medical record text data is designed and implemented. Aiming at the extraction of diabetes history in the hospital, the field verification of a single department has achieved good results.

Keywords: Information extraction · Natural language processing · Medical history

1 Background

With the continuous improvement of the level of hospital informatization in China, a large number of clinical data have been accumulated. How to make effective use of these data has become one of the focuses in the field of data science. According to 57 health industry standards related to electronic medical records issued in 2016 [1], a total of 53 items related to electronic medical records were involved. Among the 53 electronic medical record data standards, 307 pure text data items are specified as "human reading part" [1]. These unstructured data contain a lot of information about the diagnosis and treatment process, but the accurate and comprehensive extraction of information is relatively difficult. In the whole electronic medical record data set, as far as the electronic medical record data of inpatients are concerned, the information contained

H. Shen and Y. Sang (Eds.): PAAP 2019, CCIS 1163, pp. 140–146, 2020.
https://doi.org/10.1007/978-981-15-2767-8_13

in the data such as admission records [2], course records, operation records, discharge summaries is the most abundant. To investigate the hospitals that have implemented electronic medical records in China at present, the specific information contained in the above four data is shown in Table 1. Due to the different implementation strategies in the actual system, there may be slightly difference from Table 1, but the basic content is roughly similar.

Table 1. Example of description patterns for a history of diabetes

Pattern	Instance
DM*TIMEVALUE*TI MEUNIT	Past history: suffering from diabetes for 8 years, taking 5 tablets of Yishenkang capsule…….
TIMEVALUE*TIME UNIT*DM	…The cause of the patient was more than 3 months. Right eye vitreous hemorrhage 2. Right eye sugar traction 3. Left eye sugar net 4. Bilateral uveitis 5. Diabetes 6. Hypertension…
TIMEVALUE*TIME UNIT*SYMPS*DIAG*DM	Current history: 13 years ago, there was no obvious inducement for thirst, polyuria, weight loss of 5 kg, occasional foam urine, fasting blood glucose 22.9 mmol/L, urine glucose+, no numbness of hands and feet and blurred vision. To our hospital diagnosed as "type 1 diabetes"

In terms of the organization form of data, many information related to diagnosis and treatment details in electronic medical records, such as chief complaint, current medical history, past medical history, differential diagnosis, imaging diagnosis, operation records, etc., are mainly described in Chinese natural language, which is the concrete embodiment of actual diagnosis and treatment details of clinicians. While it contains a large amount of rich information, it is difficult to organize them based on unified and strict table form because its content is closely related to the thinking path of doctors in the whole diagnosis and treatment process [3]. Therefore, customized information extraction should be carried out according to specific situations and actual needs when using data (Fig. 1).

2 Data Description and Problem Definition

2.1 Data Description

At present, in Chinese electronic medical records, the description of disease history is generally described by "[disease name] [time description]". The common descriptions are "diabetes history 20 years", "diabetes 12 years", "diabetes 3 years ago" and so on.

Admission record					
name	*****	gender	*****	age	******
section	*****	bed id	*****	patient id	******
Past history	2 days before physical examination, it was found that serum creatinine increased 201umol, urea 21.1 umol, blood routine: White blood cell 7.89% 109, hemoglobin 115 g, platelet 166% 109, urine routine: occult blood negative, urinary protein negative; 1 day ago (Tongbai County people's Hospital), creatinine 203umol, urea 21.59mmol / L, uric acid 568umol, no fatigue, poor tolerance, palpitation, chest tightness and other discomfort, now in order to further treat admission, disease diet and sleep can, The stool and urine were normal, and the body weight had no significant change compared with before.				
Current medical history	Atrial fibrillation for more than 20 years, oral amiodarone, coronary heart disease for more than 20 years, oral Naoxintong; cerebral infarction for more than 10 years, no sequelae. Diabetes mellitus for more than 5 years, oral glimepiride, metformin, pioglitazone, fasting blood glucose 7 mmol / L, postprandial blood glucose 10 mmol / L, no hypertension, no history of hepatitis, tuberculosis, malaria, vaccination history with social planned immunization, More than 20 years ago, the local hospital underwent anal fistula surgery, no history of food and drug allergy.				
Physician's Signature: ******					

Medical history extraction results			
patient id	Disease	Time	Unit
************	Diabetes	5	year
************	Atrial fibrillation	20	year

Fig. 1. Schematic diagram of diabetes history extraction based on electronic medical record data

This deformation may change a lot in the writing of actual medical records. Taking the results marked by our selected corpus as an example, there are at least 10 descriptions of the history of diabetes [4]. Table 1 is an example of the first three patterns that occur frequently.

2.2 Problem Definition

For a given disease, on the basis of the selected electronic medical record data set, the following problems need to be resolved:

Table 2. Examples of medical history extraction results

Patient ID	Extraction results (section: classification $\Longrightarrow$ results)
000XXX0403_1	Past medical history: T2DM_HIS: $\Longrightarrow$ Diabetes for 7 years
000XXX1443_2	Past medical history: T2DM_HIS: $\Longrightarrow$ Diabetes for 6 years
000XXX7254_1	Past medical history: T2DM_HIS: $\Longrightarrow$ Diabetes for 10 years

To find out all the diabetes history description sentence patterns (or templates): as shown in Table 2 above, to seek out all the descriptions of diabetes history in electronic medical records, summarize them into templates according to categories, so as to eventually extract all the medical history. There are two key problems to be solved: finding out all the time statements and all the diabetes diagnosis statements; correlating the correct disease diagnosis statements with the related time statements [4].

How to extract the medical history description information of all diabetic patients and organize it into a relational table: for different templates, how to write a unified extraction rule in order to store the extracted results into the result table. The focus needs to be on accuracy, consistency, and effectiveness of rule rewriting for templates.

How to verify the accuracy and comprehensiveness of the extraction results: for the extraction results, it is necessary to determine the degree of consistency between the extraction results and the situation recorded in the data. Since it is generally impossible to achieve a comprehensive manual expert check in practice, it is a key issue to take appropriate sampling methods and assist with automated inspection tools to verify and calculate the correctness, accuracy and recall rate of the extraction results [5].

3 Methods and Steps

For the questions raised in Sect. 2.2 above, electronic medical records can be processed according to the process shown in the following figure, which can be used to extract and organize diabetes history and verify the results.

Figure 2 consists of five parts. The first step is to establish a medical history corpus, which consists of 6 people in 3 groups (2 people in each group and 2 groups for text labeling; 2 people in each group and 1 group for validation on labeling result) working in parallel. The corpus is customized and labeled according to the specifications, so as to comprehensively investigate and analyze the template for describing diabetes history; the second step is to rewrite the results of the previous step into a language-specific extraction rule base; the third step is to extract the medical history according to the rule base from unstructured text data in electronic medical records and store the results into the result table; the fourth step is to extract negative descriptions in electronic medical records and exclude possible false positive results from the results of the previous step; Finally, the results are verified by the combination of manual sampling and automatic inspection [6].

3.1 Establishment of Customized Corpus

In order to completely extract medical history information from unstructured text data in electronic medical records, it is necessary to determine the representative descriptions of specific disease history (such as diabetes history), so as to discover possible rules and construct equivalent extraction rules. The medical history part of the electronic medical record data (including current medical history, past medical history, personal history, etc.) are used as the candidate set of corpus sampling to meet the customized requirements of medical history extraction. All the data containing time unit description (year, month, day) are extracted as the basic corpus; then the basic corpus is divided into

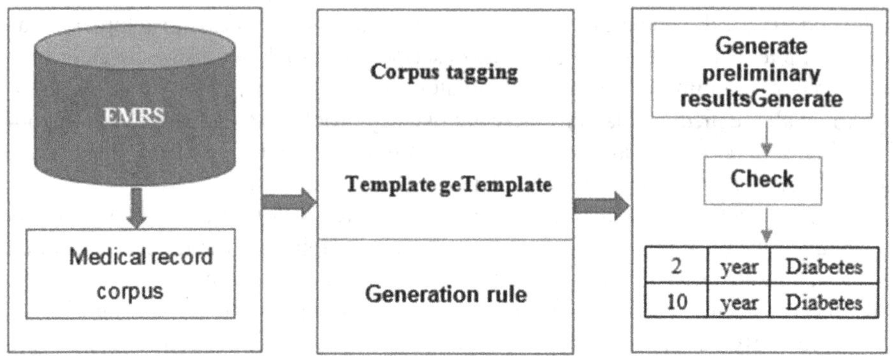

Fig. 2. Extraction and organization of diabetes history from unstructured text data in electronic medical records

groups according to hospital departments and sampled according to 5% of total volume. These sampled data are used as label candidate sets, which are labelled by professionally trained personnel.

3.2 Analysis of Annotation Results and Discovery of Medical History Description Rules

Six hundred medical history corpus were marked, and the same corpus was marked by two labelling personnel at the same time. For any results found inconsistent with the marking, the third person shall verify and negotiate with the marking personnel respectively to determine the final marking results. Because we have adopted the method of customized corpus labelling, and the marking objectives are specific and concise, there are fewer inconsistencies in all the labeling results, and inconsistencies are concentrated in the medical records with a confirmed history of diabetes. For example, some labelling personnel use "suspected diabetes" in medical records as a diagnosis of diabetes, others think that it cannot be used as a diagnosis, and finally, after discussion by consultant experts, they take it as secondary evidence to extract medical history, and the specific data users will determine whether to use it [7].

After resolving the possible problems in labeling, eight rules for extracting diabetic history were determined by combining automatic rule discovery with manual checking. According to the information extraction processing language Perl, these rules to form regular expressions for information extraction were rewritten. For example, the medical history description fragment, such as "Past medical history: suffered from 'diabetes' for 13 years, no treatment, no monitoring of blood sugar, cerebral infarction 5 years ago, recurrence 3 years ago, leaving no sequela". The corresponding regular expression of the application template "DM*DT*TIMEUNIT" is "(history of diabetes (. *?). (year, month, day, day)".

3.3 Medical History Information Extraction Based on Rule Base

After the extraction rule base which can be applied in practice is obtained through Sect. 3.2, we can extract the medical history information based on the extraction rule base. The extraction algorithm is as follows: Algorithm I. Diabetes history extraction based on rule base.

1. Read into a piece of medical history data D.
2. Read into a piece of extraction rule R.
3. Apply extraction rule R to data D (abbreviated as R (D)).
4. Merge the extraction result S = R (D) into the extraction result set.
5. Judge whether the rule base is over, if so, go to 6, otherwise go to 2.
6. Judge whether the medical history data is over, if so, go to 7, otherwise go to 1.
7. Deduplicate the result set.
8. End.

In algorithm I, step 1 refers to reading complete fragments of XML data such as current illness history and past history in a patient admission record document, and then using each rule in the rule base one by one through steps from 2 to 5. All the extracted results are entered into the initial result table; step 6 reads the next section of XML data and repeats the above steps from 2 to 5, and the entire algorithm ends (step 8) after the last XML fragment is processed and the result is deduplicated.

3.4 Negation Detection

If the generalized rule of "diabetes" mentioned above is directly used, all the similar data in the past history including "history of sugar-free urine", "history of no hypertension, diabetes" and so on will be mistakenly extracted into the history of diabetes. Therefore, we specifically extract the above cases which are clearly recorded as having no medical history and exclude them from the previous extraction results. Similar to the previous methods, the template "negative word * history of diabetes" is extracted and its corresponding rule ".* (no | denial) (.*?)is rewritten on the basis of 50 negative narrative corpus entries for the explicit negative narrative of diabetes history.

Typical negative description examples include: "past medical history: no history of hypertension, heart disease, diabetes, cerebrovascular disease, no history of hepatitis, tuberculosis, malaria, unknown history of vaccination, no history of trauma, blood transfusion, history of blood donation, being allergic to aspirin."

4 Result Analysis and Verification

The comprehensive verification on extraction results of medical history is a complicated and time-consuming task. In order to illustrate the effectiveness of the extraction results, a parallel strategy of two verification methods for the whole extraction results was adopted. The first method selects all the data from a department in 2015 to carry out manual verification based on auxiliary tools, and the verification results provide a reference basis for the index analysis of the overall extraction results; the second method is to sample 10% of the data from all departments for verification (including 5% of the labeled corpus, because the tagging corpus is actually a gold standard that can be directly verified by the extraction results. If the extraction results do not meet the specified indicators for the marked corpus results, the extraction rule base will have a high probability of poor extraction results for other non-marked data).

In order to make the description concise and to the point, the medical records with clear description of diabetes history (referring to both diabetes diagnosis and duration of diabetes) and the medical records with clear description of sugar-free urine history (see Table 3) were verified and analyzed.

Table 3. Validation indicators for extraction results

Project	Result	Indicators	Result
Number of medical records	N = 1436	PRECISION	99.5%
TP (True Positive)	765	RECALL	87.6%
FP (False Positive)	4	F-MEASURE	0.93
FN (False Negative)	108		
TN (True Negative)	558		

In this paper, the combination of natural language processing and rule-based information extraction method is used to extract customized information from unstructured electronic medical record text data, and good results are obtained in clinical application.

References

1. Circular on the issuance of 57 health industry standards, such as the specification for shared documents of Electronic Medical Records Part 1: Summary of Medical Records, State Health and Family Planning Commission of the People's Republic of China, Shanghai, September 2016
2. Feng, Z.: A Concise Course on Natural Language Processing. Shanghai Foreign Language Education Press (2012)
3. Cheng, X., Zhu, Q., Wang, J.: Principle and Application of Chinese Information Extraction. Science Press, Beijing (2010)
4. Meystre, S.M., et al.: Extracting information from textual documents in the electronic health record: a review of recent research. Yearb. Med. Inform. **35**(6), 128 (2008)
5. Hirschberg, J., Manning, C.D.: Advances in natural language processing. Science **349**(6245), 261 (2015)
6. Chang, Y.C., Manning, C.D., et al.: A hybrid method of rule and machine learning for temporal relation extraction in patient discharge summaries. J. Biomed. Inform. **46**(Suppl.), 54–62 (2013)
7. Jindal, P., Manning, C.D.: Extraction of events and temporal expressions from clinical narratives. J. Biomed. Inform. **46**(Suppl.), 13–19 (2013)

Deep Residual Optimization for Stereoscopic Image Color Correction

Yuanyuan Fan[1], Pengyu Liu[1], and Yuzhen Niu[1,2](✉)

[1] College of Mathematics and Computer Science, Fuzhou University, Fujian, China
fyybebetter@gmail.com, pengyuliufzu@gmail.com, yuzhenniu@gmail.com

[2] Key Laboratory of Spatial Data Mining & Information Sharing, Ministry of Education, Fujian, China

Abstract. The color correction algorithm is designed to eliminate color discrepancies between image pairs. Compared with the conventional algorithm, color correction for 3D stereoscopic images not only needs to achieve the color consistency of the resulting image and the reference image but also expected to ensure the structural consistency of the resulting image and the target image. For this problem, we propose a stereoscopic image color correction algorithm based on deep residual optimization. First, we get an initial result image by fusing a global color correction image and a dense matching image of the stereo image pair. Then, a residual image optimization scheme is used to improve the structural deformation and color inconsistency of the initial result caused by mismatching and fusion. By combining the target image with the optimized residual image, the structure and clarity of the target image can be retained to the maximum extent. In addition, we use the perceptual loss and per-pixel loss to improve the structural deformation and local color inconsistency while training the optimization network. Experimental results show the effectiveness of our method.

Keywords: Color correction · Structural consistency · Residual optimization

1 Introduction

In binocular stereo photography, due to the influence of camera parameters, shooting angle, diffuse reflection of the object surface and other factors, the obtained stereo images may have differences in luminance and chrominance. This difference affects not only the post-productions that are related to color consistency, but also the reconstruction of depth information, which will make the audience feel visual fatigue. Color correction is to change the color value of the target image using some mapping relationship to have a similar distribution to the reference image, also known as color transfer. It can be used to eliminate color differences between images or to transfer the color style of a reference image to the target image. The color correction algorithm is widely used in 3D stereo

H. Shen and Y. Sang (Eds.): PAAP 2019, CCIS 1163, pp. 147–158, 2020.
https://doi.org/10.1007/978-981-15-2767-8_14

image/video and multi-view video color correction, panoramic image stitching and other tasks related to color consistency.

Many color correction methods have been proposed at present. According to the number of mapping functions, color correction can be divided into global color correction algorithm [5,10–12,16,17,19] and local color correction algorithm [2,8,9,14,21]. The global color correction algorithm uses the same mapping function for all pixels in the image, and the local color correction algorithm uses different mapping functions for different regions of the image. The global method can obtain color corrected results with good performance quickly and efficiently. However, when the image is colorful or with complex textures, the global method can not correct the local color difference well. Comparatively speaking, the local correction method can better correct this difference. Still, the local method has its own imperfection. Due to the image segmentation, feature matching method as well as the application of multiple mapping functions, some local correction methods may have structure inconsistency between the resulting image and the reference image or color inconsistency within the resulting image regions, which requires post-optimization procedure and hence takes more processing time. Influenced by the reflectivity of different object materials in the scene, the difference between color and brightness of stereo image pairs is usually local, therefore the local correction algorithm can fit our requirements better compared with the global algorithm.

Deep neural networks have achieved remarkable development in many tasks related to images and videos, such as style transfer, grayscale image/video colorization, image inpainting, image dehazing/deraining, etc. These hot researches have presented us with many amazing results. And the powerful capabilities of deep neural networks have also been demonstrated. However, few researchers currently apply neural networks to color correction task. This is mainly due to the instability and randomness of the CNN model, while stereo image color correction requires strong stability and controllability. In this work, we propose a framework for incorporating deep neural networks into the stereo image color correction algorithm. The deep neural network is used as a post-processing optimization step for color correction. We try to make full use of the powerful generating ability of it while minimizing the influence of network instability.

The proposed method can be divided into two stages: initial result generation and initial result residual optimization. In the initial result generation stage, we adopt the initialization method of MO [21] which fuses a dense matching image (feature matching of the target image with the reference image) and a global color correction image to obtain the initial color correction result. In the initial result residual optimization stage, we use the residual optimization method to train the optimization network. Since the pixels of the initial result are from the global color correction image and the dense matching image. It is necessary to optimize the local color inconsistency and structure deformation caused by mismatch and region segmentation in the initialization result. Finally, the optimized residual image and the target image are combined to obtain the final result. We chose SRCNN [4] as the basic structure of the residual optimization network. Because of its simplistic fabric, the optimization process takes very little time and is more suitable for application in post-processing steps. While training the optimization network, we introduce perceptual loss [6] and per-pixel loss to improve image structural deformation and color inconsistency. The experimental results on the ICCD dataset [7] and the Middlebury dataset [3] show that our method can obtain results comparable to the state of the art methods, and also prove the effectiveness of the framework.

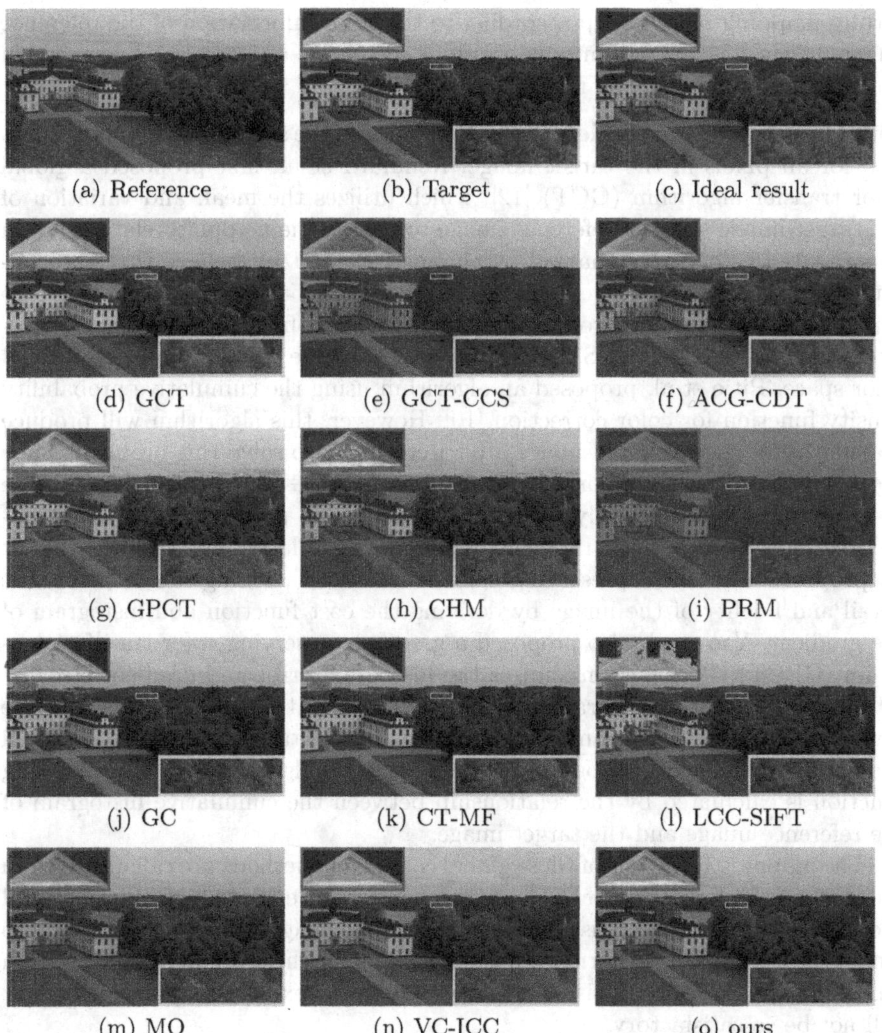

Fig. 1. An example comparing with 11 color correction algorithms on the ICCD dataset.

The rest of this paper is organized as follows: Sect. 2 describes the related work, Sect. 3 provides a detailed explanation of the proposed method, Sect. 4 introduces the specific experimental process and shows the experimental results, and Sect. 5 summarizes the paper.

2 Related Work

Color correction is a process of correcting the color of the target image by using a certain mapping relationship according to the color information of the reference image. It can be classified into global color correction and local color correction according to the number of mapping functions.

The global color correction algorithm applies the same color mapping function for all pixels in the target image. Reinhard et al. first proposed a global color transfer algorithm (GCT) [12], which utilizes the mean and variation of the target image and the reference image to obtain the mapping relationship in uncorrelated color space channel by channel. Xiao et al. believe that the conversion between color spaces of the GCT method brings extra run time. To eliminate this conversion process, they introduced global color transfer in correlated color space (GCT-CCS) [16] using the covariance matrix of images in RGB color space. Pitie et al. proposed an algorithm using the cumulative probability density function for color correction [10]. However, this algorithm will produce granularity in the corrected image after iterations. To solve this problem, They proposed an automated color grading algorithm (ACG-CDT) [11] to smooth the resulting image subsequently. Some researchers have proposed some color correction algorithms based on the histograms or cumulative histograms. Xiao et al. proposed a gradient-preserving color transfer [17], taking into account the detail and fidelity of the image by deriving the cost function and histogram of the gradient. Yao et al. also proposed a gradient-preserving color transfer algorithm (GPCT) [19] which minimizes the histogram error and gradient error by establishing a Laplacian pyramid to map the color of the reference image to the target image while maintaining the gradient of the target image. Fecker et al proposed a cumulative histogram matching (CHM) algorithm [5]. The mapping function is calculated by the relationship between the cumulative histogram of the reference image and the target image.

The mapping functions of these global correction methods are calculated from the statistical information of the images. Therefore, they have high efficiency and the correction performance is good for some simple images. However, they tend to ignore the local texture information when looking for the optimal color correction scheme, If the target image is colorful with complex texture, the corrected result will not be so satisfactory.

The local color correction algorithm can provide a more accurate mapping relationship between the target image and the reference image compared to the global color correction method. And we need this accuracy in stereo color correction exactly. Since local color correction uses different mapping functions for different regions, the region segmentation and matching between the reference image and the target image becomes a crucial link in color correction, and the stability and accuracy of the matching method also affect the correction result.

The principal regions mapping method (PRM) proposed by Zhang et al. [20] uses a registration algorithm to match the overlapping regions of the image pair and finds the principal region by the histogram peak value matching in the HSV color space. Then, Calculate an independent mapping function in each principal area. Brown et al. proposed a gain compensation algorithm (GC) [2] for color correction and stitching of panoramic images. GC performs feature matching via SIFT and RANSAC methods. Park et al. proposed a matrix decomposition based color transfer algorithm (CT-MF) [9] to optimize the color consistency among a set of images describing a common scene. The method proposed by Wang at el. (LCC-SIFT) [14] performs region matching via image segmentation and SIFT features, and then performs color correction on the regions one by one. Zheng's color correction method based on matching and optimization (MO) [21] uses the dense stereo matching image and a global color correction image to initialize the color values of the resulting image. They consider the color correction as a quadratic energy minimization problem to improve the local color smoothness and global color consistency of the initial image. When the parallax of the left and right views is large, the structural deformation between the initial image and the target image will be difficult to optimize. Therefore, Niu et al. utilizes the guided filter method and proposed the VC-ICC algorithm [8] to improve the structural inconsistency. The VC-ICC method can obtain better results when the structure is inconsistent, but it is accompanied by a slight reduction in image sharpness. The above local color correction algorithms are greatly affected by the matching algorithm, and if there exist many erroneous matches, an unsatisfactory result may appear.

3 Proposed Method

The overall architecture of our color correction algorithm is shown in Fig. 2. Given a stereo image pair, where the left view I_r is the reference image and the right view I_t is the target image to be corrected. Firstly, we preprocess the input image pair to obtain an initialized result image I_i through blending a global correction result and a dense matching image. Secondly, we calculate a difference image R_i', also named residual image in this paper, between the initialized image I_i and the target image I_t after image normalization. We get the final residual image R_i after normalizing R_i', the difference and normalization formulas are as follows:

$$R_i' = I_i - I_t \tag{1}$$

$$R_i = \frac{R_i' + 1}{2} \tag{2}$$

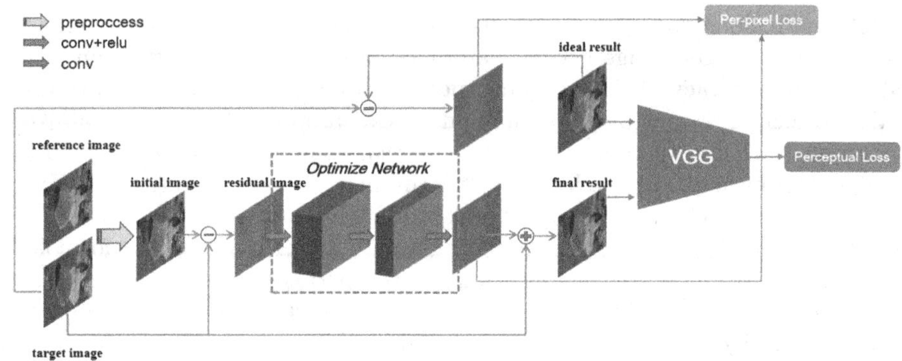

Fig. 2. The overall architecture of the proposed method.

The residual image R_i is processed by the optimization network to obtain a refined residual image R_o'. Denormalized R_o' to get the final residual image R_o:

$$R_o = R_o' \times 2 - 1 \tag{3}$$

Finally, add up the optimized residual image R_o And target image I_t to get the final correction result I_f,

$$I_f = I_t + R_o \tag{4}$$

3.1 Result Initialization

The initialized result image is generated from three images, which are the matching image, the confidence map, and the global corrected result obtained by the ACG-CDT algorithm [11]. The matching image is obtained by performing SIFT flow dense matching [21] on the target image and the reference image. It possesses similar structures with the target image and owns the same color style as the reference image. However, due to the horizontal parallax, there will be a portion of mismatched or unmatched regions in the matching image. The confidence map is obtained by using the SSIM algorithm [15] to calculate the pixel similarity between the target image and the matching image, and the pixel value of unmatched regions is set to zero. The larger the pixel value in the confidence map denotes the higher pixel consistency of the matching image and the target image. The ACG-CDT global corrected result is used to replace the unmatched or mismatched area in the matching image (ie, the areas in the confidence map whose value is lower than a threshold). A detailed implementation can be found in paper [21].

3.2 Optimization Network

The optimization network uses the SRCNN model [4], as shown in the orange dotted line in Fig. 2. SRCNN is a deep neural network model for image super-resolution. The network is very simple in structure and has a few parameters, thus it can achieve high efficiency while ensuring good optimization effect. The specific structure of the SRCNN network can be expressed as [conv1+relu1]→[conv2+relu2]→[conv3]. The convolution kernel size of conv1 is 9 × 9 and the number of input channels and output channels is 1 and 64, respectively. The convolution kernel size of conv2 is 1 × 1, and the number of output channels is 32. The conv3 has a convolution kernel size of 5 × 5. The number of output channels is 1. The three convolutions can be regarded as three operations: block extraction and representation, nonlinear mapping, and image reconstruction. Since the original SRCNN model only uses the Y channel of the YCrCb color space for image reconstruction, and we are using three-channel RGB images, so we modify the input and output channels of the network from 1 to 3.

3.3 Loss Function

The loss function of our optimization network consists of two parts, namely the perceptual loss [6] and the per-pixel loss. The perceptual loss is used to optimize the partial structural deformation in the initial result, and the per-pixel loss is used to punish the local color inconsistency in the initial result.

Perceptual loss punishes perceptually dissimilar results by the distance metric of the resulting image and the ideal image on the pre-trained network's activation layers. At present, perceptual loss is widely used in image generation tasks, including super-resolution [4,6], style transfer [6], image inpainting [18], etc. perceptual loss combines high-level/low-level features, global structure, texture, color, and other information to optimize the structural deformation and color inconsistency of the initial results. We refer to the five activation layers (relu1-1, relu2-1, relu3-1, relu4-1, relu5-1) of the pre-trained VGG19 [13] network on the ImageNet dataset [1] to calculate the perceptual loss. Input the result and the ground-truth image into the pre-trained network, then take out the feature map of the corresponding layer for distance measurement. The specific calculation is formulated as follows:

$$L_{perc} = \sum_{i=1}^{5} \frac{1}{N_i} \|\phi_i(I_{gt}) - \phi_i(I_f)\|_1 \tag{5}$$

In Eq. (5), $\phi_i()$ representing the i-th activation layer of the pre-trained VGG network. N_i indicates the total number of pixels in the i-th activation layer. I_{gt} is the ground-truth image.

Per-pixel loss is the sum of the L1 loss and the MSE loss between the output residual image and the ground-truth residual image. The MSE loss is the most commonly used loss function since it converges fast. However, it aims to minimize the quadratic sum error of the target value and the predicted value, the model will be more sensitive to the regions with larger differences (outlier point) and neglect regions with smaller differences. By contrast, the L1 loss minimizes the sum of absolute error value between the predicted value and the ground-truth, which can improve the robustness of the model and make up for the regions ignored by MSE. The calculation process is shown in Eq. (6)

$$L_{perp} = \sum_{i=1}^{n} |R_o(i) - R_{gt}(i)| + \frac{1}{n}\sum_{i=1}^{n} \|R_o(i) - R_{gt}(i)\|^2 \tag{6}$$

Where $R_{gt} = I_{gt} - I_t$ is the residual image between the ideal result image and the target image. $R_o(i)$ represetes The i-th pixel of image R_o. n is the total number of pixels in the residual image.

By combining perceptual loss with per-pixel loss, the overall objective function of our residual optimization network is defined as follows:

$$L = \lambda_{perc} L_{perc} + \lambda_{perp} L_{perp} \tag{7}$$

Here, λ_{perc} is the weight of perceptual loss and λ_{perp} is the weight of per-pixel loss, which was set to 0.1 and 1 in our experiments respectively.

4 Experiment

We used the ICCD dataset [7] and the Middlebury dataset [3] to experiment with the proposed method. The ICCD dataset contains a total of 18 original image pairs (no color difference between left and right views) describing the same scene. Each pair of images is processed by changing the brightness, contrast, exposure, RG channel, hue and saturation of the right view with photoshop to obtain 18 different image pairs with different color styles. Thus there are 324 pairs of distorted image pairs for color correction in total. Besides, we collected 68 pairs of color consistent stereo images from the Middlebury dataset and 1224 distorted stereo image pairs were obtained by the same data processing method as the ICCD dataset. The final dataset has 1548 pairs of distorted images for color correction. We divided the dataset into a training set and a test set, in which the training set contains 64 pairs of original image pairs and the test set contains 22 original image pairs. There are 6 pairs of original images from the ICCD dataset and 16 pairs of original images from the Middlebury dataset in the test set.

Due to the small amount of data, we used a data argumentation strategy in the training stage of the optimization network. First, we resize each training image pairs to let their minimal length/width be 360, and then randomly crop the left and right views of the image pair to a sub-image of size 256×256 as the input to the model. Notice that the random values in the left and right views are the same, which ensures the invariance of horizontal parallax. Nevertheless, the original size image is used directly as the input during test time. We used Adam optimizer with a learning rate of 0.001 and the batch size was set to 16.

The experimental results prove the effectiveness of our method for color correction. Figures 3 and 4 show examples of our experimental results. The color inconsistency and structural deformation in the initial images (as shown in Figs. 3(d) and 4(d)) are improved apparently after optimization. The final result

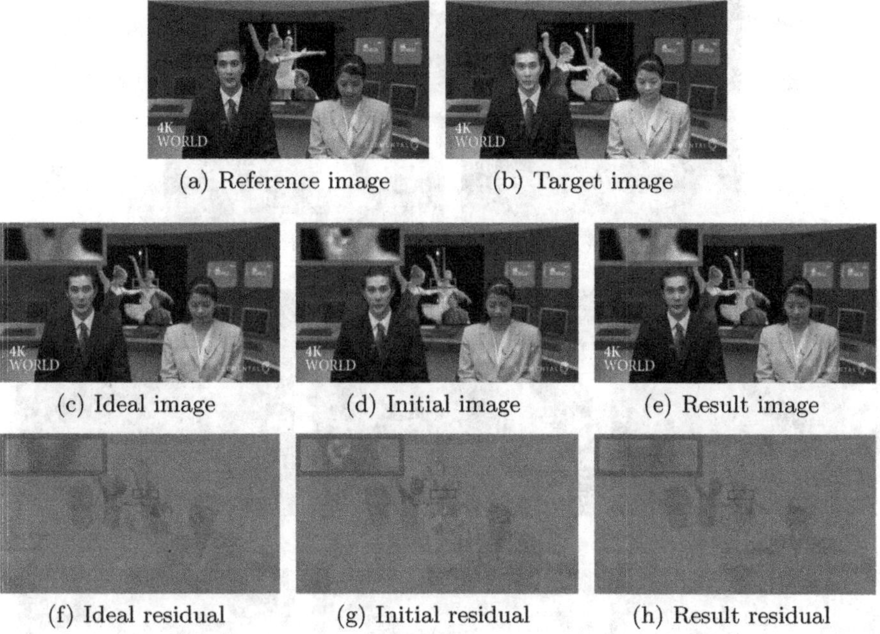

(a) Reference image (b) Target image

(c) Ideal image (d) Initial image (e) Result image

(f) Ideal residual (g) Initial residual (h) Result residual

Fig. 3. An example of our result on the ICCD dataset.

images (As shown in Figs. 3(e) and 4(e)) preferably retain the structure and clarity of the target image as well as the color style of the reference image. As can be seen from the red box in Fig. 3, the inconsistent color on the ballet dancer's arm in the initial image is eliminated after optimization. Figure 4(d) shows the structural deformation of the pen body in the red box of the initial image has been greatly improved. The optimization effect of the model can be more clearly observed from the residual images corresponding to the initial image and the resulting image. However, if the structural deformation in the initial image is too large, it is difficult to completely correct the structural difference even after the optimization step, as can be seen from Fig. 4.

The comparison of correction effect with 11 state of the art methods are shown in Fig. 1. The color correction algorithms are GCT [12], GCT-CCS [16], ACG-CDT [11], GPCT [19], CHM [5], PRM [20], GC [2], CT-MF [9], LCC-SIFT [14], MO [21], VC-ICC [8]. Figure 1(c) to (f) are the results of global color correction algorithms, Fig. 1(g) to (n) are the results of local color correction algorithms. Figure 1(o) is our correction result. It is not difficult to find out from the results that most of the algorithms do not correct the target image well, especially in the color of the wall in the red box and the color of the tree in the yellow box. Our method and VC-ICC algorithm [8] can get relatively good correction results. However, due to the blurring effect of the guided filter, the color of the leaf in the yellow frame can be observed that the sharpness of the result of the VC-ICC method is reduced, and our method can better maintain the sharpness of the image.

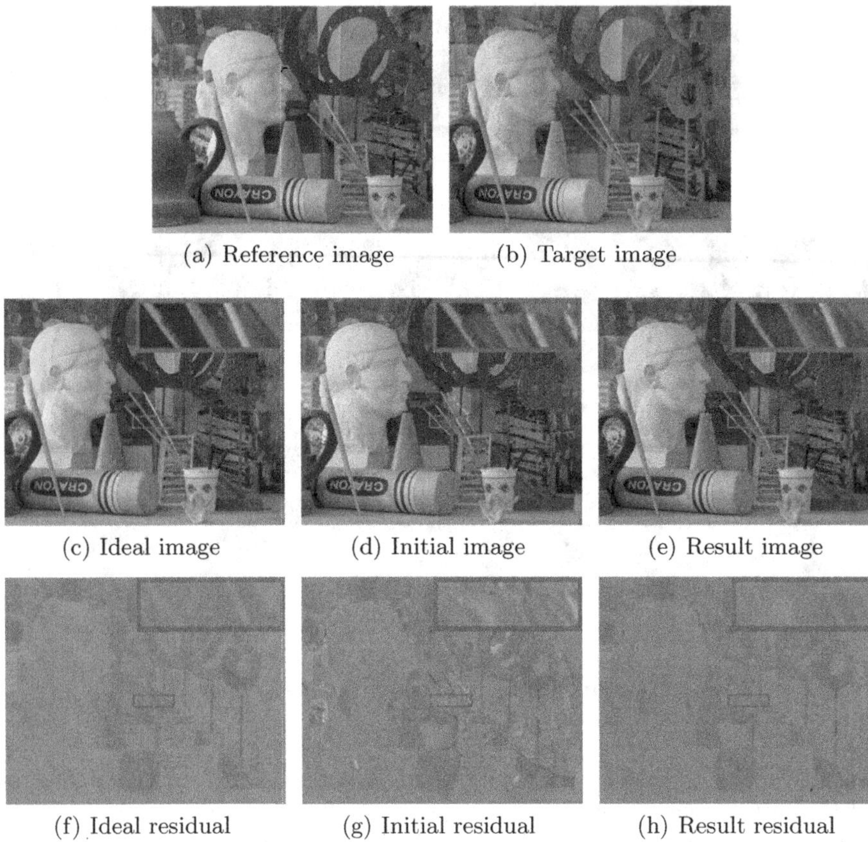

Fig. 4. An example of our result on the Middlebury dataset.

Table 1. Comparison of CSVD quality evaluation results of Fig. 1.

Methods	GCT	GCT-CCS	ACG-CDT	GPCT	CHM	PRM
Score	0.8625	0.8291	0.9046	0.8808	0.8636	0.7426
Methods	GC	CT-MF	LCC-SIFT	MO	VC-ICC	Ours
Score	0.8492	0.8677	0.8655	0.9049	**0.9161**	0.9242

Table 1 shows the performance comparison data of our algorithm with 11 the state of the art correction algorithms on the results of Fig. 1. We evaluated the results with ideal images using CSVD [7] image quality assessment index, which is specifically used to evaluate image color consistency. The best three performance methods in the table are identified by bold red, blue and green fonts respectively. The data also show that our method can get preferable result.

Moreover, since our optimization only needs to go through a simple forward network, it has more advantages in processing time than the guided filtering of VC-ICC as well as the complex optimization calculation.

5 Conclusion

In this work, we proposed a deep residual optimization for stereoscopic image color correction, which introduces deep learning into the color correction task. The entire color correction consists of two parts, the result initialization, and the residual image optimization. The comparison experiment with other methods proves that our algorithm is effective and can get a better optimization effect while speeding up the optimization. Besides, the pre-trained optimization model can also be used as a post-processing step for other stereo image color correction algorithms. We intend to replace the initialization step with a deep learning model to extend the model into an end-to-end architecture in our further study.

References

1. http://www.image-net.org/
2. Brown, M., Lowe, D.G.: Automatic panoramic image stitching using invariant features. Int. J. Comput. Vision **74**(1), 59–73 (2007)
3. Daniel, S.: http://vision.middlebury.edu/stereo/data/
4. Dong, C., Loy, C.C., He, K., Tang, X.: Image super-resolution using deep convolutional networks. IEEE Trans. Pattern Anal. Mach. Intell. **38**(2), 295–307 (2015)
5. Fecker, U., Barkowsky, M., Kaup, A.: Histogram-based prefiltering for luminance and chrominance compensation of multiview video. IEEE Trans. Circuits Syst. Video Technol. **18**(9), 1258–1267 (2008)
6. Johnson, J., Alahi, A., Fei-Fei, L.: Perceptual losses for real-time style transfer and super-resolution. In: Leibe, B., Matas, J., Sebe, N., Welling, M. (eds.) ECCV 2016. LNCS, vol. 9906, pp. 694–711. Springer, Cham (2016). https://doi.org/10.1007/978-3-319-46475-6_43
7. Niu, Y., Zhang, H., Guo, W., Ji, R.: Image quality assessment for color correction based on color contrast similarity and color value difference. IEEE Trans. Circuits Syst. Video Technol. **28**(4), 849–862 (2016)
8. Niu, Y., Zheng, X., Zhao, T., Chen, J.: Visually consistent color correctionfor stereoscopic images and videos. IEEE Trans. Circ. Syst. Video Technol. (2019)
9. Park, J., Tai, Y.W., Sinha, S.N., So Kweon, I.: Efficient and robust color consistency for community photo collections. In: Proceedings of the IEEE Conference on Computer Vision and Pattern Recognition, pp. 430–438 (2016)
10. Pitie, F., Kokaram, A.C., Dahyot, R.: N-dimensional probability density function transfer and its application to color transfer. In: Tenth IEEE International Conference on Computer Vision (ICCV 2005), Volume 1, vol. 2, pp. 1434–1439. IEEE (2005)
11. Pitié, F., Kokaram, A.C., Dahyot, R.: Automated colour grading using colour distribution transfer. Comput. Vis. Image Underst. **107**(1–2), 123–137 (2007)
12. Reinhard, E., Adhikhmin, M., Gooch, B., Shirley, P.: Color transfer between images. IEEE Comput. Graphics Appl. **21**(5), 34–41 (2001)

13. Simonyan, K., Zisserman, A.: Very deep convolutional networks for large-scale image recognition. arXiv preprint arXiv:1409.1556 (2014)
14. Wang, Q., Yan, P., Yuan, Y., Li, X.: Robust color correction in stereo vision. In: 2011 18th IEEE International Conference on Image Processing, pp. 965–968. IEEE (2011)
15. Wang, Z., Bovik, A.C., Sheikh, H.R., Simoncelli, E.P., et al.: Image quality assessment: from error visibility to structural similarity. IEEE Trans. Image Process. **13**(4), 600–612 (2004)
16. Xiao, X., Ma, L.: Color transfer in correlated color space. In: Proceedings of the 2006 ACM International Conference on Virtual Reality Continuum and Its Applications, pp. 305–309. ACM (2006)
17. Xiao, X., Ma, L.: Gradient-preserving color transfer. In: Computer Graphics Forum, vol. 28, pp. 1879–1886. Wiley Online Library (2009)
18. Yan, Z., Li, X., Li, M., Zuo, W., Shan, S.: Shift-Net: image inpainting via deep feature rearrangement. In: Ferrari, V., Hebert, M., Sminchisescu, C., Weiss, Y. (eds.) Computer Vision – ECCV 2018. LNCS, vol. 11218, pp. 3–19. Springer, Cham (2018). https://doi.org/10.1007/978-3-030-01264-9_1
19. Yao, C.H., Chang, C.Y., Chien, S.Y.: Example-based video color transfer. In: IEEE International Conference on Multimedia & Expo (2016)
20. Zhang, M., Georganas, N.D.: Fast color correction using principal regions mapping in different color spaces. Real-Time Imaging **10**(1), 23–30 (2004)
21. Zheng, X., Niu, Y., Chen, J., Chen, Y.: Color correction for stereoscopic image based on matching and optimization. In: 2017 International Conference on 3D Immersion (IC3D), pp. 1–8. IEEE (2017)

Old Man Fall Detection Based on Surveillance Video Object Tracking

Zhao Qiu[1], Xiaoquan Liang[1(✉)], Qiaoqiao Chen[1], Xiangsheng Huang[2], and Yiping Wang[3]

[1] Hainan University, Haikou 570100, Hainan, China
1872131777@qq.com
[2] Institute of Automation, Chinese Academy of Sciences, Beijing 100091, China
[3] China Unicom Hainan Branch, Haikou 570100, Hainan, China

Abstract. Image recognition technology based on deep learning has made great progress, which makes object detection technology work in many fields. The number of elderly people in China has risen year by year, proclaiming the arrival of an aging society. "The old man can't fall" is a consensus. Using object detection algorithm to detect the fall of the elderly is a research hotspot in the field of object detection. Through the analysis of the object detection algorithm and the object tracking algorithm, Deep-sort and YOLOv3 algorithms are used to achieve the real-time fall detection of the surveillance video. The experimental results prove that combined with YOLOv3 and the Deep-sort algorithms can detect the fall of the elderly.

Keywords: Fall detection · Object tracking · YOLOv3 · Deep-sort

1 Introduction

According to the latest data from the National Bureau of Statistics, China's population aged 60 and over accounted for 17.3% of the total population, which means that China is in an aging society. Recently, a sample survey released by the Beijing Municipal Center for Disease Control and Prevention showed that the annual incidence of falls for elderly people aged 60 to 69 is 9.8%. Each additional decade of the elderly age, the incidence of falls will increase by about 0.5 times. In China, about 40 million elderly people fall each year, and some elderly people may lead to the loss of mobility after falling.

The main devices used in current fall detection systems are cameras and sensors. [1] The fall detection system is divided into three categories: video image based, wearable, and environmental. The wearable fall detection system and the environmental fall detection system are based on the sensor, which mainly uses the sensor to acquire human motion data, and detects the human body fall by the threshold method or the machine learning method. This system has the advantages of low cost and wide detection range. However, Falls cannot be accurately detected when the relative relationship between the sensor and the human body is destroyed. The fall detection system based on video image mainly judges the fall according to the motion characteristics and motion trajectory of the human body. This method has the advantages of high detection accuracy, but

H. Shen and Y. Sang (Eds.): PAAP 2019, CCIS 1163, pp. 159–167, 2020.
https://doi.org/10.1007/978-981-15-2767-8_15

the calculation amount and cost are large, and the detection range has environmental restrictions. The accuracy of identifying falls in video surveillance [2] is 90%.

In recent years, deep learning has made breakthroughs in the field of object detection by virtue of the advantages of convolutional neural network in extracting image features. In order to make the object detection technology help the fallen elderly in time, this article mainly uses the YOLOv3 [3] algorithm and the Deep-sort [4] algorithm to monitor the fall of the elderly in real time.

2 Object Detection and Object Tracking Algorithm

2.1 Object Detection

(1) Object Detection Algorithm

The three major tasks of computer vision are image classification, object detection and image segmentation. Object detection can be seen as a combination of image classification and positioning. The object detection algorithm based on deep learning can be divided into two genres. The two-step algorithm first generates region proposals and then performs CNN [5] classification, represented by R-CNN [6] algorithm; One-step algorithm is directly output categories and corresponding positioning after applying the algorithm to the input image, represented by the YOLO algorithm.

The two-step object detection algorithm has experienced R-CNN, SPP-Net, Fast R-CNN, Faster R-CNN and Mask R-CNN [7–10]. In addition to these algorithms, there are many other two-step object detection algorithms also contribute. Although the two-step object detection algorithm is constantly evolving and the detection accuracy is getting higher and higher, such algorithms always have speed bottlenecks. In some real-time target detection scenarios, r-cnn series algorithm is not fast enough.

The one-step object detection algorithm is represented by the YOLO series. In 2016, YOLO algorithm proposed by Joseph Redmon et al. reached the speed of detecting video [11]. By 2018, YOLO has developed into the third generation YOLOv3. Because of its high accuracy and good timeliness, it is now one of the best algorithms in the field of object detection.

(2) YOLO Algorithm

The YOLOv1 algorithm is very simple and straightforward to process. Firstly, the size of the input image is adjusted to 448*448, then a single convolutional neural network is run on the input image, and finally the optimal result is filtered according to the confidence of the predicted bounding box.

YOLOv2 [12] improved YOLOv1 from three aspects. Firstly, YOLOv2 use those methods of batch normalization, high resolution classifier, convolutional with anchor boxes, dimension clusters, direct location prediction, fine-grained features, multi-scale training and so on. These improvements improve the recall rate of object detection, the accuracy of location and classification. Secondly, by using the new classification model Darknet-19, YOLO detection is faster. Finally, by hierarchical classification, dataset combination with WordTree, joint classification and detection, YOLO's classification ability is stronger.

YOLOv3 used logistic regression to predict the object fraction of each boundary box, binary cross entropy loss for class prediction, and new network structure darknet-53 for feature extraction. YOLOv3 has greatly improved the detection of small objects through multi-scale prediction.

2.2 Object Tracking

(1) Object Tracking Algorithm

Object tracking is an important research direction of computer vision, which can be divided into single object tracking and multi-object tracking. It is obvious that single-object tracking is to track a single object in a video, and multi-object tracking is to track multiple objects in a video. The research of single object tracking algorithm is more complete than the multi-object tracking algorithm, and the effect is better. The KCF/DCF [13, 14] algorithm based on correlation filtering, The DSST algorithm based on translation filtering and scale filtering [15], and The C-COT [16] algorithm based on deep learning have achieved good results. Compared with single-object tracking, multi-object tracking not only needs to solve the problems of background interference, light and other factors in single-object tracking, but also needs to deal with the problems of interaction between tracking objects and the recognition when the object is reappeared.

Video multi-object tracking (MOT) is an important research direction in computer vision. The problem to be solved by MOT is equivalent to processing continuous frame images, marking the detection frames belonging to the same object in consecutive frames as the same ID. MOT has applications in many areas, such as smart security, autonomous driving, medical scenes, and more. The biggest challenge facing MOT at present is occlusion. The object occlusion is easy to cause the object to be lost, the ID jump occurs, which is a difficult point in the MOT field. The object occlusion can be divided into partial occlusion and complete occlusion. There are two common solutions for solving partial occlusion. The first one is to use the detection mechanism to determine whether the object is occluded. The second one is to divide the object into multiple blocks and use the block that is not covered for effective tracking. At present, there is no effective method to completely solve the problem that the object is completely obscured.

(2) Deep-sort Algorithm

Deep-sort is an improvement of [17]. It introduces a deep learning model for offline training on pedestrian recognition dataset. In the real-time object tracking process, extracting the apparent features of the object for nearest neighbor matching can improve the occlusion. The object tracking effect in the case also reduces the problem of object ID hopping [18, 19].

The Deep-sort object tracking algorithm uses a standard Kalman filter based on a constant velocity model and a linear observation model to predict the motion state of the object. For each tracking object, record the number of frames A after the last detection result matches the tracking result. Once the detection result of one object is correctly associated with the tracking result, the parameter A is set to 0. If parameter A exceeds the set threshold, the object tracking is considered to have ended. If a object in a test result is never able to be associated with an existing tracker, then a new object may be considered. For three consecutive frames, if the potential tracker predict result of the object position which is correctly correlated with the detection result, then a new moving target is confirmed. If the above requirement cannot be met, it is considered that a "false alarm" occurs and the moving object should be deleted. Deep-sort uses the high-performance Faster R-CNN model trained in [19] for detection, and combines the residual network model of offline training in [18], which greatly improves the tracking effect of occlusion objects. Deep-sort allows for up to 30 frames of loss and speeds 20 frames per second, which meet online real-time tracking requirements.

3 Fall Detection Method Design

Collect the fall and non-fall human data sets, and after standardizing the data set, use the annotation tool to mark the data set. Using the YOLOv3 training data set, the training is stopped after the loss function tends to be stable. The weight files are tested using test sets, and the best weight file is selected by analyzing the test results. The weight file provided by the YOLOv3 official website is converted into the file required by the keras model, and the object tracking algorithm deep-sort is used to realize the human object tracking. Obtain the image of the tracked object, use the weight file of your training to detect the fall, and judge the occurrence of the fall event according to certain rules.

To facilitate the description of the process of detecting a fall, we take the object 2 in the detection video as an example. Assuming that the object 2 fall event is detected in real time, the process of detecting the fall is divided into three steps. Firstly, use yolo.h5 and deep-sort to detect object 2 and track it. If object 2 is lost, stop tracking. Secondly, extract the continuous frame image containing the object 2 in the video. Thirdly, cut out the object 2 in the extracted image, then detect the cut image, and determine the fall event according to a certain rule. In order to judge the fall more accurately, some simple rules have been formulated as follows. If five consecutive pictures are detected as falling, it is determined that a fall event has occurred. If the proportion of falls detected in 30 consecutive pictures accounts for 90%, then falls will be determined.

3.1 Data Set

In order to achieve the fall detection of the elderly, the human activities are divided into falls and non-falls, and non-falls are also called daily activities. The posture of fall is squatting, lying down and lying on the side, and the posture of non-fall is sitting, bending, walking and running.

There are three main methods of data collection: taking a photo, video conversion and network download. The first way is to use a mobile phone to take photos of 7 volunteers and get about 4,000 pictures of fall and non-fall pictures. The second way is to photographing the fall and non-fall videos, and select a picture for every 10 frames of the captured video, and get total of about 10,000 images. The third way is to download a small number of falling and non-falling images over the network. The obtained images were cleaned and normalized, and a total of about 15,000 images were obtained. For the test needs, an additional picture of two volunteers was taken to get about 600 pictures of falls and non-falls.

Use the tool of yolo_mark to mark images. The tag categories are fall and nonfall, which represent falls and non-falls, respectively. For the convenience of description, mark 15,000 images to get dataset A, and mark 600 images to get dataset B. The data set B is not included in data set A and is used only for testing.

3.2 Training

Data set A is trained using YOLOv3, a weight file is saved after per 1000 times iteration. Training is stopped when the loss function tends to be smooth. The weight file is tested using data set A and data set B respectively. The test result is shown in Fig. 1. The abscissa represents the iteration number, and the ordinate represents the mAP value.

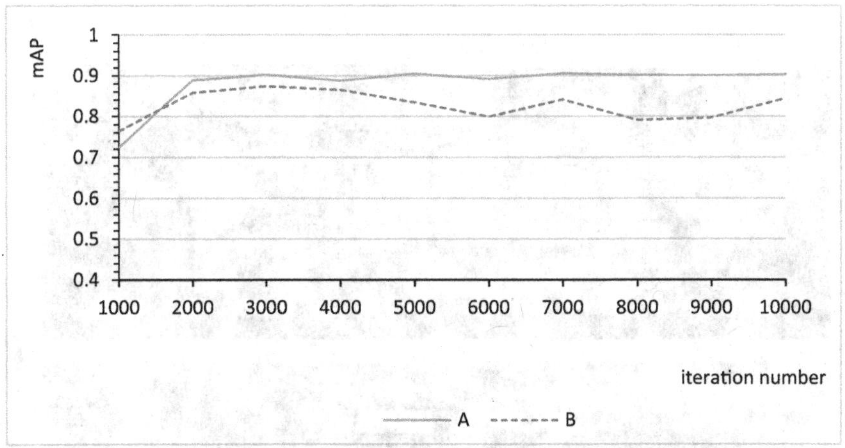

Fig. 1. Test the weight file which is obtained by different iteration number.

As can be seen from Fig. 1, when using the data set A test, the best mAP 0.901 is obtained in the iterative training 7000 times. After 2000 iterations, all mAPs are around 0.90 and the mAP values tend to be stable. When using the data set B test, iterative training 3000 times can get the best mAP 0.874%, and the mAP value is not stable enough. Because the data set B is too small, the mAP stability is insufficient. When the data set B is created, new pictures of squatting have been added, which photos are not in data set A. Because the human body posture in the data set B is different from in the data set A, so there is a slight difference between the mAP of B and the mAP of A. According to the test results, it can be judged that the training effect is basically ideal, and the expected goal is achieved. The weight file of training 3000 times is recorded as Yolo3000.weights.

3.3 Object Tracking

Because of the excellent object tracking effect of the Deep-sort algorithm, the Deep-sort algorithm is chosen as the tracking algorithm of this paper. Due to the insufficient complexity of data set A, it cannot track human targets well. Therefore, the weight of yolov3 training was used to identify the human body. First, the weight file yolov3.weights of the Darknet model is converted into yolo.h5 of Keras model, then use deep-sort to implement multi-target tracking.

4 Experiment

4.1 Fall Detection

The picture taken by the photograph is detected, as shown in Fig. 2, The walking person, the person sitting on the stool detected as non-fall, a person who lies flat or on the side, the person who accidentally fell were detected as fall. The experimental result was the same as the expected result.

Fig. 2. Fall detection

4.2 Object Tracking

In [16], the experiment done by Wojke et al. using GTX1050m proves that the speed of the deep-sort object tracking algorithm is 20 frames per second. Qidian's experiments with the GTX1060 6G show that the speed of running yolo and deep_sort is about 11.5 fps. The graphics card used in this experiment is GTX1060 6G. The object tracking is achieved by using deep-sort and yolo. The speed of detecting video shot with the mobile phone is about 7.5 fps, and The speed of real-time detection of video taken by computer camera is about 11.6 fps. As shown in Fig. 3, deep-sort algorithm can accurately track each human object.

Fig. 3. Object tracking

4.3 Fall Video Detection

Tracking and detecting the video captured by the mobile phone, the experimental results prove that the fall event can be accurately detected. There are two objects in the target tracking experiment video. After the object crosses, there is no object loss and ID jump phenomenon. It also can achieves accurate tracking that even if there is a posture conversion of fall and standing. The experimental video has been uploaded to: https://pan.baidu.com/s/13LF5Q8w1RP6wPqImt6RQLA, extraction code: eknp.

The object 2 in the video is extracted, and then each image extracted by the object 2 is detected using the weight file yolo3000.weights. The object 2 has a total of 579 images, of which 334 are falling images and 245 are non-falling images. There are 308 pictures tested true in the positive sample. There are 308 pictures tested true in the positive sample and 245 pictures tested true in the negative sample.

4.4 Evaluation of Experimental Results

Experiments show that weights file yolo3000.weights can better detect falls and non-falls, and deep-sort algorithm can better track human objects. After extracting tracking objects, falling events can be accurately judged according to the established rules.

In the experiment on GTX1060 6G graphics card, the detection speed obtained is 11.6 fps, which basically meets the real-time requirements. The sensitivity, specificity and accuracy of the experiment were 92.2%, 100% and 95.5% respectively. Literature [20, 21] is a fall detection method based on video. The sensitivity of the fall detection method is compared with the method in this paper, and the results are shown in Table 1.

Table 1. Comparison of three fall detection methods

Method	Literature [20]	Literature [21]	In this paper
Number of falls detected	479	183	308
Total number of fall samples	540	200	334
Recognition rate/sensitivity	88.7%	91.5%	92.2%

5 Conclusion

At any time, the health of the elderly is an important social problem. This paper uses the deep-sort and YOLOv3 algorithms to implement an old man fall detection system, which proves that fall detection can be realized according to the characteristics of pictures and a small number of rules. At present, the existing fall detection system for the old people, most of which is a sensor-based fall detection system, has the problem that the cost is high or the relative relationship between the old and the sensor is easily broken. Although there are some old-fashioned fall detection systems based on video images, most of the systems have a large amount of computation. The system designed in this paper can monitor the fall events in real time. The field of fall detection is still a research hotspot, and I am very happy with the work I have done.

Acknowledgment. This work is partially supported by Hainan Key R&D Program Projects (No. ZDYF2018017); Supported by Haikou Key Science and Technology Plan Project (No. 2017039); Supported by Hainan Natural Science Foundation Project (No.: 618MS028); Supported by National Natural Science Foundation of China Project (No. 61573356).

References

1. Zheng, Y., Bao, N., Xu, L., et al.: Research progress on fall detection system. Chin. J. Med. Phys. **31**(4), 5071–5076 (2014)
2. Dong, K.: Research on human body detection and abnormal behavior in video surveillance. Nanjing University of Posts and Telecommunications, Nanjing (2013)
3. Redmon, J., Farhadi, A.: Yolov3: an incremental improvement. arXiv preprint arXiv:1804. 02767 (2018)
4. Wojke, N., Bewley, A., Paulus, D.: Simple online and realtime tracking with a deep association metric. In: 2017 IEEE International Conference on Image Processing (ICIP), pp. 3645–3649. IEEE (2017)

5. LeCun, Y., Bottou, L., Bengio, Y., et al.: Gradient-based learning applied to document recognition. Proc. IEEE **86**(11), 2278–2324 (1998)
6. Girshick, R., Donahue, J., Darrell, T., et al.: Rich feature hierarchies for accurate object detection and semantic segmentation. In: Proceedings of the IEEE Conference on Computer Vision and Pattern Recognition, pp. 580–587 (2014)
7. He, K., Zhang, X., Ren, S., et al.: Spatial pyramid pooling in deep convolutional networks for visual recognition. IEEE Trans. Pattern Anal. Mach. Intell. **37**(9), 1904–1916 (2015)
8. Girshick, R.: Fast R-CNN. In: Proceedings of the IEEE International Conference on Computer Vision, pp. 1440–1448 (2015)
9. Ren, S., He, K., Girshick, R., et al.: Faster R-CNN: towards real-time object detection with region proposal networks. In: Advances in Neural Information Processing Systems, pp. 91–99 (2015)
10. He, K., Gkioxari, G., Dollár, P., et al.: Mask R-CNN. In: Proceedings of the IEEE International Conference on Computer Vision, pp. 2961–2969 (2017)
11. Redmon, J., Divvala, S., Girshick, R., et al.: You only look once: Unified, real-time object detection. In: Proceedings of the IEEE Conference on Computer Vision and Pattern Recognition, pp. 779–788 (2016)
12. Redmon, J., Farhadi, A.: YOLO9000: better, faster, stronger. In: Proceedings of the IEEE Conference on Computer Vision and Pattern Recognition, pp. 7263–7271 (2017)
13. Henriques, J.F., Caseiro, R., Martins, P., et al.: High-speed tracking with kernelized correlation filters. IEEE Trans. Pattern Anal. Mach. Intell. **37**(3), 583–596 (2014)
14. Lukezic, A., Vojir, T., ˇCehovin Zajc, L., et al.: Discriminative correlation filter with channel and spatial reliability. In: Proceedings of the IEEE Conference on Computer Vision and Pattern Recognition, pp. 6309–6318 (2017)
15. Danelljan, M., Häger, G., Khan, F.S., et al.: Discriminative scale space tracking. IEEE Trans. Pattern Anal. Mach. Intell. **39**(8), 1561–1575 (2016)
16. Danelljan, M., Robinson, A., Shahbaz Khan, F., Felsberg, M.: Beyond correlation filters: learning continuous convolution operators for visual tracking. In: Leibe, B., Matas, J., Sebe, N., Welling, M. (eds.) ECCV 2016. LNCS, vol. 9909, pp. 472–488. Springer, Cham (2016). https://doi.org/10.1007/978-3-319-46454-1_29
17. Bewley, A., Ge, Z., Ott, L., et al.: Simple online and realtime tracking. In: 2016 IEEE International Conference on Image Processing (ICIP), pp. 3464–3468. IEEE (2016)
18. Wojke, N., Bewley, A.: Deep cosine metric learning for person re-identification. In: 2018 IEEE Winter Conference on Applications of Computer Vision (WACV), pp. 748–756. IEEE (2018)
19. Yu, F., Li, W., Li, Q., Liu, Yu., Shi, X., Yan, J.: POI: multiple object tracking with high performance detection and appearance feature. In: Hua, G., Jégou, H. (eds.) ECCV 2016. LNCS, vol. 9914, pp. 36–42. Springer, Cham (2016). https://doi.org/10.1007/978-3-319-48881-3_3
20. Shen, B.: Implementation of indoor human fall detection method based on video analysis. South China University of Technology (2013)
21. Wang, Y.: Research on detection technology of falling abnormal behavior in video surveillance system. Nanjing University of Posts and Telecommunications (2014)

Electric Bicycle Violation Automatic Detection in Unconstrained Scenarios

Zhao Qiu[1], Qiaoqiao Chen[1](✉), Xiangsheng Huang[2], and Xiaoquan Liang[1]

[1] Hainan University, Haikou 570100, Hainan, China
Chen.2323@foxmail.com

[2] Institute of Automation, Chinese Academy of Sciences, Beijing 100091, China

Abstract. Object detection technology develops rapidly and has broad application prospects. There are few relevant researches on the detection of electric bicycle violation. It is of great practical significance to apply the object detection technology to the detection of electric bicycle violation. The main violations of electric bicycle are not wearing safety helmet, not install license plate, overload and so on. Use YOLOv3 to train the datasets of riding electric bike, safety helmet and license plate to detect electric bicycle violations; The technology of chineseocr is used to identify the electric bicycle license plate number. The experiment proves that the method presented in this paper has a high detection accuracy for the objects of riding electric bike, safety helmet and license plate, but the recognition accuracy for license plate number is a little less.

Keywords: Electric bicycle · Violation detection · YOLOv3 · Object detection

1 Introduction

In recent years, the city traffic congestion and transportation costs continue to increase, electric bicycles have been favored by the majority of citizens. More and more electric bicycles have brought about some new problems, such as the citizens riding electric bicycles without wearing safety helmets, not installing license plates, overloading, and occupying motor vehicle lane and so on. Since July 2018, Haikou City Traffic Management Bureau began to focus on rectifying the problem of irregular riding of electric bicycles. Although the related issues can be significantly improved during the regulation, the related issues return after the supervision is lax. A large amount of manpower and material resources have been invested to control the problem of irregular riding of electric bicycles, and the effect is very limited.

As deep learning shines in the field of object detection, object detection technology has been applied more widely. It is of great practical significance to apply the object detection technology to the automatic detection of electric bicycle violation. It can not only save a lot of manpower and material resources, but also greatly improve the supervision efficiency of electric bicycle violation.

[1] designed a fast and accurate detection algorithm for automobile violations in the city, realizing the real-time warning of the violation behavior of the automobile.

H. Shen and Y. Sang (Eds.): PAAP 2019, CCIS 1163, pp. 168–174, 2020.
https://doi.org/10.1007/978-981-15-2767-8_16

The detection accuracy of the algorithm for the violation behavior was 93.92%. [2] proposed a new automobile license plate detection and recognition method based on the maximum extremal stable region and stroke width transformation, and the recognition accuracy of this method was 96.14%. [3] proposed a automobile license plate positioning and recognition algorithm based on SVM and BP neural network. The accuracy of this algorithm was 92.46%. [4] extracted human features to detect human body through directional gradient histogram, and then used color histogram to detect safety helmet. Then, the color histogram was used to detect the hard hat. Although there are a lot of researches on the detection of automobile violation, there are few literatures on the detection of electric bicycle violation.

Comparing the violation detection of automobile with electric bicycles, there are some differences. The violation detection of electric bicycles need to judge whether or not to wear safety helmets. Because electric bicycles are small and flexible, and the degree of regulation is not high, they are more complicated in actual detection and more occluded. The detection technology used in automobile violation detection is not well used for electric bicycle violation detection. At present, there are many challenges in the detection of electric bicycle violation. The installation position of the license plate is not fixed, and the installation direction is not uniform. The safety helmet is not worn on the head but is suspended on the vehicle. Some ordinary hats and safety helmets are similar, so it is not easy to distinguish. Vehicles and human bodies are seriously blocked, which may cause misjudgment of overload.

2 Related Technologies

Object detection is one of the core tasks in the field of computer vision. Its task is to identify the class and position of the objects in the picture. Object can appear anywhere in an image and vary in size and shape, which is the difficulty of object detection. Before 2012, object detection algorithms were mostly designed based on manual features, but due to the improvement of GPU performance, the development of distributed computing and the improvement of data volume, deep neural network became hot, and the traditional detection algorithm based on manual features was gradually replaced by the detection technology based on convolutional neural network.

YOLOv3 is a object detection algorithm based on convolutional neural network, which can predict the position, size, class and confidence of several objects in the image only through a single convolutional neural network. YOLOv3 is the third version of YOLO [5–7], further improving the speed and accuracy of object detection. YOLOv3 was similar to SSD [9] in the performance indicators of AP(average precision) on the coco [15] dataset, but was three times faster and had significant improvements in detecting small objects.

YOLOv3 mainly made improvements in bounding box prediction, class prediction, predictions across scales and feature extractor. Class prediction uses multiple label classifications, replacing the softmax function with multiple independent logical classifiers to calculate the likelihood that the input belongs to a specific label. Bounding box prediction uses logistic regression to predict the goal score of each bounding box. Multi-scale fusion prediction is carried out with three different scales based on the idea of FPN [8]. Replace darknet-19 with darknet-53 as feature extractor.

The technology of chineseocr realizes Chinese natural scene text detection and recognition based on YOLOv3, CTPN algorithm [10] and CRNN algorithm [11]. The main steps of text recognition are input image, preprocessing, text detection and text recognition. CTPN uses VGG [12], RPN and line text construction algorithm to detect the location of text information in the natural environment. The technology of chineseocr replaced the convolutional network with YOLOv3. CRNN is a kind of convolutional recurrent neural network structure, which is used to solve the problem of sequence recognition based on image, especially the problem of scene text recognition.

3 Violation Detection Process

Violation detection of electric bikes mainly includes no safety helmet, overload, no license plate in this paper. Firstly, detect the object of riding an electric bike for the input image, and crop the detected object in the picture to prepare for the subsequent detection. After that, detect the person, safety helmet and license plate on the cropped image, and count the number of detected people and safety helmets separately and cut the detected license plate. If the number of people on the electric bike was more than 2, it was overload. Compare the number of helmets and the number of people to see if everyone on the electric bike is wearing a helmet; If the license plate is not detected, the electric bicycle may not be registered. Finally, chineseocr technology was used to recognize the license plate number, including Chinese characters, English letters and Numbers on the license plate. The general flow of the automatic detection system for electric bicycle violation is shown in Fig. 1.

Fig. 1. Electric bicycle violation detection system. Our system mainly uses two technologies: (1) object detection with yolov3, (2) text recognition with the technology of chineseocr.

4 Experiment and Result Analysis

4.1 Dataset

For deep learning detection tasks, the experimental dataset is the basic condition. However, there is no available public dataset required for this experiment. Therefore, this paper has made a set of datasets. The process of making this dataset mainly includes three aspects: data collection, data preprocessing and data marking.

Data Collection. Datasets are collected from two main sources: most from pictures taken on streets and overpasses, and a small amount from pictures downloaded from the Internet.

Data Preprocessing. Data preprocessing mainly includes two parts: data cleaning and normalization. First, the data is cleaned to remove some photos that do not meet the requirements. Secondly, some pictures downloaded on the Internet are not in the JPG format required by the experiment, so the image format should be unified. In addition, the safety helmet downloaded from ImageNet [14] is labeled as XML format, which needs to be converted into the format of TXT required in this article. Finally, rename the images.

Label Each Object on Images From Dataset. During the construction of the data set in this paper, labelImg tool is used to mark the image. When manually operated, it is only necessary to mark each objects in the image, and the tool can automatically generate the corresponding mark configuration file.

4.2 Training

During the experiment, there were 5,944 pictures and 15,669 marks in the dataset "riding electric bicycles", among which 5,000 were used for training and 944 for testing. There are 5,672 pictures of safety helmets, among which 4,445 are self-made and 1,227 are downloaded from ImageNet. The self-made dataset of license plate has 4,535 pieces, and another 10,000 CCPD [13] datasets have been used.

Firstly, in the actual task of automatic detection of electric bicycle violation, the prior frame dimension calculated by YOLOv3 algorithm is not suitable for the actual detection scene. Therefore, use the k-means algorithm to conduct clustering analysis on the self-made dataset. Secondly, the weight parameters provided on YOLOv3 official website were used as the initialization parameters of network training, and YOLOv3 algorithm was used to train the riding electric bicycle, safety helmet and license plate dataset respectively, and the training stopped after the loss function became stable. Finally, test the weight-file obtained by training the datasets of riding an electric bike, safety helmet and license plate, and choose weights-file with the highest mAP (mean average precision) or IoU (intersect over union). Then use this weights for detection.

4.3 Detection

In unconstrained scenarios, riding electric bicycles are in all directions, the front, side, back, and the view angle taken in the overpass is overlooking. There are also different styles and colors of safety helmets. It is found that the safety helmet is not worn on the head but hung on the electric bike, and there are also cases where people wear ordinary hats instead of safety helmets, as shown in the red box in Fig. 2. License plate suspension can be divided into four types: only hanging in front of the electric bicycle, only hanging in the back of the electric bicycle, both in front and behind the electric bicycle, suspended in the side, as shown in the green box in Fig. 2.

Fig. 2. Examples of riding an electric vehicle, a safety helmet, and a license plate. (Color figure online)

The test set is used to test the selected weight file, and the precision (formula 1), recall (formula 2) and average precision (AP) of riding an electric bike (rideEBike), safety helmet and license plate (LP) are obtained. The details are shown in Table 1.

$$Precision = TP/(TP + FP) \tag{1}$$

$$Recall = TP/(TP + FN) \tag{2}$$

T/F: the result of prediction is true or false, P/N: the prediction is positive or negative. So, TP is the number of samples that are predicted to be positive, and the result is true; FP is the number of samples predicted to be positive but the result is false. FN is the number of samples predicted to be negative and the result to be false.

For a classifier, precision and recall tend to that one falls, another rises. So it is not scientific to use precision or recall alone to measure the performance of a model. In order to better evaluate the accuracy of a model, the average precision of a single class is proposed, that is, the area of Precision - Recall curve is taken as the measuring scale.

Table 1. Evaluation index results

	rideEBike (%)	Helmet (%)	LP (%)
Precision	84.43	96.09	92.85
Recall	95.72	91.98	94.09
AP	89.88	96.05	96.57

According to the statistics of the dataset, the rate of not wearing safety helmet was 64.29%, and the overloading rate was 1.97%. The unworn safety helmet rate detected by this system is 56.20%, and the overloading rate is 1.58%.

4.4 Recognition of License Plate Number

Electric bicycle license plate recognition has a lot of variables. There are various angles. Unlike motor vehicle license plate, motor vehicle license plate installation specifications, and requirements without shielding, but the installation of electric bicycle license plate by human factors is relatively large, there is no fixed installation area, and electric bicycle license plate is easy to be affected by external force to cause deformation. As shown in Fig. 3.

Fig. 3. An example of an electric bicycle license plate

Use chineseocr technology to recognize the license plate number of electric bicycle, and the recognition rate was 64.58%.

5 Conclusion

Along with the city traffic pressure, the electric bicycle with its convenience has obtained the general public's favor. The automatic detection of electric bicycle violation behavior is imperative, and the automatic detection system can effectively supervise the violation behavior. In this paper, YOLOv3 algorithm is used to detect riding an electric bike, license plate (LP) and safety helmet, and the plate number is recognized by the chineseocr technology, and finally the detection of electric bicycle violation is realized. The experiment proves that the method in this paper has high accuracy in detecting riding an electric bike, LP and safety helmet. For the problems of human body shielding and safety helmet suspension, the follow-up work needs to further improve the accuracy of detection.

Acknowledgment. This work is partially supported by Hainan Key R&D Program Projects (No. ZDYF2018017); Supported by Haikou Key Science and Technology Plan Project (No. 2017039); Supported by Hainan Natural Science Foundation Project (No. 618MS028); Supported by National Natural Science Foundation of China Project (No. 61573356).

References

1. Wu, Y., Xiong, Y., Wu, Y.: Detection of parking violation based on convolution neural network. Mod. Comput. (Prof. Ed.) (02), 22–27 (2018)
2. Wang, Y., Xie, G., Shen, X.: A new method of vehicle license plate detection and recognition based on MSER and SWT. Acta Metrol. Sin. **40**(01), 82–90 (2019)
3. Zeng, Q., Tan, B.: License plate recognition system based on SVM and BP neural network. Electron. Sci. Technol. **29**(01), 98–101 (2016)
4. Park, M.W., Palinginis, E., Brilakis, I.: Detection of construction workers in video frames for automatic initialization of vision trackers. In: 2012 Construction Research Congress (2012)
5. Redmon, J., Divvala, S., Girshick, R., et al.: You only look once: unified, real-time object detection (2015)
6. Redmon, J., Farhadi, A.: [IEEE 2017 IEEE Conference on Computer Vision and Pattern Recognition (CVPR) - Honolulu, HI (2017.7.21–2017.7.26)]. 2017 IEEE Conference on Computer Vision and Pattern Recognition (CVPR) - YOLO9000: Better, Faster, Stronger, pp. 6517–6525 (2017)
7. Redmon, J., Farhadi, A.: YOLOv3: an incremental improvement (2018)
8. Lin, T.Y., Dollár, P., Girshick, R., et al.: Feature pyramid networks for object detection (2016)
9. Liu, W., Anguelov, D., Erhan, D., et al.: SSD: single shot multibox detector (2015)
10. Tian, Z., Huang, W., He, T., He, P., Qiao, Y.: Detecting text in natural image with connectionist text proposal network. In: Leibe, B., Matas, J., Sebe, N., Welling, M. (eds.) ECCV 2016. LNCS, vol. 9912, pp. 56–72. Springer, Cham (2016). https://doi.org/10.1007/978-3-319-46484-8_4
11. Shi, B., Bai, X., Yao, C.: An end-to-end trainable neural network for image-based sequence recognition and its application to scene text recognition. IEEE Trans. Pattern Anal. Mach. Intell. **39**(11), 2298–2304 (2015)
12. Simonyan, K., Zisserman, A.: Very deep convolutional networks for large-scale image recognition. Comput. Sci. (2014)
13. Xu, Z., Yang, W., Meng, A., et al.: Towards end-to-end license plate detection and recognition: a large dataset and baseline. In: Proceedings of the 15th European Conference, Munich, Germany, Part XIII, 8–14 September 2018 (2018)
14. Russakovsky, O., Deng, J., Su, H., et al.: ImageNet large scale visual recognition challenge. Int. J. Comput. Vis. **115**(3), 211–252 (2015)
15. Lin, T.-Y., et al.: Microsoft COCO: common objects in context. In: Fleet, D., Pajdla, T., Schiele, B., Tuytelaars, T. (eds.) ECCV 2014. LNCS, vol. 8693, pp. 740–755. Springer, Cham (2014). https://doi.org/10.1007/978-3-319-10602-1_48

Building a Lightweight Container-Based Experimental Platform for HPC Education

Zelong Wang[1,2], Di Wu[1,2(✉)], Zhenxiao Luo[1,2], and Yunfei Du[1,3]

[1] School of Data and Computer Science, Sun Yat-sen University, Guangzhou, China
{wangzl7,luozhx6}@mail2.sysu.edu.cn, wudi27@mail.sysu.edu.cn
[2] Guangdong Key Laboratory of Big Data Analysis and Processing, Guangzhou 510006, China
[3] National Supercomputer Center in Guangzhou, Guangzhou, China
yunfei.du@nscc-gz.cn

Abstract. HPC (High Performance Computing) is of great significance due to its excellent performance in computing acceleration. However, unlike other techniques in computer science, learning HPC requires advanced computing resources such as large-scale clusters which directly increase the cost of study for students. To help students to learn HPC programming easily, we design and develop a lightweight container-based experimental platform to provide students with easily accessible and customizable HPC practice environments. In our platform, we integrate multiple practical functional modules for students, teachers, and administrators respectively. It is convenient for a user to access high-performance computing resources via a web portal, use highly customizable basic environments and have nice graphical hands-on interactive HPC learning experiences from our platform.

Keywords: High-performance computing · Container-based · Web-based experimental platform

1 Introduction

As an essential branch of computer science, high-performance computing (HPC) [7] can increase the speed of computation in large-scale computing in many important fields such as climate prediction, gene sequencing, and geoscience. In an era of big data, the demand for computational ability is becoming increasingly high which directly makes HPC become more and more popular in many emerging fields.

However, the number of HPC professionals is unable to satisfy such a growing demand which indicates the lack of high-quality educational resources for HPC learners [6]. The main reason is that the cost of HPC study is much higher than other techniques in computer science. Unlike theoretical computer science, the

H. Shen and Y. Sang (Eds.): PAAP 2019, CCIS 1163, pp. 175–183, 2020.
https://doi.org/10.1007/978-981-15-2767-8_17

study and research in high-performance computing need more hands-on practice. Therefore, for an education platform, it is of great significance to provide learners and researchers with diverse educational resources in the form of both theoretical knowledge and hands-on practice. Learners and researchers usually practice with their own computing devices for most small-scale practices, while they need large-scale high-performance computing clusters to execute and optimize parallel programs for HPC study. It's overburdened and unpractical for the vast majority of common users to purchase and set up their computing clusters to study HPC programming. Consequently, it is necessary to design and develop an HPC education platform for HPC learners which provides various accessible customizable educational resources so that users can enjoy a one-stop service during their studies.

There are lots of companies and institutions that provide HPC services in many different ways. As the main force that provides HPC resources, supercomputing centers usually offer users several interfaces to access HPC services. After the resource application is approved, users will receive their username and password to access the assigned virtual machine with dedicated VPN connection, set up specific environments, submit their programs as jobs and then wait for their results. However, such kind of large-scale systems are not suitable for HPC education because of the complexity of the supercomputing systems. Non-professional users need an easier and more convenient way to learn HPC knowledge and do hands-on practice. Therefore, an HPC education resource vendor should focus on how to provide users with easily accessible and customizable environments.

Infrastructure as a Service (IaaS) [2] is one of the most popular ways to provide cloud services because of its high customizability on basic hardware facilities. It meets the needs of teaching users how to set up the environment for HPC, while it is unable to provide fast set-up environments due to its high virtualization feature. In comparison, Docker, a lightweight container-based solution, is more suitable for fast HPC practice environment establishment. Unlike those classic virtualization techniques, Docker [9] manages containers with Docker Engine which can communicate with the host operating system directly for resource allocation instead of virtualizing the whole operating systems fundamentally. Therefore, Docker has a higher startup speed and a lower storage cost [12].

In this paper, we design and develop a container-based experimental platform for HPC education to provide users with easily accessible HPC container instances that can satisfy demands for both HPC environment configuration study and HPC programming study. By leveraging the fast-start feature of Docker and the cross-platform feature of the web portal, our platform integrates various HPC educational resources and fast-loaded HPC practical environments for students. Besides, we provide teachers with customizable experimental environments. Through this platform, teachers can offer preliminary practice environments for students. And students can do hands-on practice immediately with the environment the teacher presets. This platform effectively improves the teaching and the study of HPC-related courses.

The rest of this paper is organized as follows. In Sect. 2, we discuss some techniques related to Docker and remote connection. And the system design is presented in Sect. 3 followed by implementation in Sect. 4. In Sect. 5, we introduce the system deployment and demonstration, and finally, in Sect. 6, we conclude our works and discuss future work.

2 Major Techniques

2.1 Docker

As a new virtualization technique that arose in recent years, Docker has been widely recognized as a better solution for virtualization with its faster startup speed, lower cost, and better flexibility compared with classic virtualization techniques such as Hypervisor. Such a characteristic makes it suitable for fast HPC environment establishment.

Docker mainly consists of four components including Docker daemon, Docker container, Docker image, and Docker registry.

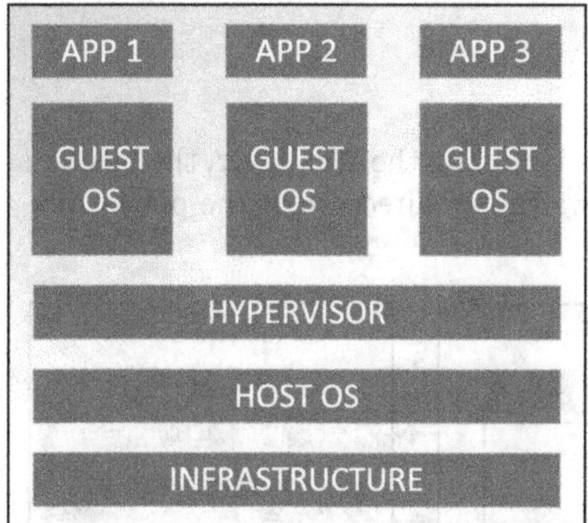

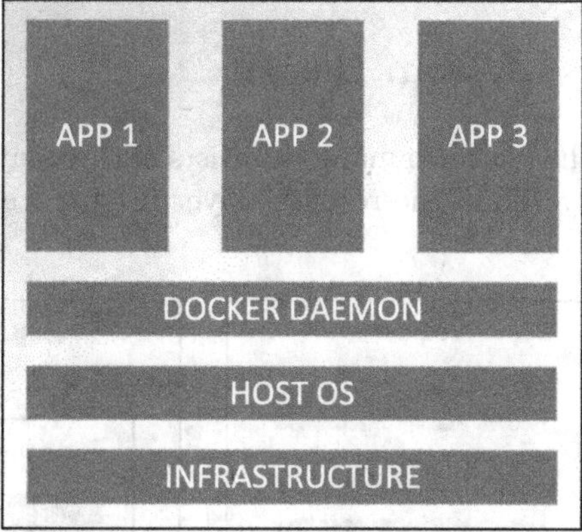

Fig. 1. The difference between classic virtualization technique (left) and Docker (right).

Docker Daemon. Docker Daemon runs on the host operating system as a background process and is used to manage the container. It collects the command sent by the user and performs corresponding operations.

Docker Container. Similar to a virtual machine, a Docker container possesses its own address space that is relatively isolated from other containers. They share the same OS kernel of the host instead of maintaining customized guest operating systems. They also share the resource of the host such as CPU, memory, and storage and can access the Internet through the host through NAT in default. Figure 1 clearly shows the difference between Docker and classic virtualization techniques.

Docker Image. Docker Image is used to create the corresponding Docker Container. The user is recommended to edit a Dockerfile to customize the image.

Docker Registry. Users can share their images by uploading images to public Docker repositories like Docker Hub or their private repositories.

2.2 Guacamole

Guacamole [1, 10] is a free and open-source software that is licensed under the Apache License, Version 2.0. It's based on HTML5 that enables the user to use a browser to access their containers through SSH [5], VNC [4] or RDP [3]. Guacamole is composed of Guacamole Client, Guacamole Server, and Guacd. Guacamole Client is a JavaScript Library. It is responsible for updating the screen content received from the server and drawing the content onto an HTML canvas. Guacamole Server is a Java-based Web server that can be regarded as a proxy for users to access their containers. Guacd is a C-based plugin that translates the protocol like SSH, VNC, and RDP into Guacamole's protocol.

3 System Design

The platform mainly consists of three layers including the Web layer, the business layer, and the resource layer. Figure 2 shows the architecture of the platform.

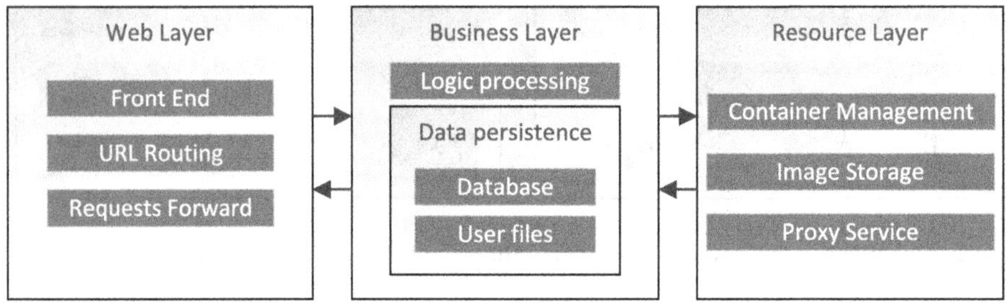

Fig. 2. The architecture of the platform.

The Web layer is responsible for providing front-end pages and forwarding requests. It verifies the validity of each request and forward the valid request to the corresponding view function according to the specified URL. The business layer is in charge of business logic processing and data persistence. And the resource layer manages the container and provides proxy service for the user to access the container. When the user chooses an experiment for the first time, he/she will get a special experiment page and there is a connection request that will be automatically sent to the business layer. After authenticating the identity of the user, the business layer will update related data and remind the resource layer to create a corresponding container resource. Then, a token will be returned to the user by which the browser will be able to access the container created before.

There are four modules in our platform including the user module, the experiment module, the administrator module, and the resource management module.

The user module is in charge of user registration, user login, and user information management. Every received request must be verified by the user module first if the business logic requires specific permissions. Users can also modify their personal information in the personal homepage.

The experiment module is mainly responsible for experiment content management. For teachers, they can create their experiment for students including creating several documents and setting up the basic environment for the experiment. Considering that the teacher may not be familiar with Dockerfile which is the key to customize a Docker image, we provide the teacher with a graphical remote desktop so that the teacher can configure the basic environment in a relatively simple manner. When completing the configuration, the teacher just needs to click the save button and the system will finish the rest of the work. For students, they can choose the experiment they are interested in and complete the experiment step by step.

The Webpage of the experiment module is composed of two parts namely the document part and the connection part. The document part displays the practice guide for users which is divided into several small study tasks. The user is asked to read the guide and finish the task by practicing it through the connection part. When a user logins, a connection request will be automatically sent, and if successful, several images of the desktop running in the container will be drawn on the canvas and updated in real-time. Besides, the user can use the clipboard, resolution selection, document hide, full screen and connection mode selection (VNC or SSH) in the toolbar to interact with the container more conveniently. The administrator module is designed for the administrator to manage the cluster. The administrator can get the information about every node including the running status, the network address and the number of the running containers. To further get the information about the specific container, the administrator can also visit the page that shows the list of the container in a specific node.

The resource management module mainly manages the container and provides the user with proxy service which separates from others and runs on a separate node. When receiving a request, the module will create a container and respond with a token. The browser will initiate a connection request and get connected if the request is valid. When the user closes the window or jumps to another page, the module will keep the container alive for several minutes considering that there may be an accidental disconnection.

4 System Implementation

All modules run on the same server except the resource management module. As Fig. 3 shows, the user module, experiment module, and administrator module are programmed into one Web server based on Flask and the resource management module provides a RESTful [11] interface which is also based on Flask [8]. Besides, it also provides the proxy service for the user based on Java Servlet that is used by Guacamole.

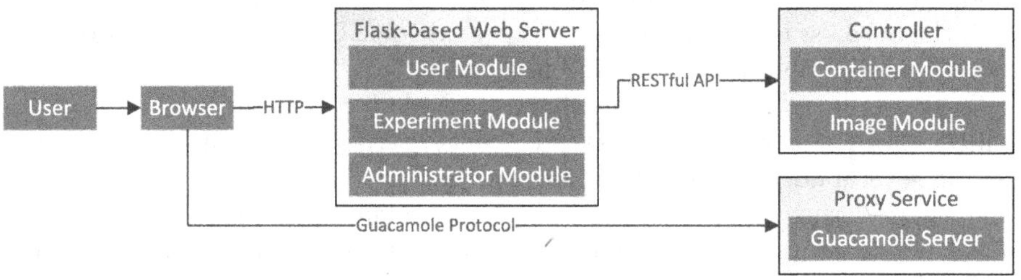

Fig. 3. The distribution of modules mentioned above.

When receiving a request from the experiment module, the module first verifies the validity of the request. If valid, it will extract the ID number of the user and the ID number of the experiment and check that if there is a container that belongs to the user. If not, the module will choose a node from the available nodes list according to specific rules to create a new container. If successful, the information on the container and the connection will be recorded. The ID number of the user, the network address of the container and the timestamp will be encrypted as a token for the following connection authentication. When the user receives the token, the browser will automatically initiate a connection request to the proxy server (programmed with the Guacamole server). After decryption and authentication, a connection will be established by the Guacamole and the user will get a desktop.

To provide different basic experimental environments for different experiments, the teacher is enabled to customize the Docker image. And to manage the Docker images, we deploy a private Docker repository and when the teacher finishes the customization, the image will be first uploaded and then distributed to all the available nodes automatically.

5 System Deployment and Evaluation

The platform is deployed in two parts that are the main business server and the resource management server. We use Nginx, Gunicorn, Supervisor, Flask, and MySQL to deploy the platform. For the resource management server, we use Flask as the logic process module and Java Servlet as the proxy module.

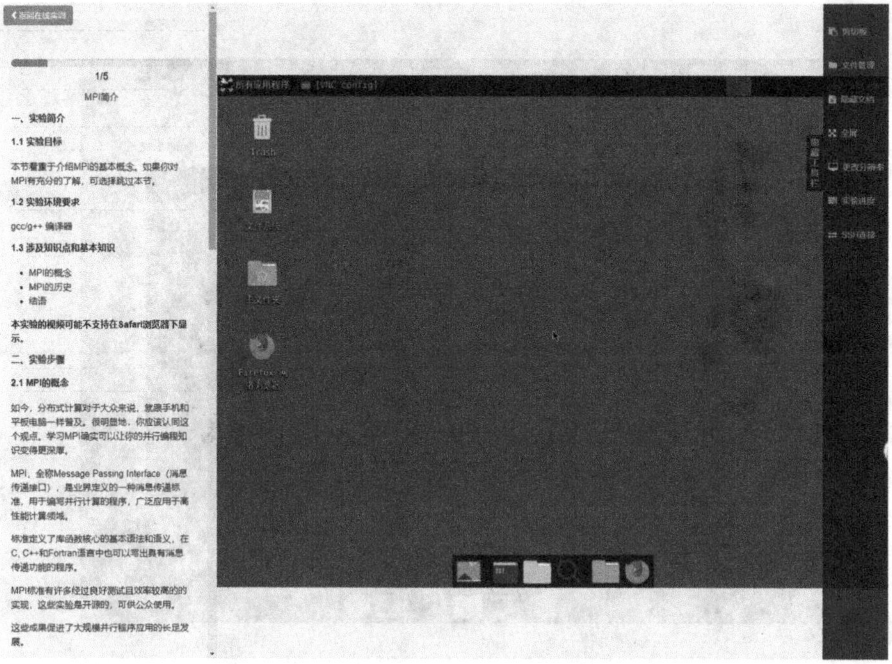

Fig. 4. The experiment page for students

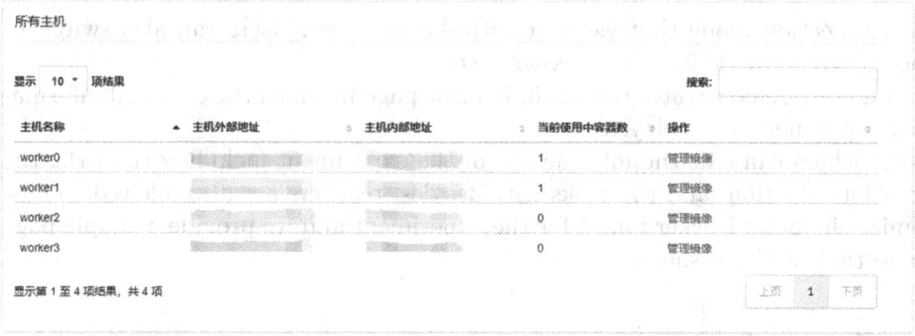

所有主机

显示 10 项结果 搜索:

主机名称	主机外部地址	主机内部地址	当前使用中容器数	操作
worker0			1	管理镜像
worker1			1	管理镜像
worker2			0	管理镜像
worker3			0	管理镜像

显示第 1 至 4 项结果，共 4 项 上页 1 下页

Fig. 5. The resource manage page for administrators

As to the Docker, we customize a basic image running at Ubuntu 18.04 in which a desktop based on Xfce4 is preinstalled. Besides, OpenSSH and VNC4SERVER are also preinstalled for different connection demands.

Figure 4 shows the experiment page of the platform. The left side of the page contains a simple knowledge point of the experiment. The right side of the page is an area for the remote desktop display. On the right side of the window, there is a toolbar for the user to choose the resolution, use the clipboard and change

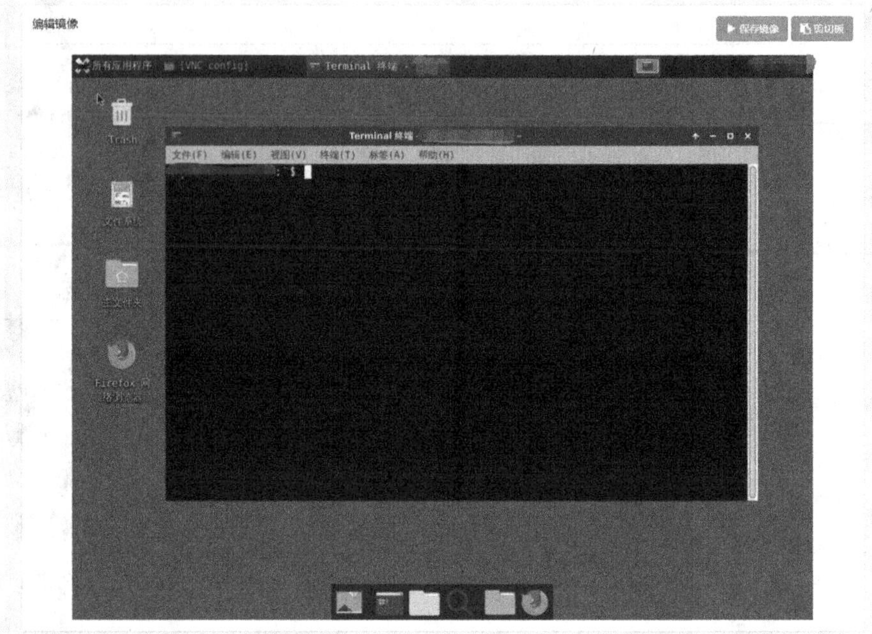

Fig. 6. The experimental environment customizing page for teachers

the connection mode that we have introduced above. Users can also switch to the fullscreen mode for better experiences.

Figure 5 demonstrates the administrator page in which the essential information of the node is displayed.

Teachers can edit the information of the experiment including the title, the brief introduction, and the tasks list. Besides, teachers are also allowed to customize the basic Docker image for the experiment and we provide a simple page to do that as Fig. 6 shows.

6 Conclusion

To meet the demand that the learner needs easily accessible HPC educational resource, we design and develop a container-based experimental platform for HPC education. Students can do hands-on practices step by step through graphical experimental environments with their browsers. Besides, we also provide the teacher and the administrator with customized management pages respectively. For teachers, we allow them to add teaching materials in the form of several tasks. And we also offer them the feature of customizing basic experimental environments. And for administrators, we provide them with a management page in which there is the information about the available nodes. To improve the current platform, we plan to support multi-node environments which satisfies the demand that users may need several resource nodes to practice. Moreover, we will add more contents to the platform for student users.

Acknowledgement. This work was supported by the National Key R&D Program of China under Grant 2018YFB0204100, Guangdong Special Support Program under Grant 2017TX04X148, the Fundamental Research Funds for the Central Universities under Grant 19LGZD37.

References

1. Apache guacamole. https://guacamole.apache.org/
2. Infrastructure as a service. https://en.wikipedia.org/wiki/Infrastructure_as_a_service
3. Remote desktop protocol. https://en.wikipedia.org/wiki/Remote_Desktop_Protocol
4. Virtual network computing. https://en.wikipedia.org/wiki/Virtual_Network_Computing
5. Barrett, D.J., Silverman, R.E., Byrnes, R.G.: SSH, The Secure Shell: The Definitive Guide: The Definitive Guide. O'Reilly Media Inc., Sebastopol (2005)
6. Basili, V.R., et al.: Understanding the high-performance-computing community: a software engineer's perspective. IEEE Softw. **25**(4), 29 (2008)
7. Dowd, K., Severance, C.: High performance computing (2010)
8. Grinberg, M.: Flask Web Development: Developing Web Applications with Python. O'Reilly Media Inc., Sebastopol (2018)
9. Merkel, D.: Docker: lightweight linux containers for consistent development and deployment. Linux J. **2014**(239), 2 (2014)
10. Mulfari, D., Celesti, A., Villari, M., Puliafito, A.: Using virtualization and guacamole/VNC to provide adaptive user interfaces to disabled people in cloud computing. In: 2013 IEEE 10th International Conference on Ubiquitous Intelligence and Computing and 2013 IEEE 10th International Conference on Autonomic and Trusted Computing, pp. 72–79. IEEE (2013)
11. Richardson, L., Ruby, S.: RESTful Web Services. O'Reilly Media Inc., Sebastopol (2008)
12. Soltesz, S., Pötzl, H., Fiuczynski, M.E., Bavier, A., Peterson, L.: Container-based operating system virtualization: a scalable, high-performance alternative to hypervisors. In: ACM SIGOPS Operating Systems Review, vol. 41, pp. 275–287. ACM (2007)

Automatic Generation and Assessment of Student Assignments for Parallel Programming Learning

Zhenxiao Luo[1,2], Zelong Wang[1,2], Di Wu[1,2](✉), Xiaojun Hei[3], and Yunfei Du[1,4]

[1] School of Data and Computer Science, Sun Yat-sen University, Guangzhou, China
{luozhx6,wangzl7}@mail2.sysu.edu.cn, wudi27@mail.sysu.edu.cn
[2] Guangdong Key Laboratory of Big Data Analysis and Processing, Guangzhou 510006, China
[3] School of Electronic Information and Communications, Huazhong University of Science and Technology, Wuhan, China
heixj@hust.edu.cn
[4] National Supercomputer Center in Guangzhou, Guangzhou, China
yunfei.du@nscc-gz.cn

Abstract. The course of parallel programming is becoming more and more important for the education of students majoring in computer science. However, it is not easy to learn parallel programming well due to its high theory and practice requirements. In this paper, we design and implement an automatic assignment generation and assessment system to help students learn parallel programming. The assignments can be generated according to user behaviors and thus able to guide students to learn parallel programming step by step. Besides, it can automatically generate an overall assessment of student assignments by using fuzzy string matching, which provides an approximate reference score of objective questions. Subjective questions can be assessed directly by comparing the answer to the reference answer. This system also provides a friendly user interface for students to complete online assignments and let teachers manage their question database. In our teaching practice, students can learn parallel programming more effectively with the help of such an assignment generation and assessment system.

Keywords: Parallel programming · Online education · Web application · Assignments generation · Assignments assessment

1 Introduction

As an important course in computer science, parallel computing can help to resolve many large-scale real-world problems such as galaxy formation, planetary movement, climate changes and so on [5]. Parallel programming uses more than one processor to perform computation at the same time. In a computation task, the instructions of a task may have a dependent relationship so we cannot simply

H. Shen and Y. Sang (Eds.): PAAP 2019, CCIS 1163, pp. 184–194, 2020.
https://doi.org/10.1007/978-981-15-2767-8_18

dispatch instructions to different processors. Now there are some programming models for parallel computing such as Pthreads [12], MPI [9], OpenMP [8], MapReduce [3], Spark [14] and so on.

In the learning process of a student, assignments allotted by teachers are based on the teaching progress because the teachers are familiar with the content of the course and the progress of the students [2]. However, it is a complex and redundant work for teachers to design the assignments each time. Besides, the assignments may be affected by the teacher's experience and habit. The assignments cannot well fit the requirements of different students. When teachers need to design a new assignment, reusing the previous work is inconvenient. The traditional management of questions and exams is low efficiency and cumbersome.

With the help of computer technology, some automatic assignment generation systems have appeared [6,13]. By using the online platform, students can do some practice in their spare time on computer and improve their knowledge skills [4,10]. As for teachers, they can make full use of digital technology to ease the burden of setting or correcting papers. Although those systems can generate tests from a question database, they can't generate a test for a specific user with high customization or set up a test paper with specific difficulty for the exam. What's more, the automatic assessment of assignments still needs more study [7]. Especially for subjective questions, it is hard to find a method to do the automatic assessment [1]. Most of the platforms don't provide the assessment of subjective questions and they just paste the reference answer to the user.

In this paper, we design and develop a system that can automate generation and assessment of student assignments based on user behaviors. This system is based on the Browser/Server mode which allows user to exploit the system by browser without installing any other client. Based on the user's past assessments, the system will dynamically adjust the difficulty of the automatically generated test paper so that the users can do practices most suited for them. Concerning teachers, the system can help them maintain a question database with a difficulty and content tag specified for each question. When a test paper is needed, the teacher can use the system automatically generate the test paper with given difficulty.

This paper is organized as follows. We first introduce the background and motivation in this section. We then give a system design in Sect. 2. In Sect. 3, we present our system implementation in detail. In Sect. 4, we show the deployment and evaluation of our system. At last, we conclude our works with a summary and point out the future work in Sect. 5.

2 System Design

The whole system contains four modules: the first one is a simple user manager, the second one is the student part which is responsible for automatic assignment generation, the third one is the teacher part which oversees the question database and the fourth one is the automatic assessment of assignments. There is a use diagram in Fig. 1 which shows the system architecture.

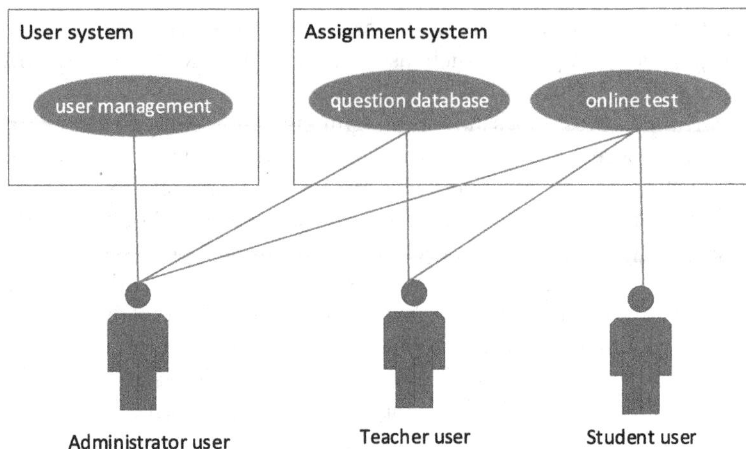

Fig. 1. Use case diagram

2.1 User Manager Module

Firstly, the system needs a simple authentication module for identity service. There are three types of users, namely, students, teachers, and administrators. As literally, a student is the user who can do the practice in the system and with no access authority to the questions management. The teacher user can not only do the practice like a student but also manage his or her question database. Administrator users can be viewed as a special teacher user who can manage all questions and user permission in the system because it is usually held by the system administrator.

When a user signs in, the user manager will query the database to determine which type of user is signing-in and then redirect the index to corresponding pages. In our design, the teacher user or administrator user will have an additional interface in the index after signing in, then they can enter the manage page and manager their questions and tag. The administrator user has an extra page to manage user permission that means it can review the teacher user applications or change user permission from student user to teacher user. In the register page, users should declare which type of account they want to register. If they want to register a teacher user, there is an additional process that is reviewed by the administrator user. As for the student users, they can use their accounts only after verifying their registration email.

2.2 Student Module

The main function of this module is assignments automatic generation. We provide two ways for student users to utilize the question database. Both approaches will provide a tag list for users to select the practice the user wants to do. After selecting a tag, the first choice is to answer all questions of the tag. There is nothing special because it just queries the database and selects all questions of this tag for the front end to render. The user selecting this option can do all the practices of this tag to improve the knowledge skills freely. It is a good way to learn the knowledge about this tag since it provides a relatively comprehensive knowledge test although it costs lots of time.

The second choice costs little time compared with the first one due to the system will only generate ten questions for the user based on user behaviors. The system will randomly select ten questions for the user for the first time. When the user finishes the ten questions, the system will provide a result analysis about this test apart from the assessment and reference answer. Meanwhile, the system will record the result of the user for the next assignments generation. If the user's grade is lower than a threshold, the difficulty of the next assignments will automatically decrease. In contrast, the difficulty will increase if the user's grade higher than the threshold. The user grade of this tag is calculated by the weighted average of the old grade and the new grade. The grade will update when the user finishes a test and be stored in the database for the next assignment generation. It provides a more targeted teaching for the reason that it will dynamically adjust the difficulty of the test according to the user's grade. As a result, the user does not meet the question which is meaningless due to it is too hard for them. When they grasp knowledge enough, the questions will become more difficult to help them learn a higher-level knowledge. It will remain some questions difficult enough to motivate the students to learn more knowledge.

2.3 Teacher Module

This part is responsible for the management of the question database. It provides an interface for a teacher user to add, modify and delete the tag or question. All teachers share a public tag library. If a tag is created, it will be visible for all teachers. Apart from the creator, the other teachers also can add some questions with this tag. When the tag is empty, there is no question with this tag, any teacher can delete this tag. But when the tag is not empty, it is not allowed to delete the tag in security considerations. The benefit of this design is that the questions can be grouped with the same knowledge point despite the questions are added by different teachers. It forms an easy way for students to find a specific kind of knowledge to do some practices and it is easy for administrator user to manage the question database. What is more, every question has its difficulty and one or more tags so that the system can generate the test paper based on that information.

The difficulty of the questions can be modified by teachers according to their needs. Every teacher can only manage his or her questions due to it can avoid some mistaken deletion made by another teacher. The system supports four kinds of questions, they are multiple-choice questions, true or false questions, fill in the blank questions, short answer questions. The answer to the multiple-choice questions can be one or more and it does affect the question structure. The true or false questions are the questions that need the user to determine the statement whether it is true. As for fill in the blank questions, those questions will leave some blanks in a statement and the student need to fill the blank of the statement. The last type of question is short answer questions which will ask the student a question directly and the student should answer the question in their understanding. It is believed that those four kinds of questions including most of the problems the student will meet. With such a plentiful question type, teachers can add the questions without obstacle.

2.4 Automatic Assessment Module

As mentioned above, the system supports multiple choice questions, true or false questions, fill in the blank questions and short answer questions. Four kinds of question all need an automatic assessment method. Those four kinds of questions can be divided into two types. They are objective questions and subjective questions. Objective questions have a standard answer without any dispute, so we can compare the student answer and the reference answer directly to determine whether the student answer is right. In contrast, subjective questions do not have a standard answer so that we cannot determine the student's answer like objective questions. Usually, the scoring method of objective questions is giving the scores by key points. In other words, if there are some keywords or key points which are in student's answer are the same as the reference answer, this student's answer can get some points. Therefore, we can use fuzzy string matching to approximate this process. It is reasonable that fuzzy string matching can provide us an approximate assessment of objective questions. Although it could be not accurate, but it is acceptable for us to provide a reference assessment automatically.

The choice questions, true or false questions, fill in the blank questions belong to subjective questions so we can simply use the reference answer to determine whether the user has submitted the correct answer. If the user's answer is completely correct, he can get all the point of this question, but he cannot get any point if his answer has any mistake. When it comes to short answer questions which belong to objective question, it is almost impossible for students to write an answer the same as the reference answer. That is why though there are some mistakes in the user's answer, he still can get some points of short answer questions. As for how many points he can get, it can be decided by the similarity between the user's answer and the reference answer through fuzzy string matching. Figure 2 is the flow chart of assignment assessment which represents this process clearly.

3 System Implementation

This section describes the database design of the question and the detailed implementation of the questions generation and assessment.

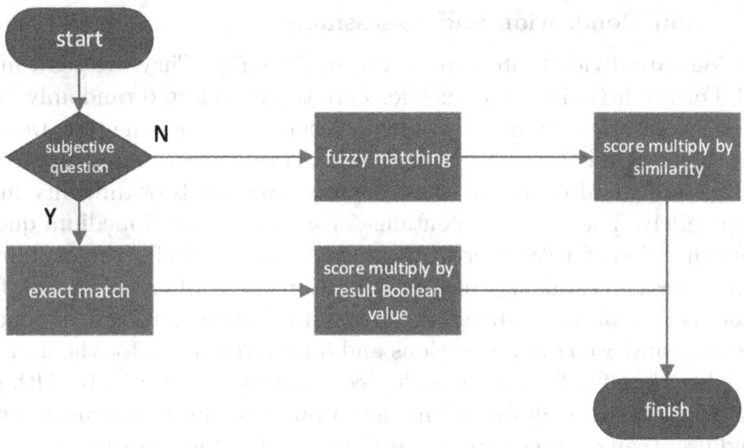

Fig. 2. Flow chart of assignment assessment

3.1 Design of Question Database

Although the four types of questions have some differences, we can make the four types of questions be a unified structure through some abstraction. It is necessary because if we don't do any process of the questions, there will be four redundancy tables in the database and it will bring some troubles when we need to operate all the questions. There are six fields in the tables. They are id, type, content, solution, analysis, and user_id.

The id field maintained by the database is the identity of the questions and is used to uniquely distinguish each question. In other words, the id is the primal key. The type filed is used for distinguishing the four kinds of questions. When it comes to content filed, thing becomes different. The multiple-choice questions have stem and options which is different from other question, so we use JSON format to store the question for multiple-choice questions. JSON are key-value pairs so it is proper to store the multiple-choice questions which may have different numbers of options. Another type of question just directly stores the question in this filed. As for the solution, multiple-choice questions use a semicolon as a separator and other questions store the solution as plaint text. All the questions store the question analysis in plaint text in the analysis filed without anything special. The last filed user_id is used for specifying which user is the owner of these questions and it was designed as a foreign key. With such a database design, we can manage the questions together which is beneficial to maintain and expand. For example, when a new kind of question is needed, it is easy to add the new type question with the content field in JSON format or plain text and after that what you need to do is just assigning a new number in the type filed.

3.2 Question Generation and Assessment

The questions are divided into three levels of difficulty. They are easy, medium and hard. For the first time, the questions are totally selected randomly because we have no information about the student. When he finishes the test, we can get a score of the test and the next test will be generated according to the score. As an early version, we also divided the test into three levels of difficulty in order to develop agilely. The easy test contains 5 easy questions, 3 medium questions and 2 hard questions for the user whose score below 70. As for the medium test, it contains 2 easy questions, 5 medium questions and 3 hard questions for the user whose score is between 70 and 90. When it comes to hard test, it contains 2 easy questions and 3 medium questions and 5 hard questions for the user whose score is higher than 90. Figure 3 has showed this process intuitively. Although it is quite simple, it is enough for a demonstration. This division forms a difficulty ladder and users can contact harder questions step by step according to the guide of the system.

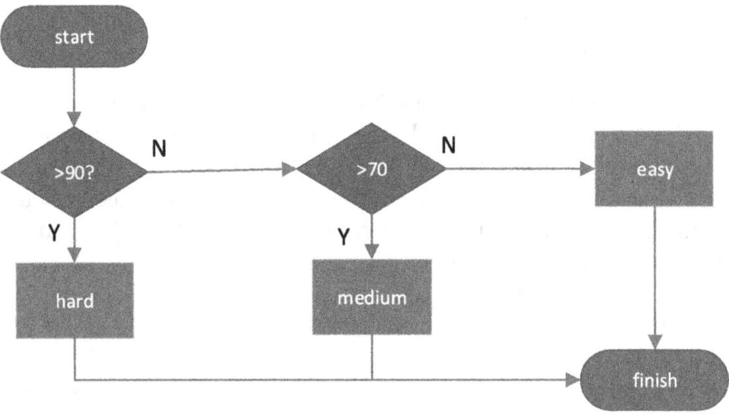

Fig. 3. Flow chart of assignment generation

The score update method is important about the question generation because it directly associates with the difficulty of the test. Therefore, the new average score is the sum of half of the old average score and half of the new test score. It is effective to combine the historical data and the newly collected data so that the average score can represent the user's knowledge level. The assessment of multiple-choice questions, true or false questions, fill in the blank questions are nothing special as mention. It just compares the user's answer and the reference answer in the database and get all point of the question if the answers are totally same with reference answer. As for the assessment of short answer questions, we use fuzzy string matching to get an approximate assessment. There is a Python library named Fuzzywuzzy [11] which can provide an implementation of fuzzy string matching so we adopt the library as the tools of assessment of short answer questions.

4 System Deployment and Evaluation

This section mainly focuses on system deployment and the demonstration of the system.

The system uses a classical python web application deployment which mainly contains the following tools: Nginx + Gunicorn + Supervisor + MySQL. The Nginx is used as a reverse proxy and it sends the HTTP requests to the WSGI server Gunicorn. The supervisor is a process management tool that can ensure the process is working properly. If the process is timeout, Supervisor will restart the process automatically. MySQL is an opensource database and we use it to achieve data persistence. What's more, we deploy the system in Ubuntu 18.04 LTS and it has no requirements for the operating system because the deployment tools are available in both Windows or Linux. Figure 4 is the performance test results of our system with a 4-core machine.

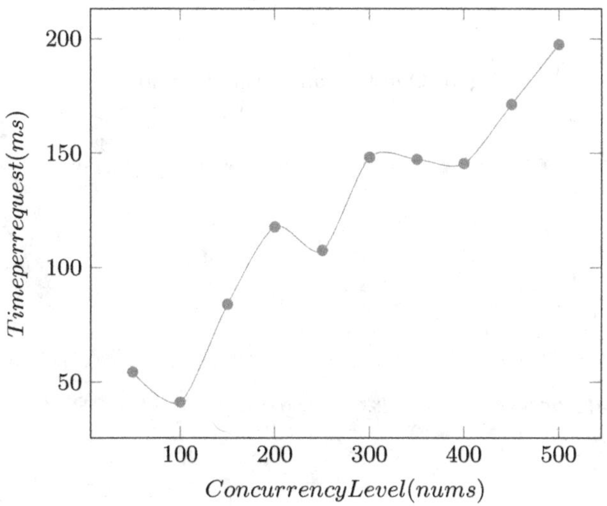

Fig. 4. Performance test

The following part is a demonstration of the system.

Figure 5 is the page which is used to answer the questions for the students. As the figure has shown, the top of the page is a process bar which indicates the finished question number and total question number. The main answer area is in the center. In the right, it is a timer and an index of the question which record the time spent and the question has been answered.

Figure 6 is the assessment page of the test. In the center, there is a statistical table for this test. In the right side, there is a radar chart and the question index with the result. The radar chart can represent the result of this test intuitively and help the user to understand the situation of this test. The index card in red indicates the user's answer is wrong and it means that the user's answer is right

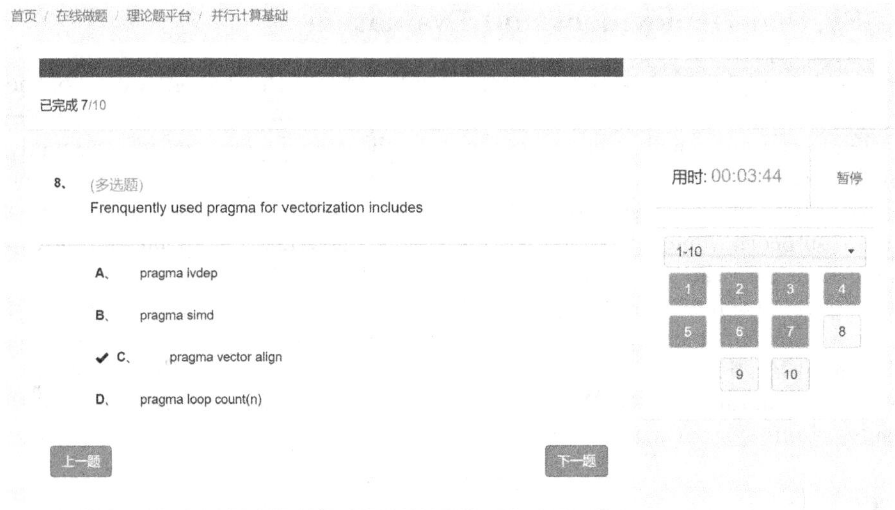

Fig. 5. Question answering function

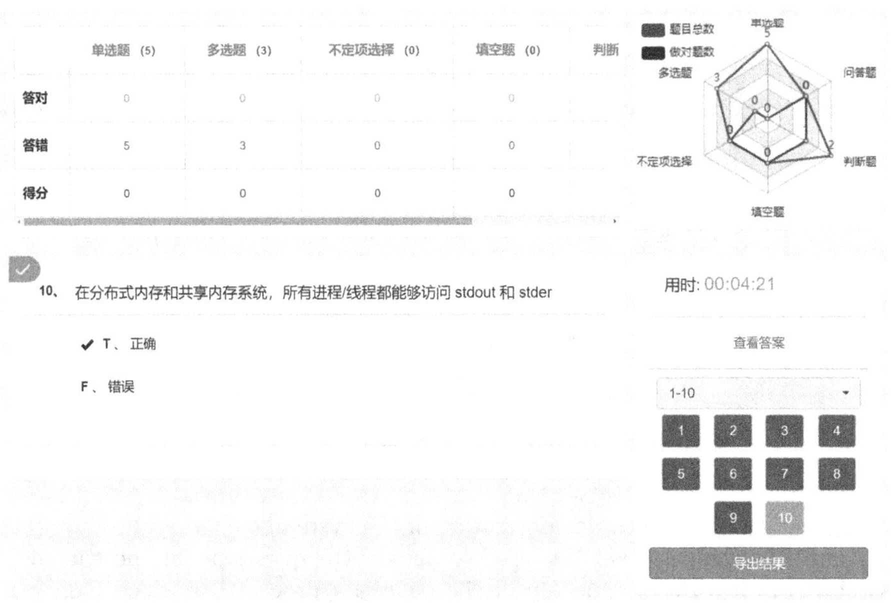

Fig. 6. Question assessment function

when it in green. Besides, there is an export result button which can download the test question with the reference answer and the user's answer after clicking it.

Fig. 7. Question editing function

Figure 7 is the multiple-choice question edit page of the teacher part. First, it can select a tag for this question in the beginning and then it is the edit area of the stem and options. You can not only add or delete the options freely but also select any number of options as the answer in your need. At last, you can add some answer analysis of this question to explain why we should choose those options.

5 Conclusion

This paper proposes an automatic generation and assessment of student assignments system with Browser/Server mode to help student learn parallel programming learning. This system can be divided into three parts, they are user management part which is used for user authentication, student part which is responsible for the assignments automatic generation and assessment, the teacher part whose main function is management of question database. The system provides a friendly user interface for students to do the assignments online and teacher to manage the question database. Besides, the assignments will be generated automatically based on the user behaviors to adapt to different levels of users. We adopt fuzzy string matching to approximate the correct of objective question and do automatic assessment of them. In the future, we will try to add more generation strategy with recommendation algorithm and consider to use some machine learning methods to assess the assignments.

Acknowledgement. This work was supported by the National Key R&D Program of China under Grant 2018YFB0204100, Guangdong Special Support Program under Grant 2017TX04X148, the Fundamental Research Funds for the Central Universities under Grant 19LGZD37.

References

1. de Assis Zampirolli, F., Batista, V.R., Quilici-Gonzalez, J.A.: An automatic generator and corrector of multiple choice tests with random answer keys. In: 2016 IEEE Frontiers in Education Conference (FIE), pp. 1–8. IEEE (2016)
2. Burch, K.J., Kuo, Y.J.: Traditional vs. online homework in college algebra. Math. Comput. Educ. **44**(1), 53–63 (2010)
3. Dean, J., Ghemawat, S.: MapReduce: simplified data processing on large clusters. Commun. ACM **51**(1), 107–113 (2008)
4. Doorn, D.J., Janssen, S., O'Brien, M.: Student attitudes and approaches to online homework. Int. J. Scholarsh. Teach. Learn. **4**(1), n1 (2010)
5. Eijkhout, V.: Introduction to High Performance Scientific Computing. Lulu. com (2013)
6. Liberatore, M.W.: Improved student achievement using personalized online homework. Chem. Eng. Educ. **45**(3), 184–190 (2011)
7. Liu, O.L., Rios, J.A., Heilman, M., Gerard, L., Linn, M.C.: Validation of automated scoring of science assessments. J. Res. Sci. Teach. **53**(2), 215–233 (2016)
8. OpenMP: The OpenMP API specification for parallel programming (2019). https://www.openmp.org/
9. OpenMPI: Open source high performance computing (2019). https://www.open-mpi.org/
10. Richards-Babb, M., Drelick, J., Henry, Z., Robertson-Honecker, J.: Online homework, help or hindrance? What students think and how they perform. J. Coll. Sci. Teach. **40**(4), 81–93 (2011)
11. Seatgeek: Fuzzywuzzy (2019). https://github.com/seatgeek/fuzzywuzzy
12. Wikipedia: Posix threads (2019). https://en.wikipedia.org/wiki/POSIX_Threads
13. Williamson, D.M., Xi, X., Breyer, F.J.: A framework for evaluation and use of automated scoring. Educ. Measur.: Issues Pract. **31**(1), 2–13 (2012)
14. Zaharia, M., Chowdhury, M., Franklin, M.J., Shenker, S., Stoica, I.: Spark: cluster computing with working sets. HotCloud **10**(10–10), 95 (2010)

HSM^2: A Hybrid and Scalable Metadata Management Method in Distributed File Systems

Yiduo Wang[1], Youxu Chen[1], Xinyang Shao[1], Jinzhong Chen[2], Liu Yuan[3], and Yinlong Xu[1(✉)]

[1] School of Computer Science and Technology, University of Science and Technology of China, AnHui Province Key Laboratory of High Performance Computing, Hefei, China
{duo,cyx1227,sxy799}@mail.ustc.edu.cn, ylxu@ustc.edu.cn

[2] East China Research Institute of Electronic Engineering, Hefei, China
chenjin_zhong@126.com

[3] China Academy of Electronics and Information Technology, Beijing, China
lyuan@csdslab.net

Abstract. In the bigdata era, metadata performance is critical in modern distributed file systems. Traditionally, the metadata management strategies like the subtree partitioning method focus on keeping namespace locality, while the other ones like the hash-based mapping method aim to offer good load balance. Nevertheless, none of these methods achieve the two desirable properties simultaneously. To close this gap, in this paper, we propose a novel metadata management scheme, HSM^2, which combines the subtree partitioning and hash-based mapping method together. We implemented HSM^2 in CephFS, a widely deployed distributed file systems, and conducted a comprehensive set of metadata-intensive experiments. Experimental results show that HSM^2 can achieve better namespace locality and load balance simultaneously. Compared with CephFS, HSM^2 can reduce the completion time by 70% and achieve 3.9× overall throughput speedup for a file-scanning workload.

Keywords: Metadata management · Distributed file systems · Namespace locality · Load balance

1 Introduction

Distributed file systems (DFS) like GFS [10], HDFS [24], Ceph [27] and Lustre [22] have intensively adopted when building highly scalable and reliable Internet services in data centers. As shown in Fig. 1, the metadata and data of DFS are managed by two sets of independent and separated servers, namely, metadata servers (MDS) and data servers. When accessing a file, a client should first fetch the file metadata from MDS to understand the layout and data location, and check the permission. Then, if the file exists and the permission check succeeds, she can read or write data content by directly interacting with data servers.

H. Shen and Y. Sang (Eds.): PAAP 2019, CCIS 1163, pp. 195–206, 2020.
https://doi.org/10.1007/978-981-15-2767-8_19

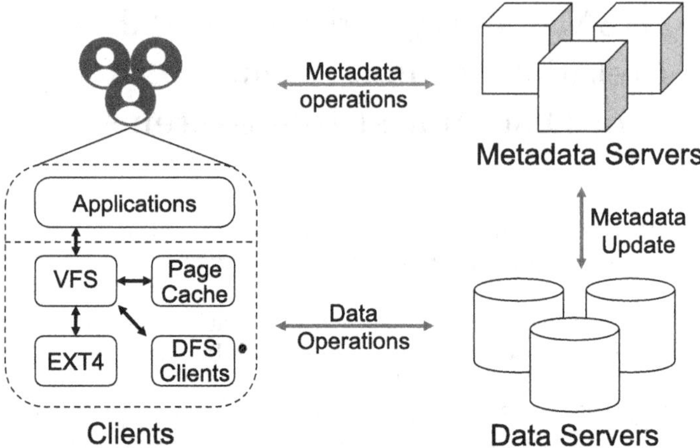

Fig. 1. The architecture of distributed file systems.

In the big data era, small files are dominating the whole file space. For instance, some studies suggest that the mean file size is around hundreds of kilobytes or smaller [4,5,8,11,32]. In addition, compared to the data operations, the metadata operations in file systems are also popular and even account for more than 50% in the overall file system operations [1,3,13,20]. These two trends introduce the design of DFS two challenges. First, the metadata service must host a huge amount of metadata information. Second, it also has to support high-performance metadata accesses.

To scale out the metadata service, more than one metadata server will be deployed to jointly host metadata and balance the workload received from clients. When designing such a metadata service, we should consider three key problems, which are the metadata partitioning, metadata indexing, and load balance strategy, respectively. Subtree partitioning is a traditional method to distribute metadata of files across multiple metadata servers at the subtree or directory granularity. The benefit of this strategy is to keep better namespace or directory locality, as the metadata of a directory and files in that directory will co-locate in the same metadata server. In addition to the subtree partitioning method, another alternative metadata management method, hash-based mapping, organizes the directories and files as a flat structure rather than a hierarchical structure. In detail, the hash-based method partitions and distributes the metadata by computing hash values of the paths or names of files and directories. Due to the randomness of hashing functions, the hash-based mapping achieves better load balance among metadata servers, compared to the subtree-based method. However, the hash-based method sacrifices the directory locality, because the metadata of files in the same directory might be placed on different metadata servers. In summary, the two traditional metadata management methods cannot achieve good spatial locality and load balance simultaneously.

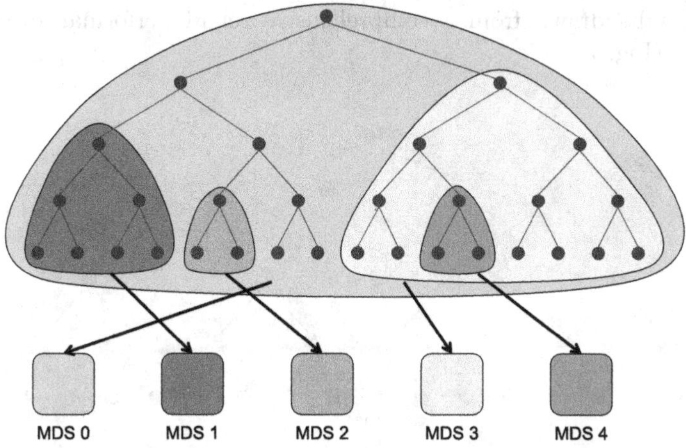

Fig. 2. Subtree partitioning metadata management.

The close the gap between maintaining good namespace locality and achieving good load balance, in this paper, we propose a hybrid metadata management method, HSM^2, which partitions metadata and balances workloads via combining both the subtree partitioning method and the hash-based mapping method. In short, this hybrid method applies different policies for namespaces at the different levels of the whole file system metadata hierarchy. For instance, with regard to directories at the lower-level of the namespace, HSM^2 will ensure their metadata integrity and keep the metadata of files under such a directory reside in the same metadata server, to keep better namespace locality. In contrast, regarding directories at the higher level of the namespace, HSM^2 adopts the hash-based mapping to randomly distribute the metadata of different directories across multiple metadata servers. To demonstrate the benefits of such a design, we implemented HSM^2 in CephFS, a widely deployed distributed file system. We conducted a comprehensive set of metadata-intensive experiments. Experimental results show that HSM^2 can achieve better namespace locality and load balance simultaneously. Compared with CephFS, HSM^2 can reduce the completion time by 70% and achieve 3.9× overall throughput speedup for a file-scanning workload.

The rest of the paper is organized as follows. We describe the background and motivation of our work in Sect. 2. Then we sketch the design and implementation details of HSM^2 in Sect. 3. In Sect. 4, we report the performance evaluation results. Finally, we conclude in Sect. 5.

2 Background and Motivation

In this section, we first introduce the two traditional metadata management methods in distributed file systems. Then we present the motivation of our work based on results drawn from a comprehensive set of performance evaluation experiments (Fig. 3).

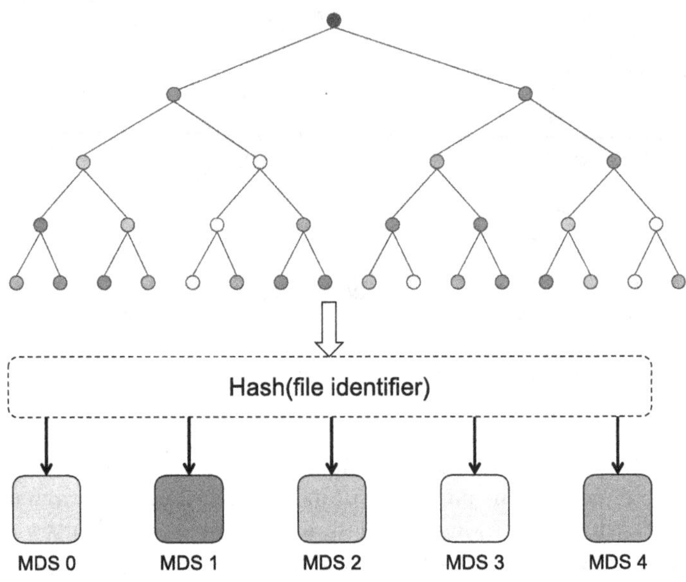

Fig. 3. Hash-based mapping metadata management.

2.1 Metadata Management Methods

Subtree Partitioning. This method splits the file system directory tree or namespace into many subtrees, as Fig. 2 shows, and then assigns subtrees to specific targeted MDS. Each MDS manages a set of subtrees. Because the metadata belongs to the same directory is assigned to the same MDS, the subtree partitioning method maintains good namespace locality. In addition, there are two variants of the subtree partitioning method, which are static and dynamic partitioning methods respectively. With regard to the static subtree partitioning method, the namespace is partitioned manually by the system administrator, like NFS [18], Sprite [17], AFS [16], Coda [21], CIFS [12] and PanFS [2]. When the system workload changes dynamically, however, this static partitioning method could introduce a load imbalance problem. To address this problem, CephFS [27] proposes a dynamic subtree partitioning method to adjust the subtree splitting granularity and migrate the metadata across MDS cluster adaptively according to the real-time workloads. But due to the variance in subtree sizes and real-time workloads, it is also challenging for this method to keep the metadata servers load-balanced.

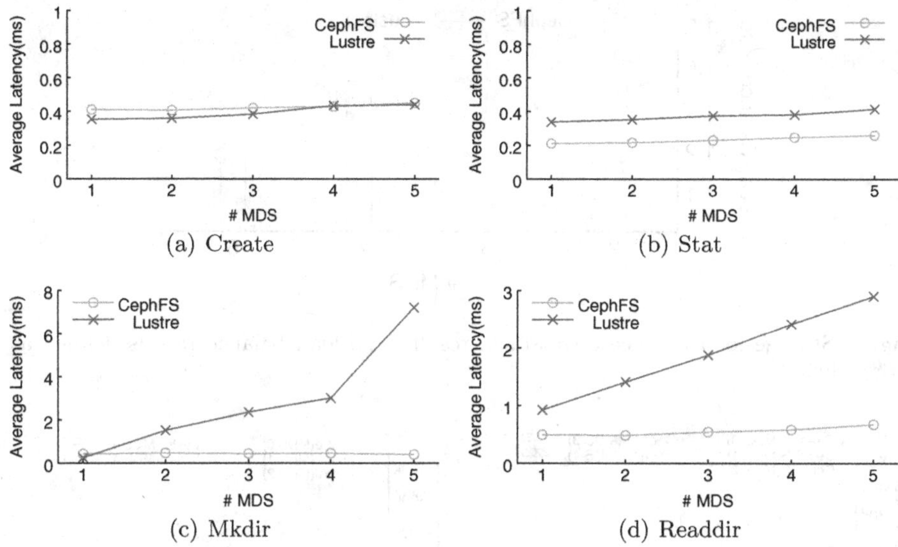

Fig. 4. File and directory metadata performance comparison under subtree partitioning and hash-based mapping metadata management methods.

Hash-Based Mapping. Unlike the subtree partitioning method, the hash-based mapping management strategy distributes the metadata according to the hash value of the unique file identifiers (i.e., file pathname or inode number). This method has been deployed in many file systems such as Vesta [9], RAMA [15], zFS [19], Lazy Hybrid [31], CalvinFS [26], SkyFS [30], Intermezzo [7], ShardFS [29], Lustre [6], and LocoFS [14]. This management method converts the file system directory tree structure into a flat namespace, thus destroying the namespace locality, despite evenly balancing workloads across metadata servers. For example, reading a directory content may need a significant number of communications between multiple metadata servers.

Next, we explore the benefits and flip-sides of both methods via running a few experiments and analyzing their results.

2.2 Namespace Locality vs. Load Balance

To understand the difference between the subtree partitioning and hash-based mapping metadata management methods deeply, we conduct a comprehensive set of experiments to evaluate the overall file/directory metadata performance and the load balance factors across multiple metadata servers. For this set of experiments, we use a popular and widely used file system benchmark, Filebench [25], to generate the metadata-intensive workload (e.g., create and stat files, create and traverse directories). The distributed file systems that we evaluate are CephFS [28] and Lustre [6], respectively, since CephFS uses the subtree partitioning method, while Lustre adopts the hash-based mapping method.

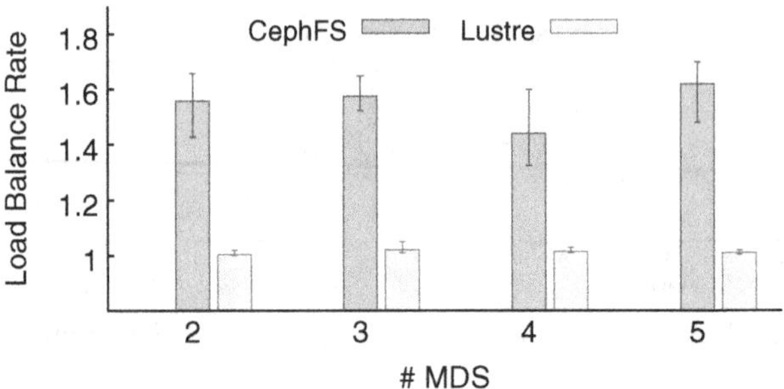

Fig. 5. Storage load balance comparison result. The load balance rate is defined as $\frac{load_{max}}{load_{avg}}$ [23].

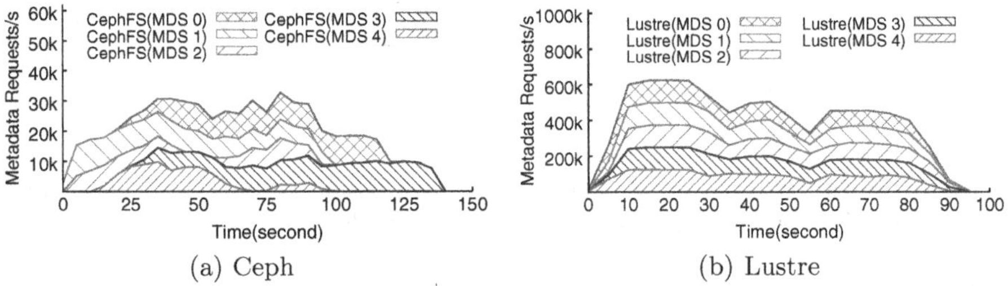

(a) Ceph (b) Lustre

Fig. 6. Workload load balance comparison result.

Namespace Locality. Figure 4 summarizes the latency results about different metadata operations achieved by two different metadata management methods. First, as shown in Fig. 4(a), for the `create` operation, the subtree partitioning method offers similar latency numbers as the hash-based mapping one. This is because this operation only contacts a single MDS. As a result, the metadata access latency of the `create` operation remains constant when the MDS cluster becomes larger. In contrast, for directory metadata operations, the subtree partitioning method performs better than the hash-based mapping method. For example, as depicted in Fig. 4(d), reading whole directory content only needs 1ms by the subtree partitioning method when deploying 5 MDS. However, with the same setup, the hash-based mapping method needs almost 5 ms. This is because, within the subtree partitioning method, the `readdir` operations only contact a single MDS, while the hash-based mapping method may have to traverse the file metadata from all 5 MDS. Consequently, the subtree partitioning method offers better namespace locality than the hash-based mapping one.

Load Balance. In addition to namespace locality, we also evaluate the storage and workload load balance performance. For this set of experiments, we run a file creation workloads via Filebench. Figures 5 and 6 (stacked presentation) show that compared to the load balance factor of the hash-based mapping method

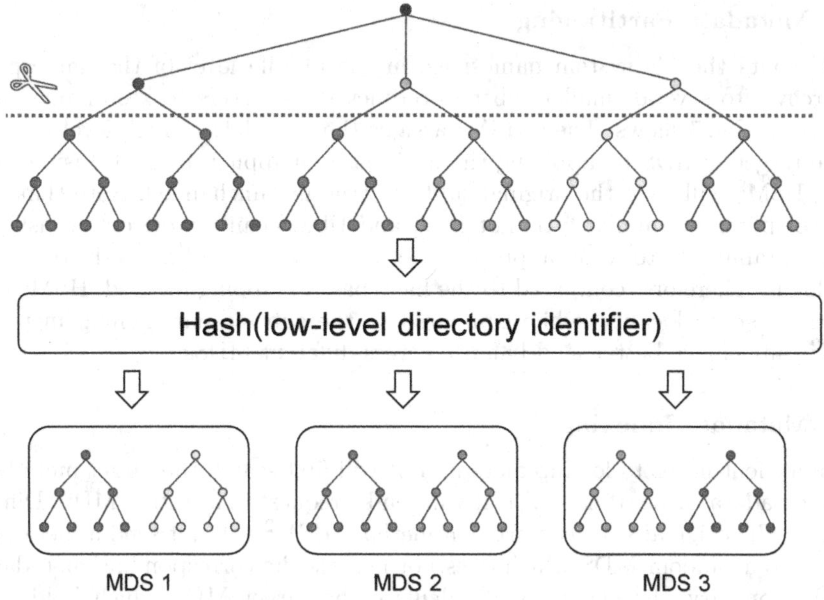

Fig. 7. HSM^2 metadata partitioning method.

outperforms the subtree partitioning method. For example, as shown in Fig. 6, the workloads were distributed evenly across 5 MDS by the hash-based mapping. However, this is not applied to the subtree partitioning method. This reason is as follows: When more workloads arrive, the migration process in the subtree partitioning method has been triggered. However, this migration does not balance well the load to all MDS, due to the complex load balance policy and metadata migration mechanism.

From these experiment results, we observe that the subtree partitioning method and hash-based mapping method cannot achieve namespace locality and load balance simultaneously. Therefore, designing an efficient metadata management method to close the gap between namespace locality and load balance is critical and challenging.

3 HSM^2

Based on the above observations and reconsideration on metadata server cluster architecture in Sect. 2, we propose an efficient metadata management method, HSM^2 to make an effective tradeoff between namespace locality and load balance. We redesign and replace the metadata management module of Ceph, using HSM^2 to determine the MDS to place instead of the original subtree partitioning method. In this section, we first introduce the metadata distribution and indexing methods, then discuss the load balance and scaling strategy.

3.1 Metadata Partitioning

HSM^2 splits the file system namespace in the middle level of the namespace hierarchy into several smaller subtrees on metadata servers to keep namespace locality, as Fig. 7 shows. Then, HSM^2 assigns the metadata of high-level subtree to the targeted MDS by applying the hash-based mapping method. Inside each MDS, HSM^2 will keep the original subtree structure unchanged. Note that the subtree splitting granularity is not fixed and HSM^2 can adaptively adjust the subtree granularity to select appropriate subtree sizes, according to the dynamic workloads. Therefore, compared to the hash-based mapping method, HSM^2 can keep namespace locality, while compared to the subtree partitioning method, HSM^2 can achieve better load balance across different MDSs.

3.2 Metadata Indexing

When a client needs to lookup metadata, it will first search the target metadata in its metadata cache. If not exist, it will send a request to a certain MDS. Different from the original subtree partition method, HSM^2 will not send a metadata request to a random MDS which does not possess the corresponding metadata. On the contrary, the client could calculate the target MDS which holds the requested metadata of the corresponding directory through a deterministic hash algorithm. By this method, unnecessary forwarding requests can be efficiently reduced. Once MDS receives the metadata request, it first checks whether the corresponding subtree of the target file already exists in the cache, and read the metadata into the cache if the check fails. Then MDS will respond to the client's request with the expected metadata.

3.3 Load Balance

For the traditional subtree partitioning method, keeping good load balance is a difficult problem to solve. In recent years, a few metadata migration methods have been proposed, but the improvement is not guaranteed. HSM^2 successfully avoids this heavy overhead because the partition method offers good load balance without sacrificing namespace locality.

3.4 Downsides

Due to splitting of subtree, the namespace locality in this level will be destroyed by HSM^2. Nevertheless, compared with hash-based mapping methods, HSM^2 successfully controlled the damage to locality to an acceptable extent. Considering the huge benefits that HSM^2 brings, we think it worthwhile.

4 Evaluation

4.1 Experiment Setup

We implement HSM^2 and integrate it with CephFS. We conduct experiments on 10 Sungon I60-G20 servers. Each server has two Intel (R) Xeon (R) E5-2650 V4

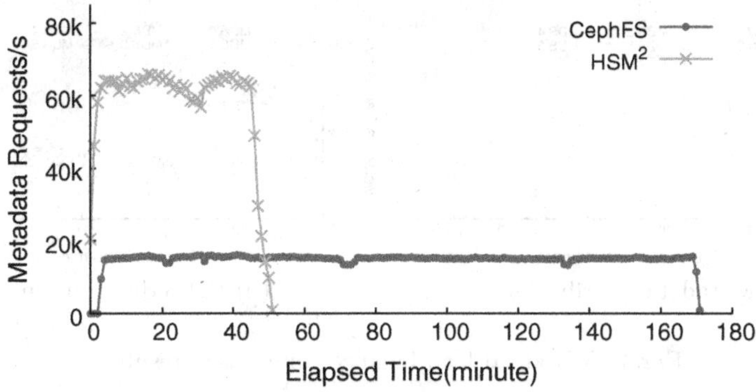

Fig. 8. The overall throughput with elapsed time.

CPUs, 64 GB 2133 MHz DDR4 memory space and 12 1TB HDDs. The operating system is CentOS 7 and kernel is Linux 3.10.0-957.1.3.el7.x86_64. All servers are connected by 56 Gbps Infiniband network and the communication protocol is IPoIB. We deploy a metadata server cluster on 2 separated nodes and each of which deploys multiple MDSs. We also deploy a data server cluster on another 3 physical nodes, each of which runs 2 data servers. The remaining 5 nodes are used to deploy clients, which issue metadata requests.

We generate a directory-scanning workload in which 100 clients perform directory traversing operations on a shared dataset which consists of 10,000 directories and almost 1.2 Million files in total, to evaluate CephFS and HSM^2 metadata performance.

4.2 Experimental Results

Figure 8 shows the system overall throughput of Ceph and HSM^2 with elapsed time respectively. According to the result, we find that traversing all directory content needs almost 175 min in CephFS. But HSM^2 only needs around 53 min and can reduce the completion time by 70% compared to CephFS. Besides, HSM^2 achieves 3.9× overall throughput speedup compared to the original CephFS. Furthermore, HSM^2 can handle 57k metadata requests per second on average, but the overall throughput of CephFS is only around 14.4k.

The second primary focus of this evaluation is to understand the load balance achieved by the new design. To this end, we collect the metadata and workload distribution on each MDS as time evolves, for both CephFS and HSM^2. Figure 9 represents the metadata distribution and IOPS distribution results on each MDS per second in HSM^2. Due to the high-level hash-based mapping method implemented in HSM^2, as illustrated in Fig. 9(a), the file system metadata were distributed evenly across all five metadata servers. In addition to the storage load balance, Fig. 9(b) highlights that the workloads were also distributed more evenly across all metadata servers, compared to CephFS (see Fig. 6(a)). As a consequence, the better load balance performance enables more metadata operations

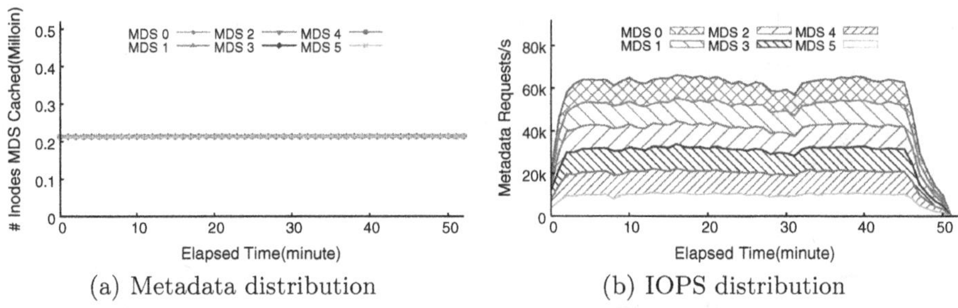

(a) Metadata distribution (b) IOPS distribution

Fig. 9. Workload load balance comparison result.

to be processed in parallel, shortens the completion time and improves the overall metadata performance.

5 Conclusion

In this paper, we proposed a hybrid and scalable metadata management method for distributed file systems, HSM^2, which combines the subtree partitioning and hash-based mapping method together to maintain both namespace locality and load balance. We implemented HSM^2 atop of CephFS. The experimental results show that, compared to CephFS, HSM^2 can reduce the completion time of a representative file-scanning workload by 70% and achieve 3.9× overall throughput speedup.

Acknowledgement. This work is supported in part by National Key R&D Program of China under Grant No. 2018YFB1003204, NSFC under Grant No. 61772484, and the Joint Funds of CETC under Grant No. 20166141B08080101.

References

1. Abad, C.L., Luu, H., Roberts, N., Lee, K., Lu, Y., Campbell, R.H.: Metadata traces and workload models for evaluating big storage systems. In: 2012 IEEE Fifth International Conference on Utility and Cloud Computing, pp. 125–132. IEEE (2012)
2. Abbasi, Z., et al.: Scalable performance of the panasas parallel file system. In: FAST 2008 Proceedings of the 6th USENIX Conference on File and Storage Technologies, pp. 17–33 (2008)
3. Alam, S.R., El-Harake, H.N., Howard, K., Stringfellow, N., Verzelloni, F.: Parallel I/O and the metadata wall. In: Proceedings of the Sixth Workshop on Parallel Data Storage, pp. 13–18. ACM (2011)
4. Anderson, E.: Capture, conversion, and analysis of an intense NFS workload. In: FAST, vol. 9, pp. 139–152 (2009)
5. Beaver, D., Kumar, S., Li, H.C., Sobel, J., Vajgel, P., et al.: Finding a needle in haystack: Facebook's photo storage. In: OSDI, vol. 10, pp. 1–8 (2010)

6. Braam, P.: The lustre storage architecture. arXiv preprint arXiv:1903.01955 (2019)
7. Braam, P., Callahan, M., Schwan, P., et al.: The intermezzo file system. In: Proceedings of the 3rd of the Perl Conference, O'Reilly Open Source Convention (1999)
8. Carns, P., Lang, S., Ross, R., Vilayannur, M., Kunkel, J., Ludwig, T.: Small-file access in parallel file systems. In: 2009 IEEE International Symposium on Parallel & Distributed Processing, IPDPS 2009, pp. 1–11. IEEE (2009)
9. Corbett, P.F., Feitelson, D.G.: The Vesta parallel file system. ACM Trans. Comput. Syst. (TOCS) **14**(3), 225–264 (1996)
10. Ghemawat, S., Gobioff, H., Leung, S.T.: The Google file system. In: ACM SIGOPS Operating Systems Review, vol. 37, pp. 29–43. ACM (2003)
11. Harter, T., et al.: Analysis of HDFS under HBase: a Facebook messages case study. In: FAST, vol. 14, p. 12 (2014)
12. Hertel, C.R.: Implementing CIFS: The Common Internet File System. Prentice Hall Professional, Upper Saddle River (2004)
13. Leung, A.W., Pasupathy, S., Goodson, G.R., Miller, E.L.: Measurement and analysis of large-scale network file system workloads. In: USENIX Annual Technical Conference, vol. 1, pp. 2–5 (2008)
14. Li, S., Lu, Y., Shu, J., Hu, Y., Li, T.: LocoFS: a loosely-coupled metadata service for distributed file systems. In: Proceedings of the International Conference for High Performance Computing, Networking, Storage and Analysis, SC 2017, Denver, CO, USA, 12–17 November 2017, pp. 4:1–4:12 (2017)
15. Miller, E.L., Katz, R.H.: RAMA: an easy-to-use, high-performance parallel file system. Parallel Comput. **23**(4–5), 419–446 (1997)
16. Morris, J.H., Satyanarayanan, M., Conner, M.H., Howard, J.H., Rosenthal, D.S., Smith, F.D.: Andrew: a distributed personal computing environment. Commun. ACM **29**(3), 184–201 (1986)
17. Ousterhout, J.K., Cherenson, A.R., Douglis, F., Nelson, M.N., Welch, B.B.: The sprite network operating system. Computer **21**(2), 23–36 (1988)
18. Pawlowski, B., Juszczak, C., Staubach, P., Smith, C., Lebel, D., Hitz, D.: NFS version 3: Design and implementation. In: USENIX Summer, Boston, MA, pp. 137–152 (1994)
19. Rodeh, O., Teperman, A.: zFS-a scalable distributed file system using object disks. In: 2003 Proceedings of 20th IEEE/11th NASA Goddard Conference on Mass Storage Systems and Technologies (MSST 2003), pp. 207–218. IEEE (2003)
20. Roselli, D.S., Lorch, J.R., Anderson, T.E., et al.: A comparison of file system workloads. In: USENIX Annual Technical Conference, General Track, pp. 41–54 (2000)
21. Satyanarayanan, M.: Coda: a highly available file system for a distributed workstation environment. In: Proceedings of the Second Workshop on Workstation Operating Systems, pp. 114–116. IEEE (1989)
22. Schwan, P., et al.: Lustre: building a file system for 1000-node clusters. In: Proceedings of the 2003 Linux Symposium, vol. 2003, pp. 380–386 (2003)
23. Shen, Z., Shu, J., Lee, P.P.: Reconsidering single failure recovery in clustered file systems. In: 2016 46th Annual IEEE/IFIP International Conference on Dependable Systems and Networks (DSN), pp. 323–334. IEEE (2016)
24. Shvachko, K., Kuang, H., Radia, S., Chansler, R., et al.: The hadoop distributed file system. In: MSST, vol. 10, pp. 1–10 (2010)
25. Tarasov, V.: Filebench (2018). https://github.com/filebench/filebench
26. Thomson, A., Abadi, D.J.: CalvinFS: consistent WAN replication and scalable metadata management for distributed file systems. In: 13th USENIX Conference on File and Storage Technologies (FAST 2015), pp. 1–14 (2015)

27. Weil, S.A., Brandt, S.A., Miller, E.L., Long, D.D., Maltzahn, C.: Ceph: a scalable, high-performance distributed file system. In: Proceedings of the 7th Symposium on Operating Systems Design and Implementation, pp. 307–320. USENIX Association (2006)
28. Weil, S.A., Pollack, K.T., Brandt, S.A., Miller, E.L.: Dynamic metadata management for petabyte-scale file systems. In: Proceedings of the 2004 ACM/IEEE Conference on Supercomputing, p. 4. IEEE Computer Society (2004)
29. Xiao, L., Ren, K., Zheng, Q., Gibson, G.A.: ShardFS vs. indexFS: replication vs. caching strategies for distributed metadata management in cloud storage systems. In: Proceedings of the Sixth ACM Symposium on Cloud Computing, pp. 236–249. ACM (2015)
30. Xing, J., Xiong, J., Sun, N., Ma, J.: Adaptive and scalable metadata management to support a trillion files. In: Proceedings of the Conference on High Performance Computing Networking, Storage and Analysis, p. 26. ACM (2009)
31. Xue, L., Brandt, S.A., Miller, E.L., Long, D.D.: Efficient metadata management in large distributed file systems. In: Twentieth IEEE/Eleventh NASA Goddard Conference on Mass Storage Systems and Technologies (2003)
32. Zhang, S., Catanese, H., Wang, A.I.A.: The composite-file file system: decoupling the one-to-one mapping of files and metadata for better performance. In: FAST, pp. 15–22 (2016)

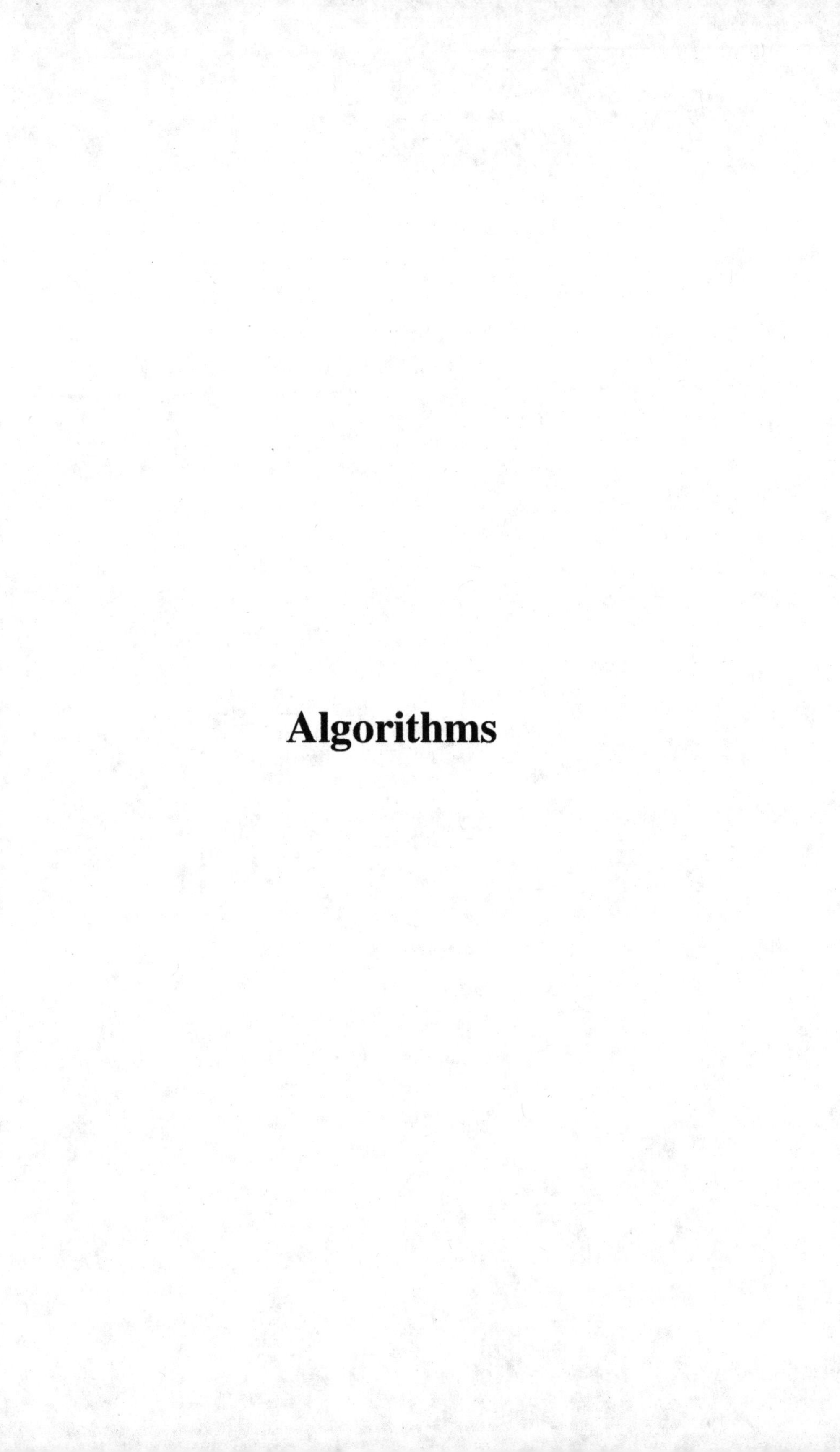

Algorithms

Heuristic Load Scheduling Algorithm for Stateful Cloud BPM Engine

Haotian Zhang, Yang Yu(✉), and Maolin Pan

School of Data and Computer Science, Sun Yat-Sen University, Guangzhou, China
zhanght9@mail2.sysu.edu.cn, {yuy,panml}@mail.sysu.edu.cn

Abstract. With the increasing popularity of cloud computing technology, the traditional Business Process Management System (BPMS) begins to transform to the architecture that deployed in the cloud. Since the traditional BPMS is often implemented as a stateful single-instance architecture, the cloud BPMS providers will encounter the stateful service load scheduling problem when they refactor the traditional BPMS to the microservice architecture that deployed on the cloud server. In order to help realize the transformation of traditional BPMS and improve the load capacity of cloud BPMS with limited computing resources, we propose a heuristic load scheduling algorithm for stateful service scheduling. The algorithm makes use of the busyness metrics of the single BPMS engine instance microservice in the cloud BPMS architecture. Because the resource scheduling problem is always defined as online bin packing problem, we improve the Best-Fit algorithm to solve this kind of problem. We come up with the Best-Fit Decreasing algorithm based on cloud BPMS engine busyness measuring and load prediction to schedule the computing resources to business process instances. Compared to some common load scheduling algorithms, our algorithm help cloud BPMS increase load level by at least 15%.

Keywords: Business Process Management System · Microservice architecture · Stateful service · Load prediction · Load scheduling

1 Introduction

With the increasing popularity of cloud computing technology, a lot of single-instance applications are transforming into multi-instance applications deployed on cloud servers gradually. Under the guarantee the quality of service (QoS), cloud computing technology helps users greatly reduce the pressure brought by operating and maintaining software systems and physical servers. The development of cloud computing technology also leads the transformation of the Business Process Management System (BPMS) towards the Software-as-a-Service (SaaS) architecture, which is called BPM as a Service (BPMaaS) architecture.

In the field of cloud computing technology, types of services are often divided into stateful services and stateless services. Stateful service is a service architecture that stores client-request context data inside the server [1]. Stateless service means that the server does not need to save the client's data inside the server, but save it in client or

H. Shen and Y. Sang (Eds.): PAAP 2019, CCIS 1163, pp. 209–220, 2020.
https://doi.org/10.1007/978-981-15-2767-8_20

external storage [2]. BPMS is an information system that deals with the definition, management, customization and evaluation of tasks that evolve from business processes and organizational structures [3]. The workflow reference model proposed by the Workflow Management Coalition (WfMC) [4] is used as a general architecture for BPMS and is the basis of most BPMS to date. Traditional BPMS often stores Business Process Model and Notation (BPMN, such as BPEL [5], YAWL [6]) in the memory allocated by BPMS at the software level. For example, Petri net is a sort of data structures which is commonly used to describe business processes. It contains data such as places, transitions, arcs and tokens [7]. More complicated business processes often correspond to more complicated data structures. In order to provide the business process parsing and response quickly, the traditional BPMS is mostly implemented as a stateful service. It means when the cloud BPMS deploys the process instance to one workflow engine, all the task execution requests contained in the process instance must be processed by this workflow engine. A mature cloud solution of microservice architecture technology can be used to help implement the cloudization of traditional BPMS. At the same time, the cloud BPMS providers will face stateful service scheduling issues when deploying traditional single-instance BPMS as a multi-instance stateful cloud BPMS.

This paper will propose a heuristic cloud BPMS engine load scheduling algorithm based on process instance stateful service scheduling. The metrics of server computing resource performance and attributes of the business process are used to schedule business process instances so that a single BPMS engine instance can manage business processes based on their workload. Compared with several common load scheduling algorithms, our load scheduling algorithm schedule business process instance requests reasonably and makes full use of computing resources to achieve the goal of improving cloud BPMS load capacity and reducing costs.

The rest of this paper includes: Sect. 2 discusses existing related work; Sect. 3 gives the detailed description of the problem; Sect. 4 gives the solution to the main problem in this paper; Sect. 5 shows experimental data and results; Sect. 6 summarizes the research and proposes the prospects for future research.

2 Related Work

Currently, there are some studies on multi-instance scheduling for stateful BPMS. Ouyang et al. [8] proposed to design a cloud-based scalable BPMS architecture, which splits BPMS into workflow engines, worklist handlers, external data storages and so on. The workflow engine and worklist handlers are implemented as a multi-instance architecture. The authors insert the router between clients and multiple workflow engines. The router calculates the busyness metrics of the workflow engine and performs load balancing of multiple workflow engines according to the busyness level. However, the authors designed the architecture to focus on the load balancing of business process requests under limited computing resources just to allow users to feel faster service response, but not to increase the load of BPMS and allow cloud BPMS providers reduce the waste of computing resources.

Rosinosky et al. [9] proposed an elastic BPMaaS based on data migration. The authors considered the future load of BPMS and used the method of migrating overload data to achieve a reasonable resource allocation status of BPMaaS. However, the author's experimental design is under an ideal condition, that is, the future load of BPMaaS is known. Actually, it is difficult to quantify the load of the business process and get the exact amount of future load. The flexible program also requires more technical research support. Other studies such as [10] have similar disadvantages.

There are also some other related works that propose a reasonable cloud BPMS architecture, such as [11] and [12], but there is no deeper exploration about the multi-instance stateful service scheduling issues, just staying at the level of the overall architectural design.

The papers like [13] and [14] propose some load scheduling algorithm. But they don't take some metrics of the process instance and possible prediction into account to give more accurate scheduling strategy.

3 Problem Statement

Since traditional BPMS is often implemented as a single stateful service, as shown in Fig. 1, there are some common issues in the single-instance architecture. First, when there are some abnormalities that cause the system to crash, the entire BPMS will not run properly. Secondly, the single-instance architecture is difficult to cope with huge traffic load. It is difficult for traditional BPMS to increase the load of the entire system platform by simply increasing the number of BPMS instance. Because of the stateful service, the relevant requests of each process instance must correspond to unique BPMS, unlike a stateless service can handle the relevant requests for each process instance with regardless of which BPMS instance.

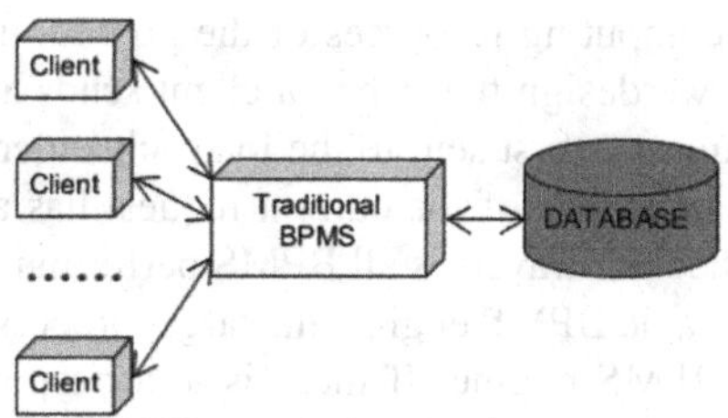

Fig. 1. Traditional single-instance BPMS architecture

To solve the above problems, it is helpful to migrate traditional BPMS on the cloud to run and maintain with the microservice architecture technology. As BPMS is often implemented as a stateful service, it is impossible to realize the cloudization of traditional BPMS by simply deploying multiple instances. Instead, it is necessary to explore a load scheduler with some scheduling strategy to help implement multi-instance stateful cloud service architecture, as shown in Fig. 2. The load scheduler runs between the clients and the BPMS engine instance microservice, and schedules the request of the specific process instance to the appropriate BPMS engine instance microservice according to a certain scheduling policy. The load scheduler not only needs to implement the migration of the traditional single-instance BPMS to the cloud BPMS of the microservice architecture, but also needs to consider increasing the load of the entire system platform as much as possible under limited computing resources. Therefore, the research goal of this paper is, assuming that the metrics of computational resource and attributes of process instances of each BPMS engine instance are known, how to design a load scheduling algorithm to improve the load of cloud BPMS under limited computing resources.

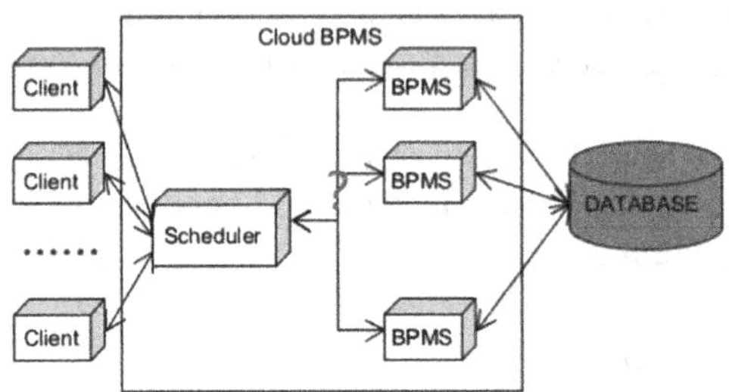

Fig. 2. Cloud BPMS architecture

4 Heuristic Cloud BPMS Engine Load Scheduling Algorithm

4.1 Load Scheduler

The single-instance architecture of traditional BPMS cannot be disaster-tolerant and has poor scalability. When the BPMS is migrated to the cloud for multi-instance microservice architecture deployment and maintenance, the load scheduler is needed to be designed to implement reasonable computing resources of the process instance scheduling and distribution. From Fig. 3, we design that when a client sends an operation request for a process instance, the request is first sent to the load scheduler. The scheduler checks whether the target process instance of the current request has a corresponding BPMS engine. If not, the load scheduler traverses all BPMS performance metrics. In this case, after selecting the most suitable BPMS engine, the target process instance of the request is bound to the selected BPMS engine. If there is a corresponding BPMS, the load scheduler obtains the parameters of corresponding BPMS according to the requested target process instance. Finally, the load scheduler routes the request to the corresponding BPMS for processing and returns the final result to the client. It can be seen that the load scheduling algorithm included in the load scheduler is the core part of the design of the load scheduler.

4.2 Simple Busyness Prediction

We import simple busyness prediction into our algorithm to figure out more accurate busyness metrics. A process instance is instantiated by the corresponding business process model, so the future load and state of the process instance can be predicted based on the results of the business process model analysis. We assume three parameters that can be used for prediction, that is, the amount of the same business process model in

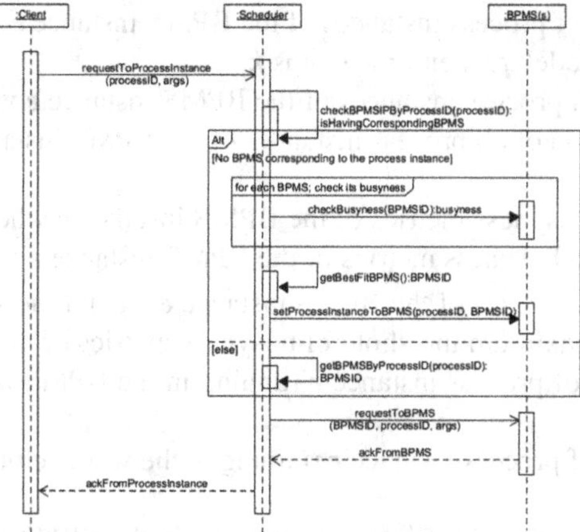

Fig. 3. Load scheduling UML sequence diagram

the same BPMS engine instance, the size of the corresponding business process model, and the progress of the current process instance. Because of caching mechanism, the more the same business process model in the same engine, the parsing execution of the business process model will take less time and improve performance. The size of the business process model determines the complexity of the life cycle of a process instance. The larger the business process model, the more complex the process instance, and the longer time it takes to consume. The progress of the process instance determines when the process instance can release the computing resources. The sooner the computing resources are released, the other and subsequent process instances will get more computing resources. The average value of these three parameters can approximate the future load of the current BPMS engine instance.

4.3 Formal Definition of Target Problem and Constraints

The implementation of the load scheduler not only provides the simple function of scheduling a request to its corresponding BPMS, but also needs to improve the cloud BPMS load capacity under the constraints of limited computing resources. Since traditional BPMS is often implemented as a stateful service, the load scheduling algorithm should be adaptive to the actual scenario of workflow. The following parameters are pre-defined:

- $\boldsymbol{E}$, the set of BPMS engine instances
- $\boldsymbol{Q}$, the set of all business process models
- $\boldsymbol{R}$, the set of process instances
- $\boldsymbol{K}$, the set of time slots
- $\boldsymbol{C_e(k)}$, the CPU usage rate of the BPMS instance $\boldsymbol{e}$ when time slot is $\boldsymbol{k}$
- $\boldsymbol{M_e(k)}$, the memory usage rate of the BPMS instance $\boldsymbol{e}$ when time slot is $\boldsymbol{k}$
- $\boldsymbol{T_e(k)}$, the active concurrent request rate of the BPMS instance $\boldsymbol{e}$ when time slot is $\boldsymbol{k}$
- $\boldsymbol{W_e(k)}$, the number of all work items of the BPMS instance $\boldsymbol{e}$ when time slot is $\boldsymbol{k}$

- $N_q^e(k)$, the number of process instances of the BPMS instance ***e*** which correspond to business process model ***q*** when time slot is ***k***
- $S_e(k)$, the size of all process instances of the BPMS instance ***e*** when time slot is ***k***
- $P_e(k)$, the completion of all process instances of the BPMS instance ***e*** when time slot is ***k***
- $b_c^e(k)$, the current busyness metrics of the BPMS instance ***e*** when time slot is ***k***
- $b_f^e(k)$, the predicted busyness metrics of the BPMS instance ***e*** when time slot is ***k***
- $B_e(k)$, the busyness metrics of the BPMS instance ***e*** when time slot is ***k***
- $Threshold_{B,\,max}$, maximum threshold of busyness metrics of the BPMS instance
- $x_r^e(k)$, the number of process instance ***r*** running in the BPMS instance ***e*** when time slot is ***k***
- $y_r(k)$, the number of process instance ***r*** running in the whole cloud BPMS when time slot is ***k***
- $z_e(k)$, the number of all process instances running in the BPMS instance ***e*** when time slot is ***k***

$$\max \sum_{\mathrm{k}}^{k \in K} \sum_{e}^{e \in E} z_e(k) \tag{1}$$

The following constraints are specified here:

$$\forall e \in E, \forall r \in R, \forall k \in K, x_r^e(k) = 1 \tag{2}$$

$$\forall r \in R, \forall k \in K, y_{\mathrm{r}}(k) = 1 \tag{3}$$

$$\exists e \in E, \forall k \in K, B_{\mathrm{e}}(\mathrm{k}) \le \mathrm{Threshold}_{B,\mathrm{max}} \tag{4}$$

Equation 1 is the optimization goal which is to maximize the number of process instances that the entire BPMS can resolve at the same time under the limited computing resource constraints. It cannot affect the time of the entire cloud BPMS response request too much. The constraint condition shown in Eq. 2 is that the number of any one of the process instances running by any one of the BPMS engine instances is unique at any one time, that is, one process instance must correspond to one BPMS engine instance. The constraint condition shown in Eq. 3 is that the number of any process instances running in the entire cloud BPMS is unique at any time, that is, only one certain process instance exists in the entire cloud BPMS. It is impossible that multiple BPMS engine instances handle the same process instance. Equation 4 indicates the constraint is that the busyness metrics of a certain BPMS engine instance is not greater than a pre-set threshold at any time. It is not only to protect the entire cloud BPMS from being crashed by suddenly request traffic. More importantly, under different threshold constraints, the maximum load of single BPMS engine instance has different performance. If the threshold is set too low, the BPMS engine instance cannot reach higher level of busyness and even the maximum load. If the threshold is set too high, the BPMS engine instance may be too busy, resulting in response time of the BPMS engine instance increasing. It will reduce the throughput and the BPMS engine instance cannot reach the maximum load either.

The busyness metrics of a BPMS engine instance is determined by the CPU usage rate, memory usage rate, active concurrent request rate, and the number of all work items generated by all process instances in the BPMS engine instance. The CPU usage rate and memory usage rate represent the physical computing resource consumption of a BPMS engine instance. The active concurrent request rate indicates the rate of connections of a BPMS engine instance which represents the busyness metrics of the BPMS engine instance handling requests. This idea refers to the existing mature load balancing algorithm which is Least-Connection algorithm. The number of work items generated by all process instances in the BPMS engine instance represents the busyness metrics in the aspect of actual business scenario of the workflow. Based on these four factors, the formula for the current busyness metrics of a single BPMS engine instance at any time is shown in Eq. 5:

$$\exists e \in E, \forall k \in K, \mathrm{b}_{\mathrm{c}}^{e}(\mathrm{k}) = (\mathrm{C}_{\mathrm{e}}(\mathrm{k}) + \mathrm{M}_{\mathrm{e}}(\mathrm{k}) + \mathrm{T}_{\mathrm{e}}(\mathrm{k}) + \mathrm{W}_{\mathrm{e}}(\mathrm{k})/10000)/4 \tag{5}$$

According to Sect. 4.3, the formula for the predicted busyness metrics of a single BPMS engine instance at any time is shown in Eq. 6:

$$\exists e \in E, \forall k \in K, \mathrm{b}_{\mathrm{f}}^{e}(\mathrm{k}) = (N_{\mathrm{e}}(\mathrm{k})/10 + \mathrm{S}_{\mathrm{e}}(\mathrm{k})/5 + \mathrm{P}_{\mathrm{e}}(\mathrm{k}))/3 \tag{6}$$

Finally, the formula for the busyness metrics of a single BPMS engine instance at any time is shown in Eq. 7. We set the ratio of current busyness metrics and predicted busyness metrics to 3:1 which means the current busyness is more important.

$$\exists e \in E, \forall k \in K, B_{\mathrm{e}}(\mathrm{k}) = \mathrm{b}_{c}^{e}(\mathrm{k}) \times \frac{3}{4} + \mathrm{b}_{\mathrm{f}}^{e}(\mathrm{k}) \times \frac{1}{4} \tag{7}$$

4.4 Best Fit Decreasing Based on Busyness Metrics Heuristic Algorithm

Because the BPMS engine instances cannot know the subsequent process instance which may arrive in the future, the research on cloud BPMS resource scheduling can be defined as online bin packing problem. The bin packing problem is a classic NP-hard problem and the approximate algorithms widely used to solve this kind of problem [15]. The most common approximate algorithms include the First-Fit algorithm and the Best-Fit algorithm, which can also be used to solve online bin packing problems. The First-Fit algorithm loads the object into the first box that satisfies the capacity condition. The Best-Fit algorithm loads the object into the smallest box that meets the capacity condition.

The scheduling algorithm is based on the Best-Fit Bin-Packing heuristic algorithm [16]. Finally, the algorithm is extended to the Best-Fit Decreasing heuristic algorithm based on busyness metrics (BFDB). The algorithm uses the busyness metrics of each BPMS engine instance as an indicator to perform scheduling process instances. The main idea is to select the busiest single BPMS engine instance that its busyness value is not more than the maximum threshold from all BPMS engine instances for scheduling. This can increase the utilization of computing resources as much as possible which is resulting in the increase of load of cloud BPMS. The value of the threshold limits the maximum busyness of a single BPMS engine instance which can to help protect the cloud BPMS from being crashed by suddenly request traffic. At the same time, different threshold values can make the maximum load of the BPMS engine instance different. The implementation of the algorithm is shown in Algorithm 1.

Algorithm 1 Best-Fit Decreasing heuristic algorithm based on Busyness Metrics

Input:
The set of BPMS instances, E_n;
Threshold of a BPMS instance, $Threshold_{B,max}$;
Output:
Qualified BPMS instance, E_{result};
for each $e \in E_n$ **do**
  if $busyness$ of $e \leq Threshold_{B,max}$ **then**
    $A = A \cup e$;
  end if
end for
$Busyness_{max} = 0$;
for each $a \in A$ **do**
  if $busyness$ of $a \geq Busyness_{max}$ **then**
    $Busyness_{max} = busyness$;
    $E_{result} = a$;
  end if
end for
return E_{result};

5 Experimental Design and Results

The cloud BPMS used in the experiment was RenWFMS [17] and the cloud BPMS microservice architecture contained three BPMS engine instance microservices. We set up a test bed on the Workflow Computing Platform that was a computing cluster consisting of four virtual machines running on a Dell PowerEdge blade server. The operating system was Ubuntu 16.04 LTS. Each virtual machine ran on a single core of an Intel E5620 CPU and 3 GB of RAM. The load test tool was Gatling v3.1.0 [18].

The main work of the experiment was to record the concurrent execution value of a simple business process in the cloud BPMS, that is the maximum number of process instances in the entire cloud BPMS that can accommodate the same business process definition, and the response time of each phase in the business process. The criterion for judging a cloud BPMS reaches the upper limit of concurrency is that if a request response time exceeds 60000 ms, the load capacity of the cloud BPMS is considered exceeded. Therefore, if all the response time of the request does not exceed 60000 ms, it means that the current concurrent quantity has not exceeded the concurrent limit of the cloud BPMS. And then the concurrent quantity can be increased to test more load. Since the cloud BPMS is still a web application service that interacts with human users, 60000 ms as the response timeout is more in line with the using habits of ordinary users [18].

Figure 4 shows the results of the load test under the different maximum threshold of busyness indicators of BPMS engine instance. The threshold determines the maximum value of busyness that a single BPMS engine instance is allowed to. Different thresholds have different effects on the load performance of the BPMS engine instance. When the threshold is small, the maximum busyness value of the BPMS engine instance is low and the maximum load cannot be reached. In this situation, the upper limit of the maximum load depends on the BPMS engine instance busyness threshold value. When the threshold is large, the maximum busyness value of the BPMS engine instance is high. However, if the BPMS engine instance is too busy, the response speed of processing will be slow. It is also unacceptable that the response of some process instance requests will be timeout and the BPMS engine instance is overloaded. In this situation, the upper limit of the maximum load depends on the amount of load given to the BPMS engine instance rather than the busyness value.

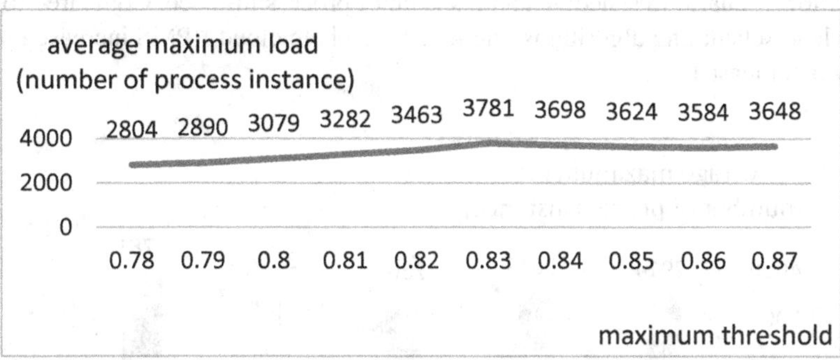

Fig. 4. The load test under the different maximum threshold of busyness indicators

As shown in Fig. 4, when the threshold is set less than 0.83, the average maximum process instance load of the cloud BPMS increases with the increase of the threshold. The threshold range that value is less than 0.83 is such that the BPMS engine instance cannot reach the maximum busyness value and load. When the threshold is set more than 0.83, the average maximum process instance load of the cloud BPMS remains at a stable level. The threshold range that value is greater than 0.83 will cause the BPMS engine instance to be in an overload state. Therefore, the maximum threshold of the busyness indicator of the BPMS engine instance with the value of 0.83 was the most appropriate in this experiment.

The experiment also compared several existing load balancing algorithms as a control group, including Random Scheduling Algorithm, Round Robin Scheduling Algorithm, Hash Scheduling Algorithm, Least Connection Scheduling Algorithm [14].

Figure 5 shows the results of simulation load test of different load scheduling algorithms. The maximum threshold of the busyness of the BFDB algorithm proposed in this paper is set to 0.83. The average maximum load of the Random Scheduling Algorithm and the Hash Scheduling Algorithm is lower because the large randomness may cause the process instance to be easily deteriorated to a certain BPMS engine instance in the cloud BPMS. Then this BPMS engine instance Excessive load greatly reduces the cloud BPMS load capability. Compared with these two load scheduling algorithms, the Round Robin Scheduling Algorithm is more balanced and it is difficult to see a part of the process instances deteriorate to a certain BPMS engine instance. However, this algorithm only performs load scheduling in the order of requests, ignoring the situation that different process instances have different levels of computational pressure. The results of the Round Robin Scheduling Algorithm is not much better than that of the Random Scheduling Algorithm and the Hash Scheduling Algorithm. The Least Connection Scheduling Algorithm considers the number of request connections for each BPMS engine instance, which is equivalent to the computational pressure brought by the request of each process instance. To some extent, the entire cloud BPMS with the Least Connection Scheduling Algorithm has better load capacity than the first three algorithms. The experimental results show that the BFDB algorithm proposed in this paper has a better effect in the workflow scenario because our algorithm not only considers the computing resource consumption of the physical machine, but also combines the complexity of the workflow scenario to schedule and dispatch of process instance. Compared to other existing load scheduling algorithms, the BFDB can help cloud BPMS increase the load capacity by at least 15%.

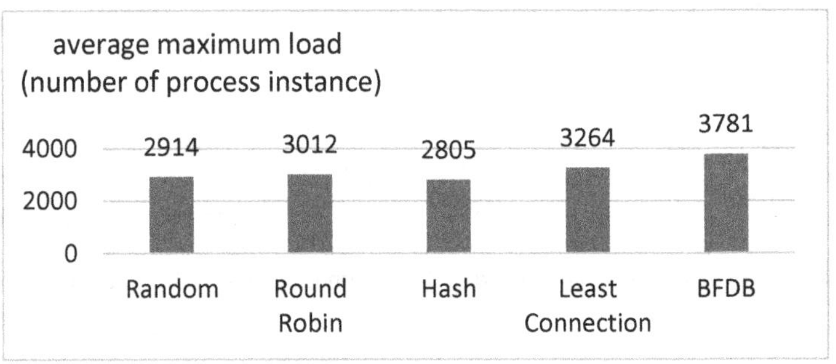

Fig. 5. Simulation load test of different load scheduling algorithms

Figure 6 shows the average response time of each phase of the business process execution during the simulated load test. The process instance initializing phase spends the most time in the entire business process because parsing the business process model into in-memory objects needs more time consuming than other phases. The work item list obtaining phase is just a simple process of database search and reading so it is less time-consuming. The process instance work item execution phase needs to call back by the behavior of the client to execute the specific work items. Then the specific work items are generated and executed according to the business process model, which will take more time than the work item list obtaining phase. Overall, under different load scheduling algorithms, the average response time trend of different phases is not much different. The only the Least Connection Scheduling Algorithm and BFDB take into account the computing stress. Therefore, it takes a shorter response time from these two load scheduling algorithms than other algorithms. In order to improve the usage of computing resources, the BFDB algorithm schedules the process instances as much as possible on the BPMS engine instance and does not exceed the busyness threshold instead of scheduling them on the least busy BPMS engine instance. Therefore, it appears to take a little more response time than the Least Connection Scheduling Algorithm.

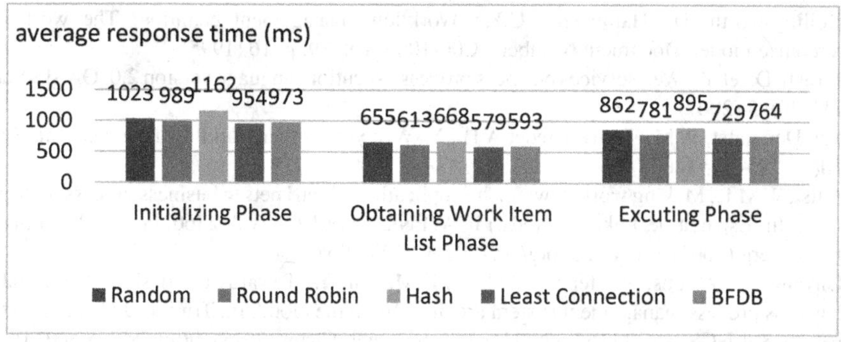

Fig. 6. Average response time of each phase of the business process execution

6 Conclusions and Outlook

In this paper, we define a heuristic cloud BPMS engine load scheduling algorithm. Our algorithm goal is to improve the load capacity of cloud BPMS with a limited computing resources. The algorithm is based on the busyness of a single BPMS engine instance calculation in the entire cloud BPMS architecture. The algorithm improves the Best-Fit algorithm and implements the Best-Fit Decreasing algorithm based on the busyness which enables the load scheduler to allocate and schedule computing resources to the business process instances according to the busyness of the BPMS engine instance. In the verification of the simulation experiment, we could see that the algorithm implemented in this paper is able to increase the process instance load capacity in the cloud BPMS by at least 15% under the constraints of limited computing resources.

The research in this article provides an algorithm for improving the load capacity of the cloud BPMS under limited computing resources. However, the cloud BPMS cannot flexibly change the number of BPMS instance microservices according to the current load to reduce the consumption of computing resources. Therefore, the next step is to realize that the cloud BPMS flexibly scale according to the busyness and even green computing architecture [19].

Acknowledgements. This work is Supported by the National Key Research and Development Program of China under Grant No. 2017YFB0202200; the National Natural Science Foundation of China under Grant Nos. 61972427, 61572539; the Research Foundation of Science and Technology Plan Project in Guangzhou City under Grant No. 201704020092.

References

1. Foster, I., et al.: Modeling stateful resources with web services. Globus Alliance (2004)
2. White, J.G.: U.S. Patent No. 6,065,117. Patent and Trademark Office, Washington, DC. U.S (2000)
3. Karagiannis, D.: BPMS: business process management systems. ACM SIGOIS Bull. **16**(1), 10–13 (1995)

4. Hollingsworth, D., Hampshire, U.K.: Workflow management coalition: The workflow reference model. Document Number TC00-1003, vol. 19, p. 16 (1995)
5. Jordan, D., et al.: Web services business process execution language version 2.0. OASIS Stan. **11**(120), 5 (2007)
6. Van Der Aalst, W.M., Ter Hofstede, A.H.: YAWL: yet another workflow language. Inf. Syst. **30**(4), 245–275 (2005)
7. Aalst, W.M.P.: Making work flow: on the application of petri nets to business process management. In: Esparza, J., Lakos, C. (eds.) ICATPN 2002. LNCS, vol. 2360, pp. 1–22. Springer, Heidelberg (2002). https://doi.org/10.1007/3-540-48068-4_1
8. Ouyang, C., Adams, M., ter Hofstede, A.H.M., Yu, Y.: Towards the design of a scalable business process management system architecture in the cloud. In: Trujillo, J.C., et al. (eds.) ER 2018. LNCS, vol. 11157, pp. 334–348. Springer, Cham (2018). https://doi.org/10.1007/978-3-030-00847-5_24
9. Rosinosky, G., Youcef, S., Charoy, F.: Efficient migration-aware algorithms for elastic BPMaaS. In: Carmona, J., Engels, G., Kumar, A. (eds.) BPM 2017. LNCS, vol. 10445, pp. 147–163. Springer, Cham (2017). https://doi.org/10.1007/978-3-319-65000-5_9
10. Rosinosky, G., Youcef, S., Charoy, F.: An efficient approach for multi-tenant elastic business processes management in cloud computing environment. In: 2016 IEEE 9th International Conference on Cloud Computing (CLOUD), pp. 311–318. IEEE, June 2016
11. Schmidt, R.: Scalable business process enactment in cloud environments. In: Bider, I., Halpin, T., et al. (eds.) BPMDS/EMMSAD -2012. LNBIP, vol. 113, pp. 1–15. Springer, Heidelberg (2012). https://doi.org/10.1007/978-3-642-31072-0_1
12. Paschek, D., Trusculescu, A., Mateescu, A., Draghici, A.: Business process as a service-a flexible approach for it service management and business process outsourcing. In: Management Challenges in a Network Economy: Proceedings of the MakeLearn and TIIM International Conference, pp. 195–203 (2017)
13. Pathirage, M., Perera, S., Kumara, I., Weerawarana, S.: A multi-tenant architecture for business process executions. In: 2011 IEEE International Conference on Web Services, pp. 121–128. IEEE, July 2011
14. Ray, S., De Sarkar, A.: Execution analysis of load balancing algorithms in cloud computing environment. Int. J. Cloud Comput. Serv. Architect. (IJCCSA) **2**(5), 1–13 (2012)
15. De La Vega, W.F., Lueker, G.S.: Bin packing can be solved within $1 + \varepsilon$ in linear time. Combinatorica **1**(4), 349–355 (1981)
16. Kenyon, C.: Best-fit bin-packing with random order. In: SODA, vol. 96, pp. 359–364, January 1996
17. RenWFMS: Business Object Oriented Workflow Environment. https://github.com/SYSU-Workflow-Lab/RenWFMS
18. Gatling load testing. https://gatling.io/
19. Kansal, N.J., Chana, I.: Cloud load balancing techniques: a step towards green computing. IJCSI Int. J. Comput. Sci. Issues **9**(1), 238–246 (2012)

An Improved Heuristic-Dynamic Programming Algorithm for Rectangular Cutting Problem

Aihua Yin, Chong Chen, Dongping Hu(✉), Jianghai Huang, and Fan Yang

School of Software and Internet of Things Engineering, Jiangxi University of Finance and Economics, Nanchang, Jiangxi, China
Dongping_hu337@jxufe.edu.cn

Abstract. In this paper, we discussed a two-dimensional cutting problem with defects. In this problem, we are given a rectangular area which contains defects. The objective is to cut some rectangles with a given shape and direction from this rectangular area, which cannot overlap the defects, maximizing some profit associated with the rectangles generating by this cutting. We present an improved Heuristic-Dynamic Program (IHDP) to solve this problem and prove the important theorem about its complexity. The algorithm reduces the size of the discretization sets, establishes one-dimensional knapsack problem with the width and height of the small rectangular blocks, constructs two discretization sets using the obtained solution and the right and upper boundaries of the defects, and performs trial cut lines for each element of the discretization set. The algorithm calculates 14 internationally recognized examples. The experimental results show that it obtains the optimal solution of these examples, and its computing time is nearly ten times higher than that of the latest literature algorithm.

Keywords: Guillotine · Two-dimension cutting · Dynamic programming · Defect · NP-hard

1 Introduction

Two-dimensional cutting problems with defects (see Fig. 1) are an important field in the cutting problem. In industrialized plants area, many cutting problems can be encountered with defects. For example, in the furniture industry, wood panels may contain breakage and the marked areas cannot be used for cutting into furniture. In the steel industry, steel coils produced may contain defects that cannot be used in construction. Natural products such as leather usually have poor quality pores or defects, and few parts that can be cut are used in the process. From the previous research, although its importance is obvious, related to the cutting problem, the algorithm for studying the large object without defects [1–4] is extensive, and there are few literatures on the problem of multiple defects. Therefore, such problems are becoming more and more important, and many researchers are working on such problems.

Scholars have proposed many algorithms on the standard two-dimensional cutting problem. In the latest literature, Lei et al. [5] proposed a heuristic search algorithm based on grouping rules, which designed the key complement of the large and small

H. Shen and Y. Sang (Eds.): PAAP 2019, CCIS 1163, pp. 221–233, 2020.
https://doi.org/10.1007/978-981-15-2767-8_21

parts division strategy and the quick recommendation of the block. Cui [6] proposed a dynamic programming algorithm for generating T-shaped layouts, and experimented with a large number of randomly generated examples, which showed that the algorithm is effective in both computation time and utilization. Song et al. [7] proposed a heuristic algorithm based on dynamic programming, which uses a subset of all possible cutting pattern and is an incomplete algorithm. Kang and Yoon et al. [8] proposed an improved version of the cutting problem for solving standard two-dimensional cutting problem, and their algorithm removes the dominated patterns efficiently and avoids duplicated patterns. Herz [9] uses a discretization set of all necessary cutting positions to propose an accurate recursive process. Beasley [10] shows how to improve the performance of the recursive process by the discretization set proposed by Herz [9], introducing a heuristic correction of the algorithm, in which the number of cuts in the discretization sets is limited.

Scholars studying the two-dimensional cutting problem with defects are rare. Carnieri et al. [11] proposed a heuristic dynamic programming algorithm, which includes branch and bound search, which assumes that large object or sub-blocks obtained from previous cuts do not contain defects, and their algorithms are reduced. The discretization sets size proposed by Herz [9], but they only studied the two-dimensional cutting problem with a defect. Vianna and Arenales [12] re-examined this problem by providing an AND/OR-based branch-qualification algorithm that further introduced a heuristic search that combines depth-first search and depth-limiting and hill-climbing strategies. Speeding up the search process, but when the authors used their method to solve some instances of defects, they only reported the value of the objective function obtained, without computing time. Neidlein and Wäscher [13] reduced the size of discretization sets in the algorithm proposed by Vianna and Arenales [12], but their algorithms could not obtain optimal solutions, and their algorithms involved several structural and computational constraints. These limitations become apparent if defects are handled. Afsharian et al. [18] modified the predecessor's heuristic dynamic programming algorithm to solve defects, but their discretization sets size is cumbersome, although the optimal solution can be obtained, but the required computational efficiency not high.

In this paper, there are many algorithms for dynamic programming of this problem. This paper only compares dynamic programming algorithms. Inspired by the previous heuristic [14–17] algorithm, an improved heuristic dynamic programming algorithm is proposed to solve the problem of multiple defects. In the case of up to 4 defects, the algorithm further reduces the discretization sets size of Afsharian et al. [18], and increases the sub-questions of the left and right edges and the upper and lower boundaries of the defects. The calculation results show that the algorithm improves the computational efficiency and is internationally recognized as the 14 most difficult optimal cutting pattern.

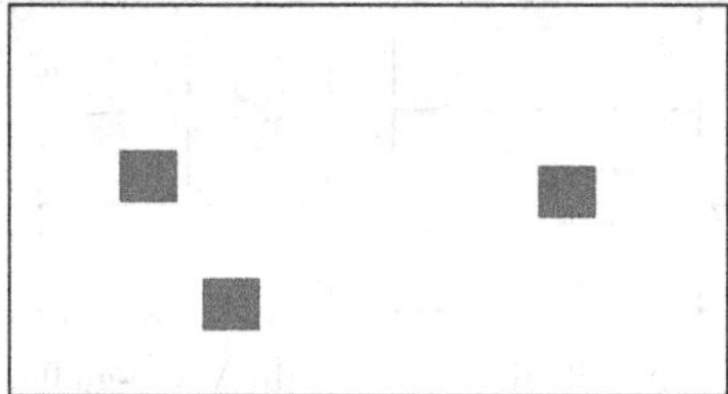

Fig. 1. A large object with defects

2 Problem Description

Let m different types of small rectangular blocks $i(i = 1, 2, \ldots, m)$, each associated with a integer width w_i^s, a integer height h_i^s, the profit value of the small rectangular block v_i, must be cut from a single non-negative integer rectangular large object with a width of W_0 and a height of H_0. To maximize the total value of the small rectangular blocks produced by the cutting process. The solution of this problem is a cutting pattern, a form of small rectangular blocks produced from large object and a description of the layout in which the small rectangular blocks are arranged on large object. In this layout, small rectangular blocks must be arranged parallel to the large object. For the issues to be considered, the following constraints should be met:

- The number of each type small rectangular block cut is not limited;
- While cutting small rectangular blocks, they must be cut according to the given width and height (that is, 90° rotation is not allowed when cutting small rectangular blocks);
- All cutting actions must be guillotine-type (see Fig. 2), that is, one side of the rectangular block extends to its opposite side, thereby producing two sub-rectangular blocks;
- The small rectangular block cut out must not contain defect or overlap with defects, otherwise it is waste.

There are n defects in the large object, where the $j(j = 1, 2, \ldots, n)$ defect have a width w_j^d and a height h_j^d. The cutting problem solved in this paper requires that all of the above constraints be satisfied, that is, it is a two-dimensional, unconstrained, guillotine, single large object cutting problem with defects (2D_UG_SLOCP_D). Let $P = (p_1, p_2, \ldots, p_m)$ be the cutting pattern, where $p_i(i = 1, 2, \ldots, m)$ represents the number of cuts of i-th small rectangular block. The goal is to maximize the value of cutting small rectangular blocks, which can be expressed as follows:

$$\begin{cases} \max V = \sum\limits_{i=1}^{m} v_i * p_i \\ s.t. P\, is\, a\ feasible\, cutting\, pattern \end{cases} \tag{1}$$

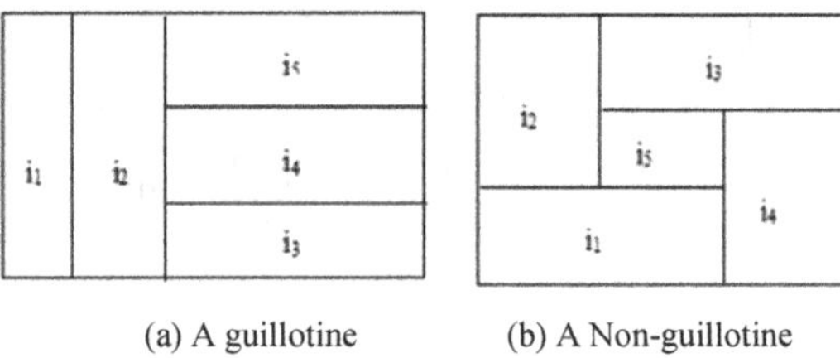

(a) A guillotine (b) A Non-guillotine

Fig. 2. Two ways of cutting

3 Algorithm Description

The algorithm proposed in this paper is called the improved heuristic dynamic programming (IHDP) algorithm. The DP algorithm generates a subset of all possible cutting patterns. The sub-problems are divided into trial cuts for each element of the discretization set.

3.1 Basic Definition

Definition 1 (sub-block). Guillotine are formed by cutting the large object or a series of cuts of the large object. Guillotine can always produce two sub-block (see Fig. 3). Unlike the problem without defect, it is unique in the coordinates and dimensions of each sub-block. Here, for the large object, the bottom left point is the origin, the x-axis is the width direction of the object, and the y-axis is the Cartesian coordinate system for the object height direction. Therefore, the large object can be represented by $(0, 0, W_0, H_0)$. The position of the sub-block from the bottom left point on the large object indicates that its coordinates are (ox, oy). Let the size of the sub-block be (x, y), and then the sub-block can be represented by $R = (ox, oy, x, y)$. By this definition, two sub-blocks $R_1 = (ox_1, oy_1, x, y)$ and $R_2 = (ox_2, oy_2, x, y)$ with different coordinates in the sub-block are different sub-problems, even if they have the same size (see Fig. 4). After performing a vertical cut (parallel to the y-axis) on the sub-block $R = (ox, oy, x, \mathrm{y})$ at the cut position z_x, the two generated sub-blocks are (ox, oy, z_x, y) and $(ox + z_x, oy, x - z_x, y)$. Similarly, for the cutting position z_y (parallel to the x-axis), two sub-blocks $\left(ox, oy, x, z_y\right)$ and $\left(ox, oy + z_y, x, y - z_y\right)$ are formed. The sub-block gets two new sub-blocks (see Fig. 5).

Definition 2 (defect definition). Defect is actually an irregular figure, approximated by a rectangle or a set of non-overlapping rectangles of integer size. Let the size of the defect j be (w_j^d, h_j^d) and let its position on the large object be represented by $\left(x_j^d, y_j^d\right)$, and then it can be represented by $(w_j^d, h_j^d, x_j^d, y_j^d)$ (see Fig. 6).

Definition 3 (C-block and D-block). If the sub-block $R = (ox, oy, x, y)$ contains defects or overlap with defects, it is called a D-block; otherwise it is called a C-block. If $\left(x_j^d + w_j^d \le ox \ or \ x_j^d \ge ox + x\right)$ or $\left(y_j^d + h_j^d \le oy \ or \ y_j^d \ge oy + y\right)$, then $R = (ox, oy, x, y)$ is a C-block. Otherwise, it is a D-block, which can be determined by the following function:

$$C\&D\,(ox, oy, x, y) = \begin{cases} 0, if\left(x_j^d + w_j^d \le ox \text{ or } x_j^d \ge ox + x\right) or \\ \quad \left(y_j^d + h_j^d \le oy \text{ or } y_j^d \ge oy + y\right) \\ 1, \quad otherwise \end{cases} \tag{2}$$

As known from the above function, if the current sub-block is a C-block, the value of C&D (ox, oy, x, y) is 0, otherwise it is a D-block, and the value is 1.

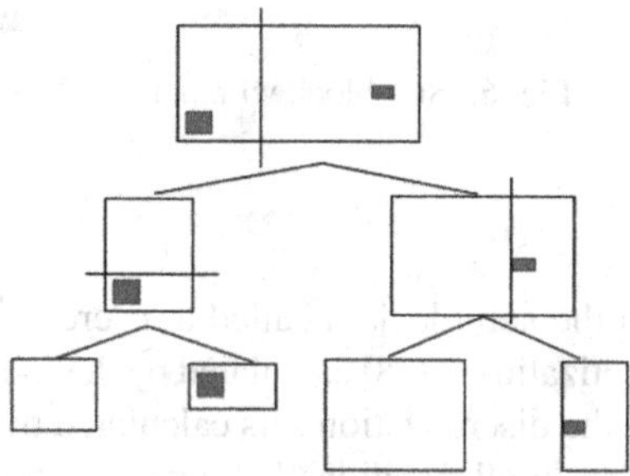

Fig. 3. A series of sub-blocks formed by guillotine cuts

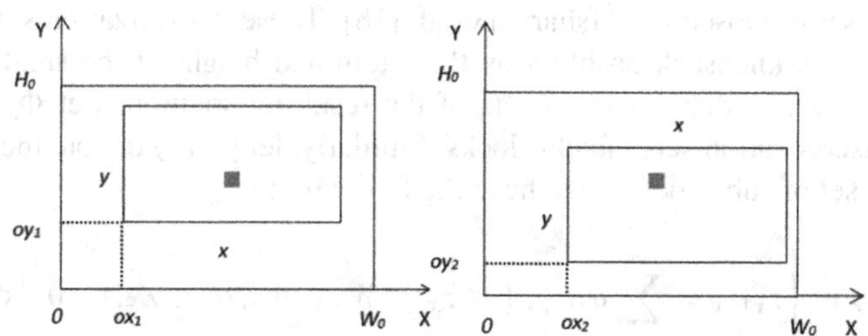

Fig. 4. Two sub-blocks with the same width and height in different positions

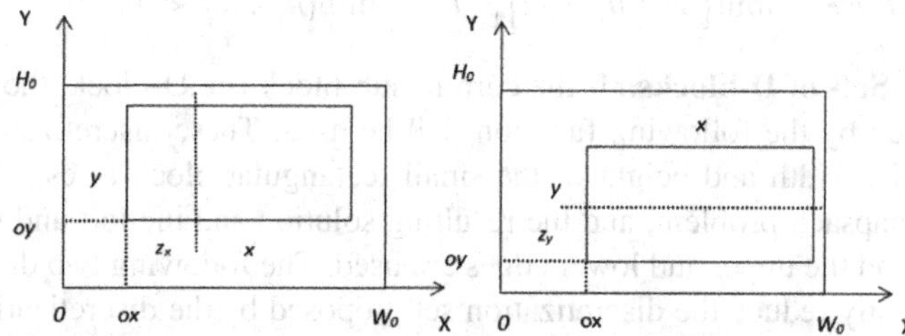

Fig. 5. After a guillotine, the sub-block gets two new sub-blocks

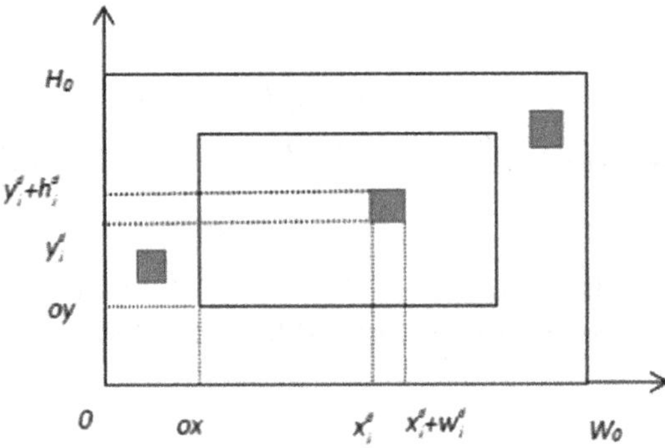

Fig. 6. Sub-block with defect

3.2 Discretization Sets

The cutting position set on the sub-block is called a discretization set. When the sub-block is a C-block, the discretization set [8] calculated by the following functions (3), (4), and (5) is used. Otherwise, the discretization sets calculated by the following functions (6), (7), and (8) are used. Z_+ in all functions belongs to a positive integer set. In this paper, the large object is regarded as the largest sub-block.

Discretization Sets of C-blocks. If the current sub-block is a C-block, the discretization set obtained by the following function is used, which is not different from the discretization set proposed by Afsharian et al. [18]. These discretization sets establish a one-dimensional knapsack problem by the width and height of the small rectangular block and the two discretization sets of the resulting solution. Let $\Phi_x(x)$ denote the vertical discretization sets of sub-blocks. Similarly, let $\Phi_y(y)$ denote the horizontal discretization set of sub-blocks, then have the following:

$$\Phi_x(x) = \left\{ z_x | z_x = \sum_{i=1}^{m} \alpha_i w_i^s,\ 1 \le z_x \le W_0 - w_0, \alpha_i \in Z_+ \cup \{0\}, \forall i \right\} \tag{3}$$

$$\Phi_y(y) = \left\{ z_y | z_y = \sum_{i=1}^{m} \beta_i h_i^s,\ 1 \le z_y \le H_0 - h_0, \beta_i \in Z_+ \cup \{0\}, \forall i \right\} \tag{4}$$

$$w_0 = \min\left\{ w_i^s : h_i^s < y \right\}_1^m, h_0 = \min\{h_i^s : w_i^s < x\}_1^m \tag{5}$$

Discretization Sets of D-blocks. If the current sub-block is a D-block, the discretization set obtained by the following function will be used. These discretization sets are composed of the width and height of the small rectangular block to establish a one-dimensional knapsack problem, and the resulting solution and the left and right edges of the defects and the upper and lower edges are used. The following two discretization sets, which greatly reduce the discretization set proposed by the discretization set size Afsharian et al. [18], so that the computing time of the example is reduced by nearly ten times in the case of obtaining the optimal solution (The following experiment will be presented):

$$\Phi_x(x) = \left\{ \begin{array}{l} z_x | z_x = \sum_{i=1}^{m} \alpha_i w_i^s, \delta_j \left(x_j^d - ox \right), \gamma_j \left(x_j^d + w_j^d - ox \right), 1 \le z_x \le W_0 \\ -w_0, \alpha_i \in Z_+ \cup \{0\}, \delta_j, \gamma_j \in \{0, 1\}, if w_i^s > x \Rightarrow \alpha_i = 0, \forall i, \forall j \end{array} \right\} \tag{6}$$

$$\Phi_y(y) = \left\{ \begin{array}{l} z_y | z_y = \sum_{i=1}^{m} \beta_i h_i^s, \mu_j \left(y_j^d - oy \right), \theta_j \left(y_j^d + h_j^d - oy \right), 1 \le z_y \le H_0 \\ -h_0, \beta_i \in Z_+ \cup \{0\}, \mu_j, \theta_j \in \{0, 1\}, if h_i^s > y \Rightarrow \beta_i = 0, \forall i, \forall j \end{array} \right\} \tag{7}$$

$$w_0 = \min\left\{ w_i^s : h_i^s < y \right\}_1^m, h_0 = \min\{ h_i^s : w_i^s < x \}_1^m \tag{8}$$

3.3 Dynamic Programming

In order to determine the optimal value of the cutting pattern of the sub-block $R = (ox, oy, x, y)$. Whether R is overlapping with defects is important. Therefore, this paper defines two recursive functions for the optimal goal, one for the C-block and one for the D-block. For D-blocks, the coordinates and dimensions on the large object must be determined, and the corresponding calculation function is represented by $F(ox, oy, x, y)$. For a C-block, it is sufficient to only determine the size, and the corresponding calculation function will simply be represented by $F(x, y)$. Note that similar $F(x, y)$ have been used by different authors in the literature (see e.g., Herz (1972), Beasley (1985a)). Furthermore, in order to determine a possible lower bound of the objective function value associated with the C-block $R = (x, y)$, use the calculation function $g(x, y)$, when $z_x \ge x/2$ or $z_y \ge y/2$, which is calculated as the maximum of all small rectangular blocks of the same type, the function is as follows:

$$g(x, y) = \max\left(0, v_i \cdot \left\lfloor \frac{x}{w_i^s} \right\rfloor \cdot \left\lfloor \frac{y}{h_i^s} \right\rfloor, w_i^s < x, h_i^s < y, i \in (1, 2, \ldots, n) \right) \tag{9}$$

That is, the optimal value of $F(x, y)$ is:

$$F(x, y) = \max \left(\begin{array}{l} g(x, y), F(z_x, y) + F(p(x - z_x), y), F\left(x, z_y\right) \\ + F\left(x, q\left(y - z_y\right)\right), z_x \in \Phi_x(x), 1 \le z_x \le x/2, z_y \in \Phi_x(y), \\ 1 \le z_y \le y/2, \Phi_x(W_0) \cup \{W_0\}, y \in \Phi_y(H_0) \cup \{H_0\} \end{array} \right) \tag{10}$$

Where $x < w_0$ *or* $y < h_0$, $F(x, y) = 0$. It is worth noting that due to the appearance of the repeated cutting pattern, the discretization set of vertical (horizontal) in (10) is limited to half the width (height) of the sub-block.

The following is used to determine the recursive function of the optimal cut pattern with the D-block $R = (ox, oy, x, y)$:

$$F(ox, oy, x, y) = \begin{cases} F(x, y) \quad if\ R = (ox, oy, x, y)\, is\ C - block, \\ \max(F(ox, oy, z_x, y) + F(ox + z_x, oy, x - z_x, y) \\ \quad F(ox, oy, x - z_x, y) + F(ox + x - z_x, oy, z_x, y), \\ \quad F(ox, oy, x, z_y) + F(ox, oy + z_y, x, y - z_y), \\ F(ox, oy, x, y - z_y) + F(ox, oy + y - z_y, x, z_y)), \\ \quad 1 \le z_x \le x - 1, 1 \le z_y \le y - 1, \\ \quad w_0 \le x \le W_0, h_0 \le y \le H_0, \\ \quad ox \in \Phi_x(W_0) \cup \{0\}, oy \in \Phi_y(H_0) \cup \{0\}, \\ \quad if\ R = (ox, oy, x, y) is\ D - block \end{cases} \tag{11}$$

Where $x < w_0\ or\ y < h_0$, $F(ox, oy, x, y) = 0$. In addition, in order to standardize the cutting pattern (see Fig. 7), $p(x), q(y)$ in the above recursive function is introduced, and the calculation function is as follows:

$$p(x) = \max(0, z_x | z_x \le x, z_x \in \Phi_x(W_0)), x < W_0, p(W_0) = W_0 \tag{12}$$

$$q(y) = \max\left(0, z_y | z_y \le y, z_y \in \Phi_y(H_0)\right), y < H_0, q(H_0) = H_0 \tag{13}$$

$p(x)$ represents the cut position nearest to the sub-block width x, and correspondingly, $q(y)$ is the cut position nearest to the sub-block height y.

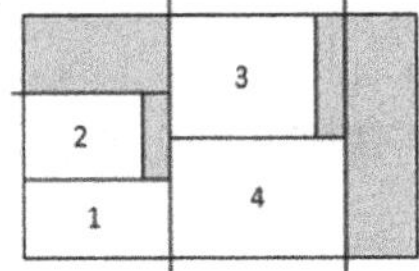

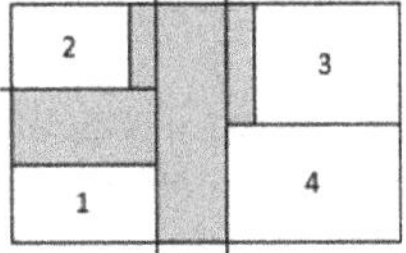

(a) Normalized cutting pattern (b) Non-normalized cutting pattern

Fig. 7. Normalized cutting pattern (shaded is scrap)

3.4 Algorithm Complexity

In this section, we study the computational aspects of the algorithm. We analyze the time complexity of its worst case.

Theorem 1. The worst case time complexity of the 2D_UG_SLOCP solution with defects by the algorithm proposed in the previous section is

$$O\left(|\Phi_x(W_0)| \cdot \left|\Phi_y(H_0)\right| \cdot \left(|\Phi_x(W_0)| + \left|\Phi_y(H_0)\right|\right)\right) \tag{14}$$

Proof. For a given single large object (W_0, H_0), the recursive function requires $O\left(|\Phi_x(W_0)| \cdot \left|\Phi_y(H_0)\right|\right)$ operations for each iteration. Therefore, the calculation involves a total of time complexity as Eq. (14).

Theorem 2. Let $w_0 = \min(\{w_i^s\}_1^m)$ and $h_0 = \min(\{h_i^s\}_1^m)$. And let $\rho_w = W_0/w_0 \leq W_0/w_0$, $\rho_h = H_0/h_0 \leq H_0/h_0$, then:

$$|\Phi_x(W_0)| = \sum_{t=1}^{\rho_w} C_{t+m-1}^t + 2n \tag{15}$$

$$|\Phi_y(H_0)| = \sum_{t=1}^{\rho_h} C_{t+m-1}^t + 2n \tag{16}$$

$$C_{t+m-1}^t = \frac{(t+m-1)!}{t!(m-1)!} \tag{17}$$

Proof. By definition, each element in $\Phi_x(W_0)$ is a viable combination of the length of a small rectangular block $\sum_{t=1}^{\rho_w}\left(\sum_{i=1}^m w_i^s\right)^t \leq W_0$ calculates the same structure of the number of terms in the polynomial. In order to obtain $\sum_{i=1}^m \alpha_i w_i^s$, in the above polynomial, t must take 1 to ρ_w. That's because if $t > \rho_w$, then there is $\sum_{i=1}^m \alpha_i w_i^s > W_0$. And $\sum_{t=1}^{\rho_w}\left(\sum_{i=1}^m w_i^s\right)^t = \sum_{t=1}^{\rho_w} C_{t+m-1}^t$. Add the above function (15) to the left and right edges of defects; similarly, the same is true for the function (16).

4 Calculation Results and Analysis

The algorithm used in this paper is implemented in the C/C++ programming language. The configuration of the computer used is: processor–Intel(R), Core(TM) i7cpu@360 Hz, RAM 8 GB, 64bit operator.

4.1 International Samples

The experiments in this paper are typical of 14 examples, Carnieri et al. [11] provide 8 examples with a single defect, and Vianna and Arenales [12] provide 6 additional examples with defects. The original object width is W0 = 200, high H0 = 100, and 5 types of small rectangular blocks. In Table 1, the objective function values (OFV) obtained by the method of this paper and the computing time are compared with other algorithms, and the OFV is the sum of the values of the small rectangular blocks cut out. The algorithm is compared with Vianna and Arenales [12]. They only give the computing time of a single defect. The computing time of defects is not given, and some of their examples do not get the optimal solution; Neidlein et al. [13] only the OFV and computing time of a single defect are given, and the partial OFV does not get the optimal solution. The examples of multiple defects are not given. Compared with the experimental results of Afsharian et al. [18], the optimal solutions are obtained. The computing time of this paper is nearly ten times higher, and they do not give the optimal cutting pattern of 14 internationally recognized examples. It can be seen that reducing the size of the discretization set greatly optimizes the operational efficiency. In this paper, the optimal cut screenshots of the two examples A11 and A12 are given (see Figs. 8 and 9). These two examples have more defects, and the more sub-problems for cutting, the more complex they are.

Table 1. Operation results and comparison of 4 algorithms.

Ins.	IHDP		Afsharian etc. (2014)		Vianna etc. (2006)		Neidlein etc. (2008)	
	OFV	Comp. time (s)	OFV	Comp. time (s)	OFV	Comp. time (s)	OFV	Comp. time (s)
A1	166	0.86	166	18.86	166	4.61	166	0.52
A2	166	0.67	166	16.43	160	3.57	160	0.77
A3	166	0.74	166	16.47	162	4.40	162	1.77
A4	164	0.25	164	18.25	160	3.15	160	0.27
A5	164	0.31	164	76.96	164	13.51	164	4.11
A6	164	0.47	164	0.90	164	1.32	164	1.44
A7	158	0.21	158	0.81	158	12.47	158	1.07
A8	154	0.13	154	1.21	154	8.07	154	0.50
A9	160	0.87	160	14.32	153	–	–	–
A10	158	0.49	158	2.22	148	–	–	–
A11	151	6.29	151	26.78	143	–	–	–
A12	156	119.30	156	1126.44	150	–	–	–
A13	150	2.19	150	9.06	142	–	–	–
A14	160	0.09	160	1.00	160	–	–	–

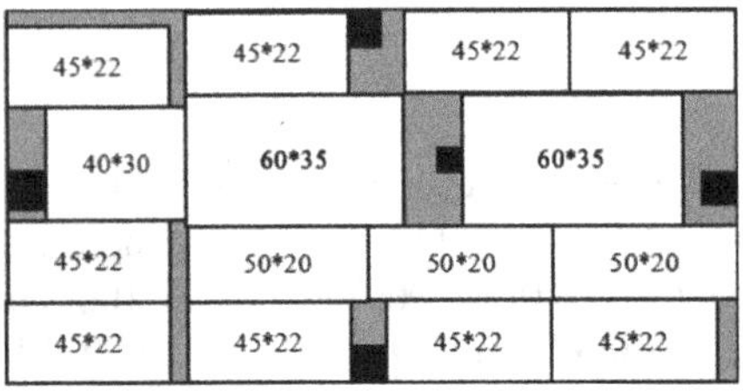

Fig. 8. A11 cutting pattern result

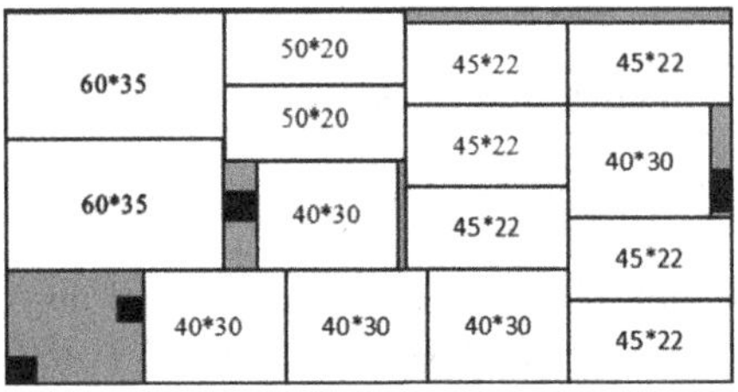

Fig. 9. A12 cutting pattern result

4.2 Randomly Generated Sample

The resulting large plate rectangles are square (75, 75) and rectangular (112, 50). These examples are set by the instance generator program of Neidlein and Wäscher (2008), and the number of types of small rectangles is set to 5. 10, 15, 20 and 25. The type width and height of the small rectangular block are uniformly obtained from $[W_0/\varpi, 3W_0/4]$ and $[H_0/\varpi, 3H_0/4]$, respectively, wherein ϖ in all categories is 6, 8, and 10. The defect is set to 1–4, 15 examples of each defect are averaged for a group. The width and height of the defect are uniformly obtained from the ranges $[W_0/10, W_0/6]$ and $[H_0/10, H_0/6]$, respectively. The position of each defect is represented by the position of the defect in the lower left corner of the large rectangular block, generated using a uniform distribution in the range of $[0, W_0 - w_0]$ and $[0, H_0 - h_0]$, and then these values are rounded. This paper implements the algorithm of Afsharian et al. The following Table 2 is a comparison of the goodness of the algorithm and their algorithm. Experiments show that the algorithm's goodness and camputing time are better than those of Afsharian et al.

Table 2. Algorithm comparison

Ins.	Number of item types	Size of item types	IHDP		Afsharian etc. (2014)	
			Ave. OFV	Ave. time (s)	Ave. OFV	Ave. time (s)
1	5	6	3825.80	0.15	3808.34	0.99
2	10	6	4381.25	0.62	4372.82	1.38
3	15	6	4567.50	0.78	4542.80	1.43
4	20	6	4726.13	1.47	4702.50	2.10
5	25	6	4842.80	1.55	4818.25	1.74
6	5	8	3997.50	0.19	3988.95	1.42
7	10	8	4630.67	1.03	4618.28	1.77
8	15	8	4793.17	1.30	4771.75	1.61
9	20	8	4863.02	1.71	4841.63	1.91
10	25	8	5047.80	2.05	5033.02	2.01
11	5	10	4166.97	0.24	4153.42	1.48
12	10	10	4707.54	1.17	4618.28	2.07
13	15	10	4864.12	1.45	4843.17	1.68
14	20	10	4981.47	2.08	4950.69	2.35
15	25	10	5099.68	2.61	5077.92	2.51
16	5	6	3700.47	0.13	3687.32	1.04
17	10	6	4366.59	0.57	4356.10	1.27
18	15	6	4504.84	0.88	4487.25	1.43
19	20	6	4600.78	0.89	4576.53	1.03
20	25	6	4697.32	1.43	4661.65	1.60
21	5	8	3838.69	0.15	3837.95	1.06
22	10	8	4560.90	0.75	4550.05	1.41
23	15	8	4769.70	1.21	4746.27	1.43
24	20	8	4826.15	1.67	4808.57	1.84
25	25	8	4944.00	2.05	4931.72	2.03
26	5	10	4033.33	0.15	4021.93	0.87
27	10	10	4562.67	0.89	4540.90	1.39
28	15	10	4781.54	1.60	4757.97	1.93
29	20	10	4959.79	2..06	4943.48	2.18
30	25	10	5014.05	2.31	4995.48	2.10

5 Conclusion

In this paper, the smaller discretization sets size is used to improve the original algorithm to solve the two-dimensional cutting problem. An improved heuristic-dynamic programming algorithm is proposed, and the important theorem about its complexity is proved. The optimal solution for a typical case of scale increases the computation time and is better than the best results published in the latest literature. Future research will be carried out on more examples, for example, to solve larger scale studies; to modify discretization set sizes such as discretization sets sparse parts to add several cutting positions.

Acknowledgements. This work was supported by the National Natural Science Foundation of China (Grant Nos. 61862027, 61702238 and 61866014), the Natural Science Foundation Project of Jiangxi (Grant No. 20192BAB207008), the Science Foundation of Educational Commission of Jiangxi Province (Grant Nos. Gjj170316 and Gjj180264).

References

1. Liu, Y., Chu, C., Wang, K.: A new heuristic algorithm for a class of two-dimensional bin-packing problems. Int. J. Adv. Manuf. Technol. **57**(9–12), 1235–1244 (2011)
2. Clautiaux, F., Jouglet, A., Hayek, J.E.: A new lower bound for the non-oriented two-dimensional bin-packing problem. Oper. Res. Lett. **35**(3), 365–373 (2007)
3. Zhang, D., Han, S.H., Ye, W.G.: A bricklaying heuristic algorithm for the orthogonal rectangular packing problem. Chin. J. Comput. **31**(3), 509–515 (2008)
4. Wäscher, G., Haußner, H., Schumann, H.: An improved typology of cutting and packing problems. Eur. J. Oper. Res. **183**(3), 1109–1130 (2007)
5. Lei, W., Qiang, L., Xin, C.: Heuristic search algorithm for the rectangular fixed-size guillotine bin packing problem. J. Softw. **28**, 1640–1654 (2017)
6. Cui, Y.D.: Recursive algorithm for generating optimal T-shape cutting patterns of rectangular blanks. J. Comput. Aided Des. Comput. Graph. **18**(1), 125 (2006)
7. Song, X., Chu, C.B., Lewis, R., et al.: A worst case analysis of a dynamic programming-based heuristic algorithm for 2D unconstrained guillotine cutting. Eur. J. Oper. Res. **202**(2), 368–378 (2010)
8. Yoon, K., Ahn, S., Kang, M.: An improved best-first branch-and-bound algorithm for constrained two-dimensional guillotine cutting problems. Int. J. Prod. Res. **51**(6), 1680–1693 (2013)
9. Herz, J.C.: Recursive computational procedure for two-dimensional stock cutting. IBM J. Res. Dev. **16**(5), 462–469 (1972)
10. Beasley, J.E.: Algorithms for unconstrained two-dimensional guillotine cutting. J. Oper. Res. Soc. **36**(4), 297–306 (1985)
11. Carnieri, C., Mendoza, G.A., Luppold, W.G.: Optimal cutting of dimension parts from lumber with a defect: a heuristic solution procedure. For. Prod. J. **43**, 66–72 (1993)
12. Vianna, A.C.G., Arenales, M.N.: Problema de corte de placas defeituosas. Pesqui Operacional **26**, 185–202 (2006)
13. Neidlein, V., Vianna, A.C.G., Arenales, M.N., Wäscher, G.: The two-dimensional guillotine-layout cutting problem with a single defect - an AND/OR-graph approach. Oper. Res. Proc., 85–90 (2008). Fleischmann, B., et al. (ed.). Springer-Verlag, Heidelberg

14. Zhang, D., Deng, A., Kang, Y.: A hybrid heuristic algorithm for the rectangular packing problem. Lect. Notes Comput. Sci. **3514**, 783–791 (2005)
15. Zhang, D.F., Kang, Y., Deng, A.: A new heuristic recursive algorithm for the strip rectangular packing problem. Comput. Oper. Res. **33**(8), 2209–2217 (2006)
16. Berkey, J.O., Wang, P.Y.: Two-dimensional finite bin-packing algorithms. J. Oper. Res. Soc. **38**(5), 423–429 (1987)
17. Alvarez-Valdes, R., Martí, R., Tamarit, J.M., et al.: GRASP and path relinking for the two-dimensional two-stage cutting-stock problem. INFORMS J. Comput. **19**(2), 261–272 (2007)
18. Afsharian, M., Niknejad, A., Wäscher, G.: A heuristic, dynamic programming-based approach for a two-dimensional cutting problem with defects. OR Spectrum **36**(4), 971–999 (2014)

Constrained Optimization via Quantum Genetic Algorithm for Task Scheduling Problem

Zihan Yan(✉), Hong Shen, Huiming Huang, and Zexi Deng

School of Data and Computer Science, Sun Yat-sen University, Guangzhou, China
ZihanYan0221@qq.com, shenh3@mail.sysu.edu.cn

Abstract. Task scheduling is one of the most important issues on heterogeneous multiprocessor systems. In this paper, the problem is defined as performance-constrained energy optimization. It is a commonly used constrained optimization problem (COP) in practice. Task scheduling for constrained optimization problem is NP problem. It is usually handled by heuristics or meta-heuristics method. Classic quantum genetic algorithm is an excellent meta-heuristics algorithm, but they are hardly ever used to handle COPs because quantum rotation gate can only deal with single objective problem. Moreover, it is difficult to model the task scheduling problems so as to be handled by quantum genetic algorithm. To handles COPs in task scheduling on heterogeneous multiprocessor systems, we propose a new quantum genetic algorithm. In our algorithm, the chromosome consists of task sequence part and mapping part. Task sequence part is generated by list scheduling algorithm which can improve the parallel of the tasks. The mapping part indicates the correspondence between the tasks and the processors which they will run on. The mapping part will be transferred to quantum bits and take part in the evolvement guided by quantum genetic algorithm. Beside, we adopt an adaptive penalty method which belongs to constraint-handling technique to transfer COP into single objective problem. The results in simulations show the superiority of our method compared with state-of-the-art algorithms.

Keywords: Task scheduling · Quantum genetic algorithm · Constrained optimization problem · Adaptive penalty method · Performance-constrained energy optimization · Heterogeneous multiprocessor system

1 Introduction

In heterogeneous multiprocessor systems, task scheduling is one of the most significant problems. It is important for improving the performance of system, and it can also be used to save the energy and optimize load balancing. With more and more people calling for green earth, performance-constrained energy optimization problem becomes a hot pot in researches. This problem belongs to

H. Shen and Y. Sang (Eds.): PAAP 2019, CCIS 1163, pp. 234–248, 2020.
https://doi.org/10.1007/978-981-15-2767-8_22

COPs and is of value in energy-saving. Task scheduling for energy optimization under performance constraint is a NP problem, so it is common to use heuristics or meta-heuristics method to handle this problem. Genetic algorithm is a popular meta-heuristics method for it is a guided-random-search-based method [1]. It uses guided search strategy that is inspired by biological evolution or biobehavioral to search the problem space directly. Numerous studies have shown that genetic algorithm usually generate output schedules of better quality than those produced by other algorithm categories. Omara et al. propose the way to use genetic algorithm to handle task scheduling problem [2]. And Xu et al. improve the genetic algorithm for task scheduling problem which makes the policy of priority queues, the way to initialize, the function of crossover and mutation more suitable for task scheduling problem [1]. The methods above have made great progress, but their modeling methods may not be suitable for quantum genetic algorithm.

The researches above are about the genetic algorithm handling task scheduling problem. However, with the development of quantum computing, many researchers start to study quantum genetic algorithm, and it is getting more and more attention because its excellent performance. As for the constrained optimization problems, most of the existed researches concentrate on how to use genetic algorithm to handle COPs rather than using quantum genetic algorithm. So we lack the researches on using quantum genetic algorithm to handle COPs.

In this paper, we propose a new quantum genetic algorithm handling a COP for task scheduling, and the COP is to minimize energy consumption under makespan-constraint. We modify the traditional chromosome to make it compatible with quantum genetic algorithm. We also find the reason why quantum genetic algorithm can not handle the COPs and come up with a method to make quantum genetic algorithm have ability to handle COPs. The contributions in this study are following:

1, To make quantum genetic algorithm become compatible with task scheduling problem, we modify the chromosome which can be seen in Fig. 3 [2]. We transfer the mapping part to quantum bits and leave the task sequence part remain natural numbers. When the evolvement is conducted, the quantized mapping parts from all the chromosomes form a population and quantum genetic algorithm guide the evolvement in the population. Meanwhile, the task sequence part is constant and does not take part in the evolvement. But when evaluating the single chromosome, the mapping part and task sequence part need to be taken into account together. The simulations show that this method to model is effective and could evolve the population until the convergence.

2, Introduce the list scheduling algorithm to generate the task sequence part. The task sequence part is constant when evolving the population, so it is necessary to ensure the quality of the sequence. In this study, we choose the list scheduling algorithm to generate the task sequence part because it can help the parallel when the tasks are executed on processors so that the workload of evolvement could be reduced.

3, We adopt an adaptive penalty method [3] as constraint-handling technique to transfer the COP to single objective problem so that it can be handled by traditional quantum genetic algorithm: To make quantum genetic algorithm capable to handle the COPs, we analyse the mechanism of it. We find that the quantum rotation gate can only handle single objective problem and this make quantum genetic algorithm not capable to handle COPs. Facing with this difficulty, we decide to adopt an adaptive penalty method [3] as constraint-handling technique to transfer the COPs to single objective problems. After this preprocessing, the quantum genetic algorithm can handle the problem of minimizing energy-consumption under makespan constraint which is a COP. Furthermore, the penalty method used in this study is adaptive, so we don't need to select an optimal penalty parameter in advance. This design makes it convenient to use the proposed algorithm in engineering. The simulations indicate that this method is better in performance than state-of-the-art algorithms.

The remainder of this paper is organized as follows. Section 2 reviews related works of handling constrained optimization problems for task scheduling. In Sect. 3, the problem is described and modeled. Then in Sects. 4 and 5, the proposed method in this paper and simulations are demonstrated. Finally, we summarize the study in Sect. 6.

2 Related Work

Task scheduling problem can be explained as searching for an optimal or approximately optimal solution to assign a set of tasks onto a set of processors. In this paper, the objective is to minimize the energy consumption under makespan constraint which is a COP. This kind of problem belongs to NP problem. For this reason, task scheduling is usually handled by heuristic algorithm because it can provide near-optimal solution in polynomial time. Heuristic algorithm could search a path in solution space at the cost of ignoring some possible paths. It can be classified to list scheduling [4], cluster scheduling [5], and task duplication-based scheduling [6].

The other common algorithm to handle NP problem is meta-heuristic algorithm which is guided-random-search-based. The well-known meta-heuristic algorithm include particle swarm optimization (PSO), ant colony optimization (ACO), artificial bee colony algorithm (ABC), simulated annealing (SA), tabu search (TS), evolution algorithm (EA), and genetic algorithms (GA). Genetic algorithm is one of the most widely used meta-heuristic algorithm in handling task scheduling problem. It can cover a larger solution space and usually find a better solution than heuristic algorithm. However, genetic algorithm usually spends considerably high computational cost.

The most mature method which can incorporate with genetic algorithm/quantum genetic algorithm to handle COPs is nondominated sorting [7], but it still has some disadvantages such as the deterioration of search ability caused by the increase of objective number, the exponential increase in the number of solutions that are used to approximate Pareto front [8]. These disadvantages are caused by the mechanism of nondominated sorting and very hard to deal with.

Another common approach to incorporate with genetic algorithm/quantum genetic algorithm to handle COPs is penalty method. Penalty method belongs to constraint handling technique and could be divided into three categories: stationary penalty method [9], non-stationary penalty method [10] and adaptive penalty method [11,12]. Penalty method is widely-used but the performance of which is too much dependent on the penalty parameter. Moreover, the optimal penalty parameter need to be selected through systematic tests which makes it bothered to use penalty method in engineering.

Moreover, there are also many other related methods from which we could learn. Chuang et al. [9] propose a simple and efficient real-coded genetic algorithm for constrained optimization. It implements some impressive operators such as ranking selection (RS), direction-based crossover (DBX) and dynamic random mutation (DRM). The model developed by Bangroo et al. [13] is also a good reference for us. Although the researches above have made great progress, they can not be used to handle the COP for task scheduling in this study.

Quantum genetic algorithm attracts many researchers' attention because of its better performance than traditional genetic algorithm. Quantum genetic algorithm is invented by Yang through introducing quantum rotation angle and quantum crossover [14]. Quantum genetic algorithm is often used to handle multi-objective problems. SPEA [15] and NSGA-II [7] are two well-known multi-objective genetic algorithms which are Pareto dominance-based. They can handle multi-objective problems but the search ability will decrease when the number of objectives increases. Moreover, the number of solutions required for its approximation exponentially increases with the dimensionality of the objective space [8]. These problems are actually caused by Pareto sorting. When dealing with COPs, the Pareto dominance-based method will also face with the problems above, so in this paper, we decide not to use Pareto dominance-based method to handle the COP.

3 Problem Formulation

In high performance computing, the COPs are frequently encountered. COPs can be explained as,

$$\begin{aligned} &\mathit{minimize} && f(\boldsymbol{x})\ \boldsymbol{x} = (x_1, x_2, ..., x_n) \in R^n \\ &\mathit{subject\ to} && g_j(\boldsymbol{x}) \leq 0, j = 1, ..., l \\ & && h_j(\boldsymbol{x}) = 0, j = l+1, ..., p \end{aligned} \tag{1}$$

where $\boldsymbol{x}$ is the solution, R^n is the space of all solutions, f($\boldsymbol{x}$) is the objective, $g_j(\boldsymbol{x}) \leq 0$ and $h_j(\boldsymbol{x}) = 0$ is the constraint.

In this section, we will describe the problem in our research. The objective is to minimize energy consumption under makespan constraint which can be expressed as,

$$\begin{aligned} & minimize \quad EC(x)\ x \in S \\ & subject\ to \quad MS(x) \leq MSC \end{aligned} \tag{2}$$

where x is the solution; S is the set of all solutions; MSC is the makespan constraint; EC(x) is the energy consumption of x; MS(x) is the makespan of x.

Task scheduling in heterogeneous system is to assign tasks onto heterogeneous processors. When tasks are assigned onto heterogeneous processors, we could obtain the makespan and energy consumption. Our objective is to minimize energy consumption under makespan constraint through optimize the solution to assign. In this section, we are going to introduce the task model and heterogeneous multiprocessor system.

3.1 Task Model

The model for task execution is represented by a Directed Acyclic Graph (DAG). The DAG is composed of n nodes, and each node represents a task. The node without any parent is called entry node and which without any child is called an exit node. The weight on a node represents the computation cost of the task, denoted by size(t_i). In DAG, there is precedence constraint which is implied by arrows. If $t_i \rightarrow t_j$, it means that t_j is child which can not start until its parent t_i has finished. For the nodes with one or more inputs, only if all inputs have arrived can it be executed. The weight of an edge in DAG represents the communication cost between two nodes, and it is denoted by c(t_i, t_j). However, when two tasks are on the same processor, the communication cost should be considered as zero [1]. The Fig. 1 is an example for a DAG.

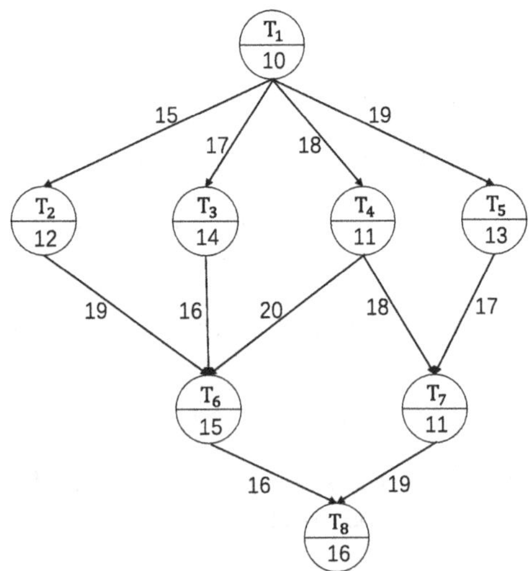

Fig. 1. An example for DAG

Table 1. Voltage-relative speed pairs

Processor	Attribute	
	Voltage	Relative speed (%)
Processor1	1.8	100
Processor2	1.7	90
Processor3	1.6	80
Processor4	1.5	70
Processor5	1.4	60
Processor6	1.3	50

3.2 Heterogeneous Multiprocessor System

The processors in the multiprocessor system are heterogeneous with different voltage and speed. In this study, there are six different processors and their attribute can be seen in Table 1. When tasks are assigned onto processors, the system can be visualized by Fig. 2.

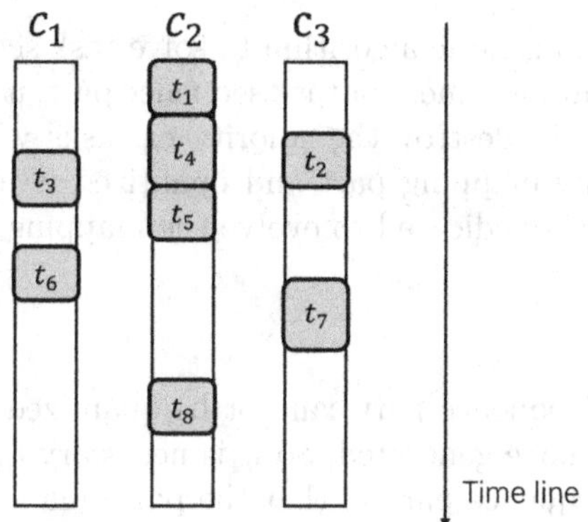

Fig. 2. Tasks are assigned onto processors

4 Proposed Method

The proposed method extends the ability of quantum genetic algorithm [14] to deal with constrained optimization problems for task scheduling. The constraint-handling technique and list scheduling algorithm have been incorporated within quantum genetic algorithm. The details are following:

4.1 Encoding

When we use quantum genetic algorithm to solve problems, the first step is encoding the solution to chromosome. In our study, the solution is assigning every task onto a processor, so we encode the solution to a chromosome as shown in Fig. 3, where a chromosome is divided into two parts, one is mapping part and the other is task sequence part. Task sequence part is the order of task execution generated from the DAG. Mapping part is the processors which the tasks will run on, respectively. For example, from Fig. 3, we can know that task t_2, t_3 and t_5 are executed on processor c_3, c_1 and c_2, respectively.

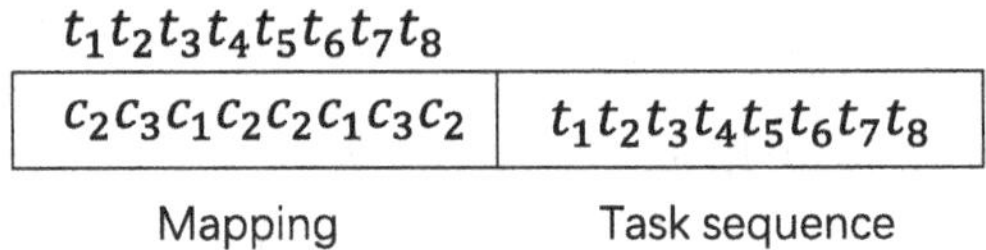

Fig. 3. Encode the solution to a chromosome

4.2 Quantization

In order to use quantum genetic algorithm to solve task scheduling problem, we need to quantize the chromosome. For task sequence part, it can not be quantized because quantization will destroy the priority of tasks which is stipulated by DAG. So we choose the mapping part and quantized it to quantum bits. The quantum rotation gate is dedicated to evolve the mapping part.

4.3 Task Sequence

As we know that task sequence part can not be quantized and take part in the evolvement. It is fixed once generated. So it is necessary to find a good method to initialize the task sequence part so that the performance can be better.

In this paper, we use list scheduling algorithm proposed in [1] to generate a task sequence. It is a heuristic rank policy called upward rank which is used to obtain a good "seeding" for the executing order of tasks. It uses $\text{rank}_b(t_i)$ to evaluate the task t_i and arrange these tasks in descending order. Intuitively, the upward rank of a task reflects the average remaining cost to finish all tasks after that task starts up. So if we arrange these tasks in descending order, we could improve the parallel of task execution. The $\text{rank}_b(t_i)$ can be computed by Eq. 3:

$$rank_b(t_i) = W(t_i) + \max_{t_j \in Succ(t_i)} (c(t_i, t_j) + rank_b(t_j)) \tag{3}$$

where the t_i is the ith task; $\text{W}(t_i)$ is the computation cost of task t_i; $\text{c}(t_i, t_j)$ is the communication cost from task t_i to t_j; the $\text{Succ}(t_i)$ is the set of immediate successors of task t_i; the $\text{rank}_b(t_i)$ is the upward rank of task t_i. The upward rank is computed recursively and starts from the exit node.

Algorithm 1. Compute the makespan of a chromosome

Input: A chromosome
Output: The makespan

/*ST[t_i] is the start time of the task t_i*/
/*RT[c_k] is the ready time of the processor c_k*/
/*FT[t_i] is the finish time of the task t_i*/
/*weight[t_i] is the executing time of the task t_i. It is equal to the quotient of the computation cost of task t_i divided by the speed of processor*/

$\forall$ RT[c_k]=0
Let TSeq be a list of tasks extracted from the Task sequence part of the chromosome;
for t_i in TSeq **do**
    Find the processor c_k which t_i is executed on;
    ST[t_i]←max{RT[c_k],DAT[t_i]};
    FT[t_i]←ST[t_i]+weight[t_i];
    RT[c_k]←FT[t_i];
makespan=max(FT);
return *makespan*

4.4 Fitness

In this section, we will introduce the method to compute fitness using constraint-handling technique. In this work, the set of processors is denoted as C = $\{c_1, c_2, c_3, ..., c_m\}$.

Makespan. The makespan of a solution can be computed by Algorithm 1 [2], where the DAT is Data Arrival Time. It can be computed by the Eq. 4:

$$DAT(t_i) = max\{FT(t_{par}) + c(t_{par}, t_i)\};\ t_{par} \in P(t_i), \tag{4}$$

where t_{par} is the parent task of task t_i; P(t_i) is the set of task t_i's parent(s).

Energy Consumption. The power model of this study is based on complementary metal-oxide semiconductor logic circuits. The dynamic power dissipation is defined by [16]

$$P = AC'\overline{V}^2 f, \tag{5}$$

where A is a parameter expressing the time of switches per clock cycle; C' is a parameter expressing the total capacitance load; $\overline{V}$ is working voltage of the processor, and f represents the frequency. The A and C' are constants, and $f \propto \overline{V}$, so we can define the dynamic power dissipation as

$$P = \phi\overline{V}^3. \tag{6}$$

The ϕ could be considered as a parameter which differs with the type of processor. In simulation, the ϕ is generated randomly from a proper range, and ϕ_k corresponds with processor c_k.

We assume that the energy consumption is 0 when processor is idle, so the energy consumption is as follow

$$E = \sum_{k=1}^{m} \sum_{t_i \in U_k} \phi_k V_k^3 W_{ki}, \tag{7}$$

where the U_k is the set of tasks running on processor c_k; V_k is the voltage of processor c_k; W_{ki} is the executing time of $task_i$ which is executed on processor c_k.

Constraint-Handling Technique. The objective of task scheduling is to minimize energy consumption under makespan constraint. It is a COP and can be expressed as Eq. 2. In order to transfer it to a single objective problem so that it can be handled by quantum genetic algorithm, we utilize the adaptive penalty method proposed in [3] which belongs to constraint-handling technique.

First, we need to define the penalty function G(x) which means the degree of violating the makespan constraint. It can be computed by Eq. 8:

$$G(x) = max\{0, MS(x) - MSC\} \; x \in S \tag{8}$$

Then, we need to normalize the penalty function G(x) and the objective function EC(x) in Eqs. 9 and 10, respectively. The Eqs. 9 and 10 are given as follow:

$$G_{norm}(x) = \frac{G(x)}{G_{max}}, \tag{9}$$

where the G_{max} is the largest penalty function in the current population.

$$EC_{norm}(x) = \frac{EC(x) - EC_{min}}{EC_{max} - EC_{min}}, \tag{10}$$

where the EC_{max}, EC_{min} is the largest and the smallest objective function in the current population.

So we obtain the modified fitness n(x) in Eq. 11,

$$n(x) = \begin{cases} G_{norm}(x), & if \; r_f = 0 \\ \sqrt{EC_{norm}(x)^2 + G_{norm}(x)^2}, & otherwise \end{cases} \tag{11}$$

where r_f is the proportion of feasible individuals in current population.

And we could also obtain a significant value p(x) given in Eq. 12,

$$p(x) = (1 - r_f)X(x) + r_f Y(x), \tag{12}$$

where

$$X(x) = \begin{cases} 0, & if \; r_f = 0 \\ G_{norm}(x), & otherwise \end{cases}$$

Algorithm 2. Main function of APMQGA

Input: Population size *popsize*, iterative time *ITR*
Output: A approximate optimal solution *best*

/**pop* means quantized mapping part*/
/**binaries* is certain binary mapping part*/
/**best* is the best chromosome in fitness*/
Initial the task sequence part using upward rank method in section 4.3;
Initial the quantized mapping part of population to obtain the *pop*;
Obtain the *binaries* from *pop*;
Evaluate the fitness of every chromosome in *binaries*;
Find out the *best*;
for e=1 to *ITR* **do**
    Obtain the *binaries* from *pop*;
    Evaluate the fitness of every chromosome in *binaries*;
    Call Algorithm 3 to evolve the population;
    Update the *best*;
return *best*

$$Y(x) = \begin{cases} 0, & for\ feasible\ individual \\ EC_{norm}(x), & for\ infeasible\ individual. \end{cases}$$

Finally, we could construct the fitness function which can be seen in Eq. 13:

$$fitness(x) = n(x) + p(x) \tag{13}$$

This fitness function could adjust the direction of evolvement according to the r_f. When the r_f is not large enough, it guide the population to search more feasible individuals. Otherwise it will guide to search the optimal solution.

4.5 Adaptive Penalty Method Quantum Genetic Algorithm

In this section, we will introduce adaptive penalty method quantum genetic algorithm (APMQGA) proposed in this study. It is improved based on the quantum genetic algorithm proposed in [14] which uses quantum bits, quantum rotation angle and quantum crossover. The main function of APMQGA is given in Algorithm 2, where the *binaries* is obtained by sampling the *pop*.

5 Experiment and Discussion

In order to evaluate the performance of the algorithm, we compute the performance of the proposed algorithm on 8 widely used benchmark problems and problems abstracted from standard workflows that are used in practical engineering [17]. The experiments are conducted using a population size of 200 for all the simulations. The number of iterations (ITR) is set to 120 for all the simulations.

Algorithm 3. Qgate algorithm

```
Input: pop, best, binaries, popsize
Output: New pop
for i=1 to popsize do
    Generate quantum rotation angle with best;
    Generate quantum rotation gate;
    Update the related chromosome;
return New pop
```

5.1 Simulation and Analyse

In this study, we choose DFG_Assign_CP(DAC) algorithm [18], NSGA-II [7] and C-MOEA/D [19] to be the algorithms for comparing.

The Simulation of 8 Benchmark Problems. The results of 8 widely used benchmark problems are shown in Table 2. For problems CTP2 to SRN, we can know that the ranking of mean (from large to small) is {NSGA-II, C-MOEA/D, APMQGA}, but the std ranking (from large to small) is {NSGA-II, APMQGA, C-MOEA/D}. From the data in tables, we can conclude that APMQGA outperforms the NSGA-II and C-MOEA/D in mean value while it has a mediocre performance when it comes to std value.

Table 2. Comparison on convergence metric

Topology	C-MOEA/D		NSGA-II		APMQGA	
	Mean	Std	Mean	Std	Mean	Std
CTP2	0.0035	**0.0007**	0.0948	0.1071	**0.0029**	0.0074
CTP3	0.0178	**0.0052**	0.1647	0.1217	**0.0142**	0.0165
CTP4	0.0995	**0.0304**	0.3063	0.2583	**0.0982**	0.0962
CTP5	0.0178	**0.0046**	0.2044	0.1864	**0.0147**	0.0253
CTP6	0.0062	**0.0012**	0.3033	0.2616	**0.0061**	0.0052
CTP7	0.0180	**0.0952**	0.2705	0.2169	**0.0162**	0.1753
CTP8	0.0180	**0.0129**	1.4573	0.9874	**0.0136**	0.0625
SRN	0.4876	**0.0109**	0.5546	0.0136	**0.4842**	0.0133

The Simulation of Problems Abstracted from Practical Engineering. After the simulation of 8 widely used benchmark problems, we need to conduct the simulation of problems abstracted from practical engineering. The key variables of the experiments abstracted from practical engineering are DAG, the processor group and the makespan constraint. The two DAGs are given in Figs. 4 and 5. The two processor groups are given in Tables 3 and 4. The makespan constraint is generated by ECS algorithm [20] in every simulation.

Table 3. Processor group 1

Members	Attribute	
	Voltage	Relative speed (%)
Processor1	1.8	100
Processor3	1.6	80
Processor5	1.4	60

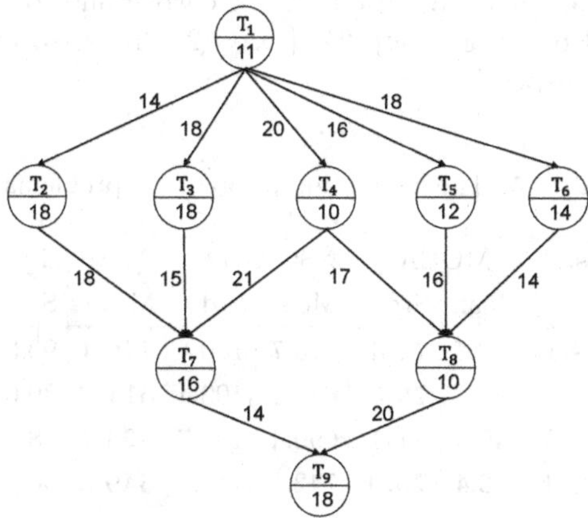

Fig. 4. The DAG 1 used for simulation

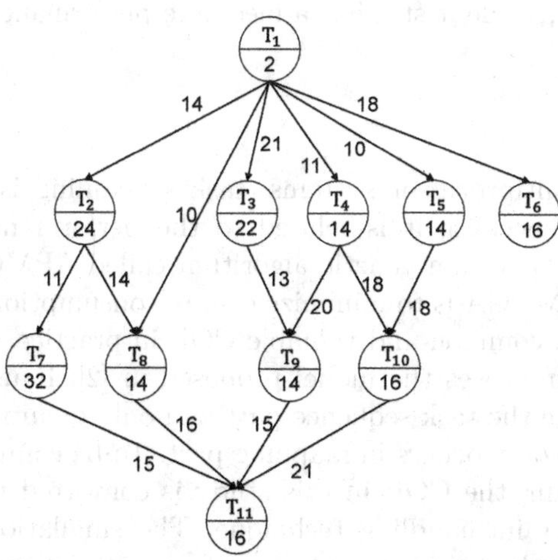

Fig. 5. The DAG 2 used for simulation

Table 4. Processor group 2

Members	Attribute	
	Voltage	Relative speed (%)
Processor2	1.7	90
Processor4	1.5	70
Processor6	1.3	50

The result of the simulation of problems abstracted from practical engineering can be seen in Table 5, where the test 1, 2, 3, 4 correspond to {DAG 1, Processor group 1}, {DAG 1, Processor group 2}, {DAG 2, Processor group 1}, {DAG 2, Processor group 2}, respectively.

Table 5. The simulation of practical problems

Test	C-MOEA/D		NSGA-II		APMQGA	
	Mean	Std	Mean	Std	Mean	Std
$Test1$	510.4	**74.4**	655.7	100.4	**449.1**	90.3
$Test2$	541.7	**79.5**	684.5	102.4	**511.2**	89.6
$Test3$	549.3	**81.1**	699.4	106.7	**524.7**	88.2
$Test4$	573.4	**79.9**	742.1	111.5	**549.3**	90.8

From the data in Table 5, we can verify that APMQGA outperforms the NSGA-II and C-MOEA/D in mean value which is energy consumption under makespan constraint, while it still has a mediocre performance in std value.

6 Conclusion

In heterogeneous multiprocessor systems, task scheduling is one of the most significant problems because it is related to the performance of the system. In this study, a new quantum genetic algorithm called APMQGA is proposed. The objective of APMQGA is to minimize energy consumption under makespan constraint which is a common and valuable COP in practice.

The APMQGA improves the model proposed in [2]. It uses list scheduling algorithm to generate the task sequence part and only quantizes mapping part. The evolvement also only occurs in mapping part. To be compatible with quantum genetic algorithm, the COP in this study is converted to single objective problem using constraint-handling technique. The simulation results indicate that the proposed method exhibits better performance compared with state-of-the-art methods (DAC, NSGA-II and C-MOEA/D). However, the performance of APMQGA in mean value is good, but the std value of APMQGA is not small enough which means the instability of the results of the algorithm, so the APMQGA still has room for improvement.

In the future, we try to figure out the principle of instability in APMQGA through experiments or theoretical proofs. Once we figure out the principle, we could improve the stability of APMQGA so that the performance of APMQGA could be improved.

Acknowledgments. This study was supported by the National Key Research and Development Plan's Program on High performance computing of China, No. 2017YFB0203201.

References

1. Xu, Y., Li, K., Hu, J., Li, K.: A genetic algorithm for task scheduling on heterogeneous computing systems using multiple priority queues. Inf. Sci. **270**, 255–287 (2014)
2. Omara, F.A., Arafa, M.M.: Genetic algorithms for task scheduling problem. In: Abraham, A., Hassanien, A.E., Siarry, P., Engelbrecht, A. (eds.) Foundations of Computational Intelligence Volume 3. SCI, vol. 203, pp. 479–507. Springer, Heidelberg (2009). https://doi.org/10.1007/978-3-642-01085-9_16
3. Tessema, B., Yen, G.G.: An adaptive penalty formulation for constrained evolutionary optimization. IEEE Trans. Syst. Man Cybern. Part A Syst. Hum. **39**(3), 565–578 (2009)
4. Topcuoglu, H., Hariri, S., Wu, M.-Y.: Performance-effective and low-complexity task scheduling for heterogeneous computing. IEEE Trans. Parallel Distrib. Syst. **13**(3), 260–274 (2002)
5. Amini, A., Wah, T.Y., Saybani, M.R., Yazdi, S.R.A.S.: A study of density-grid based clustering algorithms on data streams. In: 2011 Eighth International Conference on Fuzzy Systems and Knowledge Discovery (FSKD), vol. 3, pp. 1652–1656. IEEE (2011)
6. Shin, K., Cha, M., Jang, M., Jung, J., Yoon, W., Choi, S.: Task scheduling algorithm using minimized duplications in homogeneous systems. J. Parallel Distrib. Comput. **68**(8), 1146–1156 (2008)
7. Deb, K., Pratap, A., Agarwal, S., Meyarivan, T.: A fast and elitist multiobjective genetic algorithm: NSGA-II. IEEE Trans. Evol. Comput. **6**(2), 182–197 (2002)
8. Ishibuchi, H., Tsukamoto, N., Nojima, Y.: Evolutionary many-objective optimization: a short review. In: 2008 IEEE Congress on Evolutionary Computation (IEEE World Congress on Computational Intelligence), pp. 2419–2426. IEEE (2008)
9. Chuang, Y.-C., Chen, C.-T., Hwang, C.: A simple and efficient real-coded genetic algorithm for constrained optimization. Appl. Soft Comput. **38**, 87–105 (2016)
10. Joines, J.A., Houck, C.R.: On the use of non-stationary penalty functions to solve nonlinear constrained optimization problems with GA's. In: Proceedings of the First IEEE Conference on Evolutionary Computation. IEEE World Congress on Computational Intelligence, pp. 579–584. IEEE (1994)
11. Matias, J., et al.: Adaptive penalty and barrier function based on fuzzy logic. Expert Syst. Appl. **42**(19), 6777–6783 (2015)
12. Lin, C.-H.: A rough penalty genetic algorithm for constrained optimization. Inf. Sci. **241**, 119–137 (2013)

13. Bangroo, R., Kumar, N., Sharma, R.: A model for multi-processor task scheduling problem using quantum genetic algorithm. In: Abraham, A., Muhuri, P.K., Muda, A.K., Gandhi, N. (eds.) HIS 2017. AISC, vol. 734, pp. 126–135. Springer, Cham (2018). https://doi.org/10.1007/978-3-319-76351-4_13
14. Yang, J., Li, B., Zhuang, Z.: Research of quantum genetic algorith and its application in blind source separation. J. Electron. **20**(1), 62–68 (2003)
15. Zitzler, E., Thiele, L.: Multiobjective evolutionary algorithms: a comparative case study and the strength pareto approach. IEEE Trans. Evol. Comput. **3**(4), 257–271 (1999)
16. Chen, S., Li, Z., Yang, B., Rudolph, G.: Quantum-inspired hyper-heuristics for energy-aware scheduling on heterogeneous computing systems. IEEE Trans. Parallel Distrib. Syst. **27**(6), 1796–1810 (2015)
17. Gandhi, T., Alam, T., et al.: Quantum genetic algorithm with rotation angle refinement for dependent task scheduling on distributed systems. In: 2017 Tenth International Conference on Contemporary Computing (IC3), pp. 1–5. IEEE (2017)
18. Shao, Z., Zhuge, Q., Xue, C., Sha, E.-M.: Efficient assignment and scheduling for heterogeneous DSP systems. IEEE Trans. Parallel Distrib. Syst. **16**(6), 516–525 (2005)
19. Asafuddoula, M., Ray, T., Sarker, R., Alam, K.: An adaptive constraint handling approach embedded MOEA/D. In: 2012 IEEE Congress on Evolutionary Computation, pp. 1–8. IEEE (2012)
20. Lee, Y.C., Zomaya, A.Y.: Energy conscious scheduling for distributed computing systems under different operating conditions. IEEE Trans. Parallel Distrib. Syst. **22**(8), 1374–1381 (2010)

A Method of Business Process Bottleneck Detection

Jiexuan Chen, Yang Yu(✉), and Maolin Pan

School of Data and Computer Science, Sun Yat-sen University, Guangzhou, China
chenjx86@mail2.sysu.edu.cn, {yuy,panml}@mail.sysu.edu.cn

Abstract. In order to improve the efficiency of business processes and ensure the timeliness of cases, an approach for bottleneck detection is proposed, which gives a detailed definition of bottleneck in business process. The approach starts from the overall performance of the system and reduces process congestion by detecting and relieving bottlenecks, which is based on the event log analysis. By extracting relevant information like task arrival rate and maximum service rate etc. from the event log, this approach can analyze the historical trends of congestion rate of each task. And finally it combines the task completion time and historical congestion to detect bottleneck. Experiments show that the bottleneck detection method based on event log can better identify the bottleneck in the business process, and solving the bottleneck can effectively improve the case completion rate and average completion time of the process.

Keywords: Business process · Bottleneck · Event log

1 Introduction

Workflow technology has been widely used in standardized business process management. The development of enterprises is inseparable from the management of processes. Nowadays, industrial community is paying more and more attention to the organic combination of management and information systems. High-quality business process management, monitoring and operation and maintenance services have an important impact on the enterprise business. The completion time of the business is an important indicator for the customer to measure the quality of service. Improving work efficiency and ensuring the completion of each business on time is a major focus of the enterprise in business process management.

Efficiency and time issues are the focus of business process management research. In the past, research on improving process efficiency focused on scheduling and allocation in task dimensions. Some scholars have proposed task assignment based on task priority [1, 2], resource capability [3, 4], preference [3], and resource time availability [5], etc., to improve the efficiency of task execution under the condition of meeting time constraints. Some scholars also use heuristic algorithms [2, 6], genetic algorithms [6, 7], machine learning [8] to conduct time prediction and apply the results to task assignment. All the above studies are based on the time performance indicators of task, and each case

H. Shen and Y. Sang (Eds.): PAAP 2019, CCIS 1163, pp. 249–261, 2020.
https://doi.org/10.1007/978-981-15-2767-8_23

is completed as quickly as possible by assigning tasks to the appropriate resources. However, only pursuing the minimum average completion time of a task may not satisfy the process stability. When a bottleneck occurs due to the lack of resources, it will cause long waits for subsequent activities. In addition, the discussion or experiment in these studies only consider the case of a single process and are not verified in a multi-process scenario. However, parallel business processes are common in enterprises, and resource conflicts exist among these processes [14]. Therefore, multiple processes and multiple cases are indispensable considerations in our business process management research.

A process bottleneck will seriously limit the efficiency of the process, which will result in task congestion, large number of delayed cases and other consequences. Detecting the bottleneck accurately has a great significance to improve the time efficiency of the process. That is, we need to identify the tasks that have the strongest impact on process efficiency. By analyzing the process history information with event log, we can determine which tasks have experienced congestion that hindered the performance of the process. The event logs record information about the running of processes, including executed time, who executed the events, and so on.

In this paper, we propose an approach to detect process bottlenecks from event logs, which is simple, universal, and suitable for complex multi-process environments. By introducing the concept of bottleneck point in manufacturing system, the bottleneck in business process is defined in detail and its metrics are determined. Finally the detection of bottleneck is realized by combining the analysis of process event log. We make a series of experiments to evaluate the effectiveness of this detection method by using an actual event log. The applicability in multi-process environment is also tested by simulating its operation.

2 Related Work

2.1 Bottleneck Analysis

There are not many researches on bottleneck analysis in business process. Some scholars apply it to specific business process (such as medical and surgical process). Hyo Kyung uses continuous time markov chain (CTMC) to provide a quantitative model for MDR process and proposes an approach for bottleneck analysis in medical practice based on this model. The author assesses the impact of each task on the overall rounding time and identified the bottleneck that had the greatest impact. By improving the identified bottleneck tasks, the overall rounding time is reduced and the efficiency of the surgical procedure is improved.

In the manufacturing systems field, scholars have conducted in-depth research on bottleneck analysis, and proposed various bottleneck detection methods, which have been widely used in the manufacturing industry. Roser et al. proposed an approach to detect the bottleneck and bottleneck transferation of manufacturing system, and determined the level of the bottleneck according to the working time of the machine [9]. Kuo et al. put forward the concepts of blocking and hunger in the manufacturing system. If the upstream blocking frequency is higher than the downstream hunger frequency, then the flow between upstream and downstream is the bottleneck [11]. Li et al. proposed a data-driven bottleneck detection method based on real-time data of manufacturing system, which can determine the location of bottlenecks in short and long term [12].

Currently, there is rarely universal bottleneck detection method in business process management. Business process is similar to manufacturing system in that they all consist of a series of activities that are performed by different people (machines). Therefore, the study of bottleneck analysis in manufacturing system can be used for reference in the field of business process.

2.2 Theory of Constrain

Theory Of Constraint (TOC) was proposed by Goldratt in 1984. It was first applied to optimize production in enterprises, and now it has been applied to production, marketing, technology management and other fields.

The core idea of TOC is to manage bottlenecks that limit the functionality of the system, and this management is circular. In every system there is at least one bottleneck, and when one of the bottlenecks in the original system is relieved, the system ascends to a higher level. At this higher level, there will still be imperfections, that is, bottlenecks. In the process of solving bottlenecks, the system gets better performance. Figure 1 shows the specific process of the core idea of TOC.

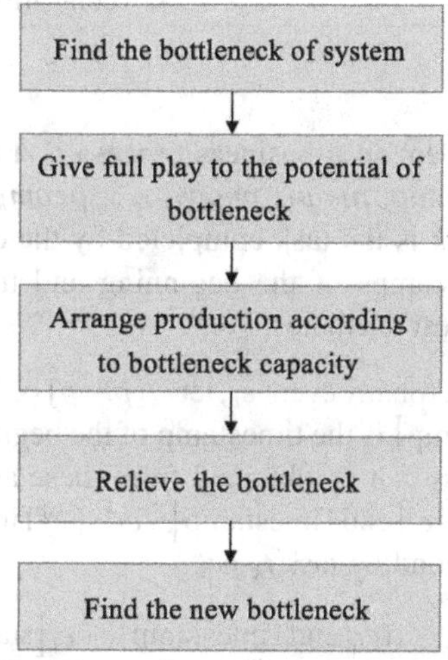

Fig. 1. The core idea of Theory Of Constraint

In this paper, TOC is introduced into business process management. One or more bottlenecks often appear in the process system when executing, which may be caused by the lack of resources, uneven resource allocation and excessive emergent tasks. Bottlenecks restrict the efficiency of the overall process, break the fluency of the process execution, and ultimately affect the completion time of a large number of cases. Based on the idea of TOC, we propose the definition and detection approach of the bottleneck, reduce the congestion of the process and finally improve the efficiency of the process by resolving bottlenecks, so as to improve the on-time completion rate of the process cases.

3 Definition and Detection of Bottleneck

3.1 Definitions

Bottleneck analysis requires extracting temporal information from event logs. There are some definitions and concepts of event log and properties of process. A typical event log consists of a unique set of identifiable use cases corresponding to the case of a business process. Table 1 shows an example snippet of an event log recorded by a business process management system. Each line refers to an event described by the case ID, start and end timestamps, resources, and so on.

Table 1. An example snippet of an event log

Case ID	Start timestamp	Complete timestamp	Activity	Resource
1	2011/01/01 06:41:00	2011/01/01 06:55:00	Analyze request for quotation	Karel
1	2011/01/01 11:43:00	2011/01/01 12:09:00	Send request for quotation to supplier	Karel
1	2011/01/01 12:32:00	2011/01/01 16:03:00	Create Quotation comparison Map	Magdalena

Definition 1 (Event). An event in a business process is a tuple e = (caseID, $task$, $start$ Timestamp, endTimestamp, $prop_1$, $prop_2$, ..., $prom_k$), In which *caseID* is the identification of the case, *task* is the task completed by the event, startTimestamp and endTimestamp are the timestamps of the beginning and the end of the event. And $prom_1, \ldots, prom_k$ are the rest attributes.

According to Definition 1, for any event e_i, let $e_i[prop]$ be its corresponding attribute. For example, $e_i[\text{startTimestamp}]$ is the timestamp of the beginning of the event. Further information about the process can be obtained from these attributes of the event. The execution time of an event e_i is $e_i[\text{endTimestamp}] - e_i[\text{startTimestamp}]$, then the average execution time of the corresponding task t_k is:

$$f_{t_k} = \frac{\sum_{\{e_i | e_i[task] = t_k\}} (e_i[\text{endTimestamp}] - e_i[\text{startTimestamp}])}{number \text{ of } e_i[task] = t_k} \quad (1)$$

Definition 2 (Process model). A process model is a directed graph P = (Ω, T, U, R), in which:

- Ω is the case arrival rate for the process.
- $T = \{t_i | i = 1, 2, 3, \ldots, K\}$ is the set of tasks. A task is a logical unit of work, which is also referred to as the node of the process, and a process is constructed from a series of tasks in a certain order.
- $\text{U} = \{u_i | i = 1, 2, 3, \ldots, K\}$ is the set of resources participating in the process, where K is the total number of resources.

- $R = \{(u_i, t_j) \mid u_i \in U且t_i \in T\}$is the set of relationships of resource and task, (u_i, t_j) indicates that the resource u_i can complete the task t_j.

Definition 3. Mapping from the relationship of resource and task to task participation rates. $\gamma : R \rightarrow [0, 1]$, for any $r \in R$, $r = (u_i, t_j)$, $\gamma\{(u_i, t_j)\}$ represents the probability of resources u_i participating in the task t_j, simply denoted as γ_{u_i,t_j}:

$$\gamma_{u_i,t_j} = \frac{total\,service\,time\;for\;task\;t_j\;of\;u_i}{total\,service\,time\text{ for all tasks of }u_i} \tag{2}$$

Definition 4 (Maximum service rate, SR). Maximum service rate of a task is the number of work items that completed by all capable resources in unit time. The maximum service rate of task t_k is calculated as follows:

$$SR_{t_k} = \frac{1}{f_{t_k}} \times \sum\nolimits_{\{u_i | (u_i, t_k) \in R\}} \gamma_{u_i,t_j} \tag{3}$$

- f_{t_k}: Average execution time of task t_k.
- γ_{u_i,t_k}: the probability of resources u_i participating in the task t_j.

3.2 Bottleneck Detection in Business Processes

According to the definitions in Sect. 3.1, we introduce the concept of bottleneck in TOC into the business process. Bottlenecks in production refer to the machines that limit the overall level of the workflow (including complete time, quality, etc.). In research on manufacturing systems, Chase and Aquilano defined the bottleneck as the resource whose capacity is lower than the demand or which limits the process throughput [13], Roser defined the bottleneck as the resource with the longest uninterrupted activity cycle [14], and Kuo et al. believed that the resource with the lowest productivity in the system was the bottleneck [11].

In a business process, when too many cases arrive, the insufficiency of some resources may cause congestion of corresponding task, preventing subsequent activities from completing on time. This is due to the fact that the execution capacity of the task is lower than process requirements, and the capacity of the task is determined by the number of its resources. Obviously, the congestion of tasks that need longer executed time has a greater impact on the throughput rate of the process. We refer to the tasks that affect process throughput due to task execution capacity below process requirements as bottlenecks of the process. Obviously, the congestion of tasks that need longer execution time has a greater impact on the throughput rate of the process. And when the execution time is similar, the higher the level of the task congestion, the greater the impact on the process throughput rate. So we measure the impact on the process by combining the level of congestion of tasks with the execution time.

Definition 5 (Congestion Rate). The congestion rate of a task in process is defined as the ratio of its task arrival rate to its maximum service rate, denote as $C_{t_k} = \frac{\Omega \times p_{t_k}}{SR_{t_k}}$.

p_{t_k} is the probability that the case performs task t_k, Ω is the cases arrival rate, so the arrival rate of the task is $\Omega \times p_{t_k}$. The ratio of task arrival rate to task maximum service rate SR_{t_k} measures the degree of task congestion. When the task arrival rate is greater than the maximum service rate of the task, it means that the completion speed of the task cannot catch up with the task arrival rate, which starts to cause congestion. The higher the ratio is, the higher level of the congestion degree is. On the contrary, when the ratio is smaller than 1, it indicates that the task resources are sufficient and there is no congestion.

Definition 6 (Congestion task). In business process, a congestion task is a task whose congestion rate (the ratio of arrival rate of task to maximum service rate of task) is greater than 1.

According to Definition 5 and the analysis of influencing factors of the process throughput, we use the product of task congestion rate and task service rate to detect the bottleneck point, which is denoted as $W_{t_k} = C_{t_k} \times f_{t_k}$. And we call W_{t_k} the bottleneck value of the task.

Definition 7 (Process bottleneck). The process bottleneck is the congestion task with the maximum bottleneck value, denoted as t_{PB}. That is, t_{PB} satisfies the following conditions:

$$\begin{cases} C_{t_k} = \frac{\Omega \times p_{t_k}}{SR_{t_k}} > 1 \\ W_{t_k} \; is \, the \, max. \end{cases} \tag{4}$$

- Ω: the case arrival rate.
- p_{t_k}: the probability that the case performs task t_k.
- SR_{t_k}: the maximum service rate of task t_k.

3.3 Bottleneck Relief Methods

As for the process bottleneck caused by unbalanced resource allocation in the process execution, it often requires enterprise personnel to look through the whole process to redistribute the resources of each task. The bottlenecks detected in this paper are due to the lack of resources of the task, and the easiest solution is to add resources to the task. Set the number of resources increased for bottleneck as M, which needs to meet the following formula:

$$C_{t_k} = \frac{\Omega \times p_{t_k}}{\frac{1}{f_{t_k}} \times \left(\sum_{\{u_i | (u_i, t_k) \in \mathrm{R}\}} \gamma_{u_i, t_j} + M \right)} < R \tag{5}$$

R is the expected congestion rate. That is, after increasing resources, the average congestion rate of this task needs to be less than the expected congestion rate. If R approaches 1, congestion is likely to occur when more cases arrive. If R is too small, it means that many resources are idle, which causes a waste of resources. So R is set as 0.7 in this paper, this is a reasonable expectation.

However, when the enterprise has no additional resources to add, it needs to reallocate resources. That is, allocate the surplus resources of other tasks to the bottleneck. From the perspective of management, reasonable allocation of limited resources and the inclination of resources to process bottlenecks within a certain period of time can make the process run smoothly. This can improve the output per unit of time, and thus improve the efficiency of the process and the on-time completion rate of cases.

Here, we propose a simple resource reallocation rule and apply it in subsequent experiments, as follows:

(1) Allocate resources that the congestion rate of corresponding task is less than 1 to the bottleneck. Resources for tasks with low congestion and short average execution time are allocated first
(2) The new congestion rate of the task after removing resources needs to be less than 1

4 Experiment and Result Analysis

4.1 Bottleneck Detection

To verify the effectiveness of the bottleneck detection method proposed in this paper, a series of bottleneck detection experiments are carried out on a procurement process log data set. The event logs we use is come from an enterprise's procurement business process, which consists of 19 tasks that take from minutes to tens of hours to execute. Through preprocessing steps, the average task execution time, task execution probability, cases arrival rate and other information can be calculated by traversing events. Then use the bottleneck detection method described in Sect. 3 to detect the bottleneck in process event log.

Figure 2 shows the historical trends of congestion rate of each task. It can be seen that the tasks 'Deliver Goods Services' (call it T1 following), 'Settle conditions with supplier' (call it T2 following) and 'Create Quotation comparison Map' all have experienced multiple congestion (the congestion rate was greater than 1). These tasks are congestion task.

Figure 3 shows the historical bottleneck value of these congestion task, and Table 2 shows the average bottleneck value of congestion tasks. Obviously, The historical bottleneck values of T1 are mostly higher than others, and its average bottleneck value W_{t1} is the largest, so T1 is the process bottleneck. Meanwhile, T2 also has a high congestion rate, and its bottleneck value is relatively large (only less than T1's and far more than others). So we regard T2 as the second bottleneck of the process.

To verify whether the detected process bottleneck is real and effective, we simulate the process from the event log in YAWL system. The verification method is to add M resources to the bottleneck and non-bottleneck tasks respectively, then detected the bottleneck using the event log of simulation. Compare process efficiency by analyzing the event log obtained from simulation. If the bottleneck is eliminated after increasing resources, and the process efficiency is significantly improved, then the detected bottleneck is effective. To improve the accuracy of the simulation and make the simulation

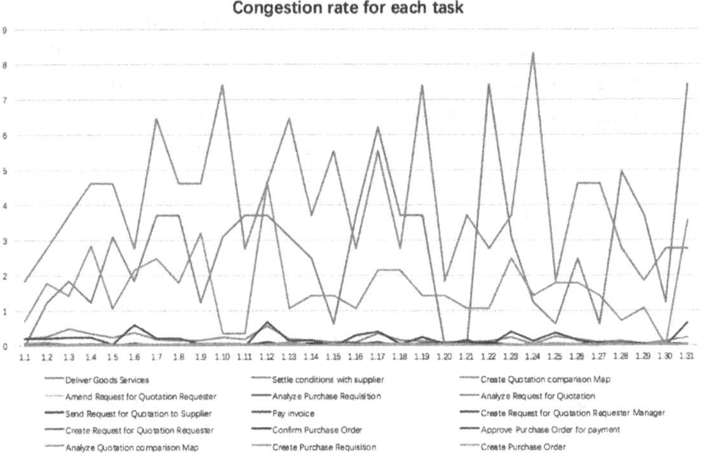

Fig. 2. Trends of congestion rate of each task in event log

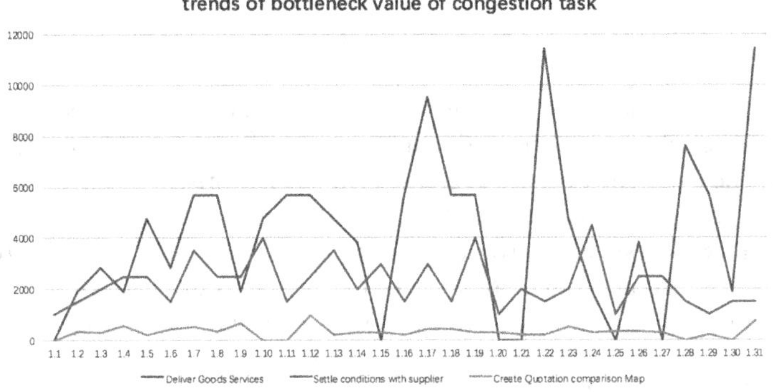

Fig. 3. Trends of bottleneck value of congestion task

closer to the real process, we obtain the case arrival rule, average execution time of each task, task execution probability and other information through the preprocessing of the event log and input it into the simulation Settings.

Our experience added M1 resources to T1 and M2 resources to T2 (M1 and M2 satisfy formula 5), and add (M1 + M2)/2 resources the three non-bottleneck tasks, then make a control group that did not add resources to any task. The simulation results are shown in follow.

Figures 4 and 5 show the trends of the congestion rate and bottleneck value of T1 and T2 of simulation. It can be seen that the congestion of T1 and T2 is significantly relieved, the congestion rates of T1 and T2 are smaller than 1 most of the time. T1 and T2 become bottlenecks only for a short time.

Table 2. Average bottleneck value of congestion tasks

Task	Average execution time (min)	Average C_{t_k}	Average W_{t_k}
Create Quotation comparison Map	204	1.8556	378.5390
Deliver Goods Services	1536	3.2211	4947.5494
Settle conditions with supplier	540	4.8030	2593.5961

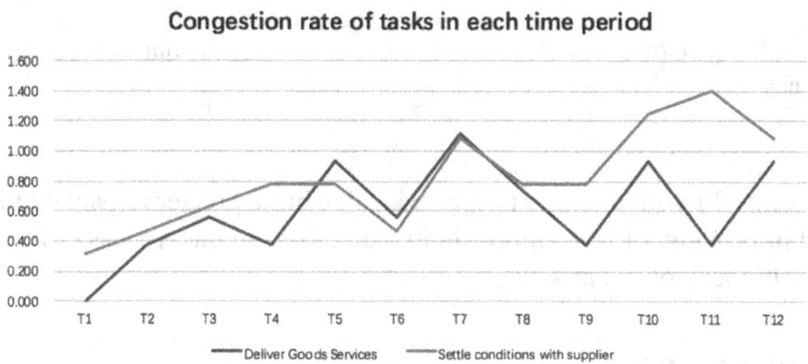

Fig. 4. Trends of congestion rate in each time period

It can be seen from Table 3 that after adding resources to T1 and T2, the on-time completion rate and average execution time of cases have significantly increased compared with the control group. However, after adding the same amount of resources to the non-bottleneck task of the other three groups, the on-time completion rate of the cases and the average execution time of the cases did not improve much compared with the control group, and the process efficiency was barely improved.

Meanwhile, when increasing the same amount of resources, the improvement of on-time completion rate and average execution time of cases obtained by resolving bottleneck T1 is higher than the improvement obtained by resolving the second bottleneck T2.

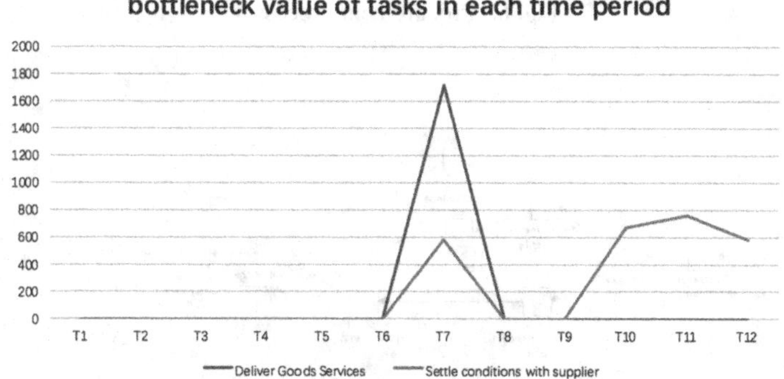

Fig. 5. Trends of bottleneck value of congestion task

Table 3. Execution result after resource allocation

The task of adding resources	Cases on-time completion rate	Cases average execution time
Control group	40%	51 min 36 s
Deliver Goods Services	90%	21 min 8 s
Settle conditions with supplier	70%	28 min 19 s
Amend purchase requisition	45%	49 min 26 s
Amend request for quotation requester	35%	47 min 19 s
Amend request for quotation requester manager	40%	50 min 57 s

It can be seen that T1 with a higher bottleneck value has a greater impact on the process than T2, and improving T1 has a more significant effect on the process efficiency. T1 is the biggest bottleneck of the process.

4.2 Application in Multi-process Environment

The goal of this paper is to propose a bottleneck detection approach suitable for multi-process environment, here we verify the approach in multi-process environments. Due to the lack of event logs obtained from the parallel execution of multiple processes, the experiment is all in the form of simulation. We designed the procurement process and maintenance process shown in Figs. 6 and 7, and carry out simulation in YAWL system, finally get the simulated event log. Similar to the experiment in Sect. 4.1, perform the bottleneck detection on the simulated event log, and reallocate the resources based on the detection result and the rule in Sect. 3.3, then simulate the process again.

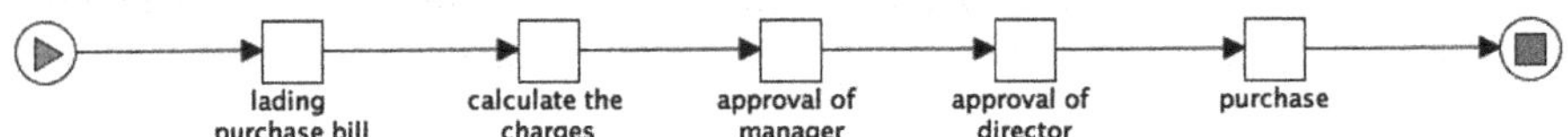

Fig. 6. Procurement process

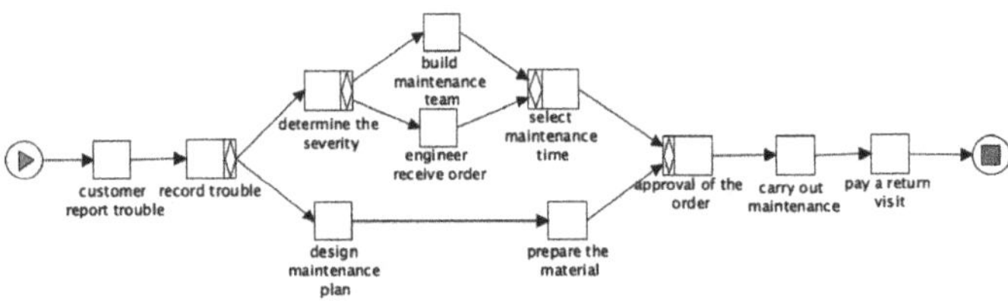

Fig. 7. Maintenance process

Compare the result of the second simulation after reallocation with the result of using Random dispatch and shortest queue priority dispatch. The allocation rules of the two task assignment algorithms in YAWL are as follows:

(1) Random Choice Dispatch (RCD): Randomly select a resource in the collection for dispatch
(2) Shortest Queue Dispatch (SQD): Select the resource with the shortest worklist for dispatch.

Suppose that the number of cases generated per unit time satisfies the Poisson distribution. If the case is not completed exceeding the deadline, timeout exception will be thrown. The experiments were carried out under three cases of low, medium and high workload respectively, and the on-time completion rates of cases of the three methods were compared as shown in Fig. 8.

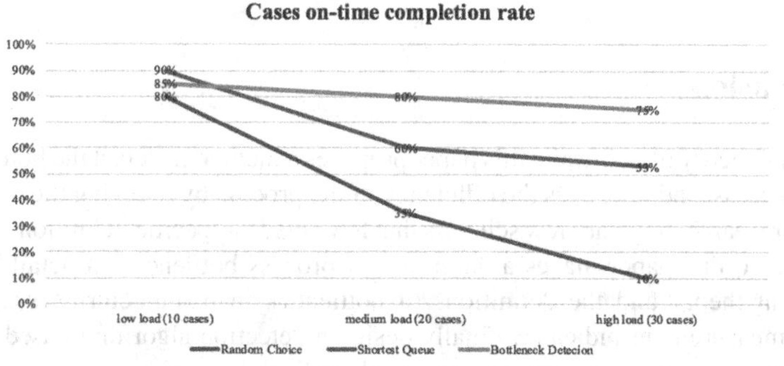

Fig. 8. Comparison of on-time completion rate

All three methods reach a high completion rate under low load, when the case load increases, the on-time completion rate starts to decline. Among them, RCD has the worst performance, with the on-time completion rate decreasing to 35% under the medium load and 10% under the high load, it can be seen that the decline range is obviously large. The resource reallocation method based on bottleneck detection has the best stability and the best performance under medium and high load, which can maintain the on-time completion rate of 70% to 80%.

Tables 4 and 5 respectively show the average case execution time of the two processes of three methods in the simulation. As you can see, SQD has the shortest average completion time of cases under each load. And the average case completion time of resource reallocation method based on bottleneck detection under each load is slightly longer than that of shortest queue priority dispatch method, but it is obviously better than that of random dispatch method.

The simulation results of the above show that the bottleneck detection method is applicable to multiple processes, which can improve the efficiency of processes and has better performance under high case load than the traditional task assignment method.

Table 4. Average execution time of purchasing process cases

	10 cases	20 cases	30 cases
Random Choice	5 min 40 s	9 min 04 s	11 min 6 s
Shortest Queue	5 min 13 s	8 min 55 s	9 min 1 s
Bottleneck detection	5 min 37 s	9 min 31 s	9 min 57 s

Table 5. Average execution time of maintenance process cases

	10 cases	20 cases	30 cases
Random Choice	5 min 45 s	10 min 43 s	13 min 54 s
Shortest Queue	5 min 2 s	7 min 15 s	8 min 20 s
Bottleneck detection	5 min 53 s	8 min 22 s	8 min 55 s

5 Conclusion

Based on the theory of constrain, this paper proposes a method to detect the bottleneck of business process, and improves the efficiency of the process by relieving the bottleneck. In the past research, there are few scholars that have made a specific definition of process bottleneck. So this paper makes a definition of process bottleneck in detail based on management theory and the definitions of bottleneck in manufacturing system, and provide a measurement indicator. Finally design a detection algorithm based on event log analysis, which is simple and has universal applicability.

Future research will be carried out in the following aspects:

(1) Improve detection methods to detect process bottlenecks more accurately.
(2) Carry out further research on resource scheduling algorithm. In this paper, a bottleneck detection method is presented. The next step is to consider the optimal solution of process resource scheduling based on the bottleneck.

Acknowledgements. This work is Supported by the National Key Research and Development Program of China under Grant No. 2017YFB0202200; the National Natural Science Foundation of China under Grant Nos. 61972427, 61572539; the Research Foundation of Science and Technology Plan Project in Guangzhou City under Grant No. 201704020092.

References

1. Zhao, W., Liu, H., Dai, W., et al.: An entropy-based clustering ensemble method to support resource allocation in business process management. Knowl. Inf. Syst. **48**(2), 305–330 (2016)
2. Byun, E.K., Kee, Y.S., Kim, J.S., et al.: BTS: resource capacity estimate for time-targeted science workflows. J. Parallel Distrib. Comput. **71**(6), 848–862 (2011)

3. Huang, Z., Lu, X., Duan, H.: Resource behavior measure and application in business process management. Expert Syst. Appl. **39**(7), 6458–6468 (2012)
4. Pika, A., Leyer, M., Wynn, M.T., et al.: Mining resource profiles from event logs. ACM Trans. Manage. Inf. Syst. (TMIS) **8**(1), 1 (2017)
5. Combi, C., Pozzi, G.: Task scheduling for a temporal workflow management system. In: Thirteenth International Symposium on Temporal Representation and Reasoning (TIME 2006), pp. 61–68. IEEE (2006)
6. Xu, J., Liu, C., Zhao, X., et al.: Resource management for business process scheduling in the presence of availability constraints. ACM Trans. Manage. Inf. Syst. **7**(3), 9 (2016)
7. Liu, L., Zhang, M., Buyya, R., et al.: Deadline-constrained coevolutionary genetic algorithm for scientific workflow scheduling in cloud computing. Concurr. Comput. Pract. Exp. **29**, e3942 (2017)
8. Liu, T., Cheng, Y., Ni, Z.: Mining event logs to support workflow resource allocation. Knowl.-Based Syst. **35**(15), 320–331 (2012)
9. Lee, H.K., Dong, Y., Pickering, B., et al.: Bottleneck analysis to improve multidisciplinary rounding process in intensive care units at Mayo Clinic. IEEE Robot. Autom. Lett. **3**(3), 2678–2685 (2018)
10. Roser, C., Nakano, M., Tanaka, M.: Productivity improvement: shifting bottleneck detection. In: Proceedings of the 2002 Winter Simulation Conference, San Diego, CA, USA, pp. 1079–1086. IEEE (2002)
11. Kuo, C.-T., Lim, J.-T., Meerkov, S.M.: Bottlenecks in serial production lines: a system-theoretic approach. Math. Prob. Eng. **2**(3), 233–276 (1996)
12. Li, L., Chang, Q., Ni, J., et al.: Bottleneck detection of manufacturing systems using data driven method. In: Proceedings of the 2007 IEEE International Symposium on Assembly & Manufacturing, Ann Arbor, Michigan, USA, pp. 76–81. IEEE (2007)
13. Chase, R.B., Aquilano, N.J.: Production and Operation Management, 6th edn. Richard D. Irwin Inc., Homewood (1992)
14. Roser, C., Nakano, M., Tanaka, M.: A practical bottleneck detection method. In: Proceedings of the 2001 Winter Simulation Conference, Arlington, Virginia, USA, pp. 949–953. IEEE (2001)

Optimized Layout of the Soil Moisture Sensor in Tea Plantations Based on Improved Dijkstra Algorithm

Manman Zhang[1], Wu Zhang[1,2](✉), Xun Hong[1], Yifan Song[1], Yuan Rao[1,2], Yujia Gao[1], and Yunyun Sun[3]

[1] College of Information and Computer, Anhui Agricultural University, Hefei 230036, China
2730055076@qq.com, 1727536969@qq.com, 2627568776@qq.com, {zhangwu,raoyuan,gaoyj}@ahau.edu.cn

[2] Anhui Province Key Laboratory of Smart Agricultural Technology and Equipment, Nanjing 21003, China

[3] School of Internet of things, Nanjing University of Posts and Telecommunications, Nanjing, China
sunyunyun0910@sina.com

Abstract. Based on the clustering center of data, this paper optimizes the data transmission path, and proposes an improved Dijkstra algorithm, which is applied to the path optimization of soil moisture sensors in tea plantations. Firstly, the date of soil moisture in tea plantation is collected under the condition of full coverage of the sensor network. Then, the AP clustering algorithm is used to cluster collected data to obtain the cluster center. Secondly, the dissimilarity values of the soil moisture data and the weighted combination of distance between the sensor nodes are used to identify the edge weights and calculate the adjacency matrix of the Dijkstra algorithm. Finally, with the clustering center as the starting point and the convergence point of wireless sensor network as the end point, Dijkstra algorithm is used to search the path. In order to verify the superiority of the proposed algorithm, the algorithm is compared with the ant colony optimization algorithm. In this paper, the data dissimilarity on the path is 25.0652, the total cost of the path is 0.3613, and the difference between the average soil moisture of the tea plantation is 0.1872 and the number of sensors required is 6, The ant colony algorithm obtained the data dissimilarity on the path of 20.4538, the total cost of the path is 0.5483, and the difference between the average soil moisture of the tea plantation is 0.7321 and the number of sensors required is 9. The test results show that the date of path obtained by this method has the largest dissimilarity and the shortest path, and the data collected by this method is representative, which can accurately reflect the distribution of soil moisture in tea plantations. At the same time, the number of sensors is reduced from 25 to 6, reducing the cost of the system.

Keywords: Soil moisture · Sensor · AP clustering · Dijkstra algorithm · Ant colony algorithm · Path optimization

H. Shen and Y. Sang (Eds.): PAAP 2019, CCIS 1163, pp. 262–274, 2020.
https://doi.org/10.1007/978-981-15-2767-8_24

1 Introduction

Soil moisture sensors are widely used in agricultural water-saving irrigation, greenhouse, crop planting, etc. The optimized layout of sensors can accurately obtain soil moisture and reduce the costs of agricultural production [1].

A lot of researches have been done on the optimized layout of sensors, which focus on areas such as set coverage and multi-objective combinatorial optimization. Wang et al. proposed a geometric coverage algorithm based on arc area, which effectively improved the planning efficiency and calculation accuracy of the sensor optimization strategy [2]. Based on the improved discrete particle swarm optimization algorithm, Zhu et al., took the sensor fault detection capability as the target to achieve the sensor layout optimization [3]. Liu et al. used the cuckoo algorithm to optimize the layout of the sensor, achieving good optimization results and improving the running speed of the optimization algorithm [4]. Lin et al. studied the K-cover algorithm and proposed an optimized layout algorithm based on simulated annealing sensors [5]. In the sensing area with obstacles, Wang et al. optimized the sensor network with the goal of achieving minimum coverage [6]. Yin et al. improved the weed monkey swarm algorithm, and applied the algorithm to the optimized layout of sensors to improve the accuracy of the algorithm [7]. In terms of the optimized layout of soil moisture sensors in farmland, Wu et al. combined the genetic algorithm with the weighted circular set layout theory to optimize the layout of soil moisture sensors under the constraints of sensor coverage accuracy and overlap restrictions, achieving good results [8]. Zhang et al. proposed the affinity propagation clustering algorithm for the distribution of soil moisture sensors in water-saving irrigation, which greatly reduced the number of sensors and saved the system cost under the premise of accurately reflecting the soil moisture in tea plantations [9].

Since the moisture of farmland soil is affected by various factors such as rainfall, topography, soil characteristics, vegetation distribution, the distribution of soil moisture is uneven [10–12]. Therefore, the optimized layout of soil moisture sensors in farmland requires consideration of various factors, including the coverage rate of sensor network and the uneven distribution of soil moisture.

This paper proposes an algorithm for optimized layout of soil moisture sensor, that is, an optimization algorithm combining AP clustering and Dijkstra algorithm. On the basis of the full coverage of the network, the soil moisture sensor nodes are deployed in the target area to detect the soil moisture of each node. The AP clustering is used to calculate the clustering center of the soil moisture in the target area, and the distance between the sensing nodes and the data dissimilarity value are weighted and combined as the edge weights to construct the adjacency matrix. An improved Dijkstra algorithm is used to search the shortest path of soil moisture data transmission, to eliminate redundant sensor nodes and reduce the number of sensors.

2 Dijkstra Algorithm and Sensor Optimization Layout

2.1 Basic Dijkstra Algorithm

In 1959, Dutch computer scientist E.W. Dijkstra proposed the Dijkstra algorithm, which is a typical method of single-source shortest path [13,14].

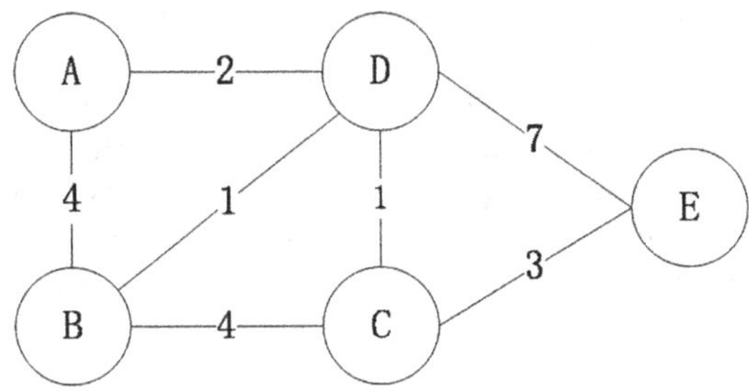

Fig. 1. Weighted graph

Algorithmic idea:

1. Specify a node, such as calculating the shortest path from 'A' to other nodes
2. Introduce two sets (**V, U**), the **V** set contains the points of the shortest path that have been found (and the corresponding minimum length), The **U** set contains the point where the shortest path is not found (and the path from point A to the point. Note that the above figure shows that A-C is not directly connected, the initial value is ∞)
3. Initialize two sets, the **V** set initially has only the node to be calculated at the beginning, A-A $= 0$, The initial set of **U** is AB $= 4$, AC $= \infty$, AD $= 2$, AE $= \infty$
4. Find the node with the shortest path from the **U** set and join the **V** set, for example, A-D $= 2$
5. Update the **U** set path, if ('D to B, C, E distance' + 'AD distance' $<$ 'A to B, C, E distance') then update **U**
6. Loop execution of steps 4 and 5 until the end of the traversal, and get the shortest path from A to the other nodes

2.2 Improving the Dijkstra Algorithm

Based on the basic idea of Dijkstra algorithm, this paper puts forward the improved Dijkstra algorithm, sets the starting node of path search, adds data redundancy factor to the edge weight, and transforms the sensor layout into the weighted graph shown in Fig. 1 above. The vertex represents the sensor and the edge weight is equal to the sum of the data redundancy and the distance length between the two sensor nodes. The specific implementation is as follows.

Calculation Path Starting Point. AP clustering belongs to semi-supervised clustering algorithm. Without setting the number of classes in advance, all data points are considered as potential clustering centers and the clustering centers are found by iteratively updating the similarity between data points. The similarity between two data points is represented by the negative of the distance, that is, the closer the distance, the greater the similarity [15–17]. The similarity is calculated according to the formula (1).

$$s(i,j) = -||m_i - m_j||^2, i \neq j \tag{1}$$

m_i and m_j are the soil mass water contents of the ith and jth sensor nodes, respectively. The data difference between AP cluster centers is the biggest, The AP clustering center is used as the starting point of the Dijkstra algorithm search path, and the convergence point of the wireless sensor network is used as the end point of the search path, which can reduce the redundancy between the sensor node data.

Soil Moisture Dissimilarity Between Sensor Nodes. In order to reflect the difference degree of soil moisture in the region, the difference values between the data of each sensor node and the data of other nodes are summed up. The equation is as in (2)

$$R_i = \sqrt{\sum_{j=1}^{n}(m_i - m_j)^2}, \quad ((i,j) \in 1, \cdots, n) \tag{2}$$

Where n is the number of sensing nodes. m_i and m_j represent the soil mass water content of the ith and jth sensor nodes. The larger the R_i value, the greater the soil moisture in this point and the soil moisture in the whole test area.

Calculation the Edge Weight Between Sensor Nodes. The Dijkstra algorithm determines the direction of the search path based on the size of the edge weight between adjacent nodes. This paper improves the traditional method of calculating the edge weight, and adds the dissimilarity index of soil moisture. The edge weight W_{ij} is obtained by weighted combination of the dissimilarity index T_{ij} and the distance index D_{ij} between the nodes, as in Eq. (3). Where T_{ij} is equal to the sum of reciprocal of the dissimilarity value of sensor node i and the reciprocal of the dissimilarity value of sensor node j, as in Eq. (4). D_{ij} represents the plane distance between the two sensor nodes, and (x_i, y_i) represents the plane coordinates, as in Eq. (5).

$$W_{ij} = \alpha T_{ij} + \beta D_{ij} \ (i,j = 1, 2, \cdots, n) \tag{3}$$

$$T_{ij} = \frac{1}{R_i} + \frac{1}{R_j} (i,j = 1, 2, \cdots, n) \tag{4}$$

$$D_{ij} = \sqrt{(x_i - x_j)^2 + (y_i - y_j)^2} \quad (i, j = 1, 2, \cdots, n) \tag{5}$$

α and β are weighting factors, which represent the proportion of T_{ij} and D_{ij} in the edge weight W, this paper $\alpha = 0.8$, $\beta = 0.2$, T_{ij} is equal to the sum of the reciprocal of the dissimilarity values of the two nodes, representing redundancy, the greater the dissimilarity between the two nodes, the smaller T_{ij}.

Improved Dijkstra Algorithm Searches for the Shortest Path. According to the starting point and boundary route convergence point set in Sect. 2.2, the Dijkstra algorithm takes $F_{min}(m_i, m_j, x_i, y_i) = \alpha T_{ij}(m_i, m_j) + \beta D_{ij}(x_i, y_i)$ as the target to search for the shortest path. The output shortest path has the minimum data redundancy and the shortest distance, and it is also the optimal path method to realize the process as shown in Fig. 2.

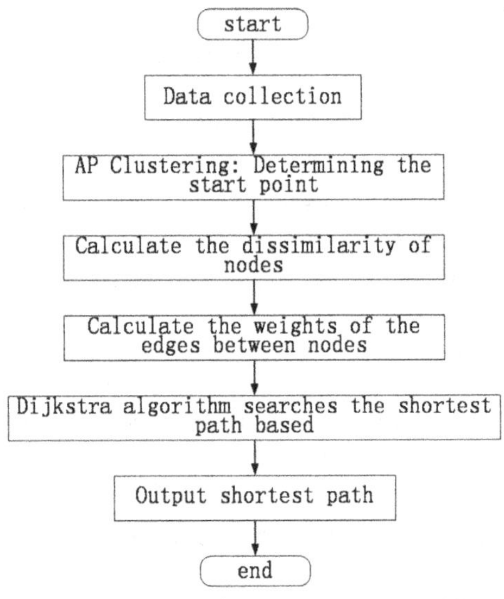

Fig. 2. Algorithmic implementation flow

3 Ant Colony Optimization

3.1 Overview of Ant Colony Optimization

Ant Colony Optimization (ACO) is a bionic intelligent algorithm [18] that mimics the process of natural ants foraging in collaboration with each other. As shown in Fig. 1 below, there are two paths from the ant nest to the source of food, namely, a path and b path. Suppose the first ants start from the ant nest to find food, and return to the ant nest after find food. Since the a path is shorter than the b path, the ants that feed through the a path return to the ant nest first, and leave the bio pheromone on the a path, guiding the subsequent ants to take a path for food; After the passage of time, the concentration of pheromone left by the ant on the a path is higher and higher, and the pheromone on the b path is volatile, there will be no more ants to choose the b path, and eventually all the ants will choose the pheromone-rich a path for foraging, in this way the ants find the optimal foraging path [19,20] (Fig. 3).

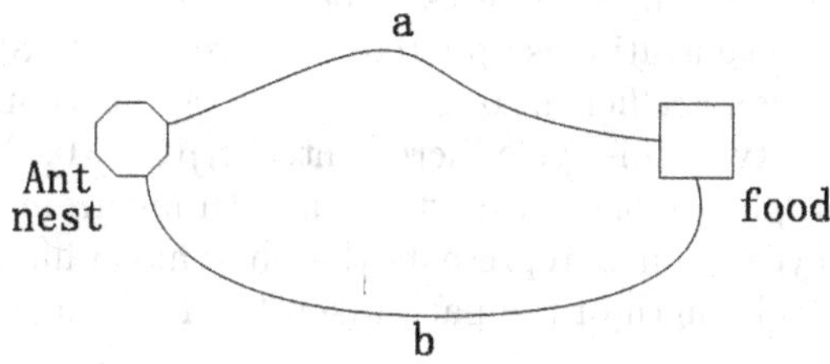

Fig. 3. Ants look for food

3.2 Basic Principles of Ant Colony Optimization

Ant Colony Optimization was first used to solve the TSP problem [21]. This paper introduces the basic principle of ant colony optimization by means of TSP.

The algorithm starts by placing m ants in n cities and sets the pheromone concentration on each path in the city to an equal constant. The heuristic function is determined by the distance between the cities.

For the visit between the cities, the ants choose the next neighboring city j, which is determined by the transfer probability. By calculating the transfer probability between the city i and all the cities to be visited, they choose the city with the most transfer probability as the next visiting city j of the i city, so as to do so until they have visited the last city and returned to the starting city. This leads to a shortest path to all cities [22,23].

Probability transfer equation

$$P_{ij}^{k}(t) = \begin{cases} \frac{[\tau_{ij}(t)]^{\alpha}[\eta_{ij}(t)]^{\beta}}{\sum_{s \in allowed_k}[\tau_{is}(t)]^{\alpha}[\eta_{is}(t)]^{\beta}}, j \in allowed_k \\ 0, \text{otherwise} \end{cases} \tag{6}$$

Heuristic function

$$\eta = 1/D_{ij} \tag{7}$$

Pheromone concentration update

$$\tau_{ij}(t+n) = (1-\rho) * \tau_{ij}(t) + \Delta\tau_{ij}(t) \tag{8}$$

$$\Delta\tau_{ij}(t) = \sum_{k=1}^{m} \Delta\tau_{ij}^{k}(t) \tag{9}$$

$$\triangle\tau_{ij}^{k}(t) = \frac{Q}{L_k} \tag{10}$$

In the above Eq. (6), τ_{ij} represents the pheromone concentration on the path between city i and city j, α is the adjustment factor, and regulates the size of the pheromone in the probability transfer; η_{ij} heuristic function, $\eta_{ij} = 1/D_{ij}$, D_{ij} is equal to the distance between city i and city j, *beta* is also an adjustment factor, adjusting the size of the heuristic function in the probability transfer; $allowed_k$ table is a collection of all cities to be visited.

The pheromone concentration is updated as above in Eqs. (8), (9), (10), is the pheromone volatilization coefficient, $0 < \rho \leq 1$; $\triangle_{ij}(t)$ represents the pheromone between i city and j city in this cycle Increment, $\triangle\tau_{ij}(0) = 0$; $\triangle\tau_{ij}^{k}$, k represents the concentration of pheromone released by the kth ant from the city i to the city j path in this cycle, and Q represents the pheromone intensity (constant), L_k represents the total length of the path taken by the k ant in this loop.

3.3 Ant Colony Algorithm Applied to Tea Plantation

The ant colony algorithm is applied to the tea plantation sensor optimization layout. The heuristic function in the ant colony algorithm is determined not only by the distance between the two sensor nodes, but also by the sum of the distance and the data dissimilarity, as shown in formula (11).

Heuristic function:

$$\eta_{ij} = \frac{1}{D_{ij} + T_{ij}} \tag{11}$$

Where T_{ij} is equal to the sum of reciprocal of the dissimilarity value of sensor node i and the reciprocal of the dissimilarity value of sensor node j, D_{ij} represents the plane distance between the two sensor nodes, The smaller T_{ij} and D_{ij}, the larger η_{ij}.

The probability transfer formula and the pheromone concentration update formula are as shown in the above formulas (6) and (8), (9), (10), It can be seen from formula (6) that probability transfer formula is related to heuristic function. The larger the value of heuristic function is, the greater the probability is. In this paper, the ant colony algorithm searches the sensor placement path with short path distance and large data dissimilarity.

4 Sensor Optimization Layout Tests

4.1 Source of Test Data

The test area is a tea plantation of the National High-tech Agricultural Park of Anhui Agricultural University. The tea plantation is about 190 m in longitudinal direction and 84 m in transverse direction. Its soil belongs to xiashu yellow brown earth. 25 sensors were selected to collect soil moisture data of 25 cm below the soil surface at intervals of about 14 m horizontally and 39 m vertically. The sensor distribution and coverage area are shown in Fig. 4. The sensor node S1 is the route convergence point.

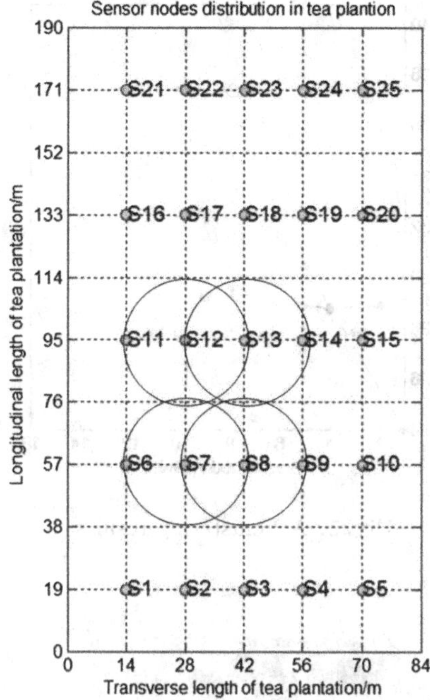

Fig. 4. Sensor nodes distribution

4.2 Test Results

The soil water content of each sensor node in the test area was collected and tested on January 18 and January 20, 2019, respectively. The test results are shown in the following chart. Figure 4 is the clustering result of two days of data, the number of clusters is 2, and the clustering center is set as the starting point of the Dijkstra algorithm path search (Fig. 5).

Based on the comprehensive test data, the spatial distribution of soil moisture in the test area is plotted by Kriging optimal interpolation estimation method, as shown in Fig. 6. It can be seen from Fig. 6 that the maximum variation range of soil moisture content is about 20%, and the distribution of soil moisture has some differences.

As can be seen from Table 1, Starting from the cluster centers S13 and S14, the route convergence point S1 is the end point. The shortest path searched by the improved Dijkstra algorithm is S14-S13-S12-S11-S6-S1, which requires 6 sensors.

Table 1 shows the test results of data collected 6 times in two days. It can be seen from the table that there are 2 AP cluster centers in 6 times, namely S13 and S14 sensor nodes, indicating that the test data has good consistency. Set the AP cluster center as the starting point and the route aggregation point S1 as the end point, and calculate 6 different path results. The results of the six tests only require reliable transmission of data through six sensor nodes. After path optimization, the number of sensors has been reduced from 25 to 6.

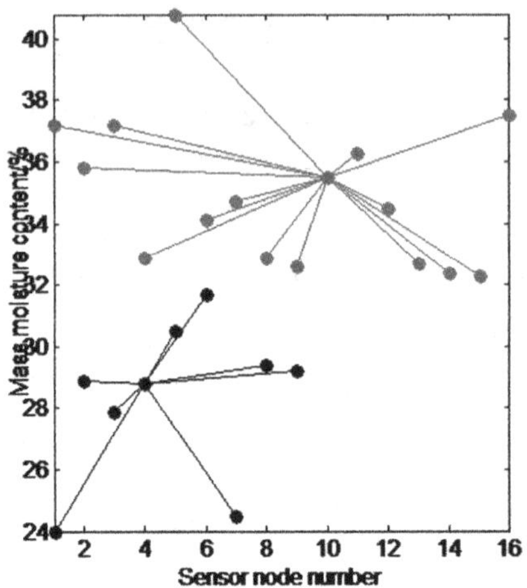

Fig. 5. AP clustering results

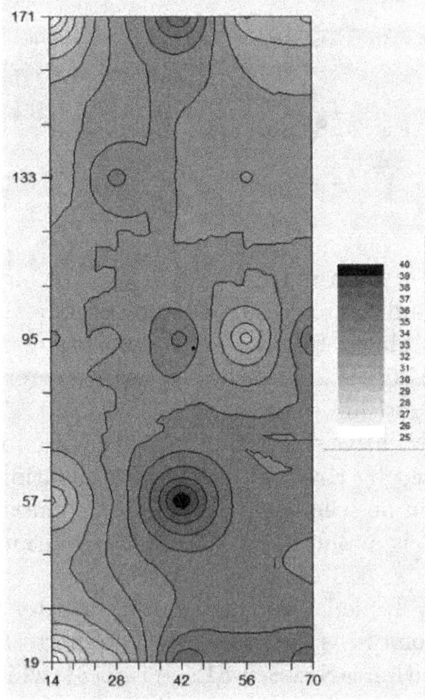

Fig. 6. Spatial distribution of soil moisture in tea plantation

Table 1. Total path cost of Dijkstra algorithms

Number of experiment	AP clustering center/number	Route	Total cost of path	Average dissimilarity
1	(S13, S14)/2	S14-S13-S12-S11-S6-S1	0.3613	25.0652
2	(S13, S14)/2	S14-S13-S8-S3-S2-S1	0.3756	22.1979
3	(S13, S14)/2	S14-S13-S8-S7-S2-S1	0.3858	21.8387
4	(S13, S14)/2	S14-S13-S8-S7-S6-S1	0.3758	24.1022
5	(S13, S14)/2	S14-S13-S12-S7-S2-S1	0.4274	20.9017
6	(S13, S14)/2	S14-S13-S12-S7-S6-S1	0.3978	23.1657

4.3 Analysis and Evaluation of Test Results

This paper analyzes and quantifies the test results by using the total cost of average dissimilarity path and the difference with the mean soil moisture content of the whole tea plantation.

Table 2. Comparison of mean values of paths passing through nodes

Number of experiment	Route	Average value of path nodes	The difference between the paths and the global mean
1	S14-S13-S12-S11-S6-S1	31.8333	0.1827
2	S14-S13-S8-S3-S2-S1	31.2833	0.7327
3	S14-S13-S8-S7-S2-S1	31.5333	0.4827
4	S14-S13-S8-S7-S6-S1	30.9333	1.0827
5	S14-S13-S12-S7-S2-S1	31.1167	0.8993
6	S14-S13-S12-S7-S6-S1	30.5167	1.4993

It can be seen from Tables 1 and 2 that the path calculated in the No. 1 test is S14-S13-S12-S11-S6-S1, the total path cost is 0.3613, and the average dissimilarity is 25.0652, and the difference between the average soil moisture and the average soil moisture of the whole tea plantation is 0.1872. The three indicators are the smallest of the six test results. The total cost of the path is the smallest, and the difference of data of the sensor nodes is the largest. Therefore, S14-S13-S12-S11-S6-S1 is the optimal path.

In addition, the path calculated by the No. 5 test is S14-S13-S12-S7-S2-S1, the total cost of the path is 0.4274, and the average dissimilarity is 20.90917, and the difference between the average soil moisture and the average soil moisture of the whole tea plantation is 0.8993. The three indicators are the largest of the six test results, and the total cost of the path is the largest and the difference of data of each sensor node is the smallest, and the data redundancy is large. So S14-S13-S12-S7-S2-S1 is the worst path.

The indicators for the results of tests No. 2, No. 3, No. 4 and No. 6 were between the two paths of tests No. 1 and No. 5. Based on the comprehensive test results, the path S14-S13-S12-S11-S6-S1 obtained by the test No. 1 is the optimal path.

Table 3. Comparison of test results between two algorithms

Algorithm	Total cost of path	Average dissimilarity	Average value of path nodes	The difference between the paths and the global mean	Route/Number of sensors
AP+Dijkstra	0.3613	25.0652	31.8333	0.1872	S14-S13-S12-S11-S6-S1(6)
Ant colony algorithm	0.5483	20.4538	32.7526	0.7321	S25-S24-S19-S18-S13-S12-S11-S6-S1(9)

It can be seen from Table 3 that the optimal path obtained by the algorithm, the total cost of the path is 0.3613, the data dissimilarity value is 25.0652, and the difference between the average soil moisture value of the tea plantation is 0.1872, and the number of sensors required is 6, The path obtained by the ant colony algorithm, the total cost of the path is 0.5483, the data dissimilarity value is 20.4538, and the difference between the average soil moisture of the tea garden is 0.7321, and the number of sensors required is 9. The method proposed in this paper reduces the number of sensors from 25 to 6, which reduces the system cost. Therefore, the proposed sensor optimization method is superior to the ant colony algorithm.

5 Summary

This paper puts forward the improved Dijkstra algorithm and applies the AP clustering to the Dijkstra algorithm to study the optimization layout of soil moisture sensor in tea plantation. On the basis of ensuring the full coverage of the sensor network, the soil moisture data of each sensor node in the tea plantation is collected in real time, and the clustering center is obtained by AP algorithm. The clustering center is regarded as the starting point of Dijkstra algorithm search path, and the routing convergence point as the end point, so as to calculate the shortest path with the minimum data redundancy and the shortest distance, And the method is compared with the ant colony optimization algorithm, which proves the superiority of this method in the optimized layout of tea plantation sensor.

The test results show that if the sensor nodes are arranged according to the optimal path obtained by the improved Dijkstra algorithm, the collected data will be highly heterogeneous, the transmission path will be short, and the soil moisture in the tea plantation can be accurately reflected. Meanwhile, on the basis of ensuring the reliable transmission of sensor node data to the sink node, the number of sensors is reduced from the initial 25 to 6, thus reducing the cost of system.

Project Fund. Key Research and Development Project of Anhui Province in 2018 (1804a0702010 8), Major Science and Technology Special Plan of Anhui Province in 2017 (1703070 1049).
2016 Ministry of Agriculture Agricultural Internet of Things Technology Integration and Application Key Laboratory Open Fund (2016KL05), Key Research and Development Projects of Anhui Province in 2019 (2 01904a06020056).
The Key Support Project of Outstanding Youth Talents in Anhui Provincial University (gxyqZD2017020).
Major Natural Science Research Projects in Colleges and Universities of Jiangsu Province (18KJA520008).

References

1. Zhang, X., Yin, C., Wu, H.: Energy-saving optimization strategy of wireless sensor networks for large-scale farmland habitat monitoring. Intell. Agric. **1**(02), 55–63 (2019)
2. Wang, H., Zhang, X., Lu, H.: Sensor coverage optimization strategy based on geometric coverage algorithm. Comput. Appl. Res. (8) (2017)
3. Zhu, X., Li, Y., Li, N., et al.: Sensor layout optimization design based on improved discrete particle swarm optimization. J. Electron. **41**(10), 2104–2108 (2013)
4. Liu, X., Zhang, X., Hu, T., et al.: Application of distributed cuckoo algorithm in layout optimization of wireless sensor networks. Comput. Appl. Res. **35**(07), 149–151 (2018). No. 321
5. Lin, F.Y.S., Chiu, P.L.: A simulated annealing algorithm for energy-efficient sensor network design. In: Third International Symposium on Modeling and Optimization in Mobile, AdHoc, and Wireless Networks, pp. 183–189 (2005)
6. Wang, Y.C., Hu, C.C., Tseng, Y.C.: Efficient placement and dispatch of sensors in a wireless sensor network. Trans. Mob. Comput., 262–274 (2008)
7. Yin, H., Du, G., Peng, Z., et al.: Study on the optimal sensor placement method of the weedy monkey swarm algorithm. Comput. Eng. Sci. **40**(04), 60–69 (2018). No. 280
8. Wu, Z., Sun, J., Wang, Y., et al.: Optimum layout strategy of soil moisture sensor based on genetic algorithm. J. Agric. Eng. **27**(5), 219–223 (2011)
9. Zhang, W., Zhang, M., Jiang, C., Jiang, Y.: Layout optimization of soil moisture sensor in tea plantation based on affinity propagation clustering algorithm. J. Agric. Eng. **35**(06), 107–113 (2019)
10. Yao, Y., Man, X.: Spatial heterogeneity of surface soil water seal of Salix psammophila with different forest ages in Maowusu sandy land. J. Soil Water Conserv. **21**(1), 112–115 (2007)
11. Huang, Q., Chen, L., Fu, B., et al.: Spatial pattern of soil moisture and its influencing factors in small watershed of loess hilly region. J. Nat. Resour. **20**(4), 483–492 (2005)

12. Pan, Y., Wang, X., Su, Y., et al.: Characteristics of soil moisture change in sandy surface layer of different vegetation types. J. Soil Water Conserv. **21**(5), 107–109 (2007)
13. Chen, S., Liu, Z.: Path coverage algorithm based on minimizing sensor moving distance. Comput. Eng. **44**(06), 106–109 (2018). No. 488
14. Fink, W., Baker, V.R., Brooks, A.J.W., Flammia, M., Dohm, J.M., Tarbell, M.A.: Globally optimal rover traverse planning in 3D using Dijkstra's algorithm for multi-objective deployment scenarios. Planet. Space Sci. **179**, 104707 (2019)
15. Yuanyihang, Z.Z.: Research on floor texture recognition based on AP clustering algorithm. Microprocessor **39**(06), 44–46 (2018)
16. Huan, R.-H., et al.: Human action recognition based on HOIRM feature fusion and AP clustering BOW. PLoS ONE **14**(7), e0219910 (2019)
17. Liu, Z., Zhang, B., Zhuning, T.H.: Self-learning application layer DDoS detection method based on improved AP clustering algorithm. Comput. Res. Dev. **55**(06), 1236–1246 (2018)
18. Liang, H.W., Chen, W.M., Shuai, L.I., et al.: ACO-based routing algorithm for wireless sensor networks (ARAWSN). Chin. J. Sens. Actuators **20**(11), 2450–2455 (2007)
19. Zheng, W., Liu, S., Kou, X.: A route restoration algorithm for sensor network via ant colony optimization. J. Xi'an Jiao Tong Univ. **44**(1), 83–86 (2010)
20. Ma, X., Cao, Z., Han, J., et al.: Routing optimization and path recovery algorithm in wireless sensor network based on improved ant colony algorithm. J. Electron. Meas. Instrum. **29**(9), 1320–1327 (2015)
21. Tong, M., Yu, L., Zheng, L.: A study on the energy-efficient ant-based routing algorithm for wireless sensor networks. Chin. J. Sens. Actuators **24**(11) (2011)
22. Yang, N., Fu, Q., Li, R., et al.: Application of ant colony algorithm based continuous space in optimizing irrigation regime of rice. Trans. CSAE **26**(Supp. 1), 134–138 (2010). (in Chinese with English abstract)
23. Omran, M.G.H., Al-Sharhan, S.: Improved continuous Ant Colony Optimization algorithms for real-world engineering optimization problems. Eng. Appl. Artif. Intell. **85**, 818–829 (2019)

Efficient Algorithms for Constrained Clustering with Side Information

Zhendong Hao[1], Longkun Guo[1], Pei Yao[1], Peihuang Huang[2(✉)], and Huihong Peng[1]

[1] College of Mathematics and Computer Science, Fuzhou University, Fuzhou, China
[2] College of Mathematics and Data Science, Minjiang University, Fuzhou, China
peihuang.huang@foxmail.com

Abstract. Clustering as an unsupervised machine learning method has broad applications within the area of data science and natural language processing. In this paper, we use background knowledge or side information of the data as constraints to improve clustering accuracy. Following the representation method as in [15], we first format the side information as must-link set and cannot-link set. Then we propose a constrained k-means algorithm for clustering the data. The key idea of our algorithm for clustering must-link data sets is to treat each set as a data with large volume, which is, to assign a set of must-link data as a whole to the center closest to its mass center. In contrast, the key for clustering cannot-link data set is to transform the assignment of the involved data points to the computation of a minimum weight perfect matching. At last, we carried out numerical simulation to evaluate our algorithms for constrained k-means on UCI datasets. The experimental results demonstrate that our method outperforms the previous constrained k-means as well as the classical k-means in both clustering accuracy and runtime.

Keywords: Constrained k-means · Minimum weight perfect matching · Side information

1 Introduction

Clustering as an unsupervised machine learning method is attracting many interest from both academical and industrial community because of its applications in machine learning related areas such as data science and natural language processing. For many problems in Machine Learning and Data Mining, there is a lot of unlabeled data that needs to be processed. In most cases, classifying this data will spend too much time and energy. Subsequently, some researchers found some background information and prior knowledge can be used to solve this problem. Therefrom, Semi-supervised clustering was proposed by *Wagstaff* and

This work is supported by National Natural Science Foundation of China under its grant number 17702005 and Natural Science Foundation of Fujian Province under its grant number 2017J01753.

H. Shen and Y. Sang (Eds.): PAAP 2019, CCIS 1163, pp. 275–286, 2020.
https://doi.org/10.1007/978-981-15-2767-8_25

Cardie [14] based on the background information and unlabeled data to improve the clustering performance. However, some background information may be the labels of some data or exists some pair-wise constraints. In order to improve the performance of clustering, constrained based semi-supervised clustering methods with background information have been proposed by *Wagstaff et al.* in [15]. In this paper, the common constrained based semi-supervised clustering methods include: search-based clustering, similarity-based clustering and search and similarity-based clustering. And they are all based on must-link (if two instances are must-link constrains, they must be in the same class in the process of clustering) and cannot-link (if two instances are cannot-link constrains, they cannot be in the same class in the process of clustering) pairwise constraints.

1.1 Related Work

Clustering is a traditional unsupervised method of data analysis and different from classification. As a supervised method, it is known that classification's tag information of the training samples and the required classes. But as an unsupervised learning method, clustering is opposite, the tag information and the classes of the training samples are unknown. It is a process of dividing data objects into subsets. Each subset is a cluster. The objects in the cluster are similar to each other, and the objects between different clusters are not similar. Clustering can be expressed formally: a data set $D = \{x_1, x_2, ..., x_n\}$ contains n data, and each data has m attributes. The purpose of the clustering algorithm is to divide the data set D into k disjoint subsets $C = \{C_1, C_2, ..., C_k\}$ that is the clusters that is proposed in the former. According to the principle of clustering, it can be applied in many fields, not only in computer science, mathematics, statistics, but also widely used in important fields such as business intelligence and image recognition [5].

Nowadays, there are various different cluster analysis methods which can be roughly divided into the followings [9]: Based on the partitioning clustering, the most famous algorithm is k-means algorithm; Based on the density clustering, the well known algorithm is DBSCAN algorithm; Based on level clustering, the more famous algorithm is AGNES algorithm.

As one of the simplest and most commonly used clustering analysis algorithms, *MacQueen* [9] was first proposed the k-means algorithm in 1967. The k-means algorithm has been widely used in various fields, such as data mining, image segmentation and information retrieval. Although the k-means algorithm has been proposed for more than 50 years, it is still one of the most widely used cluster analysis methods due to its simplicity and convenience today.

Although the k-means algorithm has the characteristics of simplicity and high efficiency, the selection of the initial cluster center and the choice of k have great influence of the clustering effect. The influence of noise and abnormal points of the k-means algorithm can also not be ignored. Because the k-means algorithm relies heavily on the selection of the initial center, a large number of k-means seeding methods have emerged base on this basis. By augmenting k-means with a very simple, randomized seeding technique, *Arthur* and

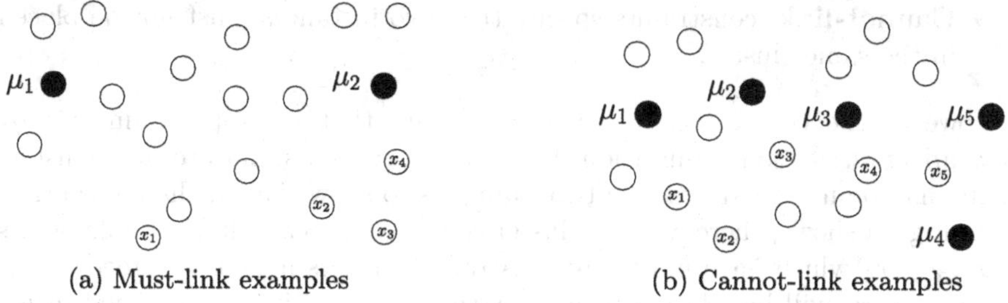

(a) Must-link examples (b) Cannot-link examples

Fig. 1. Examples for processing must-links and cannot-links

Vassilvitskii [1] proposed the k-means++ algorithm in 2007. Then *Bahmani et al.* [2] proposed the k-means|| algorithm in 2012, and the authors proved that k-mean|| is better than k-means++ in both sequential and parallel settings. The optimization of the initial clustering centers of the k-means algorithm was proposed by *Lai* and *Liu* [7] in 2008, and they used a density-based method to determine the initial clustering centers. In 2019, *Jothi et al.* [6] explored a set of probable centers through a constrained bi-partitioning approach, and proposed a deterministic initialization algorithm for k-means (Dk-means) where Dk-means has achieved a remarkable result in terms of convergence speed and stability.

There are many applications of k-means algorithm in many different fields. In order to cluster high resolution satellite images, *Chehreghan* and *Abbaspour* [4] proposed a hybrid clustering algorithm-artificial bee colony optimization approach based on k-means in 2017. On the other hand, *Marroquin* and *Girosi* [10] used the k-means algorithm to solve the efficient image segmentation and pattern classification tasks problem. Later, *Mashtalir et al.* [11] used the k-means algorithm to made a significant advance in analyzing multidimensional time series to cluster video sequences in segments, and this is a method of combining iterative deepening time warping techniques with matrix harmonic k-means. In order to cluster the skewed data, *Melnykov* and *Zhu* [12] proposed an extension of the k-means algorithm in 2019.

However, in real-world specific problems, dataset instances always have some additional data information, such as some information about the problem itself or the dataset. These information are useful for clustering, because clustering analysis can significantly improve the accuracy by using these information. But the traditional k-means algorithm cannot effectively use this information, even if these information exist.

In 2001, *Wagstaff* [15] proposed the concept of constrained k-means clustering for the first time, and successfully completed the experiments to prove that its effect is more effective than the traditional k-means. The constrained k-means algorithm utilizes pairwise constraints to improve clustering performance, these constraints are as follows:

- **Must-link:** constraints specify that two instances have to be in the same cluster.

- **Cannot-link:** constraints specify that two instances must not be placed in the same cluster.

However the constrained k-means algorithm that is proposed in [15] by *Wagstaff et al.* has some limitations for some experiments that are their clusters results may be not good, we give two examples to show that in the following:

As Fig. 1a shows, there are two cluster centers μ_1, μ_2 and four sample points x_1, x_2, x_3, x_4 which have must-link constraints, that is if x_1 is assigned to μ_1, then x_2, x_3, x_4 will be allotted to μ_1 , as well as for μ_2, if x_1 is assigned to μ_2, then x_2, x_3, x_4 will be allotted to μ_2. Hence, they will be all assigned to μ_1 or μ_2. The algorithm that is proposed in [15], these four points may be allotted to μ_1 when x_1 is firstly selected. However, it is obviously that these four points should be assigned to μ_2 such that the clustering result is better. Hence, we propose a new algorithm it calculates the center of x_1, x_2, x_3, x_4 firstly, and then determine whether it is assigned to μ_1 or μ_2 according to the distance between the center with μ_1, μ_2.

As Fig. 1b shows, there are five cluster centers μ_1, μ_2, μ_3, μ_4, μ_5 and five sample points x_1, x_2, x_3, x_4, x_5 which are cannot-link that is these five points must be assigned to different clusters. Let U be a vertex set that includes all cluster centers μ_1, μ_2, μ_3, μ_4, μ_5. Let V be a vertex set that contains all sample points x_1, x_2, x_3, x_4, x_5. The distance from each sample point to each cluster center can be calculated, so the cannot-link constrain problem can be translated into the minimum weight perfect matching problem of the bipartite graph between the two vertex sets U and V.

There are many applications about constrained k-means clustering algorithm that have achieved many important results. [3] also used constraints to improve the effect of the multi-view video data clustering. *Tang et al.* [13] applied it to social media and achieved remarkable results. *Liu et al.* [8] applied the constrained k-means algorithm to domain adaptation and had achieved remarkable results in 2018. *Zhang* and *Jin* [16] proposed a blind detector for spatial modulation based on constrained k-means algorithm in 2019.

1.2 Our Results

The results in our paper can be summarized as follows:

- We use the idea of adding constrained information to the k-means algorithm to improve the effect of the k-means clustering algorithm;
- We also redefine the must-link constraints and the cannot-link constraints. With the must-link constraints, several samples can be allocated at the same time. Using the cannot-link constraints and matching algorithm, we can find a suitable set of clusters to accommodate the cannot-link constrained sample points.

Besides the above results, experiments are also carried out to evaluate the practical performance of the proposed algorithms.

1.3 Organization

The remainder of the paper is organized as follows: Sect. 2 reports the constrained k-means clustering algorithm with incidental information; Sect. 3 introduces the performance evaluation method; Sect. 4 demonstrates experimental results for the algorithms and compares the traditional k-means and constrained k-means with our constrained k-means with incidental information algorithms; Sect. 5 concludes this paper.

2 Constrained k-means Clustering Algorithm with Incidental Information

In this section, we propose an algorithm for the constrained k-means problem (CKM). *Wagstaff et al.* [15] have proposed an algorithm for the CKM problem. However, there may exist a better classification method in some examples such as Fig. 1.

In our paper, we proposed new method that is different with [15] for the processing of must-link and cannot-link. For the must-link constraints set, we use the transitivity of all constraints such that all sample points that satisfy the must-link constraints can be grouped into one set, and then define the set as a new must-link constraint. In the process of allocation, the center of the entire set is calculated first, then the attribute value of all sample points in the set are replaced with the center value, after that the subsequent allocation is performed according to the new value for all sample points in the set. For the cannot-link constraint set, it is a set of vertices since each pair elements in this set are not allowed to be placed in a same cluster set, and the control number of samples is no more than the number of clusters. We uses the distance between each cluster center which is random obtained initially and each elements that comes from the cannot-link constraint set as their weight. Then one distance with the minimum weight will be chosen in our propose algorithm, at the same time putting the sample point into the cluster set and delete all distances that link the sample point with other cluster centers.

The key idea of our algorithm is using the must-link and cannot-link constraints to classify all data. That is the all sample points can be classified at first. Then each must-link constraint set center needs to be calculated based on the mean of all samples points, each cannot-link constraint sets seen as a vertex set which each element of one set has different cluster centers. The cannot-link constraint set are solved by using the bipartite graph minimum weight perfect matching method. After the cluster is reassigned, if any constraints are violated, the points that violate the constraints should be redistributed. Repeatedly the above steps until each constraint is not violated.

3 Evaluation Approaches

In this section, we will give the method to evaluate our algorithms. Clustering performance metrics, also known as validity metrics, are similar to performance

Algorithm 1. Constrained k-means clustering with side information

Input: A data set $D = \{x_1, x_2, ..., x_n\}$, must-link constraints $Con_{=} \subseteq D \times D$, cannot-link constraints $Con_{\neq} \subseteq D \times D$;
Output: A collection of k clusters $C = \{C_1, C_2, ..., C_k\}$;

```
Randomly pick c_1, c_2, ..., c_k as the initial cluster centers;
Repeat
    Let C_i = ∅(1 ≤ i ≤ k);
    For j = 1, 2, ..., n do
       Calculating the distance d_ij each point x_i to each cluster center C_j;
    EndFor
    For each must-link constraint set do
       Calculate all its sample mean and assign all samples to the nearest cluster
       class center;
    EndFor
    For each cannot-link constraint set do
         Assign the data of the set to the appropriate cluster class by minimum
         weight perfect matching;
    EndFor
    Assign each of the remaining data to its nearest center;
    Update the cluster centers such that c_i is the mass center of the data in C_i;
EndRepeat until cluster centers no longer change.
```

metrics in supervised learning. In our study process, the performance metrics is also need to be defined to measure the quality of clustering results. For clustering problem, the superior result is that the similarity for all sample points that they are included in the same cluster is as high as possible, and as well as the similarity between all sample points within different clusters is as low as possible. There are two types of clustering performance metrics: the first type is to compare the experimental results by cluster analysis with a reference model, called external indicators, and the other is to directly examine the clustering results without using other reference models, called internal indicators. In our paper, we mainly use external indicators to evaluate our algorithm.

We need to determine an external reference model in order to evaluate the clustering results with external indicators for the given dataset $D = \{x_1, x_2, ..., x_n\}$. For the compare performance of algorithm that is proposed in our paper, we not only need the clustering result obtained by the external reference model is $C^* = \{C_1^*, C_2^*, ..., C_k^*\}$, but also need the clustering result $C = \{C_1, C_2, ..., C_k\}$ obtained by our clustering algorithm. Let λ be the cluster center of C and λ^* be the cluster center of C^*. We firstly give the following definition that is each element in C^* can be matched with each element in C:

$$\begin{aligned}
a = |SS|,\ SS = \{(x_i, x_j)|\lambda_i = \lambda_j,\ \lambda_i^* = \lambda_j^*,\ i < j\} \\
b = |SD|,\ SD = \{(x_i, x_j)|\lambda_i = \lambda_j,\ \lambda_i^* \neq \lambda_j^*,\ i < j\} \\
c = |DS|,\ DS = \{(x_i, x_j)|\lambda_i \neq \lambda_j,\ \lambda_i^* \doteq \lambda_j^*,\ i < j\} \\
d = |DD|,\ DD = \{(x_i, x_j)|\lambda_i \neq \lambda_j,\ \lambda_i^* \neq \lambda_j^*,\ i < j\}
\end{aligned}$$

The a is the length of SS where SS is a set and each element in SS locates in the same cluster class in C and C^*; The b represents the length of SD and SD is a set whose elements locate in the same cluster class in C, but not in the same cluster class in C^*; Similarly, we can obtain the sets DS and DD and let c and d be the length of DS and DD, respectively. Due to each sample pair only belongs to one of SS, SD, DS and DD, we can get the following formula:

$$2(a+b+c+d) = m(m-1).$$

The Rand index was proposed by *Milligan* and *Cooper* in 1997. The Rand index is an indicator for evaluating clustering results and is used to measure the consistency of the clustering results and the external reference model of the data. The Rand index has a value range of $[0, 1]$. The larger the value, the better the clustering effect. The Rand index is defined as follows:

$$RI = \frac{2(a+b)}{m(m-1)}.$$

However, the Rand coefficient value is not a constant close to zero. In order to achieve the goal that the index could be close to zero in the case of random generation of clustering results, we need to adjust the Rand coefficient, which has a higher degree of discrimination. The range of ARI is $[-1, 1]$. And the larger the value, the more consistent the clustering effect is with the reference model. The ARI is defined as follows:

$$ARI = \frac{RI - E(RI)}{max(RI) - E(RI)}.$$

We used this measure to calculate accuracy for all of our experiments.

4 Experimental Results

In this section, all datasets in our experiments come from some well-known UCI datasets. The experiment uses Python language to write the program code. In Python, we use the *sklearn* library's metrics.adjusted_rand_score method to calculate automatically the ARI value of the clustering result. We iterate 20 times for each dataset in our experiments. For the k-means algorithm, after using Python's own method, we calculate its ARI in each iteration and obtain the averaged of all ARIs in the final. For the constrained k-means algorithm that is proposed in [15] and the improved constrained k-means algorithm that we propose in this paper, a certain number of constraints are generated during each iteration and added these constraints in the algorithm process. Then calculating the ARI for the constrained k-means algorithm and the improved constrained k-means algorithm, and obtaining the average of all ARIs after 20 iterations. In the end, we use *matplotlib* which is a drawing library in python to complete the comparison results of three methods that is the constrained k-means algorithm, the traditional k-means and our improved constrained k-means algorithm.

Table 1. Iris experiment results.

TNC	100	200	300	400	500
CM	0.68669	0.97119	0.99399	1.00000	1.00000
TM	0.73023	0.73023	0.73023	0.73023	0.73023
ICM	0.78485	0.97860	0.99699	1.00000	1.00000

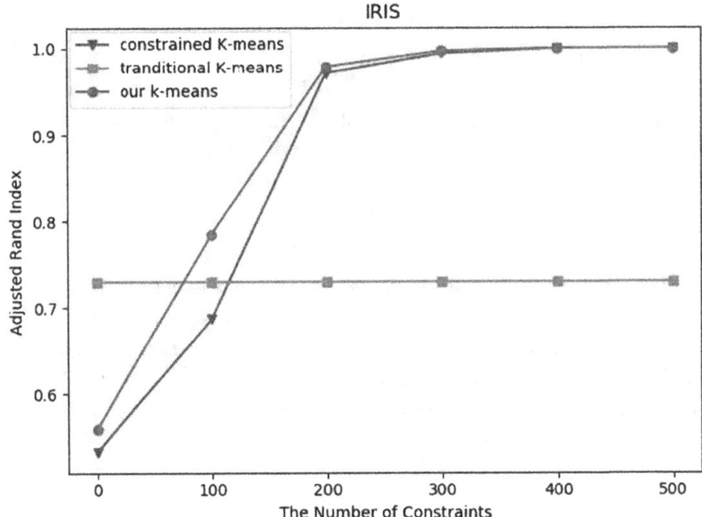

Fig. 2. Comparison of Iris experiment results about the three algorithms.

4.1 Experimental Dataset and Processing

For the UCI datasets that we select from the UCI database, each dataset has several samples, and each sample has some attributes and a decision attribute. In the data set, different samples may have the same or different decision attributes. The number of decision attributes is the number of cluster classes in the dataset. We also use decision attributes to generate must-link constraints and cannot-link constraints, in which a must-link constraint is generated between two samples with the same decision attribute, and a cannot-link constraint is obtained by the two samples which has different decision attributes. In this section, TNC stands for the number of constraints, CM means constrained k-means, TM stands for traditional k-means, and ICM means improved constrained k-means.

4.2 Experimental Specific Results

For the first dataset Iris, it has 150 samples and 5 attributes, ultimately there are 3 cluster classes are formed. For the k-means algorithm, its ARI is 0.73023. For the constrained k-means algorithm and the improved constrained k-means

Table 2. Ionosphere experiment results.

TNC	100	200	300	400	500
CM	0.44799	0.62021	0.87489	0.94606	0.99817
TM	0.17284	0.17284	0.17284	0.17284	0.17284
ICM	0.50131	0.69528	0.92172	0.96657	0.99908

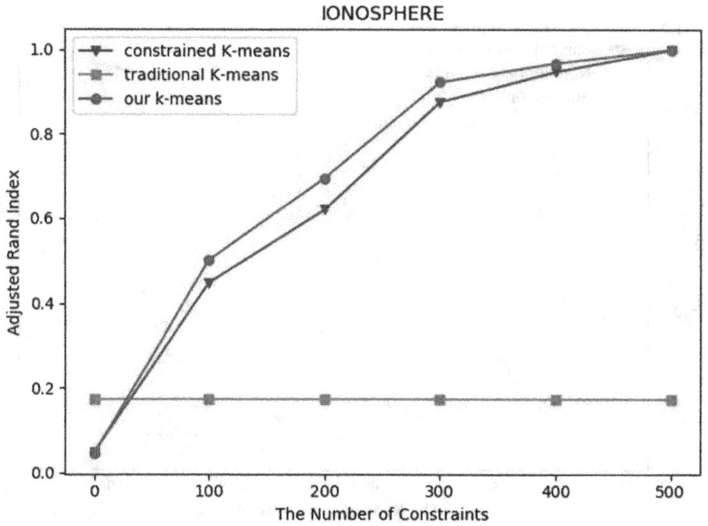

Fig. 3. Comparison of Ionosphere experiment results.

algorithm, the clustering accuracy rate increases as the number of constraints increases. When the number of constraints reaches 400 pairs, the ARI value has reached 1.0 that means the clustering result is exactly the same as the external model. All experiment results are shown in Table 1 and Fig. 2.

For the second dataset Ionosphere, it is fixed 351 samples and 34 attributes, eventually forming 2 cluster classes. The ARI of the k-means algorithm is 0.17284. The ARI value has reached 0.9 or more when 300 pairs of constraints are added for the constrained k-means algorithm and the improved constrained k-means algorithm. The ARI value almost reaches 1 when 500 pairs of constraints are added, that means the clustering results are almost identical to the reference model. The results are shown in Table 2 and Fig. 3.

For the third dataset Balance, it is 625 samples and 5 attributes, we need obtain 3 cluster classes eventually. The ARI value can be arrived 0.13234 for the k-means algorithm. It is obviously found that the clustering effect is better than k-means after adding a small number of constraints for the two different algorithms about the constrained k-means algorithm. Once the pairs of constraints is added up to 900, the ARI values of both algorithms are up to above 0.9 or more,

Table 3. Experiment results on the dataset of Balance.

TMC	100	300	500	700	900
CM	0.24879	0.35256	0.72374	0.88657	0.94483
TM	0.13234	0.13234	0.13234	0.13234	0.13234
ICM	0.26650	0.50679	0.73070	0.88045	0.95854

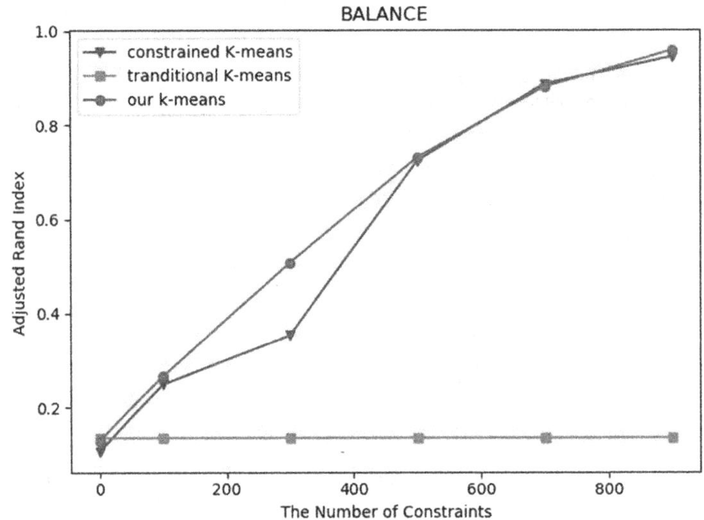

Fig. 4. Comparison of the three algorithms against Balance dataset.

that is the clustering effect is enough good compares the traditional k-means algorithm. The results are shown in Table 3 and Fig. 4.

For the fourth dataset Breast, the samples is 682 and the attributes is 11 in our experiments, there exist 5 cluster classes at last. The ARI is fixed at -0.00268 for the k-means algorithm, and the clustering effect is very poor. However, the clustering accuracy is significantly improved after the constraint is added for the constrained k-means algorithm and the improved constrained k-means algorithm. And the ARI of both algorithms reaches 0.95 or more, and the clustering effect is achieved once the pairs of constraints are increased to 800. The promotion is remarkable. The results are shown in Table 4 and Fig. 5.

According to the experimental results of the above four datasets, we can see that with the increase of constraints, the improved constrained k-means algorithm and the constrained k-means algorithm are better and better. The improved constrained k-means algorithm also outperforms the constrained k-means algorithm, which proves that our improved constrained k-means algorithm is successful.

Table 4. Experiment results on Breast.

TMC	100	300	500	700	900
CM	0.05636	0.15859	0.73693	0.97761	0.99873
TM	−0.00268	−0.00268	−0.00268	−0.00268	−0.00268
ICM	0.04795	0.42613	0.78812	0.98097	0.99970

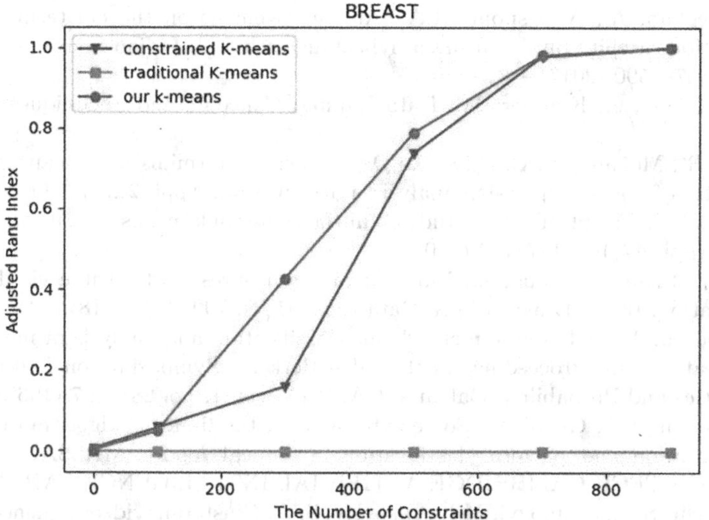

Fig. 5. Comparison of experiment results against Breast dataset.

5 Conclusion

In this paper, we first proposed an algorithm to solve the constrained k-means clustering problem. The key idea of our algorithm is first to construct must-link datasets and cannot-link datasets. Then for must-link datasets, we computed the mass center and assign the whole set to the nearest center; For the cannot-link datasets, we transformed the task into a minimum weight perfect matching of the bipartite graph. By combining the two datasets with k-means, the constrained k-means clustering problem is eventually solved. At last, numerical experiments were carried out to validate the accuracy of our algorithm, against testbed using UCI datasets such as Iris, Ionosphere, Balance and Breast. The results show that our algorithm outperforms all the other baselines that are previous existing algorithms for constrained k-means and k-means clustering.

References

1. Arthur, D., Vassilvitskii, S.: k-means++: the advantages of careful seeding. In: Proceedings of the Eighteenth Annual ACM-SIAM Symposium on Discrete Algorithms, pp. 1027–1035. Society for Industrial and Applied Mathematics (2007)
2. Bahmani, B., Moseley, B., Vattani, A., Kumar, R., Vassilvitskii, S.: Scalable k-means++. Proc. VLDB Endow. **5**(7), 622–633 (2012)
3. Cao, X., Zhang, C., Zhou, C., Huazhu, F., Foroosh, H.: Constrained multi-view video face clustering. IEEE Trans. Image Process. **24**(11), 4381–4393 (2015)
4. Chehreghan, A., Abbaspour, R.A.: An improvement on the clustering of high-resolution satellite images using a hybrid algorithm. J. Indian Soc. Remote Sens. **45**(4), 579–590 (2017)
5. Han, J., Pei, J., Kamber, M.: Data Mining: Concepts and Techniques. Elsevier (2011)
6. Jothi, R., Mohanty, S.K., Ojha, A.: Dk-means: a deterministic k-means clustering algorithm for gene expression analysis. Pattern Anal. Appl. **22**(2), 649–667 (2019)
7. Lai, Y., Liu, J.: Optimization study on initial center of k-means algorithm. Comput. Eng. Appl. **44**(10), 147–149 (2008)
8. Liu, H., Shao, M., Ding, Z., Yun, F.: Structure-preserved unsupervised domain adaptation. IEEE Trans. Knowl. Data Eng. **31**(4), 799–812 (2018)
9. MacQueen, J. et al.: Some methods for classification and analysis of multivariate observations. In: Proceedings of the Fifth Berkeley Symposium on Mathematical Statistics and Probability, Oakland, CA, USA, vol. 1, pp. 281–297 (1967)
10. Marroquin, J.L., Girosi, F.: Some extensions of the k-means algorithm for image segmentation and pattern classification. Technical report, MASSACHUSETTS INST OF TECH CAMBRIDGE ARTIFICIAL INTELLIGENCE LAB (1993)
11. Mashtalir, S.V., Stolbovyi, M.I., Yakovlev, S.V.: Clustering video sequences by the method of harmonic k-means. Cybern. Syst. Anal. **55**(2), 200–206 (2019)
12. Melnykov, V., Zhu, X.: An extension of the k-means algorithm to clustering skewed data. Comput. Stat. **34**(1), 373–394 (2019)
13. Tang, J., Chang, Y., Aggarwal, C., Liu, H.: A survey of signed network mining in social media. ACM Comput. Surv. (CSUR) **49**(3), 42 (2016)
14. Wagstaff, K., Cardie, C.: Clustering with instance-level constraints. In: AAAI/IAAI, vol. 1097, pp. 577–584 (2000)
15. Wagstaff, K., Cardie, C., Rogers, S., Schrödl, S., et al.: Constrained k-means clustering with background knowledge. In: Icml, vol. 1, pp. 577–584 (2001)
16. Zhang, L., Jin, M.: A constrained clustering-based blind detector for spatial modulation. IEEE Commun. Lett. **23**(7), 1170–1173 (2019)

Multi-objective Scheduling of Logistics UAVs Based on Simulated Annealing

Yixuan Li[1], Xiaoxiang Yuan[1,2], Jie Zhu[1], Haiping Huang[1,2](✉), and Min Wu[1,2]

[1] Nanjing University of Posts and Telecommunications, Nanjing 210003, China
hhp@njupt.edu.cn

[2] Jiangsu High Technology Research Key Laboratory for Wireless Sensor Networks, Nanjing 210003, China

Abstract. This study focuses on the issue of logistics Unmanned Aerial Vehicle (UAV) distribution in urban environment, and an automatic delivery system to support the delivery of packages. It can effectively integrate existing facilities and be easily deployed. There is a scheduling problem in this system with multiple UAVs and multiple flights. We manage to optimize the two objectives of customer satisfaction and total completion time. The scheduling problem is formulated to a Mixed Integer Linear Programming (MILP), and we propose a multiple objectives decision-making method. A special encoding method suitable for the small scale problem is presented, and Simulated Annealing (SA) algorithm framework is used to generate the approximate optimal solution for this problem. In experiments, we calibrate the important parameter and analyze the robustness of the algorithm. The experimental results show that the proposed algorithm is suitable for this problem.

Keywords: Logistics · Unmanned Aerial Vehicle · Simulated Annealing

1 Introduction

A large number of online orders have brought great pressure to the express industry. Therefore, the transformation of the production pattern needs to be carried out for traditional delivery companies. Unmanned Aerial Vehicles (UAVs) have great potential in disaster relief, environmental monitoring and logistics delivery. As one of the autonomous things, UAVs are considered to be the top strategic technology in Gartner [1]. UAV logistics is an emerging application area. It combines logistic with UAV to improve the efficiency of the logistics distribution, reduce operating costs and optimize the link of terminal distribution. In this paper, we present an automatic delivery system for logistics UAVs in urban environment. The algorithm framework based on Simulated Annealing (SA) is proposed to solve the small scale scheduling problem of this system, and we consider several important optimization objectives.

In the traditional logistics industry, all packages that need to be delivered are stored in the transshipment depot. These packages in the transshipment depot are divided by their destinations. Multiple Couriers deliver these packages, and each Courier is responsible

Y. Li and X. Yuan—Co-first author.

H. Shen and Y. Sang (Eds.): PAAP 2019, CCIS 1163, pp. 287–298, 2020.
https://doi.org/10.1007/978-981-15-2767-8_26

for the delivery of packages within a certain area. In the above system, a group of UAVs are used to replace a Courier. Some autonomous express cabinets are set up near the package's destinations. These UAVs drop some packages from the transshipment depot into express cabinets according to the task scheduling results. The aforementioned UAVs and express cabinets are all connected to the Internet. The execution status of the system is obtained by the dispatch center in real time. The dispatch center performs the task scheduling at intervals and reports the status of the system to the relevant staff. The execution process of the system is shown in Fig. 1.

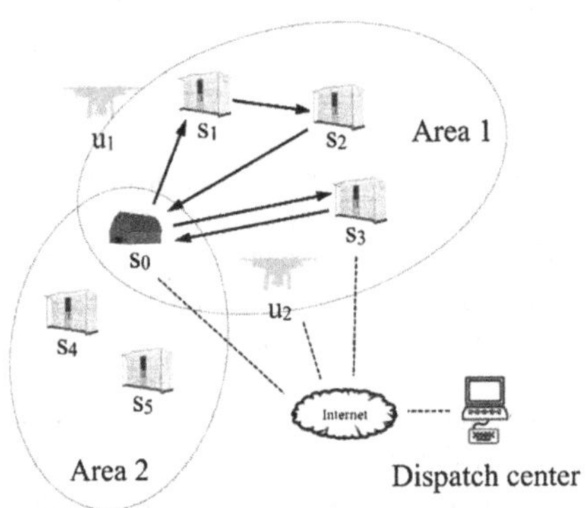

Fig. 1. The execution process of the delivery system

The scheduling problem of logistics UAVs is a special kind of unmanned aerial vehicle routing problem (UAVRP). Similar to the traditional vehicle routing problem (VRP), the UAVRP adds some new features such as limitations of flight time and load capacity. VRP is well known as an NP-hard problem. As a variant of VRP, the scheduling problem of logistics UAVs is also NP-hard. The SA algorithm framework is used to address the computational tractability and search for the approximate optimal solution of the proposed problem.

The rest of the paper is organized as follows. Related works are reviewed in Sect. 2. Section 3 describes and formalizes the problem under study. An algorithm framework is proposed for the considered problem in Sect. 4. Section 5 evaluates the performance of the proposal under different workload scenarios followed by conclusions in Sect. 6.

2 Related Works and Contributions

The traditional logistics scheduling problem is a special Vehicle Routing Problem (VRP). A great number of research has focused on the field of VRP. Dantzig and Ramser [2] first introduce the truck dispatching problem and propose a procedure to search the near-optimal solution. Chao et al. [3] consider the VRP with simultaneous pickup-delivery and time windows, and a parallel SA algorithm is proposed for the problem. Jiahai et al. [4] present a multi-objective and multi-depot VRP. They develop a two-stage multi-objective evolutionary algorithm to deal this problem.

As a special kind of VRP, UAV routing and scheduling problem is applied in various scenarios. Dorling et al. [5] propose two multi-trip VRPs for UAV delivery that minimizes cost subject to a delivery time limit or minimizes the overall delivery time subject to a budget constraint. Kim and Morrison [6] present a scenario in which UAVs are needed to provide continuous service and docking locations. They use a scheduling method to solve this problem. Zeng et al. [7] develop a nonlinear model to schedule UAV resources to the battle field.

Although UAVs can be used in many scenarios, there are few researches on the application of logistics UAV in urban environment. The scheduling method proposed in VRP related research cannot be directly applied to UAV logistics scheduling. So, a suitable logistics UAV scheduling scheme is essential to replace the work of couriers.

We refer to the methods presented in the above literatures, and the main contributions of the present study are summarized as follows. (i) We first present the automatic delivery system with logistics UAVs to improve the efficiency of the logistics distribution and reduce operating costs. (ii) Mixed Integer Linear Programming (MILP) is used to describe the scheduling problem of the system. (iii) We propose a special coding method for this small-scale problem. (iv) The algorithm framework based on SA is presented to search for approximate optimal solution and make the decision between multiple objectives.

3 Problem Description and Model

3.1 Problem Description

Packages in the transshipment depot need to be delivered to multiple areas. In the traditional logistics delivery scenario, one courier is responsible for a certain small area. Many couriers work together to complete the delivery of all packages in the transshipment depot. Multiple UAVs are being used to replace one courier. The above mentioned automatic delivery system for logistics UAVs is used to support the execution of the above workflow. Each courier's package tasks are scheduled by this system respectively.

In order to deploy the UAV delivery system on existing resources, the following components need to be used in logistics distribution. (i) Some package loading equipment in the transshipment depot, they are responsible for loading packages into UAVs and replacing UAV's battery for their next flight. (ii) Each of these UAVs will complete the delivery according to the route specified by the dispatch center. These package tasks in a certain area require multiple UAVs to collaborate. And these packages tasks are usually completed through multiple flights. (iii) Some express cabinets are placed near these package destinations. The express cabinet supports UAVs to automatically place the package inside it, and it allows customers to pick up their packages at any time. (iv) The dispatch center performs resource scheduling in units of areas. It updates the status of the transit warehouse, UAVs and express cabinets in real time, and notifies the corresponding staff in time when the system fails.

We consider the scheduling problem of the system in a certain area. Since one courier has to deliver fewer packages in a day, there is a small-scale scheduling problem in the specific area that need to be addressed. The search ability of the SA algorithm is adequate for this problem. The customer satisfaction and the total completion time, which are critical to the problem, is selected as the two optimization objectives for this problem. The scheduling problem is modeled as a MILP. Notations are summarized in Table 1.

There is a small scale problem. All packages that a courier needs to deliver are represented by $P = \{p_1, p_2, \ldots, p_n\}$. A set of stations $S = \{s_0\} \cup \{s_1, s_2, \ldots, s_m\}$ are set up in the scenario, where s_0 is the transshipment depot and the set of $\{s_1, s_2, \ldots, s_m\}$ represents these express cabinets in the area. $l_{k,f,b}$ represents the destination of the bth package delivered by u_k on f^{th} flight. We determine a minimum circle that covers all these stations, and r is the radius of the circle. According to customer requirements, the optimal delivery time t_i^0 is set for each package, and the actual delivery time of the package is represented as t_i. A set of UAVs $U = \{u_1, u_2, \ldots, u_h\}$ is used to accomplish these package tasks. S^{uav} is the solution of the task scheduling for all UAVs. It contains the scheduling results of multiple flights and is an intuitive representation of the scheduling scheme. A and B are two optimization objectives.

Based on the above descriptions and notations, the following mathematical model is established.

$$A = \sum_{i=1}^{n} \max\left(0, t_i - t_i^0\right) \quad (1)$$

$$B = \max_{1 \le k \le n} t_k^e \quad (2)$$

$$C = B^{max} \times A + B \quad (3)$$

Subject to:

$$\max_{1 \le i \le n} w_i \le c, \ \forall k, f \quad (4)$$

$$\sum_{b=1}^{T_{k,f}} w_{p_{k,f,b}} \le c, \ \forall k, f \quad (5)$$

$$\sum_{b=0}^{T_{k,f}-1} d\left(l_{k,f,b}, l_{k,f,b+1}\right) + d\left(l_{k,f,T_{k,f}}, s_0\right) \le v \times e, \ \forall k, f \quad (6)$$

$$t_k^e = t_{k,T_k} + q_{k,T_k}, \forall k \quad (7)$$

$$t_{k,f} = \begin{cases} 0, & f = 1 \\ t_{k,f-1} + q_{k,f-1}, & f \ge 2 \end{cases}, \ \forall k \quad (8)$$

$$q_{k,f} = \sum_{b=0}^{T_{k,f}-1} d\left(l_{k,f,b}, l_{k,f,b+1}\right) + d\left(l_{k,f,T_{k,f}}, s_0\right) + t^d + T_{k,f} \times t^c, \ \forall k, f \quad (9)$$

$$p_{k,f,b} = \sum_{i=1}^{n} i \times x_{k,f,b,i}, \ \forall k, f, b \quad (10)$$

$$\sum_{i=1}^{n} x_{k,f,b,i} = 1, \ \forall k, f, b \quad (11)$$

$$\sum_{k=1}^{h} \sum_{f=1}^{T_k} \sum_{b=1}^{T_{k,f}} x_{k,f,b,i} = 1, \ \forall i \quad (12)$$

$$x_{k,f,b,i} \in \{0, 1\}$$

Table 1. Notations description.

Notation	Description
h	Number of UAVs
u_k	The kth UAV
$U = \{u_1, u_2, \ldots, u_h\}$	Set of UAVs
e	Maximum flight time of UAV
c	Load capacity of UAV
v	Average speed of UAV
t^d	Time for UAV to load packages in s_0
t^c	Time for UAV to unload packages into $s_1, \ldots, s_m$
n	Number of packages
p_i	The ith package
$P = \{p_1, p_2, \ldots, p_n\}$	Set of packages
w_i	Weight of p_i
l_i	Destination of p_i
t_i^0	Best delivery time of p_i
t_i	Actual delivery time of p_i
g	Maximum weight of packages
G	Total weight of packages
m	Number of express cabinet
s_j	The jth station
$S = \{s_0, s_1, \ldots, s_m\}$	Set of stations
$d = (s_j, s_{j'})$	Distance between s_j and $s_{j'}$
r	Radius of area
t	Initial temperature of SA framework
S^{uav}	The scheduling scheme
T_k	Number of flights for u_k
$T_{k,f}$	Number of packages delivered by u_k's f^{th} flight
$p_{k,f,b}$	Number of bth package on u_k's f^{th} flight
$l_{k,f,b}$	Destination of bth package on u_k's f^{th} flight
$t_{k,f}$	Start time of u_k's f^{th} flight
$q_{k,f}$	Task execution duration of u_k's f^{th} flight
t_k^e	Time for u_k to complete all its tasks
A	Customer satisfaction
B	Total completion time
B^{max}	Maximum total completion time

Equations (1–3) describe how optimization objectives are calculated. Since A is significantly more important than B, Eq. (3) transforms the problem into a single objective optimization problem. Constraint (4) is the weight limit of packages. Constraints (5–6) ensure the maximum payload and flight distance of UAVs. Equations (7–10) present the calculation methods of the relevant parameters. $x_{k,f,b,i}$ is a decision variable, taking 1 if b^{th} package on u_k's f^{th} flight is p_i, taking 0 otherwise. Constraints associated with decision variables are 11–12.

4 Proposed Algorithm

4.1 Encoding Method

The key problem of the SA algorithm framework is to determine an appropriate encoding method for the small scale problem. A new encoding method is introduced, as $S^{uav} = \{< 5, 2, 3 >, < 4, 1 >\}$. It consists of two vectors, and each of the vector determines the order in which a UAV delivers packages. For example, the distribution scheme of the above solution S^{uav} is that u_1 delivers p_5, p_2, p_3 and u_2 delivers p_4, p_1, respectively. Each UAV completes its package tasks through multiple flights. The number of flights is determined by c.

4.2 Initialization of the Solution

We managed to find a better solution to participate in the iterations. Since the initial solution to the problem S^{uav} is essentially a sort of packages, the Initial Solution Generation Algorithm (ISG) is used to generate it. The shortest path through all express cabinets is calculated by a simple SA (Lines 1–15). According to the shortest path and the best delivery time t_i^0, the elements in S^{init} are ordered as the initial solution (Lines 16–18).

Initial Solution Generation Algorithm $ISG()$

1 $L \leftarrow \{s_1, s_2, \ldots, s_m\}$;/* L records the shortest path that traverses $\{s_1, s_2, \ldots, s_m\}$ */

2 $L^{current} \leftarrow L$;

2 $S^{init} \leftarrow P$;

3 $t \leftarrow 80$;/* t represents the initial temperature */

4 **for** $\varphi = 80; \varphi > 1; \varphi \leftarrow 0.9 \times \varphi$ **do**

5   **for** $\tau = 0; \tau < 500; \tau \leftarrow \tau + 1$ **do**

6   Swapping two random disjoint subsequences of $L^{current}$ to generate L^{new};

7   **if** $R(L^{new}) < R(L^{current})$ **then**/* $R(L^{new})$ is the path length of L^{new} */

8             $L^{current} \leftarrow L^{new}$;

9   **if** $R(L^{current}) < R(L)$ **then**

10                 $L \leftarrow L^{current}$;

else
$p \leftarrow e^{\frac{-1 \times R(L')}{0.8 \times \varphi}}$; /* Accept an inferior solution with the probability p */
A random number p' is generated between 0 and 1;
if $p' < p$ **then**
$L^{current} \leftarrow L^{new}$;
The packages in S^{init} are sorted according to L;
For packages with the same destination in S^{init}, sort by t_i^0;
return S^{init};

4.3 Local Search Algorithm Framework

Local Search algorithm (*LS*) is applied to improve the initial solution. A new solution in the local search is generated by randomly swapping. The approximate optimal solution S^{uav} is calculated by iteration (Lines 2–6).

Local Search algorithm framework *LS*()

1 $S^{uav} \leftarrow ISG()$;
2 **While** not Termination Criterion **do**
3 Generation of candidate neighbor S^{uav};
4 **if** $Fit(S^{new}) < Fit(S^{uav})$ **then**
5 $S^{uav} \leftarrow S^{new}$;
6 **return** S^{uav};

4.4 Simulated Annealing Algorithm Framework

Simulated Annealing algorithm is a greedy algorithm. It is derived from the principle of solid annealing. SA accepts an inferior solution with the certain probability, and this probability varies with the temperature. The SA algorithm framework is used to compute the integrated objective C. We obtain the approximate optimal solution by the Simulated Annealing algorithm framework. ISG is used to generate the initial solution (Line 1). The approximate optimal solution S^{uav} is calculated by iteration (Lines 2–14). In the iterative process, the global optimal solution is recorded (Lines 8–9) and an inferior solution is accepted with probability p (Lines 11–14).

Simulated Annealing algorithm framework $SA()$

$S^{uav} \leftarrow ISG()$;
$S^{current} \leftarrow S^{uav}$;
for $\varphi = t; \varphi > 1; \varphi \leftarrow 0.9 \times \varphi$ **do**
  for $\tau = 0; \tau < 1000; \tau \leftarrow \tau + 1$ **do**
    Swapping two random disjoint subsequences of $S^{current}$ to generate S^{new};
    if $Fit(S^{new}) < Fit(S^{current})$ **then**/* $Fit(S^{new})$ is the fitness of S^{new} */
      $S^{current} \leftarrow S^{new}$;
      if $Fit(S^{current}) < Fit(S^{uav})$ **then**
        $S^{uav} \leftarrow S^{current}$;
    else
      $p \leftarrow e^{\frac{-1 \times R(L')}{0.8 \times \varphi}}$; /* Accept an inferior solution with the probability p */
      A random number p' is generated between 0 and 1;
      if $p' < p$ **then**
        $S^{current} \leftarrow S^{new}$;
return S^{uav};

5 Simulation Experiments

In this section, numerical results are reported. We first calibrate the important parameter t of the SA algorithm framework. And then, the robustness of the algorithm is analyzed for all instance parameters. All experiments are coded in Java and run on a PC with an Intel(R) Core(TM) i5-7500 CPU @3.40 Ghz, 8 GB of RAM. The version of Integrated Development Environment (IDE) is eclipse Jee Oxygen April 2018 x64. Relative Percentage Deviation (RPD) is used to evaluate the performance of the algorithm.

$$RPD = \frac{Fit(C) - Fit(C')}{Fit(C')} \tag{13}$$

In Eq. (13), $Fit(C')$ represents the optimal fitness for the same instances.

5.1 Parameter Calibration

The initial temperature t is critical to the performance of the SA algorithm framework. We use a large number of instances to determine the value of t. To the best of our knowledge, no uniform testing benchmark is available for the considered problem. So we combined some practical scenarios in logistics transportation to generate test instances, such as [8] and [9].

Parameters are designed as follows. (i) We consider the regional parameters with the area radius $r \in \{1000\,\text{m}, 2000\,\text{m}, 3000\,\text{m}\}$ and the number of stations $m \in \{5, 10, 15\}$. (ii) The weight of each package w_i is generated randomly in interval $[0.05, g]$, and the parameter g represents the maximum weight of all packages. The package related parameters are set as $g \in \{3\,\text{kg}, 4\,\text{kg}, 5\,\text{kg}\}$ and $G \in \{80, 100, 120\}$. (iii) The number of UAVs $h \in \{3, 4, 5\}$. The special logistic UAV is selected with maximum flight time $e = 40\,\text{min}$, load capacity $c = 5\,\text{kg}$ and average speed $v = 800\,\text{m/min}$.

There are $3 \times 3 \times 3 \times 3 \times 3 = 243$ instance combinations. For each instance combination, we compare the algorithm performance of five different values of t. Therefore, there are $3 \times 3 \times 3 \times 3 \times 3 \times 5 = 1215$ instances for parameter calibration. One-way analysis of variance technique is used to analyze the experiment results. The mean plots of SA framework with different values of t are depicted in Fig. 2. The smaller RPD values, the better optimization effect.

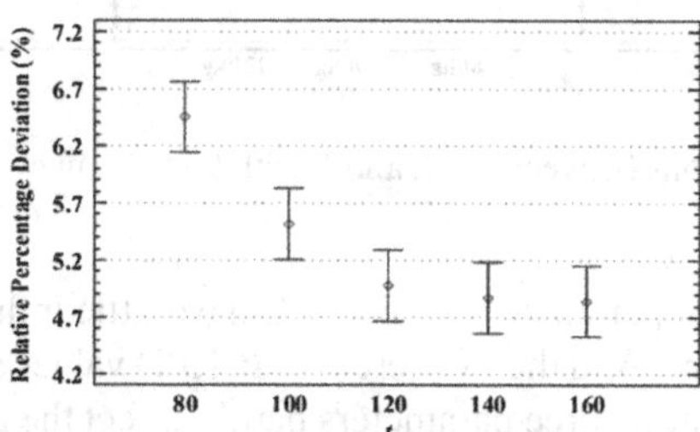

Fig. 2. The mean plot of the initial temperatures with 95.0% Tukey HSD intervals

From Fig. 2, it can be observed that the differences are statistically significant for $t \leq 120$ however tends to be flat for $t \geq 120$. So when t is set to 120, the algorithm can generate a better solution with fewer iterations.

5.2 Robustness Analysis

In terms of the parameter calibration, $t = 120$ is set to the initial temperature of the SA algorithm framework. To further demonstrate the robustness of the proposed algorithm, we analyze the influence of the five instance parameters on this algorithm. The proposed algorithm is compared with the Local Search algorithm (LS). Interactions between each parameter and the compared algorithms with 95.0% Tukey HSD intervals are depicted in Figs. 3 and 4. It can be concluded from Figs. 3 and 4 that the observed differences are not statistically significant for the proposed algorithm in most cases.

Figure 3 shows that the area radius r has a great effect on the performance of proposed SA algorithm framework. And the differences in RPD values are not statistically significant for the number of express cabinet m. This is because the radius of the region directly affects the fitness of the solution. The increase of r widens the differences between these RPD values, making it easier for the algorithm to find better solutions.

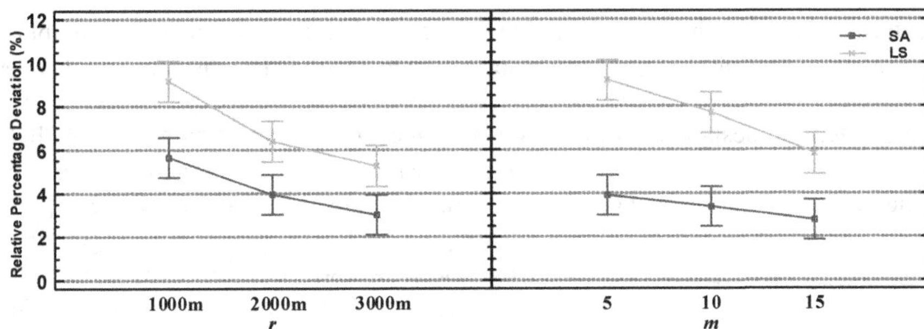

Fig. 3. Interactions between area-related parameters with 95.0% Tukey HSD intervals

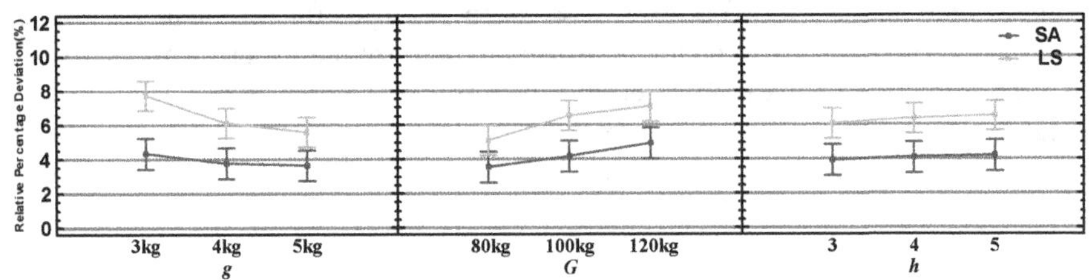

Fig. 4. Interactions between g, G, and h with 95.0% Tukey HSD interval

Figure 4 illustrates that parameters A, B and C have little influence on the execution of SA algorithm framework. And their differences in RPD values are not statistically significant. This is because these three parameters hardly affect the ability of the algorithm to search for the global optimal solution.

The experimental results demonstrate that SA is feasible and effective for the considered problem.

Average Relative Perçentage Deviations (ARPDs) are shown in Table 2 for all 243 instances. It is observed that ARPD of SA is better than LS.

From the analysis of the results, it can be seen that the proposed SA algorithm framework is robust for most parameters.

Table 2. ARPD values

		SA	LS
r	1000 m	5.647	9.136
	2000 m	3.978	6.344
	3000 m	3.084	5.212
m	5	3.891	9.235
	10	3.376	7.618
	15	2.409	5.758
g	3 kg	4.364	7.791
	4 kg	3.862	6.179
	5 kg	3.649	5.537
G	80 kg	3.416	5.097
	100 kg	4.183	6.654
	120 kg	4.878	7.086
h	3	3.907	6.103
	4	4.084	6.313
	5	4.196	6.657
Average		3.928	6.715

6 Conclusions

The delivery problem of logistics UAV in urban environment is considered to be a scheduling problem. We first present the automatic delivery system for logistics UAVs to improve the distribution efficiency and reduce costs. The Simulated Annealing algorithm framework is proposed to address the scheduling problem of the system. We use the special method of two-stage optimization to solve the optimization problem between customer satisfaction and total completion time. The parameter t in this algorithm is calibrated and the experimental results show that the proposed algorithm is robust and has better performance.

Acknowledgments. This work is sponsored by the National Natural Science Foundations of China (Grant Nos. 61672297, 71401079, 61872196), the Natural Science Foundation of the Jiangsu Higher Education Institutions of China (Grant No. 18KJB520039), the Key Research and Development Program of Jiangsu Province (Social Development Program, No. BE2017742) and the National Science Foundation for Post-doctoral Scientists of China (Grant No. 2018M640510).

References

1. Panetta, K.: Gartner's top 10 strategic technology trends for 2019. Smart with Gartner (2018)

2. Dantzig, G.B., Ramser, J.H.: The truck dispatching problem. Manag. Sci. **6**(1), 80–91 (1959)
3. Chao, W., Dong, M., Fu, Z., et al.: A parallel simulated annealing method for the vehicle routing problem with simultaneous pickup–delivery and time windows. Comput. Ind. Eng. **83**, 111–122 (2015)
4. Jiahai, W., Taiyao, W., Qingfu, Z.: A two-stage multiobjective evolutionary algorithm for multiobjective multidepot vehicle routing problem with time windows. IEEE Trans. Cybern. **49**(7), 2467–2478 (2019)
5. Dorling, K., Heinrichs, J., Messier, G.G., Magierowski, S.: Vehicle routing problems for drone delivery. IEEE Trans. Syst. Man Cybern.: Syst. **47**(1), 1–16 (2016)
6. Kim, J., Morrison, J.R.: On the concerted design and scheduling of multiple resources for persistent UAV operations. J. Intell. Robot. Syst. **74**(1–2), 479–498 (2014)
7. Zeng, J., Yang, X., Yang, L., et al.: Modeling for UAV resource scheduling under mission synchronization. J. Syst. Eng. Electron. **21**(13), 821–826 (2010)
8. Ma, Y., Li, Z., Yan, F., et al.: A hybrid priority-based genetic algorithm for simultaneous pickup and delivery problems in reverse logistics with time windows and multiple decision-makers. Soft Comput. - Fusion Found. Methodol. Appl. **23**, 1–18 (2019)
9. Jiang, X., Zhou, Q., Ye, Y.: Method of task assignment for UAV based on particle swarm optimization in logistics. In: Proceedings of the 2017 International Conference on Intelligent Systems, Metaheuristics & Swarm Intelligence, pp. 113–117 (2017)

IFME: Influence Function Based Model Explanation for Black Box Decision Systems

Benbo Zha[1(✉)] and Hong Shen[1,2(✉)]

[1] School of Data and Computer Science, Sun Yat-sen University, Guangzhou, China
zhabb@mail2.sysu.edu.cn, hongsh01@gmail.com

[2] School of Computer Science, University of Adelaide, Adelaide, Australia

Abstract. Due to the high precision and the huge prediction needs, machine learning models based decision systems has been widely adopted in all works of life. They were usually constructed as a black box based on sophisticated, opaque learning models. The lack of human understandable explanation to the inner logic of these models and the reason behind the predictions from such systems causes a serious trust issue. Interpretable Machine Learning methods can be used to relieve this problem by providing an explanation for the models or predictions. In this work, we focus on the model explanation problem, which study how to explain the black box prediction model globally through human understandable explanation. We propose the **I**nfluence **F**unction based **M**odel **E**xplanation (IFME) method to provide interpretable model explanation based on key training points selected through influence function. First, our method introduces a novel local prediction interpreter, which also utilizes the key training points for local prediction. Then it finds the key training points to the learning models via influence function globally. Finally, we provide the influence function based model agnostic explanation to the model used. We also show the efficiency of our method through both theoretical analysis and simulated experiments.

Keywords: Model explanator · Influence function · Interpretable Machine Learning · Explaining the black box

1 Introduction

Sophisticated and opaque decision systems have been adopted ubiquitously in many fields from research community to industry in recent years. These black box systems make decisions from huge volumes of data via sophisticated machine learning models such as deep neural networks. Due to their high precision and the huge demands of data processing and prediction, user maybe chooses to believe such black box. However, the lack of explanation to the prediction or model constitutes both serious practical and ethical issues. The situation is more obvious in some safety-critical fields, such as medical diagnosis, terrorism detection, self-driving cars or robotic assistants.

H. Shen and Y. Sang (Eds.): PAAP 2019, CCIS 1163, pp. 299–310, 2020.
https://doi.org/10.1007/978-981-15-2767-8_27

Users from these fields facing the black box decision systems often wonder why this prediction has been made. The best-performing models are too complicated to understand how they work. Providing human understandable explanations for these situations can help users to mitigate this kind of anxiety. Interpretable Machine Learning as a research direction that provide solutions to explain the behaviors of machine learning models has attracted more and more attentions recently. The literature [5] presents a comprehensive survey for the recent related works and categorizes the problem into four classes: model explanation, outcome explanation, model inspection, and transparent box design.

In this work, we focus on the outcome and model explanation problem, i.e. how to provide human understandable explanation to prediction and model. The common approach is utilizing an interpretable model to mimic the behavior of black box locally or globally, such as decision tree, rules, linear model [6,9]. But they didn't give an intuitional explain. Because a better understand for the given prediction via influence function through the way described in [6] can be provided, we can introduce it into the frame of LIME (local interpretable model agnostic explanation) [9] to combine their merits. The frame of LIME provides a model-agnostic interpretable and fidelity explanation, and influence function can be used to identify the key training points that have major influence for the prediction. The key training points related to a given prediction can improve the fidelity of local explanation model. In addition, we construct a global model explanation, IFME, by using the key training points for model, because the influence of these key training points is major for the parameters of model.

The major contributions in this work can be concluded as follows. (1) We design an efficient local interpretable prediction explanation via influence function. It utilizes the frame of LIME to obtain a linear model explanation for a given prediction, which trains on the sampling data based on key training points. (2) We propose a novel model explanation, IFME, which based on the key training points identified via influence function. These training points have major influence for model and the trust of explanations on them can be considered the reliability of the total model. (3) We provide the extensive theoretic analysis and simulated experiments to demonstrate our method is effective and efficient.

The rest of this article is organized as follows. Section 2 introduces the related work. Section 3 gives the detailed description about the prediction and model explanation and provides the preliminaries on the related techniques. In Sect. 4, we describe the detail implementation of local interpretable prediction explanation. And in Sect. 5, we present the design of influence function based model explanation (IFME). The experiments and results have been shown in Sect. 6, and the conclusion and future work have been presented in Sect. 7.

2 Related Work

In our work, we focus on the prediction and model explanation. The related works about this were clearly illustrated here. Meanwhile, influence function's related works also be introduced. So the entire related works in this article mainly includes three aspects: influence function, prediction explanation, model explanation.

2.1 Influence Function

The influence function is a classic technique, which has been used as a diagnostic approach originated in robust statistics in the 70s and 80s [2]. These works focus on studying the effects of removing or perturbing training points from linear models or other general models. Recently, Koh and Liang presented a new perspective to understand the black-box decision systems via the concept of influence function [6]. They used this technique to connect the key training points with a given prediction. There are some works inspired by their new perspective. In [3], Dhaliwal and Shintre proposed a new metric, Gradient Similarity, to capture the influence of training points on test input and they can use this metric to detect a variety of adversarial attacks with high accuracy.

2.2 Prediction Explanation

For a given test point and its prediction, the prediction explanation problem consists in providing an explanation for the prediction of a black box on this test point. This kind of approaches to provide a local explanation for a prediction has become the most studied in recent years. Saliency masks [4,12] has been used as an explanation of Deep Neural Network (DNN). This method provided the salient parts of the training instance as the explanation for the prediction. In [4,11], authors introduces an attention-based model to automatically identify the salient parts of an image. In [12], the authors propose a probabilistic method for explaining the prediction made by DNN.

2.3 Model Explanation

In order to explain models, the explanation should be a global description generated by a interpretable model that can globally mimic the behavior of black boxes and that can be understood by humans. The common methods for this objective are based on decision tree or decision rules. The related works can be found conveniently in a survey [5]. Other methods can be classified into model agnostic explanation, which explains any type of black box. In [7], Lou et al. proposes a Generalized Additive Models (GAMs) approach to interpret models. The explanation is returned as the importance of the contribution of the individual features together with their shape function. A feature important method has been introduced in [10,12]. Their explanation is provided by a vector of features importance.

Our work intended to provide model explanation by visualized feature importance, which is motivated by two recent works [6,9]. We then integrate our models into LIME to produce the visualized explanation.

3 Problem Formulation and Preliminaries

In this section, we depicted the model explanation problem and the related techniques in detail. The model explanation problem consists of providing a global explanation for a prediction model using a human interpretable manner. The related techniques include influence function and LIME, which motivated our work.

3.1 Model Explanation Problem

Consider a black box decision system that is supported by some machine learning models, a prediction can be assigned to a test point. The parameters of the models are trained from the training dataset. Each training point z consists of two parts: x from an input space $\mathcal{X}$ and y from an output space $\mathcal{Y}$. Assume the training dataset Z consists of N training points, $z_1, z_2, \cdots, z_N$, where $z_i = (x_i, y_i) \in \mathcal{X} \times \mathcal{Y}$. For a point z and a trained model $f \colon \mathcal{X} \rightarrow \mathcal{Y}$ with parameters $\theta \in \Theta$, the loss of point z is denoted by $L(z, \theta)$, and the total loss of training dataset is denoted as empirical risk, $\frac{1}{N}\sum_{i=1}^{N} L(z_i, \theta)$. Through minimizing the empirical risk, we can get the parameters of learning model denoted by $\hat{\theta} \stackrel{def}{=} \arg\min_{\theta\in\Theta} \frac{1}{N}\sum_{i=1}^{N} L(z_i, \theta)$. So a black box predictor b can be defined by their parameters $\hat{\theta}$.

The model explanation problem can be defined as finding an explanation $E \in \mathcal{E}$, where $\mathcal{E}$ is a human interpretable domain, through an interpretable model g. The interpretable model g can produce a prediction $c' = g(x)$ for given point x and its prediction $c = f(x)$, which can globally mimic the predictive behavior of black box. The model explanation $E \in \mathcal{E}$ is given by this interpretable model, like $E = \varepsilon(c, x)$ for some training point x and its prediction c.

3.2 Influence Function

For understanding which training points is the most important for a prediction or the whole model, we borrowed the idea introduced in [6] by Koh and Liang. They transfer the question to ask how the model's predictions change when a training point be removed. Due to removing a training point z from the training dataset Z, the parameters of the prediction model will change. The change is denoted by $(\hat{\theta}_{-z} - \hat{\theta})$, where $\hat{\theta}_{-z} \stackrel{def}{=} \arg\min_{\theta\in\Theta} \sum_{z_i \neq z} L(z_i, \theta)$. In order to find the most important set of training points, the change would be calculated for each training points. The amount of calculation is unacceptable and we need an efficient approximation. Here, we denote the most important set of training points as key training points P_{key}.

Influence functions provide the efficient approximation that upweights z by a small ϵ. Then the new parameters $\hat{\theta}_{\epsilon,z}$ can be calculated by Eq. 1. The influence of replacing z with $(1+\epsilon)z$ on the parameters $\hat{\theta}$ is given in Eq. 2 proposed in [2]. In [6], the authors provided an efficient approach to calculate Eq. 2.

$$\hat{\theta}_{\epsilon,z} \stackrel{def}{=} \arg\min_{\theta \in \Theta} \frac{1}{N} \sum_{i=1}^{N} L(z_i, \theta) + \epsilon L(z, \theta) \tag{1}$$

$$\mathcal{I}_{up,params}(z) \stackrel{def}{=} \frac{d\hat{\theta}_{\epsilon,z}}{d\epsilon}|_{\epsilon=0} = -H_{\hat{\theta}}^{-1} \nabla_\theta L(z, \hat{\theta}), \text{where} \tag{2}$$
$$H_{\hat{\theta}} \stackrel{def}{=} \frac{1}{N} \sum_{i=1}^{N} \nabla_\theta^2 L(z, \hat{\theta})$$

From Eq. 1, we come found that removing a point z is equal to set $\epsilon = -\frac{1}{N}$. So the parameter change caused by removing z can be approximated by $(\hat{\theta}_{-z} - \hat{\theta}) = -\frac{1}{N}\mathcal{I}_{up,params}(z)$. This change can be considered as the influence due to removing a training point z on the whole model.

Because we also need to find the key training points for a prediction, the influence of some training points should be expanded. As introduced in [6], through the chain rule, we can calculate the influence of upweighted z on the loss at a test point z_{test} by Eq. 3.

$$\begin{aligned} \mathcal{I}_{up,loss}(z, z_{test}) &\stackrel{def}{=} \frac{dL(z_{test}, \hat{\theta}_{\epsilon,z})}{d\epsilon}|_{\epsilon=0} \\ &= -\nabla_\theta L(z_{test}, \hat{\theta}_{\epsilon,z}) H_{\hat{\theta}}^{-1} \nabla_\theta L(z, \hat{\theta}) \end{aligned} \tag{3}$$

3.3 LIME

As a model agnostic explanation for any type of models, LIME explains the prediction c at a training input $x \in \mathcal{X}$ in an interpretable and faithful manner by locally mimicking the behavior of the whole model [9]. The interpretable model $g \in \mathcal{G}$, where $\mathcal{G}$ is a class of interpretable models, such as linear models, rules, decision tree, or falling rule lists, can produce a explanation $E \in \mathcal{E}$ based on the interpretable data representation x' that can be understand by human beings. In different tasks, the interpretable data representation has different forms. For example, text classification uses word embedding as the input format of the prediction model $f\colon \mathcal{X} \to \mathcal{Y}$, and its interpretable input representation can be a binary vector $x' \in \{0,1\}^{d'}$ to represent the presence or absence of a word. For image classification, an interpretable representation can represent the presence or absence of some salient color patches.

To ensure the interpretability of model g, the complexity $\Omega(g)$ of models can't be too high, which can be measured like the depth of tree or the number of non-zero weights for linear models. Local fidelity can be measured by $\mathcal{F}(f, g, \pi_x)$ denoting how faithful g is in approximating f in the locality defined by π_x. LIME provide an explanation interpretably and faithfully by minimizing the model complexity and maximizing the local fidelity like Eq. 4.

$$E = \varepsilon(c, x) = \arg\min_{g \in \mathcal{G}} \Omega(g) - \mathcal{F}(f, g, \pi_x) \tag{4}$$

In LIME, π_x is defined based on some distance function. x' is the interpretable representation of x. The neighbor domain of x' is defined by $\Pi_{x'}$. The interpretable model is a linear model, $g(x') = w_g \cdot x'$. So the local fidelity can be defined by Eq. 5.

$$\mathcal{F}(f, g, \pi_x) = - \sum_{x' \in \Pi_{x'}} \pi_x(x')(f(x) - g(x')^2) \tag{5}$$

A black box model can based features to predict. Explainer LIME provide an explanation. The explanation is a linear model to locally mimic the behavior of whole model.

Here we give a motivated example to show its weakness. The black box model has a very complex classified curve. When the test input is near the curve, the LIME can effectively give a explanation shown as Fig. 1(a). But when the test isn't near the curve, the explained linear model will be deviated the true curve shown as Fig. 1(b). Although sometime the explanation gives a right prediction, the weight for each feature of explanation is inaccurate, which is caused by the proximity-based sampling.

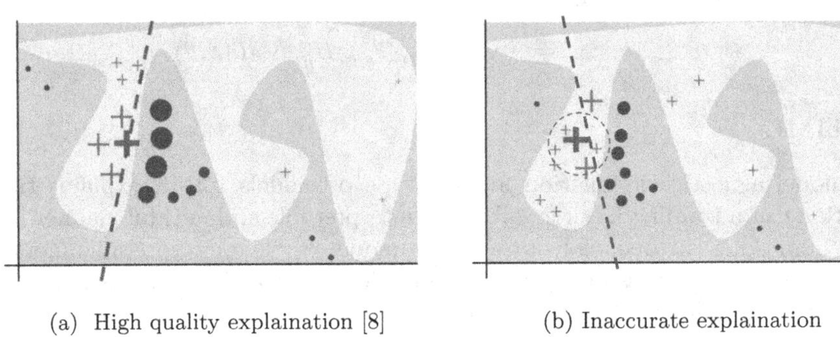

(a) High quality explaination [8] (b) Inaccurate explaination

Fig. 1. The motivation from the weakness of LIME.

4 Local Interpretable Prediction Explanation

We now present the influence function based prediction explanation (IFPE) that locally explains a prediction at a training input. The idea to solve this prediction explanation problem is fitting the black box decision curve locally. We exploit the influence function to identify the key training points of a test point, which greatly influence the parameters of the black box model. Then we present IFPE algorithm by training a linear model on the key training points.

4.1 Finding the Key Training Points

In Sect. 3, we defined the key training points as the points that have the greatest impact on the prediction or model. For local interpretable prediction explanation, the key training points is for the prediction. Given any training point z, we can calculate the influence on a test points z_{test} as $\mathcal{I}_{up,loss}(z, z_{test})$ in Eq. 3. The points that have major influence on a prediction just determine the local curve of black box model. The number of this points $|P_{key}|$ is not large. Assume there are K points selected into P_{key}, we then expand this training dataset to enough large as P_{expand} for training a interpretable model. The last step is transfering the training input $p \in P_{expand}$ to the interpretable input p'.

The algorithm generating the interpretable training dataset has shown in Algorithm 1. let Z be the training dataset for original black box model. let z be the test point that we want to explain. K is the size of the key training points set. We finally return the interpretable training dataset P_{expand}.

Algorithm 1. Generating the interpretable training dataset

Input: Z, z, K
Output: P_{expand}

function KEYTRAINSET(Z, z, K)
  for each $z_i \in Z$ **do**
    Calculate the influence $\mathcal{I}_{up,loss}(z_i, z)$ according to Eq. 3.
  end for
  Obtain the top-K training points, P_{key}, with the greatest influence.
  for each $p \in P_{key}$ **do**
    Get some neighbors around p based on distance function π_x.
    Add these neighbos to P_{expand}.
  end for
  for each $p = (x, y) \in P_{expand}$ **do**
    Transfer x to $x' \in \{0, 1\}^{d'}$.
    Replace p with $p' = (x', y)$.
  end for
  return P_{expand}
end function

4.2 Influence Function Based Prediction Explanation

In our work, we utilize the linear model , $g(x') = w_g \cdot x'$, as our interpretable model. x' is the interpretable representation of a training input x, which indicates the presence or absence of patches understood by human beings. The prediction explanation is presented visually by weighted patches, such as word or salient pixel block. We use the frame of LIME to train the interpretable training dataset P_{expand}. the locally weighted square fidelity as $\mathcal{F}(f, g, \pi_x)$ in Eq. 5. The complexity of linear model is denoted by $\Omega(g)$. For text classification,

$\Omega(g) = \infty \cdot \mathbf{I}(\|w_g\|_0 > L)$,where L is a custom constant integer, $\mathbf{I}(\cdot)$ is the indicator function, and $\|w_g\|_0$ is the number of non-zero weights.

The algorithm providing the influence function based prediction explanation for individual training input has shown in Algorithm 2. z is the training point needed to be explained. L is the maximal complexity of model g. The L-Lasso is a linear learning algorithm that first selects L features with Lasso and then learns weights via least squares.

Algorithm 2. Generating the prediction explanation

Input: z, P_{expand}, L
Output: w

function IFPE(Z, z, K)
    for each $z_i \in P_{expand}$ **do**
        Calculate the distance $\pi(z_i, z)$.
    end for
    $w \leftarrow$ L-Lasso(P_{expand}, L)
    return w
end function

5 Model Explanation

Just only giving an explanation for some individual prediction can't makes user trusting the whole model. So we pick some representative points and give their prediction explanation to decide whether trust a model. We introduce the key training points of model based on influence function, which can determine the parameters of model potentially.

In the training dataset, not all points are important for modeling the black box model. There are some points that have the most impact on the parameters of the model. If this representative points have a little change or being removed, the parameters of the model would have obviously change. Intuitively, for a complex curve, these key training points probably occur at the place where the slope of decision curve is larger. In other words, they give an effective way to represent the model. Our idea is highlighted by this phenomenon. If these key training points can be effectively explained, the model can be trusted in high probability.

In our work, we exploit the influence function into finding the key training points borrowed idea from Koh and Liang's paper [6]. The influence of some individual points can be calculated in an efficient way shown by Eq. 2. The influence $\mathcal{I}_{up,params}(z)$ of every training points z has been calculated and sorted. The top-K training points be selected as the most representative points for the model. K is a constant here and the different value of K will be studied in future. The local interpretable explanation for these key training points can be given as the model explanation. In spite of Submodule pick algorithm in LIME to choose representative points, our influence function based model explanation method (IFME) has lower computational complexity because it don't need every point's explanation. Moreover, we can combine the Submodule pick algorithm from LIME [9] into IFME and the explanations can be refined.

The algorithm about IFME has been shown in Algorithm 3. let Z be the training dataset for original black box model. K is a constant for choosing the top-K training points. P_{Key} denotes the key training points set. E_{Key} denotes the explanations for all key training points.

Algorithm 3. IFME: Influence function based model explanation

Input: Z, K
Output: P_{Key}, E_{Key}

function IFME(Z, K)
    for each $z_i \in Z$ **do**
        Calculate the influence $\mathcal{I}_{up,params}(z)$ according to Eq. 2.
    end for
    Obtain the top-K training points, P_{key}, with the greatest influence for the model.
    for each $p \in P_{key}$ **do**
        Explain the p according to Algorithm 2.
        Add the explanation for p to E_{Key}
    end for
    return P_{Key}, E_{Key}
end function

6 Experiments and Results

In this section, we present simulated user experiments to evaluate the efficiency of our proposed methods. In particular, we demonstrate our influence function based method can get high faithfulness of explanation.

6.1 Experiment Setup

In order to validate our explanation method, we conduct experiments on two sentiment analysis datasets, Books and DVDs [1]. These Sentiment Dataset contains product reviews taken from Amazon.com for different product types. Each review contain a rating (5-star) field, and has been labeled as positive for rating greater than 3, otherwise as negative. Each datasets contains 2000 instances, 1000 positive and 1000 negative. The analysis task is to classify whether the product reviews are positive or negative.

We use four common techniques to tackle this classification task. We train decision tree (DT), nearest neighbors(NN), logistic regression with L2 regularization (LR) and support vector machines with RBF kernel (SVM). All of these four models used bag of words as features. We use the implementation and default parameters of scikit-learn. Each dataset had been divided into train set (1600 instances) and test set (400 instances).

Due to lack of enough interpretability of above models, we use sparse linear model to mimic the more accurate model local for better understanding. To explain individual prediction, we compare our method (IFME) with the related method, LIME [9], which based on nearest neighbors to train a local linear model. To demonstrate the explanation performance, we also compare against a greedy procedure [8] and a random procedure introduced by [9]. In greedy procedure, we obtain the K most significant features by greedily remove them until the prediction changes. In random procedure, we randomly picks K features as an explanation. In our experiment, K is set to 10 for understanding the reasons of a prediction.

6.2 Faithfulness of Explanations

The first question to explain prediction is which features are important for explaining all prediction. These features can contribute better accuracy. To obtain these significant features, we train two interpretable classifiers (Sparse LR, DT) and then pick 10 significant features that are the most frequent features and have the most highest weight for any instances. It make sense to assume these significant features are important to these models.

To measure the faithfulness of explanations, we first generate explanations by different explanation methods for each prediction on the test set. The faithfulness is denoted to be the fraction of the covered significant features by explanation. We conducted experiments to compare the faithfulness of above four explanation methods with respect to two interpretable classifiers on above two sentiment analysis datasets. The averaged recall over all test instances has been reported in Figs. 2 and 3.

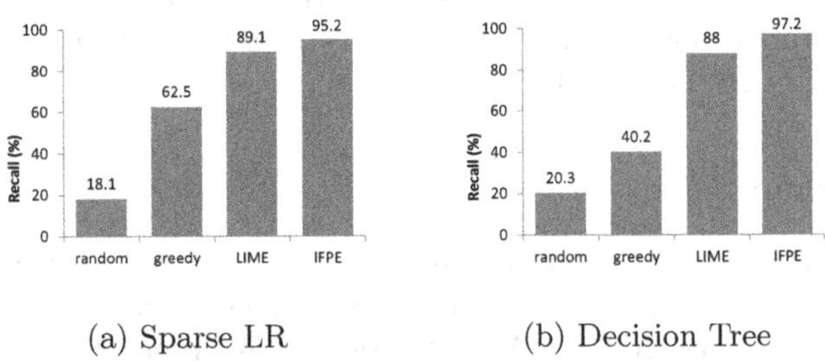

(a) Sparse LR (b) Decision Tree

Fig. 2. Recall on truly important features for two interpretable classifiers on the books dataset.

We observe that our proposed explanation method has best faithfulness since providing better local fitting. LIME is also work well, which consistently achieve exceeding 90% recall for both classifiers on two datasets. The greedy approach

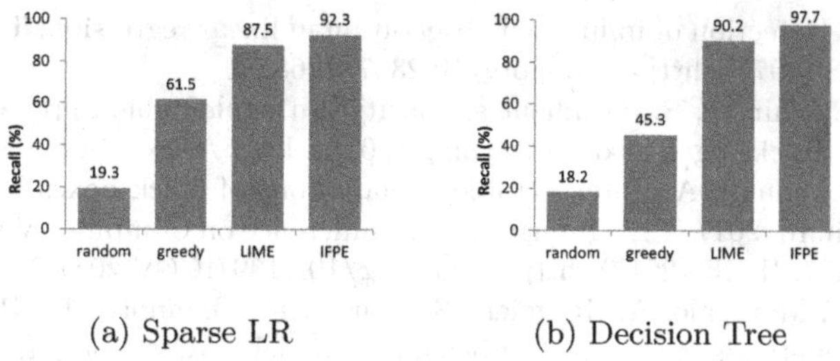

(a) Sparse LR (b) Decision Tree

Fig. 3. Recall on truly important features for two interpretable classifiers on the DVDs dataset.

just obtain better recall than random approach because it pick more important features heuristically.

7 Conclusion and Future Work

In this paper, we proposed a novel model explanation method to explain the predictions or black-box models. First, a local prediction explanation has been designed, which combines the key training points identified via influence function and the framework of LIME. This approach can give more exact explanation to a given prediction. Then we presented an agnostic method, IFME, which utilizes the key training points corresponding to a given model. The understanding about entire model provided by the key training points can be helpful for improving the confidence level. Finally, the extensive theoretic analysis and simulated experiments demonstrated our method is effective and efficient.

Influence function method provided a way to trace a prediction through the learning algorithms to the training data. It gives a high view to understand the model. In this work, we just combine it into a local explanation method and obtain more accurate and credible results. Expanding this idea to other explanation problem would also able to find more outcomes. In future work, we can introduce influence function into a global model explanation.

Acknowledgments. This study was supported by the National Key Research and Development Plan's Key Special Program on High performance computing of China, No. 2017YFB0203201.

References

1. Blitzer, J., Dredze, M., Pereira, F.: Biographies, bollywood, boom-boxes and blenders: domain adaptation for sentiment classification. In: Proceedings of the 45th Annual Meeting of the Association of Computational Linguistics, pp. 440–447. Association for Computational Linguistics, Prague, Czech Republic, June 2007. https://www.aclweb.org/anthology/P07-1056

2. Cook, R.D.: Detection of influential observation in linear regression. Technometrics **19**(1), 15–18 (1977). https://doi.org/10.2307/1268249
3. Dhaliwal, J., Shintre, S.: Gradient similarity: an explainable approach to detect adversarial attacks against deep learning (2018). http://arxiv.org/abs/1806.10707
4. Fong, R.C., Vedaldi, A.: Interpretable explanations of black boxes by meaningful perturbation. In: 2017 IEEE International Conference on Computer Vision (ICCV), pp. 3449–3457. IEEE (2017). https://doi.org/10.1109/ICCV.2017.371
5. Guidotti, R., Monreale, A., Ruggieri, S., Turini, F., Giannotti, F., Pedreschi, D.: A survey of methods for explaining black box models. ACM Comput. Surv. **51**(5), 93:1–93:42 (2019). https://doi.org/10.1145/3236009
6. Koh, P.W., Liang, P.: Understanding black-box predictions via influence functions. In: Proceedings of the 34th International Conference on Machine Learning. ICML 2017, vol. 70, pp. 1885–1894 (2017). http://dl.acm.org/citation.cfm?id=3305381.3305576
7. Lou, Y., Caruana, R., Gehrke, J., Hooker, G.: Accurate intelligible models with pairwise interactions. In: Proceedings of the 19th ACM SIGKDD International Conference on Knowledge Discovery and Data Mining - KDD 2013, p. 623. ACM Press (2013). http://dl.acm.org/citation.cfm?doid=2487575.2487579
8. Martens, D., Provost, F.: Explaining data-driven document classifications. Mis Q. **38**(1), 73–100 (2013)
9. Sonnenburg, S., Zien, A., Philips, P., Rätsch, G.: POIMs: positional oligomer importance matrices-understanding support vector machine-based signal detectors. Bioinformatics **24**(13), i6–i14 (2008). https://www.ncbi.nlm.nih.gov/pmc/articles/PMC2718648/
10. Xu, K., et al.: Show, attend and tell: neural image caption generation with visual attention (2015). http://arxiv.org/abs/1502.03044
11. Zien, A., Krämer, N., Sonnenburg, S., Rätsch, G.: The feature importance ranking measure. In: Buntine, W., Grobelnik, M., Mladenić, D., Shawe-Taylor, J. (eds.) ECML PKDD 2009. LNCS (LNAI), vol. 5782, pp. 694–709. Springer, Heidelberg (2009). https://doi.org/10.1007/978-3-642-04174-7_45
12. Zintgraf, L.M., Cohen, T.S., Adel, T., Welling, M.: Visualizing deep neural network decisions: prediction difference analysis (2017). http://arxiv.org/abs/1702.04595

GPU-Accelerated Parallel Aligning Long Reads with High Error Rate Using Enhanced Sparse Suffix Array

Hao Wei, Cheng Zhong(✉), Danyang Chen, Mengxiao Yin, and Jinxiong Zhang

School of Computer, Electronics and Information, Guangxi University, Nanning 530004, Guangxi, China
weihao_good@sina.com, {chzhong,chendanyang,ymx,zhangjx}@gxu.edu.cn

Abstract. The read alignment (sequence alignment) is one of the most basic and time-consuming problems in Bioinformatics. In this paper, a CPU-GPU parallel long-read alignment method is studied to solve this problem. A lightweight data structure using enhanced sparse suffix array is used to store the index of reference genome in order to adapt to the limited memory capacity of GPU architecture. The two-dimensional search space between the reference genome and long reads is divided into several search sub-spaces. The massive long reads alignment is further divided into the multiple long-read alignments with smaller size. A CPU-GPU parallel algorithm aligning long reads with high error rate is implemented by improving the seeds selection scheme. The experimental results show that the parallel algorithm can accelerate remarkably the long-read alignment while maintaining the alignment accuracy and recall rate as a whole.

Keywords: Long-read alignment · Seed selection · Parallel algorithm · GPU computing · Enhanced sparse suffix array · Lightweight index

1 Introduction

Over the last years, the cost of new generation sequencing has been decreasing and the sequencing flux has exploded [1]. Recently, the cost of sequencing a single human genome has been reduced remarkably [2]. The sequencing platform generated a large number of reads. The read alignment (sequence alignment) is the first and most time-consuming step in analyzing biological data. The read alignment problem is a compute-intensive task [3]. Developing efficient parallel read alignment algorithm has important practical significance.

The existing GPU-based sequence alignment algorithms include Masher [4], CUSHAW [5], pyPaSWAS [6], SOAP 3 [7], and SARUMAN [8], etc. The pyPaSWAS is a general Smith-Waterman comparison algorithm, which supports basic gap penalty and affine gap penalty method. SOAP3 uses seed and hash search table to accelerate the alignment, in which reads and reference genome are converted to numeric data by using

H. Shen and Y. Sang (Eds.): PAAP 2019, CCIS 1163, pp. 311–319, 2020.
https://doi.org/10.1007/978-981-15-2767-8_28

every 2 bit encoding. SARUMAN returns all possible alignment positions of reads occurring in the reference genome under a given error rate threshold. The SARUMAN can reduce the alignment time by filtering and CUDA computing. Masher uses an efficient memory indexing scheme to reduce the storage size of indexing human genome. When the length of the read exceeds 500 bps, Masher can speed up the alignment remarkably. In CUSHAW algorithm, the parallel read alignment is implemented by Burrows-Wheeler Transform and CUDA programming. By calculating the differences of values between adjacent elements in score matrix based on the difference recurrence relations, Suzuki et al. designed a SIMD parallel algorithm for semi-global alignment of a pair of long sequences [9]. A GPU parallel algorithm is proposed to efficiently find the maximum accurate matching between two gene sequences based on the lightweight index structure [10]. Wei et al. developed a sequential algorithm for aligning long reads with high error rate and reference genome [11]. To accelerate further comparing massive long reads with high error rate and reference genome, this paper improves the seeds selection scheme and implements a parallel long-read alignment method by hybrid CPU and GPU computing.

2 Method

2.1 Index Construction

The memory capacity of GPU architecture is very limited. So, a less memory-consuming data structure should be used to store the index information during parallel alignment. In addition, how to reduce the construction time of index for large-scale reference genome is also an important issue. In this paper, the sparse parameter s is used to reduce the size and construction time of the index. That is to say, only the locations with interval distance s in reference genome are stored in the index. In [12], the concepts for maximal exact matching (MEM) and the super-maximal exact matching (SMEM) are introduced. For all exact matches of length $>L$, the value of s satisfies $s < L - L_{index} + 1$, where L is the threshold of length of maximum accurate matching, and L_{index} is the length of the index segment corresponding to the reference genome. The number of locations to be stored in the index is $|G|/s$, where $|G|$ is the length of the reference genome.

To reduce the memory occupied by the index, the two-dimensional searching space is divided into several square blocks. During each alignment iteration, only the index of the reference genome area corresponding to the current row is used, and only $N_{locs} = \lceil L_{sq}/s \rceil$ locations are stored, where L_{sq} is the edge length of the square block. The array $locs[.]$ is used to store the starting position of the index segment of length L in sorted order, and the array $ptr[.]$ is used to store the prefix sum of the number of times that each index segment appears in the reference genome. All positions of the i-th index segment occurring in the reference genome are stored in $locs[ptr[i] \ldots ptr[i+1]-1]$. The array $locs$ will occupy $N_{locs} \lceil \log_2 L_{sq} \rceil$ bits of memory. A base is represented by 2 bits, and each index segment is represented by $2L_{index}$ bits. The array ptr is composed of $2^{2L_{index}} = 4^{L_{index}}$ elements. Hence, the array ptr requires $4^{L_{index}} \lceil \log_2 N_{locs} \rceil$ bits of memory.

The index construction is described in Algorithm 1.

Algorithm 1 Index construction

```
Input: reference genome G, star,end
Output: locs[.], ptr[.]
Begin
for each index segment i do in parallel
ptr[i] ← 0;
endfor
for each location j ∈ [star,end] in G∈ do in parallel
i ← (G_j,G_j+1,...,G_j+Gls−1);
atomicAdd(ptr[i + 1],1);
end for
Parallel computing prefix sums by calling GPUPrefixSum(ptr);
for each index segment i do in parallel
temp[i] ← ptr[i];
endfor
for each location j ∈ [star,end] in G do in parallel
i ← (G_j,G_j+1,...,G_j+Gls−1);
index ← atomicAdd(temp[i + 1],1);
locs[index] ← j;
endfor
for each index segment i do in parallel
sort locs[ptr[i],...,ptr[i + 1]-1];
endfor
End.
```

2.2 CPU-GPU Parallel Alignment Algorithm

Given the reference genome G and the set R of sequencing sequences (reads), G and R are taken as the Y axis and X axis respectively, which form a two-dimensional space. The two-dimensional space is then divided into several square blocks of size $L_{sq} \times L_{sq}$. Hence, the massive long reads alignment is divided into several long-read alignments with smaller size in order to adapt to the limited memory capacity of GPU architecture. Starting with the bottom line of a square block in two-dimensional space, the algorithm searches the maximal exact matches and the super-maximal exact matches. When the algorithm processes the square blocks in a row, it only loads this part of the index into memory until all the square blocks in the row have been processed. This part of the index is constructed by the corresponding reference genome region in the row blocks. Then, each square block is divided into N_{block} rectangular blocks of size $L_{sq} \times L_{block}$, where $L_{sq} = N_{block} \times L_{block}$. Similarly, each rectangular block contains shorter read fragments and reference genome fragments. The long-read fragments and reference genome fragments in each rectangular block will be allocated to a GPU thread block, where each thread processes ω continuous index segments. Therefore, $L_{block} = \tau \times \omega$, where τ is the size of an index segment. The index segments in locations i and $i + k\omega$ will be processed simultaneously, $1 \leq k \leq \lfloor L_{sq}/\omega \rfloor$.

The CPU and GPU collaboratively execute the following four steps to align long reads with reference genome. Firstly, the heuristic active load balancing algorithm is executed to balance the tasks of GPU threads while extracting the maximal exact matches and the super-maximal exact matches. Secondly, each GPU thread generates and extends the exact matching in related genome locations. Thirdly, the parallel combinatorial algorithms are executed to merge the continuous matches. Finally, the filtering is performed to obtain two types of seeds. The first type of seeds contains the maximal exact matches and the super-maximal exact matches in the blocks, and the second type of seeds is composed of the maximal exact matches at the block boundaries. The first type of seed is send to the CPU and added to the seed set. The maximal exact matches at block boundaries form a global list, which is sent back to the CPU for final processing. Similar to the above steps, when dealing with maximal exact matches at block boundaries, this pair of triples is merged if there is overlap between two triples.

Algorithm 2 describes a CPU-GPU parallel long-read alignment algorithm called sufKart-GPU. In Algorithm 2, the reference genome G and reads set R are transferred from CPU to GPU. A lightweight index of reference genome G is established on GPU. The algorithms for searching the maximal exact matches and super-maximal exact matches are executed by parallel threads and the search results are transferred from GPU to CPU. The candidate regions are generated by CPU. For common regions between candidate regions, the gap/no-gap alignment algorithm is executed and the alignment quality score is computed by CPU.

Algorithm 2 sufKart-GPU
Input: reference genome G, reads set R
Output: alignment results for R occurring in G
Begin
1: Transfer G and R from CPU to GPU;
2: Construct the index for G by executing Algorithm 1;
3: for each read r in R do in parallel
4: Allocate several GPU threads to the index location with large workload by heuristic active load balancing strategy to balance the load of searching the maximal exact matches and super-maximal exact matches;
5: Generate accurate matching triples (r,q,λ) and merge all pairs of overlapping triples;
6: Expand to the left and right sides from the location of seed hit until mismatch occurring or reaching block boundary
7: Transfer the results for the maximal exact matches and super-maximal exact matches in a block from GPU to CPU, and store the results for the maximal exact matches at the block boundaries to the memory of GPU;
8: Sort the results for the maximal exact matches at the block boundaries, and merge all pairs of overlapping triples to obtain the results for the maximal exact matches and super-maximal exact matches at the square boundaries
9: Sort the results for the maximal exact matches at the square boundaries and store them in the global list in GPU, and transfer the sorted results from GPU to CPU;
10: if $|seeds| \leq set_{seed}$ then
11: Reduce the threshold of seed length and goto step 3;
12: else
13: Obtain the candidate area according to the value of location difference between r and G;

14: Execute the gap/no-gap alignment algorithm and compute the alignment quality score;
15: endif
16: endfor
17: Output the alignment results;
End.

3 Experiment

3.1 Experimental Environment and Data

The experiment was conducted on the computer with qual-core Intel core i7-6700 k CPU 4 GHz processor and 32 GB memory, which equips with a NVIDIA GeForce GTX 1080 GPU with 2560 cores and 8 GB memory. The operating system is Linux ubuntu 16.04 LTS. The parallel algorithm is implemented by C++ and CUDA 8.0 programming.

The three data sets used in the experiment are Listeria monocytogenes (L. monocytogenes), Caenorhabditis briggsae (C. briggsae), and Homo Sapiensch ro mo some 2 (chr2h) respectively. The DNA sequences in three data sets are treated as three reference genomes. The simulated reads are generated by Wgsim[1]. For data sets L.monocytogenes and C.briggsae, the lengths of the three simulated reads are 100 bp, 150 bp, and 200 bp respectively, and the error rate ε of the three reads are 2%, 4%, and 6% respectively. For data set chr2h, the lengths of the three simulated reads are 200 bp, 500 bp, and 1000 bp, and the error rate ε of the three reads are 8%, 10%, and 15% respectively. The other parameters are set to the default values offered by Wgsim. We use the precision rate, recall rate, and execution time to evaluate the performance of the algorithms. Suppose that there are R_n reads in a data set R, where R_i reads are mapped into the reference genome, in other words, the R_i reads occurs in the reference genome. For each read, if the difference between the real mapping location and simulated mapping location is smaller than or equal to 30 bp, this read mapping is judged as truely mapped [13]. Let TM represents the amount of the reads that are mapped into the reference genome correctly. Similar to the existing literatures, the precision rate pr and recall rate rec are computed by $pr = TM/R_i \times 100\%$ and $rec = TM/R_n \times 100\%$.

3.2 Experimental Results

For given three species L.monocytogenes, C.briggsae, and chr2h with different error rates $\varepsilon_{L,C} \in \{2\%, 4\%, 6\%\}$, $\varepsilon_{C,H} \in \{8\%, 10\%, 15\%\}$, and different read lengths $L_{L,C} \in \{100\text{ bp}, 150\text{ bp}, 200\text{ bp}\}$ and $L_{ch} \in \{200\text{ bp}, 500\text{ bp}, 1000\text{ bp}\}$, we evaluated the performance of the sequential long-read alignment algorithm sufKart [11] and parallel long-read alignment algorithm sufKart-GPU by the precision rate and recall rate, and compared the required time of running algorithms sufKart and sufKart-GPU to evaluate the acceleration effect for sufKart-GPU.

[1] https://github.com/lh3/wgsim.

For the case in which L.monocytogenes and C.briggsae are treated as the reference genomes, the read length s is 100 bp, 150 bp, and 200 bp and the error rate ε is 2%, 4%, and 6% respectively, the precision rate pr and recall rate rec of running algorithms sufKart and sufKart-GPU are shown in Table 1.

Table 1. Precision rate and recall rate of algorithms sufKart and sufKart-GPU.

(a) read length=100bp

	L.monocytogenes				C.briggsae			
	sufKart		sufKart-GPU		sufKart		sufKart-GPU	
ε	*pr*	*rec*	*pr*	*rec*	*pr*	rec	*pr*	*rec*
2%	99.96	99.93	99.96	99.93	99.96	99.93	99.96	99.93
4%	99.95	99.91	99.95	99.91	99.95	99.91	99.95	99.91
6%	99.95	99.91	99.95	99.91	99.95	99.91	99.95	99.91

(b) read length=150bp

	L.monocytogenes				C.briggsae			
	sufKart		sufKart-GPU		sufKart		sufKart-GPU	
ε	*pr*	*rec*	*pr*	*rec*	*pr*	*rec*	*pr*	*rec*
2%	99.97	99.94	99.97	99.94	99.97	99.94	99.96	99.94
4%	99.97	99.94	99.97	99.93	99.96	99.92	99.97	99.92
6%	99.96	99.91	99.96	99.93	99.96	99.91	99.96	99.93

(c) read length=200bp

	L.monocytogenes				C.briggsae			
	sufKart		sufKart-GPU		sufKart		sufKart-GPU	
ε	*pr*	*rec*	*pr*	*rec*	*pr*	*rec*	*pr*	*rec*
2%	99.98	99.95	99.98	99.95	99.98	99.95	99.98	99.95
4%	99.96	99.93	99.97	99.92	99.97	99.94	99.97	99.94
6%	99.96	99.92	99.96	99.91	99.96	99.92	99.96	99.91

We can see from Table 1(a) that for reference genomes L. monocytogenes and C. briggsae, the precision rate and recall rate of sufKart-GPU are the same as that of sufKart. As shown in Table 1(b), when L. monocytogenes is used as a reference genome, the recall rate of sufKart-GPU is slightly lower than that of sufKart if the error rate ε is 4%. But if $\varepsilon = 6\%$, the recall rate of sufKart-GPU is higher than that of sufKart. When C. briggsae is used as the reference genome, the recall rate of sufKart-GPU is higher than that of sufKart if the error rate ε is 6%. Table 1(c) shows that for the reference genome C. briggsae, the recall rate of sufKart-GPU is a little bit smaller than that of sufKart if the error rate ε is 6%. For the reference genome L. monocytogenes, the recall rate of sufKart-GPU is slightly lower than that of sufKart if the error rate ε is 4% and 6%. In addition, for the reference genome L.monocytogenes, the precision rate of sufkart and sufKart-GPU is 99.96% and 99.97% respectively if the read length is 200 bp and the error rate is 4%. On the whole, the precision rate and recall rate of sufKart-GPU and sufKart are basically the same. This indicates that the CPU-GPU parallel long-read alignment algorithm sufKart-GPU can maintain the alignment quality.

Compared with other biological genes, human genes contain more complex errors and mutations. When human genome (chr2h) is used as a reference genome, the precision rate and recall rate of sufKart and sufKart-GPU are shown in Tables 2 and 3 if the read length is 200 bp, 500 bp, and 1000 bp and the error rate is 8%, 10%, and 15% respectively.

Table 2. Precision rate for sufKart and sufKart-GPU.

	Read length = 200 bp		Read length = 500 bp		Read length = 1000 bp	
ε	sufKart	SufKart-GPU	sufKart	SufKart-GPU	sufKart	SufKart-GPU
8%	97.81	97.81	98.66	98.66	98.92	98.92
10%	95.75	95.75	98.13	98.13	98.86	98.86
15%	94.45	94.45	97.79	97.79	97.45	97.84

Table 3. Recall rate for sufKart and sufKart-GPU.

	Read length = 200 bp		Read length = 500 bp		Read length = 1000 bp	
ε	sufKart	SufKart-GPU	sufKart	SufKart-GPU	sufKart	SufKart-GPU
8%	97.35	97.81	98.57	98.58	98.61	98.58
10%	95.02	95.03	97.81	98.13	98.57	98.53
15%	94.31	94.30	97.22	97.20	97.33	97.37

Tables 2 and 3 show that compare to aligning the reads with L. monocytogenes or C. briggsae, both of sufKart and sufKart-GPU obtain slightly lower precision rate and recall rate when aligning the reads and human genome with high error rate. This indicates that the error rate of biological sequence has an effect on the quality of the alignment results. We can also see from Tables 2 and 3 that the precision rate and recall rate of sufKart and sufKart-GPU are almost the same. When the error rate is 15% and read length is 1000 bp, the precision rate of sufKart-GPU is slightly higher than that of sufKart. When the read length is 1000 bp with error rate 8% and 10% and the error rate is 15% with read length 200 bp and 500 bp, the recall rate of sufKart-GPU is slightly lower than that of sufKart. But when the error rate is 8% with read length 200 bp and 500 bp, the recall rate of sufKart-GPU is slightly higher than that of sufKart. The above results show that for aligning longer sequences with higher error rates, the precision rate and recall rate of sufKart-GPU are almost the same as that of sufKart.

To evaluate the GPU parallel acceleration effect of sufKart-GPU, Fig. 1 shows the required time of running algorithms sufKart and sufKart-GPU when chr2h is used as the reference genome with error rate {8%, 10%, 15%} and read length {200 bp, 500 bp, 1000 bp} respectively.

As shown in Fig. 1, when the lengths of reads are 200 bp and 500 bp, although the error rates are different, the required time of running the alignment algorithms is almost

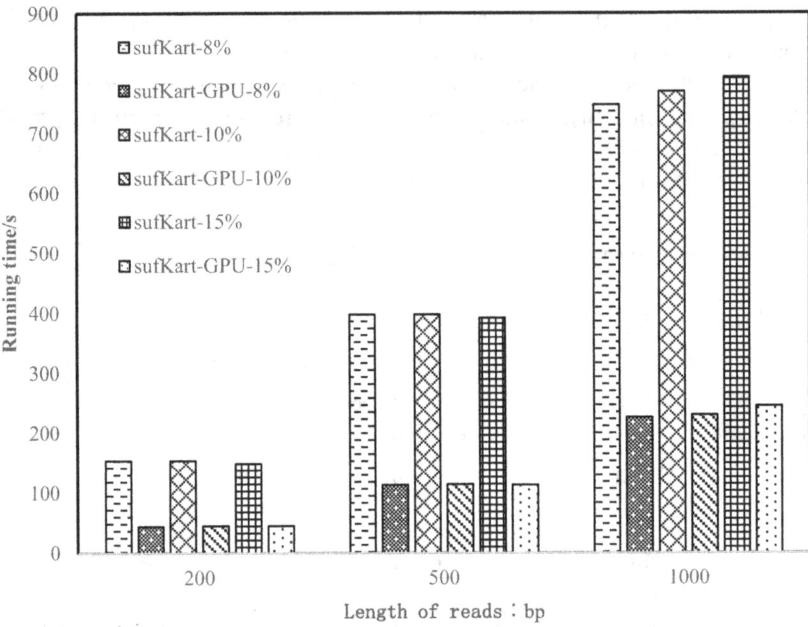

Fig. 1. Required time of running algorithms sufKart and sufKart-GPU.

the same. When the length of read is 200 bp, sufKart spends about 150 s to complete the alignment process, while sufKart-GPU spends 40 s to complete the alignment process. When the length of read is 500 bp, sufKart spends about 400 s to complete the alignment process, while sufKart-GPU takes only about 110 s to complete the alignment process. When the length of the read increases to 1000 bp, sufKart spends much more time to complete the alignment than sufKart-GPU. This is because with increase of the length of the read, the length of the segment including errors in read is increased, and the gap/no-gap alignment algorithm spends more time to process the segments including errors.

4 Conclusion

It is very time-consuming work for searching the maximal exact matches and super-maximal exact matches between long reads and reference genome in the massive long reads alignment. The implemented CPU-GPU parallel alignment algorithm constructs a lightweight index for reference genome on GPU memory, and accelerates searching the maximal exact matches and super-maximal exact matches between long reads and reference genome by improving seed selection scheme. The experimental results show that the parallel long-read alignment algorithm maintains good accuracy and recall rate on the whole, and significantly reduces the running time. The third generation sequencing platform produces longer and longer sequences. For example, the third generation sequencing platform PacBio SMRT produces a sequence with length of more than 10 kbp. This indicates that it will spend much time to align a large number of long reads with reference genome. In the future work, we will investigate the coarse-grained and fine-grained parallel algorithm for aligning massive long reads with high error rate on hybrid CPU/GPU cluster.

Acknowledgment. We thank the anonymous reviewers for their constructive comments, which help us improve the manuscript. This work is supported in part by the National Natural Science Foundation of China under Grant No. 61962004 and 61462005.

References

1. Glenn, T.C.: Field guide to next-generation DNA sequencers. Mol. Ecol. Resour. **11**(5), 759–769 (2011)
2. Hayden, E.C.: Is the $1,000 genome for real? Nature (2014). https://doi.org/10.1038/nature.2014.14530
3. Edwards, D.J., Holt, K.E.: Beginner's guide to comparative bacterial genome analysis using next-generation sequence data. Microb. Inform. Exp. **3**, 2 (2013)
4. Abu-Doleh, A., Saule, E., Kaya, K., et al.: Masher: mapping long(er) reads with hash-based genome indexing on GPUs. In: Proceedings of the International Conference on Bioinformatics, Computational Biology and Biomedical Informatics (2013). https://doi.org/10.1145/2506583.2506641
5. Liu, Y., Schmidt, B., Maskell, D.L.: CUSHAW: a CUDA compatible short read aligner to large genomes based on the Burrows-Wheeler transform. Bioinformatics **28**(14), 1830–1837 (2012)
6. Warris, S., Timal, N.R.N., Kempenaar, M., et al.: pyPaSWAS: python-based multi-core CPU and GPU sequence alignment. PLOS ONE **13**(1), e0190279 (2018)
7. Liu, C., Wong, T.K., Wu, E., et al.: SOAP3: ultra-fast GPU-based parallel alignment tool for short reads. Bioinformatics **28**(6), 878–879 (2012)
8. Blom, J., Jakobi, T., Doppmeier, D., et al.: Exact and complete short-read alignment to microbial genomes using Graphics Processing Unit programming. Bioinformatics **27**(10), 1351–1358 (2011)
9. Suzuki, H., Kasahara, M.: Introducing difference recurrence relations for faster semi-global alignment of long sequences. BMC Bioinform. **19**, 45 (2018)
10. Abu-Doleh, A., Kaya, K., Abouelhoda, M., et al.: Extracting maximal exact matches on GPU. In: Proceedings of 2014 International Parallel and Distributed Processing Symposium, pp. 1417–1426. IEEE, (2014)
11. Wei, H., Zhong, C.: Aligning high error rate reads using enhanced sparse suffix array index. J. Chin. Comput. Syst. **40**(8), 1804–1808 (2019). (in Chinese)
12. Li, H.: Aligning sequence reads, clone sequences and assembly contigs with BWA-MEM. arXiv:1303.3997.http://arxiv.org/abs/1303.3997 v2 (2013)
13. Lin, H., Hsu, W.: Kart: a divide-and-conquer algorithm for NGS read alignment. Bioinformatics **33**(15), 2281–2287 (2017)

An Improved Algorithm for Building Suffix Array in External Memory

Yi Wu[1], Bin Lao[2], Xinghui Ma[3], and Ge Nong[4](✉)

[1] State Grid Shanghai Electrical Power Research Institute, Shanghai, China
[2] School of Information Science and Technology,
Guangdong University of Foreign Studies, Guangzhou, China
[3] 21CN Corporation Limited, Guangzhou, China
[4] Department of Computer Science, Sun Yat-sen University, Guangzhou, China
issng@mail.sysu.edu.cn

Abstract. A suffix array (SA) is a data structure that has been widely used in many string processing applications, and it can be built on external memory model using the induced sorting (IS) method when the size of input and output exceeds the capacity of internal memory. In this paper, we make our first attempt to improve the performance of DSA-IS using new substring sorting and naming methods in the reduction phase. The experimental results indicate that, our program for the adapted algorithm DSA-IS+ runs as fast as eSAIS and consumes only half as much disk space as the latter on various real-world datasets.

Keywords: Suffix array · Induced sorting · External memory

1 Introduction

The suffix array (SA) [8] is a data structure that has been widely used in many string processing applications, e.g., biological sequence alignment, time series analysis and text clustering. Given an input string, traversing its suffix tree can be emulated by using the corresponding enhanced suffix array [1], which mainly consists of the suffix and the longest common prefix (LCP) arrays. It has been realized that the application scope of an index mainly depends on the construction speed and the space requirement. This leads to intensive works on designing time and space efficient suffix sorting algorithms over the past decade, assuming different computation models such as internal memory, external memory, parallel and distributed models. Particularly, to keep pace with the fast development of the data sampling techniques, several external memory algorithms have been proposed for building massive suffix arrays in recent years, e.g., DC3 [3], bwt-disk [4], SAscan [5], pSAscan [6], eSAIS [2], EM-SA-DS [10], DSA-IS [9] and SAIS-PQ [7]. Among them, the latter four algorithms are based on the induced sorting (IS) method described in SA-IS [11].

The SA-IS algorithm takes linear time and RAM space to build an SA on internal memory model. The IS method determines the lexical order of two

H. Shen and Y. Sang (Eds.): PAAP 2019, CCIS 1163, pp. 320–330, 2020.
https://doi.org/10.1007/978-981-15-2767-8_29

suffixes by comparing their heading characters and successors in sequence, where the lexical order of their successors is determined recursively following the same way. The IS method has been applied to designing several disk-based suffix sorting algorithms. These IS algorithms have linear I/O complexity better than the others designed by different methods, but they suffer from a bottleneck due to the large disk space for obtaining the heading characters of unsorted suffixes and the ranks of their sorted successors in a disk-friendly way. As reported, the average disk usage for pSAscan to build a size-n SA encoded by 40-bit integers is around $7.5n$ bytes, while that for eSAIS, EM-SA-DS, DSA-IS and SAIS-PQ are $24n$, $31n$, $18n$ and $15n$ bytes, respectively. The poor space performance for these IS algorithms is mainly because their current programs fail to free the disk space for temporary data even when the data is no longer needed. A dramatic improvement can be achieved by storing temporary data into multiple files and deleting a file immediately when the data in it is not needed anymore.

It is identified that DSA-IS reaches the peak disk usage when induced sorting substrings during the reduction phase. This reveals a need for designing new substring sorting and naming methods to improve the space efficiency in order to scale the problem size that can be tackled.

Our contribution in this paper is that we employ new substring sorting and naming methods to improve the design of DSA-IS. In our experiments, the program for the enhanced algorithm, called DSA-IS+, runs as fast as that for eSAIS while its peak disk usage is about two-thirds as that of eSAIS.

The rest of this paper is organized as follows. Section 2 introduces some notations and symbols for presentation convenience. Section 3 gives an overview of the reduction phase of DSA-IS. Section 4 describes our new substring sorting and naming methods for DSA-IS+. Sections 5 and 6 show the experimental results and the concluding remarks, respectively.

2 Preliminaries

Given an input string $x[0,n) = x[0]x[1]...x[n-1]$ drawn from a totally ordered alphabet δ, we assume $x[n-1]$ to be the smallest character in δ that appears in x only once. And $\mathsf{sub}(x,i)$ and $\mathsf{suf}(x,i)$ denote a substring running from $x[i]$ to the leftmost LMS character on its right side and a suffix running from $x[i]$ to $x[n-1]$, respectively. The basic notations used in our presentation are listed as follows.

- L-type, S-type and LMS character/substring/suffix. Let $x[i]$ be S-type if (1) $i = n-1$ or (2) $x[i] < x[i+1]$ or (3) $x[i] = x[i+1]$ and $x[i+1]$ is S-type; otherwise, $x[i]$ is L-type. Furthermore, if $x[i]$ and $x[i-1]$ are respectively S-type and L-type, then $x[i]$ is also an LMS character. Moreover, if $x[i]$ is L-type, S-type or LMS, then $\mathsf{sub}(x,i)$ and $\mathsf{suf}(x,i)$ are L-type, S-type or LMS, respectively.
- Preceding and succeeding character/substring/suffix. $x[i-1]$, $\mathsf{sub}(x,i-1)$ and $\mathsf{suf}(x,i-1)$ denote the preceding character, substring and suffix for $x[i]$, $\mathsf{sub}(x,i)$

and $\mathsf{suf}(x,i)$, respectively. Similarly, $x[i+1]$, $\mathsf{sub}(x,i+1)$ and $\mathsf{suf}(x,i+1)$ denote the succeeding character, substring and suffix for $x[i]$, $\mathsf{sub}(x,i)$ and $\mathsf{suf}(x,i)$, respectively.
- SA and STRA. Let SA and STRA be the suffix and substring arrays, respectively. Both $\mathsf{SA}(x)$ and $\mathsf{STRA}(x)$ are permutations of $[0,n)$ such that $\mathsf{suf}(x,\mathsf{SA}(x)[i]) < \mathsf{suf}(x,\mathsf{SA}(x)[i+1])$ and $\mathsf{sub}(x,\mathsf{SA}(x)[i]) \leq \mathsf{sub}(x,\mathsf{SA}(x)[i+1])$ in lexicographical order for all $i \in [0,n-1)$.
- BKT. Suffixes in $\mathsf{SA}(x)$ are naturally grouped into buckets according to their head characters. Given $\mathsf{BKT}(\mathsf{SA}(x),ch)$, the bucket occupies a consecutive range in $\mathsf{SA}(x)$ that gathers all the suffixes with a head character ch. Furthermore, a bucket, say $\mathsf{BKT}(\mathsf{SA}(x),ch)$, can be subdivided into $\mathsf{BKT_L}(\mathsf{SA}(x),ch)$ and $\mathsf{BKT_S}(\mathsf{SA}(x),ch)$ that only contain L-type and S-type suffixes in $\mathsf{BKT}(\mathsf{SA}(x),ch)$, respectively. Similarly, $\mathsf{BKT}(\mathsf{STRA}(x),ch)$, $\mathsf{BKT_L}(\mathsf{STRA}(x),ch)$ and $\mathsf{BKT_S}(\mathsf{STRA}(x),ch)$ are defined for $\mathsf{STRA}(x)$.

3 Reduction Phase of DSA-IS

The reduction phase of DSA-IS is shown in Algorithm 1. To reduce the I/O complexity, DSA-IS introduces the alternative $\mathsf{DSTRA}(x)$ for $\mathsf{STRA}(x)$ and employs I/O buffers to cache $\mathsf{DSTRA}(x)$ and other data structures for amortizing the disk access overhead, where the involved data structures are defined as below.

- DSTRA, $\mathsf{DSTRA_L}$ and $\mathsf{DSTRA_S}$. For an input x, each item of $\mathsf{DSTRA}(x)$ associates with a substring $\mathsf{sub}(x,p)$ and mainly consists of the following three components:
  - p: position index for $\mathsf{sub}(x,p)$.
  - c: head character for $\mathsf{sub}(x,p)$, that is $x[p]$.
  - t: type of the preceding character $x[p-1]$, set as 0 or 1 for L-type or S-type, respectively.

  $\mathsf{DSTRA_L}(x)$ and $\mathsf{DSTRA_S}(x)$ only contain the items of L-type and S-type substrings in $\mathsf{DSTRA}(x)$, respectively.
- LMSDATA. A string array storing the characters of an LMS substring.
- LMSNAME. An integer array storing the name of an LMS substring, where the name represents the substring's lexicographical order among all.

Notice that the above data structures organize the items in the external memory according to the lexicographical order of their corresponding substrings. Now, each step in Algorithm 1 is sketched below.

Step 1 scans x leftward to sequentially retrieve the LMS substrings and inserts them one by one into the blocks with a capacity $m = \mathcal{O}(\mathsf{M})$, where M is the size of the internal memory. In this way, each block is either a single-block composed of one LMS substring or a multi-block composed of at least two successive LMS substrings. Particularly, each multi-block contains no more than m characters such that it can be processed in the internal memory during the two phases, while a single-block may not be so.

Algorithm 1: The Reduction Phase of DSA-IS

Input: x
Output: $x1$

1 Partition x into blocks $b_1, b_2, ..., b_k$.
2 Induced sort the substrings of b_i for all $i \in [1, k]$ to compute $\mathsf{DSTRA_L}(b_i)$, $\mathsf{DSTRA_S}(b_i)$ and $\mathsf{LMSDATA}(b_i)$.
3 Induced sort the substrings of x from $\mathsf{DSTRA_L}(b_i)$, $\mathsf{DSTRA_S}(b_i)$ and $\mathsf{LMSDATA}(b_i)$ to compute $\mathsf{DSTRA}(x)$ and $\mathsf{LMSDATA}(x)$. Meanwhile, scan $\mathsf{DSTRA}(x)$ to compute $\mathsf{DSTRA_{LMS}}(x)$.
4 Scan $\mathsf{DSTRA_{LMS}}(x)$ and $\mathsf{LMSDATA}(x)$ to name the sorted LMS substrings for producing $\mathsf{LMSNAME}(x)$.
5 Compute the reduced string $x1$ from $\mathsf{LMSNAME}(x)$ and $\mathsf{DSTRA_{LMS}}(x)$.

Step 2 adopts different strategies to tackle b_i with respect to whether the block is a single-block or a multi-block. Specifically, if b_i is a multi-block, then it computes $\mathsf{STRA}(b_i)$ by conducting the substring sorting algorithm of SA-IS and scans $\mathsf{STRA}(b_i)$ and b_i to obtain $\mathsf{DSTRA_L}(b_i)$, $\mathsf{DSTRA_S}(b_i)$ and $\mathsf{LMSDATA}(b_i)$; otherwise, the substrings in the block are already sorted and it directly scans b_i to obtain the three arrays.

Step 3 also computes $\mathsf{DSTRA}(x)$ following the induced sorting method. In details, when inducing substrings in $\mathsf{DSTRA}(x)$, it retrieves the head character of the L-type/S-type preceding substring for the currently scanned substring from the external memory by using sequential I/O operations. This is feasible because the preceding substring is located at the leftmost unvisited position in $\mathsf{DSTRA_L}(b_i)/\mathsf{DSTRA_S}(b_i)$, where the subscript i of the block that contains the target item can be determined in $\mathcal{O}(1)$ time using $\mathcal{O}(\frac{n}{m})$ space [9].

Step 4 names the sorted LMS substrings according to their lexicographical order. For each pair of the neighboring substrings in $\mathsf{DSTRA_{LMS}}(x)$, it conducts a string comparison to check if they are equal, where their characters can be sequentially retrieved from $\mathsf{LMSDATA}(x)$. If yes, then the two substrings have a same name; otherwise, the name for the latter is greater than the former by one.

Step 5 sorts the names in $\mathsf{LMSNAME}(x)$ by $\mathsf{DSTRA_{LMS}}(x)[i].p$ for all $i \in [0, n1)$ to produce the reduced string $x1$.

4 Details of DSA-IS+

It was observed from our experiments that, the program for DSA-IS outperforms that for eSAIS with respect to the space efficiency, but it runs slower than the latter due to the large I/O volume for sorting and naming substrings. In this section, we present two methods that can substantially reduce the construction time and I/O volume of the reduction phase without a sacrifice in its high space efficiency. We demonstrate in Sect. 5 that, by exploiting the use of these methods, the optimized version of DSA-IS, namely DSA-IS+, runs as fast as eSAIS and its peak disk usage is two-thirds as that of the latter.

4.1 Method A

Recall that in Algorithm 1, DSA-IS first sorts LMS substrings in steps 2–3 and then names the substrings in their sorted order in step 4. These two procedures can be merged by making use of the following fact: $\forall i, j, \in [0, n)$, $\mathsf{sub}(x, i)$ and $\mathsf{sub}(x, j)$ are equal if and only if $x[i] = x[j]$ and $\mathsf{sub}(x, i+1) = \mathsf{sub}(x, j+1)$. Specifically, for any two neighboring substrings in $\mathsf{DSTR}(x)$, say $\mathsf{DSTR}(x)[p]$ and $\mathsf{DSTR}(x)[p+1]$, there must have $\mathsf{DSTR}(x)[p] \leq \mathsf{DSTR}(x)[p+1]$. Hence, the only information required for naming the two substrings is to check if they are equal or not. Following the fact describe above, this can be trivially done by adding two fields $r1$ and $r2$ to each item of $\mathsf{DSTR}(x)$, where $r1$ and $r2$ respectively record the names of the corresponding substring and the succeeding substring. More specifically, assume all the items of LMS characters are already inserted into the corresponding buckets of $\mathsf{DSTR}(x)$, it takes the following two steps to sort and name substrings at the same time:

1. Initially set $r = 0$. Scan $\mathsf{DSTR}(x)$ rightward. For each scanned item $e1$ and previously scanned item $e2$, if $e1.r2 = e2.r2$ and $e1.ch = e2.ch$ then set $e1.r1 = e2.r1$; otherwise, set $e1.r1 = r$ and increase r by one. If $e1.p > 0$ and $e1.t = 0$, then determine the block b_i that contains $\mathsf{sub}(x, e1.p - 1)$, retrieve the leftmost unvisited item $e3$ from $\mathsf{DSTR_L}(b_i)$, set $e3.r2 = e1.r1$ and insert $e3$ into the leftmost empty position of $\mathsf{BKT_L}(\mathsf{DSTR}(x), e3.c)$.
2. Initially set $r = n - 1$. Scan $\mathsf{DSTR}(x)$ leftward. For each scanned item $e1$ and previously scanned item $e2$, if $e1.r2 = e2.r2$ and $e1.ch = e2.ch$ then set $e1.r1 = e2.r1$; otherwise, set $e1.r1 = r$ and decrease r by one. If $e1.p > 0$ and $e1.t = 1$, then determine the block b_i that contains $\mathsf{sub}(x, e1.p - 1)$, retrieve the leftmost unvisited item $e3$ from $\mathsf{DSTR_S}(b_i)$, set $e3.r2 = e1.r1$ and insert $e3$ into the rightmost empty position of $\mathsf{BKT_S}(\mathsf{DSTR}(x), e3.c)$.

At the end of step 2, all the LMS substrings are already sorted and their names can be obtained by copying $r1$ from the items of $\mathsf{DSTR}(x)$.

4.2 Method B

A solution to reducing the I/O volume is to employ a multi-way merge algorithm for combining sorted LMS substrings of all the blocks, where the task of the merger is to sort and name LMS substrings by literally comparing their characters. A string comparison can be done very quickly if the involved two substrings are wholly loaded into RAM. However, there may exist some LMS substrings that cannot be accommodated in the internal memory. For these long substrings, the method described in Sect. 4.1 is employed. Following the ideas, we revise steps 2–4 of Algorithm 1 as below, where $i \in [1, k]$.

2' Induced sort the substrings of b_i to compute $\mathsf{LSA_L}(b_i)$, $\mathsf{LSA_S}(b_i)$, $\mathsf{DSTRA'_L}(b_i)$ and $\mathsf{DSTRA'_S}(b_i)$.

3' Induced sort the substrings embraced in the long LMS substrings of x from $\mathsf{LSA_L}(b_i)$, $\mathsf{DSTRA'_L}(b_i)$ and $\mathsf{DSTRA'_S}(b_i)$ to compute $\mathsf{LSA_L}(x)$.

4' Merge $\mathsf{LSA_L}(x)$ and $\mathsf{LSA_S}(b_i)$ by using a min heap to compute $\mathsf{LMSNAME}(x)$.

Before we describe each step in details, the definitions of some newly introduced notations are given below.

- long/short LMS substring and threshold value D. All the LMS substrings are classified into two categories: long and short. Specifically, an LMS substring is short if it contains no more than D characters; otherwise, it is long.
- DSTR', $\mathsf{DSTRA}'_\mathsf{L}$ and $\mathsf{DSTRA}'_\mathsf{S}$. For an input x, $\mathsf{DSTR}'(x)$ only contains the items in $\mathsf{DSTR}(x)$ that associate with substrings embraced in long LMS substrings. We say $\mathsf{sub}(x,p)$ embraces $\mathsf{sub}(x,q)$ if the two substrings end with the same LMS character and $p \leq q$. $\mathsf{DSTRA}'_\mathsf{L}(x)$ and $\mathsf{DSTRA}'_\mathsf{S}(x)$ respectively contain the items in $\mathsf{DSTRA}'(x)$ that associate with L-type and S-type substrings.
- $\mathsf{LSA_L}$ and $\mathsf{LSA_S}$. For an input x, each item of $\mathsf{LSA_L}(x)/\mathsf{LSA_S}(x)$ associates with a long/short LMS substring $\mathsf{sub}(x,p)$ and mainly consists of four components:
  - p: position index for $\mathsf{sub}(x,p)$.
  - s: leftmost D characters of $\mathsf{sub}(x,p)$, if it is long; otherwise, all the characters.
  - t: type of the last character in s, set as 0 or 1 for L-type or S-type, respectively.
  - r: name of $\mathsf{sub}(x,p)$.

Step 2' consists of two substeps:

1. Compute $\mathsf{DSTRA}'_\mathsf{L}(b_i)$ and $\mathsf{DSTRA}'_\mathsf{S}(b_i)$ by reusing the algorithm for computing $\mathsf{DSTRA_L}(b_i)$ and $\mathsf{DSTRA_S}(b_i)$ in step 2 of Algorithm 1.
2. Scan $\mathsf{DSTRA}'_\mathsf{S}(b_i)$ rightward. For each scanned item $e1$ with $e1.t = 0$, create $e2$ for the current LMS substring, compute $e2.t$ and $e2.s$ by visiting b_i, and insert $e2$ into $\mathsf{LSA_L}(b_i)$ or $\mathsf{LSA_S}(b_i)$ according to its length.

Step 3' consists of three substeps:

1. Scan x leftward with i decreasing from $n-1$ to 0. For each scanned character $x[i]$, if $x[i]$ is an ending character of a long LMS substring, insert $\mathsf{sub}(x,i)$ into the rightmost empty position in $\mathsf{BKT_S}(\mathsf{DSTRA}'(x), x[i])$.
2. Reuse step 1 of method A to sort and name the L-type substrings embraced in long LMS substrings of x by replacing $\mathsf{DSTR}(x)$ with $\mathsf{DSTR}'(x)$.
3. Reuse step 2 of method A to sort and name the S-type substrings embraced in long LMS substrings of x by replacing $\mathsf{DSTR}(x)$ with $\mathsf{DSTR}'(x)$. For each scanned item $e1$ that associates with an LMS substring, determine the block b_i that contains $\mathsf{sub}(x, e1.p)$, retrieve the leftmost unvisited item $e4$ from $\mathsf{LSA_L}(b_i)$, set $e4.r = e1.r1$ and insert $e4$ to the front of $\mathsf{LSA_L}(x)$.

Step 4' Initialize the heap by inserting the leftmost item of each sorted sequence of $\mathsf{LSA_L}(x)$ and $\{\mathsf{LSA_S}(b_1), ..., \mathsf{LSA_S}(b_k)\}$. Sequentially pop the items in the heap. For currently popped item $e1$, insert into the heap the next item $e2$ of the same sequence and compare $e1$ with the previously popped item $e3$ to determine the names of their corresponding LMS substrings. In this step, each string comparison for heap-sorting items and naming substrings observes the following rules, where $e1$ and $e2$ are items to be compared.

1. If both items belong to $\{\mathsf{LSA_S}(b_1), ..., \mathsf{LSA_S}(b_k)\}$, then literally compare $e1.s$ with $e2.s$ to determine their order.
2. If both items belong to $\mathsf{LSA_L}(x)$, then directly compare $e1.r$ with $e2.r$ to determine their order.
3. If one belongs to $\mathsf{LSA_L}(x)$ and the other belongs to $\{\mathsf{LSA_S}(b_1), ..., \mathsf{LSA_S}(b_k)\}$, then literally compare $e1.s$ with $e2.s$. If equal, then continue to compare $e1.t$ with $e2.t$.

Clearly, the time overhead of each string comparison is upper-bounded by the threshold value D.

5 Experiments

For performance comparison, we engineer DSA-IS and DSA-IS+ by using the STXXL's containers (vector, sorter, priority queue and stream). The experimental platform is a desktop computer equipped with an Intel Xeon E3-1220 V2 CPU, 4 GiB RAM and 500 GiB HD. All the programs are complied by gcc/g++ 4.8.4 with -O3 options under Ubuntu 14.04 64-bit operating system. In our experiments, three performance metrics are investigated for the programs running on the corpora listed in Table 1, where each metric is measured as a mean of two runs.

- Construction time (CT): the running time, in units of microseconds per character.
- Peak disk usage (PDU): the maximum disk space requirement, in units of bytes per character.
- I/O volume (IOV): as the term suggests, in units of bytes per character.

5.1 Performance Evaluation

Now we use eSAIS as a baseline for analyzing the performance of DSA-IS and DSA-IS+, where the program for eSAIS is also implemented by the STXXL library. Figure 1 shows a comparison between the programs for these three algorithms in terms of the investigated metrics. As depicted, the program for DSA-IS requires less disk space than that for eSAIS when running on "enwiki" and "guten". In details, the peak disk usage of DSA-IS and eSAIS are around $18n$ and $24n$, respectively. However, eSAIS runs much faster than DSA-IS due to the different I/O volumes.

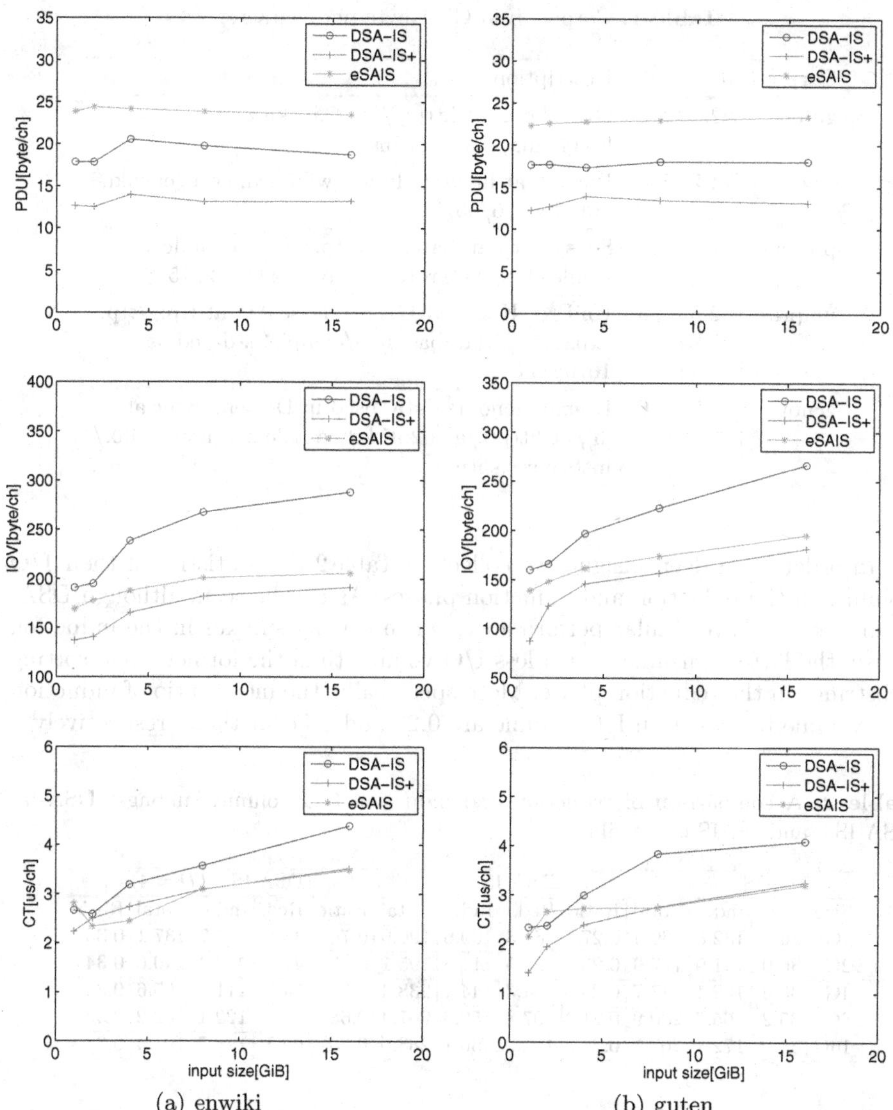

(a) enwiki

(b) guten

Fig. 1. A comparison of DSA-IS, DSA-IS+ and eSAIS on guten and enwiki in terms of peak disk usage, I/O volume and construction time, where $D = 4$ and the input size varies in {1, 2, 4, 8, 16} GiB.

Table 1. Corpus, n in Gi, 1 byte per character

Corpora	n	$\|\Sigma\|$	Description
guten	22.5	256	Gutenberg, at http://algo2.iti.kit.edu/bingmann/esais-corpus
enwiki	74.7	256	Enwiki, at https://dumps.wikimedia.org/enwiki, dated as 16/05/01
proteins	1.1	27	Swissprot database, at http://pizzachili.dcc.uchile.cl/texts/protein, dated as 06/12/15
uniprot	2.5	96	UniProt Knowledgebase release 4.0, at ftp://ftp.expasy.org/databases/.../complete, dated as 16/05/11
genome	2.9	6	Human genome data, used in Dementiev et al. [3], at http://algo2.iti.kit.edu/dementiev/esuffix/instsances.shtml

In order for a deep insight, we collect in Table 2 the statistics of their I/O volumes in the reduction and induction phases. As can be seen, although DSA-IS and eSAIS have similar performances when sorting suffixes in the induction phase, the latter consumes much less I/O volume than the former when sorting substrings in the reduction phase. More specifically, the mean ratio of induction I/O volume to reduction I/O volume are 0.23 and 0.71 for them, respectively.

Table 2. A comparison of reduction and induction I/O volumes amongst DSA-IS, DSA-IS+ and eSAIS on enwiki

	eSAIS				DSA-IS				DSA-IS+ ($D = 4$)			
Size	Red.	Ind.	Total	Ratio	Red.	Ind.	Total	Ratio	Red.	Ind.	Total	Ratio
1G	36.6	132.8	169.4	0.27	81.3	109.6	190.9	0.74	45.4	91.7	137.1	0.33
2G	36.0	141.9	177.9	0.25	83.5	111.6	195.1	0.75	47.2	93.4	140.6	0.34
4G	35.6	152.1	187.7	0.23	94.3	144.1	238.4	0.65	54.1	111.5	165.6	0.33
8G	35.2	165.7	200.9	0.21	107.8	159.6	267.4	0.68	60.1	122.1	182.2	0.33
16G	35.0	172.1	207.1	0.20	121.9	166.1	288.0	0.73	62.7	128.7	191.4	0.33

We can also see from Fig. 1 that DSA-IS+ achieves a substantial improvement against DSA-IS, it runs as fast as eSAIS and takes half as much disk space as the latter. This is because in Table 2 the reduction I/O volume for DSA-IS+ is only half as much as that for DSA-IS.

Notice that the new substring sorting and naming methods adopted by DSA-IS+ take effect when most of the LMS substrings are short. From our experiments, given D_0 and D_1 greater than 8 at the recursion level 0 and 1 respectively, Table 3 shows that the ratio of short LMS substrings in the investigated corpus nearly approaches one hundred percent, indicating that the majority of LMS substrings therein are considerably short and therefore DSA-IS+ is practical for real-world datasets.

Table 3. The ratio of short LMS substrings in the corpus for DSA-IS+

Level 0								
Corpora	D_0	Short	Total	Ratio	D_0	Short	Total	Ratio
uniprot	8	785997413	816241018	0.963	16	812390263	816241018	0.999
proteins	8	377404329	379092002	0.999	20	379081072	379092002	0.999
genome	8	773670266	793117107	0.975	20	792607109	793117107	0.999
Level 1								
Corpora	D_1	Short	Total	Ratio	D_1	Short	Total	Ratio
uniprot	10	263748775	263760624	0.995	16	263760244	263760624	0.999
proteins	10	123772731	123790857	0.996	20	123787920	123790857	0.999
genome	10	248243216	248554823	0.999	20	248400978	248554823	0.999

5.2 Discussion

Rather than designing an I/O layer for efficient I/O operations, we currently use the containers provided by the STXXL library to perform reading, writing and sorting in external memory, these containers do not free the disk space for storing temporary data even if it is not needed any more, leading to a space consumption higher than our expectation. This is an implementation issue that can be solved by storing the data into multiple files and deleting each file when it is obsolete. In this way, our program can be further improved to achieve a better space performance. Our next paper will describe a novel disk-based IS suffix sorter that only takes 1n work space excluding the disk space for storing input and output.

6 Conclusion

For better performance, we redesign the reduction phase of DSA-IS by employing two methods for sorting and naming substrings. The program of the enhanced algorithm DSA-IS+ is engineered by the STXXL library to achieve a high I/O efficiency. Our experiments indicate that DSA-IS+ requires only half peak disk usage as that for eSAIS and runs as fast as the latter on various real datasets. We are now designing and implementing a novel IS suffix sorter that takes no more than 1n work space on external memory model.

Acknowledgments. This work was funded by the National Natural Science Foundation of China (Grant number 61872391), the Guangzhou Science and Technology Program (Grant number 201802010011), and the Guangzhou Tianhe District Science and Technology Program (Grant number 201705YH075).

References

1. Abouelhodaa, M., Kurtzb, S., Ohlebuscha, E.: Replacing suffix trees with enhanced suffix arrays. J. Discrete Algorithms **2**(1), 53–86 (2004)

2. Bingmann, T., Fischer, J., Osipov, V.: Inducing suffix and LCP arrays in external memory. In: Proceedings of the 15th Workshop on Algorithm Engineering and Experiments, pp. 88–102 (2012)
3. Dementiev, R., Kärkäinen, J., Mehnert, J., Sanders, P.: Better external memory suffix array construction. ACM J. Exp. Algorithmics **12**(3), 4:1–4:24 (2008)
4. Ferragina, P., Gagie, T., Manzini, G.: Lightweight data indexing and compression in external memory. Algorithmica **63**(3), 707–730 (2012)
5. Kärkkäinen, J., Kempa, D.: Engineering a lightweight external memory suffix array construction algorithm. In: Proceedings of the 2nd International Conference on Algorithms for Big Data, Palermo, Italy, pp. 53–60 (2014)
6. Kärkkäinen, J., Kempa, D., Puglisi, S.J.: Parallel external memory suffix sorting. In: Cicalese, F., Porat, E., Vaccaro, U. (eds.) CPM 2015. LNCS, vol. 9133, pp. 329–342. Springer, Cham (2015). https://doi.org/10.1007/978-3-319-19929-0_28
7. Liu, W.J., Nong, G., Chan, W.H., Wu, Y.: Induced sorting suffixes in external memory with better design and less space. In: Iliopoulos, C., Puglisi, S., Yilmaz, E. (eds.) SPIRE 2015. LNCS, vol. 9309, pp. 83–94. Springer, Cham (2015). https://doi.org/10.1007/978-3-319-23826-5_9
8. Manber, U., Myers, G.: Suffix arrays: a new method for on-line string searches. SIAM J. Comput. **22**(5), 935–948 (1993)
9. Nong, G., Chan, W.H., Hu, S.Q., Wu, Y.: Induced sorting suffixes in external memory. ACM Trans. Inf. Syst. **33**(3), 12:1–12:15 (2015)
10. Nong, G., Chan, W.H., Zhang, S., Guan, X.F.: Suffix array construction in external memory using D-critical substrings. ACM Trans. Inf. Syst. **32**(1), 1:1–1:15 (2014)
11. Nong, G., Zhang, S., Chan, W.H.: Two efficient algorithms for linear time suffix array construction. IEEE Trans. Comput. **60**(10), 1471–1484 (2011)

In-Place Suffix Sorting on a Multicore Computer with Better Design

Jing Yi Xie[1], Bin Lao[2], and Ge Nong[1](✉)

[1] School of Data and Computer Science, Sun Yat-sen University, Guangzhou, China
issng@mail.sysu.edu.cn

[2] School of Information Science and Technology, Guangdong University of Foreign Studies, Guangzhou, China

Abstract. A suffix index built on the suffix array of data is fundamental for true full-text searches over data. The key problem for building the suffix index is how to compute the suffix array by sorting the suffixes of data time and space efficiently. According to the reported results up to date, pSACAK achieves the best suffix sorting performance on the parallel computing model of a multicore machine of internal memory. However, its naming procedure is time-consuming and constitutes a performance bottleneck. This article presents an optimized algorithm called pSACAK+ with a new naming procedure to attack this problem. Our experiments show that, pSACAK+ runs nearly 20% faster than pSACAK with a similar space consumption, which sets a new performance benchmark for suffix sorting on a multicore machine of internal memory.

Keywords: Suffix array · Induced sorting · Multicore programming

1 Introduction

Given a string $X[0 \ldots n-1]$ from a constant size-K alphabet, its suffix array (SA) [6] can be constructed by sorting all of its suffixes in ascending lexicographical order and storing their start positions in X into an integer array. The suffix array of data is a key data structure for building the suffix index to support true full-text searches over data. Theoretically, full-text searches can be performed on a suffix trie. However, suffix trie is too space costly to be applied on massive data. As a practical solution, a suffix index built on the suffix array of data is usually employed as a succinct replacement of suffix trie. Consequently, suffix array has become a fundamental data structure in many applications such as string matching, genome alignment, full-text index and etc. [12], and how to compute the suffix array time and space efficiently is a research topic receiving consistent intensive researches. In the past decade, plenty of researches have been proposed to sort suffixes in less time and space usage for various applications. These proposed algorithms can be roughly classified as three categories as follows: (1) prefix doubling, (2) recursive and (3) induced sorting (IS) [10]. By so

H. Shen and Y. Sang (Eds.): PAAP 2019, CCIS 1163, pp. 331–342, 2020.
https://doi.org/10.1007/978-981-15-2767-8_30

far, the algorithms using the IS method have been reported to achieve the best performance both in theory and practice [3].

While most of the existing IS algorithms are sequential, with motivation to utilize the increasing parallel computing resources of a modern multicore machine for higher speeds, we attempted recently the designs of two parallel IS algorithms called pSAIS [4] and pSACAK [5], by organizing the IS operations as a pipeline for parallel computations using the machine's multi-threading capability. Currently, to the best of our knowledge, pSACAK reports the fastest speeds on such a computing model. However, the naming procedure of pSACAK is not fully parallelized and constitutes a speed bottleneck. To overcome this problem, we present here an optimized algorithm called pSACAK+ with a new naming procedure of higher parallelism. To evaluate the efficiency of this new naming procedure, a set of experiments are conducted to test the running speed and space usage of pSACAK+, pSACAK and other well known sequential and parallel suffix sorting algorithms on a multicore computer. The experimental results reveal that, pSACAK+ gains the best average time performance among all the algorithms in comparison of our experiments, meanwhile, it remains in-place, saying that its space usage excluding the input and output is optimal as $\mathcal{O}(1)$.

The following sections are organized as follows. Section 2 gives preliminaries for describing the algorithms, Sect. 3 firstly analyzes the naming procedure in pSACAK and then describes our new proposal for pSACAK+. Section 4 shows our experiments and Sect. 5 gives the conclusion.

2 Preliminaries

The input string X is of size-n, each of whose character is drawn from a constant size-K alphabet. Its i-th character, i.e. $X[i]$ can be classified as L-type or S-type, respectively. It is S-type if (1) $i = n - 1$, where this ending character is assumed to be the lexicographically smallest character; or (2) $X[i] < X[i + 1]$; or (3) $X[i] = X[i + 1]$ with $X[i + 1]$ being S-type. For an S-type character $X[i]$, it is also an LMS-character if $i = n - 1$ or $X[i - 1]$ is L-type. At the same time, suffix $X[i \ldots n - 1]$ shares the same type with its head character $X[i]$, and, substring $X[i \ldots j]$ is an LMS-substring if (1) both $X[i]$ and $X[j]$ are LMS-characters while there is no other LMS-character between them, where $i \neq j$; or (2) $i = j = n - 1$. In addition, the suffixes with a same head character occupy a consecutive range in SA, which is called a bucket. The number of buckets in SA of X is bounded by K, which is $\mathcal{O}(1)$.

3 LMS-substring Naming

Naming sorted LMS-substrings is one of the performance bottlenecks of SACA-K, which consumes over 15% of the total running time according to our experiments in Sect. 4. Given that all the LMS-substrings of X have been sorted, SACA-K takes two sequential steps to produce the reduced string X_1 as presented in [8].

1. Scan SA_1 once from left to right to name each LMS-substring of X by the start position of the substring's bucket in SA_1, resulting in an interim reduced string denoted by Z_1.
2. Scan Z_1 once from right to left to replace each S-type character in Z_1 with the end position of its bucket in SA_1, resulting in the new string X_1.

3.1 Prior Art: pSACAK

The idea of LMS-substring naming in SACA-K is simple, but each step requires a size-n_1 sequential scan. Therefore, pSACAK has proposed a parallel solution for acceleration as presented in [5]. Algorithm 1 shows the process for parallel LMS-substring naming in pSACAK, which consists of three steps as follows.

Algorithm 1: Parallel LMS-substring naming in pSACAK

Input: X: input string;
SA_1: suffix array with sorted LMS-substrings;
Output: X_1: reduced string;
/* Step 1 runs in parallel. */
1 Divide the sorted LMS-substrings in SA_1 into blocks evenly;
2 **parallel foreach** *block being scanned once from left to right* **do**
3 Retrieve each LMS-substring from X;
4 Compare the LMS-substrings one by one;
5 Compute the difference bit vector for the block;
6 **end**
/* Step 2 runs in parallel. */
7 **parallel foreach** *block being scanned once from left to right* **do**
8 Using the result of step 1 to name every LMS-substring within the block by the start position of the substring's bucket in SA_1;
9 **end**
10 Get an interim reduced string Z_1;
/* Step 3 runs in sequential. */
11 Scan Z_1 once from right to left to replace each S-type character in Z_1 with the end position of its bucket in SA_1;
12 Get the new string X_1;
13 **return**

---

1. Line 1 divides the sorted LMS-substrings in SA_1 into blocks evenly, then each block computes its difference bit vector independently in parallel by one thread per block as lines 2–6. Each thread scans its block once from left to right to retrieve each LMS-substring from X. If any LMS-substring is different from its preceding one in the block, the difference bit for this LMS-substring is set as 1, or otherwise 0. After the scan, we get the difference bit vector for all the sorted LMS-substrings.

2. Using the difference bit vector, each thread scans its block once from left to right to name every LMS-substring within the block by the start position of the substring's bucket in SA_1. After the parallel scan in lines 7–9, we get an interim reduced string Z_1 as line 10.
3. Z_1 is sequentially scanned once from right to left in line 11. The type of each character in Z_1 can be determined on-the-fly, and each S-type character is replaced with the end position of its bucket in SA_1. After the scan, we get the new string X_1 as line 12.

From Algorithm 1 we can see that: (1) although both of step 1 and 2 have been parallelized, they require a data structure to store the difference bits, which brings in additional overhead for memory access; (2) the size-n_1 scan in step 3 is still sequential, and it can be parallelized for further acceleration. Therefore, it is expected to get a more competitive performance if there is a better design for the parallel LMS-substring naming in pSACAK.

3.2 New Proposal: pSACAK+

Based on the framework of prefix sum (scan) [11], we present a new proposal for the parallel LMS-substring naming in pSACAK, and the optimized algorithm is called pSACAK+. Algorithm 2 gives the details of the parallel LMS-substring naming in pSACAK+, which consists of two steps as follows.

1. The sorted LMS-substrings in SA_1 are divided into blocks evenly as line 1, then the loop in lines 2–6 scans each block once from left to right in parallel. Each LMS-substring within the block is retrieved from X and compared one by one. So the difference bits for the block are computed, and SA_1 is reused to store them. After this scan, the initial name for each block can be computed by the difference bits as line 7, where "initial name" is the name that a block should assign to its first LMS-substring in the next scan. Then the loop in lines 8–11 scans each block once again from left to right in parallel. Using the difference bits in SA_1 and the initial names, every LMS-substring within each block is named by the start position of the substring's bucket in SA_1, while the number of each name is counted and stored in SA_1 for the use of step 2. After this scan, we get an interim reduced string Z_1 as line 12.
2. The characters in Z_1 are divided into blocks evenly as line 13, then the loop in lines 14–17 scans each block once from right to left in parallel. Each character within the block is compared one by one, and the type of the leftmost character in the block is determined. After this scan, the initial type for each block can be determined as line 18, where "initial type" is the type that a block should assign to its rightmost character in the next scan. Then the loop in lines 19–21 scans each block once again from right to left in parallel. Using the number of names from step 1 and the initial types, every S-type character within each block of Z_1 is replaced with the end position of its bucket in SA_1. After this scan, we get the new string X_1 as line 22.

Algorithm 2: Parallel LMS-substring naming in pSACAK+

Input: X: input string;
SA_1: suffix array with sorted LMS-substrings;
Output: X_1: reduced string;
/* Step 1 runs in parallel. */
Divide the sorted LMS-substrings in SA_1 into blocks evenly;
parallel foreach *block being scanned once from left to right* **do**
    Retrieve each LMS-substring from X;
    Compare the LMS-substrings one by one;
    Compute the difference bits for the block, and reuse SA_1 to store them;
end
Compute the initial name for each block by the difference bits;
parallel foreach *block being scanned once from left to right* **do**
    Using the difference bits in SA_1 to name every LMS-substring within the block by the start position of the substring's bucket in SA_1;
    Count the number of each name, and reuse SA_1 to store them;
end
Get an interim reduced string Z_1;
/* Step 2 runs in parallel. */
Divide the characters in Z_1 into blocks evenly;
parallel foreach *block being scanned once from right to left* **do**
    Compare the characters one by one;
    Determine the type of the leftmost character in the block;
end
Determine the initial type for each block;
parallel foreach *block being scanned once from right to left* **do**
    Using the result of step 1 to replace every S-type character within the block of Z_1 with the end position of its bucket in SA_1;
end
Get the new string X_1;
return

Comparing with Algorithm 1, there are three major improvements in Algorithm 2 as follows: (1) SA_1 is reused to store the difference bits; (2) all the scans are parallelized by multiple threads in a blockwise manner; (3) the workload in each step is reasonably distributed to the scans, and the load balancing method in [4] can be used as well. To achieve such improvements, pSACAK+ has solved new data races brought by the space reusing method for SA_1 and the parallelization of the scans. Although the time complexity of pSACAK+ is still $\mathcal{O}(n)$, our experimental results in Sect. 4 indicate that the parallel LMS-substring naming in pSACAK+ brings acceleration to the whole algorithm. Now we proceed to discuss the parallel strategy for each step as follows.

3.3 Step 1 for Z_1

Line 1 divides SA_1 into blocks evenly. As each item in SA_1 points to the start position of an LMS-substring, the parallel scan on the blocks of SA_1 in lines 2–6 can retrieve LMS-substrings from X and compare them one by one. This is a heavy workload, but the scan runs fast because it is parallelized in a blockwise manner. Moreover, those scanned items in SA_1 can be reused to store the resulting difference bits and therefore no additional data structure is required, thus the whole algorithm is accelerated by a better memory access throughput.

Line 7 is important in the framework of prefix sum, because the initial name for each block can be computed by the difference bits now. Without initial names, the previous scan can only compute difference bits for the LMS-substrings in parallel. On the contrary, the next scan can name LMS-substrings in parallel with the difference bits and the initial names.

Lines 8–11 scan each block of SA_1 again in parallel by one thread per block. Using the difference bits in SA_1, each thread can determine whether two neighboring LMS-substrings are the same or not at low cost. If any LMS-substring is different from its preceding one in the block, it is named by the start position of the substring's bucket in SA_1. Otherwise, it is named either by the initial name or the previous name in this block. At the same time, the number of each name is counted for the use of step 2, and the scanned items in SA_1 can be reused again to store these numbers. The major workload in this scan is the naming and counting operations, which have been parallelized for acceleration. Finally, the result of step 1 is an interim reduced string Z_1 as line 12.

3.4 Step 2 for X_1

Line 13 divides Z_1 into blocks evenly, then lines 14–17 scan each block once from right to left in parallel. To determine the type of the leftmost character in the block of Z_1, each character within the block is compared one by one. On condition that all characters are the same in a block, the type of its leftmost character is unknown. This is why step 2 requires the framework of prefix sum to produce X_1 in parallel.

Based on the result of the previous scan, line 18 eliminates any "unknown" and determines the initial type for each block. Therefore, the next scan can update S-type characters in parallel with the number of names from step 1 and the initial types.

Lines 19–21 scan each block of Z_1 again in parallel by one thread per block. Using the initial type, each thread can determine whether a character within its block is S-type or not during the scan from right to left. Meanwhile, any S-type character is replaced with the end position of its bucket in SA_1, which can be computed by adding the number of its current name to the start position of its bucket in SA_1. This scan can be parallelized in a blockwise manner without any data race, because each block has already got sufficient information when the scan starts: (1) the number of each name was counted in step 1; (2) the initial type was determined on the previous scan. Finally, the result of step 2 is the new string X_1 as line 22.

4 Experiments

To investigate the performance of pSACAK+, we implemented it in C++ using Intel Cilk Plus [2]. For comparison, eight programs are evaluated in our experiments as follows, where the first five are parallel and the others are sequential.

- pSACAK+: our implementation for pSACAK+ algorithm proposed in this article, which is an optimized version of pSACAK.
- pSACAK: the implementation for pSACAK algorithm presented in [5], which is a parallel variant of SACA-K.
- pSAIS: the implementation for pSAIS algorithm presented in [4], which is a parallel variant of SA-IS.
- pDSS: the implementation presented in [3] is a hybrid parallel algorithm of libdivsufsort and prefix doubling.
- pKS: a parallel implementation for DC3 algorithm from the PBBS [13].
- SACA-K: the implementation for SACA-K algorithm presented in [8], which is an optimized version of SA-IS and uses only $\mathcal{O}(1)$ workspace.
- SA-IS: the implementation for SA-IS algorithm presented in [9].
- DSS: the sequential program of libdivsufsort [7] which is based on induced copying/sorting.

The experiments were conducted on a machine with two Intel Xeon E5-2620 CPUs of 6 cores per each and 64 GiB RAM. All the programs are complied by g++ version 5.3.1 with -O3 option on CentOS 6.8 64-bit operating system. For comparison convenience, not only the experimental platform but also the input datasets listed in Table 1 are the same with [5]. The corpora are a subset of the Pizza&Chili corpus [1] with varying size, alphabet and redundancy. The former six are from the main text corpora and the latter four are from the highly repetitive corpora.

Table 1. Corpus statistics, n in Mi, one byte per character

Corpus	n	K	Description
proteins2	2048	27	A concatenation of two copies of "proteins"
english2	2048	239	A concatenation of two copies of "english"
proteins	1024	27	The protein sequences from the Swissprot database
english	1024	239	The English text files from the Gutenberg Project
dna	385	16	The gene DNA sequences from the Gutenberg Project
sources	201	230	All the C/Java source files of linux-2.6.11.6 and gcc-4.0.0
einstein	446	139	The English article of Albert Einstein
cere	440	5	A file containing 37 sequences of Saccharomyces Cerevisiae
fib41	256	2	The Fibonacci sequence
kernel	246	160	All 1.0.x and 1.1.x versions of the Linux Kernel 6

4.1 Time and Space

We first evaluate the time and space performance of pSACAK+ versus other state-of-the-art algorithms. Table 2 and 3 list the running speed in MiBs per second and space usage in bytes per character for each program. Each parallel program ran in full parallel on the machine, and the block size of pSACAK+, pSACAK and pSAIS was set to 100Ki. Each result in the tables is the average of three runs, and each mean is the average of all results for a same program. The best results among all the algorithms are highlighted in bold text, and the normalized values are given in the last row for comparison.

Table 2. Running speed (in MiBs per second)

Corpus	pSACAK+	pSACAK	SACA-K	pSAIS	SA-IS	pDSS	DSS	pKS
proteins2	**13.836**	11.566	2.198	7.133	1.575	4.592	2.323	12.171
english2	**15.157**	12.086	2.096	7.549	1.529	4.558	2.273	13.092
proteins	**12.508**	10.555	2.644	7.626	1.960	12.421	4.890	11.970
english	**14.066**	11.337	2.507	8.159	1.912	9.903	5.130	10.723
dna	12.513	11.428	2.849	9.305	2.404	**16.211**	5.543	12.031
sources	15.201	13.631	4.413	11.323	3.901	**19.881**	8.603	11.618
einstein	**18.518**	14.082	4.575	10.875	4.240	8.173	7.407	12.186
cere	**15.665**	13.360	3.020	10.630	2.468	8.992	6.252	12.828
fib41	**18.651**	16.953	2.927	16.186	2.723	4.650	3.888	17.534
kernel	**18.344**	14.464	3.605	11.798	3.018	8.367	7.375	11.884
Mean	**15.446**	12.946	3.083	10.058	2.573	9.775	5.368	12.604
Norm.	1	0.838	0.200	0.651	0.167	0.633	0.348	0.816

Each running time of these programs used for computing running speed in Table 2 is the wall clock time measured by the shell command "time" in Linux. From the highlighted results, our program for pSACAK+ algorithm achieves the best running speed in eight corpora out of ten, and its mean speed on our experimental platform is 15.446 MiBs per second which is faster than all other programs in comparison. From the normalized values, pSACAK+ is 19.3%, 53.6%, 58.0% and 22.5% faster than pSACAK, pSAIS, pDSS and pKS, respectively. Comparing with the sequential counterpart, the acceleration brought by parallelization for each algorithm can be calculated by pSACAK+:SACA-K = 1:0.200 = 5.000, pSACAK:SACA-K = 0.838:0.200 = 4.190, pSAIS:SA-IS = 0.651:0.167 = 3.898 and pDSS:DSS = 0.633:0.348 = 1.819. These results show that the parallel strategies for pSACAK+ contribute a lot to its time performance. Moreover, pDSS may run fast on two corpora but fluctuate on the rest ones, while pSACAK+ can preform well on all corpora. The reason is that pSACAK+ is a linear-time algorithm with predictable performance.

Table 3. Space usage (in bytes per character)

Corpus	pSACAK+	pSACAK	SACA-K	pSAIS	SA-IS	pDSS	DSS	pKS
proteins2	5.012	5.012	**5.000**	5.273	5.272	6.761	**5.000**	19.833
english2	5.012	5.012	**5.000**	5.253	5.252	6.728	**5.000**	19.833
proteins	5.012	5.013	**5.000**	5.369	5.366	6.761	**5.000**	19.833
english	5.014	5.014	**5.000**	5.328	5.325	6.728	**5.000**	19.833
dna	5.019	5.019	**5.000**	5.376	5.367	6.531	5.001	19.833
sources	5.027	5.027	**5.000**	5.342	5.327	6.576	5.001	19.833
einstein	5.018	5.018	**5.000**	5.189	5.182	6.659	5.001	19.833
cere	5.018	5.018	**5.000**	5.186	5.179	6.434	5.001	19.833
fib41	5.023	5.023	**5.000**	5.215	5.202	7.198	5.001	19.833
kernel	5.024	5.024	**5.000**	5.194	5.181	6.588	5.001	19.833
Mean	5.018	5.018	**5.000**	5.273	5.265	6.696	5.001	19.833
Norm.	1.004	1.004	**1**	1.055	1.053	1.339	1.001	3.967

Each space usage in Table 3 is the heap peak measured by the shell command "memusage" in CentOS. The normalized values indicate that the space performance of pSACAK+ and pSACAK are quite close, and both of them achieve the best space usage among the parallel programs in comparison. As the difference bit vector in pSACAK is small compared to SA, the contribution of the space reusing method in pSACAK+ is not significant in the space results. However, reusing SA_1 to store the difference bits mainly contributes to the improvement of memory access throughput and therefore the acceleration of the whole algorithm. In other words, pSACAK+ is an in-place parallel algorithm with better time and space performance than pSACAK.

4.2 Time Ratio

As the major improvement of pSACAK+ is the new proposal for parallel LMS-substring naming as discussed in Sect. 3, we now evaluate its effect by comparing the time ratio of LMS-substring naming in pSACAK+, pSACAK and SACA-K. Figure 1 shows the time ratio results in percentage.

In both figures, LMS-substring naming is one of the performance bottlenecks of the sequential SACA-K algorithm, which consumes over 15% of the total running time on average. After it is parallelized in pSACAK, its mean time ratios increase to 24.2% because other parts of the algorithm are better accelerated by parallelization. For pSACAK+, the mean results drop to about 14% which is even lower than that for SACA-K. This suggests that the new proposal for parallel LMS-substring naming in pSACAK+ is more efficient than that in pSACAK.

The time ratios of all three algorithms in Fig. 1 have a relatively stable trend on the main text corpora, but fluctuate on the highly repetitive corpora due to the varying redundancy of the corpora. In spite of that, pSACAK+ keeps a

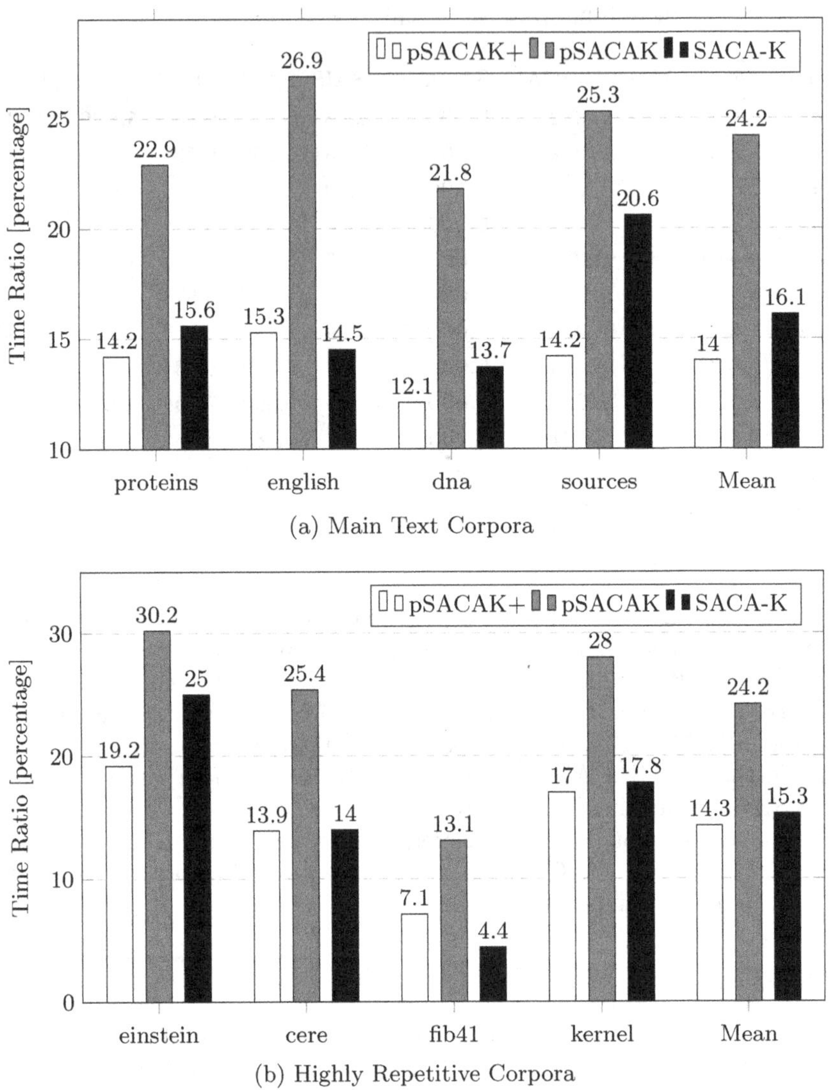

(a) Main Text Corpora

(b) Highly Repetitive Corpora

Fig. 1. Time ratio of LMS-substring naming in pSACAK+, pSACAK, SACA-K.

decrease of $24.2\% - 14.3\% = 9.9\%$ in time ratio. This indicates that pSACAK+ runs faster than pSACAK on different kinds of corpus with better design.

5 Conclusion

True full-text searches over massive data is a fundamental capability for various data processing applications. Currently, a suffix index built by sorting suffixes of data is playing an important role to provide such a capability. While a number of suffix sorting algorithms using the induced sorting method have been proposed, most of them are sequential and failed to utilize the increasing parallel computing resources of a modern multicore machine. The recently proposed parallel IS algorithms pSAIS and pSACAK change this situation by organizing the induced sorting operations as a pipeline for parallelization, and the latter reports the best time and space results so far for suffix sorting on internal memory. In this article, a new algorithm called pSACAK+ is improved from pSACAK by fully parallelizing the naming procedure that constitutes a speed bottleneck of the whole algorithm. The efficiency of this new naming procedure is verified by experiments with comparisons to a number of existing algorithms. On our experimental platform, the machine with 2 CPUs of 6 cores per each achieves a speed over 15 MiB/s. Such a hardware configuration is not high at all for a modern machine. Our experimental results here sets a new performance benchmark for suffix sorting on a multicore machine of internal memory.

Acknowledgments. This work was funded by the National Natural Science Foundation of China (Grant number 61872391), the Guangzhou Science and Technology Program (Grant number 201802010011), and the Guangzhou Tianhe District Science and Technology Program (Grant number 201705YH075).

References

1. Ferragina, P., Navarro, G.: Pizza&Chili Corpus, compressed indexes and their testbeds (2005). http://pizzachili.dcc.uchile.cl
2. Intel Corporation: Intel Cilk Plus, an extension to the C and C++ languages to support data and task parallelism (2017). https://www.cilkplus.org
3. Labeit, J., Shun, J., Blelloch, G.E.: Parallel lightweight wavelet tree, suffix array and FM-index construction. J. Discrete Algorithms **43**(1), 2–17 (2017)
4. Lao, B., Nong, G., Chan, W.H., Pan, Y.: Fast induced sorting suffixes on a multicore machine. J. Supercomput. **74**(7), 3468–3485 (2018)
5. Lao, B., Nong, G., Chan, W.H., Xie, J.Y.: Fast in-place suffix sorting on a multicore computer. IEEE Trans. Comput. **67**(12), 1737–1749 (2018)
6. Manber, U., Myers, E.W.: Suffix arrays: a new method for on-line string searches. SIAM J. Comput. **22**(5), 319–327 (1990)
7. Mori, Y.: Libdivsufsort, a software library that implements a lightweight suffix array construction algorithm (2015). https://github.com/y-256/libdivsufsort
8. Nong, G.: Practical linear-time O(1)-workspace suffix sorting for constant alphabets. ACM Trans. Inf. Syst. **31**(3), 15:1–15:15 (2013)
9. Nong, G., Zhang, S., Chan, W.H.: Two efficient algorithms for linear time suffix array construction. IEEE Trans. Comput. **60**(10), 1471–1484 (2011)
10. Puglisi, S.J., Smyth, W.F., Turpin, A.H.: A taxonomy of suffix array construction algorithms. ACM Comput. Surv. (CSUR) **39**(2), 4 (2007)

11. Santos, E.E.: Optimal and efficient algorithms for summing and prefix summing on parallel machines. J. Parallel Distrib. Comput. **62**(4), 517–543 (2002)
12. Shrestha, A.M., Frith, M.C., Horton, P.: A bioinformatician's guide to the forefront of suffix array construction algorithms. Brief. Bioinform. **15**(2), 138–154 (2014)
13. Shun, J., et al.: Brief announcement: the problem based benchmark suite. In: Proceedings of the Twenty-Fourth Annual ACM Symposium on Parallelism in Algorithms and Architectures, pp. 68–70. ACM (2012)

Security and Privacy

Any Privacy Risk if Nobody's Personal Information Being Collected?

Tingting Feng[1(✉)], Xiaoyu Li[2], Yuchun Guo[3], Ti Wang[1], Shan Yang[1], and Zhongyan Du[1]

[1] China Unicom Smart City Research Institute, Beijing, China
{fengtt13,wangti2,yangs72,duzy17}@chinaunicom.cn
[2] Customer Department, China Association for Quality, Beijing, China
lixy@caq.org.cn
[3] Beijing Jiaotong University, Beijing, China
ychguo@bjtu.edu.cn

Abstract. To alleviate the growing concern about privacy breaches in online services, some systems do not ask users for any demographic information (DI), such as gender or age. Keeping user DI private in such systems seems guaranteed. However, as a trend report, some other systems may publish statistical preference corresponding to users with different DI, e.g. 80% of buyers of one product being young females. Intuitively, such statistical preference will not raise any privacy risk in the former type of systems, since specific personal behaviour or DI cannot be reconstructed from the statistical data. However, in this paper, we will reveal that this is not the case. We propose an unsupervised transfer learning scheme to learn multidimensional DI vectors for individual users and topics with external statistical preference. To facilitate unsupervised learning, we apply it to a rating recommendation task and concatenate DI vector with the implicit preference vector. To compare the privacy risk in scenarios with/without DI available, we choose to make the DI in the datasets of real rating systems to be concealed or not. Experiments show that our unsupervised learning scheme based on external statistical preference in the DI unavailable scenario performs almost as well as the corresponding supervised learning scheme in DI available scenario in the same system. This verifies the existence of privacy risks in systems that do not collect personal information because statistical preferences in similar systems are at fingertips.

Keywords: Privacy leakage · Transfer learning · Unsupervised learning · Recommender system · Demographic information

1 Introduction

With prevailing of personalized services based on user behavior records and demographic information (DI), e.g., gender, age, profession etc., privacy leakage raises serious concern in public. A user's DI can be inferred with a supervised learning method based on the DI of other users with similar behaviors or with a classifier trained over behavior of users with known DI [1–4].

H. Shen and Y. Sang (Eds.): PAAP 2019, CCIS 1163, pp. 345–356, 2020.
https://doi.org/10.1007/978-981-15-2767-8_31

To lighten up user worries of privacy risk, some systems do not collect users' DI when they login. Although the DI inference in such systems can be facilitated via transferring individual user's DI and corresponding behavior records, e.g., ratings, on common items from a similar system [5, 6], it is usually infeasible in practice due to business interest and data legislation. Keeping user DI private in such systems seems guaranteed.

However, some consulting firms and online service systems often publish trend reports of statistical preference corresponding to users with different DI. For instance, Bain&Company, one of the world's leading management consulting firms, released a report on user preference across music, video, books etc. versus different gender, age, region and income based on an online survey [7]. Moreover, JD Research Institute released a similar report on user reading preference for different types of books versus different DI according to sales of JD shopping mall [8].

Will such external statistical preference raise any privacy risk in a system without DI available? Intuitively, the answer is negative because user DI cannot be inferred without known individual behaviours and corresponding DI labels based on traditional supervised learning methods.

However, to reveal that this is not the case, in this paper, we design an unsupervised transfer learning scheme (UTLS) with external statistical preference on aggregated topic-level.

Noticed that users of same DI aspect show similar preference towards same topic and recommendation performance relates heavily to the personal preference, we find that we can learn user feature vector by optimizing the recommendation performance. The key to learn a user's DI in an unsupervised way is to build a multidimensional DI vector for each user and each topic. For a topic, the DI vector shows the statistical preference versus different DI aspect. For a user, the DI vector shows the possibilities of a user to be male/female/youth/elder and so on.

We establish this representation in 3 steps. Firstly, for topics in the target system overlapped with the auxiliary system, we initialize their DI vectors with the transferred corresponding DI vectors in the auxiliary system. Secondly, we can establish an explicit multidimensional DI vector for each user in the target system, and initialize a user's DI vector with the weighted average of DI vectors of visited topics, taking the number of visits per topic as weight. Finally, for each user, we concatenate the explicit DI vector with the implicit preference vector as user feature vector, and optimize these vectors within a rating recommendation task.

To verify the feasibility of UTLS, we run the simple matrix factorization SVD recommendation algorithm on Flixster and MovieLens dataset. Experiment results reveal that a user's DI risks leaking no matter he has access to common items between two systems or not. A byproduct of this scheme is the obvious improvement of recommendation performance.

The remaining part is organized as follows. Section 2 introduces the related work and Sect. 3 describes the problem studied in this paper. Section 4 introduces the learning scheme in detail. And Sect. 5 evaluates performance of our work based on lots of experiments. And we make a conclusion in Sect. 6.

2 Related Work

In online service systems, there are privacy risks everywhere, since user DI can be inferred via many existing works.

User DI is often inferred based on partially known DI labels of target or auxiliary systems, and existing inference methods almost treat user DI inference as a supervised classification problem [1–4]. Specifically, existing works usually choose a classifier like the most commonly-used Logistic Regression (LR) and train the classifier with partially known user records. The records used including the user's publicly available social friends [9, 10], the user's behavioral records, e.g., the web browsing history [3], the video viewing record [1], and both social relationship and behaviors [11]. Whereas, when the target system has no associated DI labels of users, these inference attacks are invalid. Thus, many researches use transfer learning methods to infer user DI of such target systems in image domain. For instance, Su et al. estimate age of face image cross-database based on a transfer learning framework [12], and Yao et al. improves the performance of gait-based gender classification of the target view by transferring knowledge from source view [13]. In addition, transfer learning is also used to identify privacy leaks such as being pregnant and being drunk in the content of tweets [14]. Chen et al. infer dwelling address information for a user via digging such information of his friends over social network and other websites [15]. To our best knowledge, none of works can infer user DI without partially known user DI labels.

Different from above works, in this paper, to verify privacy risk raised by statistical knowledge, we will infer user DI via unsupervised learning scheme utilizing transferred statistical preference of topics versus different DI aspect.

3 Problem Description

3.1 A Common Scenario of Privacy Risk

A target system in this paper refers to an online service system with user ratings on items but without any DI information. An auxiliary system refers to an online service system sharing common ground, e.g., items, topics, with the target system.

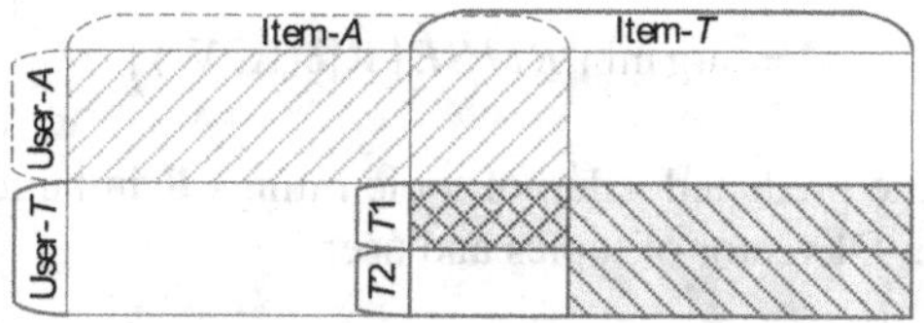

Fig. 1. The user and item distributions between target system and auxiliary system in the common scenario of overlapping behavior risk.

We describe a common risk scenario of overlapping viewing movie behaviours in Fig. 1. The sets of movie items for the target and auxiliary system are denoted as Item-*T* and Item-A, and the user sets of two systems are denoted as User-T and User-A respectively. These two systems may have some overlapping items, denoted as the intersection of Item-T and Item-A. Denote User-$T1$ as the set of users in target system who have rating records on the overlapping items, and User-$T2$ as the set of users who have no records on the overlapping items. Since it is not easy to identify overlapping users of these two systems because usually the user identification is not on a common basis across different systems, none intersection of user sets is shown in Fig. 1. In fact, privacy risk does exist even without overlapping behaviors as shown in our work.

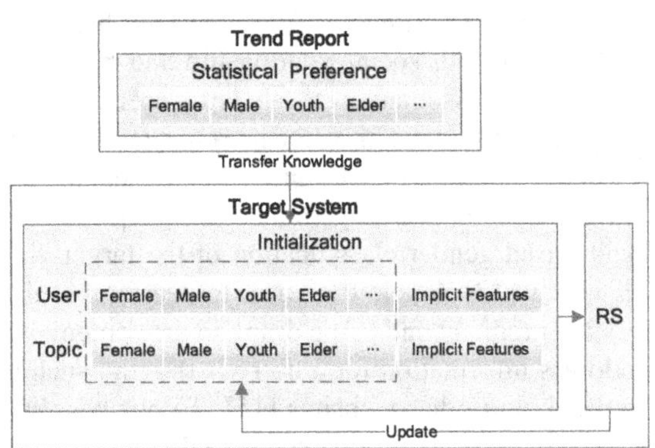

Fig. 2. The UTLS framework for DI inference.

3.2 Problem Definition

To reveal the privacy risk, the DI inference problem in this paper is defined as an unsupervised transfer learning problem. Denote D, T and U are the dimensions of DI features, the number of topics and the number of users in the target system respectively. Given the transferred DI-topic knowledge $\mathbf{W} \in \mathbb{R}^{\mathrm{D}\times\mathrm{T}}$ from auxiliary system, and the topic rating history $\mathbf{R} \in \mathbb{R}^{\mathrm{U}\times\mathrm{T}}$ in target system, find the optimal vector of the DI features for each user in the target system by minimizing the loss of recommendation accuracy, i.e., the value of *root-mean-square error* (*RMSE*) as

$$\boldsymbol{\delta}^* = \arg\min RMSE\left(\hat{\mathbf{R}}|\boldsymbol{\delta}(\mathbf{R}, \mathbf{W})\right) \tag{1}$$

where $\hat{\mathbf{R}} \in \mathbb{R}^{\mathrm{U}\times\mathrm{T}}$ is the predicted value of topic ratings $\mathbf{R}$ in target system, and $\boldsymbol{\delta}^* \in \mathbb{R}^{\mathrm{D}\times\mathrm{T}}$ is optimum, i.e., DI vector of topics and users.

3.3 Evaluation Metric

Since user DI distribution of target system is unknown, we take the commonly used F-measure F_1 of the whole users to evaluate the performance of proposed UTLS, and develop the final evaluation metric based on reference baseline $F_{1,\mathrm{Reference}}$ as

$$\Delta F_1 \geq a_0, \Delta F_1 = (F_{1,\mathrm{UTLS}} - F_{1,\mathrm{Reference}})/F_{1,\mathrm{Reference}} \tag{2}$$

where $a_0 \in [-1, 0]$ is a given threshold value which limits the tolerance of relative difference between the proposed UTLS and selected supervised learning scheme. In this paper, we take a larger value $a_0 = -0.1$ to require that UTLS has a better performance.

4 Learning Scheme

4.1 Basic Idea

We propose UTLS framework based on the accepted fact that user DI is benefit to recommendations. Besides, we take gender information as an example to show the basic idea of UTLS in Fig. 3. The horizontal and vertical axis represent the female and male preference value. The solid and hollow circulars denote the initialized and inferred DI vector of topic *t*, and the solid and hollow triangles denote the initialized and inferred DI vector of user *u* respectively. The yellow and green areas denote a set of topics visited by user 1 and user 2.

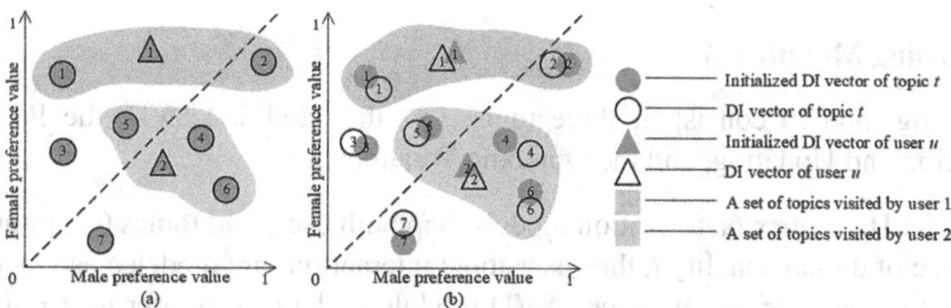

Fig. 3. The initialization and updating of DI vectors for topics and users in UTLS. (Color figure online)

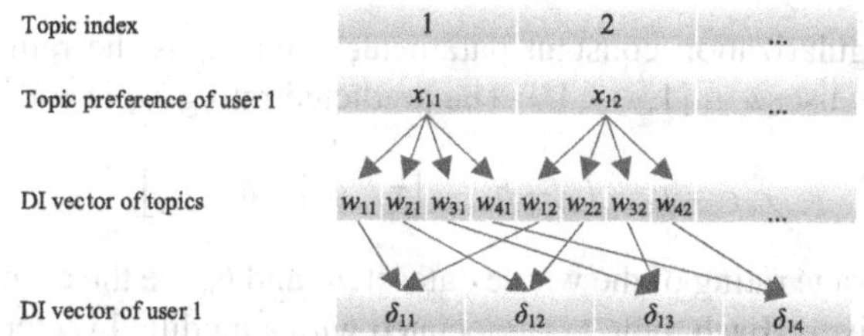

Fig. 4. An example of initialization of DI vector of user 1 in UTLS.

Since similar users usually have similar interest preferences, introducing DI to help improve recommendation performance has been shown effective. We utilize recommendation service to infer user DI. Firstly, we transfer external statistical preference to initialize the relationship between gender and topics as well as the relationship between gender and users in target system shown in Fig. 3(a). We show the details of such initialization process based on user 1 in Fig. 4. The first row lists the topic indexes. The second row displays the preference of user 1 versus topics in the yellow area in Fig. 3(a), i.e., topic 1 and topic 2. The third row gives the transferred external statistical preference, i.e., statistical preference versus female, male, youth and elder for each topic. Finally, based on inner product of above vectors, we can initialize DI vector of user 1 shown in the fourth row. Then, DI vectors of both topic and user are updated together with the implicit features via optimizing the recommendation performance shown in Fig. 3(b).

4.2 Knowledge Module

Since there are many authoritative trend report of external statistical preference provided by various online service systems, transfer knowledge can be achieved with ease. In this paper, the function of knowledge module is to collect and coordinate external statistical preference shown in Fig. 2.

Specifically, DI-topic preference matrix $\mathbf{W} = \{w_{dt}\} \in \mathbb{R}^{D \times T}$ is defined to store transferred knowledge, where $w_{dt} \in [0, 1]$ denotes the statistical preference of users with DI feature $d \in [1, \cdots, D]$ versus topic $t \in [1, \cdots, T]$, i.e., external statistical preference. In particular, denote $d = 1, 2, 3, 4$ for female, male, young and elder respectively.

4.3 Learning Module

The learning module consist of three units, i.e., the Modified SVD, the Parameter Initialization and Updating, and the Outcome Treatment.

Modified SVD. Matrix factorization models map both users and topics to a joint latent factor space of dimensionality *f*, thus user-topic interactions are modeled as inner products in that space. And in this paper, SVD module is defined to infer user ratings by minimizing the *regularized squared error* as

$$min \sum_{(u,t)} \left(r_{ut} - \hat{r}_{ut}\right)^2 + \lambda\left(b_t^2 + b_u^2 + \left\|\left[\boldsymbol{\tau}_t, \boldsymbol{q}_t\right]\right\|^2 + \left\|\left[\boldsymbol{\delta}_u, \boldsymbol{p}_u\right]\right\|^2\right) \tag{3}$$

where λ is the regularization constant parameter. And r_{ut} is the rating of topic $t \in [1, \cdots, T]$ given by user $u \in [1, \cdots, U]$. The predicted rating $\hat{r}_{ut}$ is computed as

$$\hat{r}_{ut} = \mu - b_t - b_u - \left[\boldsymbol{\tau}_t, \boldsymbol{q}_t\right]^T \left[\boldsymbol{\delta}_u, \boldsymbol{p}_u\right] \tag{4}$$

where μ is the average rating of the whole dataset. b_t and b_u are the rating bias of topic t and user u respectively. Each topic t is associated with a modified vector $\left[\boldsymbol{\tau}_t, \boldsymbol{q}_t\right] \in \mathbb{R}^f$, and each user u is associated with a modified vector $\left[\boldsymbol{\delta}_u, \boldsymbol{p}_u\right] \in \mathbb{R}^f$.$\boldsymbol{\tau}_t$ and $\boldsymbol{\delta}_u$ denote DI vectors of topic t and user u respectively, and $\boldsymbol{q}_t$ and $\boldsymbol{p}_u$ denotes the implicit feedback.

Based on transferred external statistical preference $\mathbf{W}$, $\boldsymbol{\tau}_t$ and $\boldsymbol{\delta}_u$ are initialized via the process in Fig. 4. As

$$\boldsymbol{\tau}_t = \boldsymbol{w}_t \tag{5}$$

$$\boldsymbol{\delta}_u = \boldsymbol{x}_u \mathbf{W}^T \tag{6}$$

where $\boldsymbol{x}_u$ is the normalized topic preference relevance vector of user u.

Parameter Initialization and Updating. Update b_t, b_u, $\boldsymbol{\tau}_t$, $\boldsymbol{q}_t$, $\boldsymbol{\delta}_u$, $\boldsymbol{p}_u$ in the SVD process by minimizing *RMSE* on topic-level using the following gradient descent criteria

$$\begin{cases} e_{ut} = r_{ut} - \hat{r}_{ut} \\ b_u \leftarrow b_u + \gamma \cdot (e_{ut} - \lambda \cdot b_u) \\ b_t \leftarrow b_t + \gamma \cdot (e_{ut} - \lambda \cdot b_t) \\ \boldsymbol{\delta}_u \leftarrow \boldsymbol{\delta}_u + \gamma \cdot (e_{ut} \cdot \boldsymbol{\tau}_t - \lambda \cdot \boldsymbol{\delta}_u) \\ \boldsymbol{\tau}_t \leftarrow \boldsymbol{\tau}_t + \gamma \cdot (e_{ut} \cdot \boldsymbol{\delta}_u - \lambda \cdot \boldsymbol{\tau}_t) \\ \boldsymbol{p}_u \leftarrow \boldsymbol{p}_u + \gamma \cdot (e_{ut} \cdot \boldsymbol{q}_t - \lambda \cdot \boldsymbol{p}_u) \\ \boldsymbol{q}_t \leftarrow \boldsymbol{q}_t + \gamma \cdot (e_{ut} \cdot \boldsymbol{p}_u - \lambda \cdot \boldsymbol{q}_t) \end{cases} \tag{7}$$

where γ is a constant parameter named the learning rate, and e_{ut} is the corresponding prediction error.

Outcome Treatment. According to the outcome of parameter update process, we utilize the inferred DI vector of user u, i.e., $\boldsymbol{\delta}_u$ to infer user DI.

We obtain user DI via comparing multidimensional values of $\boldsymbol{\delta}_u$, and set the one with maximum value to 1 otherwise 0. In particular, in this paper, δ_{u1}, δ_{u2}, δ_{u3} and δ_{u4} denote tendency of female, male, young and elder. For instance, if $\delta_{u1} > \delta_{u2}$, then $\delta_{u1} = 1$, $\delta_{u2} = 0$, namely, user u is inferred as female.

4.4 Availability of UTLS

To verify the availability of UTLS, we have to answer two questions. Is the final DI matrix of topics $\boldsymbol{\Gamma} \in \mathbb{R}^{\mathrm{T} \times \mathrm{D}}$, composed by DI vector of topic $\boldsymbol{\tau}$, different from the initialized $\boldsymbol{\Gamma}$, denote as $\boldsymbol{\Gamma}_0$? Does $\boldsymbol{\Gamma}$ still corresponding to DI aspect after parameter updating? To answer above questions, for each DI aspect, we compare topic vector with ground truth of DI in target system, i.e., DI-topic matrix, denoted as $\mathbf{W_{target}}$. In details, we compute the similarity between $\boldsymbol{\Gamma}_0$ and $\mathbf{W_{target}}$ as well as the similarity between $\boldsymbol{\Gamma}$ and $\mathbf{W_{target}}$ first. Then, make a comparison. According to our experiment results in next section, both answers are positive. The similarity of the later one is larger than the former one, which means that $\boldsymbol{\Gamma}$ is different from $\boldsymbol{\Gamma}_0$, and $\boldsymbol{\Gamma}$ is more like $\mathbf{W_{target}}$.

We define the similarity of vector v, $\hat{v}$ based on Euclidean distance $dist(\boldsymbol{v},\hat{\boldsymbol{v}})$ as

$$dist(\boldsymbol{v},\hat{\boldsymbol{v}}) = \sqrt{\sum_{i=1}^{n} (v_i - \hat{v}_i)} \tag{8}$$

$$sim(\boldsymbol{v},\hat{\boldsymbol{v}}) = \frac{1}{1 + dist(\boldsymbol{v},\hat{\boldsymbol{v}})} \tag{9}$$

5 Experiment and Evaluation

5.1 Data Description

For credibility, we take MovieLens and Flixster system, which are commonly used in studies on RS and DI inference, as knowledge source and target system [1, 16, 17].

All the experiments are taken by ten-fold cross validation. Besides, the ratio between training dataset and test dataset is 8:2.

MovieLens Public Dataset. MovieLens is a well-known recommendation system, which recommends movies for its users to watch based on their movie preferences. MovieLens dataset is from a project of GroupLens Research about personalized recommendation systems. The dataset contains 1,000,209 anonymous ratings of approximately 3,900 movies given by 6,040 users.

Flixster Public Dataset. Flixster is an American social movie site for discovering new movies, learning about movies, and meeting others with similar tastes in movies. The dataset contains 323,164 anonymous ratings of approximately 16,952 movies given by 6,691 users.

Table 1. User distribution based on DI.

DI	Flixster		MovieLens	
	User	Size	User	Size
Female	63.00%	4215	28.30%	1709
Male	37.00%	2476	71.70%	4331
Youth	46.90%	3140	53.00%	3199
Elder	53.10%	3551	47.00%	2841
All	100%	6691	100%	6040

Table 2. User distribution based on DI.

DI	Flixster		MovieLens	
	Rating	Mean	Rating	Mean
Female	61.4%	3.787	24.6%	3.614
Male	38.6%	3.599	75.5%	3.564
Youth	49.0%	3.667	58.5%	3.523
Elder	51.1%	3.759	41.5%	3.643
All	100%	3.714	100%	3.577

The basic statistical analysis of two datasets are listed in Tables 1 and 2. Obviously, there are similar number of users in both datasets. As shown in Table 1, MovieLens dataset is male dominated, and Flixster dataset is female dominated. The age groups also distribute oppositely. Moreover, in both datasets, the female users accustom to give higher ratings than males, and the young (age between 18 and 34) accustom to give lower ratings than elders as shown in Table 2.

Furthermore, to make a detailed analysis, we divide the users of Flixster dataset into different groups, i.e., User-$T1$, User-$T2$ and User-T as described in Fig. 1. And then we represent user popularity versus the amount of viewed movies in Fig. 5. Obviously, users in User-$T1$ (48.2% of total users) viewed more movies than users in User-$T2$ (51.8% of total users).

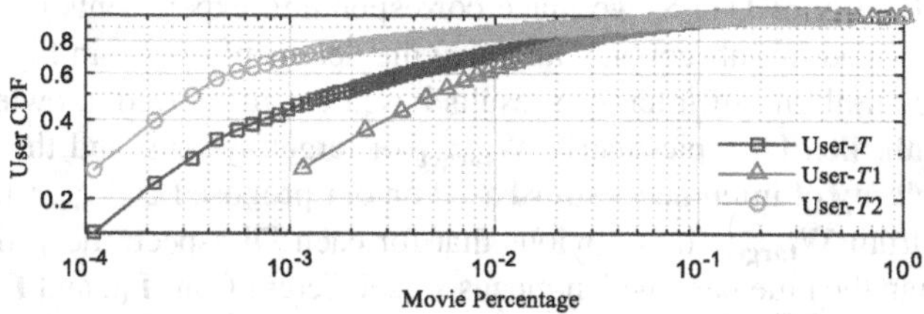

Fig. 5. User activity based on movie rating behaviors of Flixster dataset.

5.2 UTLS Process

To avoid data manipulation and ensure credibility, we take MovieLens dataset as knowledge source, and simulate statistical trend report of user preference versus different DI aspect stored in DI-topic preference matrix **W** as follow steps.

Simulate the Publicized Trend Report. To simulate trend report of external statistical knowledge, we define a topic as a synonym group extracted from item descriptions and titles based on WordNet [18, 19], which can group nouns, verbs, adverbs and adjectives into sets of cognitive synonyms interlinked by means of conceptual semantic and lexical relations. In addition, the similarity threshold of synonym groups can be adjusted to involve more items and users. And then, we take the statistical DI preference on top 500 popular topics in MovieLens dataset as transferred knowledge. In particular, DI-topic preference matrix **W** is computed by rule

$$w_{dt} = \left(\sum_{u \in \tilde{U}(d)} \tilde{r}_{ut} \Big/ \sum_{t=1 \cdots T, u \in \tilde{U}(d)} \tilde{r}_{ut} \right)^{\beta} \tag{9}$$

where $\beta \in [0, 1]$ is an adjustment parameter, $\tilde{r}_{ut}$ is the rating of topic t given by user u. The aggregated rating of group of users $\tilde{U}(d)$ with aspect d on topic t is normalized by the aggregated ratings of such users on all topics to shield the effect of uneven DI distribution.

Initialize Corresponding Parameters. We take Flixster dataset as the dataset of target system, and aggregate user behaviors from item-level to topic-level with the same process above. With **W**, we initialize regularized squared error and predicted rating.

Update Parameter. We update the parameter listed in (7) by minimizing RMSE. The iterative process runs until convergence.

Infer User DI. Finally, for each user, we compare δ_{u1} and δ_{u2} to infer user gender, and compare δ_{u3} and δ_{u4} to infer user age respectively.

5.3 Experiment Evaluation

UTLS Is Availability for DI Inference, and Can Truly Reveal Privacy Risk. To verify the availability of UTLS, we make corresponding experiments to compare the similarities described in Subsect. 4.4, and give the details pf results in Fig. 6. The blue bars denote the similarity of inference results based on transferred knowledge i.e., $\mathbf{\Gamma}_0$ and ground truth, i.e., DI-topic matrix $\mathbf{W}_{\mathbf{target}}$ of target system, and the yellow bars denote the similarity of inference results based on our proposed UTLS framework, i.e., $\mathbf{\Gamma}$ and ground truth $\mathbf{W}_{\mathbf{target}}$. It is obvious that for each DI aspect, the yellow bars are much higher than the blue bars, which means $\mathbf{\Gamma}$ is different from $\mathbf{\Gamma}_0$, and $\mathbf{\Gamma}$ is more like ground truth. In a word, the UTLS proposed framework in this paper is available and effective to show the privacy risk of user DI.

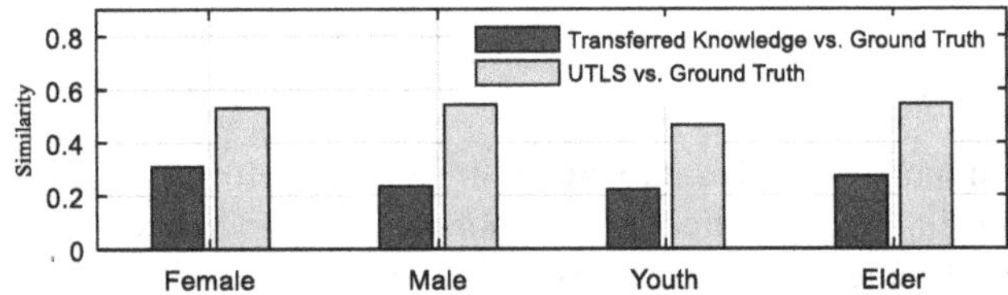

Fig. 6. Similarity comparison of topic vectors for each DI aspect. (Color figure online)

To Provide a Reference for Statistical Privacy Risk of UTLS, Logistic Regression (LR) Is Selected Among Many Existing Classical Classifiers. Existing privacy risk of DI inference cannot be separated from partially known knowledge. DI inference problem is, in essence, a classification problem that users are assigned into different groups according to their online behaviors. Since LR is the classical selection to infer user DI, e.g., gender in many existing studies [4], we take it as the reference classifier. Moreover, to verify the selection rationality, we compare LR with a series of classifiers on item-level including k-Nearest Neighbor (KNN), Random Forest (RF), Support Vector Machines (SVM) and Gradient Boosting Decision Tree (GBDT), and list results in Table 3. As same as the existing studies, the typical classifier, LR performs best with $F_1 = 0.654$. Thus, we take the DI inference results based on LR model trained on Flixster dataset as the final reference.

The Statistical Privacy Risk Is as Serious as the Existing Privacy Risk Based on Partially Known Knowledge. For users in both User-$T1$ and User-$T2$ described in Fig. 1, our proposed UTLS framework performs as well as inference reference values as listed in Table 4. According to (1), since $a_0 = -0.1$, for every results via UTLS, $\Delta F_1 \geq a_0$, which means users in a safe-seeming online service system still have to face the statistical risk of privacy leakage. In particular, even for the users in User-$T2$, the performance of gender and age inference only degrades as $\Delta F_1 = -0.079$ and -0.012 respectively, as similar as the reference values.

Table 3. Comparison based on gender.

Gender	KNN	LR	RF	SVM	GBDT
F_1	0.625	0.654	0.634	0.581	0.636

Table 4. DI inference result comparison.

DI	ΔF_1	
	Gender	Age
User-$T1$	−0.066	−0.007
User-$T2$	−0.079	−0.012

In addition, directly transferring the LR model trained on MovieLens dataset to infer user gender labels of Flixster dataset, returns $\Delta F_1 = -0.181$ much smaller than a_0. It is obvious that UTLS performs much better than such method.

Addition Product of UTLS Is the Improvement of Recommendations. Compare with the RMSE of traditional SVD based on Flixster dataset, the RMSE of UTLS decreases 0.011.

Overall, there is truly privacy risk without partially known knowledge in an online service system.

6 Conclusions

In this work, we propose an unsupervised transfer learning scheme to reveal the statistical risk of privacy leakage in a safe-seeming online environment. The statistical preference knowledge versus different DI aspect on topic-level is transferred to the target system. A user's DI features are initialized with external statistical preference, concatenated with the implicit preference features, and modified via optimizing recommendation performance. Experiment results show that UTLS infers user DI with performance close to that of the supervised learning reference. This means that user have to face the privacy risk even in a system never collected DI information.

Acknowledgment. This work was supported in part by the National Science Foundation of China under Grant No. 61572071, 61872331.

References

1. Weinsberg, U., Bhagat, S., Ioannidis, S., Taft, N.: BlurMe: inferring and obfuscating user gender based on ratings. In: ACM Conference on Recommender Systems, pp. 195–202. ACM (2012)

2. Otterbacher, J.: Inferring gender of movie reviewers: exploiting writing style, content and metadata, pp. 369–378 (2010)
3. Hu, J., Zeng, H.J., Li, H., Niu, C., Chen, Z.: Demographic prediction based on user's browsing behavior. In: International Conference on World Wide Web, WWW 2007, Banff, Alberta, Canada, May, pp. 151–160. DBLP (2007)
4. Feng, T., et al.: Tags and titles of videos you watched tell your gender. In: IEEE International Conference on Communications, pp. 1837–1842. IEEE (2014)
5. Li, B., Yang, Q., Xue, X.: Can movies and books collaborate? Cross-domain collaborative filtering for sparsity reduction. In: IJCAI 2009, Proceedings of the, International Joint Conference on Artificial Intelligence, Pasadena, California, Usa, vol.38, pp. 2052–2057. DBLP (2009)
6. Li, C.R., Sanjay, A., Yang, S.W., Lin, S.D.: Transfer learning for sequential recommendation model. In: Technologies and Applications of Artificial Intelligence, pp. 154–161. IEEE (2017)
7. Brain&Company: Seven years: Age of reason? 2005–2012: Creating value(s) in the digital age (2012). http://www.bain.com/publications/articles/seven-years-age-of-reason-avignon-report.aspx
8. JD Data Research Institute: 2018 JD National Reading Report (2018). http://research.jd.com
9. He, J., Chu, W.W., Liu, Z.: Inferring privacy information from social networks. In: Mehrotra, S., Zeng, D.D., Chen, H., Thuraisingham, B., Wang, F.-Y. (eds.) ISI 2006. LNCS, vol. 3975, pp. 154–165. Springer, Heidelberg (2006). https://doi.org/10.1007/11760146_14
10. Lindamood, J., Heatherly, R., Kantarcioglu, M., Thuraisingham, B.: Inferring private information using social network data. In: International Conference on World Wide Web, pp. 1145–1146. ACM (2015)
11. Gong, N.Z., Liu, B.: You are who you know and how you behave: attribute inference attacks via users' social friends and behaviors (2016)
12. Su, Y., Fu, Y., Tian, Q., Gao, X.: Cross-database age estimation based on transfer learning. In: IEEE International Conference on Acoustics Speech and Signal Processing, vol. 23, pp. 1270–1273. IEEE (2010)
13. Yao, Z., Zhang, Z., Hu, M., Wang, Y.: Cross-view gait-based gender classification by transfer learning. In: Huet, B., Ngo, C.-W., Tang, J., Zhou, Z.-H., Hauptmann, A.G., Yan, S. (eds.) PCM 2013. LNCS, vol. 8294, pp. 79–87. Springer, Cham (2013). https://doi.org/10.1007/978-3-319-03731-8_8
14. Castillo, S.R.M., Chen, Z.: Using transfer learning to identify privacy leaks in tweets. In: IEEE International Conference on Collaboration and Internet Computing, pp. 506–513. IEEE (2017)
15. Chen, L., Zheng, J., Gao, M., Zhou, A., Zeng, W., Chen, H.: TLRec: transfer learning for cross-domain recommendation. Comput. Sci. 167–172 (2012)
16. Yang, X., Steck, H., Guo, Y., Liu, Y.: On top-k recommendation using social networks. In: ACM Conference on Recommender Systems, pp. 67–74. ACM (2012)
17. Bilge, A., Polat, H.: An improved profile-based CF scheme with privacy. In: Fifth IEEE International Conference on Semantic Computing, pp. 133–140. IEEE (2011)
18. Feng, T., Guo, Y., Chen, Y.: A novel user behavioral aggregation method based on synonym groups in online video systems. Sci. China (Inform. Sci.) **59**(2), 1–3 (2016)
19. Bond, F., Paik, K.: A survey of wordnets and their licenses (2012)

Blockchain-Based Access Control Schemes for Medical Image Analysis System

Tonglai Liu[1,2], Jigang Wu[1(✉)], Xinpeng Zhang[1], Zhihao Peng[1], and Jingyi Li[1]

[1] School of Computer Science and Technology, Guangdong University of Technology, Guangzhou 510006, China
asjgwucn@outlook.com

[2] Guangxi Key Laboratory of Cryptography and Information Security, Guilin University of Electronic Technology, Guilin 541004, China

Abstract. Medical image analysis systems with machine learning have played an important role in the computer-aided diagnosis and treatment for diseases. However, individual privacy of user data is vulnerable since the training data is exposed to unauthorized user. Therefore, this paper designs an access control scheme to prevent illegal users from accessing medical data while achieving high accuracy of lesion classification. Specifically, in the novel lightweight consortium blockchain-based access control scheme, a chosen consortium node is utilized as key generation center instead of a trusted third party in conventional schemes. Two public retinal datasets are utilized for the classification of diabetic retinopathy (DR). Security analysis shows that the proposed scheme can prevent the user data from leakage and malicious tampering. Experimental results demonstrate that the processing of data cleaning is efficient to increase the accuracy of the classification for early lesions of DR by removing low quality images, and the accuracy is up to 90.2%.

Keywords: Access control · Consortium blockchain · Deep learning · Medical image

1 Introduction

Nowadays, medical image analysis systems with machine learning (MIASDL), especially deep learning, are widely used in computer-aided diagnosis and treatment of disease because of its high efficiency. In these systems, cloud platforms are often used to reduce the computing and storage abundant of the local terminals. A large number of electronic medical record are stored and shared on cloud servers. However, private data of users are easily exposed to adversaries

This work was supported by the National Natural Science Foundation of China under Grant Nos. 61672171 and 61902078, Guangxi Natural Science Foundation of China under Grant No. 2018GXNSFAA138082, Guangxi Key Laboratory of Cryptography and Information Security under Grant No. GCIS201816.

H. Shen and Y. Sang (Eds.): PAAP 2019, CCIS 1163, pp. 357–367, 2020.
https://doi.org/10.1007/978-981-15-2767-8_32

and being falsified in recent works, which are not implemented with access control strategy [1,2]. Thus, access control can be regarded as a significant way to protect private data by blocking unauthorized user from accessing any resource. Besides, image analysis systems are efficient concerned that patient want to access the result as fast as possible. Here comes a question that how to build a medical image analysis system with both privacy protection and reasonably efficient.

To ensure the security and privacy of medical data, various traditional access control methods have been proposed. Taking into consideration the relationship between the requestor and the owner of the resource, relationship-based access control was first developed by Gates [3]. Choi *et al.* [4] proposed risk-based access control models to decide access permissions dynamically. Furthermore, a hierarchical access control scheme using a two-layer approach was proposed in medical image transmission [5]. However, these works involve centralized trusted third party for managing user behaviour by stored control table and generate secret key for users. If these center entities encounter malicious attack or accidentally shut up, private data, such as user permissions or private key will lose or leakage.

Due to the feature of strictly sequential and anonymous, blockchain can be used to maintain consensus among untrusted or semi-trusted participants [6]. In this case, some blockchain-based access control methods have been proposed in medical information systems. A scalable and robust system using blockchain technique as an access control method was presented in [7]. Al Omar *et al.* employed the blockchain for secure privacy storage of patient healthcare, which addressed the problem of losing control while storing encrypted data [8].

In this paper, we propose an novel access control scheme to prevent medical data from unauthorized accessing. We first gather image data and patient information in hospital information system (HIS) as dataset. Then CBBAC is designed and used to store encrypted control table. Data cleaning process is introduced to filter invalid data out of dataset for training deep learning model. An improved lightweight cryptography is also used to reduce computing cost. The main contributions of this paper are listed as follows.

- We propose a blockchain-based access control scheme for medical image analysis system using three particular consortium chain.
- We propose a novel architecture that embed access control scheme into medical image analysis system with deep learning.
- We propose security goals for our systems and provide security analysis to demonstrate the proposed scheme can achieve these goals.

2 System Model

The system model consists of data cleaning and classification, as shown in Fig. 1. In order to train model in a secure environment, the stage of data cleaning is constructed to distinguish low quality images from qualified images. These images are forbidden to upload to the cloudlet. Each doctor use HIS to collect and unload medical images to the corresponding cloudlet. Then, the model of deep learning classifies and returns the low quality images to doctors. The residual images are utilized to train the model of classification. The cloudlet uploads the qualified images to the remote cloud by accessing application program interface (API) gateway at scheduled time intervals.

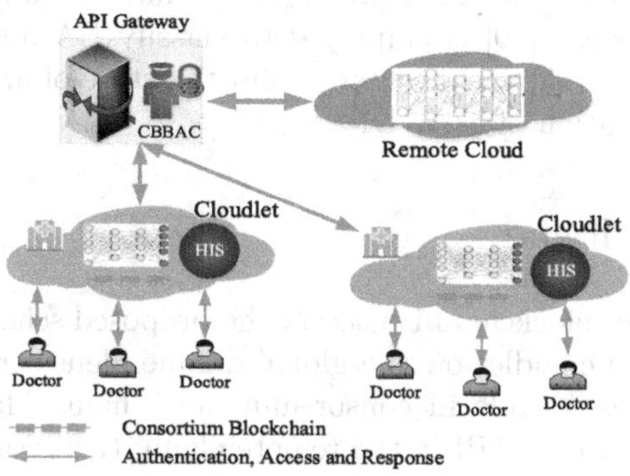

Fig. 1. System model.

In the process of model training, data among doctors, cloudlet and remote cloud are only exchanged after the authentication. For each cloudlet, the role of all participants are defined to ensures that only legitimate users can use authorized software functions and access authorized data sets in HIS. In CBBAC, the remote cloud provides services in the form of representational state transfer (REST) API. An API gateway is a channel router between cloudlet and remote cloud. Each cloudlet exchanges data with remote cloud through the API gateway. User in cloudlet can request data from remote cloud via CBBAC in an API gateway, instead of accessing data under the permissions of third-party as the traditional method does. In this case, the complexity of setting authorization permissions and validating valid users can be reduced. Three consortium blockchains are deployed on the cloudlet node and API gateway node. The first one is consortium blockchain for data cleaning model (CBDCM), which is used to store the deep learning model in the first stage. The second one is consortium blockchain for access control (CBAC), which is used to store access logs and encrypted permissions of the cloudlet in the stage of classification. The third one is consortium blockchain for classification model backup (CBCMB), which is used to save the encrypted model of deep learning for classification. The model is distributed stored among consortium blockchain nodes.

2.1 Deep Learning for Data Cleaning and Classification

The quality of medical image is uneven in clinical. For color retinal image, some images are low quality, including low contrast, over-exposed and much noise, etc. On the one hand, it is difficult for ophthalmologist to observe and diagnose early

DR lesions, such as hemorrhage (HA) and hard exudates (HEs). These images are not suitable for the early screening of DR. On the other hand, these low quality images will reduce the dirty of data to train a efficient model for computer-aided based DR detection. Therefore, convolutional neural network (CNN) is applied for data cleaning of color retinal image. The network consists of three convolution layers (Conv), one max-pooling layer and two fully connected layers (FC). Then, the network [10] is employed to classify HA and HEs, which has achieved higher sensitivity and accuracy than the-state-of-art methods for the simultaneous classification of early DR lesions.

3 Proposed Scheme

Particular consortium blockchain is used in the proposed scheme. In the consortium blockchain, each cloudlet owns a global unique identifier (ID). Meanwhile, each cloudlet work as a node in consortium blockchain. The permissions are assigned for users to access API in the remote cloud, the permissions of doctors are also pre-assigned by hospitals to access HIS.

3.1 Data Cleaning

In the proposed architecture, each cloudlet has a HIS cluster based on relational database, e.g. oracle. Meanwhile, a CNN model is constructed to cleanse the medical images in the cloudlet, and CBDCM is presented to save encrypted deep learning model. HIS is a comprehensive and integrated information platform that stores the electronic medical record of patients. We assume that only authorized users can access data in HIS. Only doctors who are responsible to specific patient can use HIS to upload related encrypted medical images to the corresponding cloudlet for data cleaning. Then deep learning model returns the results of low quality images to corresponding doctors.

We form the data chunks of deep learning model, which are uploaded and stored on CBDCM, as a ring. Data chunks are numbered in order and follow the principle of FIFO. The last data chunk connects with the first one to form a ring. Each node will write updated model trained by itself to the blockchain. In order to improve the learning ability of the model, the current node always use the latest updated model. The details are described as follows.

Step 1: All the encrypted images scanned by doctors are uploaded to the cloudlet.
Step 2: The deep learning model is used to cleanse low quality images.
Step 3: Qualified images are saved in the cloudlet, and the indexes of low quality images are returned to the doctor.
Step 4: A new model is written on the consortium blockchain CDBCM.
Step 5: The latest model of the previous node is read by the current node.

3.2 Classification

In the proposed architecture of classification, cloudlet exchanges data with remote cloud via REST API. After data cleaning process, only qualified medical images can be uploaded to the remote cloud for training and classification. Cloudlet can access data in remote cloud without the identity-authentication of a third authority through the given blockchain. We use API gateway to simultaneously validates the identity and the permissions, which can allocate proper API for the cloudlet. Then, two consortium blockchains, named CBAC and CBCMB, are constructed. Cloudlet is allowed to read data from the blockchain and write data to the blockchain through cryptography, while the API gateway can only read data from the blockchain. The classification model is backuped by all nodes in the blockchain network. Moreover, remote cloud can restore the model from any nodes participated.

Consortium Blockchain-Based Access Control. Cloudlet exchanges data with the remote cloud by microservices, each of them is deployed easily in a heterogeneous network architecture. We assume that there is a microservice '/service' including '/service/post', '/service/get', '/service/put' and '/service/delete', denoting the *Create*, *Retrieve*, *Update* and *Delete* operations, respectively. The objects are API in CBBAC. Predefined permission PE of the cloudlet is transmitted to the API gateway while the cloudlet requests services for exchanging data with the remote cloud. Specifically, PE is a series of permission codes that depend on the control table as traditional access control schemes do.

In order to avoid depending on a trusted third party KGC, we develop the lightweight certificateless public key cryptography based on ECC [11,12], and propose a blockchain-based and lightweight certificateless public key cryptography (BBL-CL-PKC) to encrypt/decrypt data and sign/verify the signature. In a consortium blockchain network, only a part of nodes can be selected to participant in the mining process, which are named as consortium nodes (CNs). In BBL-CL-PKC, KGC is a randomly selected consortium nodes.

We assume that the cloudlet A has an identifier ID_A. It requests medical data from the gateway B with an identifier ID_B. We define that only authorized node can participant in the consortium blockchain. Encrypted PE and signed message by cloudlet are written to the blockchain in advance. When the A sends a request to the B, B accesses the encrypted PE from the blockchain and decrypts it. Then, B needs to verify the digital signature. BBL-CL-PKC with a lightweight certificateless public key encryption (L-CL-PKE) scheme and a lightweight certificateless public key signature (L-CL-PKS) scheme are used to do the verification.

- L-CL-PKE

  A L-CL-PKE scheme composes of seven algorithms.

  1. Setup

     This algorithm is run by CN, which is defined by

$$(params, s, P_{mpk}) \leftarrow Setup(1^l) \tag{1}$$

where $params$, s, P_{mpk} represent the public parameters of the system, master private key and the master public key, respectively. l represents the security parameter.

2. ExtractPartialKey
This algorithm is run by CN, which is used to extract a partial key pair of d_A and R_A, calculated by 2. It returns a partial private key d_A and a partial public key R_A, which are sent to the cloudlet by a confidential and authentic channel.

$$(d_A, R_A) \leftarrow ExtractPartialKey(ID_A, s, params) \tag{2}$$

The partial private key is calculated by (3).

$$d_A = (s + r_A \times H(ID_A)) \quad mod \quad n, \tag{3}$$

where r_A is a random number from 1 to $n-1$. The partial public key R_A is calculated by (4).

$$R_A = d_A \times G \tag{4}$$

3. SetSecretValue
The algorithm is run by cloudlet, which is used to generate a secret value x_A, which should be stored securely by cloudlet. The algorithm is defined as follows.

$$x_A \leftarrow SetSecretValue(ID_A, params) \tag{5}$$

where ID represents an identifier of a cloudlet. The secret value x_A is selected randomly from $[1, n-1]$. This algorithm is also run by a gateway.

4. SetPrivateKey
This algorithm is run by cloudlet, which is utilized to set a private key SK_A for a cloudlet, formulated as follows,

$$SK_A \leftarrow SetPrivateKey(ID_A, params, x_A, d_A) \tag{6}$$

The private key SK_A is calculated by (7).

$$SK_A = (d_A + x_A \times H(ID_A)) \quad mod \quad n \tag{7}$$

This algorithm is also run by a gateway.

5. SetPublicKey
This algorithm is run by cloudlet, which is set to a public key PK_A for a cloudlet. It is defined as follows.

$$PK_A \leftarrow SetPublicKey(ID_A, params, x_A, R_A) \tag{8}$$

The public key PK_A is calculated by (9).

$$\begin{aligned} PK_A &= SK_A \times G \\ &= P_{mpk} + H(ID_A) \times (R_A + x_A \times G) \end{aligned} \tag{9}$$

From (9), PK_A is associated with ID_A and P_{mpk}. The binding relationship between ID_A and P_{mpk} do not needs to be proved. This algorithm is run by a gateway.

6. Encrypt
   This algorithm is run by cloudlet. PE is encrypted using the public key PK_B of the API gateway. Then, the corresponding ciphertext is saved on the blockchain. This algorithm is defined as follows.

$$(C, Err) \leftarrow Encrypt(PE, params, PK_B, ID_B) \tag{10}$$

   This algorithm returns C and Err, which represent a ciphertext and an encryption failure, respectively. ID_B is an identifier for an API gateway.
7. Decrypt
   This algorithm is run by API gateway. When a cloudlet requests an access from the remote cloud, the API gateway reads ciphertext C and runs this algorithm to decrypt using SK_B. This algorithm is defined as follows.

$$(PE, Err) \leftarrow Decrypt(C, params, SK_B) \tag{11}$$

   The algorithm returns PE and Err, which represent a plaintext and a decryption failure, respectively.

- L-CL-PKS
  A L-CL-PKS scheme composes of seven algorithms, including Setup, Extract-PartialKey, SetSecretValue SetPrivateKey, SetPublicKey, Sign and Verify. The algorithms of Setup, ExtractPartialKey, SetSecretValue, SetPrivateKey and SetPublicKey are the same as that of CL-PKE.
  1. Sign
     This algorithm is run by cloudlet, which signs a message M using the private key SK_A. It is defined as follows.

$$(S, Err) \leftarrow Sign(M, params, SK_A, ID_A) \tag{12}$$

     The algorithm returns signature S and an error symbol Err if the failure occurs. ID_A is an identifier for cloudlet.
  2. Verify
     This algorithm is run by API gateway, which verifies the signature S using the public key PK_A of cloudlet. This algorithm is defined as follows.

$$(True, False, Err) \leftarrow Verify(S, M, params, PK_A, ID_A) \tag{13}$$

     The algorithm returns $True$, $False$ and an error symbol Err if the failure occurs. $True$ indicates valid and $False$ indicates invalid. ID_A is an identifier for cloudlet.

3.3 Security Analysis

The proposed CBBAC scheme allows authorized cloudlets to access the remote cloud. It achieves fine-grained authorization by predefined PE. The identifier of a doctor accessing the HIS is validated by CAS using HTTPS. The permission data are also transmitted by HTTPS which has evolved into the standard for secure web browsing [13]. On the other hand, basic operations in CBBAC including *Create*, *Retrieve*, *Update* and *Delete* and the data access are also controlled strictly. In consortium blockchain network, nodes must be authorized to participate in the union. Only trusted members have the permissions to write/read data from the blockchain so that the network security is enhanced. From (9), both the identifier ID and the public key P_{mpk} are integrated into the relationship. Even if a malicious attacker can succeed in replacing the public key of victim, it cannot generate a legitimate signature or decrypt the ciphertext without the partial key, using the pseudo public key and ID of victim. Therefore, the CBBAC scheme can protect the privacy of user data.

4 Experiments and Comparisons

4.1 Running Time Based Comparisons in CL-PKE and CL-PKS

The CBBAC scheme uses BBL-CL-PKC to encrypt/decrypt and sign/verify PE. To evaluate the characteristic of lightweight, CL-PKE and CL-PKS [9] are used to compared to our scheme, in terms of time consumption. Figure 2a shows the time consumption of encrypting and decrypting the PE. Figure 2b shows the time consumption of signing and verifying. Comparing with CL-PKE, L-CL-PKE costs lower computation on encrypt and decrypt the PE. From Fig. 2b, the L-CL-PKS costs lower computation in signature and verification algorithm. CL-PKE uses bilinear pairings, the execution cost is more higher than the cryptographic operations [14]. On the contrary, L-CL-PKE is designed by integrating ID into ECC rather than identity-based encryption. It retains features of identity-based public key cryptography. Therefore, the proposed CBBAC scheme is lightweight.

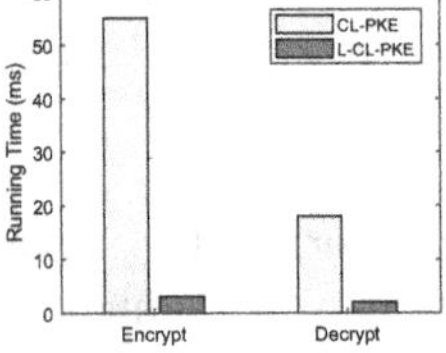

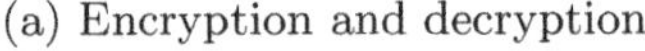
(a) Encryption and decryption.

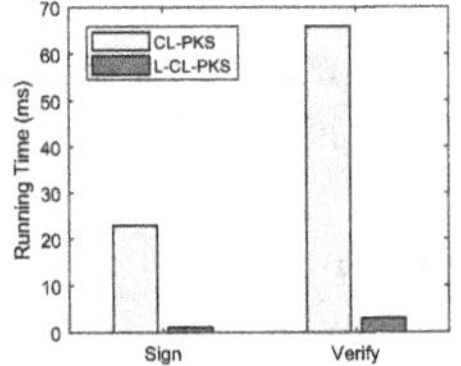

(b) Signature and verification.

Fig. 2. Comparisons in time cost.

4.2 Experiments of DR Classification

The public datasets DIARETDB0 (DB0) [15] and DIARETDB1 (DB1) [16] are introduced for data cleaning and classification of DR early lesions, respectively. The images from DB0 are divided into two categories including images with low quality and qualified images, and the training set are then generated to train the network for data cleaning. In order to verify the accuracy of this network, the images from DB1 are used to test. Experimental results demonstrate that the trained network can remove the low quality images from the source dataset, and the accuracy is up to 74.4%. DB1 dataset contains the ground truth maps of HA and HEs, thus it is utilized for classification [10]. Figure 3 shows the classification results of HA and HEs on DB1 dataset. All the lesions in color retinal image can be detected accurately. The classification results are shown in Fig. 4. The HA and HEs can be accurately recognized. The accuracy of classification is up to 90.2%. Moreover, free-response operating characteristic (FROC) curve [17] is also introduced to evaluate the whole performance of method on each lesion classification. Table 1 lists the sensitivity of each lesion and background using the network [10]. It demonstrates that the sensitivity values for HA and HEs increase after data cleaning.

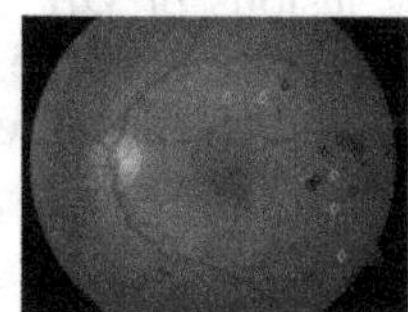

(a) Original retinal image.

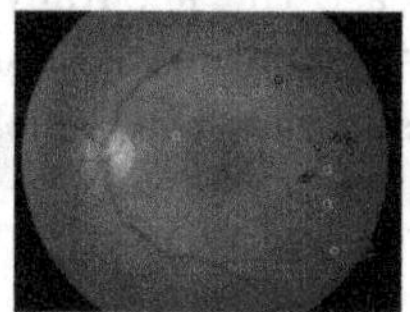

(b) Classification results.

Original images: ◇HM ◇HE
True Positive: ○HM⟶HM ○HE⟶HE
False Positive: □BG⟶HM

Fig. 3. Classification results of HA and HEs on DB1 dataset.

Table 1. Sensitivity values of the classification of DR lesions.

Process	HA	HEs	Iterations
Without data learning	0.841	0.971	2000
Data learning	0.901	0.991	2000

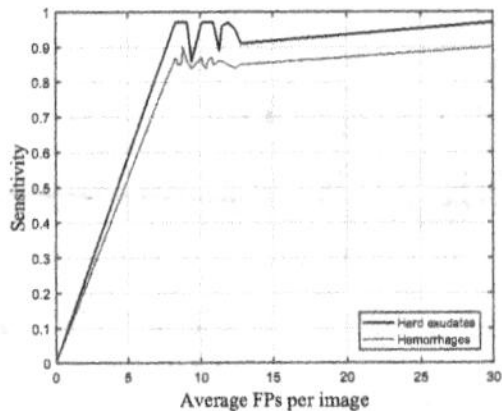

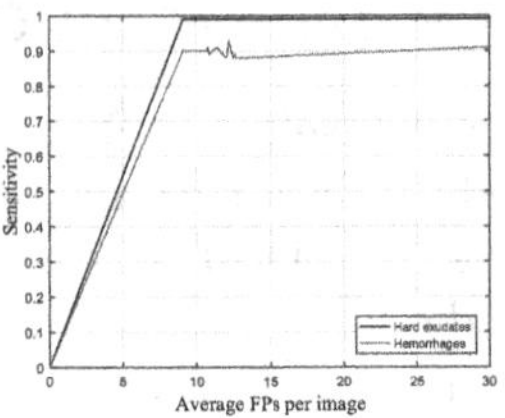

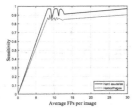

(a) FROC curves without data learning. (b) FROC curves after data learning.

Fig. 4. FROC curves for DR lesions.

5 Conclusion

This paper has proposed a MIASDL system with security and privacy concerned access control schemes. We have designed CBBAC, which is a blockchain-based access control model in terms of developed lightweight certificateless public key cryptography without the participation of a trusted third party. Security analysis demonstrates that the proposed scheme can prevent illegal users from accessing medical data to protect the private data of patients. Furthermore, data cleaning can efficiently increase the accuracy of early lesions of DR by removing low-quality images. The experimental results demonstrate that the proposed scheme can accurately classify the early lesions of DR, and the accuracy is up to 90.2%.

References

1. Anwar, S.M., Majid, M., Qayyum, A., Awais, M., Alnowami, M., Khan, M.K.: Medical image analysis using convolutional neural networks: a review. J. Med. Syst. **42**(11), 226 (2018)
2. Fan, K., Jiang, W., Li, H., Yang, Y.: Lightweight RFID protocol for medical privacy protection in IoT. IEEE Trans. Industr. Inf. **14**(4), 1656–1665 (2018)
3. Carrie Gates: Access control requirements for web 2.0 security and privacy. IEEE Web, 2(0) (2007)
4. Choi, D., Kim, D., Park, S.: A framework for context sensitive risk-based access control in medical information systems. Comput. Math. Methods Med. **2015**, 1–9 (2015)
5. Begum, J.N., Kumar, K., Sumathy, V.: Two tier protocol for hierarchical access control in medical image transmission. In: International Conference on Computing for Sustainable Global Development, pp. 769–775. IEEE (2014)
6. Kamau, G., Boore, C., Maina, E., Njenga, S.: Blockchain technology: is this the solution to EMR interoperability and security issues in developing countries? In: IST-Africa Week Conference (IST-Africa), pp. 1–8. IEEE (2018)
7. Hussein, A.F., ArunKumar, N., Ramirez-Gonzalez, G., Abdulhay, E., Tavares, J.M.R.S., de Albuquerque, V.H.C.: A medical records managing and securing blockchain based system supported by a genetic algorithm and discrete wavelet transform. Cogn. Syst. Res. **52**, 1–11 (2018)

8. Al Omar, A., Rahman, M.S., Basu, A., Kiyomoto, S.: MediBchain: a blockchain based privacy preserving platform for healthcare data. In: Wang, G., Atiquzzaman, M., Yan, Z., Choo, K.-K.R. (eds.) SpaCCS 2017. LNCS, vol. 10658, pp. 534–543. Springer, Cham (2017). https://doi.org/10.1007/978-3-319-72395-2_49
9. Al-Riyami, S.S., Paterson, K.G.: Certificateless public key cryptography. In: Laih, C.-S. (ed.) ASIACRYPT 2003. LNCS, vol. 2894, pp. 452–473. Springer, Heidelberg (2003). https://doi.org/10.1007/978-3-540-40061-5_29
10. Tan, J.H., et al.: Automated segmentation of exudates, haemorrhages, microaneurysms using single convolutional neural network. Inf. Sci. **420**, S0020025517308927 (2017)
11. Yao, X., Han, X., Du, X.: A light-weight certificate-less public key cryptography scheme based on ECC. In: 23rd International Conference on Computer Communication and Networks, pp. 1–8. IEEE (2014)
12. Yao, X., Kong, H., Liu, H., Qiu, T., Ning, H.: An attribute credential based public key scheme for fog computing in digital manufacturing. IEEE Trans. Industr. Inf. **15**(4), 2297–2307 (2019)
13. Arnbak, A., Asghari, H., Van Eeten, M., van Eijk, N.A.N.M.: Security collapse in the https market. Comput. ACM **57**(10), 47–55 (2014)
14. Karati, A., Islam, S.K.H., Biswas, G.P.: A pairing-free and provably secure certificateless signature scheme. Inf. Sci. **450**, 378–391 (2018)
15. Kauppi, T., et al.: DIARETDB0: evaluation database and methodology for diabetic retinopathy algorithms. Mach. Vis. Pattern Recogn. Res. Group **73**, 1–17 (2006)
16. Kauppi, T., et al.: The DIARETDB1 diabetic retinopathy database and evaluation protocol (2007)
17. Bunch, P.C., Hamilton, J.F., Sanderson, G.K., Simmons, A.H.: A free response approach to the measurement and characterization of radiographic observer performance. In: Proceedings of SPIE: in Application of Optical Instrumentation in Medicine, pp. 124–136 (1977)

Research on DDoS Abnormal Traffic Detection Under SDN Network

Zhaohui Ma[1,2,3] and Jialiang Huang[2](✉)

[1] Collaborative Innovation Center for 21st-Century Maritime Silk Road Studies, Guangdong University of Foreign Studies, Guangzhou 510006, China
mazhaohui@gdufs.edu.cn

[2] School of Information Science and Technology, Guangdong University of Foreign Studies, Guangzhou 510006, China
26593978@qq.com

[3] School of Computer Science, South China Normal University, Guangzhou 510631, China

Abstract. The seperation of control layer from data layer through SDN (software defined network) enables network administrators to plan the network programmatically without changing network devices, realizing flexible configuration of network devices and fast forwarding of data flows. However, due to its construction, SDN is vulnerable to be attacked by Distributed Denial of Service (DDoS) attack. So it is important to detect DDoS attack in SDN network. This paper presents a DDoS detection scheme based on the machine learning method of SVM (support vector machine) support vector machine in SDN environment. By extracting the flow table information features in SDN network, the data is detected and the data model of DDoS traffic can be trained, and the purpose of DDoS abnormal traffic identification is finally realized.

Keywords: Software defined networking · Denial of Service · SVM · Abnormal traffic detection

1 Introduction

1.1 Research Background and Significance

With the constant emergence of new computer application fields such as cloud computing [1], big data, artificial intelligence and software-defined network [2], concepts such as fast payment and smart city are becoming reality from the previous assumption. The field of artificial intelligence integrates the accumulated knowledge of mathematics and statistics in the past century, and at the same time integrates with the neural network developed in the field of biology, which gives the computer the ability to "think". However, the difficulty in the technical field of big data is how to transmit these huge and scattered data, which needs to be supported by a robust and flexible network [3].

SDN is a new network architecture proposed by the Clean Slate research group of Stanford University. It has been widely used in the field of cloud computing, promoting the high flexibility and high availability of cloud computing network, and the

H. Shen and Y. Sang (Eds.): PAAP 2019, CCIS 1163, pp. 368–379, 2020.
https://doi.org/10.1007/978-981-15-2767-8_33

deployment of security services has been greatly improved with the popularity of SDN network [4]. The SDN network decoupled the data plane from the control plane in the traditional network, and the control plane was routed by the SDN controller. Meanwhile, the interface was opened to the programmer to write routing calculation algorithm, so as to achieve programmability. The Openflow switch is responsible for packet forwarding for the data plane. Meanwhile, the controller opens the interface to the developers to develop network applications suitable for their own scenarios, such as disaster tolerance switching of services in enterprises [5]. SDN brings considerable technical convenience and promotes its own high-speed development.

In SDN network, the routing control plane is completely controlled by the controller. Therefore, the nodes of the controller are extremely easy to become the target of DDoS (Distributed denial of Service) attack, which is the most difficult attack to prevent in the current network attack [6]. DDoS has always been a research hotspot in the field of network security due to its low launching cost, high attack power and deep harm [7]. Under SDN network, how to use the characteristics of SDN network to detect DDoS attacks [8] and guarantee the stability of network services under SDN network is an important issue to be solved urgently in the field of SDN security.

1.2 Research Status

Thanks to the development of virtualization technology, the old underlying network architecture is in urgent need of revolutionary transformation, so the industry will focus more attention on SDN. Google has successfully proved the feasibility of SDN through the B4 project. With the popularization and implementation of SDN technology [9], the exploration and research of using SDN network to find defense against DDoS attack are also carried out synchronously in the engineering circle.

Cheng Jun et al. [10] proposed the link tracking method to realize the source location of DDoS attacks, but the complexity of the network scene of their experiments was limited, and the success rate of the proposed link tracking system in the real network environment would suffer from some losses. Qiong et al. [11] proposed the DDoS abnormal traffic method based on random forest algorithm, but it only collected the information entropy of source IP and destination port as three characteristic dimensions for training and recognition, and it only considered the accuracy of the algorithm but ignored the recognition time of the algorithm, which is contrary to the low delay in the network environment. Vallipuram [12] and others based on multilayer perceptron neural network is put forward, and gravity retrieval algorithm to realize the recognition of abnormal traffic detection, the study at very high recognition accuracy network anomaly traffic, but the neural network training required for large data sets and the machine performance requirements is very high, in the SDN such sensitive to network latency scenarios, if the application of the detection module in SDN will affect network latency. Van Trung et al. [13] detected DDos attacks in SDN using fuzzy logic. However, their experiments were based on the results verified by data sets generated by certain traffic.

Based on the above research status, this paper redefines the training features of recognition model according to the characteristics of DDoS attack, and obtains the best recognition model by comparing the accuracy and recognition efficiency of SVM algorithm and random forest algorithm.

The following arrangements are as follows: Sect. 1 introduces the background of SDN; Sect. 2 elaborates the detection method of DDoS attack based on SVM; Sect. 3 illustrates the prototype experiment and the analysis of experimental results systematically. Section 4 summarizes the full text and looks forward to the future research focus and development trend.

2 Technical Background

2.1 SDN Architecture

As more and more mobile devices are connected to the Internet, the influx of new data challenges the requirements of the traditional network such as fast delivery, resource allocation and path control. However, the traditional network bloated system greatly improves the network management coefficient. Therefore SDN layered concept gradually become the trend of the development of the network technology, the traditional algorithm in the network hardware, operating systems, network decouple the architecture, form the Application layer, control layer as well as the data plane, but also decide the north and south respectively two connectors, mainly for the correlation between each layer, coordinate processing network traffic, The main layered architecture is shown in Fig. 1.

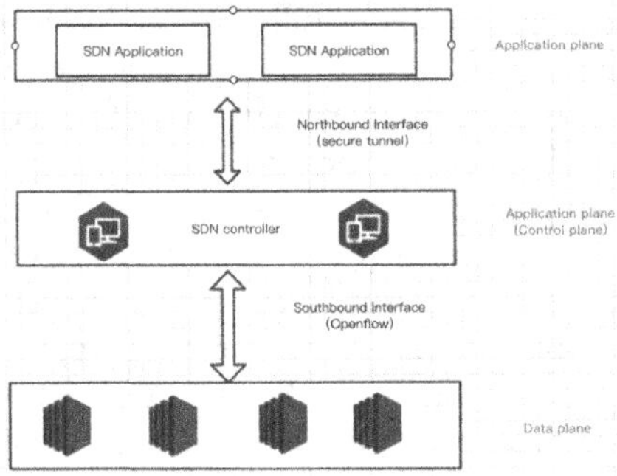

Fig. 1. SDN architecture

The control layer carries all the business logic of SDN network and maintains the topology information. Since this plane is the core plane of the control network, it must have some basic functions existing in the traditional network, such as two-three layer switching logic, VPN, DNS, DHCP and other basic routing functions to maintain the normal network operation. These basic control logic are often supported by device manufacturers and the open source community [14], and then the API is opened to the application layer for call. The application layer is a logical layer open to developers and network managers to develop self-development functions. Data plane is mainly in charge of network data flow forward, behind the clusters are often composed of hardware support Openflow switch, because the plane of the forwarding device receives from the control layer provides data stream processing results, so the interface between the data plane and control layer is also one of the important factors that affect SDN network, Openflow protocol also for statute south to the interface and the birth of a highly efficient specifically applicable to SDN architecture of south interface protocols, Its efficient and simple protocol design has also prompted many vendors to develop hardware switching devices and open source controllers that support Openflow.

2.2 Openflow Protocol

Openflow, which originated with the Stanford CleanSlate group, was originally proposed primarily to refactor traditional internet architectures. Started the project group has launched a network security project Ethane.

The protocol architecture for Openflow is shown in Fig. 2. Openflow states that the interface connection between the controller and the underlying switching equipment must establish a safe channel, and the safe channel data transmission is encrypted through TLS protocol, which is to avoid the high-risk scenario of controller hijacking (hackers impersonate authorized controller to send malicious flow table to the switch and cause network abnormalities) [15]. Data transmission in the secure channel should conform to the protocol specification standard of Openflow, which specifies the types of messages transmitted between the three controller switches. In the switch, Openflow specifies that packets are forwarded according to the rules of the flow table. Typically, we define a stream as a collection of packets with the same source/destination IP address and port number at the same time.

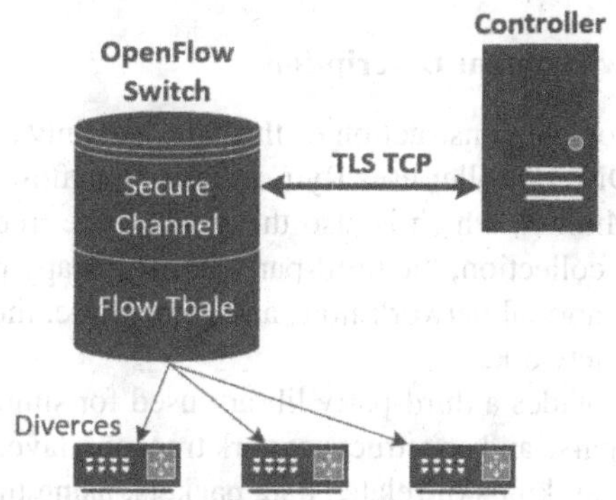

Fig. 2. Openflow protocol architecture diagram

2.3 SVM Algorithm

SVM is a supervised learning algorithm in Machine learning. The basic idea is to find an optimal decision surface that can divide two array categories in a large data set space. In order to avoid overfitting and better generalization, the decision surface to be searched should be sufficiently far away from two kinds of support vectors (data points closest to the decision surface). The SVM algorithm will keep updating iteratively to calculate the decision surface furthest away from the support vector, so as to facilitate subsequent data recognition.

The decision surface in support vector machines changes with the dimension of data. For example, the two-dimensional data features can be divided by one-dimensional straight lines, and the three-dimensional data can be divided by two-dimensional planes. In the concept of SVM, there are cases of linearly separable and linearly inseparable, but the decision surface equations of both are shown in formula (1):

$$\omega^T \chi + b = 0 \tag{1}$$

The only key coefficients in the above decision surface are omega ^T and b, where T is the transpose matrix, which need not be considered. The purpose of SVM algorithm is transformed to seek the optimal combination of omega and b. The common iterative method is the least squares error method, whose basic logic is shown as follows

Randomly select the decision surface in advance and conduct data training on the training data set. At this time, an error loss will be obtained. At this time, if the label is 0 and is recognized as 1, it is an identification error. The sum of squares of all misclassifications is calculated as shown in formula (2)

$$\sum\nolimits_i^n \omega^T \chi_i + b \tag{2}$$

.

3 Specific Analysis

3.1 Experimental Environment Description

The experimental topological construction of this study mainly uses Mininet (network simulation tool), the SDN controller uses Ryu, and the Openflow switch uses the Open vSwitch provided by Mininet, which is also the switch type frequently used in SDN. In the process of traffic collection, the third-party library Scapy provided by python is adopted to simulate the normal network flow, and meanwhile, the traffic is propagated to the established SDN network.

Python developer provides a third-party library used for simulating network traffic Scapy. The module can parse and construct network transport layer and application layer of seven layer model of all kinds of related data packets, using this feature, developers can easily implement all kinds of traffic simulation operation of network security, such as network address section scanning, network traffic pressure measurement, etc., this experiment Scapy is used to realize the TCP and UDP network traffic simulation, training for the SVM model to provide the normal network traffic data set.

3.2 Experimental Topology Description

Mininet was used to build a network topology of 3*5 (3 openflow switches +15 virtual hosts). Three switches are at the same network level, connected to the same Ryu controller, and five virtual hosts are connected under each switch. Due to the large number of network nodes in the topology, the experimental setup was built by using the python API provided by mininet, and finally started by the CLI (command line interface) of mininet.

The basic network topology is shown in Fig. 3:

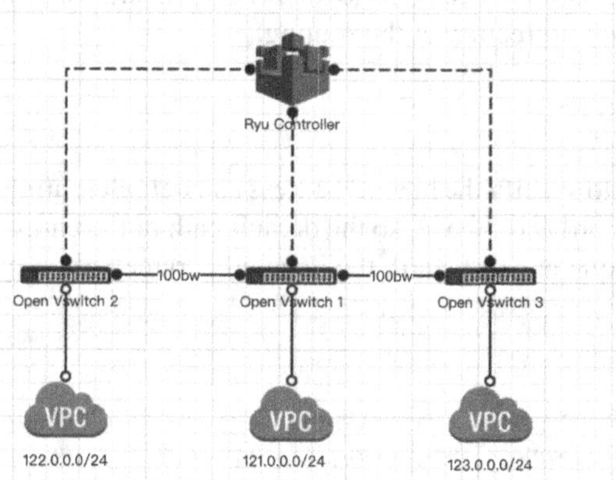

Fig. 3. Experimental topology diagram

The topology diagram uses the concept of VPC (virtual private cloud) to replace each internal private network segment, where each VPC represents a private subnet, each private network segment mask for 24 bits, are assigned the first to fifth available IP address. Take Open Vswitch1 for example, the IP address under the VPC 121.0.0.1–121.0.0.5, each IP is assigned to the VPC in the five virtual machine host, the rest of the VPC are similar to the allocation rule, and the 11th IP address is assigned to each switch as the gateway exit of VPC, such as the Open Vswitch1 gateway is 121.0.0.11. The 100bw between switches represents the link bandwidth of 100 M between them.

3.3 Topology Construction of Mininet

The key function code to add SDN network node comes from sdn_topy.py

The basic logic of this code is to build an SDN topology object with the base class of Mininet, which is the core of the whole architecture. It provides addswitch(), addhost(), addcontroller(), addlink() and other methods. By using the above method, real network topology can be simulated.

(1) Add controller node

The function of the parameter declaration forwarding devices within the topology is pointing to the controller, because mininet comes with internal controller module, if developers to write controller application as required, to declare remote controller said the connection of the controller is the remote controller, and information communication channel between the switch and controller was built using TCP transport protocol to connect, reliable transmission is to ensure a reliable communication between the transport layer protocol. In order to ensure the Security of data communication, TLS (Transport Layer Security) protocol is also used to encrypt and transmit the communication between the two, so as to avoid data being stolen by the third party, resulting in device outliers. After establishing a safe channel between the controller and the switch, the controller can use the data transmission of Openflow protocol to carry out routing, and the switch will send packets with unmatched paths to the controller, and the controller will calculate and process the routing direction of the routing.

(2) Add virtual host node

Add host node need to specify the host IP address and default routing, because the virtual host's network exit card is only one, so the default path of the entire network segment is set to the host's unique network card, the detailed parameter configuration is shown in Fig. 4:

```
h1 = net.addHost('h1', cls=Host, ip='121.0.0.1', defaultRoute=None)
h2 = net.addHost('h2', cls=Host, ip='121.0.0.2', defaultRoute=None)
h3 = net.addHost('h3', cls=Host, ip='121.0.0.3', defaultRoute=None)
    h1.cmd('ip route add 0.0.0.0/0 dev h1-eth0 scope link')
    h2.cmd('ip route add 0.0.0.0/0 dev h2-eth0 scope link')
```

Fig. 4. Description of topology node addition

3.4 Analysis of Ryu Controller Application Implementation

(1) Controller forwarding logic

In traditional network conventions, the algorithms needed for switching devices to run have been written into the device's memory when they leave the factory. Network managers only need to use the console to enter the CLI interface of the switch for configuration. But in SDN network environment, to achieve the function of traditional routing forwarding requires switch applications written in logic controller logic on the second floor and three layers, which can identify by the controller to deal with, and we also use this feature, the application of the controller, realize convection characteristics of table data collection. This part we mainly for secondary and tertiary level logic layer and the flow chart to collect pieces of code are analyzed.

The 2-layer forwarding logic mainly realizes the learning, recognition and forwarding of MAC physical addresses of network nodes. A CAM table is maintained inside the switch, which records the mapping of MAC addresses and device ports. The switch can obtain the MAC address of the machine based on the response packet, thus populating the CAM table. Packets can then be forwarded according to the CAM table, and the matching process of its mapping table is consistent with the first case.

Three-layer forwarding is mainly carried out according to the router's routing table, and its main scenario is transmission communication across network segments. For example, in this experiment, two VPCS, 121.0.0.0/24 and 122.0.0.0/24, belong to different subnet segments.In this study, three transport layer protocols, TCP, UDP and ICMP, are mainly judged to be processed by three-layer forwarding logic. Through the learning and understanding of the traditional 2-3 layer routing and switching principle, the main functions of this experiment are realized by using the API provided by the Ryu controller: to process the packet_in packets submitted by the switch to the control plane to realize the logic of switch MAC address learning and cross-subnet routing and transmission. Meanwhile, in order to monitor the flow meter rate in real time, the effective duration of the flow meter issued by the controller is set to 10 s for the convenience of subsequent flow statistics.

(2) Controller flow table collection logic

Openflow agreement, ofpts_stats message is mainly used for the controller to get flow table information exchange equipment, this experiment using ofpt_stats message request packet structure, make the frequency of the controller with 10 s periodic send switches ofpt_stats_request request link data information, report by switches ofpt_stat_reply again, put forward the key data information as abnormal flow analysis of data source. Common DDoS attackers often control a large number of target aircraft to flood the normal service and cause service paralysis. In order to achieve the attack scale that can affect the normal service operation and save efficiency, distributed flood attacks have the following characteristics: ①In order to save the machine resources of the initiator and improve the packet delivery rate, hackers often construct packets with small number of bits, so the bit size of packets in the network will be greatly reduced. ② When the traffic of hacker-controlled botnet cluster enters the SDN network, it will lead to a sharp increase in the number of source IP addresses in the network, and the source port of the data packet initiated by the machine will also rise, so as to realize single-machine multi-port data packet sending. Based on the characteristics of the above DDoS attack [16], this experiment mainly selected the information obtained from the flow table and the time period of 10 s to calculate the five features in Table 1 as the feature dimensions of SVM and logistic regression training.

Table 1. Flow table features collect indicators

Dimension	Detail info
Average packet (AP)	Average number of packets per stream
Average bytes of packets (ABP)	Average bit size of the stream packet
Ports growth rate (PG)	The growth rate of the number of ports
Flows growth rate (FG)	The growth rate of the flow
Source Ip address growth rate (SIG)	The rate of increase in the number of source IPs

3.5 Network Traffic Simulation Collection

In this experiment, the identification of DDoS abnormal traffic can be reduced to a linear separable problem, that is, a dichotomy problem. Feature samples and corresponding labels should be provided for subsequent data training using SVM. In this experiment, when simulating normal and abnormal network traffic, category records of traffic (1 means abnormal and 0 means normal) will be put into collect. Log respectively to constitute data sources. The scripts for flow simulation are all located in the flow_simulate folder, the normal_flow folder is the simulation source code for normal flow, and the netsnip-ng folder is the simulation source code for abnormal peak flow.

(1) Simulate normal flow

In the real network environment, packets are often meaningful, and the number of data bits they carry will be large and irregular, mainly for communication. To restore this feature, the use case consisting of 26 letters and 1–9 62 source character set, construct a length of 16 a string as the source of data, in which each character from 62 source character set by random function take a form, so that can highly structured transfer of content reduction in the real network packet feature.

(2) Simulate attack traffic

In 3.1, the reason why we mentioned netffin-ng is that it makes use of Linux zero-copy technology. This study USES this feature to launch Syn flood attack on our network topology to collect attack traffic data. The attack feature of Syn flood is mainly that the data bits are small and the packet growth rate increases sharply.

3.6 Traffic Characteristics

After the traffic characteristics are obtained, the data samples are divided and predicted in this study. The content of svm.py in the model directory is the training logic of support vector machine, and the content of randomforest.py is the training logic of RandomForest. GetData() implements the content to process collect_data.log. This function reads the log file and stores the feature information and traffic labels into two arrays, data1[] and data2[], according to the traffic category, to randomly scatter their contents. Subsequently, 2/3 of the data from data1[] and data2[] are taken to form training sets (train_data and train_label), and the remaining parts are taken as test sets.

Due to the characteristics of the experimental dimension into five dimensions, the dimension of the data distribution is difficult to simulate, considering the five dimensions of data distribution may not be able to use a low latitudes of the tangent plane cutting, the experiment using the linear kernel function, the data up to a higher dimensional space, easy to improve the SVM training effect, to find the best decisions, so the kernel statements chose linear kernel function (linear), trained will training results to model_tf_svm. M, the file can be embedded in the subsequent ryu controller application module, identify types of traffic. SVM is an algorithm based on geometric calculation. In order to compare with statistical methods, logistic regression was used in the experiment. Sklearn's RandomForestClassifier method was used to train the same data set.

3.7 Model Detection

In order to test the accuracy and recognition efficiency of the abnormal traffic recognition model obtained in Sect. 3.6. In the experiment, the identification application was written to the Ryu control level, detected_normal(attact).py respectively. The main logic of detected_normal.py is to get the model configuration information from detected_config.py. You just need to change the model parameters in the file, and then you can switch the detection model.

Description: RCD [0]–RCD [5] record is the flow of time and the five characteristics of the data, RCD [6] record was sponsored by the current flow type, RCD [7] is to obtain the results of the model training, training model mainly through joblib access to advance to complete the analysis of the model, five flow characteristic dimension through numpy into column type matrix is calculated to identify, predict results method returns 0 or 1, respectively, on behalf of the normal and abnormal. Finally, by comparing the traffic types initiated by itself, we can judge whether the judgment results within the time period of the current model are correct or not. To record model predicts the efficiency of the code to record before and after the timestamp, through subtraction to obtain a model to predict the time-consuming, at the same time record the time-consuming to RCD [9], facilitate subsequent statistical processing, the final record results as shown in Fig. 5.

```
2019-03-29 22:49:41 0.589285714286 177.964285714 5.3 6.3 1.5 0 normal correct 0.00372505187988
2019-03-29 22:49:51 0.575757575758 146.166666667 5.3 5.6 1.5 0 normal correct 0.00191593170166
2019-03-29 22:50:01 0.928571428571 236.171428571 5.8 6.6 1.5 0 normal correct 0.00384306907654
2019-03-29 22:50:11 0.791044776119 191.029850746 6.1 7.0 1.5 0 normal correct 0.00374484062195
2019-03-29 22:50:21 0.825396825397 190.158730159 5.8 6.7 1.4 0 normal correct 0.00255680084229
```

Fig. 5. Model detection feature record

3.8 Analysis of Experimental Results and Comparison of Efficiency

In order to measure the quality and efficiency of the model, this paper adopts the following three statistical methods to reflect the recognition effect of SVM and random forest algorithm.

(1) False alarm rate of normal flow = the number of normal flow identified as abnormal flow/The total number of normal flow
(2) Abnormal flow false alarm rate = the number of abnormal flow identified as normal flow/The total number of abnormal flow
(3) Accuracy = correctly identified traffic (including normal and abnormal)/Total traffic number

The above implementation of statistical logic has been written into result.py. The experiment takes 10 s as the time period respectively. Launch 100 times of DDoS attack traffic and 100 times of normal traffic, and then obtain three statistical rates through result.py statistics for comparison.

According to the comparison of time consumption in Fig. 6, the average time consumption of SVM is 0.24 ms, which is much lower than that of the random forest algorithm (2.56 ms). The main reason is that the SVM only records the support vector, namely the two support points closest to the decision plane, and the recognition efficiency of SVM is higher than that of the random forest. In view of the possible overfitting of SVM, the SVM algorithm can eliminate the false alarm caused by overfitting by further screening the data set and excluding some extreme points (such as network jitter, instant traffic influx, etc.).

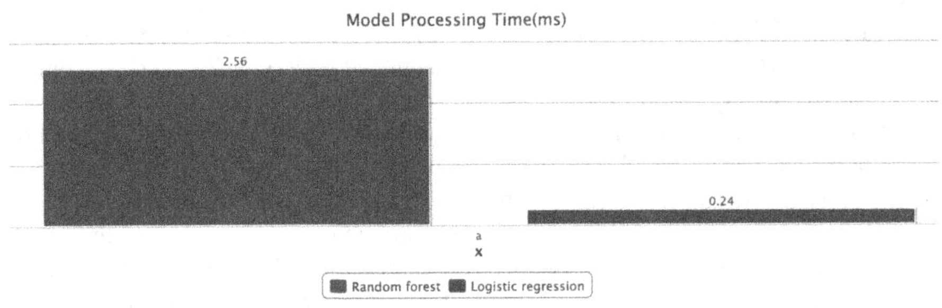

Fig. 6. The comparison of time consumption

Compared with the random forest detection method proposed by Qi Yong et al., SVM algorithm has lower recognition time. Although the recognition rate of SVM algorithm is slightly lower than that of random forest algorithm when the data set is limited and the data confoundability is high, the recognition efficiency brought by SVM algorithm is increased by hundreds of times. The improvement from millisecond to microsecond is undoubtedly more significant for the first time recognition of DDoS attacks. When the abnormal traffic attack comes, the SVM algorithm can identify it with faster efficiency to curb the network paralysis caused by the further spread of the attack. Integrated the above consideration, this study, the SVM algorithm is chosen as the final recognition model of abnormal flow, in the future research work, this research more types of attack traffic data, as well as the data of burr for further screening according to the network features, in order to obtain better DDoS attack recognition model based on SVM.

4 Conclusions

This article mainly aims at SDN network architectures and protocols for Openflow into further, by studying the mainstream open source Ryu controller programming to realize the collection of SDN network traffic, to screening, according to the features of DDos attack traffic aggregation form the characteristics of the five dimensions of sample set, from existing machine learning choose the SVM classification algorithm with random forests anomaly traffic identification module, then analyzing the actual effect and efficiency of both advantages and disadvantages are obtained. This paper adopted by the abnormal flow simulation there are some limitations of the real network environment there are different kinds of DDos attacks, this paper adopted the Syn flood as a means of attack, so in this paper, the flow chart of data has certain chanciness, model if large-scale application in the real network may be a higher rate of false positives.

DDos attack detection research has been a hot topic in the field of network security. Although machine learning training method can provide a method of training recognition model, it needs huge data set as training set to calculate in real network environment. Considering the increasing diversity of traffic in the network world, the real-time calculation of the model is inevitable to accurately judge abnormal traffic in real time, and the computing power required behind it will be greatly enhanced. It is believed that the rapid development of emerging computer technology and the emergence of quantum computing technology will make real-time streaming analysis of abnormal traffic possible.

References

1. Xiao, M.: Comparative analysis of commercial SDN schemes for cloud computing data centers. J. Mianyang Norm. Univ. **38**(02), 83–87+139 (2019)
2. Jiang, M.: Application analysis of SDN in data center. Commun. World **26**(01), 91–92 (2019)
3. Lu, W., Liu, T., Liu, X., Ye, Q.: Research on intelligent SDN wave separation network deployment. Post Telecommun. Des. Technol. (01), 26–30 (2019)
4. Zhang, Q.: Automatic deployment framework of security service chain based on SDN/NFV. Appl. Comput. Syst. **27**(03), 198–204 (2008)
5. Liu, T.: Research on node security control technology of SDN network. Beijing University of Posts and Telecommunications (2017)
6. Yang, Y., Yang, J., Sun, Y.: Research on implementation mechanism and defense of distributed denial of service attack. Comput. Eng. Des. **25**(5), 657–660 (2004)
7. Liu, S.: Link flooding attack detection and defense based on SDN and NFV. Wuhan University (2017)
8. Zheng, Z., Wang, M.: Application of k-means clustering algorithm based on big data in network security detection. J. Hubei Second Normal Univ. **33**(02), 36–40 (2016)
9. Tang, G.: Research on secure control and forwarding technology of SDN network based on password identification. University of Information Engineering of Strategic Support Force (2018)
10. Cheng, J., Gong, J., Yang, W., Zang, X.: Research on network intrusion tracking and response system based on SDN technology. J. Commun. **39**(S1), 244–250 (2008)
11. Yu, P., Qi, Y., Li, Q.: DDoS attack detection method based on random forest classification model. Comput. Appl. Res. **34**(10), 3068–3072 (2017)
12. Jadidi, J.Z, Muthukkumarasamy, V., Sithirasenan, E., et al.: Flow-based anomaly detection using neural network optimized with GSA algorithm. In: 2013 IEEE 33rd International Conference on Distributed Computing Systems Workshops, Philadelphia, PA, pp. 76–81 (2013)
13. Van Trung, P., Huong, T.T., Van Tuyen, D., et al.: A multi-criteria-based DDoS-atack prevention solution using software defined networking. In: 2015 International Conference on Advanced Technologies for Communications (ATC), Ho Chi Minh City, pp. 308–313 (2015)
14. Tang, T.A., Mhamd, L., McLernon, D., et al.: Deep learning approach for network intrusion detection in software defined networking. In: 2016 International Conference on Wireless Networks and Mobile Communications (WINCOM), Marakesh, Moroco, pp. 258–263 (2016)
15. Yu, K.: Large-scale deep learning at Baidu. In: 22nd ACM International Conference on Information & Knowledge Management, pp. 2211–2212 (2013)
16. Robinson, R.R.R., Thomas, C.: Ranking of machine learning algorithms based on the performance in classifying DDos attacks. In: 2015 IEEE Recent Advances in Intelligent Computational Systems (RAICS), Trivandrum, pp. 185–190 (2015)

An Efficient Group Signature Based Digital Currency System

Haibo Tian(✉), Peiran Luo, and Yinxue Su

Guangdong Key Laboratory of Information Security,
School of Data and Computer Science, Sun Yat-Sen University,
Guangzhou 510275, Guangdong, People's Republic of China
tianhb@mail.sysu.edu.cn

Abstract. Digital currency regulation is a hot topic. Traditional privacy-enhanced digital currency system, like the CryptoNote, seeks to protect the privacy of senders and receivers. This paper presents a digital currency system based on the group signature scheme of Boneh et al. The system can protect users' privacy and enable regulations. The system uses the one-time address technology of the CryptoNote to achieve unlinkability. It uses the group signature and an "OR" proof of the equality of two discrete logarithms to achieve untraceability. The group manager in a group signature can open a problematic transaction, restore the real identity of the sender, and revoke the private key of the sender if needed, which makes the digital currency regulatable.

Keywords: Digital currency · Group signature · Regulation · Privacy

1 Introduction

Although digital currencies such as Bitcoin have a profound impact on financial fields, they currently are not used as daily currencies. Many central banks try to follow the trend of digital currency to issue their fiat currencies. Facebook, as a company, proposes Libra, which binds legal currencies of several countries to achieve currency stability. They hope that their currency can be used in daily life, even to replace the fiat currencies of some countries. For fiat currencies of banks or currencies of companies, one of the core concerns of the government is the regulation of the currencies. The government has to prevent capital flight, enable anti-money laundering policies and so on. Some examples to show the importance of regulations are given in [2,8]. In contrast, users wish to keep their privacy. For citizens in a country, their consumption behaviors and other financial activities should be protected. Digital currencies used in daily life should not threaten privacy of users.

There are many privacy enhanced digital currency systems such as CryptoNote [16], ZCash [10], Dash [7] and Mimblewimble [15]. The CryptoNote system defines two properties of user privacy.

H. Shen and Y. Sang (Eds.): PAAP 2019, CCIS 1163, pp. 380–392, 2020.
https://doi.org/10.1007/978-981-15-2767-8_34

- Untraceability. For each incoming transaction all possible senders are equiprobable.
- Unlinkability. For any two outgoing transactions it is impossible to prove they were sent to the same person.

For the ring confidential transactions (RingCT) version of the CryptoNote, the amount of transactions are hidden too. Zcash and Dash achieve similar properties with different techniques. Mimblewimble is different since there are no addresses at all. Hinteregger and Haslhofer [9] give an analysis of Monero which is based on the CryptoNote. They show that Monero is currently mostly immune to known passive attack vectors and resistant to tracking and tracing methods applied to other cryptocurrencies. But on the other hand, their conclusion means that it is harder to regulate the XMR coins of Monero.

There are some proposals for digital currency regulations. A basic idea is to validate the legitimate of entities. In [2], a verified entity will have a certified address. In [8], an entity has an identity certificate. In [18], an entity has the membership of a group after it is registered. In [11], an entity should register their public keys. Another idea is to change the structure of a ledger. A ledger is divided into public part and private part. The public part is for user's privacy and the private part is just plain transactions, which could be regulated [13,17].

We try to balance the privacy and regulations in a scheme. We use group signatures so that all users of a digital currency system are members of a group. The group manager is an entry point of regulations. We integrate the one-time address technique and ring signature idea into the digital currency system so that user privacy is guaranteed. Comparing with other solutions, we propose the first digital currency system with enhanced privacy and regulations.

1.1 Related Works

Ateniese et al. [2] propose certified Bitcoins. They introduce an online third party to issue certified address for a user. If a user wants to spend coins in a certified address, it has to produce a signature for an embedded public key in a certified address. The identity of a user could be revealed by the third party if a certified address is used since the address is firstly generated by the third party. Lin [11] proposes a patent to specify how to reveal the identity of a transaction sender by an revocation center. A user should register their public keys to the center. A transaction sender establishes a shared secret among a sender, a receiver and the revocation center. Then a receiver could receive coins and the revocation center could reveal the identity of a transaction sender. The two proposals provides an option for a user to be regulated. However dishonest users could close the option by traditional Bitcoin address or using an unregistered key pair.

Narula et al. [13] propose a privacy preserving auditing ledger for multiple banks. Basically, transactions are stored in different banks privately. The commitments values of a transaction are added to a public ledger. From the commitments and proofs, an auditor could extract some correct statistical information. Since plain transactions are stored in banks, the identity of a transaction sender could be revealed by banks if necessary. Tian et al. [17] propose a fiat coin framework where plain transactions are also stored in different commercial banks and a central bank. Their public ledger only stores hash values. A central bank could asks a commercial bank to reveal the identity of a transaction if needed. Lampkins and Defrawy [8] propose a digital currency system based on multiparty secure computation. They suppose a set of servers that share identity certificate and public key of a user. The servers could verify the identity certificate without knowing the identity. When an address is suspected, the servers collaborate to reveal the identity of an address. The three proposals should be implemented in their framework and are not compatible to the Bitcoin unspent transaction output (UTXO) model.

Wu et al. [18] propose a linkable group signature scheme based on the well-known ACJT group signature [1]. They embed trapdoor keys for an auditor and a supervisor. An auditor could link two group signatures and a supervisor could trace the identity of a transaction sender. They did not specify how to integrate their scheme into a digital currency system. And the traceability and likability in their paper are not totally the same as those in the CryptoNote.

1.2 Contributions

Basically, we propose a group signature based digital currency system that balances the privacy and regulation requirements. It could be implemented as an alternative of the CryptoNote and are compatible to the UTXO model.

- We show how to construct a digital system based on a group signature with unlinkability property and regulation entry points.
- We further use the group signature and a ring signature to obtain untraceability.
- We show that the revocation procedure of Boneh et al. [6] is practical in the blockchain scenario.

Additionally, we show the consistency of our proposal with the CryptoNote so that techniques in the ring confidential transaction (RingCT) proposal could be integrated.

2 Preliminaries

This section defines a bilinear map, a q-strong Diffie-Hellman (q-SDH) problem and a decision linear problem. We adopt the descriptions defined in [6].

2.1 Bilinear Map

Let G_1, G_2 be two multiplicative cyclic groups of prime order p. g_1 is a generator of G_1 and g_2 is a generator of G_2. e is a computable map $e : G_1 \times G_2 \rightarrow G_T$ with the following properties:

- Bilinearity: for all $u \in G_1$, $v \in G_2$ and $a, b \in \mathbb{Z}_p$, $e(u^a, v^b) = e(u, v)^{ab}$.
- Non-degeneracy: $e(g_1, g_2) \neq 1$.

Note that $G_1 \neq G_2$ and there is no efficiently computable map from G_1 to G_2. Specially, the traditional decisional Diffie-Hellman problem in G_1 is hard. A suitable parameter set is the type D parameter in [4].

2.2 q-SDH Problem

The q-SDH problem in (G_1, G_2) is defined as follows. Given a $(q+2)$-tuple $(g_1, g_2, g_2^{\gamma}, g_2^{(\gamma^2)}, \ldots, g_2^{(\gamma^q)})$ as input where $\gamma \in \mathbb{Z}_p^*$, output a pair $(g_1^{1/(\gamma+x)}, x)$ where $x \in \mathbb{Z}_p^*$.

An adversary $\mathcal{A}$ has advantage ϵ in solving q-SDH in (G_1, G_2) if

$$Pr\left[\mathcal{A}(g_1, g_2, g_2^{\gamma}, g_2^{(\gamma^2)}, \ldots, g_2^{(\gamma^q)}) = (g_1^{1/(\gamma+x)}, x)\right] \geq \epsilon,$$

where the probability is over the random choice of γ in $\mathbb{Z}_p^*$ and the random bits of $\mathcal{A}$.

The (q, t, ϵ)-SDH assumption holds in (G_1, G_2) if no t-time adversary has advantage at least ϵ in solving the q-SDH problem in (G_1, G_2).

2.3 Decision Linear Problem

The decision linear problem in G_1 is defined as follows. Given $(u, v, h, u^a, v^b, h^c \in G_1)$ where $a, b \in \mathbb{Z}_p$ are randomly selected and $c \in \mathbb{Z}_p$, output 1 if $a + b = c$.

An adversary $\mathcal{A}$ has advantage ϵ in solving a decision linear problem in G_1 if

$$\left| \begin{array}{l} Pr\left[\mathcal{A}(u, v, h, u^a, v^b, h^{a+b}) = 1 : u, v, h \leftarrow G_1, a, b \leftarrow \mathbb{Z}_p\right] \\ -Pr\left[\mathcal{A}(u, v, h, u^a, v^b, \eta) = 1 : u, v, h, \eta \leftarrow G_1, a, b \leftarrow \mathbb{Z}_p\right] \end{array} \right| \geq \epsilon,$$

where the probability is over the random choice of the parameters to $\mathcal{A}$ and the random bits of $\mathcal{A}$.

The (t, ϵ)-Decision Linear assumption holds in G_1 if no t-time algorithm has advantage at least ϵ in solving the decision linear problem in G_1.

2.4 Group Signature

Bellare et al. [3] give three properties that a group signature scheme must satisfy. Roughly, it should be correctly verified and traced. A group signature should not reveal identity of a signer. And all group signatures should be traced to a member of the group.

This paper uses the group signature of Boneh et al. [6]. They have proved that under the (q, t, ϵ)-SDH assumption and (t, ϵ)-Decision Linear assumption, their scheme is correct, full-anonymous and full-traceable.

3 The System

We show two systems in this section. The first system enjoys the regulation and unlinkability properties. The second system additionally has the untraceability property.

3.1 System I

Basically, the system is a group signature scheme and a proof of equality of two discrete logarithms. And the proof is embedded in the group signature scheme. The system logically includes a group manager GM, many digital currency users DU_i, $1 \leq i \leq n$, many verification nodes of a blockchain VN_i, $i \in \mathbb{N}$.

System Setup. GM takes $(G_1, G_2, g_1, g_2, e, p)$ as system parameters. It then randomly selects $h, w \leftarrow G_1$ and $\xi_1, \xi_2, \lambda \leftarrow \mathbb{Z}_p$. GM computes $u = h^{\xi_1^{-1}}$, $v = h^{\xi_2^{-1}}$ and $\omega = g_2^{\lambda}$. It selects two secure hash functions $H_1 : \{0,1\}^* \rightarrow \mathbb{Z}_p$ and $H_2 : \{0,1\}^* \rightarrow G_1$. The group public key is

$$(G_1, G_2, g_1, g_2, e, p, h, u, v, w, \omega, H_1, H_2).$$

The group private key is (ξ_1, ξ_2, λ). The GM could be further divided into two logical parts. One is a register center that holds λ. The other is a revocation center that holds (ξ_1, ξ_2). The value λ could further be shared by several entities as a secret so that revocation is an operation requiring authorization from multiple departments.

User Registration. DU_i registers to GM with his own identification information. After verification, GM produces a group private key as (ID_i, x_i) where $x_i \leftarrow \mathbb{Z}_p$ is randomly selected and $ID_i = g_1^{\frac{1}{(\lambda + x_i)}}$. GM stores the identity information and their private key in a locally private database.

One-Time Address. DU_i randomly selects $\alpha' \leftarrow \mathbb{Z}_p$, sets his address as $A' = w^{\alpha'}$. DU_i stores α' locally in their wallet.

When DU_j wants to send coins to DU_i, it randomly selects $\beta' \leftarrow \mathbb{Z}_p$. DU_j computes $k_0 = H_1(A'^{\beta'})$, and computes an one-time address for DU_i as $(B = w^{\beta'}, A = A' w^{k_0})$. Figure 1 shows the one-time address in a transaction.

DU_i could check whether $A' = A / w^{H_1(B^{\alpha'})}$. If the equation holds, the coins in the output belongs to DU_i.

Coin Spending. When DU_i wants to spend some coins in an address, it simply produces a group signature in [6] and a proof of equality of two discrete logarithms.

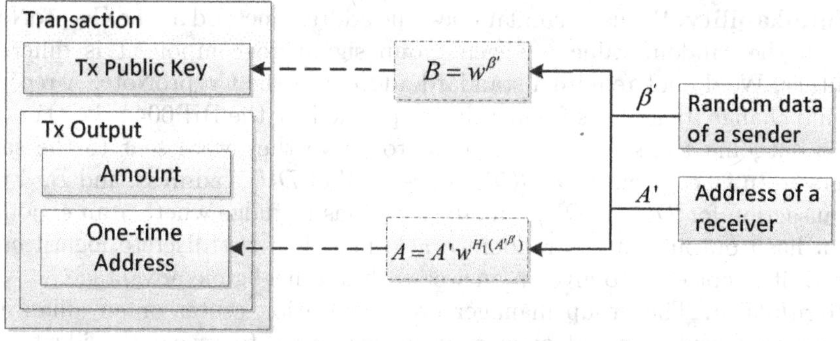

Fig. 1. Transactions with a group signature element

- DU_i selects $\beta \leftarrow \mathbb{Z}_p$, computes $T_1 = u^\alpha$, $T_2 = v^\beta$ and $T_3 = ID_i h^{\alpha+\beta}$ where $\alpha = \alpha' + H_1(B^{\alpha'})$.
- DU_i computes $\delta_1 = x_i\alpha$ and $\delta_2 = x_i\beta$. Then DU_i selects blind factors $r_\alpha, r_\beta, r_x, r_{\delta_1}, r_{\delta_2} \leftarrow \mathbb{Z}_q$ randomly.
- DU_i computes commitments $R_0 = w^{r_\alpha}$, $R_1 = u^{r_\alpha}$, $R_2 = v^{r_\beta}$, $R_4 = T_1^{r_x} \cdot u^{-r_{\delta_1}}$, $R_5 = T_2^{r_x} \cdot v^{-r_{\delta_2}}$ and

$$R_3 = e(T_3, g_2)^{r_x} \cdot e(h, \omega)^{-r_\alpha - r_\beta} \cdot e(h, g_2)^{-r_{\delta_1} - r_{\delta_2}}.$$

- DU_i then computes $c = H(T_1, T_2, T_3, R_0, R_1, R_2, R_3, R_4, R_5, M)$ where M is the other part of the transaction.
- DU_i then computes $s_\alpha = r_\alpha + c\alpha$, $s_\beta = r_\beta + c\beta$, $s_x = r_x + cx_i$, $s_{\delta_1} = r_{\delta_1} + c\delta_1$, $s_{\delta_2} = r_{\delta_2} + c\delta_2$.
- The result is $(T_1, T_2, T_3, c, s_\alpha, s_\beta, s_x, s_{\delta_1}, s_{\delta_2})$.

Node Verification. A verification node VN_i basically uses the group public key to verify the signature [6]. The additional computations are about $\tilde{R}_0$.

- A verifier computes $\tilde{R}_0 = w^{s_\alpha}/A^c$, $\tilde{R}_1 = u^{s_\alpha}/T_1^c$, $\tilde{R}_2 = v^{s_\beta}/T_2^c$, $\tilde{R}_4 = T_1^{s_x}/u^{s_{\delta_1}}$, $\tilde{R}_5 = T_2^{s_x}/v^{s_{\delta_2}}$, and

$$\tilde{R}_3 = e(T_3, g_2)^{s_x} \cdot e(h, \omega)^{-s_\alpha - s_\beta} \cdot e(h, g_2)^{-s_{\delta_1} - s_{\delta_2}} \cdot (e(T_3, \omega)/e(g_1, g_2))^c.$$

- The verifier checks whether $c = H(T_1, T_2, T_3, \tilde{R}_0, \tilde{R}_1, \tilde{R}_2, \tilde{R}_3, \tilde{R}_4, \tilde{R}_5, M)$. If the equation holds, the group signature is valid.

Properties. We give a simple analysis of the system I.

- **Double Spending.** A group member could spend some coins only when the member knows the exponent of A. In the UTXO model, if A has been used in the verification procedure and the signature is valid, the output will be removed from the UTXO set. So the usage of group signature does not introduce more double spending chances.

- **Unlinkability.** We use a similar one-time address method as the CryptoNote. With the random value β', each group signature component is different. Futher, We do not require a standard address as the CryptoNote. A receiver could change its address frequently as specified by the BIP0044 [12]. For any two outgoing transactions, it is hard to prove they were sent to the same person. In fact, given A' of DU_i's address, $\tilde{A}'$ of DU_j's address, and B, A in a transaction for DU_i or DU_j, an adversary has to judge whether an exponent is a hash output. In the random oracle model, if the discrete logarithm is hard, it is not easy to give an answer with non-negligible advantage.
- **Regulation.** The group manager or a revocation center or an alliance of revocation centers could open a group signature to reveal the identity of transaction sender. Suppose a group manager with a database storing users' information. It computes $ID = \frac{T_3}{T_1^{\xi_1} \cdot T_2^{\xi_2}}$. Then it finds the user's private key and their identity in the local database. The identity is then revealed. If it is required to revoke the user, the group manager publishes (ID, x) in the blockchain. We adopt the revocation procedure in a separate subsection.

Finally, we note that the system I only allows group members to spend coins. If a user does not register, it has no chance to participate in the system. This is different to the proposals in [2,11].

3.2 System II

The system I above does not provide untraceability. The system II does. The system I and II enjoy some same modules including system setup, user registration and one-time address generation. A new coin spending procedure and a node verification procedure are needed.

Ring Coin Spending. The system I proof the equality of two discrete logarithms. The system II provides a "OR" proof of the equality of two discrete logarithms, which forms a ring signature. DU_i draws a set of addresses with the same amount coin to form a set $\{A_l | 1 \leq l \leq m\}$ where $m \geq 2$ is the size of the set. We use A_{i^*} to denote DU_i's address. DU_i computes as follows.

- DU_i computes a group signature in the same way as the system I except that R_0 is not computed and hashed. The group signature is

$$(T_1, T_2, T_3, c, s_\alpha, s_\beta, s_x, s_{\delta_1}, s_{\delta_2})$$

  where $T_1 = u^\alpha$ and $\alpha = \alpha' + H_1(B^{\alpha'})$.
- DU_i selects randomly $(c_l, s_l \in \mathbb{Z}_p)$ for $1 \leq l \leq m$ and $l \neq i^*$.
- For $l \neq i^*$, DU_i computes $R_0^l = w^{s_l} / A_l^{c_l}$, $L_0^l = u^{s_l} / T_1^{c_l}$.
- For $l = i^*$, DU_i randomly selects $r_p \leftarrow \mathbb{Z}_p$, computes $R_0^{i^*} = w^{r_p}$ and $L_0^{i^*} = u^{r_p}$.
- DU_i then computes $c = H(R_0^1, L_0^1, \ldots, R_0^m, L_0^m)$ and $c_{i^*} = c - c_1 - \ldots - c_{i^*-1} - c_{i^*+1} - \ldots - c_m \bmod p$.

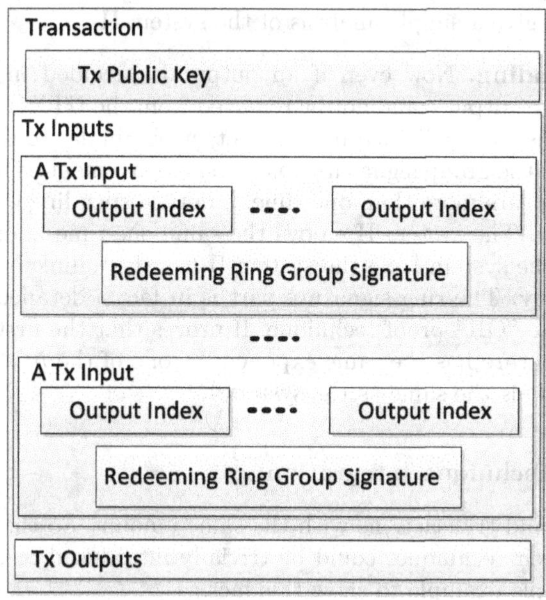

Fig. 2. An input in a transaction with ring group signature

- DU_i computes $s_{i^*} = r_p + c_{i^*}\alpha$.
- The redeeming ring group signature is

$$(T_1, T_2, T_3, c, s_\alpha, s_\beta, s_x, s_{\delta_1}, s_{\delta_2}, c_1, s_1, \ldots, c_m, s_m).$$

With the redeeming ring group signature, Fig. 2 shows a possible structure of multiple inputs. Each input should include m output indexes. For each input, there is a redeeming group signature. Note that an output index here includes a transaction identity and an output counter.

Ring Node Verification. A verification node VN_i uses the group public key to verify the group signature part and then verifies the ring signature part.

- A verifier computes $\tilde{R}_1 = u^{s_\alpha}/T_1^c$, $\tilde{R}_2 = v^{s_\beta}/T_2^c$, $\tilde{R}_4 = T_1^{s_x}/u^{s_{\delta_1}}$, $\tilde{R}_5 = T_2^{s_x}/v^{s_{\delta_2}}$, and

$$\tilde{R}_3 = e(T_3, g_2)^{s_x} \cdot e(h, w)^{-s_\alpha - s_\beta} \cdot e(h, g_2)^{-s_{\delta_1} - s_{\delta_2}} \cdot (e(T_3, w)/e(g_1, g_2))^c.$$

- The verifier checks whether $c = H(T_1, T_2, T_3, \tilde{R}_1, \tilde{R}_2, \tilde{R}_3, \tilde{R}_4, \tilde{R}_5, M)$. If the equation holds, the group signature part is valid.
- The verifier computes $\tilde{R}_0^l = w^{s_l}/A_l^{c_l}$ and $\tilde{L}_0^l = u^{s_l}/T_1^{c_l}$ for $1 \leq l \leq m$.
- The verifier checks whether $c_1 + ... + c_m = H(\tilde{R}_0^1, \tilde{L}_0^1, \ldots, \tilde{R}_0^m, \tilde{L}_0^m) \bmod p$. If the equation holds, the ring signature part is valid and the whole ring group signature is valid.

Properties. We give a simple analysis of the system II.

- **Double Spending.** Now even if an output is included in an input of a transaction, the output could not be removed from the UTXO set. In fact, the ledger is not easy to be divided into two sets now. Similar to the CryptoNote, the value T_1 in the group signature has the same exponent as the real address A. So if T_1 appears more than one time, a double spending event happens.
- **Unlinkability.** The system II enjoys the same one-time address generation procedure as the system I. So the system II has the unlinkability property.
- **Untraceability.** The ring signature part is in fact a detailed common construction of the "OR" proof technique. If proves that the first element T_1 in the group signature has the same exponent as one of the m addresses.
- **Regulation.** It is the same as the system I.

3.3 RingCT Technique Integration

It is not easy to find transactions with the same amount. So there is a RingCT proposal [14]. Their techniques could be trivially introduced to the system I or II. We give a simple example to show this fact.

In the coin spending face, suppose DU_j wants to transfer b_1 coins to DU_i from an address with coins a. Suppose the transaction fee is f. Then the value in the input address has a commitment $C_{in} = w^x v^a$ where x is a random value selected by the one who sends coins to DU_j. DU_j could obtain x by decrypt a ciphertext including x. The output to DU_i has a commitment $C_{o1} = w^{y_1} v^{b_1}$ where $y_1 \in \mathbb{Z}_p$ is a random value selected by DU_j. DU_j should encrypt y_1 for DU_j. For example, DU_j computes $H_1(A'^{\beta'}|\text{"}EncKey\text{"}) \oplus y_1$. An exchange address has a commitment $C_{o2} = w^{y_2} v^{b_2}$ where $y_2 \in \mathbb{Z}_p$ is a random value selected by DU_j. Then it is expected that $C_{in}/(C_{o1}C_{o2}v^f) = w^{x-y_1-y_2}$. Let $z = x - y_1 - y_2 \bmod p$. Next put the input address A of DU_j and the amount committed in the transaction together, one could make a value-address mixture $w^{\alpha+z}$. With the exponent value of the mixture, a ring group signature could be produced.

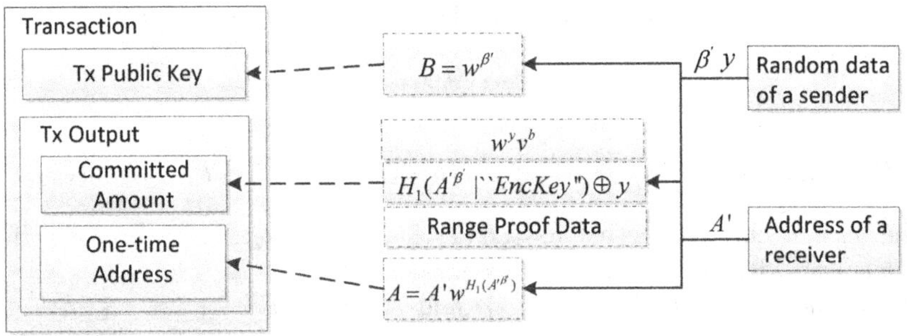

Fig. 3. An output in a transaction with RingCT technique

To further make the proposal practical, a range proof technique should be used to prove the range of committed value. We could not see any obstacles to apply the aggregate Schnorr non-linkable ring signature (ANSL) in [14] or the Bulletproofs technique in [5]. Any efficient range proof technique could be applied here. Figure 3 shows a full-fledged output with RingCT techniques. Note that in the range proof phase, the sender needs more random values except β' and y.

Note that when receivers check whether they own some coins, they should check the committed amount field in transactions.

3.4 Revocation

As the system runs, users may be revoked from the system. We integrate the revocation method in [6] into the digital currency system.

Blockchain Revocation List. A group manager with the private key λ publishes the private keys information of a revoked user in the blockchain. That is, when a new block is produced, the block may include some transactions produced by the group manager where revoked key pairs are included. The revocation information in the blockchain forms a list

$$RL_{ht} = ((ID_1, ID_1^*, x_1), \ldots, (ID_r, ID_r^*, x_r))$$

where $ID_i^* = g_2^{1/\lambda + x_i} \in G_2$ and the ht is a specified block height.

Group Public Key Update. Suppose the current block height is $1 \leq ht$, the current group public key includes (g_1, g_2, ω). Now a new revoked private key information (ID_1, ID_1^*, x_1) is added to the block $ht+1$. When the block $ht+1$ is confirmed, any verifier should produce a new group public key. The new group key includes $\hat{g}_1, \hat{g}_2, \hat{w}$ where $\hat{g}_1 = ID_1$, $\hat{g}_2 = ID_1^*$ and $\omega = g_2 \cdot (ID_1^*)^{-x_1}$.

User Private Key Update. Suppose the private key of a user is (ID^*, x) when the maximal block height is ht. When the block $ht + 1$ is confirmed, if the signer needs not spend coins, it could do nothing. However, if the signer wants to spend some coins, the signer should update their private key. The new private key of the user should be $(\hat{ID}, x)$ where $\hat{ID} = ID^{\frac{1}{x - x_1}} / ID^{* \frac{1}{x - x_1}}$. If the private key of a user is updated according to the RL_{ht-d}, and the user wants to spend some coins after block $ht + 1$ appears, then the user should update their private key according to the RL_{ht+1} where $d \in \mathbb{N}$.

When a verification node VN verifies a group signature, if should try the current group public key and its previous group public key for a block creation time to tolerate network delay. If a user is revoked at block ht, then after block $ht + 1$, the revoked user could not spend any coins.

Unfreeze Coins. If the coins the system are issued by a central organization, a revoked user may get back their coins after the user is inspected. To do this, the user should provide their private keys in the wallet so that the organization could make sure the total amount of revoked coins of the user. Then, the organization issue the same amount coins to the user with new address. The user certainly should apply new private keys from the group manager.

4 Performance

An instance of the type D parameter set is the d224 parameter set [4]. A group signature in the system I includes three elements of G_1 and six elements of $\mathbb{Z}_p$. The total length is 336 bytes. The redeeming signature in the system II depends on the number of mixed addresses. Suppose there are three extra addresses in the input script of a transaction, the total length of the signature is about 560 bytes. If there are six extra addresses, the total length is about 728 bytes.

We simulate the whole procedure in the paper based on a signature library provided in the pairing based cryptography web site. We also checks the libXSGS project in the Github web site to confirm the revocation procedure since the type D parameter has no useful map from G_2 to G_1. We use a virtual machine hosted in a notebook with a 1.8 GHz and a 1.9 GHz CPUs and 2G memory. The operation system is Ubuntu 18.04.2. The system setup step costs about 150 ms. The system I group signature generation time is about 25 ms. The node verification time of the system I is about 100 ms. The system II ring group signature generation time depends on the mixed addresses. Suppose there are six extra addresses. Then the signature generation time is about 110 ms and the node verification time is about 115 ms.

5 Conclusion

We show group signature based digital currency systems. The system I has unlinkability and regulation property. The system II additionally has untraceability. The two systems could be enhanced by the ring confidential transaction techniques to make them practical. Our systems are suitable to the UTXO model. The group signature gives us an opportunity to reveal identity of a user and freeze coins of a user. If coins are issued by a central organization, there is a chance to unfreeze coins.

Acknowledgments. This work is supported by the National Key R&D Program of China (2017YFB0802500), Guangxi Key Laboratory of Cryptography and Information Security (No. GCIS201711), Natural Science Foundation of China (61672550), Fundamental Research Funds for the Central Universities (No. 17lgjc45). Natural Science Foundation of Guangdong Province of China (2018A0303130133).

References

1. Ateniese, G., Camenisch, J., Joye, M., Tsudik, G.: A practical and provably secure coalition-resistant group signature scheme. In: Bellare, M. (ed.) CRYPTO 2000. LNCS, vol. 1880, pp. 255–270. Springer, Heidelberg (2000). https://doi.org/10.1007/3-540-44598-6_16
2. Ateniese, G., Faonio, A., Magri, B., de Medeiros, B.: Certified bitcoins. IACR Cryptology ePrint Archive 2014, 76 (2014)
3. Bellare, M., Micciancio, D., Warinschi, B.: Foundations of group signatures: formal definitions, simplified requirements, and a construction based on general assumptions. In: Biham, E. (ed.) EUROCRYPT 2003. LNCS, vol. 2656, pp. 614–629. Springer, Heidelberg (2003). https://doi.org/10.1007/3-540-39200-9_38
4. Ben, L.: On the implementation of pairing-based cryptosystems. Stanford University (2007)
5. Bünz, B., Bootle, J., Boneh, D., Poelstra, A., Wuille, P., Maxwell, G.: Bulletproofs: short proofs for confidential transactions and more. In: 2018 IEEE Symposium on Security and Privacy (SP), pp. 315–334, May 2018
6. Boneh, D., Boyen, X., Shacham, H.: Short group signatures. In: Franklin, M. (ed.) CRYPTO 2004. LNCS, vol. 3152, pp. 41–55. Springer, Heidelberg (2004). https://doi.org/10.1007/978-3-540-28628-8_3
7. Duffield, E., Hagan, K.: Darkcoin: Peer-to-peer cryptocurrency with anonymous blockchain transactions and an improved proof-of-work system (2014). https://docs.dash.org/en/stable/introduction/about.html. Accessed 2 Aug 2019
8. El Defrawy, K., Lampkins, J.: Founding digital currency on secure computation. In: Proceedings of the 2014 ACM SIGSAC Conference on Computer and Communications Security, CCS 2014, pp. 1–14. ACM, New York (2014)
9. Hinteregger, A., Haslhofer, B.: An empirical analysis of Monero cross-chain traceability (2019). https://arxiv.org/abs/1812.02808. Accessed 2 Aug 2019
10. Hopwood, D., Bowe, S., Hornby, T., Wilcox, N.: Zcash protocol specification version 2019.0.4 (2019). https://zcash.readthedocs.io/en/latest/. Accessed 2 Aug 2019
11. Lin, Q.: An anonymous digital money trading supervision method with hidden center (2019). http://pss-system.cnipa.gov.cn/sipopublicsearch/portal/uiIndex.shtml
12. Marek, P., Pavol, R.: Multi-account hierarchy for deterministic wallets, 24 April 2014
13. Narula, N., Vasquez, W., Virza, M.: zkLedger: privacy-preserving auditing for distributed ledgers. In: 15th USENIX Symposium on Networked Systems Design and Implementation (NSDI 2018), pp. 65–80, Renton, WA, April 2018. USENIX Association (2018)
14. Noether, S., Mackenzie, A., Monero Community Team: Ring confidential transactions (2016). https://www.researchgate.net/publication/311865049_Ring_Confidential_Transactions
15. Poelstra, A.: Mimblewimble (2016). http://mimblewimble.cash/20161006-WhitePaperUpdate-e9f45ec.pdf. Accessed 4 Aug 2019
16. Saberhagen, N.: Cryptonote v 2.0 (2013). https://www.mendeley.com/catalogue/cryptonote-v-20/. Accessed 1 Aug 2019

17. Tian, H., Chen, X., Ding, Y., Zhu, X., Zhang, F.: AFCoin: a framework for digital fiat currency of Central Banks based on account model. In: Guo, F., Huang, X., Yung, M. (eds.) Inscrypt 2018. LNCS, vol. 11449, pp. 70–85. Springer, Cham (2019). https://doi.org/10.1007/978-3-030-14234-6_4
18. Zheng, H., Wu, Q., Qin, B., Zhong, L., He, S., Liu, J.: Linkable group signature for auditing anonymous communication. In: Susilo, W., Yang, G. (eds.) ACISP 2018. LNCS, vol. 10946, pp. 304–321. Springer, Cham (2018). https://doi.org/10.1007/978-3-319-93638-3_18

Detecting Anomalies in Cluster System Using Hybrid Deep Learning Model

Chuming Xiao, Jiaming Huang, and Weigang Wu(✉)

School of Data and Computer Science, Sun Yat-sen University, Guangzhou, China
{xiaochm,huangjm39,wuweig}@mail2.sysu.edu.cn

Abstract. Anomaly detection is of great importance for data centers. It could help operations discover system failures and perform root cause analysis. In recent years, deep learning has achieved great results in many fields. Therefore, people begin to pay attention to applying deep learning for automatic anomaly detection. Convolution Neural Network (CNN) and Long Short-Term Memory (LSTM) are two classical structures in deep learning, which could effectively detect anomalies from system logs. However, the existing CNN-based and LSTM-based models have their shortcomings.

In this paper, we propose a novel hybrid model for detecting anomalies from system logs, which mainly consist of CNN and LSTM. Considering logs as natural language sequences, the hybrid model embeds logs first and extracts features from embedding vectors with a convolution layer. Then LSTM is used to automatically learn temporal log patterns from normal execution. The proposed model compares the log patterns that occur in practice with the log patterns it has learned before and detects anomalies when practical log patterns deviate from the model trained from log data under normal execution.

To evaluate the performance of our model, we conduct experiments over large log data. The experiment results show that the hybrid model combines the advantages of CNN and LSTM models, which is an unsupervised model, reduces the requirements of training data set, and achieves great result in anomaly detection.

Keywords: Log analysis · Anomaly detection · CNN · LSTM · Cluster management

1 Introduction

Anomaly detection is of importance for modern data centers, which can help operators run and maintain a secure and stable cluster system. When an abnormal event occurs in the cluster, it can alert the system administrators in time to take corresponding measures, so that the system would not be damaged by the abnormal event, or the damage caused by the abnormal event would be minimized. If an anomaly occurs on one machine in the data center and is not detected in time, the anomaly will quickly spread to other machines, causing significant losses [1, 2]. Therefore, the role of anomaly detection is becoming more and more important. However, with the rapid development of the Internet, the

H. Shen and Y. Sang (Eds.): PAAP 2019, CCIS 1163, pp. 393–404, 2020.
https://doi.org/10.1007/978-981-15-2767-8_35

architectures and service types of the cluster get increasingly more complex, anomaly detection is facing great challenges [3, 4].

Anomaly detection uses various data sources. Some make use of monitoring data of system resources usage [5], such as CPU utilization. Some employ system performance data [6], such as system response time. And some apply system logs [7]. System logs record system states and significant events at critical points in real-time to help debug performance issues and failures, as well as perform root cause analysis. Such log data is universally available in cluster systems, which is a valuable resource for online monitoring and anomaly detection.

Many efforts have been made to detecting anomalies from logs. The existing log-based anomaly detection algorithms can be broadly classified into three groups. The first one is statistical-based approaches [8–11], which detect anomaly based on rules or workflows. Such methods can obtain a good accuracy for anomaly detection for specific systems when rules or workflows are appropriately defined. However, they require rich domain knowledge as well as are weak on portability. The second is machine learning-based approaches [12–15], which use machine learning algorithms, for example, Support Vector Machine (SVM), to detect anomalies. Such methods avoid ad-hoc features but are more time-consuming when facing large log data. The last one is deep learning-based approaches [16–18]. Deep learning models can effectively learn the patterns from logs, which improves automation and accuracy. Convolution Neural Network (CNN) [19] and Long Short-Term Memory (LSTM) [20] are the two most classic models in deep learning. CNN is good at capturing local features, while LSTM is good at grasping the long-term dependencies in time series. Both of them have been applied in log anomaly detection. The CNN-based model [16] is a supervised model, which needs both normal and abnormal logs for training but achieves great results in log anomaly detection. The LSTM-based model [17], which is unsupervised, only requires logs under normal execution for training, but the detection accuracy is not good enough.

For the reason that CNN and LSTM have their advantages and disadvantages, researchers begin to combine these two models to achieve better results. But existing researches on combining CNN and LSTM are mainly about the natural language process. There is no similar research in the field of log anomaly detection.

In this paper, we propose a novel hybrid deep learning model combining CNN and LSTM for anomaly detection with system logs. We convert system logs into vectorized log sequences, utilize CNN to extract the features from log sequences, and then use LSTM to learn the implicit patterns in logs from normal execution. The model detects anomalies when practical log patterns deviate from the model trained from log data under normal execution. To evaluate the performance of the hybrid model, we conduct experiments on the Hadoop Distributed File System (HDFS) log data [10]. The experiment results show that the hybrid model, which is unsupervised, only needs logs under normal execution for training, as well as achieves great accuracy in anomaly detection.

In general, the main contributions of this paper are summarized below:

1. we propose a hybrid model that mainly consists of CNN and LSTM. It has both advantages of CNN and LSTM, achieves an accuracy as great as that of the CNN model, and is an unsupervised model, which only needs log data under normal execution for training like LSTM.

2. We conduct experiments on HDFS logs to evaluate the proposed model. The experiment results show that the hybrid model has both advantages of CNN and LSTM.

In Sect. 2, we introduce related works about log processing approaches as well as existing log-based anomaly detection algorithms. In Sect. 3, we describe the log processing approach we adopt, and the structure of our hybrid model in detail. We conduct experiments and present results in Sect. 4. Finally, we summarize our method and future work in Sect. 5.

2 Related Work

2.1 Log Processing Approaches

System logs are unstructured data printed in time sequence. In general, each log entry can be decomposed into two parts: constant and variable. The constant part refers to the messages printed directly from the source code, while the variable part refers to the information in the log which can reflect the current system state. We can extract log keys from constant parts, where log keys are the common constant message in all similar log entries. For example, as shown in Fig. 1, in the log entry "Running task 0.0 in stage 0.0 (TID 0)", the constant part is "Running task in stage (TID)", and the variable part is the remaining after removing constant parts, which is "0.0, 0.0, 0". From these two similar log entries, we can extract a log key, "Running task * in stage * (TID *)".

```
17/06/09 20:10:45 INFO executor.Executor: Running task 0.0 in stage 0.0 (TID 0)
17/06/09 20:10:45 INFO executor.Executor: Running task 2.0 in stage 0.0 (TID 2)
```

Fig. 1. Spark system log example

Since system source codes are usually not easy to get, we have to decompose log entries in existing log files and extract log keys from constant parts by ourselves. Log processing is to convert unstructured logs into a structured representation, usually separating log entries into constant parts and variable parts, and then extracting all the log keys from constant parts.

There are two kinds of log processing approaches [7]: clustering and heuristic. The log processing approach adopted in this article is a heuristic method. We describe it in Sect. 3.1.

2.2 Anomaly Detection Algorithm

Existing log-based anomaly detection algorithms can be broadly classified into the following three categories: statistical methods, machine learning methods, and deep learning methods.

(1) *Statistical methods*: Statistical methods mainly include rule-based methods, principal component analysis (PCA), and execution path extraction. Yen et al. [8] use keywords like "IP address" to parse logs and analyze the features based on predefined rules. Fu et al. [9] leverage a rule-based approach to identify the log keys, and detect anomalies with log keys in distributed system logs. Xu et al. [10] utilize abstract syntax tree (Abstract Syntax Tree) to generates two log variable vectors by parsing system source code, then analyze extracted patterns from the vectors using PCA. Yu et al. [11] propose a model, CloudSeer, which first builds the workflow of each management task based on normal executions, and then checks log messages against a set of automata for workflow divergences.
(2) *Machine learning methods*: To improve the applicability of log-based anomaly detection algorithms, so that an algorithm can not only be applied to a certain system log, people began to explore the application of machine learning methods in the field of anomaly detection for logs. Fulp et al. [12] use a sliding window to parse system logs and predict failures using Support Vector Machine (SVM). Yadwadkar et al. [13] utilize a Hidden Markov Model (HMM) to detect anomalies in system logs. Lou et al. [14] propose a Bayesian-based method to construct graphs from logs. Breier et al. [15] use data mining techniques to build dynamic rules for anomaly detection.
(3) Deep learning methods: In recent years, great progress has been made in the research of neural networks, and good results have been achieved in various fields, including anomaly detection for logs. Lu et al. [16] leverage convolutional neural networks (CNN) to extract features from system logs, use a multi-layer perceptron to learn the patterns from the features, and then detect anomalies with the learned patterns. Du et al. [17] leverage Long Short-Term Memory (LSTM) network to learn log patterns from logs and detect anomalies with the patterns. What's more, Brown et al. [18] learn the implicit patterns in logs with Recurrent Neural Network (RNN) and attention mechanisms.

Since CNN and LSTM have their advantages and disadvantages, we envisage whether we can combine these two models to retain their advantages and eliminate their disadvantages. In the next section, we will describe the hybrid model in detail.

3 The Hybrid Model

In this section, we first introduce how we process system logs, then provide an overview of the hybrid model and introduce its internal structure.

3.1 Log Processing

We perform log processing to generate structural input for our hybrid deep learning model. Firstly, we divide the entire logs by identifiers (defined by [10]). An identifier is an object and has a certain execution path. For example, *block_ID* is an identifier token in HDFS logs. With *block_a*, a specific identifier, we can determine the execution path of *block_a*. The execution path is a group of some logs sorted by time, recording the execution state of *block_a*. With identifiers, we can divide HDFS logs into many groups, each group corresponds to a block.

For each log entry, as demonstrated in Sect. 2.1, we divide it into a constant part and a variable part. Then, Spell algorithm [21], an unsupervised log processing approach based on the idea of the longest common subsequence, is used to find out log keys from all constant parts. By numbering logs key, we can map each unique log key to a unique number. Each log entry corresponds to a log key, that is, corresponds to a number. By this means, we convert each log entry to a number. Thus, a group of logs is converted to a series of numbers, which is called a log key sequence of an identifier.

Let $K = \{k_1, k_2, \ldots, k_n\}$ be the set of distinct log keys of a system. A log key sequence reflects an execution path that leads to that particular execution order of the log print statements. Let m_i denotes the value of the key at the position i in a log key sequence. Apparently, m_i take one of the n possible keys from K, and is strongly dependent on the recent keys that appear before m_i.

3.2 Overview of the Hybrid Model

As shown in Fig. 2, the hybrid model mainly consists of Logkey2vec layer, convolution layer, LSTM, and linear layer.

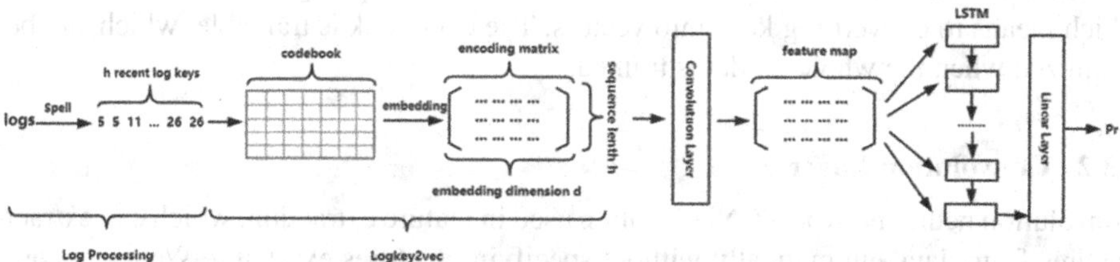

Fig. 2. Structure of the hybrid model

We model anomaly detection as a multi-class classification problem, where each distinct log key defines a class. The input is a history of recent log keys, which belong to the same identifier. We utilize the Logkey2vec layer to parse a log key sequence of several recent log keys to an embedded log matrix. Then features are extracted from the embedded log matrix by convolution layer and are fed into LSTM. Next, the LSTM layer learns log patterns from the features. Finally, the linear layer generates the output, a probability distribution over the n log keys from K, representing the probability of each log key that would appear at the next moment.

Suppose m_t is the log key that appears at time t. The input of the model is a window w of the h most recent log keys belong to an identifier, that is, $w = \{m_{t-h}, \ldots, m_{t-2}, m_{t-1}\}$, where each m_i is in K and is the log key number of the log entry e_i. For those identifiers whose log key sequence shorter that h, we pad 0 at the tail of log key sequences. The output of the model is $Pr[m_t = k_i|w]$, where $k_i \in K(i = 1, \ldots, n)$, which represents the probability of each log key in K that would appear at time t.

In the training phase, the hybrid model utilizes log history records under normal execution as the training dataset. The class label used for training is the log event that appears at time t. For example, suppose a log key sequence, $\{k_1, k_2, k_3, k_4, k_3, k_4\}$, and window size h is 3, then the input and the class label pairs will be: $\{k_1, k_2, k_3 \rightarrow k_4\}$, $\{k_2, k_3, k_4 \rightarrow k_3\}$, $\{k_3, k_4, k_3 \rightarrow k_4\}$. We use cross-entropy loss and Adam method for training.

In the testing phase, the model detects anomalies by comparing m_t, the log key that appears at time t, with the probability distribution Pr. It is worth noting that various log keys may appear at time t when under normal execution, for example, when a system tries to connect to a host, m_t may belong to log key "*Waiting for * to respond*" or "*Connected to **", both of them means the system is under normal execution. Therefore, we sort possible log keys based on their probability value. If m_t is among the top g candidates, we treat it as normal value. Otherwise, we think an anomaly has happened.

3.3 The Structure of the Hybrid Model

3.3.1 Logkey2vec Layer

To better present the correlation between log keys, we utilize a codebook of size $n \times s$, where n is dictionary dimension, i.e. the number of log keys, and s is embedded dimension, to map each log key in a log key sequence to a vector. For instance, for a window log key sequence $w = \{m_{t-h}, \ldots, m_{t-2}, m_{t-1}\}$ with length h, the whole sequence will be encoded as a matrix $M \in \mathbb{R}^{h \times s}$. We call this mapping process Logkey2vec, which means to convert log keys into vectors. The codebook is trainable, which can be optimized when the whole model is trained.

3.3.2 Convolution Layer

Convolution neural network (CNN) is often used in feature extraction, which can extract features from data automatically without specifying features explicitly. We use a convolution layer, which convolutes over the embedded matrix with a filter, to extract the features of the encoding matrix M. To avoid the loss of edge information, we fill the matrix with "Same" padding. The activation function is Leaky Rectified Linear Unit (LReLU). For the encoding matrix M, we generate feature map F with Eq. 1,

$$F = f(W \circ M + b) \tag{1}$$

where $F \in \mathbb{R}^{h \times s}$, $\circ$ denotes convolutional operation, W is a filter with size $w_1 \times w_2$, b is bias, and f is activation function LReLU. W and b are learnable parameters. After convolution operation, we feed the feature map F to the LSTM layer directly.

3.3.3 LSTM Layer

LSTM is a variant of Recurrent Neural Network (RNN), which is capable of learning long-term dependencies in time series. In system logs, the occurrence of a log if often related to the logs of the previous period. That is to say, there is a strong long-term dependency in log key sequences. To learn the pattern in log key sequences, LSTM is used to analyses the feature map F. The detailed structure of a single LSTM cell is shown in Fig. 3(a).

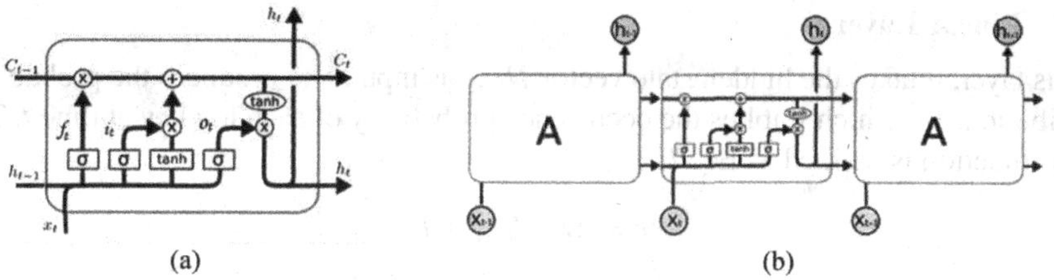

Fig. 3. (a) The detailed structure of a single LSTM cell. (b) The structure of LSTM

A single LSTM cell has two inputs, one is x_t, the data input at the current time, the other is h_{t-1}, the outputs of the previous time. After inputting data, the LSTM cell obtains the new cell state and output by updating and calculating. The cell state is the historical information saved by the LSTM cell from the previous input. Updating and computing operations are implemented mainly through a structure called gate. There are three gates in an LSTM unit, namely, forget gate, input gate, and output gate.

The first gate is the forget gate, which decides how much information from the previous time $t-1$ will be thrown away, which is formulated as:

$$f_t = \sigma\left(W_f\left[h_{t-1}; x_t\right] + b_f\right) \tag{2}$$

where $f_t \in [0, 1]$. The notation σ represents a sigmoid function, [;] represents a concatenation operation. The learnable parameters are W_f and b_f.

The second operation is the input gate, which decides how much information can be saved from the input at the current time t. It can be calculated as Eq. 3,

$$i_t = \sigma\left(W_i\left[h_{t-1}; x_t\right] + b_i\right) \tag{3}$$

where $i_t \in [0, 1]$, representing how much information would be stored in the cell state. Now, we can update the cell state as Eq. 4,

$$C_t = f_t * C_{t-1} + i_t * tanh\left(W_C\left[h_{t-1}; x_t\right] + b_C\right) \tag{4}$$

where C_{t-1} is the cell state at time $t-1$, C_t is the cell state at time t. The notation $*$ is elementwise multiplication. Finally, the output gate generates the output o_t as Eq. 5, and transforms the updated cell state into the hidden state h_t as Eq. 6.

$$o_t = \sigma\left(W_o\left[h_{t-1}; x_t\right] + b_o\right) \tag{5}$$

$$h_t = o_t * \tanh(C_t) \tag{6}$$

The above operation shows how historical information is passed to and maintained in a single LSTM cell. A series of LSTM cells form an unrolled version of the recurrent model as shown in Fig. 3(b). Each cell maintains a hidden vector h_{t-i} and a cell state vector C_{t-i}. Both are passed to the next cell to initialize its state.

In this paper, we utilize one LSTM cell for each log key of a log key sequence, that is to say, one LSTM cell for each row of feature map F. Hence, the LSTM layer consists of h unrolled LSTM cells. The hidden state $H_{t-1} \in \mathbb{R}^{1 \times d}$ of the final LSTM cell is fed into the linear layer.

3.3.4 Linear Layer

In this layer, it takes the hidden state vector H_{t-1} as input, and produces the probability distribution, Pr, which implies the occurrence probability of each log key at time t. The linear function is defined as Eq. 7.

$$Pr = W_p H_{t-1} + b_p \tag{7}$$

where $Pr \in \mathbb{R}^{1\times \mathrm{n}}$, n is the number of log keys. The learnable parameters are W_p and b_p. Each column corresponds to a log key, while the value corresponds to the occurrence probability of the log key at time t.

4 Experiments

4.1 Baseline Methods

Principal Component Analysis (PCA) [8]: It first groups log key by session and then counts the number of appearances of each log key in each session. A session vector is of size n, representing the appearance of each log key in that session. A matrix is formed where each column is a log key, and each row is one session vector. PCA detects an abnormal vector by measuring the projection length on the residual subspace of a transformed coordinate system.

Invariant Mining (IM) [22]: It constructs the same matrix as PCA. It first mines small invariants that could be satisfied by the majority of vectors, and then treat those vectors that do not satisfy these invariants as abnormal execution session.

CNNCNN-Based Model (CNN) [16]: It models anomaly detection as a two-class classification problem. It leverages CNN to learn the events relationships in system logs and detects anomalies based on the learned relationship.

DeepLog [17]: It models anomaly detection as a multi-class classification problem. It leverages LSTM to learn the pattern in logs under normal execution. When detecting, it compares logs with the learned patterns.

4.2 Dataset and Experiment Setup

We evaluate the hybrid model and other baseline algorithms over the HDFS log dataset, a widely used benchmark dataset employed by other approaches. The HDFS log is a dataset generated from running over 200 days experiment in Amazon EC2. The data was first published by Xu et al. [8], and analyzed by many approaches such as SVM and PCA. The raw log file is 1.55 GB and contains 11,197,954 log entries. HDFS log records the states of each HDFS block during job executing and includes 29 unique log keys. Furthermore, the raw data is grouped into different sessions by an identifier field, which is *block_ID*. We leverage the parsed and labeled ground truth data, which is the same as [17]. It contains normal training set (4,855 parsed sessions), normal testing set (553,366 parsed sessions), abnormal training set (1,638 parsed sessions) and abnormal testing set (15,200 parsed sessions).

The hybrid model is implemented by PyTorch. According to our experimental study, the super parameters of the model which we adopt are shown in Table 1.

Table 1. Super parameters in the hybrid model

Layer	Output
Input: log key sequence: 1 × 10	
Embedding with codebook size: 29 × 64	Embedded matrix size: 10 × 64
CNN: filter_size = 3 × 1, stride = [1, 1], padding = 'same'	Feature map: 10 × 64
LSTM: input_size = 64, hidden_size = 32, num_layers = 1	Hidden state vector: 1 × 32
Linear: in_feature = 32, out_feature = 29	Probability distribution: 1 × 29

In addition, $g = 9$, $h = 10$. Recall g decides the cutoff in the prediction output to be considered normal (i.e., the g log key values with top-g probabilities to appear next are considered normal), and h is the window size used for training and detecting.

4.3 Metrics

Those models are evaluated by the metrics listed below: True positive (TP) represents the number of real anomalies that are correctly detected as anomalies by the approach. True negative (TN) represents the normal cases that are correctly identified as normal cases. False positive (FP) presents the normal cases that are incorrectly identified as anomalies. False negative (FN) represents the abnormal cases that are incorrectly identified as normal. Based on the four metrics, we calculate the Precision, Recall, and F1-measure for each tested approach. Precision is calculated by Eq. (8), which represents the correctly detected anomalies percentage in reported anomalies. Recall is calculated by Eq. (9), which shows the detected true anomalies in all real anomalies. F1-measure is calculated by Eq. (10), which represents the harmonic average of the Precision and Recall.

$$\text{Precison} = \frac{\text{TP}}{(\text{TP} + \text{FP})} \tag{8}$$

$$\text{Recall} = \frac{\text{TP}}{(\text{TP} + \text{FN})} \tag{9}$$

$$\text{F1-measure} = \frac{2 \cdot \text{Precision} \cdot \text{Recall}}{(\text{Precision} + \text{Recall})} \tag{10}$$

4.4 Experiment Results

To compare the accuracy of our hybrid model with the CNN and LSTM model, we list all the evaluation metrics results in Table 2.

Table 2. The experiment results

Model	Precision (%)	Recall (%)	F1-measure (%)
PCA	**98**	67	79
IM	88	95	91
DeepLog	95	95	96
CNN	97.7	99.3	**98.5**
The hybrid model	97.1	**99.5**	98.3

As can be seen from Table 2, the PCA model achieves the best result on Precision, but performs badly on Recall, which results in low F1-measure. The CNN model gets the best result on F1-measure while our hybrid model achieves the best result on Recall. The results of the CNN based model and the hybrid model are very similar. Both of them achieve better results on all three metrics than DeepLog model and IM model. However, it should be noticed that the CNN based model is supervised while the hybrid model is unsupervised. In general, the CNN model and the hybrid model outperform the other models.

The experiment results prove that our hybrid model has both advantages of the CNN-based model and the LSTM-based model. The hybrid model performs well in anomaly detection, as well as is an unsupervised model, which only needs logs under normal execution for training.

4.5 Model Analysis

We explored the impacts of different parameter settings on the accuracy of the hybrid model. The specific parameters include the embedding dimension s, hidden state vector dimension d, cutoff value g, and window size h.

As can be seen from Fig. 4(a), (b), the hybrid model is less affected by the embedding dimension and hidden vector dimension. Although these two parameters are constantly changing, the scores of the evaluation indicators are all above 90, which means that we need not pay too much attention to adjusting these two parameters when applying the hybrid model in practice.

Figure 4(c) shows that a larger g value leads to a higher precision but lower recall. Therefore, g could be adjusted to achieve a higher true positive rate or lower false positive rate. As shown in Fig. 4(d), h has a large impact on the hybrid model. When the window size is too small, the hybrid model cannot effectively learn the pattern in log key sequences, which cause poor accuracy. When the window size is too large, the dependencies in log key sequences are weak, the hybrid model cannot learn log patterns correctly, which also result in poor accuracy. Therefore, it's of great importance to choose the appropriate window size.

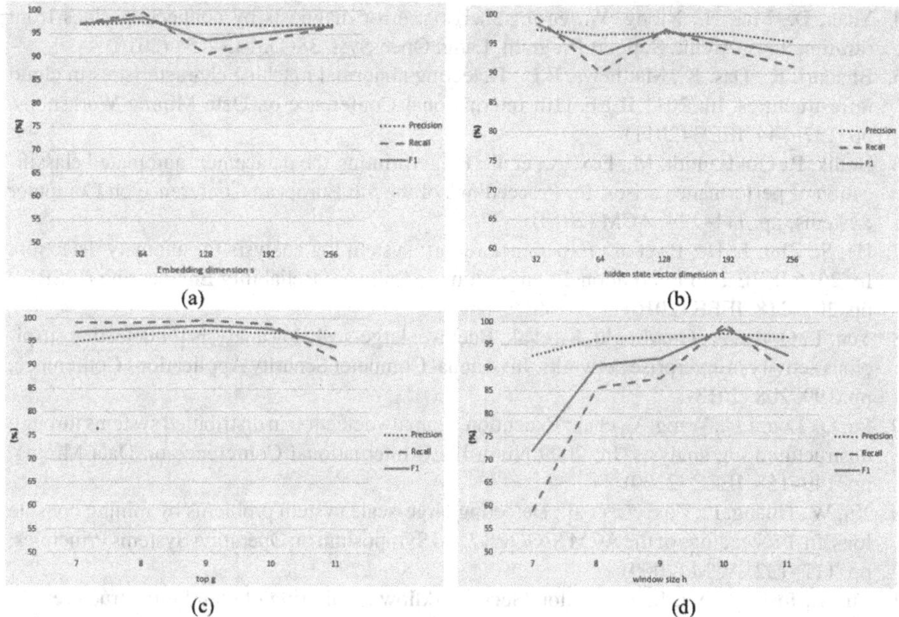

Fig. 4. The impact of parameters. (a) embedding dimension s. (b) hidden state dimension d. (c) top g. (d) window size h.

5 Conclusion

This paper presents a novel hybrid model based on CNN and LSTM for log anomaly detection. We leverage CNN to extract features from logs, which are fed into LSTM to learn the hidden patterns. The hybrid model detects anomalies by comparing the log pattern that appears in practice with the pattern it has learned before. As far as we know, this paper is the first attempt to combine CNN with LSTM model for log anomaly detection. Our experiment results demonstrate that the hybrid model has both advantages of CNN and LSTM, which is an unsupervised model, only needs logs under normal execution for training, as well as achieve great anomaly detection accuracy.

In the future, we will further improve the hybrid model by exploring different ways to combine CNN and LSTM models, or replacing CNN or LSTM with different variants, such as, utilize bidirectional LSTM instead of LSTM, or integrated with attention mechanisms. Besides, making use of both constant parts and variable parts of logs for anomaly detection is also a valuable point.

References

1. Zhang, H., Wang, L., Huang, H., et al.: SMARTH: enabling multi-pipeline data transfer in HDFS. In: International Conference on Parallel Processing, pp. 30–39 (2014)
2. Zhang, H., Sun, Z., Liu, Z., et al.: Dart: a geographic information system on Hadoop. In: International Conference on Cloud Computing, pp. 90–97 (2015)
3. Bawany, N.Z., Shamsi, J.A., Salah, K.: DDoS attack detection and mitigation using SDN: methods, practices, and solutions. Arab. J. Sci. Eng. **42**(2), 425–441 (2017)

4. Yuan, D., Mai, H., Xiong, W., et al.: SherLog: error diagnosis by connecting clues from run-time logs. Archit. Support Program. Lang. Oper. Syst. **38**(1), 143–154 (2010)
5. Bhaduri, K., Das, K., Matthews, B.L.: Detecting abnormal machine characteristics in cloud infrastructures. In: 2011 IEEE 11th International Conference on Data Mining Workshops, pp. 137–144. IEEE (2011)
6. Bodik, P., Goldszmidt, M., Fox, A., et al.: Fingerprinting the datacenter: automated classification of performance crises. In: Proceedings of the 5th European Conference on Computer Systems, pp. 111–124. ACM (2010)
7. He, S., Zhu, J., He, P., et al.: Experience report: system log analysis for anomaly detection. In: 2016 IEEE 27th International Symposium on Software Reliability Engineering (ISSRE), pp. 207–218. IEEE (2016)
8. Yen, T., Oprea, A., Onarlioglu, K., et al.: Beehive: large-scale log analysis for detecting suspicious activity in enterprise networks. In: Annual Computer Security Applications Conference, pp. 199–208 (2013)
9. Fu, Q., Lou, J.G., Wang, Y., et al.: Execution anomaly detection in distributed systems through unstructured log analysis. In: 2009 Ninth IEEE International Conference on Data Mining, pp. 149–158. IEEE (2009)
10. Xu, W., Huang, L., Fox, A., et al.: Detecting large-scale system problems by mining console logs. In: Proceedings of the ACM SIGOPS 22nd Symposium on Operating Systems Principles, pp. 117–132. ACM (2009)
11. Yu, X., Joshi, P., Xu, J., et al.: CloudSeer: workflow monitoring of cloud infrastructures via interleaved logs. Archit. Support Program. Lang. Oper. Syst. **51**(4), 489–502 (2016)
12. Fulp, E.W., Fink, G.A., Haack, J.N.: Predicting computer system failures using support vector machines. WASL **8**, 5 (2008)
13. Yadwadkar, N.J., Ananthanarayanan, G., Katz, R.: Wrangler: predictable and faster jobs using fewer resources. In: Proceedings of the ACM Symposium on Cloud Computing, pp. 1–14. ACM (2014)
14. Lou, J.G., Fu, Q., Wang, Y., et al.: Mining dependency in distributed systems through unstructured logs analysis. ACM SIGOPS Oper. Syst. Rev. **44**(1), 91–96 (2010)
15. Breier, J., Branišová, J.: Anomaly detection from log files using data mining techniques. In: Kim, K.J. (ed.) Information Science and Applications. LNEE, vol. 339, pp. 449–457. Springer, Heidelberg (2015). https://doi.org/10.1007/978-3-662-46578-3_53
16. Lu, S., Wei, X., Li, Y., et al.: Detecting anomaly in big data system logs using convolutional neural network. In: 2018 IEEE 16th International Conference on Dependable, Autonomic and Secure Computing, 16th International Conference on Pervasive Intelligence and Computing, 4th International Conference on Big Data Intelligence and Computing and Cyber Science and Technology Congress (DASC/PiCom/DataCom/CyberSciTech), pp. 151–158. IEEE (2018)
17. Du, M., Li, F., Zheng, G., et al.: Deeplog: anomaly detection and diagnosis from system logs through deep learning. In: Proceedings of the 2017 ACM SIGSAC Conference on Computer and Communications Security, pp. 1285–1298. ACM (2017)
18. Brown, A., Tuor, A., Hutchinson, B., et al.: Recurrent neural network attention mechanisms for interpretable system log anomaly detection. arXiv: Learning (2018)
19. Lecun, Y., Bottou, L., Bengio, Y., et al.: Gradient-based learning applied to document recognition. Proc. IEEE **86**(11), 2278–2324 (1998)
20. Hochreiter, S., Schmidhuber, J.: Long short-term memory. Neural Comput. **9**(8), 1735–1780 (1997)
21. Du, M., Li, F.: Spell: streaming parsing of system event logs. In: 2016 IEEE 16th International Conference on Data Mining (ICDM), pp. 859–864. IEEE (2016)
22. Lou, J., Fu, Q., Yang, S., et al.: Mining invariants from console logs for system problem detection. In: Usenix Annual Technical Conference, pp. 24–24 (2010)

Customs-Based Blockchain Solution for Exportation Protection

Hussam Juma[1,2(✉)], Khaled Shaalan[2], and Ibrahim Kamel[3]

[1] Dubai Customs, Dubai, UAE
hussam.mohammed@dubaicustoms.ae
[2] The British University in Dubai, Dubai, UAE
[3] University of Sharjah, Sharjah, UAE

Abstract. As part of the international trade supply chain, Dubai Customs acts as the gatekeeper, protecting the society and the economy. During the exportation process, one of the primary responsibilities of the Customs Authority is to authenticate the documents submitted with the exportation declaration application, to ensure the legality of the trade. Due to the lack of direct communication channel among the exportation supply chain participants, authenticating the exportation application documents is a time-consuming and challenging task. Typically, there is no direct communication paradigm among the supply chain participants. Therefore, in most cases, the authenticating process relies on human judgment. This increases the chance of non-detection of fraudulent exportation documents. In this regard, the redesign of the exportation supply chain to automate the authentication process has become an essential requirement. This paper addresses this requirement by proposing a blockchain-based system, which establishes a direct, tamper-proof information exchange mechanism among the participants. We target the car exportation supply chain; however, with slight modification, the proposed system can be easily applied to any other exportation supply chain too. To validate the performance of the proposed system, we implement a Proof-of-Concept (POC) using the IBM Hyperledger fabric.

Keywords: Dubai Customs · Luxury cars exportation · Blockchain · Hyperledger

1 Introduction

Customs Administration plays an important role in protecting the economy and society. As part of the international trade supply chain, Customs Authority monitors the flow of goods to ensure the legality of the trade, and to detect any smuggling actives. To fulfil this responsibility, Customs Authority has to communicate practically with most of the supply chain participants, in order to authenticate the trade documents. This authentication process is very time consuming since Customs Authority does not have direct communication channels with the systems of other supply chain participants. Further, authenticating documents using a paper-based communication mechanism increases the

H. Shen and Y. Sang (Eds.): PAAP 2019, CCIS 1163, pp. 405–416, 2020.
https://doi.org/10.1007/978-981-15-2767-8_36

processing time, and therefore conflicts with the Customs Authority's objective of facilitating trade World Customs Organization (WCO) [1]. The lack of connection among the supply chain participants challenges the Customs Authority's rules since it might result in failure to detect fraudulent documents.

The possibility of non-detection of fraudulent documents by Customs Authority increases the chances of exporting stolen goods, which has a significant and damaging impact on the economy. For instance, in 2017, over 30 luxury cars were exported from Dubai using fake documents[1]. As we can see from Fig. 1, at Dubai Customs, the process of car exportation commences with the submission of declaration. In this process, the exporter has to submit the ownership documents and the clearance documents from the Road and Transportation Authority (RTA). Once these documents are received, during the declaration assessment process, Customs check whether there is any case against the car in the records of the local police and the Interpol. If there is no such record relating to the car, the application would be cleared for exportation. In the current operating model, there is no direct communication between Dubai Customs system and the Road and Transportation Authority (RTA). Thus, the process of authenticating the clearance and ownership documents relies on manual verification of the authenticity of the documents, which increases the possibility of non-detection of fake documents. This problem in authenticating documents highlights the importance of designing an information-sharing mechanism that establishes a direct communication channel among the organisations (participants) involved in the exportation.

In this paper, we address the problem of automating the process of authenticating the exportation documents at the Customs Authority. Though we target the cars exportation process, the solution proposed in this work can be easily adopted by any other exportation process. To address this problem, our objective is to propose an information-sharing system, which provides participants with the ability to communicate on time in order to confirm the genuineness of the documents exchanged. To ensure the willingness of the participants to join such a system, information privacy and data immutability must also be guaranteed.

Addressing such requirements using traditional, centralised (or distributed) systems is not a straightforward task. Centralised system architecture is not typically applicable to this application domain. In such an architecture, the entire data from all the participants must be hosted at a single node (for example, Dubai Customs). In this application, records of the participants constitute highly sensitive information, and gathering these records at a single node raises significant privacy concerns. A distributed system architecture can be used in this application domain. However, ensuring the integrity and immutability of the data is not a simple task in this architecture. Complex algorithms must be applied to ensure that each participant has the latest version of the data, and no participant can manipulate the system information.

The requirement of ensuring the integrity and immutability of the data highlights the blockchain technology as an appropriate environment to host such an information-sharing system. Due to its inherited features of data tractability, integrity

[1] The Intelligence Department at Dubai Customs is the source of all statistical information provided in this paper.

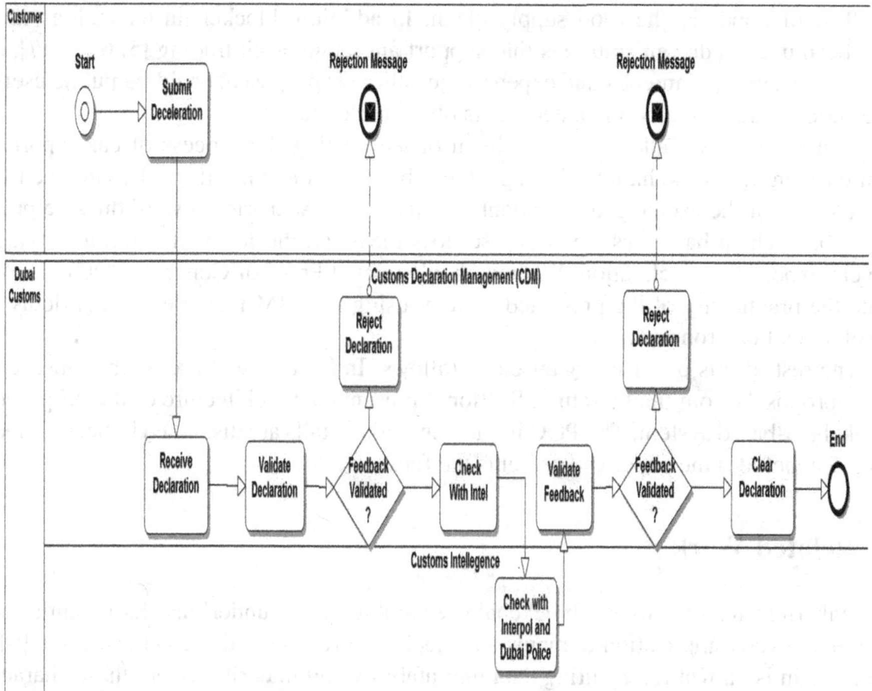

Fig. 1. The current cars exportation business process

and immutability, blockchain has emerged as a significant technology to establish trust among untrusted participants. Blockchain is a Distributed Ledger Technology (DLT), where the system logic is implemented through the use of smart contracts, which assure their enforcement through automation. In this technology, participants have identical copies of the transaction records (ledger). These records are organised as blocks, such that each block is connected to its previous block through a hash value (Fig. 2). In other words, each block stores the hash value of the previous block. Thus, if someone changes a block data, the hash value of this block will no longer match that stored inside the next block, and the link between these two blocks will be broken. This linking mechanism guarantees the immutability of the blockchain data. In addition, to add a new block to the chain, the majority of the participants have to confirm the correctness of this block data, and thus ensure the integrity of the information.

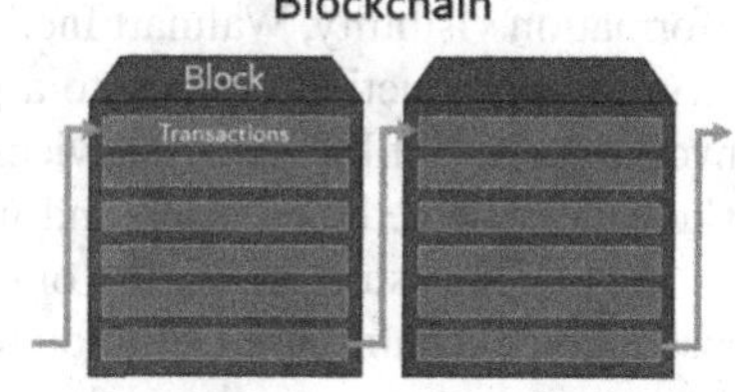

Fig. 2. Blockchain and ledger architecture

The use of blockchain technology in the international trade supply chain has been extensively studied in the literature. For instance, to address the food safety problem, several studies [2–4] have proposed blockchain-based solutions to trace and monitor the flow of goods in the food supply chain. In addition, blockchain technology has also been used to design solutions that support anti-counterfeit trading [5, 6]. In [7], a trading system for diamonds and expensive jewellery is proposed, enabling public users to ensure the authenticity and antecedents of the traded jewellery.

In this paper, we address the problem of automating the process of car exportation through the blockchain technology. Our objective is to simplify and guarantee the authenticity of the exchanged documents in this trading scenario. Toward this, we propose a blockchain-based system that is used to authenticate the documents accompanying the car exportation declaration. We have implemented Proof of Concept (POC) to validate the practicality of the presented system, using the IBM Hyperledger Fabric as a development environment.

The rest of this paper is organised as follows: In Sect. 2, we discuss the most relevant proposals from the literature. Section 3 presents the architecture of the proposed blockchain-based system. The POC implementation details are discussed in Sect. 4, and Sect. 5 concludes the paper and presents the future work.

2 Related Work

The inherited features of the blockchain technology have underlined its potential to optimise several application domains such as health [8], agriculture [2] and trade [9]. Blockchain is known for ensuring data immutability and integrity, where these characteristics result in increasing the trust among the participants in any application scenario. This revolutionises the way we address traditional problems such as food safety, trade traceability, and information exchange. In [10–13], the authors proposed blockchain-based solutions to address the problem of food safety in the food supply chain. Using these solutions, users can gain access to the required information to authenticate food quality and storage environment. For instance, to support the concept of trees to shelf information visibility, Walmart Inc. solution [11] publishes all the information gathered during the production of food to a public blockchain. Food safety solutions typically involve the use of IoT sensor devices to monitor the surrounding environment of foods, where the collected sensor data and any lab test performed are uploaded to the blockchain.

In [14], to ensure the quality of the available pharmaceutical goods, the authors proposed a blockchain-based solution to trace the status of the goods storage environment along the pharmaceutical supply chain. This proposal employs IoT devices to monitor the status of pharmaceutical goods. In [15], a relatively similar concept has been applied to trace and monitor the transportation of dangerous goods. In [16, 17], the authors presented a traceability solution named OriginChain, which aims to increase the transparency of the trading process and to ensure the compliance of the shipped goods with the trade rules and regulations. Three types of parties interact in this solution: the service user, traceability provider, and the blockchain administrator. Service users represent companies and retailers. The traceability provider is responsible for performing the test sought by the service user. The Blockchain administrator generates smart contracts, which will implement the responsibilities of traceability providers.

In [18], an industrial platform termed TRACER is presented as a traceability solution, to authenticate the diamond ownership information. This platform aims to increase trade confidence by ensuring the integrity, traceability, and immutability of the transaction. A similar concept has been adopted by the TrustChain platform also [19]. Several other proposals have investigated the use of the blockchain in the context of anti-counterfeiting measures. In [6], the authors proposed a blockchain-based solution, which uses the traceability feature of blockchain technology to detect fake products. In this solution, right from the manufacturer, all the participants in the trade supply chain have to be registered users on the blockchain. Once a participant uploads information to the blockchain, he/she has to digitally sign the information using his/her public/private keys. Therefore, the end-user can authenticate the origin of the goods, since the source of each transaction on the blockchain can be determined easily.

Several proposals have also investigated the use of blockchain technology to simplify the Customs Authority processes. In [20], the authors presented a context-aware information sharing solution, in which each of the participants can control the visibility of the information on the blockchain. Here, whenever a participant seeks access to specific information, the participant who owns this information has the option of accepting or rejecting the request. This strategy aims to increase the participants' confidence in sharing the information. Vos et al. [21] presented a blockchain-based decentralised system for freight declaration. This system aims to simplify and automate the collaboration between the economic operators and the Customs agencies. By digitizing the shipment containers through the IoT technology, this system aims to enhance the awareness of the Customs Authority about the shipped goods and their shipping path. These two systems target the international trading scenario, with participants located both inside and outside the country. The applicability of such solutions is restricted, since the willingness of the participants to join the network is a major issue.

This paper targets the car exportation scenario, where all the participants are local organisations deriving mutual benefits from joining the network. The traceability component of our solution shares some similarities with the traceability proposals discussed in this section. However, in this work, our main objective is to establish a blockchain solution that has a pre-determined set of government organisations acting as participants, which, together, can determine whether the car under consideration can be cleared for exportation or not.

3 The Proposed Blockchain-Based System

The proposed system aims to establish a communication mechanism among the participants, such that the privacy and integrity of the data are guaranteed. Participants that use the proposed system are (1) banks, (2) car rental companies, (3) Dubai Police Department, (4) Road and Transportation Authority (RTA), and (5) Dubai Customs. Generally, building a typical, distributed system that connects these participants is impractical, since such a system is expected to raise several significant privacy and security concerns. Blockchain is a technology appropriate for establishing such a system since it can ensure the privacy of the information exchanged.

3.1 Overview

In this system, only three participants are expected to have complete visibility of the information stored in the ledger, viz., Dubai Customs, Dubai Police Department, and RTA. By nature, these participants are expected to use the stored historical information in the ledger for their internal processes. They are also expected to maintain the ledger and create the consensus. Regarding the other two types of participants (banks and car rental companies), each of them can access only its information on the ledger.

In the proposed system, the main process starts once Dubai Customs submits an inquiry. This inquiry is represented as a smart contract, with information about the car being exported. Accordingly, this smart contract checks the information stored in the ledger to identify whether this car is owned by a rental company or is currently charged to a bank. Additionally, this smart contract checks with the Police Department and RTA, to determine the legal and ownership status of this car. Where there is an active case against the car in the Police Department, or the car is rented from a rental company, the exportation process will be stopped. This will also occur if the loan that with which the car is purchased is not repaid in full, or the car ownership information in RTA does not match that provided in the declaration. In such a case, the customs declaration management department will be apprised investigating the exportation further.

3.2 Architecture and Processes

Figure 3 shows the modification required in the car exportation business process model notation, after deployment of the proposed system. Once the declaration is validated, the process continues with the invocation of the proposed system. In this step, a smart contract will be triggered to process the current inquiry, which will check the information stored in the ledger. In addition, it will check the RTA and the Police Department databases, through the use of external web services. The RTA and the Police Department records are kept off-chain since they are expected to be significantly large.

If any of the participants has an issue with the exportation, the process will be stopped, and the customs declaration management will be informed. In cases of fraud, the legal authority will also be informed. This examination is performed from the perspective of each participant. Dubai Police Department checks whether there is an active case against the car. RTA validates car ownership and clearance information. Cars rental companies check whether they rented the car. Banks check whether the car is bought with a loan, which remains unpaid.

Figure 4 presents the architecture of the proposed system, which is divided into three layers, viz., the interface layer, the smart contracts layer, and the ledger layer. The interface layer defines the processes the participants can use to interact with the system. The next layer consists of several smart contracts used to store information on the ledger and to perform the inquiry process. The ledger layer represents the actual blockchain. Each participant uses functionalities related to their rule in the system. Dubai Customs performs participant registration, and this functionality deals with the process of registering banks and car rental companies. Banks and car rental companies can trigger functionalities related to loans and vehicles status, dealing with the processes of updating the vehicle or loan status on the ledger. Dubai Customs typically initiates an inquiry to determine the status of the car being exported.

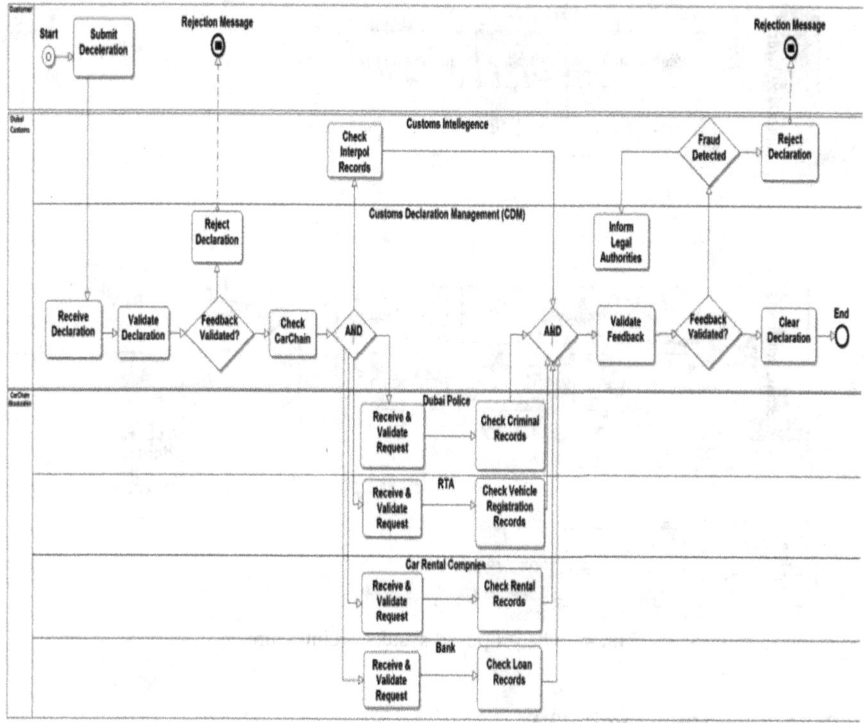

Fig. 3. The improved version of the car exportation business process

3.3 Banks and Car Rental Companies

To interact with the proposed system, car rental companies and banks need to be registered users. The registration is done through Dubai Customs, where each bank and car rental company is assigned a unique identification number. Each bank or car rental company has access to the ledger transactions originated by this participant. Once they register with the system, car rental companies and banks can start recording their car and loan activities on the ledger.

The type of transaction (activity) recorded on the ledger depends on the participant type. Transactions originated by car rental companies are related to the ownership status of their cars. Accordingly, a car rental company is allowed to register a new car under its name or change the status of any of its cars to indicate, for example, that the car had been sold, and is no longer part of this company's fleet. Banks use the system to record the cars bought using loans. In the proposed system, once a car loan is repaid, the bank has to record a new transaction to indicate the repayment. For privacy purposes, banks do not store the car owner's name on the ledger, recording only the plate number and the chassis number.

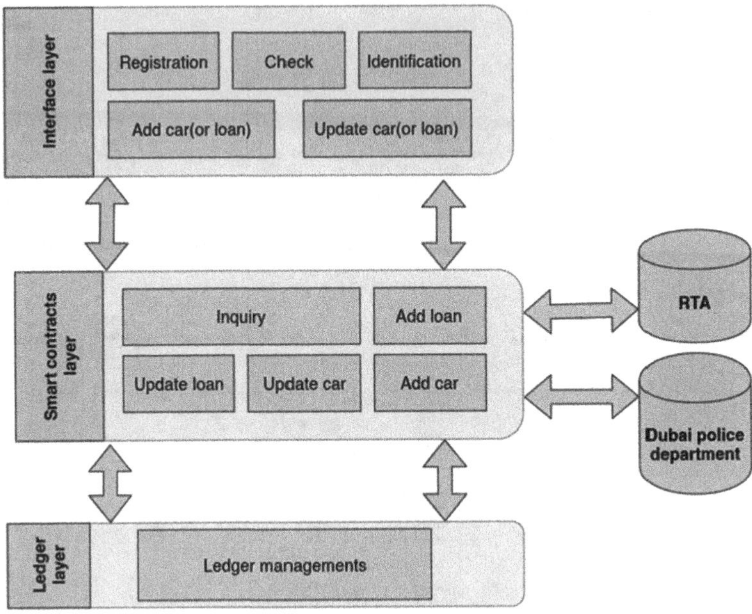

Fig. 4. The proposed system architecture

3.4 Police Department and RTA

Dubai Police Department and RTA have different types of interaction with the system. These two participants use the transactions stored in the ledger for their internal processes. For instance, the Police Department can use the ledger information to track the movement of the vehicle from/to Dubai. Once these two participants receive an enquiry about a car, each performs an examination based on its role in the system. RTA checks and validates the car ownership information, and whether there is an active case against this car in its database. These participants start their examination processes once they receive the car's information using the smart inquiry contract. If RTA examination determines that the car ownership information provided in the declaration does not match its records, Dubai Customs would be informed to stop the exportation. Dubai Customs would perform the same action if the Dubai Police Department records indicate the existence of a case against the car. Dubai Police Department and RTA records are stored off-chain.

3.5 Dubai Customs

Dubai Customs interacts with the system mainly by starting the car inquiry process. Additionally, it is responsible for registering banks and car rental companies. The inquiry process is established by passing the car information to the smart examination contract. This contract validates the declaration information by checking the transactions stored in the ledger, as well as by contacting the Police Department and RTA. Where a fraudulent activity is detected, the legal authority is informed for appropriation action.

4 Proof-of-Concept (POC)

To validate the performance of the presented system, we have implemented a Proof-of-Concept (POC) for the proposed architecture, using the IBM Hyperledger Fabric blockchain framework. Hyperledger Fabric is designed for private permissioned network, where the identity of the participants and their roles in the network are known. The objective of this POC is to test the efficiency of the proposed architecture, mainly in terms of integration. The system is designed for eventual deployment as part of the operating model of Dubai Customs. Thus, it should be easily integrated with other deployed systems, without any interruption to the business processes. In this section, we describe the POC implementation details in terms of assets, transactions, and smart contracts.

4.1 Assets

In blockchain terminology, assets could be anything of value, and in the presented system, these represent cars and loans. In this system, the ledger-stored information consists of cars bought with loans, or cars belonging to rental companies. Thus, two kinds of assets are established in our system, viz., the CLoan and the RCar. CLoan assets refer to the bank loans availed for buying cars. Banks manage CLoan assets, and loans are identified by their numbers. Each loan is associated with a Boolean variable (true/false), representing the current status of the loan. If the value of this variable is false, it indicates that the loan has been repaid. RCar refers to cars currently owned by rental companies. Rental companies manage RCar assets, where cars are identified by their chassis numbers. Each car asset is also associated with a Boolean variable, which represents the renting status of the car. If this variable value is true, it indicates that the car is currently rented to a customer.

4.2 Transactions

Banks, Dubai Customs, and car rental companies are the only participants that submit transactions to be written in the leger. Banks submit two kinds of transactions to the ledger, representing the initialisation of a new car loan and the status update of an existing loan. The status of a loan is changed to false when the customer fully repays. Car rental companies can perform two kinds of transactions: car registration and ownership update. Car registration transaction is used to register a new car with the system, and an ownership update is used to change the ownership information for the registered car. For a car exportation declaration, Dubai Customs can submit to the ledger two types of transactions: clearance for exportation and involving customs management department.

4.3 Smart Contracts

In the presented system, smart contracts are responsible for managing the assets and performing the inquiry, which is triggered by Dubai Customs. Managing the assets is performed mainly through the use of four contracts, involving registration of new bank loans, status changing of existing loans, the addition of a car to the rental company's fleet, and changing the ownership information for a car belonging to a car rental company.

The smart inquiry contract examines the ledger to obtain any information available about the car being exported and also, using web service; the smart contract contacts the RTA and Dubai Police Department to check the status of the car. This examination process can result in either clearing the exportation or blocking it. Figure 5 presents the main components of this smart contract, which starts by checking whether a loan financed the car and whether the loan is repaid (lines 2–4). Then, the contract proceeds to determine whether the car is rented from a rental company (lines 6–8). To examine whether the declared ownership information matches RTA records, a web server hosted by the RTA must be invoked. In this work, for testing purpose, we have created a local service for testing (line 10). In the official deployment, this triggered functionality must be a service hosted at RTA. The same process must be applied to trigger the Dubai Police department service (line 11).

```
   async function Inquiry(vquery) {
1    const REG = await getAssetRegistry('org.carchain.vehicle');
2    let onLoanResults = await query('selectVehicleonloan');
3    if (onLoanResults.length > 0)
4      console.log(' Vehicle is on active loan');
5    Else
6      {let onRentResults = await query('selectVehicleonrent');
7      if (onRentResults.length > 0)
8        console.log(' Vehicle is on active rent');
9      else{
10       const RTA = await request.get( {'http://RTAJUSTFORTEST/vstatus?chno=vquery.chassisnumber&eid=vquery.emiratesid',JASON:true})
11       const POLICE = await request.get( {'http://POLICETEST/vstatus?chno=vquery.chassisnumber',JASON:true});
12       if (RTA.results > 0)
13         console.log(' Vehicle is registered to correct person');
14       if (POLICE.results > 0)
15         console.log(' Vehicle has registered Police case');}}
```

Fig. 5. Code for the inquiry smart contract.

From the customs administrative perspective, we cannot assume the willingness of all banks and car rental companies to be part of our blockchain. Therefore, the use of the proposed system can be considered as a new additional service channel.

5 Conclusion and Future Works

In this paper, we presented a blockchain-based system designed at Dubai Customs to simplify and automate the process of exporting luxury cars. The proposed system aims to establish a direct and secure communication mechanism among the supply chain participants. By employing the blockchain technology, the proposed system ensures the integrity and immutability of the exchanged data. Currently, we are planning to expand the architecture of the proposed system to cover the importation scenario. Thereafter, we plan to start a pilot project, where the system will be deployed at the participating entities to monitor its performance.

Acknowledgement. Dubai Customs funded the research for this paper. The authors would also like to thank everyone from the Service Innovation department for constructive discussions and inputs.

References

1. World Customs Organization: WCO SAFE Framework of Standards, no. June (2018)
2. Hua, J., Wang, X., Kang, M., Wang, H., Wang, F.Y.: Blockchain based provenance for agricultural products: a distributed platform with duplicated and shared bookkeeping. In: Proceedings of IEEE Intelligent Vehicles Symposium, pp. 97–101 (2018)
3. Malik, S., Kanhere, S.S., Jurdak, R.: ProductChain: scalable blockchain framework to support provenance in supply chains. In: Proceedings of the 2018 IEEE 17th International Symposium on Network Computing and Applications (NCA), pp. 1–10 (2018)
4. Mao, D., Hao, Z., Wang, F., Li, H.: Innovative blockchain-based approach for sustainable and credible environment in food trade: a case study in Shandong province, China. Sustainability **10**(9), 1–17 (2018). MDPI, Open Access Journal
5. Alzahrani, N., Bulusu, N.: Block-supply chain: a new anti-counterfeiting supply chain using NFC and blockchain. In: Proceedings of the 1st Workshop on Cryptocurrencies and Blockchains for Distributed Systems – CryBlock 2018, pp. 30–35 (2018)
6. Toyoda, K., Takis Mathiopoulos, P., Sasase, I., Ohtsuki, T.: A novel blockchain-based product ownership management system (POMS) for anti-counterfeits in the post supply chain. IEEE Access **5**, 17465–17477 (2017)
7. Everledger Diamond Platform. https://diamonds.everledger.io/
8. Jiang, S., Cao, J., Wu, H., Yang, Y., Ma, M., He, J.: BlocHIE: a BLOCkchain-based platform for healthcare information exchange. In: Proceedings of the 2018 IEEE International Conference on Smart Computing (SMARTCOMP), Taormina, pp. 49–56 (2018)
9. Casado-Vara, R., Prieto, J., De La Prieta, F., Corchado, J.M.: How blockchain improves the supply chain: case study alimentary supply chain. Procedia Comput. Sci. **134**, 393–398 (2018)
10. Tian, F.: A supply chain traceability system for food safety based on HACCP, blockchain & Internet of things. In: Proceedings of the International Conference on Service Systems and Service Management, pp. 1–6 (2017)
11. Kamath, R.: Food traceability on blockchain: Walmart's pork and mango pilots with IBM. Blockchain Res. Inst. **1**(1), 1–29 (2017)
12. Cui, Y., Idota, H.: Improving supply chain resilience with establishing a decentralized information sharing mechanism. In: Proceedings of 5th Multidisciplinary International Social Networks Conference - MISNC 2018, pp. 1–7 (2018)
13. Hepp, T., Wortner, P., Schönhals, A., Gipp, B.: Securing physical assets on the blockchain linking a novel object identification concept with distributed ledgers. In: Proceedings of 1st CryBlock, pp. 60–65 (2018)
14. Bocek, T., Rodrigues, B.B., Strasser, T., Stiller, B.: Blockchains everywhere - a use-case of blockchains in the pharma supply-chain. In: Proceedings of 2017 IFIP/IEEE Symposium on Integrated Network and Service Management (IM), pp. 772–777 (2017)
15. Imeri, A., Khadraoui, D.: The security and traceability of shared information in the process of transportation of dangerous goods. In: Proceedings of the 9th IFIP International Conference on New Technologies, Mobility and Security (NTMS), pp. 1–5 (2018)
16. Lu, Q., Xu, X.: Adaptable blockchain-based systems: a case study for product traceability. IEEE Softw. **34**(6), 21–27 (2017)
17. Xu, X., Lu, Q., Liu, Y., Zhu, L., Yao, H., Vasilakos, A.V.: Designing blockchain-based applications a case study for imported product traceability. Future Gener. Comput. Syst. **92**, 399–406 (2019)
18. Rodriguez, M.A., Buyya, R.: Deadline based resource provisioning and scheduling algorithm for scientific workflows on clouds. IEEE Trans. Cloud Comput. **2**(2), 222–235 (2014)
19. trustchain. https://www.trustchainjewelry.com/

20. Van Engelenburg, S., Janssen, M., Klievink, B.: Design of a software architecture supporting business-to-government information sharing to improve public safety and security: combining business rules, events and blockchain technology. J. Intell. Inf. Syst., 1–24 (2017)
21. Vos, D., et al.: DEFenD: a secure and privacy-preserving decentralized system for freight declaration. In: Proceedings of the 1st ERCIM Blockchain Workshop 2018, pp. 1–8 (2018)

Customs-Based Distributed Risk Assessment Method

Hussam Juma[1,2](✉), Khaled Shaalan[2], and Ibrahim Kamel[3]

[1] Dubai Customs, Dubai, UAE
hussam.mohammed@dubaicustoms.ae
[2] The British University in Dubai, Dubai, UAE
[3] University of Sharjah, Sharjah, UAE

Abstract. Customs administration oversees the important processes of facilitating trade and protecting local societies and economies: the former by minimising shipment processing times and the latter by ensuring the lawfulness of trade. One of the main processes that affect the facilitation and protection of trade is the risk of the shipment assessment process. This assessment is performed by analysing available information about shipments to determine whether or not they require physical inspection. When a shipment is identified as suspicious, a physical inspection that can take hours is performed to identify and (dis)confirm the risk factors. In this process, changing trading behaviour by increasing the volume of expected shipments can be a source of pressure. This work proposes a secondary distributed risk assessment method that provides customs administration with an online risk assessment capabilities. The proposed method complements the risk assessments performed at customs administration by providing feedback from the early stage of risk analysis. The results show that the proposed method can provide classification that is 83% accurate on average.

Keywords: Customs administration · Blockchain · Risk assessment · Local outlier factor

1 Introduction

Customs administration aims to establish a trade-off between facilitating trade and protecting the public interest [1]. Of course, both of these objectives necessarily conflict, for the increased facilitation of trade increases risks for local economies and societies. At the same time, applying strong measures to ensure the protection of public interest can reduce the ease of trade. At customs administration, the process of risk assessment is expected to serve the objective of protecting local interests by, for example, confirming the authenticity of trade documents and detecting all forms of suspicious activities. For a given shipment, risk assessment involves validating available information about the shipment to determine whether it should be cleared with or without physical inspection. Although applying such risk assessment processes can further facilitate trade, optimising the accuracy of the risk assessments process remains a major challenge. From the perspective of customs administration, shipment risks can be categorised into either

H. Shen and Y. Sang (Eds.): PAAP 2019, CCIS 1163, pp. 417–429, 2020.
https://doi.org/10.1007/978-981-15-2767-8_37

value manipulation risks or undeclared goods risks. Value manipulation risks occurred when the trader falsified the trade documents in order to reduce the expected amount of duties. Undeclared goods risks occur when traders attempt to smuggle restricted or prohibited goods into a country. Whereas restricted goods such as pharmaceutical items and weapons require special permits from government authorities to enter the country. Prohibited goods represent all products not allowed to enter the country under any circumstances. The impact of shipment-related risks on local societies and economies underscore the importance of the protections provided by the customs administration.

Typically, the customs administration starts the risk assessment process once it receives the declaration application from the trader. Once the employed risk assessment process identifies a shipment as being risky, if the risk relates to suspected smuggling activity, then a customs inspection agent is expected to perform a physical inspection to determine the riskiness of the shipment. Based on the shipment volume, that inspection could take hours to perform, especially in the case of sea channel shipments. In this work, to boost the efficiency of risk assessments performed by the customs administration, we propose a lightweight distributed risk assessment method. The objective of the method is to provide customs administrations with real-time feedback about risk assessments at different stages in the international trade supply chain. The proposed method is designed as a secondary-level assessment that complements existing risk assessments processes performed by customs administrations. By using the proposed method, customs administrations can have significantly more time to investigate shipments labelled as risky.

The main idea of the proposed distributed method is to perform risk assessments for shipments at two stages of the international trade supply chain—at the manufacturer and at the shipping agent—both of which can allow the capture of value manipulation risks and undeclared goods risks. Risks related to value manipulation can be assessed by analysing the manufacturer's information (e.g. invoice and country of origin), while undeclared goods risks can be assessed using information related to the shipment's path and type. For each type of risk assessment, the proposed method represents the shipment's information as points in multi-dimensional space consisting of two kinds of subspace: safe and risky. Risky subspace encompasses shipments whose risks have been identified and confirmed, whereas safe subspace encompasses ones without any identified risks. The dimensions of each space represent the parameters used to analyse the type of risk. For instance, for value manipulation risk, the parameters are the invoice value ($), goods type, and country of origin. Figure 1 illustrates this dynamic, with the subspaces for value manipulation risk highlighted.

For each shipment, the method represents the shipment's information as points in the value manipulation and undeclared goods spaces. For each space (i.e. risk category), the primary objective is to determine whether the shipment (i.e. a point) is risky or safe based on its locality. As part of the classification step, the method employs the well-known Local-density Outlier Factor (LOF) algorithm proposed by Breunig et al. [2], which can determine whether a given point is an outlier by comparing its density against the density of points located in its neighbourhood. Next, the proposed method uses the obtained outlier factors by the LOF algorithm to determine whether the new shipment

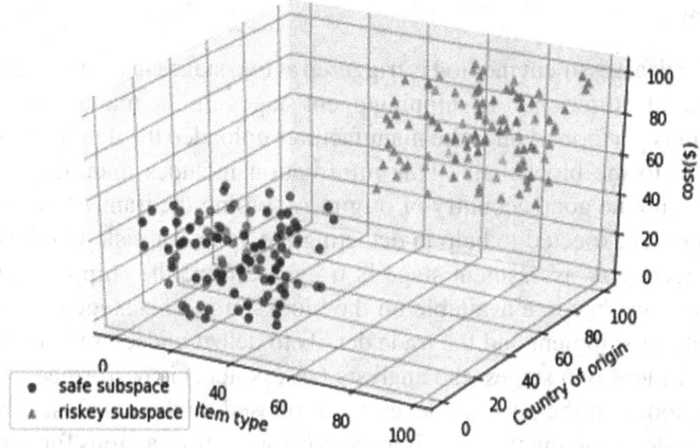

Fig. 1. The value manipulation transaction space (the manufacturer stage)

should be labelled as safe or risky. Our results show that the method can provide a classification that is 83% accurate on average.

The proposed method uses the information provided by participants in the international trade supply chain. Thus, the proposed method must be integrated with information-exchange mechanism that ensures data integrity and security. Such a mechanism can be designed using the blockchain technology. Blockchain is distributed ledger technology (DLT) that can ensure the traceability and integrity of data shared between entities. Several proposals [3–6] have highlighted the potential of optimising (international) trade supply chains by using blockchain technology. In this work, we have assumed that the proposed method is deployed with a customs-based blockchain that handles importation and exportation in the supply chain. However, using the blockchain-based information exchange mechanism is not mandatory; the method can be integrated with any information-sharing mechanism that can ensure the integrity of the information used.

The rest of the paper is organised as follows. The details of our proposed method are presented in Sect. 2. In Sect. 3, we present the evaluation for the proposed method. Section 4 presents the related proposals that use outlier mechanisms to detect suspicious (outliers) transactions, and the paper is concluded in Sect. 5.

2 The Proposed Method

The proposed method for risk assessment consists of two main steps: the transactions representation and the classification steps. These two steps are jointly triggered at each assessment stage.

2.1 Overview

The proposed risk assessment method is triggered at two stages in the trade supply chain; namely the manufacturer and the shipping agent stages. In the manufacturer stage, the risk assessment is performed once the manufacturer uploaded the details of the importer requested order to the blockchain. This information includes manufacturer location, invoice details and the goods country of origin. Assessing the transaction submitted by the manufacturer is expected to help in detecting the valuation risk. On the other hand, the shipping agent risk assessment stage is triggered once the shipping agent related information has also become available on the blockchain. This stage uses information such as the path of shipment and the trade details to detect undeclared goods risk.

For each of these two stages, the analysis (assessment) is performed at two levels: personal and global. In the personal level, the proposed method analyses the shipment under consideration by using the same importer historical transactions for benchmarking purposes. In the global step, the entire available transactions (all importers) is used for benchmarking purposes. In each stage, the assessment is performed by combining the results of both levels to determine whether the current shipment can be considered risky.

Toward this end, in each stage, the available shipments historical information is represented as points in multi-dimensional space. Each stage space is divided into risky and safe subspaces. Risky subspace is used to represent shipments, where the presence of risk is confirmed. Safe subspace represents shipments that did not have any risk issues. In each assessment stage, the outcome of the two assessments levels is represented as two outlier factors sets (personal and global). These factors are then processed to determine whether the current shipment can be considered as risky from this assessment stage perspective. Beside risky, a shipment could be classified as safe or undecidable. Undecidable shipments are expected to be reclassified by the centralised risk assessment process located at the customs administration. The introduction of the undecidable classification label aims to improve the accuracy of the proposed classification method. Accordingly, a threshold is used by the method to establish a minimum required difference (gap) between the obtained outliers' factors (safe and risky) to classify the shipments. This threshold is introduced since shipments with a relatively small gap between these outliers do not have clearly unique classification features, and therefore should be further investigated by the customs administration (undecidable shipments).

Next, we describe the transactions representation, the Local-density Outlier Factor (LOF) algorithm, and the classification process.

2.2 Transactions Representation Step

In the proposed method, shipments declaration information is represented as points in multi-dimensional spaces. Each risk assessment stage is associated with information representation space. In the manufacturer risk assessment stage, to detect the value manipulation risk, information (parameters) related to the manufacturing detailed and price are used to represent the shipments. These used parameters in the manufacturer space are the cost, the manufacturer location, and the goods Harmonized System code (HS-code). Cost represents the total amount of money paid by the importer to the manufacturer. The Harmonized System code (HS-code) is used to define a unique number for each item category. HS-code is used by customs to calculate the amount of duties; the traders are expected to pay. In addition, the HS-code is used to determine whether the shipped items can enter the country with or without permits.

In the manufacturer space, historical shipments information are represented as points in 3-dimensional space. Each point has three coordinates values (*c*: *cost*, *l*: *location*, *h*: *HScode*). Beside these coordinates, the importer identification number, the classification label (risky or safe), and a unique number to identify the shipment is also stored in the shipment point. The selection of these coordinates in the value manipulation risk assessment aims to establish a relationship between the goods cost, manufacturer location, and HS-code. This relationship can be used to analyse whether the importer manipulated the manufacturer information in order to reduce the amount of duty. Figure 1 illustrated the manufacturer space.

The shipping agent space consists of four dimensions that represent the shipping agent identification number, the goods HS-Code, the port of loading, and trading volume. These parameters (coordinates) aim to clarify whether the selection of a specific agent for the shipment under consideration is expected. Additionally, it clarifies whether such goods are expected to be delivered from the declared port. In this space, each point contains the coordinates parameters, the importer identification number, the classification label (safe or risky), and the shipment identification number.

By having two subspaces, this representation aims to simplify the problem of detecting risky shipments, since each risk category can be addressed separately.

2.3 The Local-Density Outlier Factor (LOF)

In this section, for the sake of completeness, we describe the mechanism of the LOF algorithm. For a given point *A*, this algorithm takes into consideration the density of the points located inside point (*A*) neighbourhood to determine whether this point is an outlier. By considering the local density, this algorithm can be used to capture the scenarios where the characteristics of an outlier point might change over time. Once a point is processed, this algorithm returns an outlier factor (≥ 0). In situations where the value of this factor is higher than one, the point is considered an outlier. In other situations, the point is considered as a normal point.

This algorithm starts by calculating the distance between each point (transaction), and its k-nearest neighbour. For each point, we then calculate the reachability distance between this point and all points located inside its neighbourhood. The reachability distance of point *A* from point *B* is the maximum between the actual distance between these two points or the k-nearest distance of point *A*.

Then, the algorithm proceeds to calculate the local reachability density of the points. For a given point *A*, the local reachability density is calculated by taking the inverse of the average reachability distance of all points in *A* neighbourhood to itself. Lastly, the LOF of a point *A* is calculated by dividing the average ratio of the local reachability density of point *A* neighbours over that local reachability density of point *A* itself Using this calculation it is clear that the lower the local reachability density of point *A*, the higher the LOF. This captures the situations when the distances between a point and its neighbours are relatively large (sparse). The value of this factor (LOF) determines whether the point under consideration can be considered as an outlier. The higher the LOF value ($\gg$1), the more likely that this point is an outlier.

2.4 The Classification Step

The triggering of this step is associated with the submission of the manufacturer and shipping agent transactions to the blockchain. The submission of the commercial invoice details by the manufacturer triggers the manufacturer risk assessment stage. On the other hand, submitting the shipping agent transaction to the blockchain triggers the shipping agent risk assessment stage. Once each risk assessment is performed, the result of this assessment is submitted to the customs administration via the blockchain system. Such a strategy provides the customs administration with real-time assessment of shipment during the international trade supply chain stages. Additionally, providing such information in advance gives customs the ability to investigate the shipment in more details.

For each stage, the riskiness of a point (shipment) is obtained by analysing the locality of this point in the risky and safe subspaces. For each subspace, the assessment process determines whether the new point can be categorised as normal or outlier point. This categorisation is established by considering the density of the points around the new point location, and it is performed using the LOF algorithm. The objective of using both subspaces in this risk assessment process is to provide a more accurate risk assessment.

In situations where the new point (shipment) is only considered as an outlier in one of the subspaces (safe or risky), it is easy to determine the riskiness factors of this shipment. For instance, if the new shipment is considered as an outlier in the safe subspace, and normal in the risky subspace, this point (shipment) is considered as risky. However, in situations where the new shipment is considered as an outlier in both subspaces, the outlier factor values must be taken into consideration to determine the riskiness factors of the shipments. For instance, consider the example shown in Fig. 2, where points p_1 and p_2 represent two shipments. Both of these points are expected to be outliers in the safe and risky subspaces. The safe and risky outliers' factors for point p_2 is expected to be relatively the same, since this point is located in the middle between the two subspaces. However, point p_1 is located closer to safe subspace than the risky subspace, and therefore it might be considered as safe point.

Any point with relatively the same safe and risky outlier factors is considered as an undecidable point (shipment). Figure 3 highlights the steps of the risk assessment process. This process performs risk assessment at the personal and global levels. The personal level uses only the same importer historical transactions in the assessment process (line 2), where the global risk assessment uses all importers historical transactions (line 3). The outcome of each level is represented using two variables; namely; (1) the safe outlier factor (s_f), and (2) the risky outlier factor (r_f). Both of these level factors are taken into consideration during the assessment of the shipments. In this work, we use the personal assessment level factors (Ps_f and Pr_f) to tune (increase or/and decrease) the global assessment level risk factor (Gr_f). This tuning (lines 4–5) only occurs when the value of the personal factors suggests that the current shipment is risky, and this occurs when $Pr_f \leq 1$ and/or $Ps_f > 1$. This tuning is established since the personal assessment history might be relatively small to establish an accurate classification. Additionally, the global assessment does not precisely capture the importer behaviour.

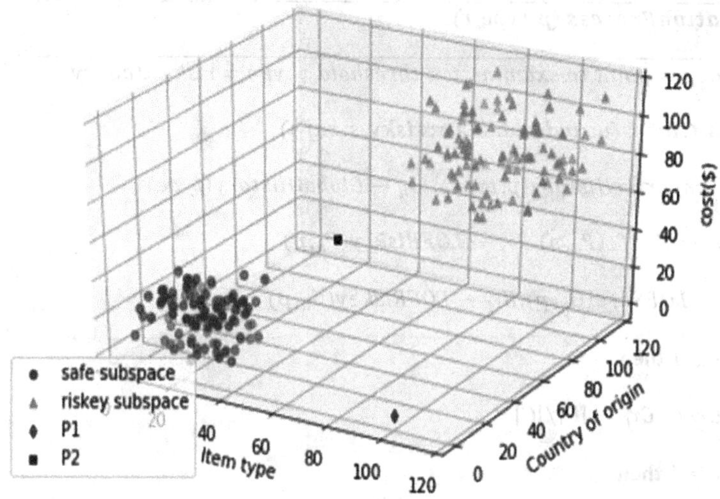

Fig. 2. Points classification example

In situations where the personal risk factor is less than or equal to one (line 4), we calculate the percentage of the personal history size from the global history size. Then, we update the global risk factor by subtracting this percentage from its value. It is clear that increasing the personal history size increases the impact of this subtraction. In other situations where the personal safe factor is greater than one, the global safe factor is updated by adding $((Ps_f - 1) \times (|P|/|G|))$ to its value (line 5). These updates occur to emphasis the situation where the personal risk assessment considers the shipment as risky.

The resultant global factors with value less that one is rounded to one (line 6). Then, we calculate the absolute difference between the global risk and safe factors (g) (line 7). As part of this process, we use a threshold (t) to determine the minimum possible acceptable gap between these two factors in order to classify the shipment. In situations where the gap is less than or equal to the threshold ($g \leq t$), the point is considered undecidable, since in this situation the global assessment factors do not clearly identify the riskiness status of the shipment.

To label a shipment as safe, this gap must be greater or equal to the threshold, and the global safe factor must be smaller than the global risk factor. A shipment is labelled as risky when the global safe factor is greater than the global risk factor by at least t value.

The threshold is introduced as a controlling parameter, were increasing the value of this threshold is expected to reduce the number of misclassified shipments. Furthermore, increasing this threshold increases the number of undecidable shipments. However, in this method, we are mainly concerned with reducing the percentage of misclassified shipments, since the undecidable shipments are expected to be re-classified using the centralised assessment strategy deployed at customs administration.

classificationProcess $(p, type, t)$

input: $p = point\ to\ examine, t = threshold\ , type = risk\ categoey$

output: $label\ (u{:}\ undecidable, r{:}\ risky, s{:}\ safe)$

$P_h \leftarrow ImporterHistory(p, type),\ G_h \leftarrow GlobalHistory(type)$

$Ps_f \leftarrow LOFSafe(P_h, p), Pr_f \leftarrow LOFRiskey(P_h, p)$

$Gs_f \leftarrow LOFSafe(G_h, p), Gr_f \leftarrow LOFRiskey(G_h, p)$

If $Pr_f \leq 1$ **then**

  $Gr_f \leftarrow Gr_f - |P|/|G|$

If $Ps_f > 1$ **then**

  $Gs_f \leftarrow Gs_f + \left((Ps_f - 1) \times (|P|/|G|)\right)$

$Gs_f, Gr_f \leftarrow RoundLowerThanOne(Gs_f, Gr_f)$

$g \leftarrow |Gr_f - Gs_f|$

Return $classifyShipment\ (g, t, Gr_f, Gs_f)$

Fig. 3. The classification process

3 Evaluation

The efficiency of the presented method is evaluated using several sets of experiments. For space limitation, we only show a subset of these experiments. The input data used in these experiments are obtained from the service innovation department at Dubai Customs. The used data consists of 12,221 shipment declaration applications submitted to Dubai Customs in 2018 (sea channel). These applications are already labelled as either risky or safe based on the outcome of the inspection performed by the customs administration. These declaration applications consist of 11% risky shipments and 89% safe shipments. The declaration applications are pre-processed to extract the required information for the value manipulation and undeclared goods risks assessments. In the presented experiments, 70% of the applications are used to represent the historical data, where the rest of the applications (30%) are used for testing purposes.

To capture the impact of the threshold (t) on the proposed method performance, we performed these experiments while varying the value of this threshold. To determine the value of k in the LOF algorithm, we have performed sensitivity analysis, where we incremented the value of k by one until the algorithm performance becomes stable. The stability is achieved when $k = 10$, and therefore in the presented experiments, the value of k is set to ten.

To calculate the overall accuracy of the presented method, the entire shipments must be classified to either risky, safe, or undecidable. Shipments are labelled as risky if any of the two risk assessments stages (manufacturer or shipping agent) identify the shipment as risky. A shipment is identified as undecidable if both risk assessments stages labelled the shipment as undecidable. In other situations, the shipments are classified as safe.

Besides accuracy, the used performance metrics in these experiments are precision, recall, and F1-score. These metrics are measured for each main classification class (safe and risky). In situations where we focus on the risky classification results, precision is defined as the percentage of correctly classified risky shipments, and it is calculated as follows:

$$P = \frac{TP}{TP + FP} \tag{1}$$

Where TP (true positive) refers to the number of correctly classified risky shipments, and FP (false positive) refers to the number of safe shipments that are wrongly classified as risky shipments. In this work, since undecidable shipments are assumed to be re-classified at the customs administration, shipments with undecidable status are not considered during the calculation of the accuracy, precision, recall, and F1-score.

Recall is defined as the percentage of correctly identified risky shipment over the total number of risky shipments. The recall is calculated as follows:

$$R = \frac{TP}{TP + FN} \tag{2}$$

Where FN (false negative) represents the number of risky shipments that are not correctly classified. F1-score is used to determine the accuracy of the test, and it is calculated as follows:

$$F1 = 2 \times \frac{R \times P}{P + R} \tag{3}$$

The value of this score ranges from zero to one, where the best accuracy occurred when the value of this score is one.

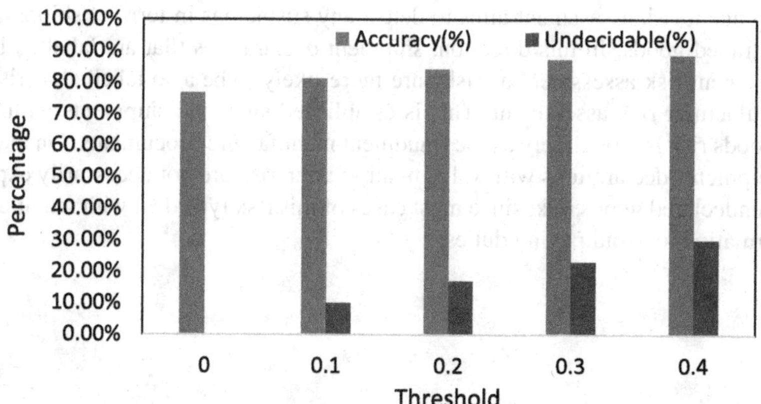

Fig. 4. Threshold value against the accuracy and the undecidable shipments percentages

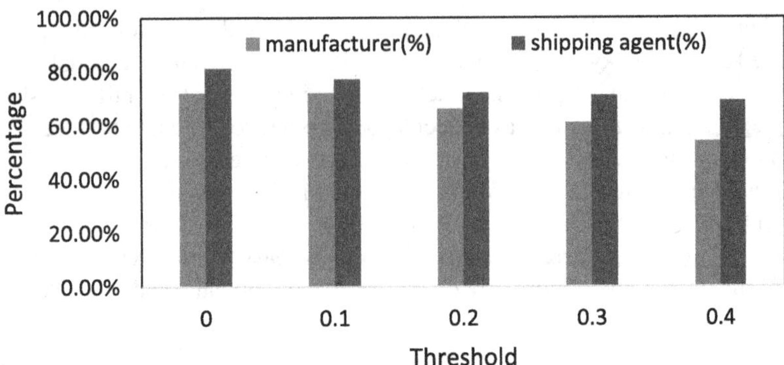

Fig. 5. Threshold value against the percentage of risky shipments captured by the manufacturer and the shipping agent assessment stages

To investigate the impact of the threshold value on the accuracy and the percentage of the undecidable shipments, we ran the experiment, while varying the value of the threshold. Figure 4 shows the results of these experiments. The result shows that increasing the threshold value increases classification accuracy. This is expected, since increasing the threshold results in increasing the percentage of shipments, which are labelled as undecidable, and this increases the probability of correctly classifying the rest of the shipments. Additionally, increasing the threshold value results in increasing the acceptable gap between the shipments safe and risked outlier factors, and therefore the shipments that will be examined are expected to have more distinct features that simplify the classification process.

Next, to clarify the percentage of truly risky shipments detected by each risk assessment stage, we ran the experiment while varying the threshold values (Fig. 5). The results show that the shipping agent assessment stage (undeclared goods risk) is always able to detect a higher percentage of risky shipments compared to the manufacturer risky assessment stage (value manipulation). This highlights the relationship between the two risk categories. To clarify this relationship, let us consider the objective of each risk assessment stage. Manufacturer risk assessment stage aims to detect any manipulation in the original invoice that is submitted by the manufacturer (value manipulation risk). Shipping agent risk assessment aims to detect any suspicions in term of shipping path and the traded goods. In this direction, shipment declarations that are labelled by the shipping agent risk assessment as risky are more likely to be also labelled as risky by the manufacturer risk assessment. This is established since the shipments with undeclared goods risk is more likely to use fraudulent manufacturer documents. On the other hand, shipments declarations with value manipulation risk are not necessarily expected to have undeclared goods risk, since most cases of this risk type deal with manipulating the information to avoid paying duties.

To investigate the performance of the proposed method in term of accuracy factors (precision, recall, and F1-score), we ran the experiments for threshold value equal to 0.2. In these experiments, we calculate the performance factors for both the risky and safe classifications. The results of these experiments are shown in Table 1. From the results, we can see that the precision score for the safe shipment classification is significantly higher compared to the risky shipments classification. In our scenario, the shipments with risky classification label are further examined by the centralised risk assessment process at customs administration, whereas shipments with safe classification label are expected to be quickly cleared by the customs administration. Thus, achieving a high precision score for the safe shipments' classification is desirable in our situation. About the risky shipment classification precision, from the results, we can see that 27% of the risky classified shipments were safe shipments. This occurs because the distance between these safe shipments and the risky subspace is expected to be relatively small. In this direction, the proposed method labelled these shipments as risky to be re-classified by the centralised risk assessment functionality located at the customs administration.

Table 1. Performance measures

	Precision	Recall	F1-score
Risky	73%	85%	79%
Safe	90%	81%	85%

The performance of the proposed methods depends mainly on the threshold value, and the employed risk assessment stages. One of the main advantages of this method is that new risk assessment stages can be designed and deployed without interrupting the rest of the stages. In addition, since we assume that the method is implemented on top of a blockchain solution for international trade, any risk assessment stage can be modified by deploying a new smart contract (newer version of the code) to replace the current active one. The mechanism of adopting the threshold strategy aims to take advantage of the fact that regardless of the deployed distributed risk assessment method, a centralised risk assessment strategy is also required to be deployed at the customs administration. Beside re-examining risky classified shipments, the centralised risk assessment process is designed to capture the intelligence information provided by external departments (Interpol and police department). Therefore, the proposed method works well in situations where it is employed as a secondary assessment level to provide real-time feedback about the shipments risk assessment at different stages in the trade supply chain.

4 Related Work

The use of outlier detection algorithms has advanced the detection of abnormal activities in different application domains such as network traffic intrusion [7], money laundering [8, 9], and fraud detection [10–12].

In computer network domain, the detection of abnormality in network traffic is performed by analysing the network traffic periodically to capture any irregularity in traffic flow. To address this problem, Gan et al. [7] proposed an improved version of the LOF algorithm that attempts to capture the irregularity in the traffic pattern, where network traffic is represented as points in multi-dimensional space. In this improved version, the authors combined LOF with a clustering approach to optimise the identification of the neighbourhood.

To address the money laundering problem, Zengan et al. [8] proposed a LOF-based mechanism that applies a clustering approach to reduce the complexity of the outlier detection problem. In this solution, the distance between any two transactions belong to the same cluster must be less than or equal a pre-determined threshold. In this context, threshold is used as a measurement of similarity between transactions. Once clusters are established, the proposed solution apply LOF algorithm to identify outliers.

In the credit card domain, several proposals [10, 11] have addressed the importance of using outlier detection algorithms (such as LOF and k-Nearest Neighbours) to detect fraudulent activities. In these papers, the authors show that the behaviour of the transaction can be efficiently determined, and therefore fraud detection mechanism can be established using outlier detection algorithms.

Badriyah et al. [12] have applied the k-Nearest Neighbours outliers detection mechanism to identify frauds in cars insurance application domain. To identify fraud, this mechanism compares the features of the new transaction (attributes) against the features of its k-nearest neighbours. In this direction, if a transaction does not share similarity with the majority of its neighbours, it is considered as an outlier.

In this paper, as part of the proposed risk assessment method, the LOF algorithm is used to detect whether a given point can be considered as an outlier. Other outlier detection mechanisms could also be used for this purpose. However, the LOF algorithm is selected since the density of the trade transactions is expected to change over the financial year. Therefore, employing local density-based outlier detection mechanism such as LOF is expected to capture the variation in the data pattern over time.

5 Conclusion

In this paper, we proposed a distributed risk assessment method that employs the well-known LOF algorithm to detect whether the new shipment can be considered risky (outlier). The proposed method is designed to reduce the pressure on customs administration by performing an early-stage risk assessment. This gives the customs administration the advantage of investigating the shipment in more detail if required. By considering the safe and risky historical shipment information, the proposed method attempts to improve its classification accuracy. Using this method, points are classified as either safe, risky, or undecidable. The undecidable point (shipments) are required to be investigated further (re-classified) by the customs administration. The results show that the proposed method can achieve around 83% accuracy.

Acknowledgement. Dubai Customs funded the research for this paper. The authors would also like to thank everyone from the Service Innovation department for constructive discussions and inputs.

References

1. World Customs Organization: WCO SAFE Framework of Standards, June 2018

2. Breunig, M., Kriegel, H.-P., Ng, R.T., Sander, J.: LOF: identifying density-based local outliers. In: Proceedings of the 2000 ACM SIGMOD International Conference on Management of Data (SIGMOD), pp. 93–104 (2000)
3. Yuan, C., Xu, M., Si, X.: Research on a new signature scheme on blockchain. Secur. Commun. Netw. **2017**, 1–10 (2017)
4. Macedo, L.: Blockchain for trade facilitation: Ethereum, eWTP, COs and regulatory issues. World Cust. J. **12**(2), 87–94 (2018)
5. Deloitte: Global Blockchain Survey - Blockchain Gets Down to Business. Deloitte Insights (2019)
6. Loklindt, C., Moeller, M., Kinra, A.: How Blockchain could be adopted for exchanging documentation in the shipping industry. In: Lecture Notes in Logistics, pp. 194–198 (2011)
7. Gan, Z., Zhou, X.: Abnormal network traffic detection based on improved LOF algorithm. In: Proceedings of the 2018 10th International Conference on Intelligent Human-Machine System and Cybernetics, IHMSC 2018, vol. 1, pp. 142–145 (2018)
8. Gao, Z.: Application of cluster-based local outlier factor algorithm in anti-money laundering. In: Proceedings of the 2009 International Conference on Management and Service Science, Wuhan, pp. 1–4 (2009)
9. Chen, M.C., Wang, R.J., Chen, A.P.: An empirical study for the detection of corporate financial anomaly using outlier mining techniques. In: Proceedings of the 2007 International Conference on Convergence Information Technology, ICCIT 2007, pp. 612–617 (2007)
10. Ceronmani Sharmila, V., Kumar, K., Sundaram, R., Samyuktha, D., Harish, R.: Credit card fraud detection using anomaly techniques. In: Proceedings of the 2019 1st International Conference on Innovations in Information and Communication Technology (ICIICT), pp. 1–6 (2019)
11. Malini, N., Pushpa, M.: Analysis on credit card fraud identification techniques based on KNN and outlier detection. In: Proceedings of the 3rd IEEE International Conference on Advances in Electrical, Electronics, Information, Communication and Bio-Informatics, AEEICB 2017, pp. 255–258 (2017)
12. Badriyah, T., Rahmaniah, L., Syarif, I.: Nearest neighbour and statistics method based for detecting fraud in auto insurance. In: Proceedings of the 2018 International Conference on Applied Engineering, ICAE 2018, pp. 1–5 (2018)

Pufferfish Privacy Mechanism Based on Multi-dimensional Markov Chain Model for Correlated Categorical Data Sequences

Zhicheng Xi(✉), Yingpeng Sang(✉), Hanrui Zhong, and Yongchun Zhang

Sun Yat-Sen University, Guangzhou, China
{xizhch,zhonghr3,zhangych65}@mail2.sysu.edu.cn,
sangyp@mail.sysu.edu.cn

Abstract. Differential privacy is a rigorous standard for protecting data privacy and has been extensively used in data publishing and data mining. However, because of its vulnerable assumption that tuples in the database are in-dependent, it cannot guarantee privacy if the data are correlated. Kifer et al. proposed the Pufferfish Privacy framework to protect correlated data privacy, while till now under this framework there is only some practical mechanism for protecting correlations among attributes of one individual sequence. In this paper, we extend this framework to the cases of multiple correlated sequences, in which we protect correlations among individual records, as well as correlations of attributes. Application scenarios can be different people's time-series data and the objective is to protect each individual's privacy while publishing useful information. We firstly define privacy based on Pufferfish privacy framework in our application, and when the data are correlated, the privacy level can be assessed through the framework. Then we present a multi-dimensional Markov Chain model, which can be used to accurately describe the structure of multi-dimensional data correlations. We also propose a mechanism to implement the privacy framework, and finally conduct experiments to demonstrate that our mechanism achieves both high utility and privacy.

Keywords: Pufferfish privacy · Multi-dimensional Markov Chain · Time series · Data correlations

1 Introduction

Big data era has come and it is called the "fourth paradigm" of scientific research. More and more databases are used in various fields such as healthcare, education, finance, population, transportation, science and technology, and have created huge social benefits. However, privacy concerns hinder the wildly use of these data. People would refuse to provide their sensitive information such as salary, diseases and user behavioral information. To this end, how to release useful information without revealing the individual's privacy has become a hot issue.

Dwork proposed the concept of differential privacy [2–5], which is still the state-of-the-art standard notion in data privacy. It provides a rigorous privacy guarantee that

H. Shen and Y. Sang (Eds.): PAAP 2019, CCIS 1163, pp. 430–439, 2020.
https://doi.org/10.1007/978-981-15-2767-8_38

it will not influence the outcome of any analysis when removing or adding a single database item. However, The initial framework of differential privacy is only effective for independent data records.

In practice, tuple correlation occurs naturally in datasets. User activity streams like time-series data, GPS trajectories and social networks typically generate records which are correlated. It has been shown that the data correlations can be utilized by attackers to improve their inferences about individuals and cause privacy leakage [7]. Group differential privacy has been proposed to solve this problem [5], which extends the privacy protection on individual to a group of correlated individuals. But the required noise may greatly destroy data utility.

Pufferfish was proposed by [8], which is based on differential privacy but can accommodate more situations. There are 3 important components in Pufferfish, a set of potential secrets S, a set of discriminative pairs S_{pairs}, and a set of data evolution scenarios $D(\theta \in D)$. It promises that the secret pairs are indistinguishable to the adversary. D captures how much knowledge the potential attackers have and then it can take the correlation of data into consideration. But the framework did not propose any specific perturbation algorithm to handle the correlation. Song et al. adopted the framework and used it to protect the privacy of time-series data such as physical activity measurements and power consumption data [11].

However, the prior work focuses on the correlations among individuals with only one attribute [14], or multiple attributes but only for one individual [12]. In this paper, we consider the correlations among individuals as well as the correlations among multiple attributes inside each sequence, such as different people's time-series data. These databases have wide applications, including stock markets, disease surveillance and real-time traffic monitoring. For example, in a database which records physical activities of members from the same family or company across time, there are different individual's records, and each record is a data sequence. Our goal is to publish aggregate statistics on individuals' activities without leaking the privacy of a specific individual, and here privacy is the activity at any given moment.

The contributions of our paper can be summarized as follows:

- We consider the simultaneous privacy protection for two types of correlations among categorical data sequences. One is the correlations among individuals, and the other is correlations inside each sequence.
- We propose a protection mechanism based on Pufferfish privacy by modelling correlations among variables employing the multi-dimensional Markov Chain.
- We conduct experiments on simulated data and demonstrate that our privacy mechanism provides both high privacy and utility guarantees.

2 Related Work

In the past decade, a growing body of work has been published on differential privacy [2–5]. As we explain earlier, differential privacy assumes that records are independent so it is not the right framework for the scenarios where records are correlated.

Correlated differential privacy has emerged to solve this problem. Kifer [7] was the first to raise the issue that differential privacy may not guarantee privacy without consideration of data correlations, and then proposed Pufferfish privacy [8], a generalization of differential privacy. It provides some specific instances of Pufferfish framework but is lack of specific mechanisms for many practical applications.

Existing privacy mechanisms for correlated data publishing can be classified into two types. The first one replaces the global sensitivity with new correlation-based parameters, such as dependence coefficient [9] and correlated sensitivity [15], and [10] used Maximal Information Coefficient to measure the correlations and achieved correlated differential privacy for big data publication. The other one uses appropriate models to describe the correlations between variables. [14] uses a modification of Pufferfish and proposed Bayesian differential privacy, which represents the data correlations by a Gaussian correlation model. Song proposed Markov Quilt Mechanism representing data correlation via a Bayesian Network [11]. There are also some efforts on time-series release such as [13] and high-dimensional data releasing based on Markov network [12]. However, these efforts only considered one-dimensional correlations of data. Therefore, they cannot be applied to simultaneously protect the two types of correlations. One type is the correlations among various sequences, and the other is the correlations inside each sequence.

3 Preliminaries

We will introduce some basic concepts in this section, including Pufferfish privacy mechanism, Multi-dimensional Markov Chain models, global sensitivity and Laplace mechanism. To start with, Table 1 lists notations and their explanations used across this paper.

3.1 Pufferfish Privacy Mechanism

We use Pufferfish framework as our privacy definition and extend it to apply in our cases. A Pufferfish framework consists of three parts, a set of potential secrets S, a set of discriminative pairs S_{pairs}, and a set of data evolution scenarios $D(\theta \in D)$. S captures what is protected, which is the set of secrets that refer to individual's private data. S_{pairs} captures how to protect, which means that the attackers cannot distinguish between the secret pairs. Finally, D captures how much knowledge the potential attackers have, which is a collection of plausible data generating distributions. In this paper, the correlations of data are controlled. Each $\theta \in D$ represents an adversary's belief about how to generate the data, and we should promise the indistinguishability.

Definition 3.1 (ϵ-Pufferfish(S, S_{pairs}, D) Privacy). Given set of potential secrets S, a set of discriminative pairs $S_{pairs}\left((s_i, s_j) \in S_{pairs}\right)$, a set of data evolution scenarios $D(\theta \in D)$, and a privacy parameter $\epsilon > 0$, M satisfies ϵ-Pufferfish(S, S_{pairs}, D) privacy if

$$P(M(X) = \omega | s_i, \theta) \leq e^{\epsilon} P(M(X) = \omega | s_j, \theta) \tag{1}$$

$$P(M(X) = \omega | s_j, \theta) \leq e^{\epsilon} P(M(X) = \omega | s_i, \theta) \tag{2}$$

Table 1. Table of notations

Symbol	Description
X	A database instance $\left\{x_n^k, k = 1, 2, \ldots, s\right\}$
$y_n^{(k)}$	The state probability distribution vector of the kth sequence at time n
S	Set of potential secrets
S_{pairs}	Discriminative pairs. $S_{pairs}(s_i, s_j) \subset S \times S$
D	The set of evolution scenarios: a conservative collection of plausible data generating distributions
M	A privacy mechanism over X
$P^{(jk)}$	The transition probabilities from the state of kth sequence at time n to the state of jth sequence at time $(n+1)$
λ_{jk}	The weights between columns
F	A query function on X
GS_f	The global sensitivity of a query function on X
ϵ	The privacy budget

Equivalently,

$$e^{-\epsilon} \leq \frac{P(s_i|M(X) = \omega, \theta)}{P(s_j|M(X) = \omega, \theta)} / \frac{P(s_i|\theta)}{P(s_j|\theta)} \leq e^{\epsilon} \tag{3}$$

when s_i and s_j are such that $P(s_i|\theta) \neq 0$, $P(s_j|\theta) \neq 0$.

3.2 Multi-dimensional Markov Chain Models

Markov Chain models are widely used in the modeling of data sequences [1]. In our work, we use a multi-dimensional Markov Chain model for correlated data sequences such as sales demand data, stock index data and physical activities of a group individual. We assume that there are s sequences $\left\{y_n^{(k)}, k = 1, 2, \ldots, s\right\}$, and $y_n^{(k)}$ is the state probability distribution vector of the kth sequence at time n. Each sequence has m possible states in M. If the kth sequence is in state j with probability one at time n then we write $P\left\{y_n^{(k)} = j\right\} = 1$ or

$$y_n^{(k)} = \left(0, \ldots, 0, \underbrace{1}_{j}, 0, \ldots, 0\right)^T \tag{4}$$

The following conditions are satisfied in a multivariate Markov Chain model:

$$y_{n+1}^{(j)} = \sum_{k=1}^{s} \lambda_{jk} P^{(jk)} y_n^{(k)}, (j = 1, 2, \ldots, s) \tag{5}$$

where $\sum_{k=1}^{s} \lambda_{jk} = 1, \lambda_{jk} \geq 0, 1 \leq j, k \leq s$. $P^{(jk)}$ are the transition probabilities from the state of kth sequence at time n to the state of jth sequence at time (n + 1), and λ_{jk} are the weights between columns.

The state probability distribution of the jth Chain at time (n + 1) is related to the state distribution of the s sequences at time n, but independent of the state before time n, which only hinges on the weighted average of $P^{(jk)} y_n^{(k)}$. The following is the matrix notation:

$$\begin{pmatrix} y_{n+1}^{(1)} \\ y_{n+1}^{(2)} \\ \vdots \\ y_{n+1}^{(s)} \end{pmatrix} = \begin{pmatrix} \lambda_{11} P^{(11)} & \lambda_{12} P^{(12)} & \cdots & \lambda_{1s} P^{(1s)} \\ \lambda_{21} P^{(21)} & \lambda_{22} P^{(22)} & \cdots & \lambda_{2s} P^{(2s)} \\ \vdots & \vdots & \vdots & \vdots \\ \lambda_{s1} P^{(s1)} & \lambda_{s2} P^{(s2)} & \cdots & \lambda_{ss} P^{(ss)} \end{pmatrix} \begin{pmatrix} y_n^{(1)} \\ y_n^{(2)} \\ \vdots \\ y_n^{(s)} \end{pmatrix} \tag{6}$$

Let $y_n = \left(y_n^{(1)}, y_n^{(2)}, \ldots, y_n^{(s)}\right)^T$, then $y_{n+1} = Q y_n$.

Lemma 1. For $1 \leq j, k \leq s$, if $\lambda_{jk} \geq 0$, then the matrix Q has a eigenvalue that is equal to 1, and the eigenvalues of Q are smaller than or equal to 1.

Lemma 2. For $1 \leq j, k \leq s$, assume that $\lambda_{jk} \geq 0$ and $P^{(jk)}$ is irreducible. Then there exists a stable vector $y = \left(y^{(1)}, y^{(2)}, \ldots, y^{(s)}\right)^T$ such that y $= Qy$ and $\sum_{i=1}^{m} \left[y^{(j)}\right]_i = 1, 1 \leq j \leq s$.

In order to obtain the values of parameters, the transition probability matrix of each data sequence must be determined. Let $f_{i_j i_k}^{(jk)}$ represent the transition matrix from the state i_k in the sequence $\left\{y_n^{(k)}\right\}$ to the state i_j in the sequence $\left\{y_n^{(j)}\right\}$. Then the transition frequency matrix can be written as follows:

$$F^{(jk)} = \begin{pmatrix} f_{11}^{(jk)} & \cdots\cdots & f_{1m}^{(jk)} \\ f_{21}^{(jk)} & \cdots\cdots & f_{2m}^{(jk)} \\ \vdots & \vdots \; \vdots & \vdots \\ f_{m1}^{(jk)} & \cdots\cdots & f_{mm}^{(jk)} \end{pmatrix} \tag{7}$$

And the following rule:

$$\hat{p}_{i_j i_k}^{(jk)} = \begin{cases} \dfrac{f_{i_j i_k}^{(jk)}}{\sum_{i_k=1}^{m} f_{i_j i_k}^{(jk)}}, & \sum_{i_k=1}^{m} f_{i_j i_k}^{(jk)} \neq 0 \\ 0, & in\, the\, other\, cases \end{cases} \tag{8}$$

Using this transition frequency matrix $F^{(jk)}$ and the normalized rule, one obtains the estimations of the matrix of transition probabilities $P^{(jk)}$:

$$\widehat{P}^{(jk)} = \begin{pmatrix} \hat{p}_{11}^{(jk)} & \cdots\cdots & \hat{p}_{1m}^{(jk)} \\ \hat{p}_{21}^{(jk)} & \cdots\cdots & \hat{p}_{2m}^{(jk)} \\ \vdots & \vdots \; \vdots & \vdots \\ \hat{p}_{m1}^{(jk)} & \cdots\cdots & \hat{p}_{mm}^{(jk)} \end{pmatrix} \tag{9}$$

We also need to obtain the parameters λ_{jk}. There is a stable probability vector y in the multi-dimensional Markov Chain. We can estimate the vector y by calculating the probability of each state in each sequence, and is denoted as $\widehat{y} = \left(\widehat{y}^{(1)}, \widehat{y}^{(2)}, \ldots, \widehat{y}^{(s)}\right)^T$, then $\widehat{y} = Q\widehat{y}$. The values of λ_{jk} can be obtained by solving the following optimization problem:

$$\begin{cases} \min\limits_{\lambda} \max\limits_{i} \left| \left[\sum_{k=1}^{m} \lambda_{jk} \widehat{P}^{(jk)} \widehat{y}^{(k)} - \widehat{y}^{(j)} \right]_i \right| \\ subject\ to\ \sum_{k=1}^{s} \lambda_{jk} = 1,\ and\ \lambda_{jk} \geq 0,\ \forall k \end{cases} \tag{10}$$

This problem can be formulated as a linear programming problem. Let B be the condition-$B = \left[\widehat{P}^{(j1)}\widehat{y}^{(1)} \middle| \widehat{P}^{(j2)}\widehat{y}^{(2)} \middle| \ldots | \widehat{P}^{(js)}\widehat{y}^{(s)}\right]$, the model can be written as follows. For each j:

$$\min_{\lambda} w_j$$

Subject to

$$\begin{cases} \begin{pmatrix} w_j \\ w_j \\ \vdots \\ w_j \end{pmatrix} \geq \widehat{y}^{(j)} - B \begin{pmatrix} \lambda_{j1} \\ \lambda_{j2} \\ \vdots \\ \lambda_{js} \end{pmatrix}, \\ \begin{pmatrix} w_j \\ w_j \\ \vdots \\ w_j \end{pmatrix} \geq -\widehat{y}^{(j)} + B \begin{pmatrix} \lambda_{j1} \\ \lambda_{j2} \\ \vdots \\ \lambda_{js} \end{pmatrix}, \\ w_j \geq 0, \\ \sum_{k=1}^{s} \lambda_{jk} = 1,\ and\ \lambda_{jk} \geq 0,\ \forall j \end{cases} \tag{11}$$

3.3 Additional Notion

We introduce some additional definitions and notation to conclude this section.

Definition 3.4 (global sensitivity). Let f be a function that maps a dataset into a fixed-size vector of real numbers (i.e.$X \to R^d$). For any two neighboring databases X and X', the sensitivity of f is defined as

$$GS_f = \max_{X,X'} \left\| f(X) - f(X') \right\|_p \tag{12}$$

Where p denotes L_p norm used to measure Δf, and we usually use L_1 norm. For any query function $F: X \to R^d$, the privacy mechanism M

$$M(X) = f(X) + Z \tag{13}$$

Satisfies ϵ-differential privacy, where $Z \sim Lap(\Delta f/\epsilon)$. We use $Lap(\sigma)$ to denote a Laplace distribution with mean 0 and scale parameter σ. Recall that this distribution satisfies the density function: $h(x) = \frac{1}{2\sigma} e^{-|x|/\sigma}$.

4 A Mechanism for 2-Dimensional Correlated Data

4.1 Problem Statement

We consider a more restricted setting when the database X are several categorical data sequences. We assume that there are s categorical sequences and each has m possible states in M. Their dependence can be described by multi-dimensional Markov Chain model, and the goal is to keep the value of each x_i^k private. We next use two examples to illustrate the problem.

Example 1: A Group Physical Activity Measurement. A is the set of activities such as {walking, sleeping, working} and s_t^{k*a} denotes the event that the kth person's state is activity a at moment t, i.e., $x_t^k = a$. In the Pufferfish framework, we set S as $\{s_t^{k*a} : k = 1, \ldots, s, t = 1, \ldots, T, a \in A\}$, so the activity at any specific moment t of each person is a secret. S_{pairs} is the set of all pairs (s_t^{k*a}, s_t^{k*b}) for a, b in A and for all t and each person; in other words, for all pairs a and b, the attackers cannot tell whether this person is doing activity a or activity b at any time. D is a set of possible distributions to generate the data, which captures how people switch between activities and how people influence each other. A plausible belief is to set D be a set of multi-dimensional Markov Chains where each state is an activity in A. Each multi-dimensional Markov Chain can be represented by an initial distribution y_1 which represents the initial state of each sequence, the transition probabilities $P^{(jk)}$ and the weights between columns λ_{jk}. For example, we have two activities {walking, working} and use $(1, 0)^T$ to represent walking. There are two sequences in the dataset. Thus, a distribution $\theta \in D$ is represent by a tuple

$$\left\{y_1, \begin{bmatrix} P^{11} & P^{12} \\ P^{21} & P^{22} \end{bmatrix}, \begin{bmatrix} \lambda_{11} & \lambda_{12} \\ \lambda_{21} & \lambda_{22} \end{bmatrix}\right\}$$

Then such D can be the set:

$$\left\{\begin{array}{l} \left(\begin{bmatrix} (0,1)^T \\ (1,0)^T \end{bmatrix}, \begin{bmatrix} \begin{bmatrix} 1 & 0.5 \\ 0 & 0.5 \end{bmatrix} & \begin{bmatrix} 0.7 & 0.6 \\ 0.3 & 0.4 \end{bmatrix} \\ \begin{bmatrix} 0.8 & 0.5 \\ 0.2 & 0.5 \end{bmatrix} & \begin{bmatrix} 0.9 & 0.6 \\ 0.1 & 0.4 \end{bmatrix} \end{bmatrix}, \begin{bmatrix} 0.5 & 0.5 \\ 0.5 & 0.5 \end{bmatrix}\right), \\ \left(\begin{bmatrix} (1,0)^T \\ (0,1)^T \end{bmatrix}, \begin{bmatrix} \begin{bmatrix} 0 & 0.5 \\ 1 & 0.5 \end{bmatrix} & \begin{bmatrix} 0.5 & 0.5 \\ 0.6 & 0.4 \end{bmatrix} \\ \begin{bmatrix} 0.4 & 0.3 \\ 0.6 & 0.7 \end{bmatrix} & \begin{bmatrix} 0.9 & 0.6 \\ 0.1 & 0.4 \end{bmatrix} \end{bmatrix}, \begin{bmatrix} 1 & 0 \\ 0 & 1 \end{bmatrix}\right) \end{array}\right\}$$

Example 2: Sales Demand Data Sequences. The database consists of a soft-drink company's sales demand data. The company has 5 products {A, B, C, D, E} and each product is labeled as its moving rate of sales volume - {very fast-moving, fast-moving, standard, slow-moving, very slow-moving, no sales volume}. Each customer of the company has 5 sales demand data sequences. We can use the database to reduce the company's inventory and maximize the needs of each customer, but we cannot reveal customer's privacy which means the adversary cannot infer the customer's demand for all products at a specific time. Let M be the moving states set and let s_t^{k*m} denote the event that the kth product's state is m at time t, namely, $x_t^k = m$. In the Pufferfish framework, we set S as $\{s_t^{k*m} : k = 1, \ldots, 5, t = 1, \ldots, T, m \in M\}$, so the state at each time t of each product is a secret. S_{pairs} is the set of all pairs (s_t^{k*m}, s_t^{k*n}) for m, n in M and for all t and each product. Similarly, D can also be a set of multi-dimensional Markov Chains.

4.2 Our Mechanism

In our mechanism, we first use multi-dimensional Markov Chains to describe the 2-dimensional correlation and get the set of all possible distributions which can generate the data. Then we adopt the Pufferfish framework and customize our privacy definition for our application. At last, we use the concept of interpretation by adding appropriate noise to the result and then achieve both utility and privacy.

Our mechanism is based on the Laplace mechanism in differential privacy which adds noise to the result of F proportional to the global sensitivity. In our mechanism, we use the worst-case distance between the distribution $P(F(X)|s_i, \theta)$ and $P\big(F(X)|s_j, \theta\big)$ for a secret pair (s_i, s_j). First, we use the idea of Earth Mover's Distance (EMD) to represent two probability distributions' distance.

Definition 4.1. Let μ, ν be two probability distributions on R, and let $\Gamma(\mu, \nu)$ be the set of all joint distributions. The distance between μ and ν is defined as:

$$Distance_\infty(\mu, \nu) = inf_{\gamma \in \Gamma(\mu,\nu)} \max_{(a,b) \in support(\gamma)} |a - b| \tag{14}$$

The Earth mover's distance is the minimum shift probability mass between μ and ν which in our mechanism is $P(F(X)|s_i, \theta)$ and $P\big(F(X)|s_j, \theta\big)$. To guarantee the Pufferfish privacy, we add Laplace noise to the result of the query F proportional to the $Distance_\infty\big(P(F(X)|s_i, \theta), P\big(F(X)|s_j, \theta\big)\big)$. We describe the full mechanism in Algorithm 1.

Algorithm 1 : A Mechanism for 2-dimensional Correlated Data

Given Database X, query F, Pufferfish framework(S, S_{pairs}, D), privacy parameter ϵ

for all $(s_i, s_j) \in S_{pairs}$ and all $\theta \in D$ such that $P(s_i|\theta) \neq 0$ and $P(s_j|\theta) \neq 0$ **do**

  Set $\mu_{i,\theta} = P(F(X) = \cdot\ |s_i, \theta)$, $\mu_{j,\theta} = P\big(F(X) = \cdot\ |s_j, \theta\big)$.

  Calculate $Distance_\infty(\mu_{i,\theta}, \mu_{j,\theta})$

end for

Set $Distance = sup_{(s_i,s_j) \in S_{pairs}, \theta \in D}\ Distance_\infty(\mu_{i,\theta}, \mu_{j,\theta})$.

`return` $F(X) + Z$, where $Z \sim Lap(\frac{Distance}{\epsilon})$

For given Database X, query F, Pufferfish framework (S, S_{pairs}, D), and privacy parameter ϵ, we find the supremum of the distance (EMD) between $\mu_{i,\theta}$ and $\mu_{j,\theta}$ through all S_{pairs} and D. Then, we add the Laplace noise to the result of F proportional to the distance we find. The mechanism for 2-dimensional correlated data satisfies the pufferfish privacy.

5 Experiments

We apply our mechanism to the simulated data which is generated by a multi-dimensional Markov Chain of two sequences ($s = 2$) and each sequence with length $T = 100$ and states $\{0, 1\}$. We employ this prototype simulation in order to achieve an efficient implementation of our algorithm.

First, we generate the database X which is determined by initial distribution for two sequences with two parameters $q_0^1 = P\left(X_1^1 = 0\right)$ and $q_0^1 = P\left(X_1^2 = 0\right)$, the transition probabilities $P^{(jk)}$ and the weights between columns λ_{jk} which are equal to 0.5 in our setting. The transition probabilities are determined by four transition matrices and each matrix such as $P^{(11)}$, $P^{(12)}$, $P^{(21)}$, *or* $P^{(22)}$ is determined by parameters p_0^{jk} and p_1^{jk}, in which $p_0^{jk} = P(X_{i+1}^j = 0|X_i^k = 0)$ and $p_1^{jk} = P(X_{i+1}^j = 1|X_i^k = 1)$.

The query $F(X) = \frac{1}{T*s}\sum_{k=1}^{s}\sum_{i=1}^{T} X_i^k$. Then we calculate the conditional probability $P(F(X) = \cdot|s_i, \theta)$ and $P\left(F(X) = \cdot|s_j, \theta\right)$ and measure the distance between them by Earth Mover's Distance. The privacy budget ϵ varies in $\{0.2, 0.5, 1, 2, 5\}$. We compare the actual *F(X)* with our output result and show the average L_1 error between them. We use group differential privacy as our baseline which assumes that all variables are correlated and adds $Lap(1/\epsilon)$ noise to each bin. Table 2 shows the result of our experiments.

Table 2. L_1 error of frequency of state 1

ϵ	0.2	0.5	1	2	5
Our mechanism	3.1498	1.4735	0.4326	0.1252	0.0243
Group DP	4.3157	2.3584	0.6324	0.1432	0.1025

From Table 2, we can see that our mechanism is more accurate than group differential privacy. As expected, the L_1 error decreases as the private budget ϵ increases which shows that smaller ϵ means more privacy. The experiments show that our mechanism achieves both higher utility and privacy than group differential privacy.

6 Conclusion

We propose a Pufferfish privacy mechanism for correlated categorical data sequences, such as a group of physical activity measurements, sales demand data sequences, and other time-series datasets. We use the multi-dimensional Markov Chain model to represent the correlations among individuals and inside each sequence. Experiments with simulated data show that our mechanism achieves both high utility and privacy.

There are still some aspects for our work to be improved in the future. The computational efficiency can be improved by exploiting structural information of multi-dimensional Markov Chains. Experiments also need to be conducted on real-world datasets. Some other types of correlated data, such as semi-structured data, graph data and large-scale data, also requires novel models and privacy mechanisms.

Acknowledgements. This work was supported by the National Key Research and Development Program of China (No. 2017YFB0203201), the Science and Technology Program of Guangdong Province, China (No. 2017A010101039), and the Science and Technology Program of Guangzhou, China (No. 201904010209).

References

1. Ching, W., Zhang, S., Ng, M.: On multi-dimensional Markov chain models. Pac. J. Optim. **3**(2), 235–243 (2007)
2. Dwork, C., Kenthapadi, K., McSherry, F., Mironov, I., Naor, M.: Our data, ourselves: privacy via distributed noise generation. In: Vaudenay, S. (ed.) EUROCRYPT 2006. LNCS, vol. 4004, pp. 486–503. Springer, Heidelberg (2006). https://doi.org/10.1007/11761679_29
3. Dwork, C., McSherry, F., Nissim, K., Smith, A.: Calibrating noise to sensitivity in private data analysis. In: Halevi, S., Rabin, T. (eds.) TCC 2006. LNCS, vol. 3876, pp. 265–284. Springer, Heidelberg (2006). https://doi.org/10.1007/11681878_14
4. Dwork, C.: Differential privacy: a survey of results. In: Agrawal, M., Du, D., Duan, Z., Li, A. (eds.) TAMC 2008. LNCS, vol. 4978, pp. 1–19. Springer, Heidelberg (2008). https://doi.org/10.1007/978-3-540-79228-4_1
5. Dwork, C., Roth, A.: The algorithmic foundations of differential privacy. Found. Trends® Theor. Comput. Sci. **9**(3–4), 211–407 (2014)
6. Humbert, M., Trubert, B., Huguenin, K.: A Survey on Interdependent Privacy (2019)
7. Kifer, D., Machanavajjhala, A.: No free lunch in data privacy. In: Proceedings of the 2011 ACM SIGMOD International Conference on Management of Data, pp. 193–204. ACM (2011)
8. Kifer, D., Machanavajjhala, A.: Pufferfish: a framework for mathematical privacy definitions. ACM Trans. Database Syst. (TODS) **39**(1), 3 (2014)
9. Liu, C., Chakraborty, S., Mittal, P.: Dependence makes you vulnberable: differential privacy under dependent tuples. In: NDSS, vol. 16, pp. 21–24 (2016)
10. Lv, D., Zhu, S.: Achieving correlated differential privacy of big data publication. Comput. Secur. **82**, 184–195 (2019)
11. Song, S., Wang, Y., Chaudhuri, K.: Pufferfish privacy mechanisms for correlated data. In: Proceedings of the 2017 ACM International Conference on Management of Data, pp. 1291–1306. ACM (2017)
12. Wei, F., Zhang, W., Chen, Y., Zhao, J.: Differentially private high-dimensional data publication via Markov network. In: Beyah, R., Chang, B., Li, Y., Zhu, S. (eds.) SecureComm 2018. LNICST, vol. 254, pp. 133–148. Springer, Cham (2018). https://doi.org/10.1007/978-3-030-01701-9_8
13. Wang, H., Xu, Z.: CTS-DP: publishing correlated time-series data via differential privacy. Knowl.-Based Syst. **122**, 167–179 (2017)
14. Yang, B., Sato, I., Nakagawa, H.: Bayesian differential privacy on correlated data. In: Proceedings of the 2015 ACM SIGMOD International Conference on Management of Data, pp. 747–762. ACM (2015)
15. Zhu, T., Xiong, P., Li, G., et al.: Correlated differential privacy: hiding information in non-IID data set. IEEE Trans. Inf. Forensics Secur. **10**(2), 229–242 (2014)

Lattice Based Multi-replica Remote Data Integrity Checking for Data Storage on Cloud

Yongchun Zhang(✉), Yingpeng Sang(✉), Zhicheng Xi, and Hanrui Zhong

School of Data and Computer Science, Sun Yat-sen University, Guangzhou, China
{zhangych65,xizhch,zhonghr3}@mail2.sysu.edu.cn,
sangyp@mail.sysu.edu.cn

Abstract. With the development and popularity of cloud computing, it is of crucial importance to guarantee cloud security and privacy. Remote data integrity checking (RDIC) makes cloud server capable of proving to users that their data store in the cloud is intact. To ensure the availability and reliability of critical data, users may generate multiple replicas for those data and deploy those replicas on the cloud. However, it is a problem how to check all replicas' integrity of data saved in cloud. In previous works, some PDP schemes were proposed to solve the auditing problem of multi-replica data's integrity on cloud servers. In this paper, we proposed a novel lattice based certificateless RDIC scheme to public auditing of outsourced data with multiple replicas. This scheme can eliminate certificate management issue and burden in PKI (Public Key Infrastructure) using users own identity to support the whole verification. Finally, our analysis demonstrates our scheme is efficient and secure.

Keywords: Cloud storage · Remote data integrity checking · Lattice · Multiple replicas

1 Introduction

With the development of cloud computing techniques and the rapid increase in data volume, cloud service becomes so popular that many clients tend to deploy their data on the cloud. However, cloud, which keeps plenty of users' data and supplies on-demand services, might occurs problems like human errors or software faults, which cause data corrupted or lost. Hence, it is necessary to make Remote Data Integrity Checking (RDIC) to ensure the data in the cloud is intact.

To ensure the correctness of the RDIC result and reduce the computation and communication overhead of users, it is essential to enable public auditing service where users employ a Third Party Auditor (TPA), who has the capabilities and expertise to complete the auditing job, to check the integrity of users' data uploaded in the cloud periodically. However, TPA may be curious and eager

H. Shen and Y. Sang (Eds.): PAAP 2019, CCIS 1163, pp. 440–451, 2020.
https://doi.org/10.1007/978-981-15-2767-8_39

to learn knowledges about user's data during the verification process. For data privacy as well as data ownership, the users also do not want their data leaked to external parties. Hence, it is of critical importance to protect data privacy from TPA during the auditing process.

To avoid the data loss due to hardware or software failures, users may deploy multiple replicas of one data file on the cloud so that they can retrieve the raw data file from just one correct replica. Then, as an extension of normal RDIC scheme, how to check the integrity of those replicas efficiently and securely is also a highly desirable research topic.

In 2007, Ateniese *et al.* [1] proposed a model for provable data possession to check that a file is correctly retained in an outsource storage site. Curtmola *et al.* [2] are the first to propose a multiple-replica version of provable data possession. To eliminate the heavy overhead of public key certificates, the identity-based cryptosystem was employed to construct certificateless schemes [3–5]. Sasikala *et al.* [6] designed a certificateless, privacy-preserving RDIC protocol using lattice-based cryptosystem. The scheme avoids the overhead of PKI and reduce the computation overhead over the public verifier, while they did not provide any solution to scenarios of multi-replica integrity verification.

Our Contributions. The contribution of this paper is summarized as follows:

(1) We propose a novel multi-replica RDIC protocol for verification on all replicas at once based on the lattice signature. Using the lattice signature, our protocol provide public verification for remote data and capability of resisting quantum computer attacks. To the best of our knowledge we are the first to solve the multi-replica integrity verification based on the lattice signature.
(2) We present a formal security model which has two properties: soundness and privacy-preserving. Then we give a detailed security proofs for our protocol. Finally, the performance analysis shows the efficient of our protocol.

The rest of the paper are organized as follows: Sect. 2 overviews the related work of privacy-preserving public auditing. Section 3 introduces the system and security models. In Sect. 4, we present the preliminary knowledge of our scheme. Then, we give a detailed description of our protocol in Sect. 5. Section 6 gives the security analysis, followed by Sect. 7 that provides the perfomance analysis. Finally, we conclude the whole paper in Sect. 8.

2 Related Work

There are many RDIC schemes proposed in recent years [1,2,7–12]. In 2007, Ateniese *et al.* [1] proposed a data integrity verifying method namely provable data possession(PDP). This probablistically accurate method allows a client of cloud service to check whether the cloud server possesses his data intactly without retrieving the whole file. In 2010, Wang *et al.* [7] proposed a security model which achieves both public auditability and dynamic data operations. In [10], Wang *et al.* proposed a privacy-preserving public auditing scheme, and they also realized batch auditing and data dynamics in the cloud storage system they proposed. In 2014, Liu *et al.* [9] presented a novel RDIC scheme namely MuR-DPA. With less communication overhead, the scheme not only supports dynamic data updates auditing with data block indices checking, but also achieves integrity verification for multiple replicas. However, to identify the data owners, the aforementioned schemes resort to the public key certificates issued by Public Key Infrastructure(PKI). The PKI runs the management of certificates, which is a heavy burden. Besides, the security of PKI could be vulnerable [13].

To eliminate the overhead aforementioned, some RDIC schemes resorted to the identity-based cryptosystem, like [3–5]. Based on those research, Peng *et al.* [14] proposed an identity-based multi-replica PDP scheme. In 2019, Peng *et al.* [15] proposed a dynamic and identity-based RDIC scheme for multiple replicas without the overhead of PKI. Besides, they extended their scheme to support batch auditing for multiple users and cloud servers efficiently. In [6], Sasikala *et al.* designed a certificateless, secure and privacy-preserving RDIC protocol using lattices. The scheme resorts to lattice signature to avoid the overhead of PKI and reduces the computation overhead between cloud servers and verifiers.

3 System and Security Models

3.1 System Model

The system model of our scheme is shown on Fig. 1. It consists of four entities: private key generator (PKG), user, cloud server and third-party auditor (TPA). The PKG generates the partial private keys for users according to their user ID. Users have plenty of data files stored on cloud without possessing files locally. The cloud server has large capacity storage and significant computing ability to provide data storage service to users. TPA has the capabilities and expertise users do not have, and is authorized by users to verify the integrity of the cloud files for users upon their requests.

3.2 Security Model

We assume that the cloud server does not want to expose users' data to external parties due to financial and reputational reasons. Although the TPA is honest to users and reports the correct result of the data integrity checking to users, the TPA is curious and eager to learn the knowledge about users' data during the auditing process. Meanwhile, we assume that the cloud server is untrusted that it may store a single copy of user data rather than multiple copies in the cloud or decide to keep data corruption incidents concealed and unreported for its own benifits. In conclusion, there are two security requirements: soundness indicates that the scheme is secure against cloud servers and privacy-preserving indicates that the scheme preserves the privacy of stored data against the verifiers.

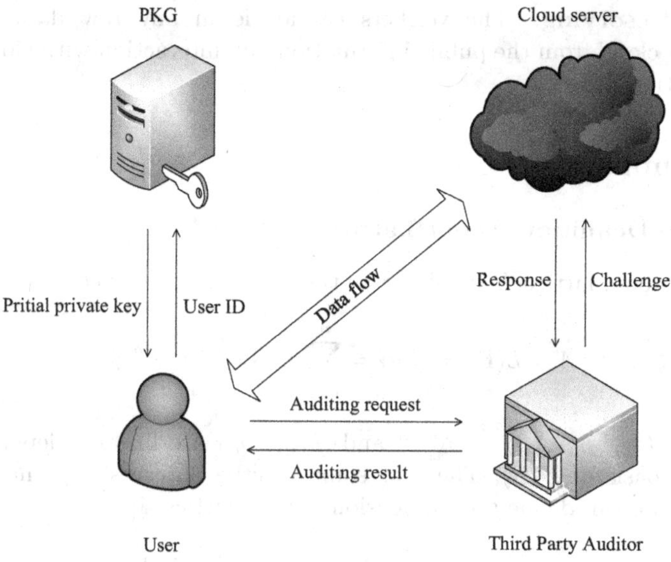

Fig. 1. The system model of our scheme.

Soundness. The proof of security against cloud servers is based on [16]. It contains two roles: challenger and adversary. In this scene, challenger represents cloud user or TPA and the adversary represents the cloud server. The security game should prove that an adversary can pass the verification only because it possesses all the challenged data blocks correctly. The game is defined as following phases:

Setup. The challenger initializes public parameters and generates the master secret key msk. Then the challenger sends the public parameters to the adversary while keeping msk secret.

Queries. In this phase, The adversary can generate some queries and send them to the challenger, such as extract query and tag query. Then the challenger calculates the tag for each data block and returns the set of tags to the adversary.

Challenge. The challenger generates a challenge according to a file on the cloud and forwards it to the adversary.

ProofGen. Once receiving the challenge, the adversary computes the proof based on the challenge and forwards it as a response to the challenger.

ProofVerify. After receiving the proof, the challenger verifies the proof. If the proof is valid, the adversary passes the verification and wins the game.

Privacy Preserving. The verifiers cannot learn any raw data file users deployed on cloud from the public information and interaction with cloud during the verification process.

4 Preliminaries

4.1 Some Definition About Lattice

A m-dimensional lattice L is defined as the set of all integer combinations:

$$\Lambda = L(\mathbf{B}) = \{\mathbf{B}\alpha = \sum_{i=1}^{n} a_i \cdot \mathbf{b_i} : \alpha \in Z^m\}$$

where $\mathbf{B} = (b_1, b_2, ..., b_n) \in R^{m \times n}$ and $(b_1, ..., b_n)$ are linearly dependent. We say B is a basis of $L(B)$. Then for some positive integers n, q and a matrix $A \in Z_q^{n \times m}$, we can define a m-dimensional q-ary lattice:

$$\Lambda_q^{\perp}(\mathbf{A}) = \{\beta \in Z^m : A\beta = 0 \bmod q\}$$

In the meantime, we can define the coset of $\Lambda_q^{\perp}(\mathbf{A})$ with a fixed vector $\mathbf{v} \in Z_q^n$:

$$\Lambda_q^{\mathbf{v}}(\mathbf{A}) = \{\mathbf{e} \in Z^m : \mathbf{Ae} = \mathbf{v} \bmod q\} = \Lambda_q^{\perp}(\mathbf{A}) + \mathbf{t}.$$

where $\mathbf{t}$ is an integral solution to $\mathbf{At} = \mathbf{v} \bmod q$.

4.2 Discrete Gaussian on Lattices

For any vector $\mathbf{r} \in R^m$, $s > 0$, the Gaussian function on R^m centered at $\mathbf{r}$ with parameter s is defined as:

$$\forall \mathbf{x} \in R^m, \rho_{s,\mathbf{r}}(\mathbf{x}) = exp(-\pi||\mathbf{x} - \mathbf{r}||/s^2)$$

Then we can define the discrete Gaussian distribution over m-dimensional lattice L as:

$$\forall \mathbf{x} \in L, D_{L,s,\mathbf{r}}(\mathbf{x}) = \frac{\rho_{s,\mathbf{r}}(\mathbf{x})}{\rho_{s,\mathbf{r}}(L)},$$

where $\rho_{s,\mathbf{r}}(L) = \sum_{\alpha \in \mathbf{A}} \rho_{s,\mathbf{r}}(\alpha)$.

4.3 Trapdoors for Lattices and Sample Basis Algorithm

The algorithms we use to generate signature in [17] is as follows.

TrapGen(n, m, q) (Lemma 3.1 in [17]). $\forall n, q, m \in N^*$ with $q \geq 2$ and $m \geq 5n \lg q$, we can generate a matrix $\mathbf{A} \in Z_q^{n \times m}$ and $\mathbf{B}$ as the short basis of the lattice $\Lambda_q^{\perp}(\mathbf{A})$ with $||B|| \leq m \cdot \omega(\sqrt{\log m})$, where $\omega(\sqrt{\log m})$ represents the number of distinct prime factors of $\sqrt{\log m}$.

SamplePre(A, $\mathbf{T_A}$, u, *i*) (Lemma 3.2 in [17]). Given $n, q, m \in N^*$ with $q \geq 2$ and $m \geq 5n \lg q$, input a matrix $\mathbf{A} \in Z_q^{n\times m}$ and trapdoor basis $\mathbf{T_A}$ of the lattice $\Lambda_q^{\perp}(\mathbf{A})$, a vector $\mathbf{u} \in Z_q^n$ and an integer $i \geq ||\mathbf{T_A}|| \cdot \omega(\sqrt{\log m})$. There exists a PPT algorithm SamplePre which could generate a vector $\mathbf{v} \in \Lambda_q^{\mathbf{u}}(A)$ that $\mathbf{v}$ will satisfy $||\mathbf{v}|| \leq \mathbf{i}\sqrt{\mathbf{m}}$ with an overwhelming probability, where $\Lambda_q^{\mathbf{u}}(A) = \{\mathbf{e} \in Z^m : \mathbf{Ae} = \mathbf{u} \bmod \mathbf{q}\}$.

SampleBasis(A, *S*, $\mathbf{T}_S$, *I*) (Theorem 3.3 in [17]). Let n, m, q, k be positive integers with $q \geq 2$ and $m \geq 5n \lg q$. On input of $\mathbf{A} \in Z^{n\times km}$, a set $S \subseteq [k]$, trapdoor basis $\mathbf{T}_S$ of $\Lambda_q^{\perp}(\mathbf{A})$, and an integer $I \geq ||\mathbf{T}_S|| \cdot \sqrt{km} \cdot \omega(\sqrt{\log km})$, The algorithm outputs a matrix $\mathbf{B}$ as a basis of the lattice $\Lambda_q^{\perp}(\mathbf{A})$ with $||\mathbf{B}|| < I$.

4.4 SIS Hard Problem

Small integer solution (SIS) hard problem is described as follows: Given an integer q, a real β and a matrix $\mathbf{A} \in Z_q^{n\times m}$ with $\beta = \text{poly(n)}$ and $q \geq \beta \cdot \omega(\sqrt{n \log n})$, it is hard to get a nonzero vector $\mathbf{v} \in \Lambda^{\perp}(\mathbf{A})$ that $\mathbf{Av} = 0 \pmod q$ and $||\mathbf{v}|| \leq r$.

5 Our Construction

We designed our protocol to achieve multiple replica public auditing which satisfies security and privacy-preserving aforementioned against cloud server and TPA respectively. Our protocol consists of the following algorithms: {Setup, Extract, KeyGen, ReplicaGen, TagGen, Challenge, ProofGen, ProofCheck}. The details of our scheme is as follows:

Given a constant c, on input a security parameter n, let $m > c \cdot n \log q$ with $q \geq \sigma\omega(\log n)$, which q is a big prime for $\sigma = \text{poly}(n)$. Then calculate Gaussian parameter $g = \Omega(\sqrt{n \log q})$, where $\Omega(\sqrt{n \log q})$ represents the number of prime factors of $\sqrt{n \log q}$.

Setup. Given a security parameter n, by running TrapGen(n, m, q) respectively, the PKG generates a matrix $\mathbf{A} \in Z_q^{n\times m}$ with a short trapdoor basis $\mathbf{T_A}$ of lattice $\Lambda_q^{\perp}(\mathbf{A})$ and the cloud server generates a matrix $\mathbf{B} \in Z_q^{n\times m}$ with a short trapdoor basis $\mathbf{T_B}$ of lattice $\Lambda_q^{\perp}(\mathbf{B})$. After that, the PKG chooses two hash functions $H_1 : \{0,1\}^* \rightarrow Z_q^m, H_2 : \{0,1\}^* \times Z_q^{n\times m} \rightarrow Z_q^*$ and a pseudo-random function $\psi : Z_q^m \times \{0,1\}^* \rightarrow Z_q^m$. In the end, the PKG sets $params = \{n, m, q, g, \mathbf{A}, \mathbf{B}, H_1, H_2, \psi\}$ as the public parameters and sets $msk = \mathbf{T_A}$ as the master secret key.

Extract(*params*, *ID*, *msk*). Given the user ID, the PKG runs the algorithm SampleBasis$(\mathbf{A}, \mathbf{T_A}, g, H_1(ID))$ to generate a matrix $\mathbf{M}_1 \in Z_q^{n\times k}$ and sends it as partial private key to the user.

KeyGen(*params*, *ID*). After receiving partial private key $\mathbf{M}_1$, the user randomly chooses a matrix $\mathbf{M}_2 \in Z_q^{m\times k}$ which must satisfy $||\mathbf{M}_2|| \leq b$ and set his private key $sk = (\mathbf{M}_1, \mathbf{M}_2)$. Then the user computes the public key $pk = \mathbf{A} \times \mathbf{M}_2$.

ReplicaGen(*params*, *F*, *fname*, τ, *c*). The user splits the raw data file F into l blocks $\mathbf{f}_1, \mathbf{f}_2, \cdots, \mathbf{f}_l, \mathbf{f}_i \in Z_q^m$, in which $\mathbf{f}_i \in Z_m^q$ and chooses $fname \in \{0,1\}^*$ as the tag of file F. For the file F, the user produces c replicas $\{F_1, F_2, \cdots, F_j\}$. Firstly, the user randomly chooses a vector $\tau \in Z_q^m$. Secondly, for each $\mathbf{f}_i, i = 1, \cdots, l$, and for $j = 1, \cdots, c$, the user computes $\mathbf{b}_{i,j} = \mathbf{f}_i + \psi_\tau(fname||i||j) \bmod q$. Note that for any replica $F_j = (\mathbf{b}_{1,j}, \cdots, \mathbf{b}_{l,j})$, the user can recover the raw data file by computing $\mathbf{f}_i = \mathbf{b}_{i,j} - \psi_\tau(fname||i||j)$. Then the user sends $\{F_1, \cdots, F_j\}$ to the cloud and keeps τ private. Note that τ must keep secret from the cloud.

TagGen(*params, ID, sk, F, fname*). The user executes the algorithm TagGen to get the tags $\Phi = \{\sigma_1, \sigma_2, \cdots, \sigma_l\}$ for the file F where σ_i is the tag for $\mathbf{f}_i$. Then the user stores the file F together with $\{\Phi, r, \mathrm{IDS}(r||fname)\}$ where $\mathrm{IDS}(r||fname)$ is an identity-based signature [18] on the value $r||fname$. The algorithm to generate tag $\{\sigma_i\}$ is as follows:

Algorithm 1. TagGen

---

input: $params, ID, sk, F, fname$
output: $\{\sigma_i\}$
1. Compute $\mathbf{u}_j = H_1(ID||fname||j) \in Z_q^m, j = 1, \cdots, n$. Let $\mathbf{N} = (\mathbf{u}_1, \mathbf{u}_2, \cdots, \mathbf{u}_n)^{\mathrm{T}} \in Z_q^{m\times n}$.
For each $\mathbf{f}_i$:
2. Calculate $\mathbf{v}_i = H_1(fname||i) \in Z_q^m$. Let $\mathbf{v}_i$ be a row vector such that $\mathbf{v}_i \in Z_q^{1\times m}$.
3. Compute $\mathbf{e}_i = \mathbf{v}_i \cdot \mathbf{N}$.
4. $\sigma_i = \mathrm{SamplePre}(\mathbf{A}, sk, \mathbf{e}_i, g)$.

Challenge(*F*, *fname*, τ). In this phase, the user sends the auditing request with $fname, \tau$ to TPA. After receiving the request, TPA randomly chooses a subset I from $\{1, \cdots, l\}$. Then for each $i \in I$, TPA randomly chooses a value $v_i \in Z_q$. So the challenge token $chal = (\{i, v_i\})$. Then, TPA forwards the challenge token to the cloud server.

ProofGen(*params*, $\{b_{i,j}\}$, $\{\sigma_i\}$, chal). After receiving the challenge from TPA, the cloud server calculates

$$\mu' = \sum_{i\in I}\sum_{j=1}^{c} v_i \mathbf{b}_{i,j} \bmod q, \text{where } \mu' \in Z_q^m$$

$$\sigma = \sum_{i\in I} v_i \sigma_i \bmod q, \text{where } \sigma \in Z_q^m$$

Then the cloud server randomly selects $\mathbf{w} \in Z_q^m$ with $||\mathbf{w}|| \leq \beta$. After that, the cloud server calculates $\mathbf{C} = \mathbf{B}\mathbf{w} \bmod q$, where $\mathbf{C} \in Z_q^{n\times 1}$ and $\gamma = H_2(\mathbf{C})$. Then, it calculates $\mu = \mathbf{w} + \gamma\mu' \bmod q$, sets the response $proof = (r, \mathrm{IDS}(r||fname), \mu, \sigma, \mathbf{C})$ and returns it to TPA.

ProofCheck(*params, fname, proof*). After receiving the proof, TPA firstly checks the validation of IDS($r||fname$). If not valid, it returns 0 to the user. Otherwise, TPA calculates $\gamma = H_2(\mathbf{C})$ and verifies whether the following equation holds:

$$\gamma c \cdot \mathbf{A}\sigma + \gamma \mathbf{B} \sum_{i \in I} \sum_{j=1}^{c} v_i \psi_\tau(i||j) + \mathbf{C} = \mathbf{B}\mu \bmod q.$$

If it holds, TPA outputs 1(valid). Otherwise, TPA outputs 0 (invalid).

6 Security Analysis

In this section, we show that the correctness of our scheme, the soundness that our scheme is secure against cloud servers and privacy-preserving that our scheme keeps users' data private against TPA.

6.1 Correctness

Suppose both cloud server and TPA are honest, then for any random challenge if the cloud server keeps the challenge blocks right, it will always pass the verification. The correctness of our scheme is as follows:

$$\begin{aligned}
\gamma c \mathbf{A}\sigma + \gamma \mathbf{B} \sum_{i \in I} \sum_{j=1}^{c} v_i \psi_\tau(i||j) + \mathbf{C} &= \gamma c \sum_{i \in I} v_i \mathbf{A}\sigma_i + \gamma \sum_{i \in I} \sum_{j=1}^{c} v_i \mathbf{B}\psi_\tau(i||j) + \mathbf{C} \\
&= \gamma c \sum_{i \in I} v_i \mathbf{B}\mathbf{f}_i + \gamma \sum_{i \in I} \sum_{j=1}^{c} v_i \mathbf{B}\psi_\tau(i||j) + \mathbf{B}\mathbf{w}, \bmod q \\
&= \gamma \sum_{i \in I} v_i \mathbf{B}(\sum_{j=1}^{c} \mathbf{f}_i + \psi_\tau(fname||i||j)) + \mathbf{B}\mathbf{w}, \bmod q \\
&= \gamma \mathbf{B} \sum_{i \in I} \sum_{j=1}^{c} v_i \mathbf{b}_{i,j} + \mathbf{B}\mathbf{w}, \bmod q \\
&= \gamma \mathbf{B}\mu' + \mathbf{B}\mathbf{w}, \bmod q \\
&= \mathbf{B}(\gamma\mu' + \mathbf{w}), \bmod q \\
&= \mathbf{B}\mu \bmod q
\end{aligned}$$

6.2 Soundness

In this paragraph, we assume SIS hard problem in lattices to prove the security of our scheme against untrusted cloud server.

Proof. Let $\mathcal{A}$ be a generic adversary and $\mathcal{C}$ be a challenger. $\mathcal{C}$ simulates the auditing process and answers the queries received from $\mathcal{A}$. If there exists a PPT $\mathcal{A}$ wins the security game aforementioned in Sect. 3.2, then we have the demonstration below:

We set the SIS distance of $\mathcal{C}$ as $(A \in Z_q^{m\times n}, m, n, q, g)$. If $\mathcal{C}$ figures out a non-zero vector $\mathbf{v} \in Z_q^m$ as the solution of $\mathbf{Av} = 0 \pmod q$ which satisfies $||\mathbf{v}|| \leq 2\sigma\sqrt{m}$, $\mathcal{C}$ wins the game.

For a file F with a file name $fname$, $\mathcal{C}$ generates c replicas of F as $\{\mathbf{b}_{i,j}|i = 1,\cdots l; j = 1,\cdots,c\}$ and computes the tags $\{\sigma_i\}$ for $\{\mathbf{f}_i\}$. In this game, the tags $\{\sigma_i\}$ of each data vector $\mathbf{f}_i$ are public to both $\mathcal{A}$ and $\mathcal{C}$. After receiving the $H_1(fname||i)$ query, $\mathcal{C}$ returns the vector corresponding to the ith row of $\mathbf{A}$. After that, $\mathcal{C}$ generates a challenge and sends it to $\mathcal{A}$.

$\mathcal{A}$ forwards a hash query $H_2(\mathbf{C})$ to $\mathcal{C}$. After receiving the $H_2(\mathbf{C})$ query, $\mathcal{C}$ calculates $\gamma = H_2(\mathbf{C})$ and forwards it to $\mathcal{A}$. Then, $\mathcal{A}$ returns $(\mu, \sigma, \mathbf{C})$ that

$$\mu = \gamma \sum_{i\in I} \sum_{j=1}^{c} v_i \mathbf{b}_{i,j} + \mathbf{w}$$

Suppose that $\mathcal{C}$ is able to communicate with $\mathcal{A}$ before the $H_2(\mathbf{C})$ query. In this case, $\mathcal{C}$ chooses a random number γ^* as the result of $H_2(\mathbf{C})$, where $\gamma^* \neq \gamma$, and returns it to $\mathcal{A}$. Then $\mathcal{A}$ outputs $(\mu^*, \sigma, \mathbf{C})$ such that

$$\mu^* = \gamma^* \sum_{i\in I} \sum_{j=1}^{c} v_i \mathbf{b}_{i,j} + \mathbf{w}$$

Then we know

$$\sum_{i\in I} \sum_{j=1}^{c} v_i \mathbf{b}_{i,j} = (\mu - \mu^*)/(\gamma - \gamma^*)$$

Finally, $\mathcal{C}$ can compute $\mathbf{w}$ by

$$\mathbf{w} = \mu - \gamma \cdot (\mu - \mu^*)/(\gamma - \gamma^*)$$

In this case, since $\mathcal{A}$ chooses $\mathbf{w}$ by the condition that $\mathbf{w}$ satisfies $||\mathbf{w}|| \leq \beta$ and $\mathcal{A}$ computes $\mathbf{C}$ by $\mathbf{C} = \mathbf{Bw}$, then we have the solution to the SIS instance $\mathbf{w}$. If there exists an adversary $\mathcal{A}$ wins the game aforementioned, then we can set up a challenger $\mathcal{C}$ to figure out the solution of the given SIS instance. However, our scheme is built based on SIS hard problem in lattices, which indicates that it is hard to find the solution $\mathbf{w}$, implies that $\mathcal{C}$ cannot win the game. Thus our scheme is secure against the cloud server.

6.3 Privacy Preserving

In this case, we assume that TPA is eager to know the data user stores in the cloud during verification phase. In another words, TPA tries to get information from $F = (\mathbf{f}_1, \mathbf{f}_2, \cdots \mathbf{f}_l)$. In our protocol, the cloud server calculates the aggregation of replica blocks μ', and confuses μ' with a vector $\mathbf{w}$ by computing $\mu = \gamma\mu' + \mathbf{w}$. According to SIS hard problem in lattices, TPA cannot figure out the vector $\mathbf{w}$ and computes μ by knowing μ' and γ. Without knowing the aggregation of replica blocks, TPA cannot get any data block with messages that TPA knows. Therefore, our protocol satisfies the privacy-preserving property.

7 Performance Analysis

In this section, we analyze the performance of our protocol numerically from computation cost as well as communication cost. To get a baseline method for comparisons, we also have a trivial extension of the single replica RDIC scheme in [6] to the multi-replica problem, and compare it with our solution on the computation cost.

7.1 Computation Analysis

Let l, c, $\tilde{l}$ be the number of data blocks, the number of replicas and the number of challenge blocks respectively. Let ψ be the time cost of pseudo-random functions ψ_T, $Hash_{H_1}$ and $Hash_{H_2}$ the time cost of Hash function H_1 and H_2 respectively, Mul_{Mat} the time cost of multiplication of two matrices, $Mul_{Z_q^m}$ the time cost of multiplication between a number and a vector, $Add_{Z_q^m}$ the time cost of the summation of two vectors, Sam the time cost of algorithm SamplePre($\mathbf{A}, \mathbf{T_A}, \mathbf{u}, i$).

We omit the time costs in Setup, Extract and KenGen phases because they cost less time than the other phases (Setup phase just runs the algorithm TrapGen and Extract phase just runs the algorithm SampleBasis) and they have the same costs in the compared scheme. The comparation can be shown in Table 1.

Table 1. The computation overhead of our protocol and [6] in different phases

Phase	Our protocol	[6]
ReplicaGen	$lc\psi$	–
TagGen	$(n+l)Hash_{H_1} + lMul_{Mat} + lSam$	$(n+l)cHash_{H_1} + lcMul_{Mat} + lcSam$
ProofGen	$(2\tilde{l}+1)Mul_{Z_q^m} + [\tilde{l}(c+1)+1]Add_{Z_q^m} + Mul_{Mat} + Hash_{H_2}$	$(2\tilde{l}+1)cMul_{Z_q^m} + (2\tilde{l}+1)cAdd_{Z_q^m} + cMul_{Mat} + cHash_{H_2}$
ProofCheck	$3Mul_{Mat} + (\tilde{l}+2)Mul_{Z_q^m} + (\tilde{l}c+2)Add_{Z_q^m}$	$2cMul_{Mat} + cMul_{Z_q^m} + cAdd_{Z_q^m}$

By Table 1, we can have the following analysis and draw a conclusion that our protocol has less time cost than [6]:

(1) Our protocol has faster TagGen phase with $c > 1$ than [6]. No matter what value c is, our protocol only needs to generates one set of tags for all replicas, while the time cost in TagGen phase in [6] depends on c.
(2) Our protocol has faster ProofGen phase with $c > 1$ than [6]. The time cost in ProofGen phase of [6] depends on c, especially in Mul_{Mat} and $Mul_{Z_q^m}$, which may have high costs.
(3) In ProofCheck phase, our protocol costs more time than [6] in $Mul_{Z_q^m}$ and $Add_{Z_q^m}$, but less time in Mul_{Mat}, which dominates the time cost in [6]. Therefore, our protocol spends less time in ProofCheck phase than [6].

7.2 Communication Analysis

In the challenge phase, TPA sends the challenge set $\{i, v_i\}$ to the server. In practice, we can employ two pseudo-random function ρ and ϕ as public parameters. Instead of sending the challenge set, TPA can send a key k_1 for rho and a key k_2 for phi as the challenge, which can reduce the communication cost [5]. So the communication cost in the challenge phase is of binary length $\log_2 k_1 + \log_2 k_2$. In the ProofGen phase, the cloud server returns $proof = (r, \mathrm{IDS}(r||fname), \mu, \sigma, \mathbf{C})$ to TPA. The signature $(r, \mathrm{IDS}(r||fname))$ usually comprises two points of elliptic curves, which length is 320 bits. And an element in Z_q^m costs $m \log_2 q$ bits, hence the communication cost in ProofGen phase is of binary length $320 + 3m \log_2 q$.

8 Conclusion

In this paper, we propose a novel lattice-based multi-replica integrity checking protocol for data storage in cloud. We introduce a security model including properties of soundness and privacy-preserving. We propose our construction and prove that it is soundness and privacy-preserving, following the requirements of our security model. The performance analysis of our construction also demonstrates its efficiency, both in computation and communication.

Acknowledgement. This work was supported by the National Key Research and Development Program of China (No. 2017YFB0203201), the Science and Technology Program of Guangdong Province, China (No. 2017A010101039), and the Science and Technology Program of Guangzhou, China (No. 201904010209).

References

1. Ateniese, G., et al.: Provable data possession at untrusted stores. In: Proceedings of the 14th ACM Conference on Computer and Communications Security, pp. 598–609. ACM (2007)
2. Curtmola, R., Khan, O., Burns, R., Ateniese, G.: MR-PDP: multiple-replica provable data possession. In: 2008 the 28th International Conference on Distributed Computing Systems, pp. 411–420. IEEE (2008)
3. Wang, H., Wu, Q., Qin, B., Domingo-Ferrer, J.: Identity-based remote data possession checking in public clouds. IET Inf. Secur. **8**(2), 114–121 (2013)
4. Wang, H.: Identity-based distributed provable data possession in multicloud storage. IEEE Trans. Serv. Comput. **8**(2), 328–340 (2014)
5. Yu, Y., et al.: Identity-based remote data integrity checking with perfect data privacy preserving for cloud storage. IEEE Trans. Inf. Forensics Secur. **12**(4), 767–778 (2016)
6. Sasikala, C., Shoba Bindu, C.: Certificateless remote data integrity checking using lattices in cloud storage. Neural Comput. Appl. **31**(5), 1513–1519 (2019)
7. Wang, Q., Wang, C., Ren, K., Lou, W., Li, J.: Enabling public auditability and data dynamics for storage security in cloud computing. IEEE Trans. Parallel Distrib. Syst. **22**(5), 847–859 (2010)

8. Wang, C., Wang, Q., Ren, K., Lou, W.: Privacy-preserving public auditing for data storage security in cloud computing. In: 2010 Proceedings IEEE Infocom, pp. 1–9. IEEE (2010)
9. Liu, C., Ranjan, R., Yang, C., Zhang, X., Wang, L., Chen, J.: MUR-DPA: top-down levelled multi-replica merkle hash tree based secure public auditing for dynamic big data storage on cloud. IEEE Trans. Comput. **64**(9), 2609–2622 (2014)
10. Wang, C., Chow, S.S.M., Wang, Q., Ren, K., Lou, W.: Privacy-preserving public auditing for secure cloud storage. IEEE Trans. Comput. **62**(2), 362–375 (2011)
11. Wang, C., Ren, K., Lou, W., Li, J.: Toward publicly auditable secure cloud data storage services. IEEE Netw. **24**(4), 19–24 (2010)
12. Yang, K., Jia, X.: An efficient and secure dynamic auditing protocol for data storage in cloud computing. IEEE Trans. Parallel Distrib. Syst. **24**(9), 1717–1726 (2012)
13. Ellison, C., Schneier, B.: Ten risks of PKI: what you're not being told about public key infrastructure. Comput. Secur. J. **16**(1), 1–7 (2000)
14. Peng, S., Zhou, F., Wang, Q., Xu, Z., Xu, J.: Identity-based public multi-replica provable data possession. IEEE Access **5**, 26990–27001 (2017)
15. Peng, S., Zhou, F., Li, J., Wang, Q., Xu, Z.: Efficient, dynamic and identity-based remote data integrity checking for multiple replicas. J. Netw. Comput. Appl. **134**, 72–88 (2019)
16. Shacham, H., Waters, B.: Compact proofs of retrievability. In: Pieprzyk, J. (ed.) ASIACRYPT 2008. LNCS, vol. 5350, pp. 90–107. Springer, Heidelberg (2008). https://doi.org/10.1007/978-3-540-89255-7_7
17. Cash, D., Hofheinz, D., Kiltz, E.: How to delegate a lattice basis. IACR Cryptology ePrint Archive 2009:351 (2009)
18. Choon, J.C., Hee Cheon, J.: An identity-based signature from gap Diffie-Hellman groups. In: Desmedt, Y.G. (ed.) PKC 2003. LNCS, vol. 2567, pp. 18–30. Springer, Heidelberg (2003). https://doi.org/10.1007/3-540-36288-6_2

Secure Multi-Party Computation on Blockchain: An Overview

Hanrui Zhong(✉), Yingpeng Sang(✉), Yongchun Zhang, and Zhicheng Xi

School of Data and Computer Science, Sun Yat-sen University, Guangzhou, China
{zhonghr3,zhangych65,xizhch}@mail2.sysu.edu.cn,
sangyp@mail.sysu.edu.cn

Abstract. Secure multi-party computation (SMPC) is a hot topic in the field of cryptography. It focuses on finishing computation tasks without revealing users' inputs and outputs in decentralized scenarios. Although many researches have been conducted to perform SMPC protocols, it is hard to obtain fairness while most participants in SMPC are dishonest. Recently, the foundation of cryptocurrency, blockchain has attracted the attention of many scholars. Since blockchain's ability to provide security and incentives, researchers start to make use of blockchain to provide fairness in SMPC protocols and increase efficiency. In this paper, we present a brief survey on how to use blockchain technology to perform SMPC protocol. We start by introducing the concept of secure computation and its security requirements. Then, we explain how we can utilize blockchain to provide fairness and present the basic model. We summarize state-of-the-art blockchain based SMPC applications and conclude this paper.

Keywords: Secure multi-party computation · Blockchain · Access control · Privacy-preserving technology

1 Introduction

With the rapid development of information technology, Internet is becoming more and more important in people's daily life. Internet applications and services spring up in recent years. Big data, cloud computing, machine learning and artificial intelligence, these technologies play important roles in Internet because of hardware development, which has a great impact to both people's lifestyle and situation of Internet. Although these technologies bring gigantic convenience to people's life, it also gives rise to concern about privacy information leakage since many of these services are data-driven. It means that they need huge amount of data to work correctly. In reality, many companies have been collecting users' information from all aspects to provide more suitable services, which actually divulge users' privacy since they are reluctant to share it. Privacy-preserving technology is thus in urgent need.

For many years, researchers have developed several technologies to protect users' personal data from leakage, secure multi-party computation (SMPC) is one of the most significant of them. SMPC was proposed in 1982 by Yao [1] to perform secure computation between two parties. It addresses the problem how to finish computation using

H. Shen and Y. Sang (Eds.): PAAP 2019, CCIS 1163, pp. 452–460, 2020.
https://doi.org/10.1007/978-981-15-2767-8_40

private information of participants without a trusted third party in distributed scenarios. Since the input data is personal and users do not want to share them, it requires the task must be finished while keeping input secret to others. Many works have been conducted to perform SMPC, such as garbled circuit, oblivious transfer, linear secret share scheme, homomorphic encryption. However, these technologies have their limitations including lack of scalability, low efficiency. Moreover, some unrealistic assumptions in security models make it difficult to apply SMPC and achieve fairness in practice.

In this paper, we introduce a model to perform SMPC using blockchain technology. Blockchain is the fundamental component of cryptocurrency like bitcoins, Ether etc. It is a powerful tool to help decentralized system to achieve byzantine agreement. Informally blockchain is a distributed database. With consensus mechanism, encryption algorithm and other technologies, blockchain maintains the consistency of the data in the database and realizes decentralization and non-tampering in peer-to-peer network. It perfectly suits SMPC since both of them work in distributed scenarios and focus on the problem of trust and security. In Sect. 2, we give a brief introduction of SMPC, including its security requirement and related work. Then we introduce blockchain technology in Sect. 3. In Sect. 4, we conduct blockchain based SMPC model and present related work. In Sect. 5, we conclude this paper and future work.

2 Secure Multi-Party Computation

Secure Multi-Party Computation (SMPC) has been discussed for decades since it was put forward. It was first proposed by Yao [1] with the problem of two millionaires. Consider two millionaires wish to know who is richer, how could they find out the answer without revealing their wealth, which they want to keep private? Yao also formalized the millionaires' problem as a secure computation model and proposed a solution. SMPC focuses on the solutions that allow distributed participants to compute desired results corporately while participants' inputs remain private. In the SMPC scenario, two or more parties with their private inputs wish to cooperate to compute objective results in distributed network. Figure 1 shows that three parties compute desired outputs via communication. An SMPC protocol must figure out how to finish the computation while preserving users' private inputs in distributed scenarios with adversaries.

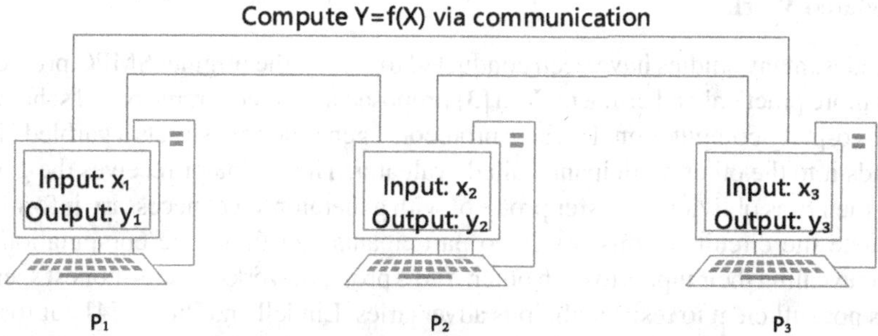

Fig. 1. Secure three-party computation overview

2.1 Security Model

The security of SMPC focuses on ensuring the right computation while protecting participants' private information. The protocol should meet the following requirements: (1) Privacy: participants' input must keep secret to others at all time. (2) Correctness: the protocol ensures that the final result of computation is correct when everyone in the system behaves honestly. (3) Fairness: a corrupted party cannot get its output while denying other parties to get their outputs. The whole procedure should not be interrupted by adversaries in the network, and it should be detected when adversaries try to break the protocol. In the past study, the security model of SMPC can be divided into following types:

- Semi-honest adversary model: in the semi-honest adversary model, an adversary does not try to break the protocol, but it collects all related messages and attempts to analyze more useful information from them. Adversaries in this model correctly follow the protocol so it only provides weak security guarantees.
- malicious adversary model: in the malicious adversary model, apart from collecting information as much as possible, adversaries behave arbitrarily beyond the protocols, try to interrupt the protocol, sending wrong input or disturbing the protocol while communication. Malicious model provides strong security guarantees because honest parties in the system must be protected from dishonest ones.
- covert adversary model: covert adversary model was proposed by Aumann [2] since security guarantees in semi-honest model are too weak and unrealistic, and protocols with malicious model are so inefficient with too strict security guarantees. Covert model is between semi-honest and malicious. Adversaries in covert model still collect information and cheat, but only if they are not caught. Every time when they cheat, honest parties are able to detect it with probability at least ε.

The scenario in reality is more complicated than that in theory. Participants in real world perform rational. They are not just simply honest or dishonest. In the distributed settings, participants are more likely to maximize their benefits regardless of behaving honest or not, especially in financial fields.

2.2 Related Work

For decades, many studies have been conducted to extend the original SMPC protocol to make it more practical and efficient. Yao [3] proposed a garbled circuit-based scheme for secure two-party computation. In Yao's protocol, a generator constructs a garbled circuit and sends it to the other participant, called evaluator. The evaluator receives the garbled circuit, then runs oblivious transfer protocol with generator to get necessary information to evaluate the circuit. In this way, two participants can finish the computation task without revealing their inputs to each other. Yao's protocol works in semi-honest scenario and it is not sufficient to resist malicious adversaries. Lindell and Pinkas [4] put forward the cut-and-choose paradigm against malicious generators. It forces the generator to construct correct garbled circuits that preserve evaluator's privacy because it requires the generator to generate multiple independent garbled circuits, and the evaluator only reveals some of them to check whether the generator cheat or not.

Cloud-aided SMPC was proposed to increase efficiency for situation that some parties in the system may not have enough computing resources. Kamara [5] proposed two single-sever-aided SMPC protocols based on garbled circuits with fairness and better efficiency, where the circuit evaluation work is outsourced to the sever. Kerschbaum [6] introduced oblivious outsourcing where outsourced severs are not aware of each other, and presented an outsource scheme for garbled circuit generation based on lattice to decrease circuit generation time.

3 Blockchain Technology

Blockchain is the foundation of cryptocurrency like Bitcoin and Ether. It gains increasingly attention because Bitcoin achieved great success since it was implemented in 2009. Blockchain helps to achieve agreement in decentralized scenarios without a trusted third party. It consists of a group of participants following the same consensus protocol. In general, Blockchain is a public ledger shared among the nodes in distributed network. With consensus algorithm, participants in blockchain are able to maintain the same copy of the data, promising ledger consistency and its security is guaranteed by cryptography. Since its great potential of ability to provide security and privacy in decentralized network, more and more researchers have been devoted to apply blockchain in practice.

3.1 Blockchain Architecture

Blockchain is a kind of chain data structure which combines data blocks in a sequential order. Blocks in blockchain consist of block header and block body [7]. Block header contains information including block version, Merkle tree hash, timestamp, nonce, hash of previous block, etc. Block body is composed of a transaction counter and transactions. By adding the hash of previous block in the current block, blocks become connected and form an ordered chain as Fig. 2 shows. This makes the data in the blockchain immutable. If someone wants to change data in one block, it means that he has to change all blocks behind since they are chained with hash code. However, it is almost impossible with consensus algorithm used in blockchain. Take Bitcoin as an example. Miners in the Bitcoin system compete with each other by solving the proper nonce that makes hash of this block legal and they only work on the longest chain. So, attackers can never succeed unless they control at least half computing resources in blockchain because their block generation speed is slower than the majority.

Incentives mechanism is another reason why blockchain is popular. In Bitcoin system, miners will get paid with new bitcoin if they succeed in calculating the hash of next block. In other blockchain systems, incentives mechanism like Bitcoin's also exist, and this prompts participants to act honestly to get profit. Although some malicious users may try to get more gain, relative measures have been promoted to provide better efficiency and fairness.

Blockchain is decentralized and persistent with transparency and auditability, which makes it an ideal party that suits decentralized applications which need both privacy

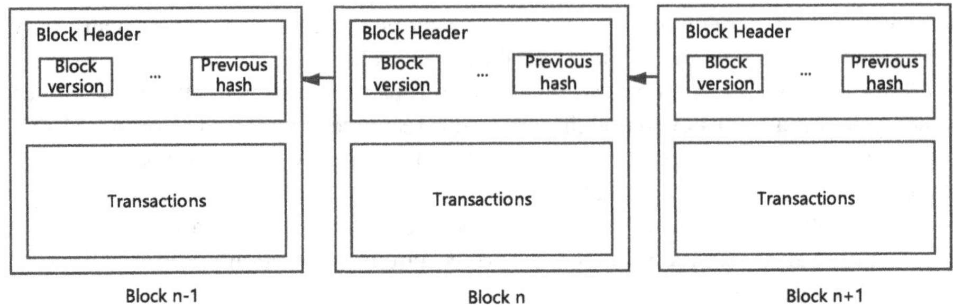

Fig. 2. Blockchain architecture

and security. Aitzhan et al. [8] proposed an energy trading scheme PriWatt enabled by blockchain and multi-signatures. Zyskind et al. [9] used blockchain for access control to protect user data in mobile application. Liang et al. [12] combined blockchain and cloud auditing by embedding the provenance data into blockchain transactions to enhance privacy and availability in cloud environment.

4 SMPC on Blockchain

4.1 Overview

Blockchain based SMPC model is showed in Fig. 3. It consists of the following parts: data owner, services user, blockchain, computing party, storage party.

- Owner: owner is the one who possesses the data. He is responsible for encrypting his data before uploading them to blockchain. Also, an owner decides who can query his data by deploying related access policy.
- User: user is the one who wants to execute computation and gets desired results. User sends computation request and function to blockchain with reference of data and payment. When computation is finished or interrupted, user gets desired output or refund.
- Blockchain: blockchain is responsible for access control, delivering computation tasks and managing the incentives and refunds.
- Computing party: parties for computation receive inputs from storage and then execute computation.

The framework serves as a cloud service with both privacy and fairness. It begins with data owner, who encrypts his data and then shares it to the blockchain. Data owner is the only one who can get in touch with raw data. At any time when the owner has data stored in the blockchain, he is allowed to decide who can query his share secret. He can send a new transaction to the blockchain to alter permission to his data. A user can query the data to start a computation task if he is approved. He should get access to his necessary data before sending a computation request and provide enough reward. After the computation is finished, user gets his desired result without learning anything else. If computation task fails, user can take back his refund. Parties in the framework

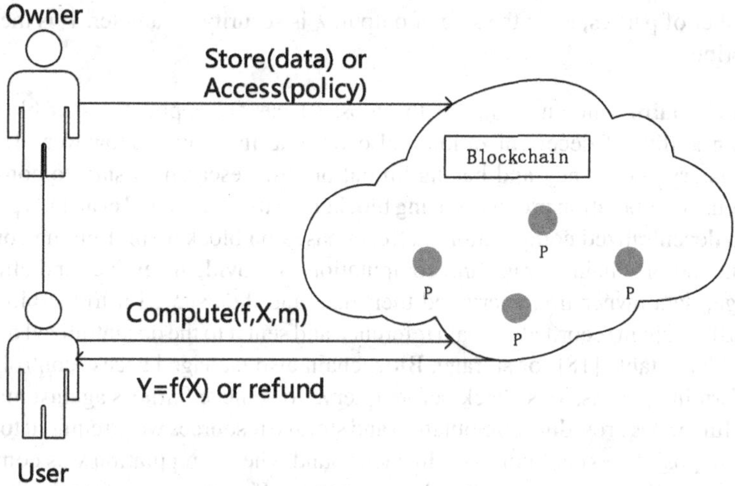

Fig. 3. Blockchain based SMPC framework (P means computing parties)

provide computing and storage resources. Each party is required to have enough funds to be locked in the blockchain ledger. When a computation task is finished, the blockchain will determine whether involved parties cheat, and honest parties will get their rewards while dishonest ones get penalties.

4.2 State-of-the-Art Researches

Using Bitcoin. Andrychowicz et al. [13] first utilized Bitcoin to construct a version of timed commitments, where the committer has to reveal his secret within a certain time. While the committer starts committing phase, he must combine his commitment with some deposit, which will be given to other parties if he refuses to open his commitment within the promised time. Based on the timed commitment, they also proposed a lottery protocol using Bitcoin transaction. Users with deposit in Bitcoin ledger commit their secrets by generating a commitment transaction and post it on ledger. Then they construct computation transaction and post it within an agreed period of time to get back their deposit. Whoever fails to reveal his secret with transaction in time will lost his pledge, which will be divided and sent to honest parties. Bentov et al. [17] proposed a claim-or-refund functionality and constructed a secure computation protocol with penalties using Bitcoin. By sending transactions to the Bitcoin network, protocols in [17] guaranteed that honest parties received compensation when adversaries aborted the protocol after they got output, which provided a kind of fairness to protect honest parties. Kumaresan et al. [15] extended [17] and provided a general framework for ladder mechanism. In [15], they used this framework to propose a protocol which offered better security. It ensures complete fairness when corrupted parties are less than half and achieves fairness with penalties when corrupted parties are more than half. Additionally, Kumaresan reduced script complexity from $O(n^2|z|)$ to $O(n\lambda)$ in non-reactive setting and achieved improvement to script complexity from $O(n^2T)$ to $O(nT)$ in reactive setting, where n

is the number of parties, $|z|$ is the size of output, λ is security parameter, T is the size of the transcript.

Using Blockchain. Bitcoin is one of the most successful applications of blockchain with strong ability of decentralization and economic incentives. However, Bitcoin is designed as cryptocurrency and has its limitation. So, researchers start to consider to deploy secure computation protocols using blockchain itself. Zyskind et al. [14] proposed Enigma, a decentralized computation platform based on blockchain. Enigma combined blockchain and off-chain storage and computation to provide incentives and efficiency. For storage, data owner first encrypted their data and then shared it to the blockchain network. Blockchain recorded the data reference and sent it to the decentralized off-chain distributed hash-table [18] for storage. Blockchain also managed access control to user data, performing permissions check before query. To achieve fairness against malicious behavior, full nodes providing computation and storage resources were required to submit a security deposit to a smart contract. In each round when computation was completed, the contract verified whether nodes cheated or not. If nodes were found lying, their deposit would be split between honest nodes. After the computation task was finished, honest nodes would receive compensation for providing resources. Zyskind [10] used the same framework in [14] but extended it with more detailed security analysis. It also presented more detailed constructions such as linear secret sharing scheme and re-sharing with mobile proactive secret sharing while [14] proposed a high-level framework. Besides, Zyskind presented a modified comparison protocol which required only 1 round and 1 communication for small integer. The protocol also had advantages when it referred to larger values.

Benhamouda et al. [11] focused on the Hyperledger Fabric, an open source permissioned blockchain architecture. Different from previous works, they addressed providing private data option on Hyperledger Fabric, integrating secure computation protocol as part of the smart contract. Parties encrypted their private data with secret key and then uploaded it on the ledger. When private data was needed, parties with secret key were able to decrypt it as input of secure computation. Unlike [10] and [14], Benhamouda et al. integrated SMPC protocols within the blockchain itself instead of using off-chain computation resource. In this way, they utilized blockchain facilities for identity verification and communication, so it was unnecessary to rebuild them in practice. They also added local configuration and inter-peer communication to Fabric to perform secure computation.

Choudhuri et al. [16] used bulletin board like Google's certificate transparency project or blockchain to construct fair SMPC protocols. It reduced fairness in SMPC to fairness in decryption using witness encryption. As described in [16], the proposed protocol included 2 phases. First, participants executed an unfair MPC protocol to get a witness encryption of function values they wanted. Each party needed to release tokens with shares of all parties to the bulletin board, so the other parties could use the posted information and authentication to decrypt ciphertext. In the next phase, each party sent their secret to the other parties in limited time. If there was no valid post on bulletin board in time, no party got output. For implementation, Choudhuri et al. used Bitcoin as the bulletin board and SGX as the witness decryptor, deploying a search protocol with SPDZ-2 framework [19]. Results showed that achieving fairness only needed little overhead in linear search over 1000 entries.

5 Conclusion

For decades of SMPC research, the fundamental theories of SMPC have been mature and researchers start to seek how to implement SMPC in practice. Many scholars attempt to design their SMPC platforms and try to deploy protocols on them. In recent years, the rapid development of blockchain has attracted interest of researchers. The decentralization characteristic of blockchain makes it an ideal model in applications that needs privacy and trust. Aiming at problems of fairness and scalability of SMPC, researchers utilize blockchain as a core component in their new model. Although blockchain has great potential in decentralization, there are many challenges such as balance between efficiency and privacy. Also, blockchain based SMPC needs more further research both in theory and practice.

Acknowledgements. This work was supported by the National Key Research and Development Program of China (No. 2017YFB0203201), the Science and Technology Program of Guangdong Province, China (No. 2017A010101039), and the Science and Technology Program of Guangzhou, China (No. 201904010209).

References

1. Yao, A.C.: Protocols for secure computations. In: Proceedings of the 23rd Annual Symposium on Foundations of Computer Science (SFCS 1982), pp. 160–164. IEEE Computer Society, Washington (1982)
2. Aumann, Y., Lindell, Y.: Security against covert adversaries: efficient protocols for realistic adversaries. In: Vadhan, S.P. (ed.) TCC 2007. LNCS, vol. 4392, pp. 137–156. Springer, Heidelberg (2007). https://doi.org/10.1007/978-3-540-70936-7_8
3. Yao, A.C.: How to generate and exchange secrets. In: Proceedings of the 27th Annual Symposium on Foundations of Computer Science (SFCS 1986), pp. 162–167. IEEE Computer Society, Washington (1986)
4. Lindell, Y., Pinkas, B.: An efficient protocol for secure two-party computation in the presence of malicious adversaries. In: Naor, M. (ed.) EUROCRYPT 2007. LNCS, vol. 4515, pp. 52–78. Springer, Heidelberg (2007). https://doi.org/10.1007/978-3-540-72540-4_4
5. Kamara, S., Mohassel, P., Riva, B.: Salus: a system for server-aided secure function evaluation. In: Proceedings of the 2012 ACM Conference on Computer and Communications Security (CCS 2012), pp. 797–808. ACM, New York (2012)
6. Kerschbaum, F.: Oblivious outsourcing of garbled circuit generation. In: The 30th Annual ACM Symposium. ACM (2015)
7. Zheng, Z., Xie, S., Dai, H., Chen, X., Wang, H.: An overview of blockchain technology: architecture, consensus, and future trends. In: 2017 IEEE International Congress on Big Data (BigData Congress), Honolulu, HI, pp. 557–564 (2017)
8. Aitzhan, N.Z., Svetinovic, D.: Security and privacy in decentralized energy trading through multi-signatures, blockchain and anonymous messaging streams. IEEE Trans. Dependable Secure Comput. **15**, 840–852 (2016)

9. Zyskind, G., Nathan, O., Pentland, A.: Decentralizing privacy: using blockchain to protect personal data. In: 2015 IEEE Security and Privacy Workshops, San Jose, CA, pp. 180–184 (2015)
10. Guy, Z.: Efficient secure computation enabled by blockchain technology (2016)
11. Benhamouda, F., Halevi, S., Halevi, T.: Supporting private data on hyperledger fabric with secure multiparty computation. In: 2018 IEEE International Conference on Cloud Engineering (IC2E). IEEE (2018)
12. Liang, X., Shetty, S., Tosh, D., Kamhoua, C., Kwiat, K., Njilla, L.: ProvChain: a blockchain-based data provenance architecture in cloud environment with enhanced privacy and availability. In: 2017 17th IEEE/ACM International Symposium on Cluster, Cloud and Grid Computing (CCGRID), Madrid, pp. 468–477 (2017)
13. Andrychowicz, M., Dziembowski, S., Malinowski, D., Mazurek, L.: Secure multiparty computations on bitcoin. In: 2014 IEEE Symposium on Security and Privacy, San Jose, CA, pp. 443–458 (2014)
14. Zyskind, G., Nathan, O., Pentland, A.: Enigma: Decentralized Computation Platform with Guaranteed Privacy. Computer Science (2015)
15. Kumaresan, R., Vaikuntanathan, V., Vasudevan, P.N.: Improvements to secure computation with penalties. In: ACM SIGSAC Conference 2016 (2016)
16. Choudhuri, A.R., Green, M., Jain, A., Kaptchuk, G., Miers, I.: Fairness in an unfair world: fair multiparty computation from public bulletin boards. In: Proceedings of the 2017 ACM SIGSAC Conference on Computer and Communications Security (CCS 2017), pp. 719–728. ACM, New York (2017)
17. Bentov, I., Kumaresan, R.: How to use bitcoin to design fair protocols. In: Garay, J.A., Gennaro, R. (eds.) CRYPTO 2014. LNCS, vol. 8617, pp. 421–439. Springer, Heidelberg (2014). https://doi.org/10.1007/978-3-662-44381-1_24
18. Maymounkov, P., Mazières, D.: Kademlia: a peer-to-peer information system based on the XOR metric. In: Druschel, P., Kaashoek, F., Rowstron, A. (eds.) IPTPS 2002. LNCS, vol. 2429, pp. 53–65. Springer, Heidelberg (2002). https://doi.org/10.1007/3-540-45748-8_5
19. Multiparty computation with SPDZ online phase and MASCOT offline phase. Github (2017). https://github.com/bristolcrypto/SPDZ-2

A Survey of Privacy-Preserving Techniques on Trajectory Data

Songyuan Li[1(✉)], Hong Shen[1,2], and Yingpeng Sang[1]

[1] School of Data and Computer, Sun Yat-sen University, Guangzhou, Guangdong, China
lisy36@mail2.sysu.edu.cn, hongsh01@gmail.com, sangyp@mail.sysu.edu.cn
[2] School of Computer Science, University of Adelaide, Adelaide, Australia

Abstract. How to protect user's trajectory privacy while ensuing the user's access to high quality services is the core of the study of trajectory privacy protection technology. With the rapid development of mobile devices and Location Based Service (LBS), the amount of locations and trajectories of moving objects collected by service providers is continuously increasing. On one hand, the collected trajectories contains rich spatial-temporal information, and its analysis and mining can support a variety of innovative applications. Since trajectories enable intrusive inferences which may expose private information, such as individual habits, behavioral patterns, social relationships and so on, directly publishing trajectories may result in individual privacy vulnerable to various threats. On the other hand, the existing techniques are unable to prevent trajectory privacy leakage, so the complete real-time trajectories of individuals may be exposed when they request for LBS, even if their location privacy is protected by common data protection mechanisms. Therefore, specific techniques for trajectory privacy preserving have been proposed in accordance with different application requirements. In the trajectory data publishing scenario, privacy preserving techniques must preserve data utility. In the LBS scenario, privacy preserving techniques must guarantee high quality of services. In this survey, we overview the key challenges and main techniques of trajectory privacy protection for the above requirements respectively.

Keywords: Trajectory data · Privacy protection · LBS

1 Introduction

With the development of computer technology and positioning technology, mobile users enjoy information services anytime and anywhere. Mobile users provide their own online locations and query requests through the server. The location service handles the corresponding location based query and returns the processing results to the users. The more accurate the location information is, the better the service experience for users will be received. However, if the location server is not credible, it will cause a great threat to the position and

H. Shen and Y. Sang (Eds.): PAAP 2019, CCIS 1163, pp. 461–476, 2020.
https://doi.org/10.1007/978-981-15-2767-8_41

trajectory privacy of mobile users. Therefore, while providing accurate location services, how to ensure location and trajectory privacy of mobile users, is an urgent problem that needs to be solved [1,2].

A trajectory is a series of location data based on time series, and trajectory privacy preservation is generated and developed on the basis of Location Based Services (LBS). It is found that although the location privacy of mobile users is protected, the trajectory privacy of mobile users can not be protected safely. In LBSs, the user sends a query that contains location information to the location server. If the attacker intercepts the information or the location server is monitored by the attacker, the attacker will get the user's location information. If the mobile user is constantly asking for a location query, the attacker will continuously acquire the locations of the user and link these locations, so it is easy to get the user's trajectory [3–5]. Through the analysis of these trajectories, combined with other relevant background knowledge, the attacker can infer a lot of user privacy information, such as work, family address, behavior habit, the place most often to go, and it will lead to even a threat to personal safety. Therefore, how to protect the trajectory privacy of mobile user has become an important issue [6,7].

2 Key Issues in Trajectory Privacy Protection

2.1 Basic Concept

Privacy refers to information that individuals, institutions and other entities do not want to be known externally. For example, the individual's behavior patterns, hobbies, and health conditions. Under different privacy requirements, the definitions of privacy also vary. In general, man is not willing to disclose information that can be referred to as personal privacy [8]. Trajectory is the position information sequence of a mobile user, which changes with time, and can be formalized as:

$T = \{uuid, (x_1, y_1, t_1), (x_2, y_2, t_2), ..., (x_i, y_i, t_i) ..., (x_n, y_n, t_n)\}$

The *uuid* is the identifier of the mobile user or identifier of the data item, (x_i, y_i, t_i) indicates the mobile user is at the position coordinates (x_i, y_i) at the moment t_i. With the location information of the mobile user connected, the trajectory information of the mobile user can be obtained.

2.2 Types of Trajectory Privacy Protection

At present, trajectory privacy protection mainly solves two aspects of privacy problems. One is trajectory privacy protection in continuous location query, and the other is trajectory privacy protection in data publishing. The advent of mobile location devices spawns a variety of location-based data applications. These applications can be broadly divided into two categories:

The first is online application, as shown in Fig. 1, which refers to the location of the moving object to provide corresponding services to it. The second type is offline application. As shown in Fig. 2, a location service provider or other institution collects and analyzes trajectory, or releases mobile objects for using by third parties.

(1) Trajectory privacy protection in continuous location queries [9,10]
Preserving the location privacy of mobile users can not completely preserve the real-time running trajectory of mobile users. Attackers can obtain the running trajectory of mobile users by other means. In LBS services, in order to obtain high-quality location services, users must provide accurate location information. If you want to obtain continuous location services, you must continue to provide location information, that is, continuous location queries.

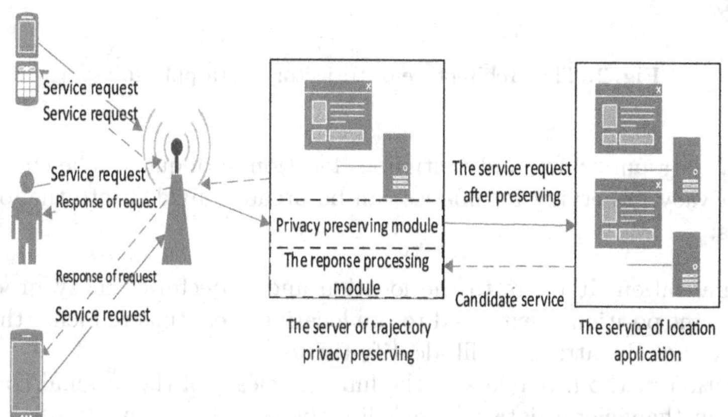

Fig. 1. The architecture of trajectory privacy protection in location queries

(2) Privacy protection for Trajectory Data Publishing
Trajectory data itself contains detailed spatial-temporal information, and plenty of useful information can be obtained from the analysis and research of trajectory data. In trajectory data release, privacy protection is the simplest way to hide or delete sensitive trace data and attributes from the published information. However, these methods are sometimes not effective, an attacker using anonymous spatial-temporal data can infer the mobile user's privacy information, and delete some properties, which will influence the data usability [11,12].

2.3 The Classification and Measurement Standards of Trajectory Privacy Preserving Techniques

The Classification of Trajectory Privacy Preserving Techniques. Trajectory privacy protection is accompanied by the development of location protection technology. It mainly solves the problem of trajectory privacy protection in

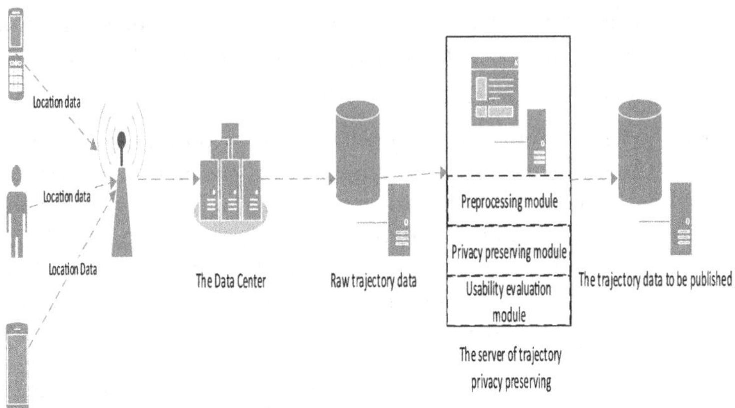

Fig. 2. The architecture of trajectory data publishing

trajectory data publishing and continuous location data query. The current trajectory privacy preserving techniques can be broadly divided into the following categories:

(1) Generalization. It refers to the location and trajectories fuzzy processing. The point position is extended to the location area, thus reducing the probability that the attacker will identify the user.
(2) Inhibition method. It refers to the limited release of the original trajectory data on the general data released directly, issued or converted to sensitive data after processing.
(3) False data method. It is the method of distorting the real data by replacing the real trajectory with the false trajectory or adding false data in the real data.

The Measurement Standards of Trajectory Privacy Protection. The purpose of trajectory privacy protection is to protect the user's privacy while ensuring that the released data has higher availability and that the mobile users can get good experience. In order to evaluate the level of trajectory privacy protection and the effect of privacy preserving technologies in practical applications, we mainly measure the trajectory privacy preserving method from the following aspects.

(1) Degree of privacy protection. Generally speaking, the higher the level of privacy protection is, the smaller the risk of privacy disclosure is.
(2) Service quality. In the trajectory privacy protection, the smaller the information distortion is, the better the service quality is.
(3) Information entropy. Suppose that attackers can identify mobile users by combining their knowledge with the probability of $p_i (i = 1, 2, 3, \ldots, k)$, the intensity of privacy protection can be weighed with information entropy.

$$H = -p_1 logp_1 - p_2 logp_2 - \ldots - p_k logp_k$$

The greater the information entropy is, the better the degree of privacy protection is.

(4) Anonymization success rate. The number of successfully anonymized trajectories in all sent trajectories reflects the performance of the privacy protection algorithm.
(5) Anonymization time. Anonymization processing time reflects the privacy preserving algorithm's implementation efficiency.
(6) Query time. The anonymous server spends time in anonymous query, and the query time is mainly used to measure the query cost.
(7) Candidate result size. It refers to the size of the query result set returned after anonymization processing, and is used to measure the communication cost between the data server and the anonymous server. The smaller the candidate result is, the smaller the communication cost is.

2.4 The Architecture of Trajectory Privacy Protection

Trajectory privacy preserving model based on mobile users proposes location service request, terminal mobile node location service request in different ways. It can be divided into distributed structure and central server structure [13,14].

(1) The distributed structure. The distributed structure consists of two parts, the client and the database server. The client itself completes the trajectory anonymity and the refinement of the query results. Each mobile user queries the appropriate anonymization region according to an anonymization algorithm, which is constructed by other users.
(2) The central server structure. The central server consists of the database server and the anonymization server. The server is responsible for the collection of accurate trajectory information of users, the anonymization of the trajectories, and the query refinement.

3 Generalization Method

Samarati and Sweeny et al. first proposed the k–anonymity privacy-preserving model for relational data publishing [15,16]. The k–anonymity model requires that any record in the table be at least the same value as any other $k - 1$ record about the quasi-identifier (QI). After years of research, k–anonymity model is becoming more and more mature. Unlike relational data, it is difficult to define quasi-identifiers and sensitive attributes in moving trajectory data. At present, the definition of quasi-identifier for moving trajectory data is still an open question.

The generalization method is the extension point, line position for location surface, area. Trajectory k–anonymity technology first proposed by Sweeney [15] is the most basic generalization method, which is mainly used to protect the privacy of data in a relational database. Its essence is the generalization processes identifier attributes in a database record, making specific $k-1$ records and other records can not be distinguished [17].

3.1 k^m–Anonymity Trajectory Data Privacy Preserving Methods

The user's identity information is leaked by recording its moving data. Sometimes deleting identity information can also lead to disclosure of trajectory privacy information. On the basis of k–anonymity method, Giorgos proposed an improved k^m–anonymity method to preserve the trajectory privacy of mobile users by generalizing the locations of the trajectories that do not satisfy the k^m–anonymity metric [18].

The k^m–anonymity method is a generalization of the privacy preserving model, to reduce the transaction data released in the user identity information that may be leaked, where k stands for the strength of privacy protection and m for the relevant information on m points that the attacker may have acquired. This method uses the generalization method to minimize the distance between the original trajectory and the anonymous trajectory, and uses the distance based inductive method to realize the k^m–anonymity of the trajectory data. The biggest advantage of the model is that it does not require detailed information about the attributes of quasi identifiers before the trajectory data is published, nor does it need to distinguish sensitive information from non sensitive information.

3.2 Privacy Preserving Method Based on Prefix Tree

In view of the existing disclosure risk of the trajectory privacy in mobile social network service, Huo et al. proposed PrivateCheckIn, a privacy preserving method based on prefix tree. Firstly, the prefix tree is constructed according to the attendance sequence, and after the pruning, reconstruction and traversal operations are carried out, a new k–anonymity login sequence is obtained to protect the trajectory privacy [19].

(1) The architecture of PrivateCheckIn
The method is based on the structure of the central server, and its architecture is composed of 3 parts, the client, the privacy protection server and the data server. Privacy protection server in the client and server data quality control, as a trusted third party server, is mainly responsible for the registration of mobile users, the storage parameters set by the user privacy and signature according to mobile user's submitted location type signature. It will produce a signature sequence generation of k–anonymity prefix tree execution. The runing, reconstruction operations and traversal on the tree will be generated with privacy protection requirements and sent to the data server to complete the inquiry service.

(2) The privacy preserving method of PrivateCheckIn
The essence of this method is to change the k–anonymity process of data trajectory into the process of generating k–anonymity prefix tree. Therefore, the prefix tree structure generates a signature sequence, firstly starting from the root node of the tree k–anonymity along a path with a reduced support less than the privacy protection degree k, in order to reduce the

actual attendance trajectory sequence loss and improve the availability of trajectory data. Finally, the traversal generates the k–anonymity signatures in sequence.

3.3 A Method of Trajectory Privacy Protection Based on Semantic Anonymous agent

Geng et al. proposed trajectory privacy preserving method based on semantic anonymization proxy, incorporating semantic location into the protection of trajectory privacy. Firstly, the model of city map is modeled as an undirected weighted graph with semantic, and then a regional semantic map is constructed [20]. Each structure must meet the requirements of regional privacy threshold τ. When the user makes request in the current location area, the probability of obtaining sensitive position in the area of the current user must be less than τ, so as to realize the semantic trajectory of the user's privacy protection.

This method introduces the concept of semantic anonymity, which can effectively prevent association attacks. It producess a semantic map building area achieving k–anonymity using an anonymization box by randomly selecting user's u anonymous set forwarded to the server. This method reduces the relevance between the user and the position, so that the attacker can't distinguish between the locations and users, fo the purpose of improving the privacy protection degree [21,22].

3.4 Dynamic Trajectory Privacy-Preserving Publishing

At present, the methods to deal with dynamic trajectory release are basically to recalculate the results of the last release. This will increase the computational cost of dynamic trajectory publishing. In addition, the static trajectory data publishing method takes the trajectory as the basic unit of the cluster. Therefore, there are many different basic units in the trajectory, and the k–equivalence class formed in this way will have a large trajectory generalization area, which will seriously reduce the utility of the released trajectory data [23,24].

Dynamic trajectory data privacy preserving algorithm designed a dynamic location generalization method. This method is a two-stage clustering method based on trajectory data k–anonymity, including the stages of representing region and the generalized region. In the first stage, the representative areas were clustered and adjusted in the continuous time slice by the dynamic Gibbs sampling clustering method. The second stage is to cluster the generalized region.

The generalized function of the algorithm is expressed by fitness function, which can be used to evaluate the effect of clustering.

The number and area size of internal links have a negative impact on information loss, because internal links are inhibited in clustering and have the opportunity to be published. At the same time, the greater the region, the greater the uncertainty. According to this rule, the fitness function is designed based on LFM method to cluster the generalized region.

$$fitness = (\frac{C_{out}}{C_{in} + C_{out}})^{\frac{R}{\alpha r D}} p_k$$

Among them, the α is the control factor, C_{out} is generalized area outside, C_{in} is generalized area in degrees, R is the radius of the generalized area, r is the radius of the representative area, D is a generalized area system, the importance of the ith generalized area is the importance of the system.

3.5 Grid Based l–Diversity Principle

The trajectory k–anonymity model ensures that any anonymization region covers at least k tracks and their corresponding sampling points. Therefore the probability of the attacker acquiring the real trajectory of the target is $1/k$. However, in reality, each trajectory contains the moving characteristics of the position, such as the directional trend of the trajectory movement in sensitive areas, for instance Banks and shopping malls in specific locations. If the two trajectories are highly similar, it means that the two trajectories also have high feature similarity. When similar trajectories are anonymized in the same region through the trajectory anonymization algorithm, the generated anonymization regions may still contain these feature information, thus leading to the risk of privacy leakage [18,25].

In order to prevent privacy leaks due to too little diversity, any anonymization group must satisfy l–diversity. In order to provide data utility, the trajectories that are close to each other must be as anonymous as possible while satisfying l–diversity.

Guo et al. put forward an improved l–differential method, for two-dimensional trajectory protection. This method divides the space into equal cells and corresponds the trajectory to these cells so that the similarity relationships among the locations on the trajectory can be displayed by the sequence of cells in the space in order to judge whether the trajectory meets the principle of anonymity with l-difference [26].

3.6 A Trajectory Privacy Preserving Method Based on Time Obfuscation

At present, many privacy preserving techniques simply divide trajectory information into sensitive and non-sensitive information, without considering the time, scene and other information. Huang et al. put forward the trajectory privacy preserving method of a time of confusion with the current context information of users. The method uses the temporal obfuscation method to integrate the

3 privacy protection parameters, r–anonymity, k–anonymity, s–segment paradigm, to hide the true trajectory privacy of the user.

(1) Privacy parameters
In order to solve the problem that LBS may disclose user's trajectory information, this method introduces four privacy protection parameters, r–anonymity, k–anonymity, s–segment paradigm and time obfuscation.
Anonymization server does not send query requests according to the logical sequence formed by the time sequence of query requests, but completely disrupted queries, and then randomly send them to the LBS server, reducing the possibility of an attacker to reconstruct the actual trajectory of the user, so as to prevent leakage privacy of the user's trajectory information.
(2) Architecture of privacy preserving algorithm
The main structure of the privacy preserving technology can be divided into 3 parts: map network construction, r–anonymity and time obfuscation.

4 Suppression Method

Suppression is the most common method of trajectory privacy protection. It achieves the goal of privacy protection by selectively publishing the original trajectory data, that is, restricting the release of certain sensitive information. Suppression method is a simple and efficient privacy preserving method based on background knowledge [27–30].

4.1 Trajectory Privacy Preserving Method Based on Disturbance

At present, the publication of trajectory data privacy protection based on disturbance is to reconstruct the trajectories within each cluster group. It generally includes point-based and verge-based disturbance.

According to the usability problems, Weng et al. put forward the trajectory privacy protection method based on the perturbation frequency, with similar minimum nodes to replace the existing node, which can suppress the node with the risk of loss of privacy.

4.2 Trajectory Privacy Preserving Method Based on Trajectory Frequency Suppression

Inhibition method is an important method of trajectory privacy protection, by limiting the release of sensitive points in the trajectory data to achieve privacy protection, but how to choose the appropriate balance to inhibit the privacy protection and data availability is an important research topic. Zhao et al. proposed trajectory privacy preserving method based on path frequency suppression, adding false data or local suppression problem trajectory.

(1) Add dummy data method. According to the privacy protection parameters set by the mobile user, the number of false track data needed to be added in the original trajectory is calculated when the privacy protection requirement reaches to Sum_add.
(2) Trajectory suppression method. According to the degree of privacy protection set by users, the local or overall suppression of trajectory data is calculated, and the number of trajectories needed by privacy protection requirements is calculated as sum_delete.
(3) Choose the right method. When $sum\_add > sum\_delete$, data suppression method is adopted. On the contrary, the dummy data method is added.

5 Pseudo Data Method

The basic idea of pseudo data method is to generate false trajectory data for each trajectory using a false path instead of the real, or form a group of false trajectory data through the real data, and add it to the original data [31,32].

At present, there are two main methods to generate pseudo data, incluiding random pattern generation and rotation mode generation.

(1) Random generation method. A random data is generated from the start point to the end of the connection, in continuous operation and consistent operation mode.
(2) Rotation mode generation. Based on the real trajectory of the mobile user, some sampling points in the real trajectory are rotated as the axis points, and the trajectories are generated as pseudo trajectories.

6 Privacy Protection Effectiveness Metric and Comparative Analysis

In trajectory privacy preserving data publishing, the performance of privacy preserving algorithms is mainly measured in two aspects: data utility and privacy protection degree [33].

6.1 Privacy Protection Effectiveness Metric

There are several methods for evaluation of privacy protection, such as discernibility metric, classification metric, normalization certainty punishment and so on [34,35].

(1) Discernibility metric
In the given data table T, the final published data is assumed to be processed $T^{'}(p_1, p_2, ..., p_m)$, $p_1, p_2, ..., p_m$ is m anonymization sets. $P_1, P_2, \ldots, P_m$ is m anonymization groups. Then, according to the Discernibility Metric (DM) measure function, the table is punished by the following values.

$$DM(T^{'}) = \sum\nolimits_{1 \le i \le m} |P_i|^2$$

The meaning of the formula is to compute the sum of the square values of all anonymization group sizes. The smaller the punishment value is, the smaller the information loss of the anonymization groups have, the higher the quality of the published data is.

(2) Classification metric

The classification metric first uses a criterion to divide the records of the entire original data table into two sets. In the given data table T, the final published data is assumed to be processed $T^{'}(p_1, p_2, ..., p_m)$, $p_1, p_2, ..., p_m$ is m anonymization sets. Each $P_i (1 \le i \le m)$ record also belongs to the two sets. Among them, a larger number is recorded as $majority(P_i)$, while a smaller number is recorded as $minority(P_i)$. According to the Classification Metric (CM) measurement function, the table is punished as follows.

$$CM(T^{'}) = \sum\nolimits_{1 \le i \le m} |minority(P_i)|$$

(3) Normalized certainty punishment

In the given data table T, the final published data is assumed to be $T^{'}(t_1, t_2, ..., t_m)$, where $t_1, t_2, ..., t_m$ are m anonymization sets. Suppose that $T^{'}$ has d QI attributes, and if the j-th attribute A_j of t_i is a numeric property and its value is $[y_{ij}, z_{ij}]$, then t_i receives the following Normalized Certainty Punishment (NCP) on property A_j:

$$NCP(t_{ij}) = \frac{|z_{ij} - y_{ij}|}{|A_j|}$$

where $|A_j|$ is the size of the domain of attribute A_j. If A_j is a numeric property and its value is X_{ij}, then t_i receives the following punishment on property A_j:

$$NCP(t_{ij}) = \frac{|X_{ij}|}{|A_j|}$$

where $|X_{ij}|$ is the number of leaf nodes in the semantic expression tree of t_i containing X_{ij}. Then, t_i receives the following punishment of records:

$$NCP(t_i) = \sum\nolimits_{1 \le j \le d} NCP(t_{ij})$$

Then, the overall publishment of table $T^{'}$ is as follows:

$$NCP(T^{'}) = \sum\nolimits_{1 \le i \le n} NCP(t_i)$$

6.2 Comparative Analysis

This paper classifies and compares the methods proposed in the study of trajectory privacy protection, and lists the main advantages and disadvantages of these methods as well as the representative techniques. Through comparative analysis, we can find that the three kinds of methods have their own advantages and disadvantages.

(1) Pseudo data method. The computation cost is small and the implementation is simple, but the algorithm is not transplantable, the data utility and service quality are poor.
(2) Generalization method. The adaptability of the algorithm, the utility of data and the quality of service have been improved, and the cost of implementation has been greatly improved.
(3) Suppression method. The suppression method is simple to realize and has high degree of privacy protection, but the distortion is serious.

7 Future Research Directions

7.1 The Optimization of Privacy Location and the Reasonable Construction of Anonymization Box

In privacy protection, if we do not consider the user's environment and background information, we can divide the user's positions into sensitive and non-sensitive points directly, then preserve sensitive points before the release, and release the non sensitive points directly. In fact, this approach is not realistic, sensitivity position depends on the situation and context, e.g., the hospital is sensitive to some patients, but not to the doctor. The privacy of the location should be classified according to the user's personal information and the environment, scene and contextual information, so as to provide personalized privacy protection [36].

Therefore, it is necessary to optimize the privacy location and construct the anonymization frame scientifically and effectively.

7.2 Protect the Trajectory Information in Continuous Location Queries

Based on the continuous query location, a method was proposed [37] to protect positions according to order of the queries. In fact, each user presents a query service request at each time point, and the requirements of k–anonymity can be met in every moment, but if the user sends a query request according to the time sequence, the attacker can still infer that the running trajectory of users. Therefore, we should propose a new model based on the proposed time of service request, to preserve the trajectory privacy information.

7.3 Research on Privacy Preserving Technology in Big Data Environment

Anonymization technology is the most common privacy preserving technology, and it has better privacy protection for single data source. However, in the era of big data, the attacker has some other public or private data sources. Through the integration of multiple data sources, using link attack of anonymity data sources, the attacker can infer the vast majority personal sensitive information, causing the individual privacy leakage.

Therefore, how to break through the existing privacy preserving technology in the big data environment, and how to prevent the threats brought by resource data integration, are important directions for future research.

7.4 Other Issues that Need to Be Addressed

At present, the trajectory data privacy-preserving algorithms can effectively prevent the attacker using a specific location information for trajectory privacy attack, and at the same time, ensure released trajectory data with high quality. However, most algorithms only focus on the privacy protection of individuals corresponding to each trajectory, but neglect the protection of the characteristics of trajectory clustering. Through theoretical analysis and experimental verification, there is a risk of secondary cluster attack on trajectory data processed by clustering technology. How to prevent secondary cluster attack needs further study.

The existing trajectory release models and algorithms can prevent privacy leakage in trajectory data release to a certain extent. However, these models and methods assume that all trajectories have the same privacy requirements. In the real world, individuals corresponding to different trajectories often have different privacy requirements, and even the same individuals have different privacy requirements at different times or places. How to effectively meet the needs of personalized privacy protection also needs further in-depth study.

8 Conclusions

With the development of mobile location devices, wireless sensor networks and location-based services, people are at risk of privacy leakage when they conveniently access location-based services. On one hand, based on the location of online inquiry service, the trajectory information of mobile users will be in the hands of the location service providers, which may misuse the trajectory information. On the other hand, some location-based service providers need to release data periodically and may reveal information about users' privacy. At present, researchers have done a lot of work on trajectory privacy preserving methods. This papers reviews and summarizes the main research achievements in the field of trajectory privacy protection in recent years, and summarizes the current status of privacy preserving techniques in data publishing and location-based services. Various methods are analyzed and compared, and some major research directions for the future are proposed. In general, The study of trajectory privacy protection technology is still in its infancy, and there are still many key issues to be studied.

Acknowledgment. This work is supported by National Key R & D Program of China Project #2017YFB0203201, Science and Technology Program of Guangdong Province, China (No. 2017A010101039).

References

1. Ghasemzadeh, M., Fung, B.C.M., Chen, R., Awasthi, A.: Anonymizing trajectory data for passenger flow analysis. Transp. Res. Part C Emerg. Technol. **39**(2), 63–79 (2014)
2. Domingo-Ferrer, J., Trujillo-Rasua, R.: Microaggregation- and permutation-based anonymization of movement data. Elsevier Science Inc. (2012)
3. Rowe, M.: Applying semantic social graphs to disambiguate identity references. In: Aroyo, L., et al. (eds.) ESWC 2009. LNCS, vol. 5554, pp. 461–475. Springer, Heidelberg (2009). https://doi.org/10.1007/978-3-642-02121-3_35
4. Kaplan, E., Pedersen, T.B., Savas, E., Saygin, Y.: Discovering private trajectories using background information. Data Knowl. Eng. **69**(7), 723–736 (2010)
5. Thimmarayappa, S., Megha, V.: Big data privacy and management. Int. J. Comput. Appl. **107**(6), 13–16 (2014)
6. Shokri, R., Theodorakopoulos, G., Troncoso, C., Hubaux, J.P., Le Boudec, J.Y.: Protecting location privacy: optimal strategy against localization attacks. In: ACM Conference on Computer and Communications Security, pp. 617–627 (2012)
7. Terrovitis, M., Mamoulis, N., Kalnis, P.: Local and global recoding methods for anonymizing set-valued data. VLDB J. **20**(1), 83–106 (2011)
8. Gao, S., Ma, J., Sun, C., Li, X.: Balancing trajectory privacy and data utility using a personalized anonymization model. J. Netw. Comput. Appl. **38**(1), 125–134 (2014)
9. Tramp, S., Frischmuth, P., Arndt, N., Ermilov, T., Auer, S.: Weaving a distributed, semantic social network for mobile users. In: Antoniou, G., et al. (eds.) ESWC 2011. LNCS, vol. 6643, pp. 200–214. Springer, Heidelberg (2011). https://doi.org/10.1007/978-3-642-21034-1_14
10. Bonchi, F., Lakshmanan, L.V.S., Wang, H.: Trajectory anonymity in publishing personal mobility data. ACM Sigkdd Explor. Newsl. **13**(1), 30–42 (2011)
11. Pingley, A., Zhang, N., Fu, X., Choi, H.A.: Protection of query privacy for continuous location based services. In: 2011 Proceedings IEEE INFOCOM, pp. 1710–1718 (2013)
12. Li, H., Shen, Y., Sang, T.: An efficient method for privacy preserving trajectory data publishing based on data partitioning. J. Supercomput. (2019)
13. Lin, Y., Lin, C., Kong, X., Feng, X., Wu, G.: A clustering based location privacy protection scheme for pervasive computing. In: Green Computing and Communications, pp. 719–726 (2011)
14. Sang, Y., Shen, H., Tian, H.: Privacy preserving tuple matching in distributed databases. IEEE Trans. Knowl. Data Eng. **21**(12), 1767–1782 (2009)
15. Sweeney, L.: k anonymity a model for protecting privacy. Int. J. Uncertain. Fuzziness Knowl.-Based Syst. **10**(05), 557–570 (2002)

16. Li, S., Shen, H., Sang, Y.: An efficient model and algorithm for privacy-preserving trajectory data publishing. In: Park, J.H., Shen, H., Sung, Y., Tian, H. (eds.) PDCAT 2018. CCIS, vol. 931, pp. 240–249. Springer, Singapore (2019). https://doi.org/10.1007/978-981-13-5907-1_25
17. Sun, X., Sun, L., Wang, H.: Extended k anonymity models against sensitive attribute disclosure (2011)
18. Poulis, G., Skiadopoulos, S., Loukides, G., Gkoulalas-Divanis, A.: Distance based km anonymization of trajectory data. In: IEEE International Conference on Mobile Data Management, pp. 57–62 (2013)
19. Aslam, B., Amjad, F., Zou, C.C.: Pmtr, privacy enhancing multilayer trajectory-based routing protocol for vehicular ad hoc networks. In: MILCOM 2013 2013 IEEE Military Communications Conference, pp. 882–887 (2013)
20. Yigitoglu, E., Damiani, M.L., Abul, O., Silvestri, C.: Privacy preserving sharing of sensitive semantic locations under road-network constraints. In: IEEE International Conference on Mobile Data Management, pp. 186–195 (2012)
21. Sanchez, D., Castella Roca, J., Viejo, A.: Knowledge based scheme to create privacy preserving but semantically related queries for web search engines. Inf. Sci. **218**(1), 17–30 (2013)
22. Chow, C.Y., Mokbel, M.F., Liu, X.: Spatial cloaking for anonymous location based services in mobile peer to peer environments. Geoinformatica **15**(2), 351–380 (2011)
23. Xin, Y., Xie, Z.Q., Yang, J.: The privacy preserving method for dynamic trajectory releasing based on adaptive clustering. Inf. Sci. **378**, 131–143 (2017)
24. Al-Hussaeni, K., Fung, B.C.M., Cheung, W.K.: Privacy preserving trajectory stream publishing. Data Knowl. Eng. **94**(PA), 89–109 (2014)
25. Lefevre, K., Dewitt, D.J., Ramakrishnan, R.: Incognito: efficient full-domain k-anonymity. In: Proceedings of 2005 ACM SIGMOD International Conference on Management of Data, SIGMOD 2005, New York, NY, USA, pp. 49–60 (2005)
26. Cao, J., Karras, P., Kalnis, P., Tan, K.L.: SABRE: a sensitive attribute bucketization and redistribution framework for t closeness. VLDB J. Int. J. Very Large Data Bases **20**(1), 59–81 (2011)
27. Lee, K.C.K., Zheng, B., Chen, C., Chow, C.Y.: Efficient index based approaches for skyline queries in location based applications. IEEE Trans. Knowl. Data Eng. **25**(11), 2507–2520 (2013)
28. Chen, R., Fung, B.C.M., Mohammed, N., Desai, B.C., Wang, K.: Privacy preserving trajectory data publishing by local suppression. Inf. Sci. Int. J. **231**(1), 83–97 (2013)
29. Sang, Y., Shen, H.: Efficient and secure protocols for privacy preserving set operations. ACM Trans. Inf. Syst. Secur. **13**(1), 1–35 (2009)
30. Xu, Q., Shen, H., Sang, Y., Tian, H.: Privacy preserving ranked fuzzy keyword search over encrypted cloud data. In: International Conference on Parallel and Distributed Computing, Applications and Technologies, pp. 239–245 (2013)
31. Mano, K., Minami, K., Maruyama, H.: Privacy preserving publishing of pseudonym based trajectory location data set. In: Eighth International Conference on Availability, Reliability and Security, pp. 615–624 (2013)
32. Gao, S., Ma, J., Shi, W., Zhan, G., Sun, C.: TrPF, a trajectory privacy preserving framework for participatory sensing. IEEE Trans. Inf. Forensics Secur. **8**(6), 874–887 (2013)
33. Zhou, L., Ding, L., Finin, T.: How is the semantic web evolving, a dynamic social network perspective. Comput. Hum. Behav. **27**(4), 1294–1302 (2011)

34. Bayardo, R.J., Agrawal, R.: Data privacy through optimal k anonymization. In: International Conference on Data Engineering, 2005, ICDE 2005, Proceedings, pp. 217–228 (2005)
35. Xu, J., Wang, W., Pei, J., Wang, X., Shi, B., Fu, W.C.: Utility based anonymization using local recoding. In: ACM SIGKDD International Conference on Knowledge Discovery and Data Mining, pp. 785–790 (2006)
36. Sang, Y., Shen, H., Tian, H., Zhang, Z.: Achieving probabilistic anonymity in a linear and hybrid randomization model. IEEE Trans. Inf. Forensics Secur. **11**(10), 2187–2202 (2016)
37. Xu, Q., Shen, H., Sang, Y., Tian, H.: Privacy preserving ranked fuzzy keyword search over encrypted cloud data. In: International Conference on Parallel and Distributed Computing, Applications and Technologies, pp. 239–245 (2014)

Big Data Processing and Deep Learning

Minimizing Off-Chip Memory Access for Deep Convolutional Neural Network Training

Jijun Wang(✉) and Hongliang Li

Jiangnan Institute of Computing Technology, Wuxi 214083, China
wjjxjtu@mail.ustc.edu.cn

Abstract. When training convolutional neural networks, a large amount of operations and memory access are in need, which easily lead to the bottleneck of "memory wall" and decrease the computational performance and efficiency. Batch Normalization (BN) can effectively speed up the deep network training convergence, but it has complex data dependence and causes more serious "memory wall" bottleneck. Aiming at the "memory wall" problem occurred in the training for convolutional neural network using BN algorithm, the training method with splitting BN layer and multi-layer fusion calculation is proposed to reduce the memory access in model training. Firstly, by reordering "CONV+BN+RELU" (CBR) block, we trade computation for memory access with extra computation to reduce data accessed during training. Secondly, according to the memory access characteristics of the BN layer, the BN layer is divided into two sub-layers, which are respectively fused with the adjacent layers and the CBR block is recombined into "BN_B+RELU+CONV+BN_A" (BRCB), which further reduces the read-write of the main memory during training and alleviates the "memory wall" bottleneck to improve accelerator computational efficiency. The experimental results show that when using the NVIDIA TESLA V100 GPU to train ResNet-50, Inception V3 and DenseNet models, compared with the original training method, the amount of data accessed using BRCB multi-layer fusion optimization method is reduced by 33%, 22% and 31% respectively, and the actual computing efficiency of V100 is improved by 19%, 18% and 21% respectively.

Keywords: Convolutional neural network · Multi-layer fusion · BN reconstruction · Memory access optimization

1 Introduction

Convolutional Neural Network (CNN) is one of the most popular deep neural network models, being widely used in image recognition, natural language processing, biology and autopilot, etc. Heavy computing burden and large off-chip memory bandwidth demand are key characteristics for CNN training. Generally, the memory bandwidth demand far exceeds the accelerator's bandwidth, leading to the reduction of accelerator performance. Therefore, memory access optimization for CNN training has attracted extensive attentions.

H. Shen and Y. Sang (Eds.): PAAP 2019, CCIS 1163, pp. 479–491, 2020.
https://doi.org/10.1007/978-981-15-2767-8_42

Intermediate results produced by each layer in forward propagation should be stored to main memory for use in back propagation [1]. Training convolution layer and BN layer depend on results of adjacent layer, and require the same intermediate data several times, causing serious "memory wall" bottleneck. Besides, BN layer's computing density is much lower than other layers, further exacerbating "memory wall" bottleneck. To alleviate this problem, we propose an effective method through multi-layer fusion computing with BN reconstruction, where BN layer is split into two sub-layers.

This rest of this paper is organized as follows. Section 2 analyses the data dependence in BN layer and its impact on memory access. Section 3 presents the proposed optimization method, builds a memory access model and computational model. Section 4 quantitatively analyzes the optimization effect. Section 5 summarizes the related work. Final section concludes this paper.

2 Data Dependence of BN Layers and Memory Access Characteristics

When the depth of the convolutional neural network reaches tens or even hundreds of layers, it is prune to "gradient explosion" or "gradient disappearance", which leads to model training cannot converge. BN algorithm proposed by Sergey loffe et al. in 2015 is one of the most effective way to solve this problem [2], and has been widely used in state of art CNN models. Table 1 summarizes the depths of ResNe-50 [3], Inception V3 [4], DenseNet [5] and Yolo V3 [6] models, as well as the number of convolution and BN layers.

Table 1. The layer amount of different type in convolutional networks

Layer	ResNet-50	InceptionV3	Yolo V3	DenseNet
Convolution layer	53	107	75	121
BN layer	53	107	72	121
RELU layer	49	109	72	121
Depth	177	369	318	547

2.1 Data Dependence of BN Layer

BN algorithm includes two-part operations. Firstly, calculating the mean and variance of input data from convolution layer; Secondly normalizing and scaling the input data based on mean and variance. Figure 1 illustrates data dependence of BN in forward propagation.

As is seen in Fig. 1, X indicates input data of BN, μ and σ^2 indicates the mean value and variance value of X respectively, and γ, β represent parameter of BN, Y indicates the result of BN. μ and σ^2 depend on all input data from adjacent convolution layer; Normalization and scaling operations require X, μ, σ^2 and parameters γ, β. Consequently, the two-part operations of BN in forward propagation is serial in time.

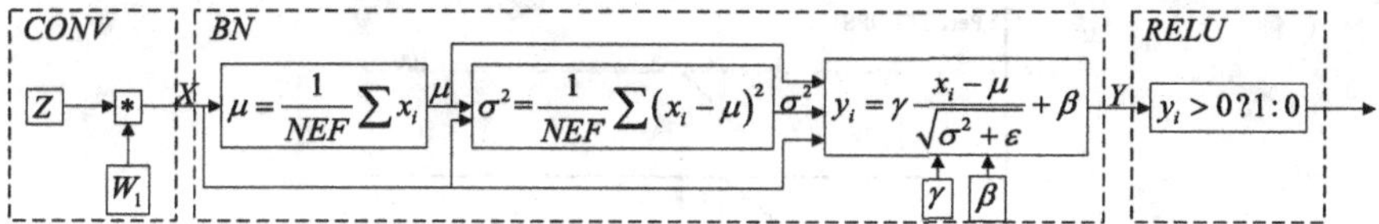

Fig. 1. BN calculation data dependence during forward-propagation

Figure 2 illustrates data dependence of BN in backward propagation. ΔY indicates the result error, Δγ, Δβ indicate the parameters error, ΔX indicates the input data error. Obviously, Δγ, Δβ depend on X, ΔX depends on Δγ, Δβ, X and ΔY. As a result, the two-part operation of BN in backward propagation is serial in time as well.

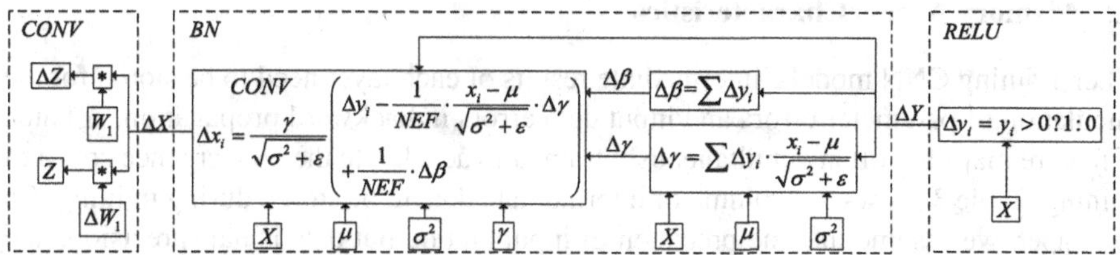

Fig. 2. BN calculation data dependence during Backward-propagation

The amount of input and output data of the BN layer is the same during training. Assume that the amount of input data stored in main memory is D, and the BN layer is calculated by single precision (4B) [7]. We make a statistic on amount of data accessed and computing density of BN during forward and backward propagation in Table 2.

Table 2. Analysis on operations, data accessed and computing density of BN layer

Category	μ, σ^2	Normalization and scaling	Operations (FLOP)	Memory access (BYTE)	Computing density
Forward pass	$\frac{3}{4}D$	$\frac{D}{2}$	$\frac{5}{4}D$	$2D$	0.61
Backward pass	$\frac{5}{4}D$	D	$\frac{9}{4}D$	$4D$	0.55

The computing density of forward and backward propagation is 0.61FLOP/B and 0.55 FLOP/B respectively, can exacerbate "memory wall" bottleneck when off-chip memory bandwidth is not large enough.

Figure 3 depicts the single-precision compute ability roofline of NVIDIA Tesla V100 [8] and P100 [9]. Ideally, when the computing density of application reaches 22 FLOP/B and 25 FLOP/B, V100 and P100 can reach up to peak performance when running the application [11]. However, the computing density of BN algorithm is far from 22FLOP/B and 25FLOP/B, which means lower computing efficiency of V100 and P100 for BN algorithm.

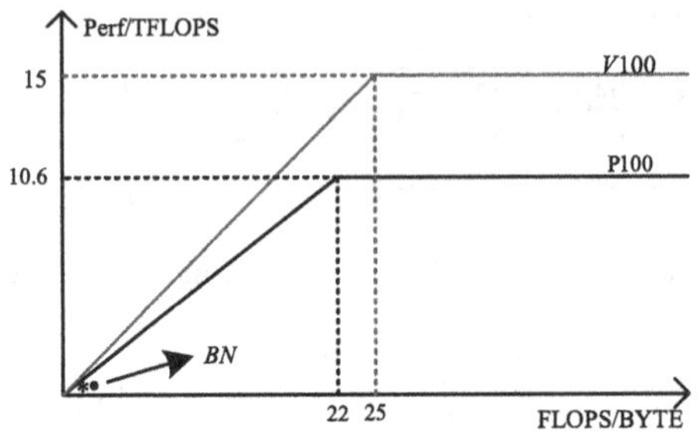

Fig. 3. NVIDIA V100 and P100's ROOFLINE curve

2.2 Memory Access Characteristics

When training CNN models, intermediate results of each layer need to be stored for the calculation of parameter errors and input data errors in backward propagation. A batch of feature maps are often simultaneously trained to accelerate the convergence speed of training. Table 3 shows the volume of intermediate data to be stored during training. (In this paper, we assume that the precision of input and output data is half-precision, and the precision of parameter is single-precision).

Table 3. Volume of intermediate results and parameters during training

CNN models	PIC SIZE	BATCH	Intermediate data and parameters (MB)
AlexNet	224 × 224 × 3	16	119
VGG-16	224 × 224 × 3	16	1761
ResNet-50	224 × 224 × 3	16	2202
Inception V3	299 × 299 × 3	16	2523

Table 3 shows that a large amount of intermediate results and parameters need to be stored and accessed during the training of CNN models, and as the depth of model increases, the amount of data stored and accessed increase rapidly. For example, the depth of AlexNet [11] model is 8 layers and its amount of data to be stored and accessed is only 199 MB in contrast with 2202 MB of ResNet-50. As the on-chip buffer capacity of accelerator is limited, it is impossible to store such large amount of data. Therefore, the intermediate results and parameter during training need to be written or read from off-chip memory. In general, the accelerators for training have a large-capacity off-chip memory, such as NVIDIA Tesla V100 equipped with 16 GB and 32 GB HBM memory.

The state-of-art CNN models have a large amount of "Convolution-BN-RELU" (CBR) block, such as ResNet-50, Inception V3, DenseNet and other models. Therefore, CBR block determines the memory access characteristic of the whole model during training. Figure 4 details the memory access of CBR block in forward and backward propagation.

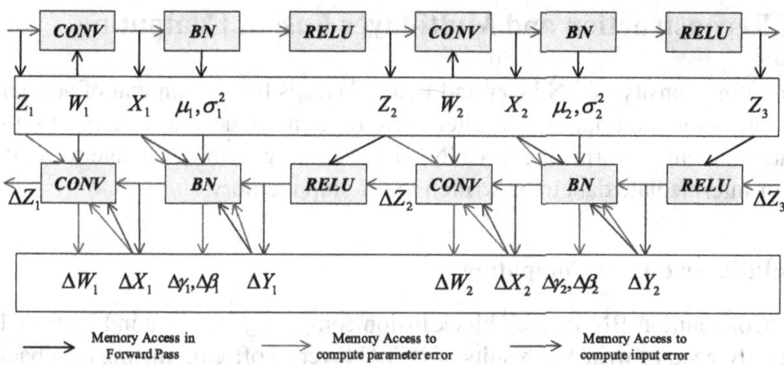

Fig. 4. Memory access of CBR block in forward and backward propagation

In Fig. 4, X indicates the output of convolution layer (the input data of BN layer), Y indicates the output of BN, Z indicates the output of RELU. The results of backpropagation need to be written to off-chip memory, as both BN layer and convolution layer need to calculate parameter errors and input errors using the output errors, as shown in Fig. 4.

Assuming that the input and output data volume of convolution is equal and the kernel parameter volume is too much smaller to consider, that is, $Z_1 \approx X_1 = Z_2 \approx X_2 = D$. Based on the assumption, the amount of data accessed during training of convolution, BN and RELU is $6D$, $7D$ and $2D$ respectively. Obviously, the convolution layer is much more computationally intensive than the BN layer and RELU layer, further proving that BN layer is the bottleneck of improving training efficiency. Figure 5 shows the computing density distribution of different convolution layer, BN layer and RELU layer of ResNet-50.

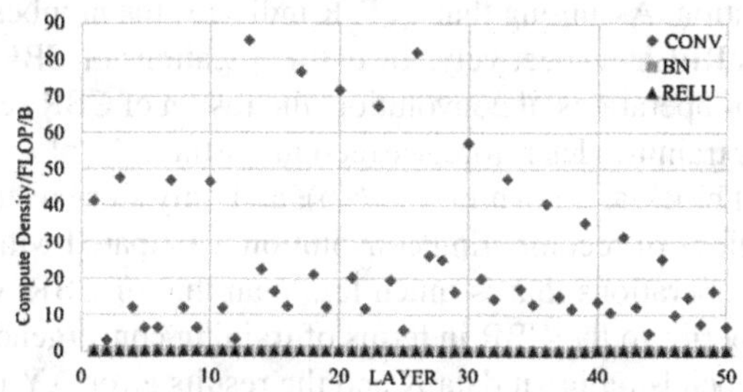

Fig. 5. Computing density distribution of ResNet-50

As is shown in Fig. 5, the computing density of convolution layer is greater than that of BN layer and RELU layer. Compared with convolution layers, the amount of operations of BN layer and RELU layer is extremely small while they require a large amount of data for computation. Therefore, memory access optimization on BN layer and RELU layer can effectively improve the accelerators' efficiency.

3 BN Reconstruction and Multi-layer Fusion Computing

The computing density of BN layer and RELU layer is lower than that of accelerators, we consider "more computation as alternative of memory access" strategy to improve accelerators actual performance in CNN model training with advantage to reduce the amount of intermediate data to be written to off-chip memory.

3.1 Multi-layer Fusion Computing

Ideally, "Convolution-BN-RELU" block fusion computing is shown in Fig. 6(a). In this way, we only need to write the results of RELU layer to off-chip memory. In backward propagation, when BN layer results or convolution layer results are in need, the required data will be recomputed by performing the forward pass again with the closest recorded data. For example, when performing backpropagation of BN layer in Fig. 6(a), the results of convolution layer is recomputed by performing convolution with recorded data Z1.

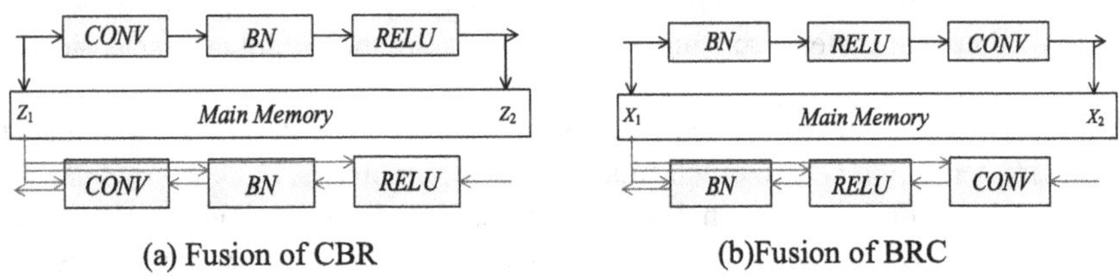

Fig. 6. Training process of "CONV+BN+RELU" (CBR) and "BN+RELU+CONV" (BRC)

CBR block fusion significantly reduces the intermediate results to be stored during training, while it needs extra computations to calculate the required data for BN layer in backward propagation. Assuming that Q, P, R indicates the number of operations for convolution, BN and RELU respectively, the extra operations of CBR block is 2Q. Due to the large amount of operations of convolution, the fusion of CBR seriously affects the convergence speed of training. Therefore, we recombine the CBR block into "BN-RELU-Convolution" (BRC) block as shown in Fig. 6(b), and only store results of convolution to avoid extra operations of recomputing convolution. Compared with CBR, BRC only needs P+R+Q extra operations that is much less than that of CBR. Consequently, the fusion of BRC is superior to the CBR in terms of training convergence speed.

BN algorithm depends on input data X and the results error ΔY in backward propagation, as shown in Fig. 1(b). When using CBR or CRB block fusion computing, BN still needs to access X and ΔY multiple times, so the training bottleneck caused by BN remains unresolved. In Fig. 4, we observed that some data can be multi-layer multiplexed. For example, X can be used for computing mean value μ and variance value σ^2 before written to off-chip memory; ΔY can be used for computing parameter errors $\Delta\gamma$, $\Delta\beta$ before written to off-chip memory. Based on the above analysis, BN can be split into two sub-layers, which are respectively integrated into the adjacent layer to reduce the amount of memory access.

"BN_B+RELU+CONV+BN_A" Forward (BRCB-F). In forward propagation, BN is split into BN_A and BN_B (BN_A calculates the mean value μ, variance value σ^2 and BNB is responsible for the normalization and scaling), which are respectively fused to the convolution and RELU layer, as shown in Fig. 7. In forward propagation, "BN_A+RELU+CONV+BN_B" reads previous convolution layer results X and μ, σ^2 to complete normalization and scaling, then directly calculate RELU with BN layer results Y, RELU layer results are used for convolution, and convolution results are used for calculation of the mean value μ, variance value σ^2. In summary, BRCB only needs to read X and write X' once as well as some related parameters.

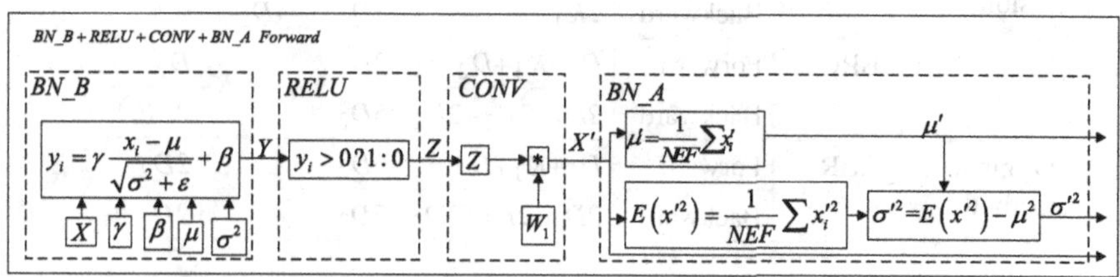

Fig. 7. Fusion of "BN_B+RELU+CONV+BN_A" (BRCB) in forward propagation

"BN_A+RELU+CONV+BN_B" Backward (BRCB-B). In backward propagation, BN is also split into BN_A and BN_B (BN_A calculate the parameter error Δγ, Δβ, and BN_B calculates the input data error $\Delta X'$), which are respectively fused into adjacent layer, as shown in Fig. 8. "BN_A+RELU+CONV+BN_B" in backward propagation reads $\Delta Y', X'$ and related parameter γ, β to calculate $\Delta X'$, which are used for calculation of ΔZ, and ΔZ are used to calculate ΔY, which is used for calculation of parameter error Δγ, Δβ before written out to off-chip memory. Besides, $\Delta Y', X'$ should be read again to calculate $\Delta X'$, which is used for calculation of ΔW_1.

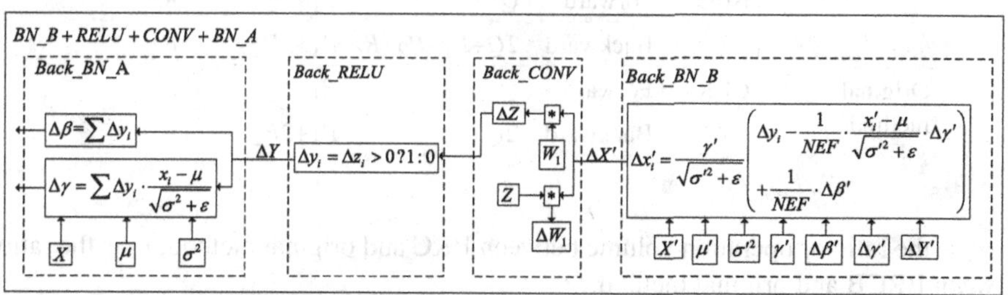

Fig. 8. Fusion of "BN_B+RELU+CONV+BN_A" in backward propagation

3.2 Data Volume Model and Operation Volume Model

Table 4 shows the data accessed volume of BRC and BRCB when used for training. It is assumed that the D_1 and D_2 indicate input and output data volume of convolution layer respectively, and K_1 indicates the kernel volume. In forward propagation, the ratio of data volume between BRCB and BRC is $\frac{D_1+K_1+D_2}{D_1+K_1+3D_2}$, and the ratio is $\frac{3D_1+2K_1+4D_2}{2D_1+2K_1+7D_2}$ in backward propagation. If D_1 is close to or much smaller than D_2, BRCB fusion computing can effectively reduce the amount of data accessed from off-chip memory during model training.

Table 4. The volume of data accessed with different methods during training

Method	Process		CONV	BNA	BNB	RELU
Multi-layer fusion	BRCB	Forward	K_1	D_2	D_1	0
		Backward	$2K_1$	$3D_1$	$4D_2$	0
	BRC	Forward	D_1+K_1+D_2	$2D_2$		D_2
		Backward	$2D_1$+$2K_1$+$2D_2$	$5D_2$		0
Original method	CBR	Forward	D_1+K_1+D_2	$3D_2$		$2D_2$
		Backward	$2D_1$+$2K_1$+$2D_2$	$5D_2$		$2D_2$

Table 5 counts the operations volume of BRC and BRCB (Assuming that Q, P_1, P_2, R indicates the amount of required operations of convolution, BNA, BNB and RELU respectively in forward propagation).

Table 5. The volume of operations with different methods during training

Methods	Process		CONV	BNA	BNB	RELU
Multi-layer fusion	BRCB	Forward	Q	P_1	P_2	R
		Backward	$2Q$+$4P_2$	P_1	$2P_2$	R
	BRC	Forward	Q	P_1+P_2		R
		Backward	$2Q$+P_1+P_2+R	P_1+$2P_2$		R
Original method	CBR	Forward	Q	P_1+P_2		R
		Backward	$2Q$	P_1+$2P_2$		R

r_1 is the ratio of operation volume between BRC and original method; r_2 is the ratio between BRCB and original method.

$$r_1 = \frac{3Q + 7P_2 + 2P_1 + 2R}{3Q + 3P_2 + 2P_1 + 2R} \tag{1}$$

$$r_2 = \frac{3Q + 4P_2 + 3P_1 + 2R}{3Q + 3P_2 + 2P_1 + 2R} \tag{2}$$

As there are facts that $Q \geq (P_1 - P_2)$ and $Q \gg R$, $r_1 \approx r_2 \approx 1$. The extra volume of operations of BRC and BRCB during training is too small to impact on training speed.

4 Evaluation

In order to evaluate the effects of BRC and BRCB block fusion computing training methods, we perform experiment on ResNet-50, Inception V3 and DenseNet model.

4.1 Quantitative Evaluation on BRC and BRCB

Based the model in 3.2, we develop a memory access analysis tool which can automatically output the memory access of different layer when there is an model structure file as tool's input. Taking ResNet-50 model as an example, the amount of data accessed from off-chip memory is counted for CBR (origin method), BRC and BRCB, as shown in Fig. 9.

In Fig. 9, the BRC and BRCB curves respectively indicate the optimization ratio of memory access when using BRC and BRCB methods. It is obvious that the data volume using BRCB is smallest, and the data volume of resnet4.1.3 is reduced by 60%. However, as the depth of ResNet-50 increases, the optimization effects of the two optimization methods are gradually decreased. The reason is that the kernel volume gradually increases as the depth of ResNet-50 increases, approaching or even exceeding the volume of input and output data. For example, in resnet5.2.2 in Fig. 9, the kernel volume is nearly 45 times of input feature map. According to the analysis model in Sect. 3.2, optimization effects of BRC and BRCB is not obvious.

The curves in Fig. 9 show a "sawtooth" shape because the kernel size of resnet4.1.2, resnet4.2.2, resnet4.3.2, etc. is 3 × 3, which leads to a smaller size of output feature map than input feature map. According to the analysis in Sect. 3.2, optimization effect of BRC and BRCB is weakened in this case.

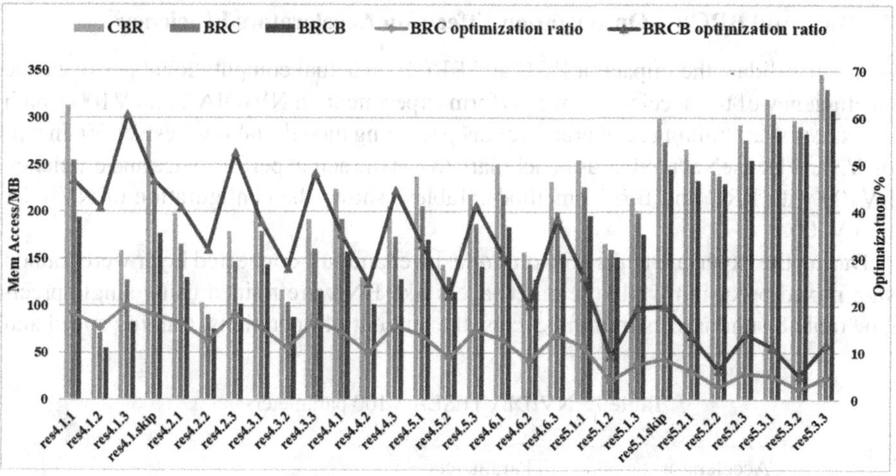

Fig. 9. Memory access of "CONV-BN-RELU" block for CBR, BRC and BRCB of Resnet50

4.2 BRC and BRCB's Optimization on Memory Access

In order to further evaluate the memory access optimization effect brought by the proposed method, we make statistics on the amount of accessed data in training for ResNet-50, Inception V3 and DenseNet models in Table 6.

Table 6. Statistics of memory access of ResNet-50, Inception V3 and DenseNet

Models	CBR(GB)	Data accessed and optimization ratio			
		BRC(GB)	Ratio (%)	BRCB(GB)	Ratio (%)
ResNet-50	18.18	14.3	22%	12.27	33%
InceptionV3	11.51	9.82	15%	8.93	22%
DenseNet	25.07	20.45	18%	17.19	31%

Table 6 shows that compared with CBR, the memory access of ResNet-50, Inception V3, and DenseNet in training is significantly reduced with BRC and BRCB optimization method. As seen in Table 6, the amount of data accessed for the three models is reduced by 22.3%, 14.7% and 18.4% respectively with BRC, while the amount of data accessed for the three models is reduced by 32.5%, 22.4% and 31.4% respectively with BRCB. Compared with BRC method, there was a further optimization by 11%, 7% and 13% respectively.

As the different number of BN layers in different models, the optimization effect is different. The experimental results show that proposed method in this paper can significantly reduce the amount of data accessed in training, effectively alleviating the increasingly serious "Memory Wall" bottleneck.

4.3 BRC and BRCB's Optimization Effects on Accelerators Efficiency

To further validate the impact of BRC and BRCB on actual computational performance and efficiency of the accelerator, we perform experiment on NVIDIA Tesla V100 which is the state-of-art training accelerator for deep learning models, taking ResNet-50, Inception V3 and DenseNet models as benchmark to test the actual performance and efficiency of V100 with BRC and BRCB methods. Table 7 shows the configuration of NVIDIA Tesla V100.

During the experiment, the convolutional layer and full-connected layer were trained using mixed precision while the other layers like BN were trained using single precision. Table 8 summarizes training cycles, the amount of operations, training speed and

Table 7. NVIDIA TESLA V100 parameters

Accelerator	Parameters
NVIDIA TESLA V100	Frequency: 1455 MHz
	HBM2: 16 GB HBM
	BandWidth: 900 GB/s
	Half-precision performance: 120TFLOPS

actual computational performance, efficiency when training ResNet-50, Inception V3 and DenseNet using BRC and BRCB with V100 GPU.

Table 8. Statistics of ResNet-50, Inception V3, DenseNet training with V100 GPU

Model	OP/PIC	Training speed (PIC/S)			Performance (TFLOPS)			Efficiency (%)		
		CBR	BRC	BRCB	CBR	BRC	BRCB	CBR	BRC	BRCB
ResNet-50	2.3×10^{10}	2074.7	2852.7	3060.2	48	66	**70.8**	40	55	**59**
InceptionV3	3.7×10^{10}	1131.9	1519.9	1714	42	56	**63.6**	35	47	**53**
DenseNet	1.8×10^{10}	2377.7	3277.4	3727.2	44.4	61	**69.6**	37	51	**58**

As shown in Table 8, when training models on V100, the performance of the V100 is not fully exploited. One of the main reasons for this phenomenon is that the bandwidth of V100 cannot satisfy the model training. When using BRC, actual efficiency of V100 is increased by 15%, 12% and 14% for the three CNN models compared with that of CBR, indicating that there are a large number of layers in CNN models with computational density much less than 25FLOP/B. When using BRCB, real performance efficiency increased by 19%, 18%, 21% respectively, indicating that the splitting BN layers into two sub-layers and recombining them into BRCB block further improve the efficiency of accelerator.

5 Related Works

Existing work are divided into two categories, namely promoting data reuse on chip and intermediate result compression, mainly focusing on model inference.

5.1 Promoting on-Chip Data Reuse

Parameter sharing is a typical feature of CNN, is the basis for on-chip data reuse. The accelerating core "systolic array" of TPU uses "Weight Stationary" scheme to increase parameters reuse [12]. TNPU uses "Output Stationary" to increase partial results reuse [13]. Escher selects the optimal batch size to balance the input and output for the limited on-chip buffer, reduces the memory bandwidth requirement [14]. Li et al. designed a automation framework to select different types of data reuse with input dimension changes, but it is only oriented to inference [15]. Due to the limited on-chip buffer and variability of inputs, the reduction of off-chip memory access through promoting on-chip data reuse is limited.

5.2 Intermediate Results Compression

Chen et al. segmented the convolutional neural network into "CONV-BN-RELU", each segment only stores the convolution result to reduce the volume of data stored during training, but there is no consideration about how to reduce the data accessed [16]. Sharan proposed mixed-precision training method, by which way the intermediate data volume stored during training is reduced by nearly 1/2 [17]. Animeh Jain et al. proposed a compression method to reduce the intermediate results stored during training, however, it suffers from a certain precision loss [18].

6 Summary

Large amounts of data need to be accessed in the computation of convolutional neural network, leading to "Memory Wall" bottleneck. And BN layer can effectively speed up the convergence of model training and is widely used in state-of-art convolutional neural networks, but the global data dependence of BN algorithm leads to more serious "Bandwidth Wall" bottleneck. However, there are few researches on memory access optimization for model training.

To alleviate this problem, we propose "BNB-RELU-CONV-BNA" (BRCB) multi-layer fusion computing method to reduce the data accessed during training. By splitting BN into two sub-layers and merging them with adjacent layers respectively, the demand for memory access is further effectively reduced. When using NVIDIA Tesla V100 to train ResNet-50, Inception V3 and DenseNet models, the data volume accessed from off-chip memory decreased by 33%, 22% and 31%, respectively, and the actual performance efficiency of V100 increased by 19%, 18% and 21%. It reduces the main memory access requirement during model training and improves the efficiency of the accelerator.

The optimization method of BRCB multi-layer fusion computing is orthogonal to the previous research, such as promoting on-chip data reuse and intermediate results compression. Therefore, in the future, we will explore combination of multiple optimization methods for model training, to further alleviate "Memory Wall" bottleneck.

References

1. Schmidhuber, J.: Deep learning in neural networks: an overview. Neural Netw. **61**(4), 85–117 (2015)
2. Ioffe, S., Szegedy, C.: Batch normalization: accelerating deep network training by reducing internal covariate shift. In: Proceedings of the 32nd International Conference on Machine Learning, pp. 448–456. IEEE, Lile (2015)
3. He, K., Zhang, X., Ren, S., et al.: Deep residual learning for image recognition. Comput. Vis. Pattern Recognit. **53**(2), 770–778 (2016)
4. Szegedy, C., Vanhoucke, V., Ioffe, S., et al.: Rethinking the inception architecture for computer vision. In: Proceedings of the IEEE Conference on Computer Vision and Pattern Recognition, pp. 2818–2826. IEEE, Las Vegas (2016)
5. Huang, G., Liu, Z., Van Der Maaten, L., et al.: Densely connected convolutional networks. In: Proceedings of the IEEE Conference on Computer Vision and Pattern Recognition, pp. 4700–4708. IEEE, Honolulu (2017)
6. Redmon, J., Farhadi, A.: YOLOv3: an incremental improvement. Comput. Vis. Pattern Recognit. **53**(2), 125–136 (2018)
7. Narang, S., Diamos, G., Elsen, E., et al.: Mixed precision training[OL], 25 December 2018. https://arxiv.org/pdf/1710.03740.pdf
8. NVIDIA TESLA V100 GPU architecture. The world's most advanced data center GPU[EB/OL], 10 October 2018. https://devblogs.nvidia.com/inside-volta/

9. NVIDIA TESLA P100. the most advanced datacenter accelerator ever built featuring Pascal GP100[OL], 7 June 2018. https://www.nvidia.com/o-bject/pascal-architecture-whitepaper.html
10. Williams, S., Waterman, A., Patterson, D.: Roofline: an insightful visual performance model for floating-point programs and multicore architectures. Commun. ACM **52**(4), 65–76 (2009)
11. Krizhevsky, A., Sutskever, I., Hinton, G.E.: Imagenet classification with deep convolutional neural networks. In: Advances in Neural Information Processing Systems, pp. 1097–1105. IEEE, Lake Tahoe (2012)
12. Google Inc.: TPUv2[OL], 7 January 2019. https://www.tomshardware.com/ne-ws/tpu-v2-google-machine-learning-35370.html
13. Li, J., Yan, G., Lu, W., et al.: TNPU: an efficient accelerator architecture for training convolutional neural networks. In: Proceedings of the 24th Asia and South Pacific Design Automation Conference, pp. 450–455. ACM, Tokyo (2019)
14. Chen, Y., Luo, T., Liu, S., et al.: Dadiannao: a machine-learning supercomputer. In: Proceedings of the 47th Annual IEEE/ACM International Symposium on Microarchitecture, pp. 609–622. IEEE, Cambridge (2014)
15. Shen, Y., Ferdman, M., Milder, P.: Escher: a CNN accelerator with flexible buffering to minimize off-chip transfer. In: 2017 IEEE 25th Annual International Symposium on Field-Programmable Custom Computing Machines (FCCM), pp. 93–100. IEEE, Napa (2017)
16. Li, J., Yan, G., Lu, W., et al.: SmartShuttle: optimizing off-chip memory accesses for deep learning accelerators. In: 2018 Design, Automation & Test in Europe Conference & Exhibition (DATE), pp. 343–348. IEEE, Dresden (2018)
17. Chen, T., Xu, B., Zhang, C., et al.: Training deep nets with sublinear memory cost[OL], 5 January 2019. https://arxiv.org/pdf/1604.06174.pdf
18. Jain, A., Phanishayee, A., Mars, J., et al.: Gist: efficient data encoding for deep neural network training. In: 2018 ACM/IEEE 45th Annual International Symposium on Computer Architecture (ISCA), pp. 776–789. IEEE, Los Angeles (2018)

Resultant Gradient Flow Method for Multiple Objective Programming Based on Efficient Computing

Bao Feng[1], Peixin He[1], Yunyao Li[1], Junfeng Wu[1], Peng Li[2], Haichang Yao[2], Yimu Ji[2], Chao Min[3], Jiekui Zhang[4], Youtao Li[4], Peizhuang Wang[5], Yong Shi[5], Jing He[1,3,6(✉)], Hui Zheng[6], and Yang Wang[3]

[1] Nanjing University of Finance and Economics, Nanjing, China
480245@qq.com
[2] Nanjing University of Posts and Telecommunications, Nanjing, China
[3] Southwestern Petroleum University, Chengdu, China
[4] Jingqi Smart Healthcare Pty Ltd., Hefei, China
[5] Research Centre on Fictitious Economy and Data Science, Beijing, China
[6] Swinburne University of Technology, Melbourne, Australia

Abstract. The process of blending gas transmission contains multiple kinds of influence factors that are related with the achievement of maximal overall profit for a refinery gas company. It is, therefore, a multiple objective optimization problems. To maximize overall profit, we proposes a multiple objective resultant gradient descent method (RGDM) to solve fractional, nonlinear, and multiple objective programming problems. Resultant gradient descent requires a proper direction of multiple objective functions. The proper direction in this paper is computed by gradient flow to approach to the global maximum values. Gradient flow is one of the forms of geometric flow, which is widely used in linear programming, least-squares approximation, optimization, and differential equation. It is the first time to be used in mathematical programming. Resultant gradient flow is calculated in linear programming, and the extremum can directly affect the extremum of the our multiple objective functions. Such steps can indirectly simplify the non-linear objective function by separate the single objective functions so that we can use the gradient flow method to solve the multi-objective problem of non-linear programming. It also embodies the stability and efficiency of the proposed gradient flow.

With the case study of a refinery gas company, this paper build a overall profit model. Also, we apply the proposed resultant method to solve this multi-objective problem by a planned strategy of how to supply natural gas to the residential area and schedule the initial coordination. Moreover, its solutions are displayed and compared with a genetic algorithm-based solver in our experimental study.

Keywords: Resultant gradient flow · Multiple objective programming · Maximum profit

H. Shen and Y. Sang (Eds.): PAAP 2019, CCIS 1163, pp. 492–506, 2020.
https://doi.org/10.1007/978-981-15-2767-8_43

1 Introduction

In the general pursuit of the market economy, profit is regarded as the primary goal of economic behaviors for enterprises. Ideally, an enterprise would like to achieve the goal of "exchanging the minimum investment for the maximum profit". For example, if an enterprise wants to make the maximal profit of a project, then this enterprise should reduce the cost of the project and increase the as more as possible. When the cost can not be reduced any more, the cost can be regarded as the lowest cost. When the benefits can not be increased anymore, the benefits can be regarded as the highest benefits. At this time, the profit is generally regarded as the maximal profit. In a refining natural gas company, one of the essential profit issues includes: (1) choosing the lowest cost way from different strategies of blending crude oil in the range of general standard before the gas transmission procedure, (2) balancing the maximum gas volume and the cost of pipelines of the gas transmission and, (3) selling strategy after the gas transmission procedure. Then, It can be represented as a multi-objective optimization problem for maximum profit in the problem of blending gas transmission.

The multi-objective optimization problem is a contradiction between each target, and improved sub-targets may cause one or the other performance of several sub-targets [1]. Making more sub-targets at the same time to achieve the optimal value is unlikely, so we can coordinate and compromise among them, to make each goal to optimize as much as possible. There is no unique global optimal solution for the multi-objective optimization problem, and too many non-inferior solutions cannot be directly applied.

Multiple objective programming could be used to find an approximated solution for fractional programming by maximizing numerator and minimizing denominator simultaneously in the range of a positive feasible solution. For generalized fractional programming, Charnes proposed the application and algorithm of form P: $\bar{\theta} = inf \max_{x \in S \, i \leq P} \left\{ \frac{f_i(x)}{g_i(x)} \right\}$ in [1], but the convergence is not proved yet. Moreover, the problem is limited to the case that f_i and g_i are only linear, and S are affine sets. In [2], Schaibe gave some algorithms and applications and C'rouziex [3] proposed the same algorithms for solving general nonlinearity P and proved the global convergence. Besides, the authors of [4] and [5] have claimed that the generalized fractional programming is solved by using the programming with $P + 1$ parameter. However, up to now, there is no global convergence and strongly-polynomial time algorithm for solving P. For minimax fractional programming, many scholars have studied the optimality and duality of minimax fractional programming according to the different convexity and differentiability of functions. Lai and Huang [6] discussed minimax fractional programming based on generalized (p, θ) nonconvex n-set functions. Hanson and Pini [7] studied multi-objective programming based on generalized V-type-I functions. According to this idea, the concept of generalized (p, p^*, θ) V-type-I function is proposed in [8]. And the optimality conditions of minimax fractional programming under this function are given, thus enriching the optimality theory of minimax programming.

Utilizing set functions, we can extend the minimax fractional programming of n-set functions. The authors [8] have discussed this. Preda [9] have studied the important theory of multi-objective programming under generalized V uniform invariant convexity. Inspired by [6, 9], paper [10] has proposed type-I (p, p^*, θ) nonconvex functions, and under such convexity. Also, sufficient optimality conditions for Minimax programming are given. Besides, the generalized convex order minimax fractional programming problem is discussed. Yada, Mukherjee [11], Handra and Kumar [12] studied the minimax fractional programming problem when $(p1)$ differentiable, i.e., $A = D = 0$. Mond studied the problem of $(p1)$ non-differentiable numerical programming when Y is a unit set. Zalmai [13] studies the problem of generalized minimax programming and obtains necessary and sufficient optimal conditions. More than this, Zalmai used Gordan theorem to obtain the first and second-order optimal necessary conditions for a class of continuous minimax programming problems in Banach spaces and produced Wolfe type duality.

Multi-objective programming problems have different ways of solutions in different periods. Early nonlinear constrained optimization problems were solved by transforming them into unconstrained ones by the penalty function method [14]. The developed successive quadratic programming (SQP), successive multi-objective programming, and generalized reduced gradient method (GRG) have broken away from the dependence on unconstrained optimization methods. Above are more effective methods for solving non-linear constrained optimization problems. Later, the hybrid algorithm of chaotic search and conjugate gradient method proposed in [15], and the Lagrange method is proposed in [16]. While the particle swarm optimization algorithm [17] is displayed for solving mixed-integer nonlinear programming problems and the genetic algorithm, which is often used to improve the solver in many applications.

The author of paper [18] solves the problem of crude oil blending and maximum profit, mainly using the genetic algorithm and building a nonlinear model. However, for multi-objective planning oil, it has some limitations. So for the same original blending and maximum profit problem, we use the proposed resultant gradient flow method for multiple objective programming based on parallel computing to solve them. The synthetic gradient flow method can not only solve the nonlinear programming problem but also solve the multi-objective programming problem by parallel computing. We will explain it further in the following sections.

However, existing algorithms have their drawbacks, such as they are not accurate, efficient. We, therefore, propose a resultant gradient method to optimize multiple objectives accurately and efficiently. The contributions of this paper conclude (1) Our work has improved the efficiency and efficiency (2) We propose a flow-based sliding gradient algorithm to solve the multi-objective optimization problem accurately. It is a new way. (3) It jumps out of the local solution to finding the global optimal solution.

The remainder of this paper is organized as follows. In Sect. 2, we explain our resultant gradient flow-based method to solve the problem of multiple objectives optimization. It is more efficient and accurate. In Sect. 3, we represent the maximum profit problem of blending gas transmission and build a multi-objective optimization model to solve it. In Sect. 4, we compare the experimental results with each other. Finally, we conclude our work in Sect. 5.

2 Resultant Gradient Flow Method

In this section, we propose our resultant method to solve the multi-objective optimization problem. We first introduce the flow-based method to prove its convergence and sustainability by referring to the concept of "flow". Secondly, the result gradient descent method is based on the flow direction of water droplets of gravity is represented, which leads to the iterative direction of the solution. Thirdly, we explain how to find effective results for multi-objective problems.

2.1 Flow-Based Method

Many mathematical problems have the problem of convergence, and non-linear programming problems are no exception. To achieve this problem, an iterative process is needed, such as the lambda required in the previous section. From the engineering point of view, we can regard the iteration process as a flow. We usually connect the problems through ordinary differential equations to form a flow. So we have this definition [19–25]: Given a smooth function $\mathcal{F}$, differential equation: $\frac{dx}{dt} = -\nabla f(x)$ Its flow is called the gradient flow of $f(x)$. Among $\mathcal{F}$: $\mathbb{R}^n \rightarrow \mathcal{R}$, we can find the minimum value of $f(x)$. According to the definition and those mentioned above, the reason why the gradient flow method can become a "flow" is that it is continuously differentiable, whether it is an objective function or a constraint condition. This is the first step, and the second step is iteration. We have already explained that iteration is necessary to achieve this process in practice. The main idea of iteration is to repeatedly explore the heuristic points (i.e. iterate the heuristic points under constraints to achieve the extreme requirements of the objective function). Therefore, it can also prove that the parallel gradient flow method proposed by us has convergence and continuity.

2.2 Resultant Gradient Descent Method for Multiple Objective Programming

Resultant gradient descent is a first-order iterative optimization algorithm for finding the minimum of two functions. In coordinates, a vector field on a feasible solution domain in n-dimensional Euclidean space can be represented as a vector-valued function that associates an n-tuple of real numbers to each point of the feasible solution domain. Given a feasible solution for mathematical programming as a subset S in R^n, a feasible solution vector field is represented by a vector-valued function $V : S \rightarrow R^n$ in standard Cartesian coordinates $(x_1, \ldots, x_n)$. If each component of V is continuous, then V is a continuous vector field. To find a local minimum of two objective functions using gradient descent, one takes steps proportional to the negative of the gradient (or approximate gradient) of the function 1 at the current point, and the function 2 at the current point as well. Then the parallelogram law applies to calculate the joint direction of two gradients. If we have more than two functions, say multiple objective programming, we keep going with more functions by pairwise. Vector fields can be constructed out of scalar fields using the gradient operator (represented by the delta: ∇ [26]). A vector field V defined on an open set S is called a gradient filed if there exists a real-valued function (a scalar field) f on s such that $V = \nabla f = \left(\frac{\partial f}{\partial x_1}, \frac{\partial f}{\partial x_2}, \frac{\partial f}{\partial x_3}, \ldots, \frac{\partial f}{\partial x_n}\right)$. In this paper, a vector field is an assignment of a vector to each point in a subset of feasible solution space. A vector field of feasible solution for mathematical programming in the plane (for instance), can be visualized as a collection of arrows with a given magnitude and direction, each attached to a point in the feasible solution plane. These vector fields are to model, the speed and

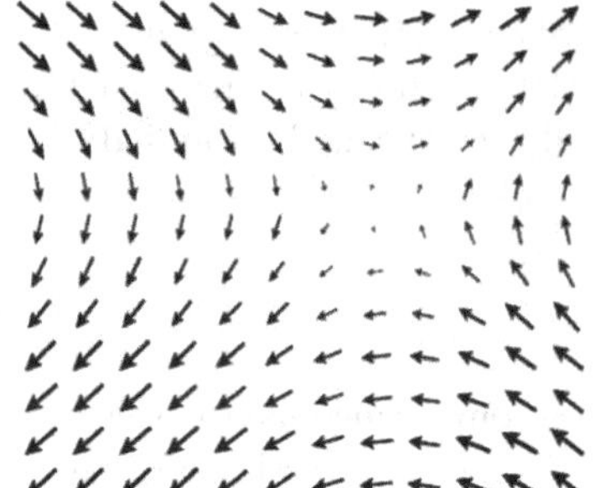

Fig. 1. Moving fluid throughout the space in RGFM [26].

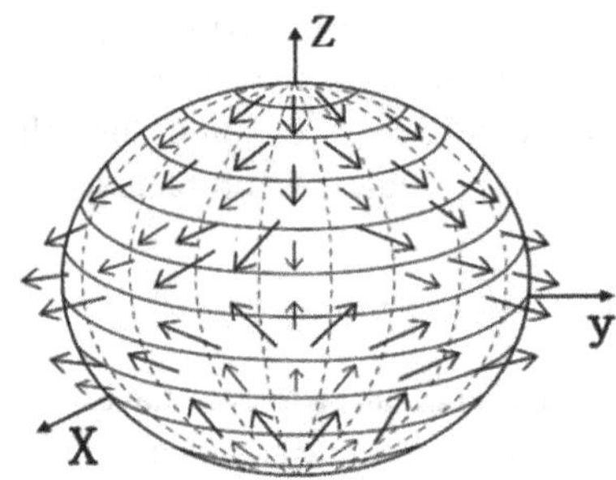

Fig. 2. A vector field on the sphere [26].

direction of a moving fluid throughout the feasible solution space, as it changes from one possible solution point to another possible solution point. It was called a resultant gradient flow method (RGFM) for mathematical programming (Fig. 1).

The associated flow is called the gradient flow and is used in the method of gradient descent [26].

A representation of a vector field depends on the coordinate system, and there is a well-defined transformation law in passing from one coordinate system to the other. Vector fields are often discussed on open subsets of Euclidean space, but also hold on other subsets such as surfaces, where they associate an arrow tangent to the surface at each point shown in Fig. 2.

2.3 Multiple Objective Programming

Resultant Gradient descent is based on if the multi-objective function $F_N(x)$ is defined and differentiable in a neighborhood of a point a, then $F_1(x)$ decreases fastest if one goes from a in the direction of the negative gradient of F_1 at a, $-\nabla F_1(a)$. And then $F_2(x)$ decreases fastest if one goes from a in the direction of the negative gradient of F_2 at a, $-\nabla F_2(a)$ [27]. Assume that $-\nabla F_1(a)$ and $-\nabla F_2(a)$ are not necessarily equal vectors, but that they may have different directions. If F has m dimensions, the sum of $-\nabla F_1(a)$ and $-\nabla F_2(a)$ is $(-\nabla F_1(a)) + (-\nabla F_2(a)) = ((-\nabla F_{11}) + (-\nabla F_{21}))e_1 + ((-\nabla F_{12}) + (-\nabla F_{22}))e_2 + \ldots + ((-\nabla F_{1m}) + (-\nabla F_{2m}))e_m$. The addition may be represented graphically by placing the tail of the arrow $-\nabla F_2(a)$ at the head of the arrow of $-\nabla F_1(a)$. And then drawing an arrow from the tail of $-\nabla F_1(a)$ to the head of $-\nabla F_2(a)$. This addition method for resultant gradient flow is called the parallelogram rule. This is because $-\nabla F_1(a)$ and $-\nabla F_2(a)$ form the sides of a parallelogram, and $(-\nabla F_1(a)) + (-\nabla F_2(a))$ is one of the diagonals. $(-\nabla F_1(a)) + (-\nabla F_2(a))$ are bound vectors that have the same base point a. This point will also be the base point of $(-\nabla F_1(a)) + (-\nabla F_2(a))$. The new arrow drawn represents the vector $(-\nabla F_1(a)) + (-\nabla F_2(a))$, as illustrated below (Figs. 3 and 4):

We use this pairwise way to figure out the resultant gradient $-\nabla F(a)$ as $(-\nabla F_1(a)) + (-\nabla F_2(a)) + \ldots + (-\nabla F_N(a))$. It follows that, if

$$a_{n+1} = a_n - \beta \nabla F(a_n)$$

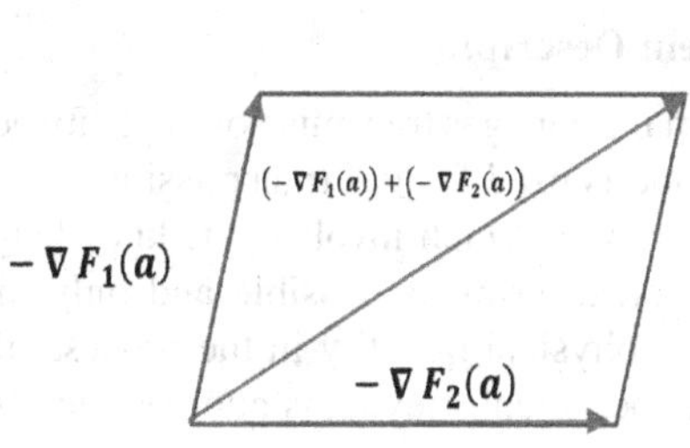

Fig. 3. Demonstration of resultant gradient flow.

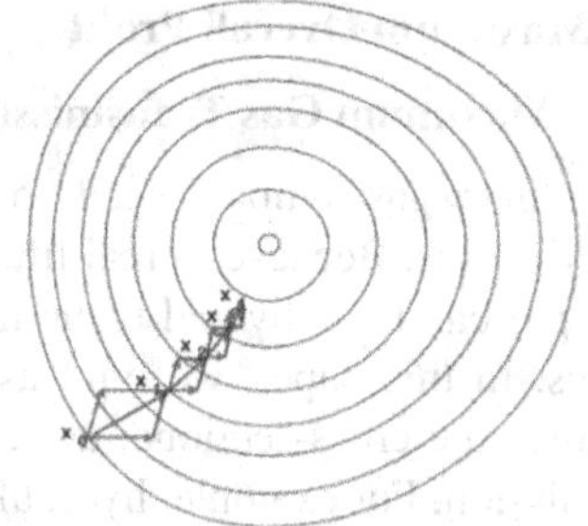

Fig. 4. Illustration of Resultant gradient descent on a series of level sets [26]. (Color figure online)

For β ∈ $\mathbb{R}_+$ small enough, then $F(a_n) \geq F(a_{n+1})$. $\beta\nabla F(a_n)$ is subtracted from a because the objective function was moved against the gradient, and toward the minimum [28]. The solution starts with an initial value x_0 for a local minimum of F, and considers the sequence $x_0, x_1, x_2, \ldots$ such that

$$\boldsymbol{x_{n+1} = x_n - \beta_n \nabla F(x_n), n \geq 0.}$$

The sequence is monotonic as follows: $F(x_0) \geq F(x_1) \geq F(x_2) \geq \ldots$. It is supposed that the sequence (x_n) converges to the desired local minimum. The value of the step size β is allowed to change at every iteration. If F convex and ∇F Lipschitz, and particular choices of β. Convergence to a local minimum can be possible. When the function F is convex, all local minima are also global minima, so in this case, resultant gradient descent can converge to the global solution. This process is illustrated in the following figure. Here F is supposed to be defined on the plane and that its graph has a bowl shape. The blue curves are the contour lines, that is, the regions on which the value of F is constant. A red arrow originating at a point shows the direction of the resultant negative gradient at that point. The resultant descent will lead us to the bottom of the bowl, that is, to the point where the value of the function F is minimal.

3 A Case Study and Its Profit Modeling

In this section, we apply the proposed multi-objective based Resultant Gradient flow method on a case study. It can maximise the overall profit with multiple aspects.

For a refining natural gas company, there are three main objectives to maximize the profit of blending gas transmission. The first objective is to find out the way to minimize the prime cost of different kinds of oil from the possible assembles of blending crude oil in the range of general standards. The second objective is to balance the maximum gas volume and the lowest cost of pipelines of the oil transmission. The third objective is to decide the price of selling. So in this section, we will describe these three objectives before we build the maximum profit of gas transmission model. And then, we find out a solution to maximize the overall profit and minimize the cost to schedule different oil blending assembles.

3.1 Maximum Overall Profit

3.1.1 Maximum Gas Transmission Problem Description

The Refinery gas company needs to study the maximum gas transmission capacity before delivering gas. Because in real life, the pipeline is used for gas transmission, and how much gas can be delivered is the first consideration, which involves the knowledge of physics. In this paper, we omit as many physical terms as possible and only model and solve the cross-sectional area, length, and physical quantity in the process of gas transmission. For example, hydraulic friction coefficient, Reynolds number, etc.. In the modeling chapter, we will elaborate.

3.1.2 Oil Blending Problem Description

Refinery gas company needs to mix the appropriate different kinds of crude oil with additives before gas transmission. A proper blending means it satisfies the public standard and has the lowest cost. In this case, to find a proper blending, the following indicators are considered: cetane number, sulfur content, viscosity, flash point, and solidification point. Petroleum refining and gas companies mainly focus on gasoline refining. Taking the octane number model as an example, Table 1 shows the indicators of the additives to be mixed. Table 2 shows the indicators of the oil which meets the requirements.

Table 1. Consolidated component data.

Component	Reforming oil	Straight-run oil	Butane	Catalytic oil	Alkylated oil
RON	94.1	70.7	93.8	92.9	95
MON	80.5	68.7	90	80.8	91.7
RVP (psi)	3.8	12	138	5.3	6.6
Paraffin wax (%)	1	1.8	0	48.8	0
Aromatic hydrocarbons (%)	58	2.7	0	22.8	0
Output (ton/day)	6500	800	5500	12000	3000
Cost (Dollar/barrel)	34.0	26.0	10.3	31.3	37.0

How to match the components of gasoline to form the best refining model is a crucial step for gas companies to maximize profits. If the refining components are well-matched, we can get the objective function of the cost of refining gasoline, so that the objective function of profit can be obtained by subtracting the cost from the total sale price.

The relationship between the octane number of producing oil and the octane number of component oil is not simple superposition, but a rather complicated non-linear relationship. To estimate the octane number of blended products, we use the double correlation method. This method can accurately estimate the research octane number and motor octane number of blended products.

$$RON = \bar{r} + a_1(\overline{rs} - \bar{r}\bar{s}) + a_2\left(\overline{O^2} - \bar{O}^2\right) + a_3\left(\overline{A^2} - \bar{A}^2\right) \tag{1}$$

Table 2. Consolidation of product data.

	Price (Dollar/barrel)	Upper limit	Lower limit	Min RON	Min MON	Max RVP
Ordinary gasoline	33.0	8000	7000	88.5	77	10.8
Advanced gasoline	37.0	10000	10000	91.5	80	10.8

$$MON = \bar{m} + b_1(\overline{ms} - \bar{m}\bar{s}) + b_2\left(\overline{O^2} - \bar{O}^2\right) + b_3\left(\frac{\overline{A^2} - \bar{A}^2}{100}\right)^2 \quad (2)$$

There are some notations for formula (1) and (2). $\bar{r}$ is the sum of RON volume fraction of component oil. $\bar{s}$ is the sum of the sensitivity volume fraction of component oil. $\bar{O}$ is the sum of the wax volume fraction of component oil. $\bar{A}$ is the sum of the volume fraction of component oil. $\bar{m}$ is the sum of the volume fraction of component oil. Among Constants, $a_1 = 0.03224$; $a_2 = 0.00101$; $a_3 = 0$; $b_1 = 0.0445$; $b_2 = 0.00081$; $b_3 = -0.0645$.

3.1.3 Gas Sales Problem Description

After blending crude oil, refinery gas company need deliver gas to people for use. Assuming there are four residential districts *A1*, *B1*, *C1*, *D1*. Refinery gas company has three gas supply stations *A*, *B* and *C*. To ensure that each district can be dispatched enough essential daily gas consumption $(10^4\ \mathrm{m}^3)$, the three gas supply stations should be adjusted according to different consumption of gas. Then the sufficient supply of natural gas can be guaranteed every day. Assuming that the gas supply station *A* sells to the district *A1* is called a_{11}, and the gas supply to the district *B1* is called a_{12}, and so on. Table 3 can be obtained. The sales and costs prices charged by the three gas supply stations *A*, *B*, and *C* to the district are as shown in Table 4. The demand of four districts could increase, so the gas transmission (cost) from three gas supply stations to each district will correspondingly increase, as shown in Table 5.

Table 3. Sales volume (demand) of gas supplied from gas supply station to each district.

Gas capacity (m^3)	*A1*	*B1*	*C1*	*D1*
A	a_{11}	a_{12}	a_{13}	a_{14}
B	a_{21}	a_{22}	a_{23}	a_{24}
C	a_{31}	a_{32}	a_{33}	a_{34}

Table 4. Sales and costs prices of three gas supply points.

Sales	*A1*	*B1*	*C1*	*D1*	Costs
A	p_{11}	p_{12}	p_{13}	p_{14}	p_{15}
B	p_{21}	p_{22}	p_{23}	p_{24}	p_{25}
C	p_{31}	p_{32}	p_{33}	p_{34}	p_{35}

Table 5. Gas transfer from gas supply points to residential areas.

Distance	*A1*	*B1*	*C1*	*D1*
A	x_{11}	x_{12}	x_{13}	x_{14}
B	x_{21}	x_{22}	x_{23}	x_{24}
C	x_{31}	x_{32}	x_{33}	x_{34}

3.2 Modeling of Maximization Overall Profit

3.2.1 Maximum Gas Transmission Model

For a refining natural gas company, obtaining the maximal profit means finding the maximal gas transmission. Fractional programming is applied to solve this problem. It generally refers to the ratio of two non-linear functions. It is also the concept of efficiency in a certain system. Let $\mathcal{F},\ g,\ h_j,\ j = 1, \ldots$, m is a set of defined real-valued functions $S_0 \subset \mathbb{R}^n,\ S = \{x \subset S_0 : h_j(x) \leq 0,\ j = 1, \ldots m\}$. The Nonlinear Programming: $\max_{x \subset S} \frac{\mathcal{F}(x)}{g(x)}$, where $g(x) > 0$ on S is called fractional programming. Fractional programming is a form of solving fractions consisting of two non-linear functions.

For a hydraulic calculation of gas pipeline in an actual situation. When the gas supply station delivers natural gas to residents, it is necessary to consider to maximize the gas transmission capacity as follows:

$$\max q_v = 1051[\frac{(P_1^2 - P_2^2)d^5}{\lambda Z \Delta T L}]^{0.5}, \tag{3}$$

where $P_1(9 < P_1 < 12)$ is the starting pressure of the gas pipeline; $P_2(6 < P_2 < 8)$ is the end pressure of the gas pipeline; d is the inner diameter of the gas pipeline; $\lambda(0 \leq \lambda \leq 1)$ is the hydraulic friction coefficient; Z is the average compression factor of the natural gas transported; Δ is the relative density of the natural gas transported; T is the average temperature of the gas in the gas pipeline; L is the length of gas pipeline. In our experiments, we implemented the fractional programming in a parallel environment with non-linear programming in Hadoop ecology.

From the formula (3), we can see that there are three variables, P_1, P_2 and λ (the constraints in parentheses). P_1 and P_2 can be regarded as two unknowns in $\mathcal{F}(x, y)$ function. They are mutually restricted, so they are not able to apply for fractional programming directly. λ can be regarded as the only unknown in function $g(x)$, so we can take $g(x)$ as the goal of fractional programming. For λ $(0 \le \lambda \le 1)$, it is a hydraulic friction coefficient [29]. Then, we have a real-time model of λ as follows:

$$\frac{1}{\sqrt{\lambda}} = -2.01lg\left(\frac{K}{3.71d} + \frac{2.51}{Re\sqrt{\lambda}}\right), \tag{4}$$

where K is the absolute roughness of the inner wall of the steel pipe; d is the inner diameter of the gas pipeline; *Re* is the Reynolds number. The general expression of the hydraulic friction coefficient in physics is (4), but we have not converted it. The main factor affecting lambda is *Re*. Then, we have a real-time model of *Re* as follows:

$$Re = 1.536\frac{Q\Delta *}{D\mu}, \tag{5}$$

where Q is the designed transportation capacity; Δ_* is the relative density of natural gas transported; D is the inner diameter of the gas pipeline, and μ is the dynamic viscosity of natural gas. The special feature of *Re*'s formula is that Q and μ have the initial values, so the *Re* obtained is also the initial value for hydraulic friction coefficient λ. The initial value of λ is selected as 0.01. If the error of λ is less than 10^{-5} [30], then we can stop our iteration and obtain the final acceptable value of λ. After calculating the value of λ, we go back to formula (3) and substitute λ for other constant values. In this situation, we can have an expression of the maximum gas flow as follows:

$$\max q_v(P_1, P_2) = 1431.752\left(P_1^2 - P_2^2\right)^{0.5} \tag{6}$$

3.2.2 Oil Blending Model

To choose a good blending strategy, it must save the total cost of different oil. In this way, A high price of the end product of gas and a low price of crude oil could benefit our overall profit. Otherwise, A low price of the end product of gas and a high price of crude oil could reduce our overall profit. Suppose we already have the gas sales price and the oil cost price so that we can subtract the total oil cost from the total sales price directly. Then we can get the objective function of different gas sales. Sales volume is the amount of natural gas required by a residential area, which is a demanded requirement [32]. The maximum amount of gas transported can be regarded as the maximum supply. That is the maximum amount of natural gas transported by a gas supply station. In this way, we can have a clear objective and how to treat these variables. From this point of view, we can conclude that the objective function of sales is as follows:

$$\max w\left(a_{ij}, x_{ij}\right) = \sum_{i=1}^{3}\sum_{j=1}^{4} p_{ij}a_{ij} - \sum_{i=1}^{3}\sum_{j=1}^{4} p_{i5}x_{ij} \tag{7}$$

This formula is a simple general expression, where we can see that there are two different variables: a_{ij}, x_{ij}. They contain a total of 24 variables as $a_{11} \ldots a_{34}$, $x_{11} \ldots x_{34}$. The sum of the former is the total gas sale price, and the sum of the latter is the total oil cost price. The most important constraints are the relationship between gas flow, demand, and maximum gas flow. Gas transmission must be larger than demand, and gas transmission must not exceed the maximum gas transmission. The main problem is the maximum gas flow ($k1$, $k2$, $k3$). This is easy to be overlooked because in general, the maximum gas flow is not considered, but in practice, it needs to be carefully put into consideration, which is an essential connection between mathematics and physics. We already have (6) of maximum gas flow, so that we can set up objective functions together, and then construct constraints according to the knowledge of physics as follows:

$$\begin{cases} \max\ q_v(\mathrm{P}_1, P_2) = 1431.752\left(P_1^2 - P_2^2\right)^{0.5} \\ \max\ w\left(a_{ij}, x_{ij}\right) = \sum_{i=1}^{3}\sum_{j=1}^{4} p_{i1}a_{ij} - \sum_{i=1}^{3}\sum_{j=1}^{4} p_{i2}x_{ij} \end{cases} \tag{8}$$

$$\begin{aligned} \text{s.t}\quad & 9 < P_1 < 12 \\ & 6 < P_2 < 8 \\ & a_{11} + a_{12} + a_{13} + a_{14} \le x_{11} + x_{12} + x_{13} + x_{14} \le q_v \\ & a_{21} + a_{22} + a_{23} + a_{24} \le x_{21} + x_{22} + x_{23} + x_{24} \le q_v \\ & a_{31} + a_{32} + a_{33} + a_{34} \le x_{31} + x_{32} + x_{33} + x_{34} \le q_v \\ & w > 0,\ \Delta h \le 200,\ a_{ij} > 0,\ x_{ij} > 0 \end{aligned}$$

where, a_{ij} is demand; x_{ij} is gas supply; p_{11}, p_{21}, p_{31} is three sales prices; p_{12}, p_{22}, p_{32} is three cost prices. In the next section we will present simulation values and solutions.

3.2.3 Gas Sales Model

According to the octane number model mentioned above, we can build similar models of other components. Thus, we apply the formula (7) to establish the final maximum profit objective function:

$$\max Profit = w\left(a_{ij}, x_{ij}\right) - \sum_{j=1}^{m} C_j Y_j, \tag{9}$$

where $w\left(a_{ij}, x_{ij}\right)$ is the total sales price; C_j is the cost price of component oil j; Y_j is the consumption of component oil j; M represents the types of gasoline products and component gasoline, respectively.

To solve this model, we should consider the total output value of gasoline products and the cost of component oil, rather than the relatively fixed cost of blending equipment and human resources, and the energy loss of oil products in the blending pipeline. In this way, we combine the objective function (8) and the constraint function (9) of harmonic scheduling to the following values:

$$\begin{cases} \max\ q_v(P_1, P_2) = 1431.752\left(P_1^2 - P_2^2\right)^{0.5} \\ \max\ Profit = \sum_{i=1}^{3}\sum_{j=1}^{4} p_{i1}a_{ij} - \sum_{i=1}^{3}\sum_{j=1}^{4} p_{i5}x_{ij} - \sum_{j=1}^{m} C_j X_j \end{cases} \tag{10}$$

$$
\begin{aligned}
s.t \quad & 9 < P_1 < 12 \\
& 6 < P_2 < 8 \\
& a_{11} + a_{12} + a_{13} + a_{14} \le x_{11} + x_{12} + x_{13} + x_{14} \le q_v \\
& a_{21} + a_{22} + a_{23} + a_{24} \le x_{21} + x_{22} + x_{23} + x_{24} \le q_v \\
& a_{31} + a_{32} + a_{33} + a_{34} \le x_{31} + x_{32} + x_{33} + x_{34} \le q_v \\
& Y_j \le q_v \, j = 1 \ldots m \\
& w > 0, \, \Delta h \le 200, \, a_{ij} > 0, \, x_{ij} > 0 \\
& 88.5 < RON_{nor} < 89 \\
& 91.5 < RON_{high} < 93 \\
& 82.7 < (RON_{nor} + MON_{nor})/2 < 83.7 \\
& 85.7 < \left(RON_{high} + MON_{high}\right)/2 < 86.7 \\
& (RVP)_{nor} < 10.8 \\
& (RVP)_{high} < 10.8
\end{aligned}
$$

Among them, P_1 is the starting pressure of gas pipeline; P_2 is the end pressure of gas pipeline; q_v is the maximum gas transmission capacity; a_{ij} is the demand; x_{ij} is the gas supply; p_{11}, p_{21}, p_{31} is the three different kinds of selling prices (gas supply stations *A*, *B* and *C*); p_{12}, p_{22}, p_{32} is the three different kinds of cost prices; C_j is the cost price of component oil *j*; Y_j is the consumption of component oil *j*, *N* and m are the representatives respectively. The types of gasoline and component gasoline [30–34]; RON_{nor} is the octane number constraint of ordinary gasoline; RON_{high} is the octane number constraint of high-quality gasoline; $(RON_{nor} + MON_{nor})/2$ is the anti-riot index of ordinary gasoline; $\left(RON_{high} + MON_{high}\right)/2$ is the anti-riot index of high-quality gasoline; $(RVP)_{nor} < 10.8$ is reed vapor pressure constraints for ordinary gasoline and $(RVP)_{high} < 10.8$ is for high-quality gasoline.

4 Experimental Study

We build up two isolated clusters to implement our algorithms based on Hadoop ecology at Nanjing University of Posts and Communications and TH-2 respectively, shown in Fig. 5. After the model is established, and we need some specific numerical values to solve the real-time. In this section, we simplify the solution by substituting the constant (i.e., sales price and cost price) into the function. The computation environment is a PC with CPU as Intel(R) Core(TM) i7-6700 CPU @ 3.40 GHz, RAM 8.00 GB, 64 bits operating system (Win10) and Matlab (R2014b).

The simulation values are shown in Table 6 and sales objective function is simplified as follows:

$$
\begin{aligned}
w\left(a_{ij}, x_{ij}\right) = {} & (2.8 * a_{11} + 3.1 * a_{12} + 3 * a_{13} + 3.2 * a_{14}) + (3 * a_{21} + 3 * a_{22} + 2.9 * a_{23} + 3 * a_{24}) + 0.4 \\
& * (2.9 * a_{31} + 3.1 * a_{32} + 2.8 * a_{33} + 3.1 * a_{34}) - 0.3 * (x_{11} + x_{12} + x_{13} + x_{14}) - 0.1 \\
& * (x_{21} + x_{22} + x_{23} + x_{24}) - 0.2 * (x_{31} + x_{32} + x_{33} + x_{34})
\end{aligned}
$$

With the three builded models of maximum gas transmission, oil blending and gas sales, we can solve the multi-objective function. For our gradient flow method, we set

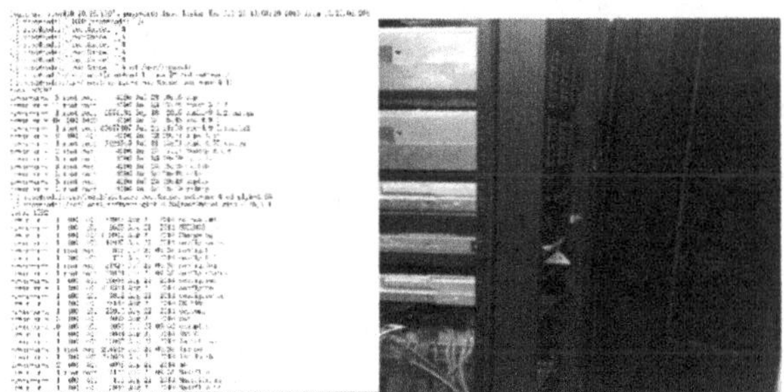

Fig. 5. Parallel computing based on Hadoop

Table 6. Sales and cost prices of three gas supply points.

Sales	*A1*	*B1*	*C1*	*D1*	Costs
A	2.8	3.1	3	3.2	0.3
B	3	3	2.9	3	0.1
C	2.9	3.1	2.8	3.1	0.2

a detection point, i.e., the initial value, and iteratively detect. The constraints can be satisfied until the maximum of the objective function is satisfied. According to formula (7) and maximum profit objective function formula [35], we can solve the differential equation of two variables according to the definition of $q_v(P_1, P_2)$. Also a detection point is obtained from the constraint condition $9 < P_1 < 12, 6 < P_2 < 8$. We assume the initial value P_0 is (9, 6). Then we obtain the maximum value by iterations. At the next point of iteration, we use the adjustment programming algorithm of factor space. The main formulas [36] are: $tj := [cj - (tj, Ps)]/(tj, d)$; $j^* = Argminj\{tj|TJ > 0\}$; $Ps + 1 := Ps + TJ^*D$. At the end of iterations, we have $P_1 = 9.118$, $P_2 = 7.994$, $q_v = 6263.329$.

In the case of q_v, we also use gradient flow method to solve the profit function. The result $a_{11} \ldots a_{34} = \{0.4, 0.1, 0.2, 0, 0, 0, 0.1, 0, 0.2, 0, 0.3, 0\}$; $x_{11} \ldots x_{34} = \{0.8, 1, 1.8, 0, 0, 0, 1.3, 0, 1.5, 0, 1.5, 0\}$; $\mathrm{Y}_1 \ldots \mathrm{Y}_9 = \{2108.078, 2409.711, 91.003, 3309.029, 2.178, 7632.406, 965.608, 144.241, 1150.127, 106.850\}$ The final profit was 67097.38. The blending capacity of ordinary gasoline is 7919.537, and that of high-quality gasoline is 10001.038. We compare the results from paper [18] with our own. The result of the genetic algorithm (crossover probability is 0. 8, mutation probability is 0. 015) is shown as follows:

From Table 7, we can template the advantages of such methods.

Table 7. Profit comparison between the two methods

Method	Profit	Ordinary gasoline	High-quality gasoline
Result of genetic algorithm	66288.7	7920.107	10000.394
Result of resultant gradient flow method	67097.38	7919.537	10010.038

5 Conclusion

A gradient flow method for solving fractional and non-linear programming problems is proposed. It can approach to global optimal solution with a gradient flow-based iteration direction. This paper not only solves the problem of multi-objective optimization but also adjusts the factor space of crude oil blending scheduling. Also, this paper solves the problem of maximizing gas transmission and its overall profit through refinery adjustment and scheduling. Moreover, the results of the overall profit are compared in the experimental study and obviously a higher profit value is obtained by our method. That is to say, the performance of our method outperforms that of the corresponding method.

References

1. Charnes, A., Cooper, W.W.: Goal programming and multi-objective optimization, part I. Eur. J. Oper. Res. **1**, 39–54 (1977)
2. Schaible, S.: Fractional programming. Eur. J. Oper. Res. **12**, 325–338 (1983)
3. Grouzeix, J., Ferland, J.A., Schaible, S.: An algorithm for generalized fractional programs. J. Optim. Theory Appl. **47**, 35–49 (1985)
4. Xu, Z.: Solution of a fractional programming problem. J. Shanghai Univ. Technol. **1**, 66–72 (1983)
5. Xu, Z.: Solving Generalized Fractional Programming by Programming with P+1 Parameters. Zhejiang Normal University (1986)
6. Lai, H.C., Huang, T.Y.: Minimax fractional programming for n-set functions and mixed-type duality under generalized convexity. J. Optim. Theory Appl. **139**, 295–313 (2008)
7. Hanson, M.: Multi-objective programming under generalized type. J. Math. Anal. Appl. **261**, 562–577 (2001)
8. Wang, W.: Sufficient optimality conditions for minimax fractional programming of set functions. Xi'an Univ. Electron. Sci. Technol. **27**, 5 (2010)
9. Preda, V., Stancu-Minasian, I., Beldiman, M.: Generalized V-Type-I for multi-objective programming with N-set functions. J. Glob. Optim. **44**, 131–148 (2009)
10. Wang, W.: Sufficient optimality conditions for minimax fractional programming of n-set functions. Xi'an Univ. Electron. Sci. Technol. **33**, 2 (2011)
11. Yadav, S.R., Mukherjee, R.N.: Duality for fractional minimax programming problem. J. Aust. Math. Soc. (Ser. B) **31**, 484–492 (1990)
12. Chandra, S., Kumar, V.: Duality in fractional minimax programming. J. Aust. Math. Soc. (Ser. A) **58**, 376–386 (1995)
13. Zalmai, G.J.: Optimality criteria and duality for a class of minimax programming problems with generalized conditions. Utilitas Mathematica **32**, 35–37 (1987)
14. Luo, C.: Solving Nonlinear Constrained Optimization Problem by Chaotic Search, p. 8. Shanghai Jiaotong University (2000)

15. Qian, F.: A hybrid algorithms for global optimum search by chaos. **27**(3), 232–235 (1998)
16. Hestenes, M.R.: Multiplier and gradient method. J. Optim. Theory **4**, 303–320 (1969)
17. Liu, D.: Solving Mixed Integer Nonlinear Programming Problem by Improved Particle Swarm Optimization. Wuhan University of Science and Technology, p. 6 (2005)
18. Chi, T.: Solving of Gasoline Blending Nonlinear Model and Oil Online Blending. Dalian University of Technology, p. 12 (2007)
19. Wang, P.Z., He, J., et al.: Linear adjusting programming in factor space. Submitted to CCPE
20. Singh, A., Forbes, J.F., Vermeer, P.J., Woo, S.S.: Model-based real-time optimization of automotive gasoline blending operations. J. Process Control **10**(10), 43–58 (2000)
21. Wang, P.Z., Sugeno, M.: Factorial field and the background structure of fuzzy sets. Fuzzy Math. **02**, 45–54 (1982)
22. Dantzig, G.B.: Linear programming. Oper. Res. **50**(1), 42–47 (2002)
23. Wang, P.Z.: Cone-cutting: a variant representation of pivot in Simplex. Inf. Technol. Decis. Making **10**(1), 65–82 (2011)
24. Wang, P.Z.: Discussions on Hirsch conjecture and the existence of strongly polynomial-time simplex variants. Ann. Data Sci. **1**(1), 41–71 (2014). https://doi.org/10.1007/s40745-014-0005-9
25. Wang, P.Z., Lui, H.C., Liu, H.T., Guo, S.C.: Gravity sliding algorithm for linear programming. Ann. Data Sci. **4**(2), 193–210 (2017). https://doi.org/10.1007/s40745-017-0108-1
26. Hubbard, J.H., Hubbard, B.B.: Vector Calculus, Linear Algebra, and Differential Forms. A Unified Approach. Prentice-Hall, Upper Saddle River (1999). ISBN 0-13-657446-7
27. Roll, J., Chang, J.J.: Analysis of individual differences in multidimensional scaling via an n-way generalization of 'Eckart-Young' decomposition. Psychometrika **35**, 283–319 (1970)
28. Harshman, R.A.: Foundations of the PARAFAC procedure: models and conditions for an explanatory multi-modal factor analysis. UCLA Working Pap. Phonetics **16**(1), 84 (1970)
29. Chang, B.B., Zhang, Q.L., Xie, L., et al.: The application of NIR in oil blending. Chin. J. Sci. Instrument **22**(3), 408–410 (2001)
30. Xiong, F., Zhang, X., Li, S., Gai, Y.: Nonlinear planning for oilfield development based on profit maximization. School of Information and Control Engineering, University of Petroleum, vol. 28, no. 1 (2004)
31. Belokvostov, M.S., Okorokov, V.A.: System for blending gasoline distiliates. Chem. Pet. Eng. **32**(6), 543–544 (1996)
32. Mamat, H., Aini, I.N., Said, M., Jamaludin, R.: Physicochemical characteristics of palm oil and sunflower oil blends fractionated at different temperatures. Food Chem. **91**(4), 731–736 (2004)
33. Guo, Y., He, J., Xua, L., Liu, W.: A novel multi-objective particle swarm optimization for comprehensible credit scoring. Soft Comput. **23**, 9009–9023 (2018). https://doi.org/10.1007/s00500-018-3509-y. (Impact Factor: 2.367)
34. Zhang, Z., He, J., Gao, G., Tian, Y.: Sparse multi-criteria optimization classifier for credit risk evaluation. Soft. Comput. **23**(9), 3053–3066 (2019)
35. He, J., Zhang, Y., Shi, Y., Huang, G.: Domain-driven classification based on multiple criteria and multiple constraint-level programming for intelligent credit scoring. IEEE Trans. Knowl. Data Eng. **22**(6), 826–838 (2010). (ERA A, 2011 Impact Factor: 1.657, SNIP 3.576)
36. Shi, Y., He, J., et al.: Computer-based algorithms for multiple criteria and multiple constraint level integer linear programming. Comput. Math. Appl. **49**(5), 903–921 (2005). (ERA Rank A, ISI Impact Factor: 1.472, SNIP 1.248)

Barrage Video Recommendation Method Based on Convolutional Recursive Neural Network

Siyuan Ma and Ping He(✉)

Institute of Information Technology, Hebei University of Economics and Business, Hebei, China
11112082@bjtu.edu.cn

Abstract. Aiming at solving the problems of traditional video recommendation process, such as low time efficiency and low accuracy, this paper proposes a convolutional recursive neural network video recommendation method based on barrage. Firstly, according to the number of barrage in video, the method selects the preferable video fragments of users, and adopts the k-means clustering method to extract key frames. Secondly, we construct a convolutional recursive neural network model (RCNN) to classify the similar video fragments. Finally, the recommendation can be achieved by the similarity between video fragments. The experimental results show that the proposed recommendation method improves the accuracy of recommendation by 0.22 compared with CTR, 0.18 compared with CDL, and 0.31 compared with ConvMF. So it improves the accuracy of recommendation in a certain extent.

Keywords: Barrage · Convolutional neural network · Recursive neural network · Video

1 Introduction

With the rapid development of digital technology and network technology, the domestic and foreign appear many big video websites. After more than ten years of exploration and practice, major video sites (domestic video sites such as iQIYI, Tencent, Youku, foreign video sites such as YouTube and Netflix, etc.) have already occupied a majority position in the field of video website. And watching the video has been integrated into people's daily life. Nevertheless, it is an important problem that how to timely recommend video that the users may be

This work is supported by Key Project of Hebei Educational Committee (Higher Education Research Project of Hebei Province) No. ZD2019017, 2019 School Level Graduate Innovation Funding Project, Natural Science Foundation of Hebei Province under Grant No. F2019207061, Science and Technology Research Project of Higher Education of Hebei Province under Grant No. QN2018116, Research Foundation of Hebei University of Economics and Business under Grant No. 2018QZ04.

H. Shen and Y. Sang (Eds.): PAAP 2019, CCIS 1163, pp. 507–518, 2020.
https://doi.org/10.1007/978-981-15-2767-8_44

interested, moreover it also becomes a key problem that needs to solve actively for each big video website.

In recent years, video that the users can send the barrage has become the mainstream [1], and researchers pay more and more attention to the barrage video. The barrage text sent by the users can reflect the feelings of users about the current segment of video, and the number of barrage can reflect the degree that the current segment of video is favored by users. Therefore, this paper studies the number of barrage in the video to improve the accuracy of video recommendation.

At present, a larger number of domestic researches are based on the analysis of barrage content. For example, according to the topic model to classify the word of barrage, the literature [2] combined with the theme distribution of each word and emotional dictionary and proposed the algorithm that can measure the emotional vector of dynamic evaluation words. It uses the "global + local" context-related emotion similarity calculation method to calculate the emotional similarity, and finally obtain the recommended video segments by the emotional similarity scores, however, the emotional classification of bullet screen content without emotional color or irony is a little insufficient.

The literature [3] firstly processed the barrage text data, calculated the emotional value of these texts, improved the traditional k-means algorithm, calculated the distance between the data by using the dynamic time normalization algorithm. And then, the emotional values are classified so as to distinguish the similarities and differences in users' emotions when they watching video, however, the literature only calculates the positive and negative emotions of the users who send a large amount of barrage data, and cancels the users who send a small amount of barrage data, so it is impossible to classify the users who prefer this video but send a small amount of barrage data. In the emotional value analysis of barrage text, there is a problem that it is seriously relying on the barrage content, therefore this paper proposed a video recommended model that is based on the number of barrages and combined with the recursive convolutional neural network. The model uses the number of barrages to analyze the fragments favored by users in video, and adopts the K-means clustering method to extract the key frames of video clips. Furthermore, the key frames can be processed to the valid static images that can be used to the input of the recursive convolutional neural network model. Finally, the important human behavior characteristics can be extracted, and on this basis the method can be recommended to the users by looking for video with similar video frames.

The remainder of this paper is organized as follows. In Sect. 2 we describe some related studies on video recommendation and video recommendation based on convolutional neural network. Section 3 defines the problem of video recommendation on the basis of barrage. Section 4 formally describes the work flow of video recommendation that contains the data preprocessing and RCNN model. Section 5 illustrates the data sources and experimental sets, and gives the experimental results. Finally, Sect. 6 concludes this paper and explains the next researching direction of video recommendation based on barrage.

2 Related Works

This section introduces the related research results of video recommendation and video recommendation method based on convolutional neural network.

2.1 Traditional Video Recommendation

Traditional video recommendations are generally divided into content-based video mixed recommendation method and collaborative filtering based video mixed recommendation method.

(1) Content based video recommended methods: the literature [4] proposed a recommendation method based on label weight score that each label is set the corresponding score, where the score represents the weight of the item or the user on the label, in order to reduce the influence of objective factors on user ratings and improve the accuracy and authenticity of the score. On the basis of context, Lin [5] proposed a recommendation model based on user decision that selects the required features or feature combinations according to the factors affecting user decision, and takes the preference of users' interests as the direct influencing factor of decision. Tzamousis [6] uses various machine learning algorithms to learn the efficient combination method of various recommendation algorithms, and can select the best hybrid method according to the given input. This method can be easily extended to the other recommendation methods.

(2) Video based on collaborative filtering recommendation method: Nguyen [7] proposed a probability model that combines the displayed and hidden feedback. The method firsty adopts the users and projects based the displayed feedback to represent the matrix decomposition model, secondly adopts the embedding model of projects to find the representation of goods, so as to capture the relationships among the projects based on hidden feedback. In order to solve the problem that a single user is only interested in some fields, Zhang [8] proposed a collaborative clustering recommendation method that adopts clustering algorithm to group the users and items according to their interests or characteristics, and then makes corresponding recommendations on the basis of each group. Zhang [9] improved the original frequency-based and ranking-based information kernel extraction methods, and proposed a method that considers the similarity between users and fully utilizes the scoring information of users and goods when seeking the list of neighbors for optimizing the process of finding the most similar neighbors.

2.2 Video Recommendation Based on Convolutional Neural Network

Li [11] proposed a method that computes video correlation directly from the content, rather than as the sub conditions of user behavior matrix decomposition. The method uses the deeping convolution neural network to process the video information (such as the pixels, audio, subtitles and metadata) in order to build a video link table, and reduce the behavior requirement of the new video user. In addition, in order to improve the applicability of the convolutional neural network, the literature [11] uses the condition convolution to extraction the behavior features of users. The method introduces the feature vector of goods as the convolution kernel and does not set training parameters. Moreover, this method only needs one convolution layer to get the higher order combination between N attributes of user and N attributes of items. On this basis, the method integrates user and item attribute information in the neural collaborative filtering.

Cai [12] proposed an improved recommended method that combines the matrix decomposition and cross channel convolution neural network, and add the influence factors of the user and the project to the traditional matrix decomposition. Then, the information matrix composed of word vectors is input into the convolutional neural network. Finally, the eigenvalue of evaluation information is combined with the regularization term of the improved matrix decomposition model. The literature [13] applies the dynamic convolution probability matrix decomposition model to group recommendation, integrates the text representation method of convolutional neural network into the potential factor model, and integrates the state space model into the potential factor model.

3 Problem Formulation

This section introduces the related background of this paper, including the characteristics and mechanism of barrage video, and the relevant definition s. When a user sees a scene in video, he or she may write some texts and send it to the video in the period of time. The other users may send the texts to this video when they watch the same scene of video later. So when the number of barrage in this time is more than a certain number during a period of time, and it can be concluded that those users who send the video barrage are more interested in this scene. By analyzing these interested video segments, we can find the similar video in order to recommend to the users. The above questions can be summarized as Definition 1.

Definition 1 (The video recommendation model based on barrage). Given the set of video is $V = \{v_1, v_2, \cdots, v_n\}$, where $|V|$ denotes the number of video in V and the time of the video v_i is T_{v_i}, the set of users is $C = \{c_1, c_2, \cdots, c_m\}$, the video set contains the number of barrages in various times for n video v_i is d_{i,t_j} and the number of views is g_{ij} et al. The model firstly takes the time point t_j when the barrage numbers $d_{ij} > \lambda$ (λ is obtained after testing) in the video set v_i. According to the t_j, secondly extracts the video fragments $f_i = \{q_{i,1}, q_{i,2}, \cdots, q_{i,|v_i|}\}$, where $q_{i,k}$ denotes the *k-th* video segment in the *i-th* video. Next, uses K-means clustering scheme to extract the key frame in the extracted fragment set f_i. The extracted data set S is processed to the structured data set D by introducing the recursive convolutional neural network model for improve the accuracy ε of the recommendation system. The mathematical model of the problem is shown in Eq. (1).

$$\begin{aligned}
Input: \quad & V = \{v_1, v_2, \cdots, v_n\} \\
& C = \{c_1, c_2, \cdots, c_m\} \\
& v_i = \{d_{ij}, g_{ij}\} \\
& d_m \subseteq V \\
& T = \{t_1, t_2, \cdots, t_e\} \\
& f_i = \{q_{i,1}, q_{i,2}, \cdots, q_{i,|v_i|}\} \\
Output: \quad & S \\
Goal: \quad & D, max\ \varepsilon \\
s.t.: \quad & (1)\, 1 < i < n \\
& (2)\, 1 < j < e \\
& (3)\, n, m, e \in N
\end{aligned} \tag{1}$$

4 Video Recommendation Structure

Video recommended workflow consists of two sub-modules: (1) data preprocessing; (2) RCNN model, as shown in Fig. 1.

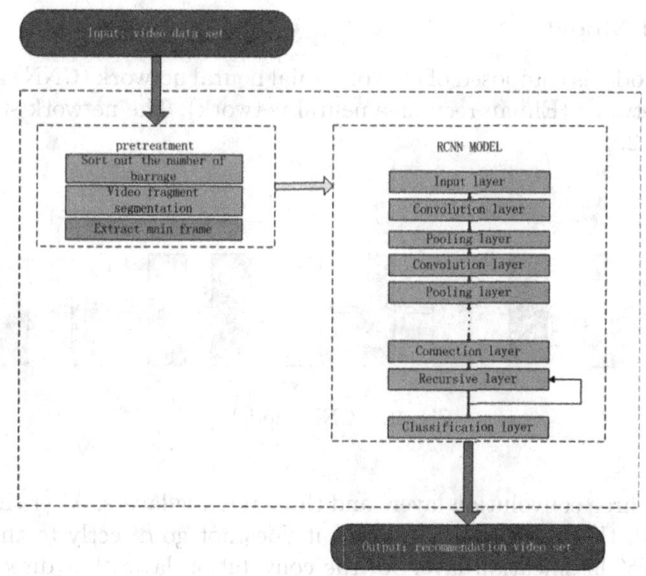

Fig. 1. The process of video recommendation

4.1 Barrage Data Preprocessing

The data preprocessing stage mainly includes three steps: sorting out the number of bullet screens, cutting video fragments, and extracting the main frame. The barrage is presented in the form of dynamic text, scroll or static, so the number of barrage in the same video playing video at the same time is the number of barrage on the same screen. The rolling time and stationary time of each barrage of Bilibili are 7 s, and it is found by test that there are few cases when the number of barrages of the same screen is more than 50 [14]. Literature [15] drew the "time-barrage" polyline graph with coordinates t_j, d_{i,t_j}) at an interval of 5 s. This paper firstly counted the number of barrages d_{i,t_j} of each video, found the time point t_j of the barrage number $d_{ij} > \lambda$ in video v_i, and then cut video segment f_i according to the time point t_j, where λ is simply computed in Eq. (2).

$$\lambda = \frac{1}{|T_{v_i}|} \sum_{t_j=1}^{T_{v_i}} d_{i,t_j} \tag{2}$$

Considering the interference at the beginning and end of video, it is necessary to remove the number of barrages in some times, such as when music plays at the start and end stage. The key frame extraction algorithm based on k-means clustering method is used to extract the main frames from video fragments and select the video frames that can fully represent video characteristics.

4.2 RCNN Model

The RCNN model is composed of convolutional neural network (CNN) and recursive neural network (Elman recursive neural network). The network structure is shown in Fig. 2.

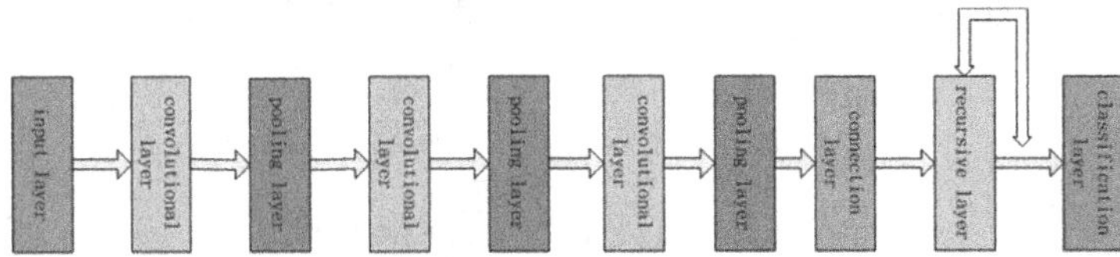

Fig. 2. RCNN model

CNN has three convolution layers and three pooling layers. After the network passes through the full connection layer, it does not go directly to the softmax function layer (classification layer) of the convolution layer, but directly to the added recursive neural network layer. Relu function is used as nonlinear mapping function in the network.

The construction steps of video recommendation model based on recursive convolutional neural network proposed in this paper are as follows:

Step 1: extract the necessary information in the spatial features of video frames that have been selected to represent video characteristics by using the convolutional neural network in the RCNN model. Then, convert the image into low-dimensional feature information, and output the low-dimensional feature information. The calculation form of convolution layer is generally shown in Eq. (3).

$$S_j^l = f\left(\sum_{i \in M_j} Kernel_{ij}^l \times S_j^{l-1} + b_j^l\right) \tag{3}$$

Where, the S_j^l is the result obtained by convolution at l layer, $f(\circ)$ is an activation function, S_j^{l-1} is the output feature of the previous layer, $Kernel_{ij}^l$ is the convolution kernel matrix, b_j^l is the bias of the feature graph after convolution, M_j is the number of feature inputs, that how many image features are selected as the input of the convolution layer.

Step 2: Input the low-dimensional feature information into the RNN model in the RCNN model. The output relation between input layer, hidden layer, connection layer and output layer of RNN network is calculated by Eqs. (4, 5 and 6).

$$v_i(k) = \sum_{j=1}^{n} w_{ij}^E(k-1)\, s_j^E(k) + w_i^u(k)\, u(k) \tag{4}$$

$$s_i(k) = f(v_i) \tag{5}$$

$$s_j^E(k) = s_j(k-1) \tag{6}$$

The output of the network $D(k)$ is calculated by Eq. (7).

$$D(k) = \sum_{j=1}^{n} w_i^D(k-1)\, s_i(k) \tag{7}$$

Where $v_i(k)$ represents all inputs of the *i-th* hidden layer unit, and $f(\circ)$ represents the activation function. w_{ij}^E, w_i^u, w_i^D represents the weights from the input layer to the hidden layer, the connection layer to the hidden layer, and the hidden layer to the output layer.

Step 3: according to the parameters set, the loss function model σ_j in this paper uses the error back propagation algorithm for the partial derivatives of the weight and bias of each layer in the network. Then update the parameters, and at the same time adjust the feedback weights of Elman respectively. When the model reaches the maximum number μ of iterations or loss function within a reasonable range, stop the training, or return to the second step.

Step 4: after ending the model train, get the feature vectors of specific video that users interests. According to these feature vectors, sort video similarity by descending. Finally, the users can be recommended some projects.

In summary, the recursive neural network recommendation algorithm based on barrage is described as Algorithm 1.

Algorithm 1. A recursive neural network recommendation algorithm based on barrage

Input :

video training set S_{train}, *video test set* S_{test}

Output :

video recommendation set D

for each video S_{train} *do*
  calculate S_j^l
    calculate σ_j
      calculate w_{ij}
        if $\sigma_j < \mu$ *then*
          update w_{ij} *and* b_j^l
        end if
  calculate $s_i(k)$
    calculate $s_j^E(k)$
      calculate σ_i
        if $\sigma_i < \mu$ *then*
          update w_{ij}^E, w_i^u, w_i^D
        end if
end for
return $D(k)$

5 Experimental Results

This section briefly introduces the data sources and experimental environment used in the experiment. Video of this experiment is downloaded from the domestic barrage website "bilibili" by "jiji" Down software. From the classic video set to choose multiple types of video, such as the modern comedy-Home With Kids, ancient costume comedy-Bronze teeth Ji Xiaolan, humanities war drama-Bright sword, historical costume drama-Youth bao zheng, action comedy-World for the Monkey King, martial arts love drama-The Heaven Sword and Dragon Saber By Jin Yong respectively. We choose the first 5 episodes of each drama, so the total number of episodes is 30. Since bilibili.com maintains the barrage pool and limits the amount of barrage data, so video with more than 20 min has about

3,000 barrages in per episode, and video with more than 40 min has 6,000–8,000 barrages in per episode. The results is shown in Fig. 3, where <p= "when the barrage appears at video (second), the mode of barrage (such as 1..3 denotes rolling barrage, 4 denotes bottom barrage, 5 denotes top barrage, 6 denotes the reverse barrage, 7 denotes the specified bits, 8 denotes the advanced barrage), font size (px), font color (HTML color (decimal)), the generating time of barrage (Unix format), barrage pool, the sender id of barrage, barrage id in barrage database"> barrage content.


```
<chatid>3473629</chatid>
<mission>0</mission>
<maxlimit>6000</maxlimit>
<state>0</state>
<real_name>0</real_name>
<source>e-r</source>
<d p="466.52100,1,25,16777215,1537589892,0,eed5d550,5477613164298244">真是年轻啊</d>
<d p="695.31600,1,25,16777215,1537590121,0,eed5d550,5477733165432832">故意说不会水</d>
<d p="758.83500,1,25,16777215,1537590185,0,eed5d550,5477766523256832">本来就是少女</d>
<d p="786.32700,1,25,16777215,1537590212,0,eed5d550,5477780895039488">和珅大头</d>
<d p="953.97900,1,25,16777215,1537590380,0,eed5d550,5477868729008128">真会拍马屁</d>
<d p="26.35200,1,25,16777215,1537590839,0,51671930,5478109172727808">真的停不下来 本来只打算看一集</d>
<d p="863.71700,1,25,16777215,1537593776,0,51671930,5479649300185090">和大人你是不是回去复习了哈哈哈哈</d>
<d p="930.55300,1,25,16777215,1537593861,0,51671930,5479693672775680">[illegible]</d>
<d p="1026.55900,1,25,16777215,1537593971,0,51671930,5479751557840896">和珅的武功还不赖呢</d>
<d p="2385.80300,1,25,16777215,1537608030,0,373b0528,5487122667012100">扇子戏很多</d>
<d p="1517.79900,1,25,16777215,1537613903,0,7186a5fe,5490201565593604">ooo</d>
<d p="1279.42500,1,25,16777215,1537614966,0,bf745471,5490758836551680">四姑娘，我看你是想做皇后啊</d>
<d p="1811.69900,1,25,16776960,1537616845,0,40e8d4fc,5491744182370308">住手！</d>
<d p="1576.88700,1,25,16777215,1537619719,0,3cb9249f,5493250977169408">猴才是本体</d>
<d p="1832.32400,1,25,16777215,1537620005,0,3cb9249f,5493400705433600">怎么感觉文豪撩文盲都是从名字开始的</d>
<d p="2003.00300,1,25,16777215,1537620192,0,3cb9249f,5493499065532416">老板好淡定</d>
<d p="2598.63900,1,25,16777215,1537620809,0,3cb9249f,5493822558044160">教你写字的时候你就写倒了</d>
<d p="1855.50100,1,25,15138834,1537624402,0,b3e2015b,5495706352615424">赫</d>
......
```


Fig. 3. Barrage-list

By python program, it crawls the sending time, content and sender id of the barrage. Then, the barrage data is processed, and is visualized, as shown in Fig. 4.

Barrage transmission time	Barrage sender id	Barrage content
00:00:50	9.51E+07	oh亲爱的上帝 快看看我发现了什么
00:00:54	1699353	下冰雹
00:00:54	85df764b	我叫夏雨，我叫夏雪，我叫下冰雹
00:00:54	5bfd1ca2	小猴猴！
00:00:55	b7f1c21a	b站竟然有这个
00:00:56	849f240f	夏东海秒变刘新建
00:00:56	9acff6d	从组家庭
00:00:57	e86c7df3	合影！
00:00:57	2f1cb5d8	合影
00:00:58	552d84c2	合影
00:00:59	1eb025be	合影
00:00:59	d6fd0afb	好暖啊
00:00:59	b8bda1cd	小雪美的勒
00:00:59	b749017e	居然已经15年了
00:00:59	d6b55f0c	合影
00:00:59	66de1888	合影！
00:01:00	407b7aca	合影！
00:01:00	70bb9da8	合影
00:01:00	15819157	合影
00:01:00	14550831	合影
00:01:01	46ed6115	合影
00:01:01	2a01391f	合影!
00:01:01	b693a27d	合影！！
00:01:01	74238a05	希望所有二婚家庭都这么美满鸭!
00:01:01	2b0e5b12	合影
00:01:01	e535b27c	合影
00:01:01	d6992e63	合影
00:01:01	2ab2ef26	合影
00:01:01	b3fbcc72	合影
00:01:01	[illegible]	合影

Fig. 4. The list of processed barrage

In this paper, the number of barrage removed the barrage at the beginning and end of video, reducing the noise barrage, as shown in Fig. 5.

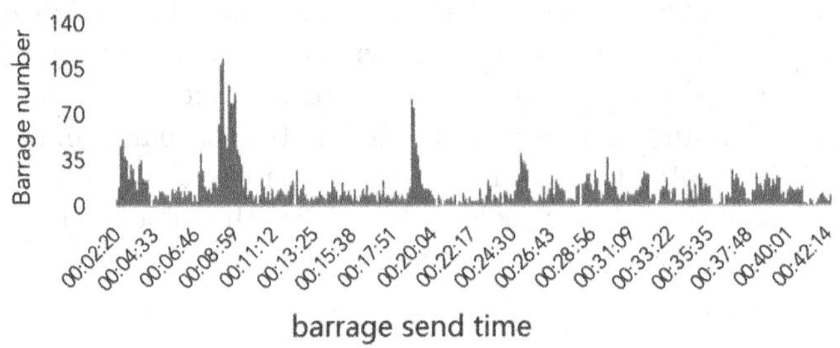

Fig. 5. The changing number of barrages

Besides data preprocessing in this paper, we set the training model and some parameters, as follows:

(1) The operating system is Windows 7, Intel core i5 processor and 16 GB RAM.
(2) The programming environment is python3.0, and the keras library environment is built. In order to train the weight of RCNN, the random gradient descending algorithm is used.
(3) In order to evaluate the overall performance of the model, the data set was randomly divided into a training set(80 and the Mean Absolute Deviation (MAE) [16] is adopted as the evaluation merit, as shown in Eq. (8).

$$M_{MAE} = \frac{\sum_{i=1}^{N} |p_i - q_i|}{N} \tag{8}$$

Where N is the number of recommended video, p_i is the predicted results of the experiment, and q_i is the actual results. MAE reflects the difference between the predicted value and the actual value of the algorithm. The smaller MAE value is, the more accurate the recommended algorithm is. In order to verify the effectiveness of this model, the proposed algorithm of this paper is compared with collaborative filtering thematic regression algorithm (CTR) [17], collaborative filtering deep learning algorithm (CDL) [18] and convolutional matrix decomposition algorithm (ConvMF) [19] on the same data set of this paper.

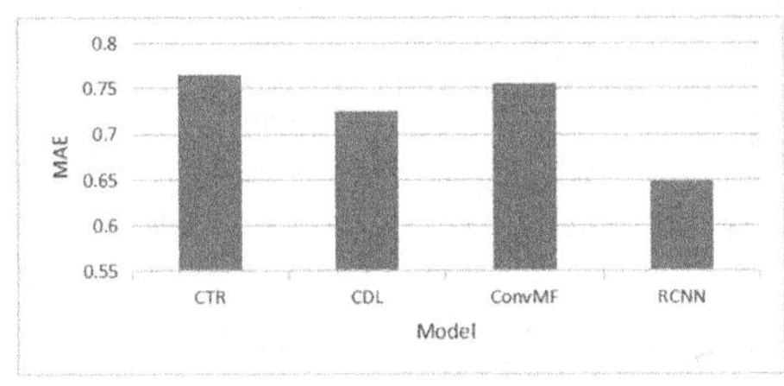

Fig. 6. The experiment results of model comparison

This paper uses the data set crawlled from the bilibili website, In order to reduce herd effect in video barrage, we preprocess the data, the experimenta l results obtained in the experiment test set are shown in Fig. 6.

From the figure, we can see that the performance of proposed method compared with the CTR, CDL, ConvMF respectively increases by 0.22, 0.18 and 0.31. From the comparison results in this data set, the proposed methode in this paper owns higher accuracy.

6 Conclusion

In order to improve the accuracy rate of the recommendation model, this paper proposes a video recommendation method that adopts the convolutional recursive neural network based on barrage. The barrage video can quickly capture the preference features of users by barrages, and improve the overall recommendation performance of prediction model with the help of convolutional recursive neural network. Experimental results show that the proposed convolutional recursive neural network recommendation method based on barrage can increase the selectivity of users. However, video without motion features has a weak recognition ability. Therefore, the next research based on the video key frame is to add video content-related descriptive statements, and improve the recursive neural network [20–22] for further improving the accuracy of the prediction model.

References

1. Ma, S., He, P.: Review of recommended methods for application. Comput. Sci. Appl. **9**(7), 1317–1327 (2019)
2. Deng, Y., Zhang, C., Li, J.: Video fragment recommendation model based on barrage emotion analysis. Comput. Appl. **37**(04), 1065–1070+1134 (2017)
3. Hong, Q., Wang, S., Zhao, J., Li, J., Rao, W.: Video user group classification based on barrage emotion analysis and clustering algorithm. Comput. Eng. Sci. **40**(06), 1125–1139 (2018)
4. Kong, X., Su, B., Wang, H., Gao, H., Li, J.: Research on recommendation model and algorithm based on tag weight score. J. Comput. Sci. **40**(06), 1440–1452 (2017)
5. Lin, X., Sang, Y., Long, C.: Personalized recommendation based on user decision mechanism. Libr. Inf. Work **63**(02), 99–106 (2019)
6. Tzamousis, E., Papadopouli, M.: On hybrid modular recommendation systems for video streaming (2019)
7. Nguyen, T.B., Aihara, K., Takasu, A.: A probabilistic model for collaborative filtering with implicit and explicit feedback data (2017)
8. Zhang, F., Zhang, L., Luo, T., Wu, Y.: A feature-based collaborative clustering model. Comput. Res. Dev. **55**(07), 1508–1524 (2018)
9. Zhang, W., Li, J., Yang, J.: An improved information kernel extraction method in collaborative filtering recommendation. Comput. Appl. Res. 1–6 (2019)
10. Li, Y., Wang, H., Liu, H., Chen, B.: A study on content-based video recommendation. In: IEEE International Conference on Image Processing, Beijing, 17–20 September 2017, pp. 4581–4585 (2017)

11. Li, N., Sheng, Y., Ni, H.: Conditional convolution implicit factor model for personalized recommendation [J/OL]. Comput. Eng. 1–10 (2019)
12. Cai, N., Liu, G., Cai, H.: A recommended model for the combination of improved matrix decomposition and convolutional neural network [J/OL]. Comput. Eng. Appl. 1–8 (2019)
13. Wang, H., Dong, M.: Potential group recommendation based on dynamic convolution probability matrix decomposition. Comput. Res. Dev. **54**(08), 1853–1863 (2017)
14. Liu, S.: Research on human-computer interaction efficiency of modern web barrage. Sun Yat-sen University (2015)
15. Guo, K.: Research on barrage data mining algorithm based on quantitative characteristics. Huazhong University of Science and Technology (2017)
16. Zhou, J., Huo, H.: Multi-dimensional video recommendation algorithm in social network service. Comput. Eng. **41**(01), 245–250 (2015)
17. Zhang, M., Ding, B.-Y., Ma, W.-Z., et al.: Mixed recommendation method based on deep learning enhancement. J. Tsinghua Univ. (Nat. Sci. Ed.) (10), 9–16 (2017)
18. Wang, C., Blei, D.M.: Collaborative topic modeling for recommending scientific articles. In: ACM SIGKDD International Conference on Knowledge Discovery and Data Mining, pp. 448–456. ACM (2011)
19. Kim, D., Park, C., Oh, J., et al.: Convolutional matrix factorization for document context-aware recommendation. In: ACM Conference on Recommender Systems. ACM (2016)
20. Xiong, M.T., Feng, Y., Wu, T., Shang, J.X., Qiang, B.H., Wang, Y.N.: TDCTFIC: a novel recommendation framework fusing temporal dynamics, CNN-based text features and item correlation. IEICE Trans. Inf. Syst. **E102.D**(8), 1517–1525 (2019)
21. Liu, E., Chu, Y., Luan, L., Li, G., Wang, Z.: Mixing-RNN: a recommendation algorithm based on recurrent neural network. In: Douligeris, C., Karagiannis, D., Apostolou, D. (eds.) KSEM 2019. LNCS (LNAI), vol. 11775, pp. 109–117. Springer, Cham (2019). https://doi.org/10.1007/978-3-030-29551-6_10
22. Hsieh, C.K., Campo, M., Taliyan, A., et al.: Convolutional collaborative filter network for video based recommendation systems (2018)

A Pipelining Strategy for Accelerating Convolutional Networks on ARM Processors

Xin Zhou(✉), Rongchun Li, Peng Zhang, Yuntao Liu, and Yong Dou

National Key Laboratory for Parallel and Distribution Processing, National University of Defense Technology, Changsha 450001, China
zhouxin17a@nudt.edu.cn

Abstract. Convolutional neural networks (CNN) is playing an important role in many fields. Many applications are able to run the inference process of CNN with pre-trained models on mobile devices in these days. Improving performance of embedded processors such as ARM-based CPUs makes it possible to meet the requirement of real-time processing. In this paper, a pipelining strategy is proposed to accelerate convolution networks on ARM processors. We implement a 3×3 convolution with Neon instructions which are single instruction and multiple data (SIMD) instructions supported by ARM processors. In order to reduce stalls in the pipeline, issue orders of instructions are rearranged according to the out-of-order execution and dual-issue mechanism on ARM processors. A tiling method is exploited to increase data reuse. The input feature map is divided into multiple 6×6 tiles, and the computations within the tile is highly optimized using our proposed pipelining strategy. The speedup of proposed method is 2.88 compared with gcc compiled codes on RK3288. The effect of our optimizing method is measured by a performance profiling tool, cycles and cache misses are decreased significantly. The multi-thread version implemented with openMP achieve speedup of 6.8 compared with single-thread gcc complied version.

Keywords: Convolutional neural network · Pipeline · ARM · Instruction level parallelism embedded processor

1 Introduction

Convolution neural networks (CNNs) are playing an important role in many fields such as object detection, image classification and face recognition. The accuracy of CNN is growing while the number of its layers and parameters is also increasing. Deeper networks often introduce more computations, and some CNN applications like autonomous driving and face detection require real-time processing. There are two solutions for these scenarios. The traditional solution is transmitting the data to servers which have higher performance and better computing ability. Then the servers send the results to the front-end

H. Shen and Y. Sang (Eds.): PAAP 2019, CCIS 1163, pp. 519–530, 2020.
https://doi.org/10.1007/978-981-15-2767-8_45

devices. This solution reduces performance requirements of front-end devices but requires higher transmitting speed and wider bandwidth. The alternative solution becomes common with improvements of front-end devices. In this solution, front-end devices are not only responsible for collecting data, they also process data. We call this solution as edge computing, because these front-end devices are usually the edge nodes which are the closest to the data and knowledge and the furthest to the central servers in a computing network. The concept of edge computing is proposed to reduce the overhead of transmission and accelerate data processing. Applications of CNNs also get benefit from growing performance of embedded devices. More implementations of CNNs can be ported to mobile devices and embedded devices.

Embedded processors like ARM provide an efficient and flexible platform with good energy efficiency. Newly released Cortex-A series of ARMv7 processors have 4 cores and dual-issue pipelines. They also support out-of-order execution and multi-thread processing. Neon units on these processors provide the capability of single instruction and multiple data (SIMD). Neon operations give us an opportunity to achieve higher computing efficiency when implementing CNN applications.

Convolution is a primary operation in most neural networks. Many studies are focusing on improving computing efficiency of convolution on different platforms [1,2]. The original convolution is a sliding window method. This method is easy to implement but has poor memory access efficiency. A general way to speed up convolution operation is rearranging the input feature map to columns according to the accessing sequence of the sliding window. By doing this, the input feature map is transformed to a matrix and the convolutional operation is transformed to matrix multiplications. There are many existed pre-tuned libraries for matrix multiplication such as general matrix multiplication (GEMM) [3]. Another optimizing method is replacing multiplications with additions. Multiplications of floating number usually cost more than one cycle on a CPU. Total amount of computation can be reduced significantly by decreasing the number of multiplications. This method is called winograd algorithm [4,5]. Winograd algorithm requires transformation before and after the matrix multiplication, and it is an approximate method with some loss of precision.

For an embedded platform with limited computing resources and memory, it is reasonable to implement convolutions by the sliding window method. Sliding window method is not fast because it consists many branches and reductions if compiled by a common compiler like gcc. Optimizing convolution operations on an ARM CPU is usually based on the Neon instructions. Four floating numbers are calculated simultaneously by using Neon instructions on an ARMv7 processor and the speedup is 4 theoretically. However, gcc does not support optimization for Neon operations. Most implementations optimize convolution by hand-writing assembly codes. Although there are some existed frameworks for accelerating inference of CNNs like Arm compute library (ACL) [6], ncnn and Tengine [7], and these libraries support most operations in a CNN, there is still strong need for faster inference on an embedded device. It is useful and meaningful to make the most efficient use of the resources on the embedded CPU which has limited computing capability.

This paper introduces a pipelining strategy to achieve faster inference from the perspective of instruction level parallelism (ILP). The sliding window method is highly optimized by using the character of dual-issue and SIMD on the ARMv7 CPU. A memory access strategy is designed to make sufficient use of registers and computing units on the ARM CPU. We implement the optimized 3×3 convolution on the RK3288 chip with an ARM Cortex-A17 CPU. The speed of optimized 3×3 convolution operation is faster than the ncnn framework which is designed to speed up inference of CNNs on ARM CPUs.

The remainder of this paper is organized as follows. Section 2 presents related works about accelerating methods of convolution on ARM-based processors. In Sect. 3, the convolution operation and the architecture of ARM processors are introduced. The details of proposed pipelining strategy and efficient memory access strategy are introduced in Sect. 4. In Sect. 5, we carry out the experimental results and analysis the effect of proposed method. Eventually conclusion is drawn in Sect. 6.

2 Related Work

Both vendors and application service providers are focusing on solutions for accelerating inference of CNNs. Most operations in a convolutional neural network are optimized by these libraries [3,6,8,9]. Many works like quantification and optimizing memory allocation are done in order to reach the target of real-time processing on ARM-based processors.

The Arm Compute Library [6] is a software library for computer vision and machine learning proposed by ARM. It provides optimized functions of convolutional building blocks, such as convolution, pooling and softmax operation, using SIMD technologies. It supports parallel computing on Cortex-A CPUs and Mali GPUs.

Ncnn [10] is a lightweight open source inference framework designed for ARM-based processors. It has no third-party library dependencies, does not rely on BLAS/NNPACK or any other computing framework. The convolution operation in ncnn is highly optimized. The speed of inference can be faster by using 8-bits quantification and half-precision floating point storage.

3 Convolution and Pipelines on ARM CPUs

3.1 Convolution

Convolution is widely used in CNNs. The kernel size of convolution ranges from 1×1 to 11×11 [11,12]. The representative sizes are 1×1 and 3×3. Large filters can be replaced with multiple 3×3 convolutions without loss of precision. Combinations of multiple 3×3 convolutions can also have the same receptive

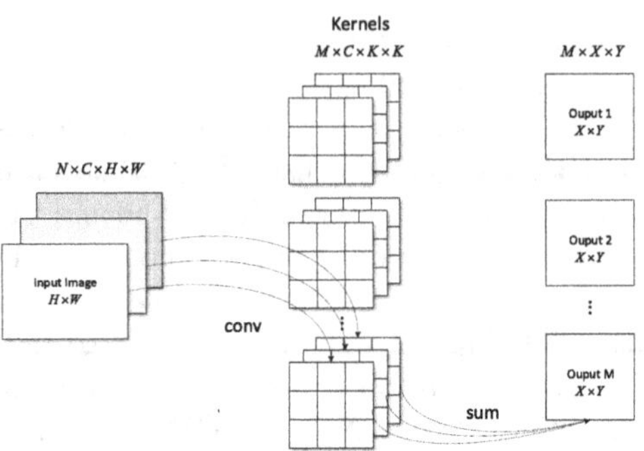

Fig. 1. Convolution layer (N = 1)

field as big filters' with less parameters. Therefore, 3×3 convolution is adopt by many popular networks such as VGG16 [13] and Mobilenet [14].

The common storage order of feature map is NCHW, where N is the number of inputs, C is the number channels, H and W represent the height and width of the feature map respectively. We denote the kernel size as $K \times K$ and there are M kernels for a single convolution layer. Denote I as the input feature map and F as the kernel. The computation of a single convolution layer can be described as follows:

$$Y_{n,m,x,y} = \sum_{c=1}^{C} \sum_{u=1}^{K} \sum_{v=1}^{K} I_{n,c,x+u,y+v} F_{m,c,u,v} \tag{1}$$

where n is the index of input images and m is the index of the output. The relationship between input feature maps and the outputs in a convolution operation is described in Fig. 1. The kernel size is 3×3 and the number of input images $N = 1$, and M is the number of output feature maps in this figure.

3.2 Instruction Pipeline on ARMv7 CPUs

ARMv7 architecture is a reduced instruction set computing (RISC) architecture. It supports 32-bit computing and Neon operations. Figure 2 shows the simplified functional diagram of the Cortex-A17 processor. There are two dispatch stages and three instruction issue queues on A17 processor. One dispatch stage is for Address Generation Unit (AGU) and integer executions, and another is for Neon and floating executions. The issue queues includes integer execution queue, load/store queue and Neon and vector floating point (VFP) units execution queue. Because this ARM processor supports dual-issue, each queue is able to issue up to two instructions. The instruction is executed in a pipeline on the CPU. It takes one or more cycles to get the results from the computing units. The number of cycles required by an operation is static if all the data for calculating are ready [15]. However, there are some stalls in a pipeline caused by data dependencies. In this case, current instruction must wait until the result of former instruction has been loaded or calculated. In addition, stalls can also

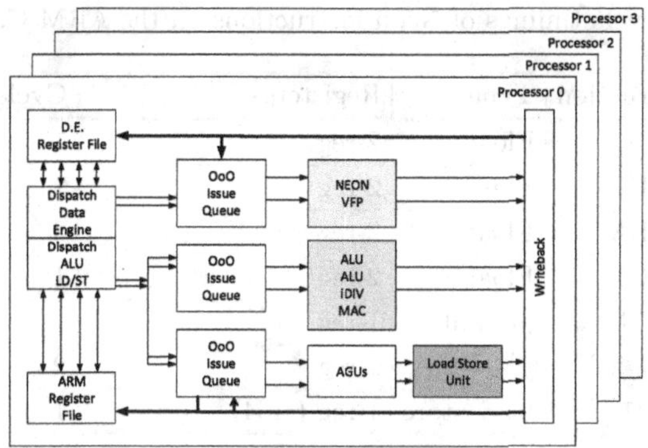

Fig. 2. ARM A17 processor diagram (simplified)

be caused by more than one instructions asking for the same unit on the CPU. Modern compilers are able to avoid most stalls for a common program, but some compute-intensive applications still require optimizing to achieve higher speed.

There are 16 128-bit SIMD registers for Neon operations on ARM A17. The issue queues and computing units are independent. For example, the processor support a floating-point multiplication instruction and a load/store instruction being issued simultaneously. If all the data are prepared in the SIMD registers, there will always be two instructions being issued from two different issue queues.

Table 1 shows the cycles required by frequently-used Neon instructions on Arm Cortex-A8 [16], which is also an armv7-based processor. A SIMD register on ARM is 128-bit, it can be regarded as four 32-bit registers or two 64-bit registers. Registers in this table is 64-bit so 2-reg represents two 64-bit registers. Operations for unaligned data require one extra cycle. The total cycles required by a piece of codes can be evaluated according to cycle timings of relative instructions. In addition, it is possible to fill up the pipeline theoretically, because the processor supports out-of-order executions. However, the compiler is not smart enough to fill all the idle cycles by instructions which have no dependencies. Therefore, it can be found that there are still many stalls in practical cases even if the compiler has optimized the codes. On the other hand, the effect of reorganizing the executing order is limited because the number of registers is limited. Therefore, it is necessary to exploit some optimizing strategies to make the most efficient use the resources on the ARM processor.

4 Methods

The convolution with a 3×3 kernel size is adopt in most convolutional networks. Computations of 3×3 convolution on an ARM processor are often optimized by using SIMD instructions. Four 32-bit floating-point numbers can be calculated simultaneously and the theoretical speedup is 4. However, there are branches

Table 1. The cycle timings of Neon instructions on the ARM Cortex A8 [16]

Instruction	Type	Registers	Cycles
VADD	Float	2-reg	1
VMUL	Float	2-reg	2
VMLA	Float	2-reg	3
VMOV	Float	2-reg	1
VEXT	permute	1-reg	1
		2-reg	2
VLD1	load/store	1-reg (@64)	1
		2-reg (@128)	1
		3-reg (unaligned, @64)	3
		4-reg (@128, @256)	2
VST1	load/store	1-reg (@64)	1
		2-reg (@128)	1
		3-reg (@64)	2
		4-reg (@128, @256)	2

when implementing convolutions. Moreover, the overhead of memory access during this process can also not be ignored. All the methods that aim at speeding up computation of convolution can be summarized as two types. One is achieving more parallelism by SIMD technologies and multi-thread processing. The deeper level one is avoiding stalls in a pipeline by reasonable order of instructions and memory access.

4.1 Pipelining of SIMD Instructions

Traditional compilers like gcc are not able to finely optimize convolution with Neon instructions. SIMD computations are often implemented by Neon intrinsics. Each row of a 3×3 kernel can be loaded into a 128-bit SIMD register. And corresponding floating numbers from the feature map can also be loaded into the SIMD registers according to the computing order. Then the MLA instruction is used to calculate the product of two vectors. Overlapping of calculating and load/store is the most efficient way to avoid stalls in a pipeline. We can reorder the load instruction to ensure all parameters of a computing instruction have been loaded into corresponding registers before calculating. The calculating processes are not affected by load/store instructions because Neon instructions and load/store instructions occupy different units on the processor. In addition, computations of integers and Neon operations are also independent. Therefore, we can organize the instructions of convolution operation to make sure that all the data flow to respective computing units without interruption based on the features described above.

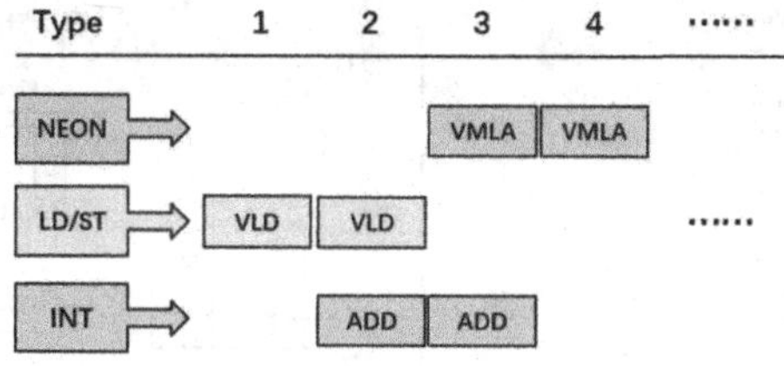

Fig. 3. Pipelining of SIMD instructions

This pipelining pattern is presented in Fig. 3. ADD instructions are used to compute addresses of required data. VLD instructions are used to load data from L1 cache. Notice that the data loaded by VLD instructions must exist in L1 cache, or it would cost multiple cycles to load the data from L2 cache and the memory. The PLD instruction can help preload required data to the cache before calculating. This pipelining pattern has been adopt by [10]. Moreover, computations of convolution in ncnn exploits some optimizing strategies such as unrolling of loops and data reusing skills to achieve higher parallelism. Although many optimizing methods have been used in ncnn, we still find a more efficient way to feed data to the pipeline.

The execution of a MLA instruction requires 3 cycles as shown in Table 1. If a MLA instruction is issued at the first cycle, then its result can be used for next operation at the 5th cycle, the $2^{nd}, 3^{rd}, 4^{th}$ cycles are in its executing duration. Therefore, at most three MLA instructions can be filled into the pipeline in this duration. This four MLA instructions can be organized as a minimum computing group. Once the first MLA instruction is calculated, its result can be used as the parameter of the MLA instruction issued at 5th cycle. The 5th MLA instruction is issued to calculate the product of two row vectors of 3×3 kernel and input feature map of next position.

The implementation of 3×3 convolutions in ncnn unrolls the loop to reduce branches and increase reuse of data. In its implementation, two channels of the 3×3 kernel are loaded into SIMD registers in each iteration. Each kernel have $C \times K \times K$ numbers and there are M kernels in total, where M is the number of outputs. This two channels are from two different kernels, but the index of two channels is identical to the channel index of input feature map. By doing this, the number of iterations for calculating outputs is reduced to $M/2$. There is another advantage to unroll the loop. The four MLA instructions group can not be filled up if there is only one channel of data being calculated. Two channels being calculated in one iteration increases usage of SIMD registers while the computing efficiency if improved. Meanwhile, this strategy avoids stalls in the pipeline. In order to gather a 4-MLA instructions group, ncnn fill more computations into the pipeline. It preloads a row of input feature map with 6 elements at each step. The 3×3 kernel slides 4 steps in row direction when calculating these 6 elements. So 4 outputs are calculated in this process. It can be found that only 3 steps are needed if we use SIMD instructions, and we name

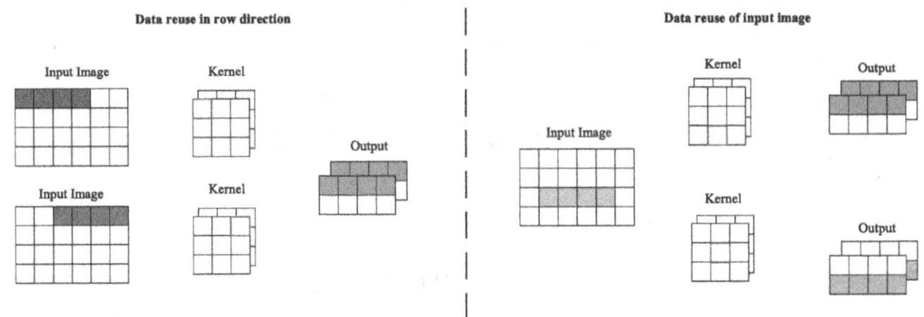

Fig. 4. Data reuse of input feature map

them as *r-left*, *r-mid* and *r-right*, *r* means operations in row direction. Figure 4 shows the relationship between the 6 elements of input and the 4 elements of output. Two SIMD steps of two channels in the row direction are filled into the pipeline in ncnn's implementation, then the 4-MLA instructions group is filled up.

In these three steps, *r-mid* step overlaps the elements of *r-left* step and *r-right* step. Ncnn uses a permute instruction VEXT to combine elements from *r-left* and *r-right*. This operation avoids load operation because it is a data transfer process between registers. However, the permute instruction requires 2 cycles for two 64-bit registers cases. Moreover, the permute operation occupy at least two SIMD registers, two source registers and one destination register. We found that it is more efficient to use a VLD1 instruction instead because VLD1 only requires 1 cycle for two registers cases. Although load operations may cause cache misses, the input row has already been preloaded to cache in this process. In addition, VLD1 only need one SIMD register. Therefore, in our implementation of convolution operation, we replace VEXT with VLD1 to load elements of *r-mid*. This replacement saves SIMD registers while cache references are increased. In order to keep the Neon units busy and decrease stalls in the pipeline, it is necessary to feed the required data as fast as possible. And the number of SIMD registers is limited on the ARM processor, we can utilize the saved registers and spare cycles to achieve higher parallelism.

4.2 Optimizing 3 × 3 Convolution

As Fig. 4 shows, there are two kinds of combinations of the 4-MLA group.

1. combination of *r-left* and *r-right*, generates one row of output.
2. *r-mid* generates two rows of output.

r-mid is the last row of the 3 × 3 sliding window at first and the second row of the window when the sliding starts from the second row. So it can be used to calculate two rows of the output once loaded into a SIMD register. This strategy is adopt by ncnn and increases reuse of data when calculating convolutions.

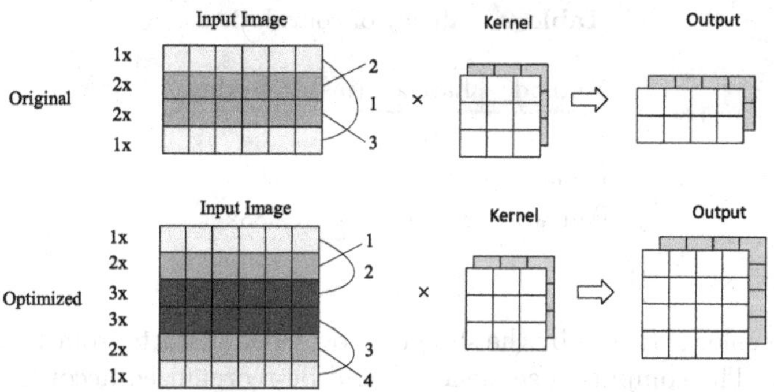

Fig. 5. 4 × 6 tiling and 6 × 6 tiling.

The target of data reusing is reducing cache misses. Cache misses would cause many stalls in a pipeline so the access order need to be reasonable. Similarly, intermediate rows of *r-left* and *r-right* can also be reused to calculate results of two positions.

The input map is divided into many 4×6 tiles in ncnn as presented in Fig. 4. The tiling strategy is proved to have good effect when calculate 3×3 convolutions. First, it reduces overhead of load and store. Secondly, the 4-MLA instructions group fills up the pipeline so the computing efficiency is improved. Eventually, this tiling strategy increases reusing of input data. As shown in Fig. 5, we replace the 4×6 tile with a 6×6 tile. A 4×6 tile generates a 2×4 output in each iteration, and a 6×6 tile generate a 4×4 output each time. The 6×6 tile is equivalent to a 3×3 kernel slides four steps on row direction and four steps on the column direction.

In the original process in ncnn, six SIMD registers store two channels of kernel's weights. Four registers store outputs of two channels and four registers store input feature map. Fourteen registers are used frequently during this process. In our implementation, all 16 SIMD registers join the computing. 6 SIMD registers store the output, 2 SIMD registers store weights of kernel, and the rest 8 SIMD registers are used to store elements of input map. The output is 4×4 so 6 registers are not enough. It is unnecessary to always store the results in the registers. Once all calculations of one row are completed, the results can be stored to the memory. For example, in the 6×6 solution, the calculating of 5th row is not start when results of first row are all calculated. Therefore, we can store results of first row to the memory and two registers are emptied for the rest computations. Then 6 SIMD registers are able to store 8 rows by using this method. SIMD registers are always scarce on an ARM processor. In our implementation, we load the input map more frequent because more rows would be calculated.

It is apparent in Fig. 5 that more data reusing is implemented by using our method. The original 4×6 method reuse the intermediate input rows at most 2 times. Our 6×6 method reuses the intermediate input rows at most 3 times.

Table 2. Latency of convolutions

Method	Latency (ms)	Speedup
gcc	301.4	-
ncnn	114.8	2.62x
Our work	104.6	2.88x

Rows in red color is reused by the slide window when it starts from 1st to 3rd row respectively. The computing sequence should be reorganized according to times of reusing. Because if one row is reused for multiple times, it should be stay in a SIMD register once loaded from cache. However, if one row is only used for one time, such as 1st and $6th$ row in the tile, it would be overwritten by next row once the result is calculated. Therefore, the computing sequence is rearranged to make time for load of input rows. The input rows in the tile is divided into four combinations as Fig. 5 shows. For convenience, we name a row being reused for one time as 1x row, and reused for two times as 2x row. We combine a 1x row with a 3x row, and 2x rows are combined by oneself. Combining of 1x row and 3x row helps make enough time for load operations. Because 3x row is reused for three times and the saved load cycles can be used to load a 1x row.

The 6×6 tiling method is implemented with 16 SIMD registers by exploiting pipelining strategies described in Sect. 4.1, and it reduces number of iterations and increases reuse of input data significantly.

5 Experimental Results

5.1 Experimental Settings

The experiments are based on a Firefly RK3288 development board. The processor of RK3288 is based on ARM Cortex-A17 architecture, which has 4 cores and 1.8 GHz frequency. The operation system is ubuntu 14.04 and the compiler is gcc-arm-linux-gnueabihf 4.9.4. We use inline assembly codes to implement proposed optimizing methods.

5.2 Latency of 3 × 3 Convolution

We measured the convolution programs on RK3288. Size of input map is $1 \times 32 \times 114 \times 114$, and size of output is $1 \times 64 \times 112 \times 112$. The kernel size is 3×3. We use $perf$ tool to measure the effect of our proposed method. *Perf* is a profiling tool that can generate performance information of CPU by reading the performance monitoring unit (PMU) on the ARM processor.

Table 2 shows the latency of three methods, including unoptimized codes that are compiled by gcc, ncnn inferencing framework, and our proposed optimizing method. The unoptimized does not exploit instruction level parallelism (ILP), and ncnn and our method use Neon instructions to implement SIMD.

Table 3. CPU information when calculating

Method	Cycles	Instructions	CPI	Cache references	Miss rate
gcc	482495936	590878144	0.82	258286384	0.0099
ncnn	181076240	118399144	1.53	73678160	0.0362
Our work	161192736	135627568	1.19	100844032	0.0277

Table 4. Latency of convolutions using openMP

Method	Thread = 2		Thread = 4	
	Latency (ms)	Speedup	Latency (ms)	Speedup
gcc	146.6	-	117.9	-
ncnn	54.7	2.68x	46.6	2.53x
Our work	50.6	2.90x	44.4	2.65x

The speedup of our method is 2.88 times compared with the gcc version. And it is faster than ncnn, the improvement is around 8.8%.

Table 3 shows information of the CPU when executing these three programs. It can be found that cycles of our method is less than ncnn. Because we replaced VEXT instruction with VLD instruction, VLD requires one cycle but VEXT requires two. And it is also the reason why cache references are increased. In addition, we exploited 6×6 tiling method and there are less iterations in our codes. In order to load $r - mid$ elements by using VLD instruction, the address of $r - mid$ should have been calculated. So increased instructions are ADD instructions which are executed independent of load/store instructions and Neon instructions. The CPI is reduced significantly because there are less stalls in the pipeline. Moreover, more reusing of input map reduced cache miss rate compared with ncnn.

We also measured latency of the convolutions when openMP is used. OpenMP supports multi-thread processing and two different numbers of threads are measured in our implementations. When the number of thread is 4, improvement of our optimizing method is not very apparent compared with ncnn, the speed is just 4.7% higher than ncnn. But when thread number is 2, the improvement achieves 7.5% in the same case. Because L2 cache are shared by 4 cores on A17 [17], the speed of L2 cache becomes the bottleneck when the number of threads increases. Extra overhead of memory access reduces the improvement. It can be found in Table 4 that the speedup of ncnn is also decreased compared with the single-thread version. The speedup of 4-thread case is 6.8 compared with the single-thread gcc version.

6 Conclusion

In this paper, we exploit a pipelining strategy to accelerate convolution computations based on an ARM platform. In order to increase data reuse, we use a

6×6 tiling method. One input row can be reused at most three times when calculating. The proposed method has significant effect on our CPU, the speedup is 2.88 compared with the codes compiled by gcc, and it is faster than the inference framework ncnn. The speedup of multi-thread processing implemented by openMP achieves 6.8 compared with the single-thread codes that compiled by gcc.

Our future work will focus on accelerating convolutions on armv8-based processors, which have higher performance than armv7-based CPUs. Optimizing methods for 8-bit integer numbers will also be considered.

Acknowledgment. This paper is supported by the National Key Research and Development Program of China (Grant No. 2018YFB1003405) and the National Natural Science Foundation of China (Grant No. 61802419).

References

1. Liu, Z., Chow, P., Xu, J., Jiang, J., Dou, Y., Zhou, J.: A uniform architecture design for accelerating 2D and 3D CNNS on FPGAs. Electronics **8**(1), 65 (2019)
2. Qiao, Y., Shen, J., Xiao, T., Yang, Q., Wen, M., Zhang, C.: FPGA-accelerated deep convolutional neural networks for high throughput and energy efficiency. Concurrency Comput.: Practice Exp. **29**(20), e3850 (2017)
3. Dongarra, J.J., Cruz, J.D., Hammarling, S., Duff, I.S.: Algorithm 679: a set of level 3 basic linear algebra subprograms: model implementation and test programs. ACM Trans. Math. Softw. (TOMS) **16**(1), 18–28 (1990)
4. Winograd, S.: Arithmetic Complexity of Computations, vol. 33. SIAM, Philadelphia (1980)
5. Lavin, A., Gray, S.: Fast algorithms for convolutional neural networks. In: Proceedings of the IEEE Conference on Computer Vision and Pattern Recognition, pp. 4013–4021 (2016)
6. Arm compute library. https://github.com/ARM-software/ComputeLibrary
7. Tengine. https://github.com/OAID/Tengine
8. Chetlur, S., et al.: cuDNN: Efficient primitives for deep learning. arXiv preprint arXiv:1410.0759 (2014)
9. Mkl-dnn. https://github.com/intel/mkl-dnn
10. Ncnn: a high-performance neural network inference framework optimized for the mobile platform. https://github.com/Tencent/ncnn
11. Krizhevsky, A., Sutskever, I., Hinton, G.E.: Imagenet classification with deep convolutional neural networks. In: International Conference on Neural Information Processing Systems (2012)
12. Szegedy, C., et al.: Going deeper with convolutions (2014)
13. Simonyan, K., Zisserman, A.: Very deep convolutional networks for large-scale image recognition. arXiv preprint arXiv:1409.1556 (2014)
14. Howard, A.G., et al.: Mobilenets: efficient convolutional neural networks for mobile vision applications (2017)
15. Patterson, D.A.: Computer Architecture: A Quantitative Approach (2008)
16. Cortex, A.: A8 technical reference manual. Revision: r3p2, p. 64, May 2010
17. Cortex, A.: Arm Cortex-A17 MPCore processor. Revision: r1p1, September 2014

Prediction Model of Suspect Number Based on Deep Learning

Chuyue Zhang, Manchun Cai(✉), Xiaofan Zhao(✉), Luzhe Cao, and Dawei Wang

People's Public Security University of China, Beijing, China
caimanchun@ppsuc.edu.cn

Abstract. With the development of public security informatization, crime prediction has become an important tool for public security organs to carry out accurate attacks and effective governance. In this paper, we propose an algorithm to predict the number of suspects through the feature modeling of historical data. We use Deep Neural Networks (DNN) and machine learning algorithms to extract features of different dimensions of case data. We also use Convolutional Neural Networks (CNN) to extract the text features of case description. These two types of features are combined and fed into fully connected layer and softmax layer. Compared with the DNN model which only uses numeric data, the DNN-CNN model combined with text data has improved the precision rate by 20%. The addition of text data significantly improves the precision and recall rate of prediction. To the best of our knowledge, it is the first time to combine numerical and textual data of case information in crime prediction.

Keywords: Crime prediction · Deep learning · Feature selection

1 Introduction

At present, big data and artificial intelligence have become national strategies. Informationization revolution is fast and steady. The informationization of public security is also in full swing. Crime prediction provides assistance for crime prevention, public security prevention and control, case detection and police decision-making and has become a hot research topic nowadays. More than 25% of the criminal suspects prosecuted by prosecutors were burglars, ranking first [1]. The occurrence rate and quantity of theft crime is high. It causes the state, the collective and the citizen's individual property to suffer heavy loss.

Nowadays, the detection of theft crimes relies on traditional detection ideas and police experience. However, the police experience has limitations, subjectivity and one-sidedness. In this paper, we use the deep learning algorithm to predict the number of thieves through historical data. When a new crime occurs, it can provide the police with a prediction of the number of people involved in the crime.

This work is supported by National Key R&D Program Project (Grant No. 2018YFC0809802), the Fundamental Research Funds for the Central Universities (Grant No. 2018JKF609), Specialized Research Fund of Higher Education of China (Grant No. 2019ssky012).

H. Shen and Y. Sang (Eds.): PAAP 2019, CCIS 1163, pp. 531–540, 2020.
https://doi.org/10.1007/978-981-15-2767-8_46

2 Related Works

Crime prediction has gone through a process from qualitative to quantitative, from simple to complex. The qualitative research of crime prediction includes Delphi method, correlation factor analysis and so on. According to the different object scope, the quantitative research of crime prediction can be divided into two aspects: macro prediction of crime and micro prediction of crime. Macro prediction of crime mainly reveals the dynamic regularity of crime phenomenon in terms of quality and quantity. It is primarily a broad and comprehensive forecast of the number of long-term crimes. Predicting the number of crimes based on historical crime data and Geographic Information System data. Methods include grey model, markov chain, association rule mining [2], Support Vector Machine, hybrid model of Long Short-Term Memory and Spatial-Temporal Auto Regressive and Moving Average [3] etc. It is applied in the service command of prevention and control patrol. Micro-prediction is mainly the prediction of individual behaviors and attributes under certain space-time conditions. It is applied to the key personnel of the crime risk analysis, auxiliary case detection, suspects features identification. For example, based on criminal population conviction histories of recent offenders, Tollenaar and van der Heijden [4] use statistical method to predicate general recidivism, violent recidivism and sexual recidivism. Based on the case information and victim information, Li, Sun and Ji [5] use Support Vector Machine algorithm to predict the suspect's gender, age, race, etc. Based on date and location, crime type, criminal ID and the acquaintances, Vural and Gök [6] use Naive Bayesian Model to predict criminal of particular crime incident. Based on the features of criminals in criminal case, Sun, Cao and Xiao [7] uses random forest model to predict possible suspects. But some of the input data in these studies is only known after solving the case, such as suspect age, criminal history, acquaintances, etc. In most cases, the identity of the suspect is unknown after the theft. In this paper, we only use case information to predict the number of suspects.

This paper focuses on the micro-prediction of individual behavior. Extract case features such as the time of the case, loss amount, method, places and so on, and covert them to discrete values. For numerical features, machine learning methods are used to rank and delete the features with lower contribution. After feature selection, Deep Neural Networks (DNN) algorithm is used for feature processing. Some information may be lost if only discrete numerical values are used to represent case information. Therefore, text information of case description is added. We use the natural language processing method to extract the case information in the text and combine them to predict the number of suspects. When a new case occurs, the model can provide investigators with a prediction of the number of suspects.

3 Data Preprocessing

Statistics show that about 90% of the total number of thefts are "pickpocketing", "theft of property in the car", "household theft" and "theft of non-motor vehicles". In this paper, we selected more than 20,000 cases of "pickpocketing", "theft of property in vehicles", "housebreaking" and "theft of non-motor vehicles" detected in X city as experimental data. The case category is numerically coded in this paper. That is 1, 2, 3, 4 code for "pickpocketing", "theft of property in the car", "household theft", "theft of non-motor vehicles" respectively.

3.1 Time Data Processing

According to different time scales, the time information extracted in this paper includes year, quarter, month, ten days, day, week and time period. The data processing rules of time period are shown in Table 1:

Table 1. The data processing rules of time period.

Label	Time (24 h)	Note
1	0:00–8:00	Including 8:00
2	8:00–12:00	Including 12:00
3	12:00–14:00	Including 14:00
4	14:00–18:00	Including 18:00
5	18:00–22:00	Including 22:00
6	22:00–24:00	Including 24:00

3.2 Location Data Processing

In the criminal case information system, the location of the crime is recorded as the longitude and latitude of the place and the location name of crime. By the location name of the crime, the region of the crime and the place of the crime can be obtained. The region where the case occurs is the administrative division of the place. In the data set of this paper, X city is divided into 16 administrative districts. Therefore, this paper encodes the districts 1–16. There are more than 90 original categories of places involved, such as subway stations, shopping malls, Internet cafes, hotels and so on. According to the police's individual experience, this paper divides the places involved into four categories, namely residential, traffic area, office area and entertainment area. The data processing rules of places are shown in Table 2:

Table 2. The data processing rules of places

Label	Categories	Instructions
1	Residential	Residence, dormitory
2	Traffic area	Subway station, bus, roadside, expressway, etc.
3	Office area	Schools, hospitals, parking lots, offices, etc.
4	Entertainment area	Shopping malls, vegetable markets, street shops, catering places, Internet cafes and so on

3.3 Method Data Processing

The method of theft refers to the method used by thieves when they steal, such as technical method unlocking, climbing over walls, smashing glass, etc. Considering the different crime experience of different types of suspects, the methods may be different. This paper divides the theft methods into 12 categories. The data processing rules of methods are shown in Table 3.

Table 3. The data processing rules of methods

Label	Categories	Instructions
1	Others	Stolen goods from trucks, Unarmed climbing, Decoy
2	Pickpocketing	Pickpocketing, By the way to steal
3	Technical unlock	Insert card unlock, Poke the lock, Tin foil unlock, Technical unlock
4	From the window to enter	Break Windows, Break glass
5	From the roof to enter	From the roof, From the vent
6	From the wall to enter	Climb over the wall, Break walls
7	From the door to enter (Door damage)	Expand seam, Destroy anti-theft net (column), Destroy the door body
8	From the door to enter (No damage to the door)	Deceive into the door, Follow others into the door
9	Violence unlocked	Break the lock core, Pliers cut the lock, Break the lock
10	Violence hit the car	Smashing car windows, Pry the trunk of the car
11	Theft through the window	Get the key through the window with a pole, Open the window and steal
12	Stolen vehicle	Towing, dragged, Traction

3.4 Loss Amount Data Processing

The amount of damage is the value of the stolen goods. It has the best effect by comparing min-max normalization, zero-mean normalization and feature normalization of loss amount. Therefore, this paper uses the feature encoding method to process the loss amount data. We take 1/4, median and 3/4 of the loss amount as the dividing point and divide the loss amount into four categories. The data processing rules for loss amount are shown in Table 4.

Table 4. The data processing rules of loss amount.

Label	Money (RMB)	Note
1	0–900	Including 900
2	900–1880	Including 1880
3	1880–3600	Including 3600
4	3600–1000000	More than 3600

3.5 Weather Data Processing

In order to consider all kinds of factors when the case happened, the data of day weather, night weather, day temperature, night temperature, day wind and night wind were added in this paper. For day temperature, night temperature, day wind, and night wind, we extract their values by regularization. For the text description information of daytime weather and night weather, this paper uses keyword matching method, and the data processing rules for weather are shown in Table 5.

Table 5. The data processing rules of weather.

Weather	Sunny	Rain or snow	Others
Daytime weather	1	2	3
Night weather	1	2	3

4 Model Building

4.1 Feature Selection

In numerical data, this paper describes the case from 20 dimensions. If the information in the data is irrelevant or noisy, the prediction results will be affected. In this paper, the random forest classification (RFC) and Linear Regression recursive feature elimination (LR_RFE) are used to calculate the feature contribution and filter the variables so as to optimize the prediction model. The processing of numeric data is shown in Fig. 1.

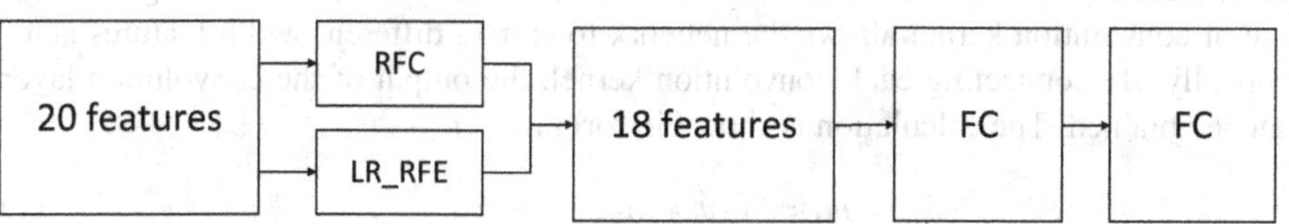

Fig. 1. Model flow for numeric data

4.1.1 Feature Ranking of Random Forest

Random forest is an integrated learning algorithm based on decision tree. It has good effect on classification and regression. In this paper, the grid search method is used to find the optimal solution of random forest parameters and return the contribution ranking of each feature. The experimental results show that the optimal parameters of grid search are criterion = 'gini', max_depth = 50, min_samples_leaf = 2, min_weight_fraction_leaf = 0.0 and n_estimators = 1000. Under the current parameter setting, the least contributing feature is night temperature.

4.1.2 Feature Ranking of Recursive Feature Elimination

Recursive feature elimination (RFE) is used in this paper to train Linear Regression in several rounds. After each round of training, the feature with low weight coefficient is removed, and the next round of training is carried out based on the new feature set until the remaining feature number reaches the required feature number. In this algorithm, the least contributing feature is night temperature.

By deleting the feature with the lowest contribution in the above two algorithms, this paper describes the case through 18 dimensions. They are Longitude, Case classification, Latitude, Quarter, Places, Loss amount, Years, Months, Methods, Days, Daytime wind, Ten days, Regions, Time period, Night weather, Night wind, Daytime weather and Week.

4.2 Text Data Model Construction

This paper uses 18 characteristics to describe case information. DNN algorithm is used to further explore the relationship. However, the data after numerical dispersion is easy to cause the loss of features. For example, the name, type and victim information of the stolen item cannot be represented. Therefore, the text description information of the case is added in this paper.

Brief case is a simple description of the case, ranging from 5 to 150 words. After transforming text information into word vectors, the feature is extracted by using convolution neural network algorithm [8]. CNN has two main operations: convolution and pooling. Convolution focuses on local features. Each hidden layer node only connects to an input point that is small enough, instead of connecting to every input point. At the same time, the weights of some neurons in the same layer are shared, which can greatly reduce the weight parameters that need to be trained.

The convolution layer uses multiple n*h convolution kernel (n is the dimension of the embedding vector, h is the dimension of the filter's window size). Using different size of convolution kernel allows the network to extract different width features automatically. By connecting each convolution kernel, the output of the convolution layer can be obtained. The calculation is shown in formula (1).

$$m_i = f(w * x_{i:i+h-1} + b) \tag{1}$$

m_i represents the i-th feature of the convolution operation, f represents the activation function. w represents the weight of a filter. It performs a convolution operation on the input feature x whose window size is h, and get a new feature. The output features of the convolution layer are obtained by connecting all the features obtained above. The calculation is shown in formula (2).

$$M = [m_1, m_2, \ldots, m_{l-h+1}] \tag{2}$$

l represents the input length. The max-pooling used in this model is to take the maximum value for each vector of the convolutional layer output. The calculation is shown in formula (3).

$$z = \max\{M\} \tag{3}$$

z represents the output of max-pooling. By connecting all the maximum pooling results, the output of the pooling layer Z is obtained. k represents the number of convolution kernel.

$$Z = [z_i, z_2, \ldots z_k] \tag{4}$$

The model in this paper uses convolution kernel size of 2, 3 and 4 to acquire features of different widths, and then putting into max-pooling layer. After that, the full connection layer is added. The text data model structure is shown in Fig. 2.

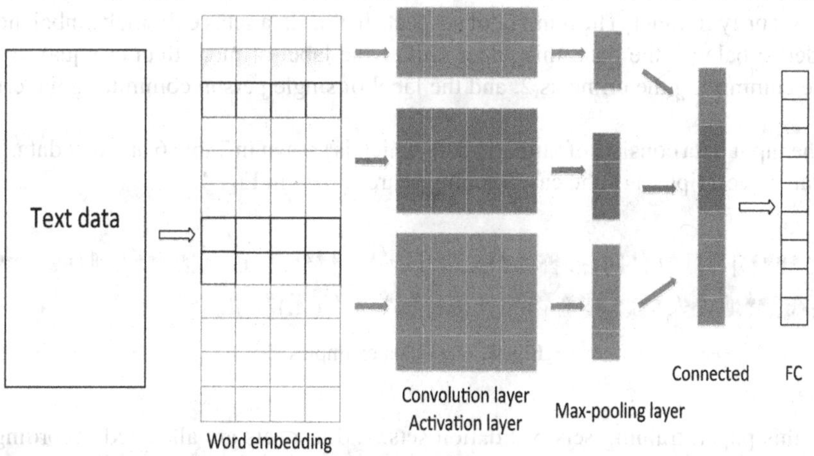

Fig. 2. Text data model structure

4.3 Model Construction

In this paper, numerical features processed by deep neural network and text features processed by convolutional neural network are combined and input into the full connection layer. Finally, classification tasks are completed through softmax layer. The model structure is shown in Fig. 3.

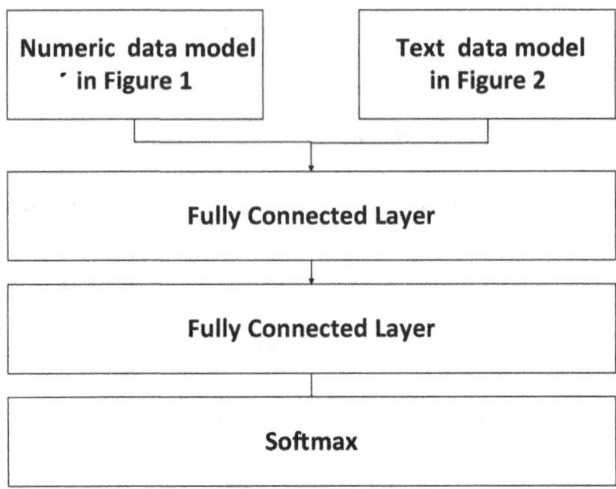

Fig. 3. Model structure

5 Experimental Results and Analysis

5.1 The Experimental Data

The data sets used in this paper are all from the criminal case information system of public security Intranet. The number of suspects in this data set is extremely unbalanced. In order to balance the data, this paper unifies the label of more than or equal to two people committing the crime as 2, and the label of single person committing the crime as 1.

The input data consists of numeric data which is shown in Table 6 and text data. The text data is description of the case, examples are shown in Fig. 4.

****年*月*日*时,报警人***,身份证号*****,联系电话****,现住址****,称其在***地丢失****,被盗物品预估价值***,有(无)发票。

Fig. 4. Text data examples

In this paper, training sets, validation sets, and test sets are allocated according to the ratio of 7:2:1. The optimal model is determined by training set and cross validation set. The precision rate, recall rate, and F value of the test set are calculated as model evaluation.

5.2 DNN Parameter Setting

This paper uses the grid search method to adjust and optimize the parameters in DNN network. Parameter value optimal parameter values in 3-layer DNN network are shown in Table 6.

Table 6. Parameter value and optimal parameter value

Parameter	Parameter value	Optimal parameter value
batch_size	16, 32, 64, 128	64
epochs	10, 20, 30, 40, 50	10
init_mode	'he_normal', 'he_uniform', 'glorot_normal', 'glorot_uniform', 'lecun_normal'	'glorot_normal'
learning_rate	0.001, 0.01, 0.0001	0.001
momentum	0.0, 0.2, 0.4	0.2
activation	'relu', 'tanh', 'softmax', 'linear', 'hard_sigmoid', 'softplus', 'selu'	tanh
dropout	0.0, 0.1, 0.2, 0.3, 0.4, 0.5	0

5.3 Experimental Results and Analysis

Two comparative experiments are designed in this paper. One is an algorithm without text data, and the other is an algorithm with text data but only one convolution size in CNN. The experimental results are shown in Table 7.

The experimental results are analyzed as follows:

(1) How to convert case information into values is the most important part of this paper. The experimental results show that it is feasible to convert the case information into the corresponding value according to the method presented in this paper. By modeling the features of the case data, good results can be achieved.
(2) Through feature modeling, case information can be described with numerical data, but the information description is incomplete. The accurate in predicting the number of people who committed the crime is 71%. There is still room for improvement.
(3) After adding text information, the precision rate and recall rate of the algorithm has been greatly improved. Especially in terms of precision rate, it has increased by 20%. In the experimental results, the precision rate and recall rate are relatively balanced, which indicates that the model is good at predicting the number of suspects.
(4) Compared to the size of a single convolution, the model that has different sizes of convolution cores is better to extract feature information.

Table 7. Experimental results

Algorithm	Precision rate	Recall rate	F-values
DNN	71	73	72
DNN-CNN (filter size = 3)	90	90	90
DNN-CNN (filter size = [2, 3, 4])	91	91	91

6 Conclusion

In this paper, the number of suspects is predicted by modeling the features of real case information. As far as we know, this is the first time to combine the numerical and textual features of the case information. In terms of experimental results, this model has a better effect, with 91% precision and recall rate. When new cases occur, it can provide the police with more reliable prediction results. This model has a strong practical significance.

In terms of text data processing, how to use natural language processing algorithm to minimize text information in a deeper level is the next step of research. In addition, the application of this model in predicting other characteristics of suspects can be further explored. For example, suspect age, suspect domicile place.

References

1. Jin, G., Zhu, S., Lin, X.: Analysis and prediction of criminal situation in China (2017–2018). J. Chin. People's Public Secur. Univ. (Soc. Sci. Ed.) **2**(5), 99–110 (2016)
2. Asmai, S.A., Roslin, N.I.A., Abdullah, R.W., et al.: Predictive crime mapping model using association rule mining for crime analysis. Sci. Int. **26**, 1703–1706 (2014)
3. Liu, M., Lu, T.: A hybrid model of crime prediction. J. Phys: Conf. Ser. **1168**(3), 032031 (2019). https://doi.org/10.1088/1742-6596/1168/3/032031
4. Tollenaar, N., van der Heijden, P.G.M.: Which method predicts recidivism best: a comparison of statistical, machine learning and data mining predictive models. J. Roy. Stat. Soc. **176**(2), 565–584 (2013)
5. Li, R., Sun, C., Ji, J.: Suspect characteristics prediction based on support vector machine. Comput. Eng. **43**(11), 198–203 (2017)
6. Vural, M.S., Gök, M.: Criminal prediction using Naive Bayes theory. Neural Comput. Appl. **28**(9), 2581–2592 (2017)
7. Sun, F., Cao, Z., Xiao, X.: Application of an improved random forest based classifier in crime prediction domain. J. Intell. **33**(10), 148–152 (2014)
8. Kim, Y.: Convolutional neural networks for sentence classification. Eprint Arxiv (2014)

A Sequence-to-Sequence Transformer Premised Temporal Convolutional Network for Chinese Word Segmentation

Wei Jiang, Yuan Wang, and Yan Tang(✉)

School of Computer and Information Science, Southwest University, No. 2, Tiansheng Road, Chongqing, China
jw2312@email.swu.edu.cn, 645763395@qq.com, ytang@swu.edu.cn

Abstract. The prevalent approaches for the task of Chinese word segmentation almost rely on the Bi-LSTM neural network. However, the methods based the Bi-LSTM have an inherent drawback: the Vanishing Gradients, which cause the little efficient in capturing the faraway character information of a long sentence for the task of word segmentation. In this work, we propose a novel sequence-to-sequence transformer model for Chinese word segmentation, which is premised a type of convolutional neural network named temporal convolutional network. The model uses the temporal convolutional network to construct an encoder, and uses a fully-connected neural network to build a decoder, and applies the Viterbi algorithm to build an inference layer to infer the final result of the Chinese word segmentation. Meanwhile, the model captures the faraway character information of a long sentence by adding the layers of the encoder. For achieving a superior result of word segmentation, the model binds the Conditional Random Fields model to train parameters. The experiments on the Chinese corpus show that the performance of Chinese word segmentation of the model is better than the Bi-LSTM model, and the model has a better ability to process a long sentence than the Bi-LSTM.

Keywords: Natural Language Processing · Chinese word segmentation · Temporal convolutional network · Transformer model

1 Introduction

Chinese word segmentation (CWS) is a preliminary task for Natural Language Processing (NLP) of Chinese. The CWS has regarded as a sequence labeling problem since Xue [21]. Previous research of the CWS focussed on statistical methods based on supervised machine learning algorithms, such as Maximum Entropy [3] and Conditional Random Fields [13]. However, those methods heavily depend on the selecting of handcrafted features.

Recently, the neural network models have widely adhered to solving the NLP tasks for their ability to minimize the effort in feature engineering. The

H. Shen and Y. Sang (Eds.): PAAP 2019, CCIS 1163, pp. 541–552, 2020.
https://doi.org/10.1007/978-981-15-2767-8_47

research attention in the CWS has shifted to deep-learning [4–6,16,18,22,23]. Deep-learning practitioners commonly regard the recurrent architectures as a default starting point for sequence modeling tasks. Chen built a recurrent neural network (RNN) for the CWS and applied Long short-term memory (LSTM) as the cell operator of the RNN [5]. Cai employed gate combination neural network and LSTM to establish a word-based model of the CWS [4]. Ma Proposed a relatively simple and efficient model by stacking forward and backward LSTM cell chains, which is one of the best models based the Bi-LSTM for the CWS [16].

However, the models based on the Bi-LSTM have an inherent drawback: the Vanishing Gradients. The Vanishing Gradients means that the gradient values of the recurrent neural network parameters go to zero when the network propagates the gradients of faraway words or characters in corpora. While the Bi-LSTM is an updated recurrent neural network and can relieve this problem, it is not the solution to entirely solve the problem. For the word segmentation task, the Bi-LSTM is little efficient in capturing the faraway character information of a long sentence. Contrasted the Bi-LSTM, Convolutional Neural Network (CNN) has more advantages in parallel computing and extraction of features.

It is difficult that using the traditional convolutional neural network builds a sequence model. For language modeling task, the extraction of the information of context is a key obstacle in the traditional convolutional neural network. Kim used CNN to extract features from character-based embeddings and concatenate the features as the input of the LSTM neural network that is used to predict the next word in a sentence [11]. Gehring proposed an architecture composed of an encoder and a decoder for machine translation that the encoder was a primitive temporal convolutional network [8,9]. Bai proposed a generic temporal convolutional network architecture for numerous tasks, which is a systematical description of the temporal convolutional network firstly [2]. However, The temporal convolutional network that Bai proposed is weak to the tasks of language modeling.

In this paper, we propose a sequence-to-sequence transformer model for the task of Chinese word segmentation. The base of the model is the temporal convolutional network, which derives from Bai's model. The model uses the temporal convolutional network to construct an encoder and uses a fully-connected neural network to build a decoder. Meanwhile, the model captures the faraway character information of a long sentence by adding the layers of the encoder. The most key points are that the model binds the Conditional Random Fields model to train parameters, and the model uses the Viterbi algorithm to build an inference layer to infer the final result of the task of Chinese word segmentation.

In summary, the contributions of this paper are concluded as follows:

- We construct a novel transformer model for the task of Chinese word segmentation and achieve the outstanding result comparing to the Bi-LSTM model.

- We introduce the Conditional Random Fields and the Viterbi algorithm to our model. It mends the shortcoming of Bai's model in the task of Chinese word segmentation. The shortcoming is that ignores the correlation of segmentation labels of successive characters. Comparing to Bai's model, our model achieves a tremendous growth in the performance of the task of Chinese word segmentation.

2 The Transformer Model

Chinese word segmentation task is usually regarded as a sequence labeling task. Specifically, each character in a Chinese sentence is classified as a segmentation label of $L = \{B, M, E, S\}$, B indicating the begin site of a word, M indicating the middle site of a word, E indicating the end site of a word, and S indicating the words with a character. A sentence with m characters can be described as $X = \{x_1, x_2, \ldots, x_m\}$. The aim of the CWS is to figure out the labels of the characters that can be described as $Y = \{y_1, y_2, \ldots, y_t, \ldots, y_m\}, y_t \in L, t = 1, 2, \ldots, m$.

The transformer model that we propose, as shown in Fig. 1, consists of the embedding layer, the encoder, the decoder, and the inference layer. The embedding layer has a responsibility to convert original characters to pre-trained embedding vectors. The encoder is composed of numerous temporal convolution layers. A temporal convolution layer has three operations to each vector inputting to the layer. The operations are **dilated convolution**, **convolutional blocks**, and **residual connection**. The dilated convolution captures a receptive field of input vectors and offers the vectors in the field to the convolutional blocks. Both the result of the convolutional blocks and the original input vector of the layer are inputted to the residual connection so that the residual connection generates a final output vector of the layer. The result of the residual connection is served as the input of the next temporal convolution layer or the decoder. All temporal convolution layers are stacked to construct a temporal convolutional network, which is the encoder. The decoder transforms the vectors that are produced by the encoder to 4-dimensions vectors where each vector indicates the probability distribution of the segmentation labels.

In common, the segmentation label of a character has an impact on the labels of the character's adjacent characters. This situation is called as the **correlation**. For example, the label of the first character of a word is B so that the label of the next character of the word has a tremendous probability equivalent to M or E. When we train the parameters of the transformer model, we combine the Conditional Random Fields to the model so that the model has a sensitivity to the relevance of segmentation labels of successive characters. In the inference layer, a vector of the 4-dimensions vectors that are produced by the decoder is applied to infer the segmentation label of the character by the Viterbi algorithm so that the final segmentation labels have a sensitivity to the correlation.

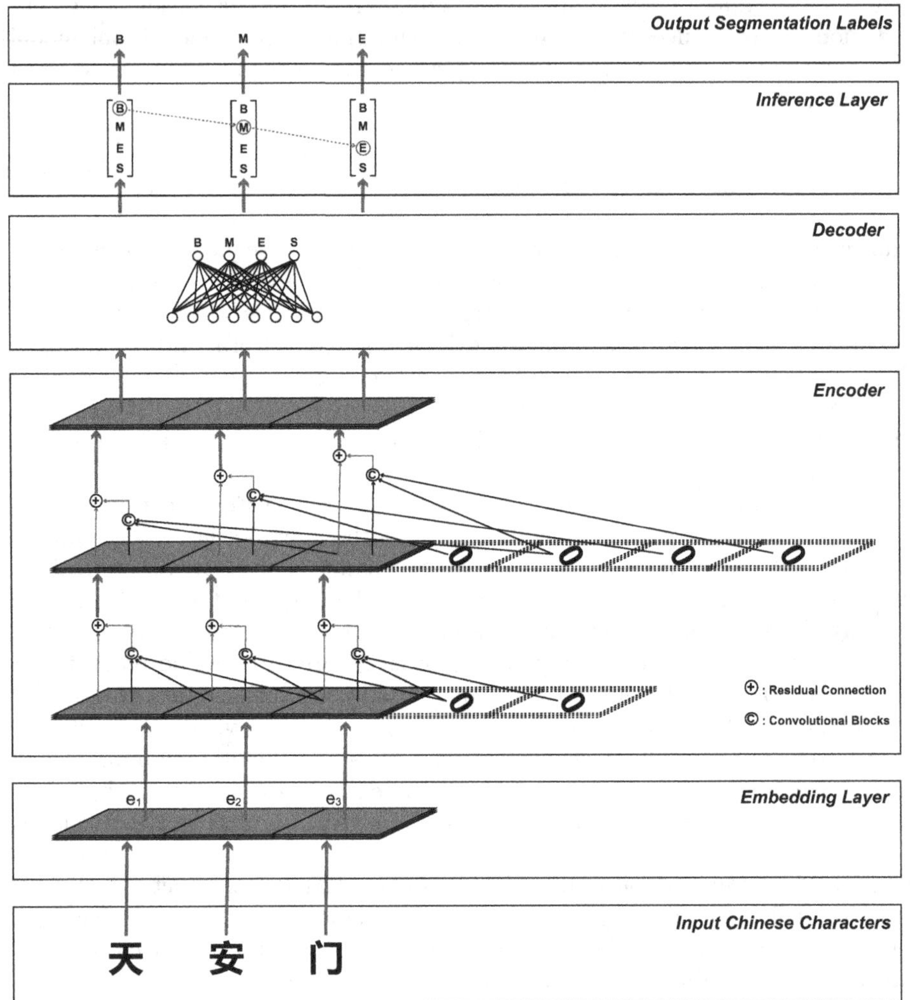

Fig. 1. The architecture of seq-to-seq transformer model. For example, inputting a Chinese sentence with three characters to the model, every character is converted to an embedding vector in the embedding layer. The encoder transforms these vectors to encoded vectors by the dilated convolution where the dilation factors are set as $d = 0, 1$. The dimension of an encoded vector are equivalent to an embedding vector. The decoder transforms the encoded vectors to decoded vectors. A decoded vector, which is bound to a character, has 4 dimensions and a dimension is a probability of a word segmentation label. The inference layer applies the Viterbi algorithm to infer final labels of the sentence from the decoded vectors.

2.1 Embedding Layer

In neural models, the first step usually is to map discrete language symbols to distributed embedding vectors. For generating the pre-trained embedding vectors, We apply **wang2vec**[1] to pre-train the character-based embedding vectors [15]. Formally, The pre-trained embedding vectors can be described as $E = \{e_1, e_2, \ldots, e_t, \ldots, e_m\}, e_t \in R^n$, n indicating the dimension of a pre-trained embedding vector, and R indicating the set of Real numbers. In our model, the dimension of a pre-trained embedding vector is set as 100.

2.2 Dilated Convolution

The convolution neural network has two essential concepts: receptive field and convolution filter. In our model, A receptive field is a set of input vectors that are produced by the previous temporal convolution layer or the embedding layer. A convolution filter, or kernel, is a convolutional operator with independent parameters and has the sliding mechanism from left to right of a Chinese sentence to travel each character. The dilated convolution captures the vectors that a receptive field needs. Formally, for a sentence X inputting to the model, the vectors are described as a set of $v_{t+d \cdot i}$, t indicating the index of the vector that is processing by a convolution filter and corresponding to the index of the character. d means the dilation factor that indicates the interval between two vectors of a receptive field. The dilation factors of temporal layers are exponents of 2 except the first layer of the encoder, but the power of the exponents is incremental. The dilation factor of the first layer is 0. i indicating an index of the receptive field.

The dilated convolution causes that a receptive field cannot gain sufficient vectors when the filter slides to the rear of the input sequence. So, it is necessary for adding zero-padding blocks to the tail of the input. A zero-padding block has the same dimensions as an input vector and the value at each dimension is zero. As the layers of the encoder adding, the transformer model can capture the character information at the distant site of a long sentence by the dilated convolution.

2.3 Convolutional Blocks

A convolutional block is a concatenation of three transformations for the vectors in a receptive field. The transformations are Convolutional Operator, Layer Normalization, Dropout. Numerous convolutional blocks are stacked as an integral operation named **Convolutional Blocks**. In our model, we only stack two convolutional blocks.

The Convolutional Operator is the traditional convolutional operator of one-dimension in the CNN, which can describe as (1):

$$ReLU(w \cdot x + b) \tag{1}$$

1 https://github.com/wlin12/wang2vec.

w and b are the parameters of a convolution filter and x is a one-dimension vector. *ReLU* is the rectified linear unit that is used as the activation function [17]. The Layer Normalization is a simple normalization method to improve the training speed for various neural network models, which is proposed by Jimmy and designed to overcome the drawbacks of batch normalization [1,10]. The Dropout is a prevalent method to inhibit the Overfitting, which is used in numerous neural network language models [20].

2.4 Residual Connection

The Residual Connection is a connection way between different layers of a neural network, which was first applied in computer vision study [14,24]. Traditionally, the input of a layer of the neural network is the output of the previous layer directly. However, by the Residual Connection, The input of a layer of the neural network is the sum of the input of the previous layer and the output after all operations of the previous layer. In our model, an output of an element of a temporal convolution layer corresponding to a character is described as (2):

$$output = ReLU(ve + cblocks) \tag{2}$$

In (2), we use *ReLU* as the activation function [17], and *ve* is the output of the element at the previous layer that has the same index with the character of a sentence where a convolutional filter is processing, and *cblocks* is the output of the Convolutional Blocks for the element, and *output* is the final output for the element.

2.5 The Decoder

The decoder is composed of an input layer and an output layer. It receives an input sequence composed of the vectors that are produced by the encoder. The number of neurons of the input layer is the dimension of the input vector. The number of neurons of the output layer is 4 that indicates the four segmentation labels for the CWS. The decoder transforms a vector of the input sequence to the output vector indicating a probability distribution for the segmentation labels.

2.6 Inference Layer

The vectors that are produced by the decoder are the input of the inference layer. In common, for inferring the segmentation labels, it is a simple way to infer the labels by directly hitting the label that has the maximum probability on the vector. However, this way is not taking the interaction of two successive labels into account, which is described as the **correlation** problem. So, we use the *Viterbi algorithm* that is a dynamic programming algorithm to infer the labels.

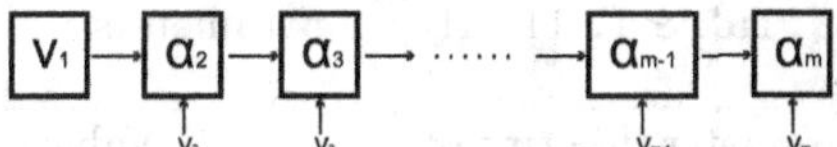

Fig. 2. The computing procedure of α. The V_1 is the vector that is produced by the decoder corresponding to the first character of an inputted sentence. The value of α_1 is set as V_1. Except α_1, the solution of the value of α_t at t step needs the V_t that is the vector corresponding to the character at t and the value of α_{t-1}. The α_m is the final result that can reflect the segmentation labels probability distribution of the whole sentence that is inputted to the model.

3 Training

We bind the Conditional Random Fields (CRF) to train the parameters of our model. The CRF is a simple and effective model for the task of sequence labeling. The idea of the CRF is that seeing adjacent labels in a sequence is dependent instead of independent. In common, the CRF has a transform matrix indicating the transfer weight of two adjacent labels and holds two paths at forward-path (from the previous character to the next) and backward-path (from next character to the previous) for an input sequence. The transform matrix is a parameter that needs to infer by the training and it is initially set from the Gaussian distribution. In our model, for simple in practice, we only consider the interaction of two successive labels at forward-path. For a training sample $(x_t, y_t)^m$ to our model, where y_t is the true label for x_t and m is the length of the sentence inputted to the model, the $\hat{Y}$, the probability for all labels, is designed as (3):

$$\hat{Y} = \frac{exp\left(\sum_{t=1}^{m} (vector_t(y_t) + \varphi(y_{t-1}, y_t))\right)}{\sum\limits_{l \in L} exp(\alpha_m(l))} \tag{3}$$

In (3), The *vector* is a vector of the vectors that are produced by the decoder, and $vector_t(y_t)$ means the probability of the true label of the character at t of an input sentence of the training set. The φ is the function indicating the probability from the label of the previous character to transfer the next one and $\varphi(y_0, y_1)$ is zero, which means that it is without the dependent relationship for the first character, and $\varphi(r, c)$ is the mapping to the transform matrix that r indicates the row of the matrix and c indicates the column of the matrix.

It is hard to sum over an exponential number of state sequences for the CRF because it requires to compute a score based on the whole sentence. The score is the sum over all possible labeling schemes. The *Forword-Backward* algorithm is a key solution to compute the score [7], where α indicates the score in the forward direction. In our model, we only compute the score at forward-path. It is an iterative procedure to compute the α value. The α value at the index t for the label l is described as (4):

$$\alpha_t(l) = vector_t(l) + log \sum_{l' \in L} exp(\alpha_{t-1}(l') + \varphi(l', l)) \tag{4}$$

Table 1. The Hyper-parameters

Parameter description	Value
Dimensions of embedding vector	100
Learn rate	0.001
Filters number	100
Hidden layers	4
Kernel size	3
Dropout rate	0.3
Dilation factors	$0, 1, 2, 4$
Stride length	1
Epochs	100
Batch size	32

The initial value of $\alpha_1(l)$ at the first character is equal to the $vector_1(l)$. The α_m means the score at the last index m, which is the final score and describes the whole sentence. The procedure to compute α is shown at Fig. 2.

We employ the Adam optimizer with $\beta_1 = 0.9$, $\beta_2 = 0.999$ and $\epsilon = 10^{-8}$ to optimize the model parameters [12], which can avoid the training plateauing early. Then, we use the cross-entropy loss to train the model, and the loss function for a sentence is designed as (5):

$$loss = -log\left(\hat{Y}\right) \tag{5}$$

4 Experiments

4.1 Datasets

We use the NLPCC2016, a shared corpus for Weibo segmentation that the data are collected from Sina Weibo, as our main dataset [19]. It is split as training data and test data. Both the training and the test are UTF-8 encoded. There are 22187 sentences in the corpus. The training data possesses 20135 sentences and the test data possesses 2052 sentences. To train our model and get a set of suitable hyper-parameters, we divide the training data into two sets, a training set and a development set. The development set contains 2000 sentences and the training set contains 18135 sentences.

4.2 Hyper-parameters

Hyper-parameters of neural network model significantly impacts its performance. The hyper-parameters of our model are shown in Table 1. For the dropout rate, it is only available in the training procedure but has no impact on the test procedure. The kernel size and the dilation rate are set by commonly configuration

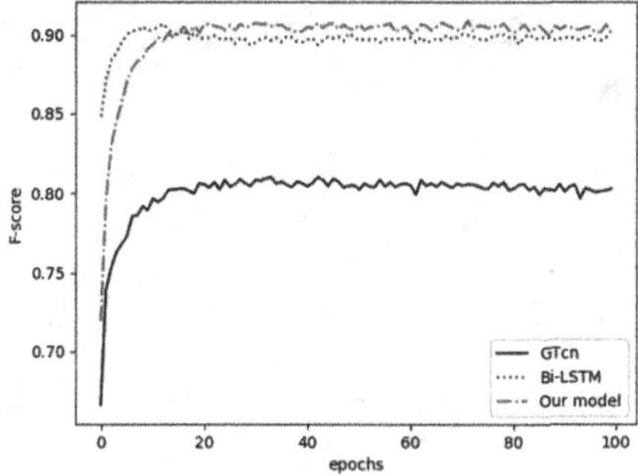

Fig. 3. The F-score values of three models at each training epoch.

Table 2. Performance comparison of three models.

Model	P	R	F
GTcn	82.50	83.28	82.89
Bi-LSTM	90.34	91.27	90.81
Our model	91.74	92.94	92.34

policy. The stride length is the stride of a convolutional filter sliding to next spot, and it is only set as 1. Other hyper-parameters are trained by hand-manipulated.

4.3 Experiment Environment and Evaluation Criteria

The hardware environment is composed of an Intel Core i5 3.2 GHz CPU with 8 GB RAM and an Nvidia GeForce GTX 1050 Ti GPU. The software environment is composed of the Linux operating system, Tensorflow, Numpy. We apply the **F1** score to evaluate the performance of the CWS, which can be described as a **F** score. The F1 score is the harmonic average of the precision (**P**) and recall (**R**), where an F1 score reaches its best value at 1 (perfect precision and recall) and worst at 0.

4.4 The Performance Evaluation of the CWS

One of the current state-of-the-art models for the task of Chinese word segmentation is the model that Ma proposed [16], which mostly based the Bi-LSTM and can be named **Bi-LSTM**. The generic temporal convolutional network that Bai proposed can be named **GTcn**. For evaluation our model, we select the Bi-LSTM and the GTcn as the baseline models, and experiment these models on NLPCC2016 dataset, and show the performance comparison between our model with the baseline models on the test set. As shown in Fig. 3 and Table 2, our model boosts the performance of the CWS approximately 10% contrasted the GTcn. Meanwhile, the performance of our model is better than the performance of the Bi-LSTM in the CWS approximately 1%.

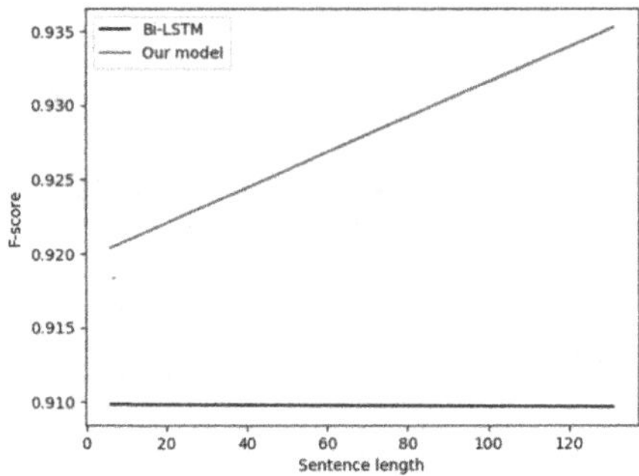

Fig. 4. The trend of the model performances as the length of sentence adding.

As shown in Fig. 3, the F-score values of the three models are achieved on the development set. The models have trained 100 epochs that an epoch means a training on the corpus based the previous epoch parameters. The training speed of the GTcn is fast than the other models but its performance of the CWS is massively lower than the other models for the reason of that the GTcn ignores the labels correlation of the adjacent characters. The Bi-LSTM has the ability to process the labels correlation with its natural advantage in processing sequence data. However, it has an inherent drawback that is the Vanishing Gradients discussed before so that it is little efficient than our model in processing long sequences.

4.5 The Ability in Processing Long Sentences

For evaluation the ability in processing long sentences, we experiment our model and the Bi-LSTM on numerous length sentences of the test set. We split the test set by the length of sentences and experiment the split sentences separately and get a set of scattering spots. We apply the Linear Regression to fit the scatter spots and achieve the trend of the model performances as the length of sentence adding. As shown in Fig. 4, the horizontal axis means the length of a sentence, and the vertical axis means the F1 score, and each spot indicates the F1 score at the length, the black indicating the Bi-LSTM and the red indicating our model. Our model has a tremendous ascending trend and the Bi-LSTM has a slowly descending trend. Therefore, our model has an advantage in processing long sentences than the Bi-LSTM.

The Bi-LSTM is little efficient in capturing the faraway character information of a long sentence for the reason of the Vanishing Gradients. However, For the reason of the dilated convolution, as the layers of the encoder add, our model can capture the faraway character information of a long sentence by adding the layers of the encoder.

5 Conclusion

In this paper, we propose a sequence-to-sequence transformer model that is a novel method to address the task of Chinese word segmentation. The model uses the temporal convolutional network to construct an encoder, and uses a fully-connected neural network to build a decoder, and applies the Viterbi algorithm to build an inference layer to infer the final result of the Chinese word segmentation. Meanwhile, the model captures the faraway character information of a long sentence by adding the layers of the encoder. For achieving a superior result of word segmentation, the model binds the Conditional Random Fields model to train parameters. Experiments show that our model has a better word segmentation performance than the Bi-LSTM and has a better ability to process a long sentence than the Bi-LSTM.

References

1. Ba, J.L., Kiros, J.R., Hinton, G.E.: Layer normalization. arXiv:1607.06450 (2016). Version 1
2. Bai, S., Kolter, J.Z., Koltun, V.: An empirical evaluation of generic convolutional and recurrent networks for sequence modeling. arXiv:10803.01271 (2018). Version 2
3. Berger, A.L., Pietra, V.J.D., Pietra, S.A.D.: A maximum entropy approach to natural language processing. Comput. Linguist. **22**(1), 39–71 (1996)
4. Cai, D., Zhao, H.: Neural word segmentation learning for Chinese. In: Proceedings of the 54th Annual Meeting of the Association for Computational Linguistics, pp. 409–420. Association for Computational Linguistics (2016)
5. Chen, X., Qiu, X., Zhu, C., Liu, P., Huang, X.: Long short-term memory neural networks for Chinese word segmentation. In: EMNLP, pp. 1385–1394. Association for Computational Linguistics (2015). https://doi.org/10.18653/v1/D15-1141
6. Chen, X., Shi, Z., Qiu, X., Huang, X.: Adversarial multi-criteria learning for Chinese word segmentation. In: Proceedings of the 55th Annual Meeting of the Association for Computational Linguistics, pp. 1193–1203. Association for Computational Linguistics (2017). https://doi.org/10.18653/v1/P17-1110, https://doi.org/10.18653/v1/P17-111
7. Collins, M.: The forward-backward algorithm. http://www.cs.columbia.edu/~mcollins/fb.pdf
8. Gehring, J., Auli, M., Grangier, D., Dauphin, Y.N.: A convolutional encoder model for neural machine translation. In: Proceedings of the 55th Annual Meeting of the Association for Computational Linguistics, pp. 123–135. Association for Computational Linguistics (2017a). https://doi.org/10.18653/v1/P17-1012
9. Gehring, J., Auli, M., Grangier, D., Yarats, D., Dauphin, Y.N.: Convolutional sequence to sequence learning. In: ICML, pp. 1243–1252 (2017b)
10. Ioffe, S., Szegedy, C.: Batch normalization: accelerating deep network training by reducing internal covariate shift. In: ICML (2015)
11. Kim, Y., Jernite, Y., Sontag, D., Rush, A.M.: Character-aware neural language models. In: Proceedings of the Thirtieth AAAI Conference on Artificial Intelligence, pp. 2741–2749. Association for the Advancement of Artificial Intelligence (2014)

12. Kingma, D.P., Ba, J.L.: Adam: a method for stochastic optimization. arXiv:1412.6980 (2014). Version 9
13. Lafferty, J., McCallum, A., Pereira, F.C.: Conditional random fields: probabilistic models for segmenting and labeling sequence data. In: Proceedings of the Eighteenth International Conference on Machine Learning (2001)
14. Lea, C., Flynn, M.D., Vidal, R., Reiter, A., Hager, G.D.: Temporal convolutional networks for action segmentation and detection. In: The IEEE Conference on Computer Vision and Pattern Recognition (CVPR), pp. 156–165 (2017)
15. Ling, W., Dyer, C., Black, A., Trancoso, I.: Two/too simple adaptations of Word2Vec for syntax problems. In: The 2015 Annual Conference of the North American Chapter of the ACL, pp. 1299–1304. Association for Computational Linguistics (2015)
16. Ma, J., Ganchev, K., Weiss, D.: State-of-the-art Chinese word segmentation with Bi-LSTMs. In: Proceedings of the 2018 Conference on Empirical Methods in Natural Language Processing, pp. 839–849. Association for Computational Linguistics (2018)
17. Nair, V., Hinton, G.E.: Rectified linear units improve restricted Boltzmann machines. In: Proceedings of the 27th International Conference on Machine Learning (2010)
18. Pei, W., Ge, T., Chan, B.: Max-margin tensor neural network for Chinese word segmentation. In: ACL, pp. 293–303. Association for Computational Linguistics (2014). http://aclweb.org/anthology/C04-1081
19. Qiu, X., Qian, P., Shi, Z.: Neural word segmentation learning for Chinese. In: Overview of the NLPCC-ICCPOL 2016 Shared Task: Chinese Word Segmentation for Micro-Blog Texts. pp. 901–906. International Conference on Computer Processing of Oriental Languages (2016)
20. Srivastava, N., Hinton, G., Krizhevsky, A., Sutskever, I., Salakhutdino, R.: Dropout: a simple way to prevent neural networks from overfitting. J. Mach. Learn. Res. **15**(1), 1929–1958 (2014)
21. Xue, N.: Chinese word segmentation as character tagging. Comput. Linguist. Chin. Lang. Process. **8**(1), 29–48 (2003)
22. Yang, J., Zhang, Y., Dong, F.: Neural word segmentation with rich pretraining. In: Proceedings of the 55th Annual Meeting of the Association for Computational Linguistics, pp. 839–849. Association for Computational Linguistics (2017). https://doi.org/10.18653/v1/P17-1078
23. Zheng, X., Chen, H., Xu, T.: Deep learning for Chinese word segmentation and POS tagging. In: EMNLP, pp. 647–657. Association for Computational Linguistics (2013). http://aclweb.org/anthology/D13-1061
24. He, K., Zhang, X., Ren, S., Sun, J.: Deep residual learning for image recognition. In: The IEEE Conference on Computer Vision and Pattern Recognition (CVPR), June 2016

Author Index

Printed in the United States
By Bookmasters